SCHOOL PSYCHOLOGY

Past, Present, and Future

Thomas K. Fagan
The University of Memphis

Paula Sachs Wise
Western Illinois University

THIRD EDITION

From the NASP Publications Board Operations Manual

The content of this document reflects the ideas and positions of the authors. The responsibility lies solely with the authors and does not necessarily reflect the position or ideas of the National Association of School Psychologists.

Published by the National Association of School Psychologists

Copies may be ordered from:
NASP Publications
4340 East West Highway, Suite 402
Bethesda, MD 20814
(301) 657-0270
(301) 657-0275, fax
e-mail: *publications@naspweb.org*
www.nasponline.org

ISBN 978-0932955-71-5

Printed in the United States of America

Third Printing, Fall 2010

10 9 8 7 6 5 4 3

NATIONAL ASSOCIATION OF SCHOOL PSYCHOLOGISTS

To:

Ruth and Paul Fagan
Susan Fagan
Shannon, Lance, and Colleen

Bella and Milton Sachs
Dan Wise
Ben

and to past, present, and future
generations of school psychology students

Table of Contents

Preface

For several years prior to the publication of the first edition of this book, each of us had searched for an appropriate textbook for graduate students just starting out in the field of school psychology. We, and our students, had been particularly unhappy with the so-called introductory texts of the recent past, which were actually edited books of in-depth chapters that seemed more suitable for specific advanced courses or seminars than for a general introductory course. Other available texts for an introductory course seemed more concerned with conveying an author's particular theoretical viewpoint than with providing a realistic overview of the past, present, and future of the profession of school psychology. The first edition of this text, then, was an effort to find a book that each of us could use in our own Introduction to School Psychology classes.

When we first discussed coauthoring an alternative to the books available on the market, we found that we were in strong agreement about the type of book for which each of us was searching. Such a book would provide general information about the many facets of school psychology without overwhelming readers with details and references that are mandatory for more advanced students but less important and often confusing at this introductory level. Such a book would also provide an overview of some of the most important issues and challenges facing psychologists currently working in the schools. Such a book would be readable and thought provoking, challenging excellent students to look forward to continuing their studies in school psychology while portraying the profession in an honest and realistic manner. We wanted a book that represented a "best lectures in school psychology" philosophy. We were reasonably satisfied that the first edition of *School Psychology: Past, Present, and Future* was the type of book we had sought. Judging from the reactions we received from book reviewers, from the number of program adoptions, from our colleagues, and, most important, from our students, the first edition was a success.

For the second edition we changed publishers, added two chapters, and modified the existing chapters, beefing up sections that we felt needed additional clarification and introducing new information that had been published in the years since the first edition appeared. The two additional chapters were those related to school psychology in Canada and international school psychology. We wanted the book to cover school psychology issues beyond the borders of the United States.

We now offer the third edition of the book. We continue to address what we consider to be the most important topics and issues relevant to the history, the current status, and the future of the profession of school psychology. We are delighted that the National Association of School Psychologists has agreed to continue its relationship with us in this endeavor.

Throughout its history, the book has been developed around certain assumptions. First, we assume that the book will be used primarily as a text in courses designed to be the students' first examination of the profession of school psychology. Second, we assume that readers have had some undergraduate psychology coursework. Third, we assume that readers have come to school psychology training from a variety of backgrounds. Some students will have had limited experience in grade schools and high schools aside from their own 12 or so years as students and perhaps as parents of schoolchildren. Others have had experience in a variety of capacities within the school system. Our fourth assumption in our writing is that this book is only a small part of each student's total professional preparation. The information that students will be introduced to in this text will be discussed, expanded upon, and perhaps demonstrated through other classes and field experiences. Finally, we assume that those reading the book are bright and capable students, interested in the subject matter of school psychology.

Some readers may be wondering if school psychology is the right profession for them to pursue. Our experiences as trainers of school psychologists and as advisers to undergraduate psychology majors have taught us that some students are certain they want to become school psychologists, occasionally even as entering freshmen. They seem convinced from the start that school psychology is the best possible career option for them. They like children, they are interested and have done well in the subject matter of psychology, and they see school psychology as a logical way to combine these two interests. Other students remain skeptical, sometimes throughout their graduate training and beyond. They debate the advantages of clinical psychology versus school psychology or of school counseling versus school psychology. Many students are concerned about the amount of time they will spend testing relative to the amount of time they will spend counseling children. Others worry about the amount of time they will spend consulting with adults rather than working directly with children and adolescents.

Although both of us are strong proponents of school psychology, we recognize that it is not the ideal profession for everyone. Each student must make a personal decision, carefully weighing the advantages and disadvantages of the profession before making a final selection. Although career decisions are in no way irreversible, spending 3 years or more in training to gain knowledge and to acquire skills you may never use is neither efficient nor advisable. We hope, among other things, that this book will help in the decision-making process for those students who are struggling to determine whether school psychology is an appropriate professional identity for them. Our intention is to present a candid view of the past and present of school psychology while offering some educated hunches as to what school psychology may become in the future. We have attempted throughout the book to link the history of school psychology with current developments and with future professional directions.

The profession of school psychology does not operate in a vacuum. When schools are under attack, when laws change or new legislation is adopted, when events bring about societal changes, the impact of each of these developments is felt within school systems in general and within the profession of school psychology specifically. Changes from within the field of school psychology influence teachers and supervisors also. When leading school psychologists support changes in professional roles and functions, when new intervention techniques are presented in the literature, when new and revised tests are published, the practice of school psychology is changed. We have attempted to provide a balance of the formal information that students need in their training with less formal information that students want. Throughout the book we have attempted to draw our readers into the discussion, to get them actively involved as trainees within the profession of school psychology. We recognize that many of the readers of this book will be our colleagues of the future. With that thought in mind, we have provided some hints or guidelines to expedite the passage from student to professional.

Throughout this book we examine fundamental questions and dimensions regarding the nature and delivery of psychological services within the public schools. In this manner, chapter 1 is organized around 14 basic questions that are often asked by beginning and prospective school psychologists. The importance of professional accountability and evaluation is emphasized.

Chapter 2 presents an overview of the history of school psychology. The chapter summarizes the development of psychological services in schools in the context of the development of psychology and education and the changing treatment and status of children in America. A major premise of the chapter is that the history of school psychology can be divided logically into two eras: the hybrid years (1890–1969) and the thoroughbred years (1970–present).

Chapter 3 examines the unique opportunities and challenges available to those who choose to practice psychology within the educational context. Included is a discussion of the goals and purposes of education; the structure of regular education, special education, administration, and special services; arrangements for the delivery of psychological services; and the significance of power and authority relationships in the system. The chapter also addresses the issue of clientage: Who is the client of the school psychologist? The child? Parents? Teachers or administrators? The school board? The notion of the school psychologist as a "guest in the house of education" is first presented in chapter 3. In addition to the traditional public school setting for the school psychologist, alternative employment settings are explored, such as clinics and hospitals.

Chapter 4 examines the various roles and functions of school psychologists and discusses which roles are most common and most appropriate. The roles and functions of school psychologists are presented within the context of the ultimate goal of school psychology, that is, helping children. The variables that influence the roles and functions of individual psychologists are addressed as well. In this edition, readers are shown the differences between the traditional role, which relies heavily on traditional assessment techniques, and an emerging role, which relies heavily on curriculum-based measurement and the response-to-intervention movement. References are suggested that should enable readers to learn more about many of the topics presented briefly in chapter 4.

Chapter 5 focuses on the topics of professional evaluation and accountability. The chapter examines how school psychological services are planned and evaluated and suggests methods for improving not only the effectiveness of school psychology but also the means by which school psychology and school psychologists are judged. The importance of professional accountability is emphasized, that is, being able to demonstrate that methods are effective and outcomes are accurate.

Chapter 6 examines topics such as the training of school psychologists, professional standards, and issues of accreditation. We present various models of training and introduce readers to the types and levels of training that coexist in school psychology. Opportunities for continuing professional development are also discussed.

Chapter 7 focuses on professional control and the regulation of school psychology through three spheres of influence: accreditation, credentialing, and practice. The section on practice regulations discusses the influences of litigation, legislation, credentialing, and ethics on professional roles and functions.

Chapter 8 presents information about field experiences in school psychology, including practicum placements and internship settings, as well as postinternship employment in traditional and nontraditional settings. It also addresses some of the factors involved in selecting and obtaining an internship and eventually more permanent employment. A discussion of internship guidelines and provider standards expands on earlier discussions of credentialing and training guidelines. Readers can learn how to prevent or deal with professional stress and burnout.

Chapter 9 discusses the past, present, and future of school psychology in Canada. It explores roles and functions, training, and regulation that readers can compare with U.S. systems of practice. We hope that this information will be of particular interest not only to those thinking about practicing in Canada but to other readers as well.

Chapter 10 expands the scope of the book to the practice of school psychology around the world. This international perspective should provide an interesting view for all readers in the United States, Canada, and elsewhere. As with the Canadian chapter, topics discussed include the past, present, and future of roles and functions, training, and regulation. The chapter also describes the development of the International School Psychology Association.

Chapter 11 presents some ideas as to what the future of school psychology may be like. We return to the past to read how those who contributed to the field saw the future of the profession, and see how those predictions turned out. We also examine our own predictions from previous editions of this book to see if the predictions have come to pass. Our hope is the lessons in this chapter will inspire ideas and discussion about how to bring about a positive future for school psychology.

One unique feature of this book is the attention we have paid to presenting the information our students want to know. From the 14 questions posed in chapter 1, to the exercises included in section 5, to the worksheets in appendix A, to the rules and regulations that govern the practice of school psychology, we have tried to be aware of who our readers are and what they want and need to know to become successful professionals.

We designed this text to be read within the context of a total school psychology curriculum or program. Although we have emphasized particular areas—history, demographics, and roles and functions—we have also tried to include other important ideas. Readers will notice frequent references to areas of study such as consultation, intervention, and assessment. In writing an introductory book in a field, it is necessary to discuss many vital issues quite briefly. We are confident that readers will learn more about these concepts and issues throughout their training.

Acknowledgments

Special thanks go to the following individuals who have contributed their time and talents:

Tracy Cruise, Western Illinois University
Carl DiMartino, National Association of School Psychologists
Denise Ferrenz, National Association of School Psychologists
Ruth Kelly, Western Illinois University
Linda Morgan, National Association of School Psychologists
Jack A. Naglieri, Ohio State University
Natasha Reeves, University of Memphis
Jessica Roesch, University of Memphis
Nancy Sherer, Western Illinois University
Mark Swerdlik, Illinois State University, Dan Olympia, University of Utah, and their students

We also thank the following alumni of Western Illinois University's School Psychology Program for their invaluable suggestions for the scenarios in chapter 4. All have been gainfully employed as school psychologists since graduating from our program!

Judith Ormerod Assmann
Vicki Boyer
Kate Pietscher Cole
Jon Jacobus
Michelle Marshall
Joanna Rinaldo
Dee Ring
Kris Sanders
Jaimee Steele
Deb Vensel
Nicole Weaver

Chapter 1

Introduction to the Field of School Psychology

School psychology is a complex specialty of professional psychology that is not easily described to those just entering the field or to parents and other professionals. This introduction to the field of school psychology begins by answering several questions that are frequently asked by prospective and new students and by others seeking information about the field. Much of this information is explored in greater detail in other parts of the book. The following questions and responses provide a quick synopsis of the major aspects of professional school psychology.

1. What is a school psychologist?
2. What are the most common services provided by school psychologists?
3. What are the most common settings in which school psychologists are employed?
4. At what levels are school psychologists trained?
5. How do school psychologists differ from other psychologists?
6. How are practitioners credentialed for practice?
7. How many school psychologists are there?
8. How are school psychologists dispersed geographically?
9. What is the typical service ratio of school psychologists to school-age children?
10. To what professional associations do school psychologists belong?
11. What are the major journals and other publications in the field of school psychology?
12. Do school psychologists have standards for professional practice?
13. What contract and salary arrangements are most common?
14. What does the employment market look like?

In addition to answering questions about the who, what, when, where, and why of school psychology, this book discusses the debate over the primary roles and functions of the school psychologist. It is the authors' opinion that among the primary roles of school psychologists is their role as assessment specialist in the educational setting. Broadly construed, that role consists of the assessment of children, systems, programs, and families and is not limited to testing.

RESPONSES TO COMMON QUESTIONS ABOUT SCHOOL PSYCHOLOGY

The questions asked here are not about how to do school psychology, a subject covered in other sources, especially the National Association of School Psychologists' *Best Practices in School Psychology* series. In many instances data from surveys are used to present the most representative and reliable demographic and practice information available, including data from NASP membership surveys or its National School Psychology Certification System.

1. What Is a School Psychologist?

Most professions elude precise definition. This is because such definitions are difficult to write and achieve consensus on and because, by defining a profession (e.g., who they are and what they do), professionals fear giving the impression that the rest of the field of practice belongs to someone else. Such so-called turf issues are at the core of the American Psychological Association's position: to treat training and credentialing issues generically. Even the APA's "Specialty Guidelines for the Delivery of Services by School Psychologists" were couched in complicated policies of training, titles, and broad areas of function (APA, 1981). Though less concerned with generic issues, the National Association of School Psychologists (NASP) also has defined the school psychologist in terms of its own policies and standards (NASP, 2000b).

Definitions

On its website (*www.nasponline.org*), NASP answers the question, "Who are school psychologists?" as follows:

> School psychologists help children and youth succeed academically, socially, and emotionally. They collaborate with educators, parents, and other professionals to create safe, healthy, and supportive learning environments for all students that strengthen connections between home and school. School psychologists are highly trained in both psychology and education. They must complete a minimum of a post–master's degree program that includes a year-long internship and emphasizes preparation in mental health, child development, school organization, learning styles, and processes, behavior, motivation, and effective teaching. School psychologists must be certified and/or licensed by the state in which they work. They also may be nationally certified by the National School Psychology Certification Board (NSPCB).

The NASP description does not name specific services provided and concentrates on the school psychologist's training and credentialing consistent with its standards.

In 1998, APA's Commission for the Recognition of Specialties and Proficiencies in Professional Psychology approved the *Petition for Reaffirmation of the Specialty of School Psychology.* The lengthy document provided an abundance of viewpoints about the field. The petition was reapproved in 2005 (*Petition for Reaffirmation*, 2005). A shorter archival description defines school psychology as follows:

> School psychology is a general practice and health service provider specialty of professional psychology that is concerned with the science and practice of psychology with children, youth, families; learners of all ages; and the schooling process. The basic education and training of school psychologists prepares them to provide a range of psychological diagnosis, assessment, intervention, prevention, health promotion, and program development and evaluation services with a special focus on the developmental processes of children and youth within the context of schools, families, and other systems. School psychologists are prepared to intervene at the individual and system level, and develop, implement, and evaluate preventive programs. In these efforts, they conduct ecologically valid assessments and intervene to promote positive learning environments within which children and youth from diverse backgrounds have equal access to effective educational and psychological services that promote healthy development. (Archival Description of the Specialty, 2006, p. 1)

The petition is perhaps the most complete description of the specialty of school psychology available, although it reflects the APA's links to doctoral-level professional psychologists.

Another comprehensive description appears in *School Psychology: A Blueprint for Training and Practice III* (Ysseldyke et al., 2006). To the extent the document serves as a definition of school psychology, it does so by describing the functions of school psychologists in eight domains:

1. Interpersonal and collaborative skills
2. Diversity awareness and sensitive service delivery
3. Technological applications
4. Professional, legal, ethical, and social responsibility
5. Data-based decision making and accountability
6. Systems-based service delivery
7. Enhancing the development of cognitive and academic skills
8. Enhancing the development of wellness, social skills, mental health, and life competencies

The *Blueprint* is a description of what the school psychologist should strive to be in the future rather than a description of the contemporary school psychologist. The authors do not present a concise definition of the field of school psychology. The *Blueprint* domains serve as a basis for the NASP training and program approval content standards.

Other definitions tend to be brief and general. For example, an early description by Walter (1925) simply referred to the purpose of the school psychologist as "to

For the purposes of this book, the term *school psychologist* is defined as follows: A school psychologist is a professional psychological practitioner whose general purpose is to bring a psychological perspective to bear on the problems of educators and the clients educators serve. This perspective is derived from a broad base of training in educational and psychological foundations as well as specialty preparation, resulting in the provision of comprehensive psychological services of a direct and indirect nature.

bring to bear upon educational problems the knowledge and technique which have been developed by the science of psychology" (p. 167). A similar viewpoint was expressed by Bardon and Bennett (1974): "School psychology differs from other psychological specialties in that it brings psychological knowledge, skills, and techniques to bear on the problems presented by the school as a total, unique place in which people live and work and on the problems of the people living in the school" (p. 8). Magary (1966) identified more than a dozen brief statements attempting to define the school psychologist that were published in the early 1960s. Each of them would be, in part at least, true today. The International School Psychology Association (ISPA) published a set of guidelines that help to define school psychology (Oakland & Cunningham, 1997). These guidelines are described in chapter 10.

This definition draws upon existing viewpoints, links training to the field's educational and psychological foundations as well as specialty training, and stresses the importance of comprehensive service provision. The profession's overarching identity reflects the setting in which it is practiced. The definition is not specifically linked to issues of credentialing and levels of training, which guide the definitions of the APA and NASP, nor is the specialty confined to school settings. This definition includes the provision of comprehensive direct and indirect services, which allow a broad range of roles and functions and do not imply narrowly limited services. Other definitions and descriptions of the school psychologist often exist in state-level credentialing and practice regulations and in published training program descriptions.

Demographic Descriptions

School psychology also can be defined by demographic descriptions of professionals in the field, including gender, ethnicity, degrees, levels of experience, and other characteristics (see Table 1.1). The following figures are from the NASP membership renewal survey of November 1999 and NASP's demographic survey of 2004–2005 (Curtis, Lopez, Batsche, & Smith, 2006).

Representation by women has increased by at least 7 percentage points since the first edition of this book (Fagan & Wise, 1994, p. 3). The comparability of the two data sets provides support for the NASP sampling method, while confirming that minority representation is a continuing issue. Reschly and Wilson (1992) reported that 62% of practitioners were married, 24% were divorced, and 14% were unmarried. Sixty-eight percent reported having children (20% with preschool-age children and 40% with school-age children). The studies provide a fairly consistent picture of school psychology in the United States as a field that is largely female and largely Caucasian, and whose practitioners have more than a decade of experience,

Table 1.1 Demographic Description of School Psychology Professionals

Gender (%)	**1999 (*N* = 14,949)**	**2004–2005 (*N* = 1,750)**
Female	72.3	74
Male	27.7	26

Years of Experience	11–15 (median)	14.76 (mean)

Ethnicity (%)	**1999 (*N* = 14,489)**	**2004–2005 (*N* = 1,750)**
White	92.04	92.6
African American	2.14	1.9
Other Hispanic	1.46	3.0
Other (Unspecified)	1.36	0.8
Asian American/Pacific Islander	0.93	0.9
American Indian/Alaskan Native	0.40	0.8
Chicano/Mexican American	0.91	N/A
Puerto Rican	0.76	N/A

Sources: NASP membership survey (1999); Curtis, Lopez, Batsche, & Smith (2006).

are usually married, and have children. The field has a persistently small representation of minorities, in disproportion to the school population served (Loe & Miranda, 2005).

The median and mean ages of practitioners reported in Reschly and Wilson (1992) were 40.3 years and 41.4 years, respectively. Curtis, Hunley, Walker, and Baker (1999) reported a median age category of 41 to 45. The Curtis et al. (2006) data revealed an average age of 46.2 years for 2004–2005, 45.2 for 1999, and 38.8 for 1980. The data reflect an increasing average age over the past 25 years. Reflecting the more recent development of the field internationally, earlier data from 54 countries indicated that "school psychologists were typically between ages 31 and 39, and female (62%)," with 10 years of experience (Oakland & Cunningham, 1992, p. 109).

2. What Are the Most Common Services Provided by School Psychologists?

Several surveys on the role and function of the school psychologist were reported in the first edition of this book (e.g., D. K. Smith, 1984; D. K. Smith & Mealy, 1988; Reschly & Wilson, 1992. Overall, the surveys found that school psychology practitioners reported spending their time in the following ways: 52–55% in psychoeducational assessment, 21–26% in interventions (e.g., counseling and remediation), 19–22% in consultation, and 1–2% in research and evaluation. Reschly and Wilson (1995) studied role changes from 1986 to 1991–1992. Basing their observations on a 40-hour work week, they concluded that "over one-half of the time [was] devoted to psychoeducational assessment, about 20% to direct interventions, 16% to problem-solving consultation, and 5% or less to systems-organizational consultation and research-evaluation" (p. 69). A subsequent analysis by Reschly (1998) comparing 1997 data to that of 1992 found virtually the same percentage of time allocations. That is, slightly more than half of practitioners' time was spent on psychoeducational assessment, 20% of time continued to be in direct interventions, 17% was devoted to problem-solving consultation, 7% to systems/organizational consultation, and 2% to research/evaluation. However, the period 1986–1997 showed a decline of 8% in the amount of time spent on special education eligibility services. In 1997 it was 59.9%.

The results reported by Curtis et al. (1999), which were based on data from the 1994–1995 school year, did not report percentage allocations. However, school psychologists reported spending considerable time on special education evaluations, with 59.1% spending more than 70% of their time on such evaluations, and only 2.7% reporting that they did not complete such evaluations at all. More than three fourths of respondents also reported doing evaluations for purposes other than special education. They concluded that "school psychologists continue to spend the majority of their time conducting psychoeducational evaluations related to special education" and "relatively little time conducting psychoeducational evaluations for purposes other than special education" (p. 113). Although not reporting time spent in such activities, they also found that most respondents reported being engaged in consultation (97.4%), individual counseling (86.4%), in-service education programs (77.8%), and student group counseling or other group sessions (53.5%). These studies are also consistent with 1992 and 1993 surveys by Bontrager and Wilczenski (1997) and a time study analysis of practitioners in San Diego (McDaid & Reifman, 1996).

A study by Bramlett, Murphy, Johnson, Wallingsford, & Hall (2002, p. 329) found the percentage of practitioners' time allocated to several areas of practitioner services:

assessment (46%)
consultation (16%)
interventions (13%)
counseling (8%)
conferencing (7%)
supervision (3%)
in-servicing (2%)
research (1%)
parent training (1%)
other (3%)

The most recent data are from a comparison of 2004–2005 data and data from previous studies (Curtis et al., 2006). For example, in 2004–2005, school psychologists were spending more time in special education activities than they did in 1989–1990 (80.1% of their time vs. 52.3%). Compared with 1999–2000, they were conducting fewer initial special education evaluations (34.5 evaluations vs. 39.9) and reevaluations (34 vs. 37), fewer 504 plans (5.9 vs. 9.3), fewer in-service programs (3.4 vs. 2.6), and fewer student groups (3.2 vs. 1.7). In 2004–2005, school psychologists were counseling an average of 1 to 10 students per year and had 42 consultation cases. It appears that they were devoting more time to fewer cases. This comparison may also reflect personnel shortages, the time required for conducting alternative nontraditional assessments (e.g., curriculum-based measures), and the administrative duties that accompany special education services.

Collectively, the research findings reveal a consistent pattern of activities for school psychologists over the past two decades, with school psychologists providing a variety of services, many of which are connected to the special education sector of school districts. It is clear that school psychologists spend the largest amount of their time in assessment-related duties, and less of their time involved in direct intervention and consultation. Research and evaluation functions have consistently carried the least weight in surveys of school psychologists. Thus, even though school psychologists may be active consumers of research and evaluation through journals and conferences, their active involvement is infrequent. These patterns of roles and functions were also observed in a survey of services to charter schools, a relative newcomer to the education industry (Nelson, Peterson, & Strader, 1997). An international survey by Jimerson et al. (2004), which revealed that more practitioner time was devoted to services other than assessment, especially counseling, perhaps reflects an overlapping of school psychology and school counseling roles.

The research findings reveal a consistent pattern of activities for school psychologists over the past two decades, with school psychologists providing a variety of services, many of which are connected to the special education sector of school districts. It is clear that school psychologists spend the largest amount of their time in assessment-related duties, and less of their time involved in direct intervention and consultation.

3. What Are the Most Common Settings in Which School Psychologists Are Employed?

The 1999 NASP membership renewal survey and 2004–2005 demographic survey reported a stable distribution of employment settings, as shown in Table 1.2.

School settings of all types (except colleges and universities) appear to represent about 80–90% of the employment setting data. Reschly (1998) reported data over three time periods, as shown in Table 1.3.

Table 1.2 Distribution of School Psychology Employment Settings

Setting	1999	2004–2005*
Public school	76.58	83.1
Private school—sectarian	1.11	2.1
Private school—nonsectarian	1.27	5.2
Residential institution	1.15	N/A
Private practice	4.54	4.1
State department of education	0.45	0.8
Mental health agency	1.41	N/A
Preschool	1.18	N/A
College/university	6.92	6.5
Other	5.40	2.8
Hospital/medical setting	N/A	1.3

Sources: NASP membership survey (1999); Curtis et al. (2006).
*Total exceeds 100% because multiple choices were possible.

Table 1.3 Percentage Distribution of School Psychologists

Year	Public School	College/ University	Private Practice	Residential Institution	Clinic/Hospital/ Other
1997	89.0	2.9	3.6	0.5	3.9
1992	86.0	1.3	4.2	1.0	7.5
1986	88.0	0.0	2.8	2.0	7.1

Source: Reschly (1998).

Curtis et al. (1999) reported that 11.9% of school psychologists were engaged in some private practice, but only 2.8% worked in private practice full-time (40 or more hours per week). An earlier sample of nationally certified school psychologists (NASP, 1989) indicated that school psychologists most often worked in elementary and secondary school settings with both regular and special education programs. A division along lines of school and nonschool settings suggested that nonschool settings represented about 10% of the respondents' (N = 647) settings. Thus, over the 25 years, school settings have been the dominant employment setting (80–90% of respondents), with private practice consistently in the 3–5% range and other settings making up the difference. Curtis et al. (2006) indicated that 22.5% of respondents engaged in secondary employment, the most common sites being independent practice, colleges or universities, and public schools.

School Settings

The most common employment setting for school psychologists is the single school district. Here the school psychologist serves the entire elementary and/or secondary school system, including regular and special education programs. The next most common setting appears to be the cooperative agreement district, sometimes called a special education cooperative. Cooperatives have the advantage of combining the services and personnel of several districts to maximize service options at less overall cost than each district attempting to do the same individually. Such options are especially useful to small rural and suburban districts. Another service option is one in which the same school psychologist serves multiple school districts, perhaps under more than one contract. These three service options have been the traditional settings for school psychologists throughout the profession's history. In the Bramlett et al. (2002) survey, respondents identified themselves as working with all ages of students (47%), elementary-age (20%), secondary-age (15%), preschool-age (6%), and other (12%).

Nonschool Settings

As the surveys reveal, school psychologists also work in nontraditional settings such as public and private community or state agencies, including community mental health centers, developmental disability centers, or rehabilitation centers; independent and church-related private schools; and private practice, either individually or in groups of service providers. Although traditional school settings dominate the field, the number (not necessarily the percentage) of school psychologists in nontraditional settings continues to grow (D'Amato & Dean, 1989). Practice settings are discussed in chapters 3, 4, and 8.

4. At What Levels Are School Psychologists Trained?

School psychology training programs exist in all but a few states (e.g., Alaska, New Hampshire, Vermont, and Wyoming do not have programs), but their geographical distribution is based largely on historical patterns of program development of earlier decades. The last NASP *Directory of Graduate Training Programs* (Thomas, 1998) in 1996–1997 identified and briefly described 218 program institutions in 46 states. Eight states (California, Illinois, New Jersey, New York, Ohio, Pennsylvania, Texas, and Wisconsin) accounted for 47% of all training institutions, with New York having 20 and California having 21 such institutions. The increasing availability of freestanding and online programs will no doubt translate into the availability of training in all states. The 218 institutions, which offer 294 programs, reported a total of 8,587 students enrolled in training and 1,897 students who were graduated or recommended for certification. Almost all programs required field experiences, including both a practicum and an internship. In 2005, NASP changed to an online data-based list of training programs. Although participation has been insufficient to provide overall training program data, it appears that the total number of program institutions is still in the range of 210–220. Subspecialty training in several areas (e.g., neuropsychology, preschool, and vocational) is available at many institutions, though typically at the doctoral level only.

Training is available at the master's, specialist, and doctoral degree levels, corresponding roughly to 36, 60, and 90 semester hours. However, the actual average number of semester hours required of programs was reported to be 40, 68, and 106, respectively (Thomas, 1998). Although more recent data are not available, it is unlikely that the lengths of these degree programs have changed. Compared to the master's and doctoral degrees, the specialist degree is a relative newcomer to higher education, but it is popular among school psychology programs. Though the EdS degree is granted most often by colleges of education, several psychology departments in colleges of arts and sciences now grant the education specialist degree. The hourly requirements for the specialist degree are about midway between the traditional master's and doctoral degree requirements and usually include credits for practicum and internship. There may be a thesis or research report, or other culminating experience near the end of the degree, but the internship often substitutes for this requirement (Fagan, 1997, 2005c). The specialist degree is considered the equivalent of the master's degree plus 30 hours and fits conveniently into school district salary schedules that often include a level of MA plus 30 semester hours. Doctoral degrees include the doctor of philosophy (PhD), doctor of education (EdD), and doctor of psychology (PsyD). The availability of PsyD programs has increased in recent years, and the degree is often available from freestanding professional schools of psychology (e.g., Illinois School of Professional Psychology).

In the 2004–2005 NASP membership survey, 32.6% held master's degrees, 34.9% specialist degrees, and 32.4% the doctoral degree; and 80.5% held the specialist level or above.

The 1999 NASP membership renewal survey (N = 14,650) found that 54% held the specialist degree or equivalent training and 26% held a doctoral degree. Curtis et al. (1999) reported that almost 79% of school psychologists were prepared at the specialist level or higher. Earlier studies of practitioners (D. K. Smith, 1984) found that 17% held the master's degree, 45% the master's plus 30 hours, 22% the specialist degree, and 16% the doctoral degree. Reschly and Wilson's (1992) data found 23% held the master's, 56% the specialist, and 21% the doctoral. Graden and Curtis (1991) found 28% doctoral representation in a sample that included university faculty as well as practitioners. In the 2004–2005 NASP survey (Curtis et al., 2006), 32.6% held master's degrees, 34.9% specialist degrees, and 32.4% the doctoral degree; and 80.5% held the specialist level or above.

It is NASP policy that the education specialist degree is the appropriate level for entry into the profession. APA policy contends that the doctoral degree is appropriate for entry as a professional psychologist, but the APA has made some concessions in its policy for school psychologists trained at the specialist level. Most state education agencies allow entry with the master's or specialist degree, whereas entry into non-school and private independent practice is most often limited to professionals holding doctoral degrees. The policies influence the accreditation and state credentialing expectations discussed in chapter 7. The content of programs is discussed in chapter 6.

5. How Do School Psychologists Differ From Other Psychologists?

The many types of psychologists are differentiated along lines of research and application. The most visible types of psychologists are those referred to as professional psychologists and include school, clinical, and counseling psychologists. Industrial or organizational psychologists are also considered to be among the applied psychologists, but they are less identified with the role of health-services provider that is associated with professional psychology. Industrial or organizational psychologists work with the applications of psychology with respect to problems of business and industry, including organizational development, systems analysis, personnel selection, program evaluation, and human factors.

Clinical and Counseling Psychology

Few clear-cut dividing lines separate school, clinical, and counseling psychologists, and overlap in training and practice is common. Bardon and Bennett (1974) identified as a unique feature of school psychology its focus on the school setting and the problems of those who work in the school. In contrast, *clinical psychologists* "assess and treat mental, emotional, and behavioral disorders... [that] range from short-term crises, such as difficulties resulting from adolescent rebellion, to more severe, chronic conditions such as schizophrenia" (APA, 2003, p. 2). Clinical psychologists usually are employed in medical facilities, clinics, and private practice. *Counseling psychologists* "help people recognize their strengths and resources to cope with their problems." They provide counseling and psychotherapy, teach, and do scientific research with individuals, families, and groups. Counseling psychologists "help people understand and take action on career and work problems. They pay attention to how problems and people differ across life stages" (APA, 2003, p. 2). Counseling psychologists often work in settings similar to those of clinical psychologists.

School psychologists are distinguished from other professional psychologists by their background and training in educational foundations and applications, their concern for the individual learning and behavioral problems of students, their school-age clientele, and the educational settings in which they are most often employed. However, clinical and counseling psychologists occasionally work in school settings, and school psychologists occasionally work in clinical or counseling settings. Of course, many clinical, counseling, and school psychologists are involved in teaching and research in higher education.

Educational Psychology

Because many school psychologists are trained in educational psychology departments, they are sometimes confused with educational psychologists. The confusion is understandable, and in some locales the term *educational psychologist* is synonymous with *school psychologist.* Generally, however, educational psychologists are trained as research psychologists and not as professional psychologists. They study the learning process generally rather than how individual children or groups of children adjust to that process. Thus, educational psychologists share much with other psychologists in the study of motivation, learning and cognition, and human development, and of how these can be applied to the improvement of education. School psychologists, who are interested in such matters as well, concentrate on the study of individuals and groups of children and youth (and sometimes adults) who have difficulty with the process of education, including both the learning and mental health aspects. Educational psychologists often conduct research and evaluation on matters of school curriculum and are directly involved in teacher preparation programs in academic settings. Historically, school psychologists have a kinship with both educational and clinical psychologists. The APA's *Psychology: Careers for the Twenty-First Century* (2003) and the APA website have more information on the many types of psychologists, career resources, and careers in psychology. A historical treatment of these specialties and their differences is presented by Benjamin and Baker (2004).

Guidance and Counseling

Although the boundaries between school psychologists and guidance counselors are sometimes blurred, significant differences in training and practice exist. School counselors historically have worked primarily with secondary school students to provide academic and vocational guidance. In recent years, the trend has been for counselors to implement comprehensive developmental guidance programs throughout all school grades. In this role, counselors provide a total program that includes individual, group, and crisis counseling; developmentally appropriate classroom presentations; and teacher and parent consultation. Though decreasing in emphasis, school counselors are usually required to possess a teaching certificate, and often teaching experience, in order to be credentialed for school-based practice. They are usually hired to provide services to only one or two school buildings. Their training programs are nearly always housed in education colleges or departments. Trainees typically take few, if any, courses in the psychology departments, and there is much less emphasis on working with children who have disabilities.

However, some of the guidance counselor's functions overlap with those of the school psychologist, including group testing, testing of student achievement, individual and group counseling, and teacher and parent consultation. In some districts, a secondary school may have building-based school psychologists and guidance counselors working together, and their functions may overlap. Many states now require school districts to have elementary counselors, and they too may be building-based. Generally, school psychologists work for entire districts or sets of schools and are not building-based. A few school systems have taken a broader pupil services approach, employing personnel trained in both guidance counseling and school psychology (e.g., Charlotte-Mecklenburg schools in North Carolina).

School Social Work

School psychologists' services overlap with the work of school social workers, who provide services directly to children and their parents. School social workers also offer consultation with teachers and intervention services with students and parents, individually and in groups. School social workers and school psychologists often have similar training in counseling, interviewing, and psychotherapy; are assigned to several buildings or districtwide services; and do not need a teaching credential to acquire a credential in school social work (Constable, McDonald, & Flynn, 1999).

6. How Are Practitioners Credentialed for Practice?

School psychology practice is regulated in school and nonschool settings by different agencies, typically a state department of education (SDE) and a state board of examiners in psychology (SBEP), respectively. The SDE issues a certificate (the trend is to call this a license), whereas the board of examiners in psychology issues a license (sometimes called a certificate). Types of credentials tend to follow degree levels. Although almost all basic SDE credentials are available to practitioners holding master's or specialist-level training, non-school-setting licensing is most commonly available only to those holding doctoral degrees. There are usually major differences in the criteria for obtaining a practice credential from these agencies.

As discussed in chapter 7, credentialing is a complex but very important aspect of professional psychology. Credentialing titles and requirements vary from state to state. A candidate applies for the respective credential after completion of training, including field experiences such as a practicum and internship. NASP's *Credentialing Requirements for School Psychologists* (NASP, 2000d) is a valuable source of information on certification and licensing, and updates can be found through links at NASP's website. In some states school psychologists are eligible to apply for credentials as mental health counselors, certified professional counselors, and so on. New Hampshire credentials specialists in the assessment of intellectual functioning, and several states credential educational diagnosticians. A nonpractice credential, Nationally Certified School Psychologist (NCSP), is issued by the NASP National School Psychology Certification System and may aid in acquiring a practice credential. The American Board of School Psychology offers a nonpractice credential, but it is reserved for doctoral practitioners.

Of practitioners surveyed in 2004–2005, 91.3% held SDE credentials and 36.7% held nonschool licensure.

Curtis et al. (1999) found that among practitioners, 94.1% held state education agency certification as school psychologists, 11.3% held separate doctoral-level licenses as psychologists or school psychologists, and 17.4% held separate nondoctoral licenses (e.g., school psychologist, psychometrist, and psychological associate). Curtis et al. (2006) found that 91.3% held SDE credentials, and 36.7% held nonschool licensure. Sixty-two percent held the NCSP, a considerably lower figure from the 76% reported by Reschly and Wilson (1992). The figure for NCSPs is currently about 50% of NASP members. A small percentage of doctoral practitioners hold the American Board of School Psychology diploma.

7. How Many School Psychologists Are There?

Highly reliable nationwide estimates of school psychology practitioners have never existed, and state estimates are seldom available. However, reasonable estimates have been made from surveys taken in several states or from NASP and APA surveys, and studies of the international school psychology community have yielded estimates. For several years it was believed that there were about 40,000–45,000 school psychologists in the world (Catterall, 1979b). Another study, based on 54 reporting countries (including the United States), estimated 87,000 school psychologists worldwide (Oakland & Cunningham, 1992). In the United States, a consensus figure of 35,000 school psychologists has been estimated in recent years. Table 1.4 provides state and regional estimates of the state-by-state distribution of school psychologists, based on NASP membership for June, 2006. A recent NASP study sampling 10 states estimated a nationwide total of 37,893 credentialed school psychologists, with 29,367 working in the public schools (Charvat, 2005). This estimate and the NASP state member data in the table (omitting about 6,200 student members) suggest that about half or fewer of all credentialed school psychologists belong to NASP.

8. How Are School Psychologists Dispersed Geographically?

A good estimate of how school psychologists are dispersed can be observed from NASP membership data. Table 1.4 presents a breakdown of that data as of June 30, 2006 (June data represent the largest membership for the year).

The NASP regional structure, established in the early 1970s, was revised in the late 1990s and provides greater balance among the regions. The study reflects the school population in these states and reveals the concentrations of practitioners across the United States. The six states with at least 1,000 members (New York, California, Pennsylvania, Illinois, Florida, and New Jersey) have 41.45% of the entire membership. A much earlier study of the APA Division of School Psychology members (Hyman, Bilker, Freidman, Marino, & Roessner, 1973) suggests the relatively greater professional influence of these states in the development of school psychology over the past several decades. Several metropolitan areas contribute to these concentrations, including several hundred school psychologists in major urban areas such as Los Angeles, New York City, and Chicago.

Findings are consistent with the NASP survey for 2004–2005, in which respondents identified their locales as urban (28.6%), suburban (49.9%), and rural (28.8%).

Table 1.4 State and Regional NASP Membership Data

Region	Members (% of Total by Region)	States (Members)
Northeast	7,848 (32.89%)	CT (709), DC (48), DE (95), MD (617), ME (172), MA (800), NH (148), NJ (1,028), NY (2,503), PA (1,450), PR (63), RI (158), VT (57)
Southeast	5,184 (21.72%)	AL (119), AR (129), FL (1,070) GA (542), KY (268), LA (198), MS (101), NC (516), SC (323), TN (389), TX (888), VA (567), WV (74)
Central	5,200 (21.79%)	IL (1,203), IN (409), IA (207) KS (207), MI (553), MO (153), MN (366), ND (48), NE (285), OH (987), OK (155), SD (91), WI (536)
West	5,271 (22.09%)	AK (79), AZ (600), CA (2,488), CO (547), HI (53), ID (109) MT (102), NV (189), NM (126), OR (253), UT (175), WA (500), WY (50)
Other (international)	360 (1.51%)	
Total membership	23,863 (100%)	

Source: NASP membership database, June 2006.

Another measure of dispersion is provided by Reschly and Wilson (1992) and Reschly (1998), whose survey respondents were employed in settings as follows: largely urban (27–28%), largely suburban (33–38%), largely rural (21%), and combination settings (14–17%). Another survey indicated 30.3% urban, 44.8% suburban, and 24.9% rural (Curtis et al., 1999). In the Bramlett et al. (2002) survey, respondents identified themselves as working in suburban settings (43%), urban (30%), and rural (27%). These findings are consistent with the NASP survey for 2004–2005, in which respondents identified their locales as urban (28.6%), suburban (49.9%), and rural (28.8%; Curtis et al., 2006). Despite consistent results, the data do not necessarily represent the situation in a particular state. For example, in Ohio, which might be considered by some to be a fairly urban and populous state, the dispersion was identified as approximately 29% urban, 39% suburban, and 32% rural (Mcloughlin, Leless, & Thomas, 1998). How school psychologists are dispersed geographically can influence their practice and organization, especially at the state level.

In Canada, school psychologists are available in all the provinces and territories, but their distribution tends to cluster in the southern portions of the provinces and in major population centers. From an international perspective, school psychologists are dispersed predominantly in North America, Europe, and the Mediterranean, and in some historically British colonies of Africa and the Far East. The availability of school psychological services tends to correspond to the availability of educational and special educational services (Catterall, 1979b) and to a country's level of economic development (Oakland & Cunningham, 1992). Chapters 9 and 10 discuss in greater detail the Canadian and international distributions, respectively.

9. What Is the Typical Service Ratio of School Psychologists to School-Age Children?

An estimated ratio of one school psychologist to 1,500 school-age children nationwide seems reasonable, acknowledging wide variations within and between states.

The ratio of practitioners to children has served as a barometer for judging quantitatively the acceptability of services. Although only rough indicators of the quality of service provision, the ratio has been an important index of services for several decades (see, e.g., Charvat, 2005; Feinberg, Nujiens, & Canter, 2005).

Reported Service Ratios

The ratio of school psychologists to school-age children continued to improve throughout the 20th century (Curtis et al., 1999; Curtis et al., 2006; Fagan, 1988b), although with wide variation within and among states. The range may be as high (favorable) as one school psychologist to 535 schoolchildren (1:535) or as low (unfavorable) as 1:7,946 in some settings (Charvat, 2005). The NASP (1999) membership renewal survey reported that 56% of 13,441 respondents worked with a ratio of 1:1,000 or less, and only 15% reported a ratio greater than 1:3,000. A survey based on the 1994–1995 school year (Curtis et al., 1999) reported approximately 49% of 1,430 respondents working with a ratio of 1:1,500 or less, and approximately 12% reported a ratio greater than 1:3,000. This estimate is consistent with an earlier survey finding of 1:1,875, which suggested the ratio had remained the same between 1989 and 1993 (Lund et al., 1998). Curtis et al. also reported regional estimates and discussed factors influencing the ratio (e.g., per pupil expenditures by state). Bramlett et al. (2002) reported a median ratio of 1:1,500 (26% were 1:1,000 or better; 49% were 1:2,000 or worse). In summary, an estimated ratio of one school psychologist to 1,500 students nationwide seems reasonable, acknowledging wide variations within and between states.

Professional Guidelines

Professional associations have recommended ideal ratios. For example, NASP (2000b) recommended 1:1,000, whereas the APA (1981) recommended 1:2,000. However, few state education agencies mandate a ratio in any form. NASP has recommended the ratio of 1:1,000 since 1984 (NASP, 1984b), but it no longer qualifies its ratio by also recommending a maximum of one school psychologist for four schools. Given the number of public school buildings in the country (i.e., about 94,000), the ratio already is approximately one school psychologist for every four school buildings, but only on a nationwide basis. At the local district level, many school psychologists serve more than four buildings and some serve only one. By comparison, the recommended ratio for school counselors is 1:250 and for school social workers it is 1:800 (Allensworth, Lawson, Nicholson, & Wyche, 1997). The national average for counselors, however, was reported as 1:477 (Feller, 2004), almost twice the recommended ratio.

Ratios by Setting

A comparison of ratios in rural and urban settings was done by Reschly and Connolly (1990), and historical comparisons of urban ratios were studied by Fagan and Schicke (1994). These studies suggest that the best ratios are in suburban settings and that rural and urban ratios do not differ significantly from each other or from the overall national ratio. Internationally, the median ratio was reported as 1:11,000 (Oakland & Cunningham, 1992; see chapter 10 for more details), and wide variation is observed (Jimerson et al., 2004).

10. To What Professional Associations Do School Psychologists Belong?

School psychologists belong to associations at the international, national, state, and local levels. The International School Psychology Association (ISPA) is the best source of information about school psychology in other countries. NASP and the APA's Division of School Psychology (Division 16) are the primary national organizations in the United States, with approximately 24,000 and 2,500 members, respectively. The Division of School Psychology is one of the APA's 56 divisions (150,000-plus members as of 2006). The Canadian Association of School Psychologists (CASP) is the primary association for school psychologists in Canada, although many belong to the Canadian Psychological Association. School psychologists belong to numerous secondary organizations as well (e.g., American Counseling Association and Council for Exceptional Children). Irrespective of their mission statements, the range of matters in which the APA and NASP are involved is enormous and beyond concise definition.

NASP and the APA's Division of School Psychology (Division 16) are the primary national organizations in the United States.

The APA Division of School Psychology

Division 16 was founded in 1945 and is the oldest national organizational entity for school psychologists. Its parent organization, the American Psychological Association, was founded in 1892 and is the oldest national psychological organization in the United States. The Division of School Psychology has an elected set of officers, representatives to the APA Council of Representatives (the APA's major governing body), and vice presidents for professional affairs; membership; education, training and scientific affairs; publication, communications, and convention affairs; and social, ethical, and ethnic affairs. Collectively they constitute the division's executive council, which along with several appointed positions (e.g., editors and student representatives) manages all aspects of the division except those reserved for the parent organization. Although without a central office of its own, the division has many business services provided by the APA and is housed in a large building in Washington, DC.

The National Association of School Psychologists

NASP was founded in 1969 and is the world's largest organization to exclusively serve the interests of school psychologists. It is governed by nationally elected officers and state-elected representatives to the NASP Delegates Assembly, NASP's primary legislative body. Each of its four regions has two delegate representatives, who with the elected officers and program managers constitute the executive council. The entire governing structure, including committee members, editors, etc., within program manager areas, exceeds 200 individuals. The policies and business of NASP are implemented through its central office staff in leased facilities in Bethesda, Maryland. Both NASP and the APA Division 16 have representatives to each other's governance meetings.

State and Regional Groups

Each state also has an organization of school psychologists that is usually an affiliate of NASP. In most instances, the state organization for school psychologists is independent of the state psychological association, though in a few states school psychologists are organized as part of the state psychology group. The network of state APA and state NASP affiliates is a product of, and contributor to, the two worlds of school psychology (education and psychology) that pervade the field's history. As discussed in other chapters, these two largely independent affiliate networks influence many state and national policies on training, accrediting, credentialing, and practice. Curtis et al. (2006) found that among NASP members, 72% belonged to a state school psychology association, 18% belonged to the APA, and 11% belonged to its Division of School Psychology. School psychologists are seldom organized regionally, but within states it is common for there to be regional and local groups affiliated with the state organization. Several state associations have descriptive and historical publications.

Association Membership

The cost of association membership varies considerably. Although annual dues of national associations are typically in excess of $100, state association dues may range from as little as $15 to as much as $100 (F. Smith, 1997). Most organizations have special student membership rates. Other classes of membership include associate, retired, and honorary. Faculty in school psychology training programs are typically members of Trainers of School Psychologists (TSP) or Council of Directors of School Psychology Programs (CDSPP). For information about professional associations and their development see Cummings (2005); Fagan (1993, 1996a, 2005d); Fagan, Gorin, and Tharinger (2000); Fagan, Hensley, and Delugach (1986); Oakland (1993, 2005); Phelps (2005); and Phillips (1993).

11. What Are the Major Journals and Newsletters in the Field of School Psychology?

Many journals are available to school psychologists either through professional associations or on related issues.

Primary Journals

School psychology journals are available to association members or on a subscription basis. Journals received as part of membership in NASP include NASP's *School Psychology Review* and *School Psychology Forum: Research in Practice* (an electronic publication). APA members receive Division 16's *School Psychology Quarterly* (an official APA journal as of 2007) and the *American Psychologist*. CASP members receive *Canadian Journal of School Psychology*. The ISPA has as its official journal *School Psychology International*, which is provided to members at a reduced subscription rate. Unaffiliated school psychology journals available by subscription include the *Journal of School Psychology, Psychology in the Schools, Journal of Applied School Psychology*, and *Journal of Educational and Psychological Consultation*. The content of school psychology journals is similar, though editorial policies vary (Wilczenski, Phelps, & Lawler, 1992).

Secondary Journals

Many other journals also may be of interest to school psychologists. Some deal with broad issues and practices in professional psychology (e.g., *Journal of Consulting and Clinical Psychology, Professional Psychology: Research and Practice*), some cover foundational research (e.g., *Developmental Psychology, Journal of Educational Research*), and some cover specific orientations or practices (e.g., *Behavior Therapy, Exceptional Children, Journal of Learning Disabilities, Journal of Psychoeducational Assessment,* and *Mental Retardation*). Although state associations commonly publish newsletters, they rarely publish a journal; however, one is the *California Journal of School Psychology* (Fagan, 1986a).

Newsletters

National and international groups publish newsletters several times each year. These include the APA's *Monitor on Psychology* and its Division of School Psychology's *The School Psychologist*, NASP's *Communiqué*, and the *Trainers' Forum* from the TSP. The *CDSPP Press* has not been published since 2002. An independent newspaper, *The National Psychologist*, is a useful source of information, especially for psychologists in private practice. NASP publishes many other newsletter-type formats, including its *NASP Announce* and several newsletters for special interest groups within the organization. Although school psychology newsletters are typically published by professional associations, *Today's School Psychologist,* published monthly by LRP publications, has been a private venture since 1997.

Online electronic versions of journals and newsletters are becoming more common. More information on the literature of school psychology can be found in Fagan, Delugach, Mellon, and Schlitt (1985); Fagan and Warden (1996); French (1986); and Whelan and Carlson (1986).

12. Do School Psychologists Have Standards for Professional Practice?

Two codes of ethics are employed by school psychologists in the United States: the American Psychological Association's *Ethical Principles of Psychologists and Code of Conduct* (APA, 2002) and the NASP Professional Conduct Manual, *The Principles for Professional Ethics: Guidelines for the Provision of School Psychological Services* (NASP, 2000a; also see appendixes C and D in this book). In some instances, a state association of school psychologists will adopt one or both of these codes or may prepare its own. Ethics codes also have been developed or adopted by CASP (see chapter 9) and by ISPA (see chapter 10). In addition, standards for the provision of school psychological services attempt to specify acceptable levels at which services should be provided (APA, 1981; NASP, 2000b). These standards are expressed in terms of service ratios, employment conditions, breadth of services, agency relationships, and so on. Ethics and standards are discussed in chapter 7.

13. What Contract and Salary Arrangements Are Most Common?

Contracts, salaries, and benefits vary with setting and position. The following sections describe ranges and other considerations.

Terms of Appointment

Full-time employment of at least 40 hours a week is the most common employment arrangement. Curtis et al. (2006) reported that 50.4% of practitioners held contracts of 180–190 days, and 33.6% held contracts of 200 days or more. Reschly and Wilson (1992) reported that the average number of days in the school psychologist's contract was 202, and the median was 192. Curtis et al. (1999) reported similar data based on the 1994–1995 school year. The 1999 NASP membership renewal survey reported that 55% had contracted for 180–199 days and 20% for 200–219 days. Because a school year is typically about 180–185 days, the survey data translate into a school year plus 2–4 weeks. These data are consistent with earlier data (Graden & Curtis, 1991) and suggest that the trend has been toward increased numbers of 10-month contracts despite the continued popularity of 9-month contracts.

Salaries

A paper presented at the NASP 2006 Annual Convention reported an average salary of $60,581, which included faculty, practitioners, and others in the NASP membership survey of 2004–2005 (Curtis et al., 2006). APA salary studies of full-time school-based psychology employees in 2001 revealed a median salary of $61,000 for non-doctoral-degree holders and $77,000 for doctoral licensed school psychologists, 70% of whom were in precollege educational settings (Singleton, Tate, & Randall, 2003). The APA study of 2003 doctorates employed in 2003–2004 found that school psychologists in school settings had median and mean salaries of $47,000 and $48,129, respectively (Wicherski & Kohout, 2005).

A paper presented at the NASP 2006 Annual Convention reported an average salary of $60,581.

According to the Bureau of Labor Statistics the median salary of school psychologists was $54,480 in 2002. In comparison, teachers that year had a median salary of $44,499. On the basis of the 1999 NASP membership renewal data, Thomas (1999a) reported median and average practitioner salaries of $48,000 and $49,089, respectively. In 1994 the average salary was reported to be $43,000 (Dawson, Mendez, & Hyman, 1994). Earlier, Reschly and Wilson (1992) reported a median salary for practitioners of $35,800 and an average salary of $37,587. It appears that salaries grew by about 50% in the period 1992–2002. Chamberlin (2006) reported very favorable salary data from various sources, including an APA survey indicating that the average school psychologist salary in 2003 was $78,000, among the highest in the psychology subfields. The varied findings of the studies may reflect smaller numbers of respondents and salaries for 11- and 12-month positions rather than the 9-and 10-month positions held by most practitioners.

Factors Influencing Salaries

Thomas (1999b) presented salary data in combination with years of experience and education, revealing that salaries rose as a function of both. Dawson, Mendez, and Hyman (1994) provided data for a full-time practitioner's salary by age, gender, degree, and NCSP status, but not in combination (it is still a useful source of earlier data). Thomas and Witte (1996) made similar comparisons from a sampling of 10 states. Factors influencing salaries is a frequent topic on the NASP Listserv. Salaries appear to range widely as a function of graduate degree, contract length, years of experience, teacher versus nonteacher pay schedules, NCSP status, critical-shortage pay, and bilingual competence. Although additional pay for NCSP status is of interest to practitioners, and some states pay several thousand more for this, most provide no additional compensation and the issue is controversial across Listserv respondents. Gender differences in salaries, if any, are confounded by indications that men and women differ in the distribution of their experience and degrees (Thomas & Witte, 1996). Differences often are not large between specialist- (EdS) and doctoral-level salary schedules. Of course, the principles of supply and demand operate as well, with some areas willing to pay considerably higher salaries owing to the relative scarcity of practitioners. A starting salary for a fully trained and credentialed beginning school psychologist in a school setting could range from $35,000 to $65,000. In most instances, an administrative position would provide higher pay partly because such positions involve 12-month contracts.

Collective Bargaining

Some school psychologists may belong to unions or other collective bargaining groups, which may also affect salaries. Collective bargaining is more common in urban areas, where the school psychologists more often belong to the teachers' association and/or bargaining unit or may have their own bargaining unit. Curtis et al. (1999) reported that 38.4% of respondents belonged to a union. The relative stability of such affiliation is observed in the findings of Curtis et al. (2006), where the figures were 34.4% (National Education Association), 9.7% (American Federation of Teachers), and 29.5% (local unit).

Nonschool Practice

The relationship of salary and setting is not clear, though salaries in nonschool settings may be higher. The additional salary, however, may be attenuated by the costs of liability insurance, equipment, travel, and the length of the contract. This is especially true of private practice settings. Some school psychologists choose to work part-time, a phenomenon that may become more popular as a larger number of practitioners retire but seek continued employment. Reschly and Wilson (1992) reported that part-time employment was typically a personal preference rather than a necessity. They also reported that 35% of school psychologists were engaged in some amount of outside secondary employment, averaging about $6,800 in additional income. However, as was mentioned earlier (see employment settings), only a small percentage of school psychologists engage in private practice and even fewer engage in this full-time. More recent nonschool salary data are not available.

14. What Does the Employment Market Look Like?

Despite occasional economic downturns, employment opportunities for school psychologists have been consistently favorable throughout the history of the field (Fagan, 2004b). Substantial vacancies existed for the 1987–1988 school year, and an updated report for 1989–1990 by Connolly and Reschly (1990) identified more than 500 vacancies for that year. Although the recessionary times of the early 1990s tightened school district budgets, the job market continued to be characterized by greater demand than supply, and the personnel shortage may have lessened (Lund et al., 1998). Reschly and Wilson (1992) found that of the 23% reporting that they had not worked for 1 or more years since being certified as a school psychologist, only 15% of those individuals indicated "job not available" as the reason. The three more prevalent reasons were other professional work (32%), family responsibilities (20%), and graduate school (16%). A special 2004 issue of *Psychology in the Schools* covered the 2002 school psychology Futures Conference, which discussed concerns about personnel shortages in practitioner and academic settings (Vol. 41, No. 4). A 2004 listing of APA-accredited programs showed that 24% were seeking new faculty. In fall 2006, it was reported that 72 school psychology positions existed at 63 institutions; about half were at the assistant professor level (Tingstrom, 2006). Academic psychology positions were ranked among the top 10 of 50 positions in *Money* magazine, and school psychology positions were expected to be "particularly fast growing because of increased public understanding of the link between mental health and learning" (Chamberlin, 2006, p. 7).

School psychology has been listed among the top areas on GradSchool.com and was featured in the online APA magazine *GradPsych* as a postgraduate growth area (Greer, 2005). According to the magazine, "The Bureau of Labor Statistics reports that school psychology will be among the five fastest growing doctoral-level occupations through 2012" (p. 32). Personnel turnover and retirements are factors in continued job opportunities. The most favorable opportunities will be in rural and geographically isolated areas, in school systems that are under pressure to increase psychological services, and in many urban locales. The shortages exist in practitioner and in academic settings, and the employment market continues to look favorable for doctoral as well as nondoctoral personnel. Although market forces have made private practice a more challenging employment sector, continued opportunities are expected to be favorable.

Employment opportunities for school psychologists have been consistently favorable throughout the history of the field.

PRIMARY ROLES OF THE SCHOOL PSYCHOLOGIST

For the past 80 years school psychology practitioners and their trainers have considered the roles school psychologists play in the educational setting and how those roles should expand. Some believe that school psychologists should do more than merely

It is the school psychologist's assessment expertise, viewed in its broadest context, that has been the basis of the growth and success of school psychology.

administer and score the psychoeducational tests used by the educational bureaucracies to remove children from the educational mainstream and place them in special educational programs. The literature of this group contends that the schools, not to mention the school psychologists themselves, would be better served by taking on nontesting roles such as interventions, including individual and group therapy, consultation, research and evaluation, and in-service education. University trainers often espouse the nontraditional model. Interns and first-year practitioners are apt to experience shock when they realize that the many roles for which they had been prepared are viewed as secondary to the psychoeducational evaluations and reevaluations they are expected to complete on the job.

The predominance of the assessment role of school psychologists has continued into the 21st century, but it has expanded to include two other major roles: interventions and consultation. These three roles account for most of the school psychologist's time. However, all the roles of the school psychologist are based on assessment. Educational placement decisions require assessment data, yet so do effective case consultations, which require consultants to assess the relevant characteristics of the context and parties involved. Effective family therapy requires assessment of the family members individually and as a group. Effective staff or system development requires assessment of the strengths and weaknesses of the individuals in the system. Thus, all roles have underlying assessment functions.

It is the school psychologist's assessment expertise, in the context of the expanded roles of intervention and consultation, that has been the basis of the growth and success of school psychology. Where criticism of the assessment or *child study* role is expressed, the concern is not that it involves testing and other assessment-related tasks. Rather, the criticism is that too often the assessment ends when the results of testing are presented; the data are not used in the next phases of intervention at individual, group, family, and system levels.

The California Association of School Psychologists (1991) approved a formal position on assessment that states in part,

> Assessment is the cornerstone of educational and psychological services delivery. Assessment is required to define pupil needs, guide children's education, and to provide data which may be used to evaluate educational outcomes. Educational research shows that assessment is necessary because individualized interventions and educational programs conducted without ongoing assessment may be detrimental to children, because (a) programs not based on empirical data are often based on flawed assumptions regarding the nature and causes of problems; (b) programs often raise unrealistic expectations, which impair future intervention efforts; and (c) programs without data are unaccountable, and cannot be adequately evaluated to determine whether resources are appropriately allocated. (p. 4)

The California association's position embraced traditional school psychologist functions, including psychoeducational testing, but it also emphasized the importance of assessment at all levels, for individuals, programs, and systems.

More recently, there are organized efforts to involve school psychologists in the broader mental health and prevention roles, with less traditional normative assessment functions and increased use of nontraditional models that are linked more directly to interventions, such as criterion-referenced and curriculum-based models and functional-behavioral assessment models (also called problem-solving assessment models; see, e.g., Grimes, Kurns, & Tilley, 2006). These roles and applications are consistent with the legacy of psychoeducational assessment among school psychologists.

In summary, this publication endorses a model of school psychology practice that combines the complementary assessment and intervention roles that agree with ideas expressed in *School Psychology: A Blueprint for Training and Practice III* (Ysseldyke et al., 2006); the *helping process* put forth by Maier (1969); the positions of Susan Gray (1963b) and of Roger Reger (1965), who viewed the school psychologist as a "data-oriented problem solver" and as an "educational programmer," respectively; the views on alternative delivery systems (see, e.g., Ysseldyke & Christenson, 1988); and broader ecological service models (Sheridan & Gutkin, 2000). The future of the profession, therefore, is to not lose sight of the fact that school psychologists have been, and will continue to be, the professionals who are best trained in assessment in most educational settings and therefore logically the best qualified for intervention as well.

Chapter 2

Historical Development of School Psychology

Study of the history and development of psychology illustrates where modern school psychology fits in the overall evolution of U.S. society and education. In the opening segment of the respected Public Broadcasting System's television series *Cosmos*, Carl Sagan described the evolution of the universe in a 1-year cosmic calendar in which each month represented 1.25 billion years, each minute 30,000 years, and each second 500 years (also see Sagan, 1977). Sagan noted that not until 10:30 p.m. of the last day of the cosmic calendar year do the first humans appear, and the emergence of cities did not occur until 11:59:35! From Sagan's analogy, everything important to the history of school psychological services and the structure of U.S. schooling has occurred in the last quarter of a second of Sagan's calendar. No significant aspect of contemporary school psychology, including its practitioners, training programs, or credentials, existed before the 1890s. Thus, although the histories of school psychology and education are fairly long in some respects, they are quite short in the broader development of society. Such a perspective is a reminder that schooling and psychological services are quite recent, often untested, and subject to improvement.

The centennial celebration of the American Psychological Association (APA) in 1992 served as a stimulus for the historical study of psychology. Several investigations have clarified origins, trends, events, and individuals significant to the development of school psychology, but although considerable research has been done, numerous areas of research continue to be worthy of attention (Fagan, 1990c). This chapter is a synopsis of that ongoing research and of the development and growth of school psychology in the United States. The discussion only touches on the concurrent social, economic, and political history, and the historical development of related professional fields. A chronological discussion of school psychology organizes the major developments that occurred over several decades within two periods: the *hybrid* years and the *thoroughbred* years. For a general analysis of the history of professional psychology in America, see Benjamin and Baker (2004).

Note: Portions of this chapter are excerpted from a chapter by Fagan (1990a) and cited here with permission of the National Association of School Psychologists, from a chapter by Fagan (1990b) and cited here with permission of Lawrence Erlbaum Associates, Inc., and from an article by Fagan (1992) and cited here with the permission of the American Psychological Association.

THE HYBRID YEARS AND THE THOROUGHBRED YEARS DEFINED

School psychology's period of historical development can be divided into the hybrid years (1890–1969) and the thoroughbred years (1970–present). These are arbitrary timelines between two overlapping but different historical periods. The first was a period when "school" psychology often was a blend of many education and psychology practitioners loosely mobilized around a dominant role of psychoeducational assessment for special class placement. Even in the latter decades of the hybrid years, school psychology was a mix of practitioners certified in various fields, many from teacher education or guidance and counseling, who entered school psychology as an "add on" to their existing education credentials. The thoroughbred years, though certainly not void of the earlier theme, differ from the hybrid years because of the growth in the number of training programs, practitioners, and state and national associations, and the expansion of literature and regulations, all of which have contributed to a stabilized professional entity called school psychology.

During the hybrid years, although some states had established a professional identity for school psychology, that identity was not consistent across the United States. The more developed states such as California, Connecticut, Illinois, Ohio, New Jersey, New York, and Pennsylvania provided leadership and direction that other states then followed into the thoroughbred years. Even in developed states, however, the professional identity and development were more noticeable in urban and suburban locales (Mullen, 1967). Though some rural services existed, the growth of psychological and special educational services was confined mainly to urban schools. Surveys by Van Sickle, Witmer, and Ayres (1911) and Wallin (1914) revealed that special education and psychological services were most prevalent in the northeast and Great Lakes regions and in large urban and city school districts. The urban settings, having the most schoolchildren, were most pressed for adjustments to meet district and children's needs. Many rural settings lagged behind in the provision of services for several decades. Not until the latter decade of the hybrid years and the era of the Education for All Handicapped Children Act of 1975 (now IDEA) were widespread rural services observed. In the thoroughbred years states began offering school psychology credentials for professionals who completed accredited school psychology training programs.

School psychology's historical development can be divided into the hybrid years (1890–1969) and the thoroughbred years (1970–present).

Box 2.1 provides a chronology of school psychology's historical events and landmarks. Each chronological period is labeled according to its most salient characteristics and not necessarily the accomplishments of that decade. In this format, the activities of a particular decade can be linked to the accomplishments seen in later decades. For example, the decade of the 1950s was an era of strong effort toward professional identity, even though that identity was not generally accomplished across most of the United States until the 1970s.

Box 2.1 A Chronology of Events and Landmarks in the History of School Psychology

I. The Hybrid Years (1890–1969)

1890–1909 Origins of Practice

1890 Cattell publishes article on mental tests
1892 Founding of the first U.S. organization for psychologists, the American Psychological Association
1896 First psychological clinic is established by Lightner Witmer at the University of Pennsylvania
1898 Term *school psychologist* first appears in English language literature
1899 First school-based psychological clinic is founded in Chicago public schools
1905 First version of the Binet-Simon Scales is published
1907 First practitioner journal, *The Psychological Clinic,* is founded and published
1908 First internships in clinical psychology at the Vineland Training School in New Jersey
1909 Rochester, New York, public schools appoint a Binet examiner

1910–1929 Expansion and Acceptance

1910 Cincinnati public school district starts Vocational Bureau
1910 Term *school psychologist* appears in the German language literature
1911 Term *school psychologist* again appears in English language literature following German translation
1912 First psychoeducational clinic (University of Pittsburgh)
1913 First survey of practitioners/examiners (Wallin)
1915 Gesell is first person appointed with title *school psychologist* and serves in Connecticut until 1919
1916 Terman publishes Stanford revision of the Binet-Simon Scales (Terman, 1916)
1917 Founding of first organization for clinical psychologists (American Association of Clinical Psychologists)
1919 APA Section of Clinical Psychology is founded
1923 First journal article with *school psychologist* in title is published (Hutt, 1923)
1925 New York City school district establishes first psychologist licensing exam
1928 New York University offers first training program in school psychology

1930–1939 Emerging Regulation

1930 First book on school psychology is published (Hildreth, 1930)
1932 Association of Consulting Psychologists is founded
1935 New York establishes first state department of education certification standards
1937 Pennsylvania establishes state department of education certification standards
1937 First applied psychology association with subdivisions is founded (American Association of Applied Psychologists)
1938 Pennsylvania State University initiates PhD in school psychology

continued

Box 2.1 *Continued*

1940–1949 Organizational Identity

1942 Special issue of *Journal of Consulting Psychology* on school psychology is published
1943 First state association is founded (Ohio School Psychologists Association)
1945 APA reorganizes into divisional structure and provides first organizational identity for school psychologists (Division 16, APA)
1945 Connecticut enacts first psychologist licensure
1947 First accreditation of clinical psychology programs by APA
1947 Division 16 publishes first national school psychology newsletter
1949 Boulder Conference on clinical psychology is held in Colorado

1950–1959 Professional Identity

1951 Northwestern Conference for counseling psychology is held in Illinois
1952 APA accreditation is extended to counseling psychology
1953 University of Illinois starts first recognized/organized doctoral program in school psychology
1953 APA publishes its first code of ethics
1954 National Council for Accreditation of Teacher Education is established
1954 Ohio State Department of Education establishes first state-approved internships
1954 Thayer Conference in West Point, New York, is first national conference on school psychology

1960–1969 Training and Practitioner Growth

1962 First school psychology journal is founded in Ohio (*Journal of School Psychology*)
1962 National Council for Accreditation of Teacher Education (NCATE) has first reference to school psychology programs
1963 Second school psychology journal founded (*Psychology in the Schools*)
1963 Peabody Conference on the school psychology internship is held in Tennessee
1968 Ohio hosts invitational conference on school psychology
1969 Organizational meeting to form a national group is held in St. Louis
1969 First national organization exclusively for school psychologists is founded (National Association of School Psychologists)

II. The Thoroughbred Years (1970–Present)

1970–1979 Trainer and Practitioner Regulation, Association Identity and Growth, Professional Division

1971 APA gives first accreditation of a school psychology program at University of Texas–Austin
1972 NASP founds journal, *School Psychology Digest* (now *School Psychology Review*), and renames its newsletter *Communiqué*
1973 Section 504 of Rehabilitation Act is enacted

continued

1974 NASP publishes its first *Principles for Professional Ethics*
1975 Public Law 94-142, Education for All Handicapped Children Act of 1975, is enacted
1976 NASP affiliates with NCATE
1977 First training and certification directories are published by NASP
1978 APA/NASP Task Force is established
1978 NASP publishes standards for training, field placements, credentialing, and service provision
1979 *School Psychology International* journal is founded

1980–1989 Professional Reorganization

1980 Spring Hill Symposium is held in Wayzata, Minnesota
1981 Olympia Conference is held in Oconomowoc, Wisconsin
1981 APA publishes specialty guidelines, including those for school psychology
1982 International School Psychology Association founded
1983 First joint APA/NCATE accreditation of a school psychology program occurs (University of Cincinnati)
1985 Canadian Association of School Psychologists is founded
1985 *Canadian Journal of School Psychology* is founded
1985 *Professional School Psychology* (now *School Psychology Quarterly*) journal is founded by APA Division 16
1988 NASP initiates folio review system for training program approval and approves first programs through NCATE
1988 American Psychological Society is founded (becomes the Association for Psychological Science in 2005)
1988 NASP initiates National Certification System
1988 First National School Psychology Examination is administered
1989 First National Certification in School Psychology is granted

1990–1999 Stable Growth, Reform, Identity Reconsidered

1991 Concern builds about personnel shortages
1991 First APA-accredited school district internship occurs in the Dallas, Texas, public schools
1992 American Board of Professional Psychology creates specialty boards, including American Board of School Psychology (ABSP)
1993 American Academy of School Psychology is founded
1994 Society for the Study of School Psychology is founded
1996 APA Division 16 reconsiders its name and the definition of school psychology
1997 Official specialty recognition by APA is granted to school psychology, through the Commission on the Recognition of Specialties and Proficiencies in Professional Psychology (CRSPPP)
1998 Implementation of NASP governance changes

2000–Present: Prosperity, and Broadening Identity and Practice

2001 Concern for personnel shortages continues

continued

Box 2.1 *Continued*

2001	Passage of No Child Left Behind (NCLB) Act draws practice further into regular school arena
2002	Futures Conference is held at Indiana University
2002	APA/NASP Interorganizational Committee (formerly Task Force) is disbanded
2002	*Journal of Applied School Psychology* is founded
2004	Reauthorization of IDEA is predicted to have substantial effect on practice, for example, learning disability diagnoses, evidence-based interventions, and response to intervention
2005	CRSPPP reapproves school psychology specialty recognition
2006	NASP establishes online journal, *School Psychology Forum: Research in Practice*

THE HYBRID YEARS (1890–1969)

This arbitrary historical period marked the first appearance of school psychology. Though not a true profession, it would emerge as education and psychology practitioners loosely mobilized around a common goal of helping children within the schools.

Origins of Practice and Expansion (1890–1920)

The origins of school psychological services can be traced to an era of social reform in the late 19th and early 20th centuries. Several reform movements were related to the emergence of school psychological services. Among these movements were compulsory schooling, juvenile courts, child labor laws, mental health, vocational guidance, the growth of institutions serving children, and an array of other child-saving efforts (Cohen, 1985; Cravens, 1985; Siegel & White, 1982).

Changing Status of Children and Youth

In contrast to earlier generations, which viewed the father as savior of the child (the child as redeemable), there was at the turn of the century strong sensitivity to the proposition that in children lay the salvation of society (the child as redeemer; Wishy, 1968). Thus, by improving the conditions of children's lives, particularly through systematic education, society hoped to overcome many of the problems of the urban United States and stem the fearful erosion of U.S. moral and economic values in the wake of immigration, urban growth, and industrialization (Cohen, 1985; Cravens, 1985; Cremin, 1988; Cubberley, 1909).

The notion that by properly educating children society could rise above its problems has been a pervasive theme in U.S. education.

The "child-savers" operated from the assumption that "children constituted a special, vulnerable group in the population whose members should be protected through public policies" (Cravens, 1987, p. 159). According to Hoag and Terman (cited in Cubberley, 1920): "The children of today must be viewed as the raw material of a new State; the schools as the nursery of the Nation. To conserve this raw material is as logical a function of the State as to conserve the natural resources of coal, iron, and water power" (p. 683). This viewpoint toward children evolved over a long period, during which attitudes and practices about schooling shifted from the home to community agencies outside the home, and the model of the family shifted from primarily patriarchal to separate spheres for father and mother. The meaning of children and childhood changed from an economic source of labor to a psychological source of love and affection (Zelizer, 1985). Children were important not just for their potential labor asset but also for their psychological meaning as representatives of the next generation of American adults.

The notion that by properly educating children society could rise above its problems has been a pervasive theme in U.S. education. At least in theory, even when problems were known not to be intrinsic to children, it would be the proper instruction of children that would alleviate the problems of society (e.g., delinquency, unemployment, and poverty). Because children held the key to the future, and the schools were places in which all children congregated for several years, the school curriculum came to represent a major opportunity for societal intervention.

Compulsory Schooling

The preeminent force behind the need for school psychological services was compulsory schooling, which reciprocally influenced child study and clinical psychology. Field (1976) suggests two complementary explanations for the growth of compulsory schooling. The "human capital" explanation contends that compulsory schooling emerged in response to the need for a more educated labor force to coincide with increasing industrialization, whereas the "structural reinforcement" explanation contends that issues of social order and the need to maintain the character and social structure of society drove the growth of compulsory schooling. Related to the human capital explanation is the possibility that labor unions encouraged compulsory schooling as part of their resistance to the use of children in the workplace. Also, along with the structural reinforcement and human capital explanations, a humanistic motive must be considered (Cohen, 1985). Tyack (1976) divided the compulsory schooling movement into a "symbolic" stage (1850–1890) and a "bureaucratic" stage (after 1890). In the latter stage, "school systems grew in size and complexity, new techniques of bureaucratic control emerged, ideological conflict over compulsion diminished, strong laws were passed, and school officials developed sophisticated techniques to bring truants into schools" (p. 359). It was an era in which scientific and bureaucratic experts were on the rise as specialists and administrators worked in increasingly segmented school systems. School systems included divisions for "elementary, junior high, and high schools; vocational programs of several kinds; classes for the handicapped; counseling services; research and testing bureaus" (p. 374). The first state to enact a compulsory attendance law was Massachusetts in 1852, and the last was Mississippi in 1918.

The condition of education created the need for specialized school services to work in conjunction with the small but growing services in remedial and special education.

The increasing enactment and enforcement of compulsory attendance laws between 1870 and 1930 dramatically changed public education. Table 2.1 reveals the unprecedented growth in enrollment and financial commitment the nation made to public education during this period. The condition of U.S. education in that era of heavy immigration, compulsory education, and child labor laws created the need for specialized school services to work in conjunction with the small but growing services in remedial and special education. School enrollment increased dramatically and included many children who had not been in school previously or had been unsuccessful in school, and yet whose attendance was now required.

With regard to the origins of school psychology, the change in the scope of schooling was even more important than the change in its size. The combination of compulsory attendance, large numbers of immigrant children, and poor child health and hygiene forced upon the schools a large segment of the population that had only occasionally, if ever, regularly attended school. Not only were more children, of more diverse backgrounds, attending school for longer periods, many had little or no prior record of schooling, and a child's age was not a reliable estimate of proper grade placement (Thorndike, 1912). A single classroom might have children whose ages differed by 6 years.

Prevalence of Physical and Mental Defects

Compulsory schooling quickly necessitated adjustments of the educational system. Among these were mandatory medical examinations, or "inspections." A survey by Wallin (1914) provided a vivid description of the poor general health of the school population. Wallin contended that "physical defects in children are not restricted to any clime, race, environment or social condition" (pp. 5–6). Summarizing his nationwide surveys he stated:

> The percentage of pupils of various defects are as follows: defective teeth (one or more cavities, serious malocclusion), from 50 to 95%; defective vision and adenoids and nasal obstruction, from 5 to 20%; seriously enlarged or diseased tonsils, 5 to 15%; curvature of the spine, 2 to 7%; malnutrition, 1 to 6%; weak or tubercular lungs and defective hearing, 1 to 2%. It is estimated that 12,000,000 of the pupils in the public schools of the country are to some extent handicapped by one or more physical defects. (pp. 5–6)

The attention to physical defects is understandable in an era of much poorer medical knowledge and practice. It was widely regarded that defects of physical

Table 2.1 Comparison of Attendance and Enrollment Data for 1890 and 1930

	1890	1930
Average days in school year	135	173
Average days attended per pupil	86	143
Public school enrollment	12,723,000	25,678,000
Public secondary school enrollment	203,000	4,399,000
Total Expenditures	$140,507,000	$2,316,790,000

Source: Snyder, Hoffman, and Geddes (1997).

health could be symptomatic of defects in ability, school achievement, and behavior as well. In addition to noting physical defects, Wallin noted that mental defects and related educational problems necessitated psychological inspections. Because good physical hygiene was considered a precursor to mental hygiene and educational attainment, both medical and psychological inspections were important. Thus medical and psychological inspections were among the early adjustments to compulsory schooling made by school districts. According to Wallin, failing students should be given a physical examination to detect

> defects of the eyes, ears, nose, throat, teeth, glandular system, lungs, heart, nutrition, nervous disorders, etc.; and a psychological examination . . . for the detection of intellectual retardation and anomalies of sensation, movement, memory, imagination, association, attention, imitation, color perception, speech, number sense, fatigue, and for the determination of indices of stature, weight, vitality and dynamometry, etc. (p. 17)

Wallin's data also provided a basis for extending the logic of compulsory schooling to the provision of services for the exceptional child. If the child was to be compelled to attend school, "is it not his right, under a parity of reasoning, to demand that the state put him in such condition that he can assimilate those contents demanded of him by a compulsory attendance law?" (Wallin, 1914, pp. 17–18). Here was the ideology for why children having physical and mental handicaps should have special treatment. Thus compulsory schooling necessitated the management of children with varied mental and physical conditions and demanded that ways be found to cope with such conditions for a longer period of time, typically ages 7–14. During this same period, concerns for the general health of all children encouraged the rise of pediatric medicine (King, 1993).

Medical and psychological inspections were among the early adjustments to compulsory schooling.

Emergence of Special Education

Compulsory schooling laws ushered in the need for enforcement, resulting in the training and hiring of truancy officers to carry out the law. Concern quickly developed about dropouts and their future. The issue of truancy has pervaded education since the enactment of compulsory attendance laws and continues to be a concern for both regular and special education students (Christie, 2005). Enforcement of compulsory attendance came about gradually and only for "normal" schoolchildren, because many states did not provide comprehensive services for the handicapped, which would enable them to attend school, until legislative initiatives of the post–World War II era. Nevertheless, the schools were inundated with unanticipated children with disorders and forced to cope by using unproven interventions. These conditions were particularly acute in the school systems of major cities, which enrolled large percentages of students with "mental, physical, and moral" impairments, the three primary categories of exceptionality used at that time.

During this period special education programs emerged, and although they were small in number by current comparisons, they were available in many urban and some rural school systems by 1910 (Van Sickle, Witmer, & Ayers, 1911; Wallin, 1914). These sources do not provide figures about the total number of children then served in special education. However, the Van Sickle et al. (1911) study concluded that the top and bottom 4% of the school population were gifted and feebleminded, respectively, and that large numbers of students were normal intellectually but were students "for whom the present school curriculum and regime are ill adapted" (p. 18). This last group was mostly boys who made slow progress in school, and in the average city the group constituted one third of the student population. Dunn's (1973) figure for 1922 mostly included children with mental retardation. The studies suggest that the number of children in need of services and those enrolled were vastly discrepant. Dunn's figures are therefore conservative and based only on the numbers being served. The studies suggest that approximately the same percentage of the school population (10–12%) were in need of special services throughout the 20th century. However, the makeup of the exceptional child population and the related problems of these children would change considerably. As medical and public health technology improved, fewer children would be handicapped by physical health conditions. An example of this change is the decline in the use of open air classes for children having respiratory distress and the virtual disappearance of school physicians by mid-century.

Approximately the same percentage of the school population (10–12%) were in need of special services throughout the 20th century.

The early categories of special education and their nomenclature were considerably different from those of recent times. Special classes were provided for truant, delinquent, backward, adult education, and other categories that today are outside the legislated scope of special education and that reflected the "human capital" and the "structural reinforcement" explanations of compulsory schooling. That is, special educational arrangements were offered by the schools for adults and children to enhance both their employability (human capital) and their adjustment to U.S. society (structural reinforcement).

Corresponding to the segregationist ideology of the period, seriously atypical children most often were "educated" in facilities apart from the regular school, and most school psychologists were hindered from making contributions to regular education programs owing to heavy caseloads with referrals for special class placement. Hall (1911) put the segregationist position quite bluntly, stating, "Habits of stupidity and ineptness are often more contagious than are the examples of the best workers. This is why the elimination of the stupids is so urgent and so often effected today by segregating them in various ways" (p. 607). Wallin (1914) believed the psychological clinic should serve as an educational clearinghouse for the segregation of feebleminded and backward pupils from average and bright pupils—some to be segregated temporarily, others permanently, often through institutionalization. Such segregationist practices have been observed throughout the twentieth century, although they declined as the ideology shifted toward mainstreaming of handicapped children, and their placement in what is now called the least restrictive environment, both of which were required by the Education for All the Handicapped Children Act of 1975 (Public Law 94-142) and subsequent reauthorizations of this law (IDEA). The trend also is reflected in a gradual shift in practices in several sectors including mental health, education, public health, medicine, and corrections (Pfeiffer & Reddy, 1999).

Emergence of School Psychological Services

Compulsory schooling was among the most potent forces in the emergence of special educational services. The subsequent need for experts to assist in the process of child selection, and their educational segregation, led to an increasingly bureaucratic segmentation of the public schools. The increased school enrollments and subsequent need for specialized programs provided fertile ground for the emergence of pupil personnel services (PPS), including truancy or attendance officers, guidance counselors, school nurses and physicians, school psychologists, school social workers, speech and language clinicians, and vocational counselors. With required attendance, attendance officers were among the earliest PPS workers. Concerns about dropouts led to the emergence of vocational and guidance counselors. The need for special education programs and assistance in determining eligibility quickly involved school psychological personnel. As the concept of PPS spread across regular and special education, other PPS workers emerged to deal with atypical children.

Early use of the term *school psychologist* in the English literature appears to have emanated from Munsterberg's (1898) discussion in the *Educational Review* and from Stern's (1911) article translated from the German literature (Fagan, 2005a). There is also evidence that Binet and Henri (1894) used the term in the context of experimental psychology research in the school setting (J. Cunningham, personal communication, 2005). Nevertheless, the term was not widely used for many years. The term *clinical psychologist* was in greater use, reflecting the generic orientation of Witmer's conceptualizations in which clinical psychology was considered to be a methodology used by psychologists in many settings with a variety of clients as opposed to a separate specialization per se (Witmer, 1907). The development of distinct specialties occurred after the 1920s (Fagan, 1993).

School psychological services existed only to a limited extent and were delivered directly or indirectly to children by agencies inside or outside the school. They were based on the available methodologies of child study and clinical psychology, and were provided by the pioneers in these new fields. It is reasonable, therefore, to hypothesize that among the primary reasons for securing and employing school psychologists was the specific notion of having them help educators sort children reliably into segregated educational settings where they might be more successful individually and where their absence would help the system itself function better for the masses of "average" children. In essence, pupil personnel services that included school psychologists were not central to the system of schooling; rather, the services furthered the system's goals of educating the masses more efficiently while dealing with the problems such goals presented (see, e.g., Kaplan & Kaplan, 1985).

The concept of the school psychologist as an ancillary member of the system, and as a "gatekeeper" for special education, has a long historical precedent.

The concept of the school psychologist, therefore, as an ancillary member of the system, and as a "gatekeeper" for special education, has a long historical precedent. These images of the school psychologist are reflected in the analogy of school psychologists as "guests" in the house of education (Elliott & Witt, 1986b), and there are many historical and current accounts of discrepancies between school psychologists' perceptions of their role and function and those held by school administrators (e.g., Hughes, 1979; Moss & Wilson, 1998; Symonds, 1933). The guest analogy is discussed in chapter 3. A similar impact of compulsory schooling at the international level can be observed in Turkey following their recent increase in compulsory attendance laws from 5 years to 8 years of elementary education (Albayrak-Kaymak & Dolek, 1997).

Psychological services in the United States had their source in the activities of the psychologist Lightner Witmer at the clinic he founded at the University of Pennsylvania in 1896 (the first in the United States). Considered by many to be the father of clinical and school psychology, Witmer advocated the training of a "psychological expert who is capable of treating the many difficult cases that resist the ordinary methods of the school room" (Witmer, 1897, p. 117). Witmer also is credited with coining the term *clinical psychology* and publishing an early journal related to clinical services and handicapped children, *The Psychological Clinic* (Brotemarkle, 1931). The journal served as an outlet for disseminating Witmer's ideas of practice, the work of the first psychology clinic, and the work of other significant psychologists. The journal was considered to be a major publication for clinical psychologists until the time it ceased publication in 1935. It was widely circulated to practitioners and to college or university libraries. Witmer (1907) stressed an individualized approach that would use psychological knowledge to solve children's problems, especially problems related to schooling. A comprehensive account of Witmer's life and contributions appears in McReynolds (1997) and in a 1996 centennial tribute section of the *American Psychologist* (Vol. 51, No. 3).

Another major early figure was G. Stanley Hall, who founded the American Psychological Association (APA) in 1892, as well as several journals, including *American Journal of Psychology* and *Pedagogical Seminary* (now the *Journal of Genetic Psychology*). Hall was the father of the child study movement. Though Hall was not directly involved, the child study movement in Illinois influenced the establishment and functions of the Department of Scientific Pedagogy and Child Study in the Chicago Public Schools in 1899, the first clinic facility operated within the public schools (Slater, 1980). Wallin and Ferguson (1967) described the mix of normative and clinical casework conducted in the early years of this facility. Initiated with a research orientation, the Chicago clinic evolved quickly into a major school service agency. In contrast to Witmer's idiographic clinical method, Hall espoused a nomothetic approach that also was observed in the later work of his Clark University students Henry Goddard, Arnold Gesell, and Lewis Terman. English and English (1958) define *nomothetic* as "characterizing procedures and methods designed to discover general laws" and *idiographic* as "attempts to understand a particular event or individual" (p. 347). Slater (1980) contended that the relationship between psychology and education at that time was essentially symbiotic, with each needing the other to

Lightner Witmer (1867–1956)

Source: Reprinted by permission of the Archives of the History of American Psychology, University of Akron, Akron, Ohio.

advance. He surmised that Hall was the stimulus for education's response and that Witmer was a response to the stimulus provided by education. Both were important influences in establishing the 20th century as the first century in which the scientific study of children and adolescents occurred. Witmer and Hall were the bellwethers of early school psychology (Fagan, 1992). It was the intellectual descendants of Witmer and Hall who bridged their different concepts and practices and thus influenced the wider acceptance of school psychological services. A comprehensive account of Hall's life and contributions appears in Ross (1972).

Granville Stanley Hall (1844–1924)

Source: Reprinted by permission of the Archives of the History of American Psychology, University of Akron, Akron, Ohio.

Thus, early models of school psychological services evolved primarily from two orientations: idiographic clinical psychology and nomothetic educational psychology. These orientations can be seen in the variety of practices of the emerging clinics in the United States. Some of these clinics provided individualized services organized around case studies, whereas others were at least in part organized around research, studying individuals in terms of normative characteristics. At least in the early years of operation, the idiographic model could be observed in the practices of the clinic at the University of Pennsylvania and the nomothetic model in the Chicago Public Schools' Department of Scientific Pedagogy and Child Study.

These two orientations, singly or in combination, are observed throughout our history of training and practice. For example, school psychologists have continued to provide individualized psychological services while making categorical decisions for special education along normative lines of deviance. Thus the individual child study model, employing idiographic and nomothetic data, has been the primary identity of school psychologists and often has served to distinguish the field from related fields. School psychology's knowledge base and practice continue to be heavily influenced by developments in education and psychology and the research in these fields (Fry, 1986). The dual influences are further reflected in the recently reapproved specialty document for school psychology (Petition for reaffirmation of specialty of school psychology, 2005) and the most recent edition of *School Psychology: A Blueprint for Training and Practice III* (Ysseldyke et al., 2006).

Rise of Clinics and Psychoeducational Testing

Following the efforts of Witmer, Hall, and others, school-based and non-school-based clinics (sometimes called research bureaus or child study departments) spread quickly between 1900 and 1930, with most large-city school systems having access to some form of what was most often called *clinical psychology.* Child study services also were provided by clinics located in juvenile institutes, courts, universities, hospitals, vocational guidance bureaus, and other settings. These services were a mixture of educational and clinical psychology but were more akin to modern-day school psychology than to either current educational or clinical psychology. Late 19th-century developments in measurement and psychological science had laid the groundwork for the study of individual differences and test standardization. The spread of psychological services was spurred by the development of psychological and educational tests and the interest of school systems in segmenting their student population, especially according to what was considered intelligence.

Wallin's (1914) survey described the availability of clinics, the examiners' backgrounds, tests and inspection methods employed, and financial resources allocated to the task of early psychological inspections. His study identified clinics in several settings under various names, including 19 school-based clinics and their dates of establishment between 1899 in Chicago and 1914 in Detroit. He concluded that there were 26 clinics in institutions of higher learning; that more than 20 clinics were affiliated with correctional facilities, mental health institutions, vocational centers, and so on; and that 84 of the 103 city school systems that responded to the survey "report that psychological tests are given either by employees of the school boards or by outside agencies" (Wallin, 1914, p. 393). The clinic often was nothing more than a small room and a single examiner, and the psychological examination usually involved only the use of the Binet-Simon intelligence scale, a precursor of Goddard's Binet and Terman's Stanford-Binet examinations, or form board tests (Fagan, 1985). After reviewing the backgrounds of the 115 examiners identified as working in school-based clinics, Wallin concluded that only about one-fourth were qualified and the rest were nothing but amateur Binet testers (e.g., special class teachers, supervisors, or administrators, including school superintendents). Wallin's study revealed the variable conditions of psychological services, but he predicted the following:

> Psychology is destined to have not only a pedagogic but a clinical value for education. Eventually we shall have an independent science of clinical psychology or clinical education, instruction in which will be afforded in all of the large progressive normal schools and colleges of education. And we shall also have psychological or psycho-educational clinics in the large school systems, manned by psychological and educational experts, for the purpose of classifying the educational misfits. (pp. 20–21)

Following the introduction of Binet's scales in 1905 and especially the adaptations by Goddard and Terman, psychological testing was widespread by the 1920s. This led Hollingworth (1933) to comment that the situation "within the past 25 years has transformed Binet's name into a verb (nearly all teachers now know what it is to 'binet' a pupil)" (p. 371). The early years of the testing movement demonstrated the utility of ability and achievement tests for segregating individuals for specialized treatment. Although school personnel had been familiar with 19th-century work in phrenological and anthropometric measurement, it was the work of Binet and Simon in France, and the many adaptations of their tests in the United States, that truly spurred new conceptualizations within the individual testing movement. Phrenology had been the study of character and mental capacity from the conformation of the skull; certain brain segments were thought to control various characteristics, and protrusions were thought to represent strengths associated with that area. Phrenology was popular in the late 18th and much of the 19th century, but then lost credibility. Anthropometry was the study and technique of human body measurement for use in anthropological classification and comparison. It included such measures as a cephalic index (ratio of length to width of head), lung capacity, grip, and ratio of upper limb to lower limb. Anthropometric measurement was very popular in early school psychological assessment and could still be observed in practices of the 1920s.

The early years of the testing movement demonstrated the utility of ability and achievement tests for segregating individuals for specialized treatment.

World War I had a major influence on the development of standardized tests and their public acceptance. The Army Alpha and Beta tests demonstrated the utility of group devices in screening large numbers of army inductees in a short period of time, and the success of this effort brought public attention and acceptance of tests. Several versions of the Binet-Simon scales were available between 1910 and 1920, but it was Terman's Stanford Revision (Terman, 1916) that captured the attention of educators and psychologists for several decades. School achievement and aptitude tests also developed rapidly with the growth of educational psychology after 1910. The reliability of these scales and their associated levels of ability and achievement facilitated the development of categorical special education. A report on the services in the Cleveland (Ohio) Public Schools from 1918 through 1928 showed that test results were identifying children in the categories of bright, above average, normal, slow, dull, moron, imbecile, and idiot (Cleveland Public Schools, ca. 1928).

School Psychologist Roles and Functions

The development of group and individual ability and achievement tests in the early decades of the 20th century fulfilled educators' need for student differentiation. The tests also became the forte of psychologists serving educational settings. Although dissenters certainly existed, there was widespread acceptance of these tests and their use by educators and psychologists. Thus, psychological and educational tests quickly became the major tools of psychologists employed in school settings, and the administration and interpretation of these tests became the primary role and function of early school psychologists (see, e.g., Kehle, Clark, & Jenson, 1993).

Prior to World War II, interventions were only a modest aspect of many psychologists' roles, in or out of school settings, though some psychologists even then were engaged in intervention and consultation activities. Overall, testing had given applied psychologists, including school psychologists, a respectable methodology for practice, in part because many tests had developed out of earlier laboratory procedures that connected practitioners to academics. As applied psychology evolved, testing procedures developed along more pragmatic lines and were influenced by the interaction of applied psychologists and their clients (van Strein, 1998). That is, school psychologists' tools were developed and selected to answer specific questions of predictive validity needed by school districts rather than to simply provide a descriptive report of children's strengths or weaknesses. In this early period, therapeutic activities were not well accepted by the scientific psychology community, and therapy functions of psychologists often were thwarted by the psychiatric community. Behaviorism, linked to experimental psychology, was more readily accepted and was quite popular with educators early in the century. Educational literature of this period suggests an acceptance of learning and behavioral principles decades in advance of the widespread influence of B. F. Skinner's applications familiar to contemporary school psychologists. Interventions were influenced by many ideas, including Edward L. Thorndike's learning principles and educational psychology, the educational philosophies of John Dewey and William James, Freudian therapeutic conceptualizations, and John B. Watson's behaviorism.

Early Literature, Organizations, and Training

The period from 1890 to 1920 provided a framework for many later developments. In addition to the origination of services, the period also included the founding of several journals (e.g., *Journal of Educational Psychology*, Witmer's *The Psychological Clinic*, and Hall's *American Journal of Psychology* and *Pedagogical Seminary*), the establishment of organizations for applied and clinical psychologists, individual and group tests, and special education classes. Other literary benchmarks included the first appearance of the term *school psychologist* in U.S. literature and several early articles and manuals that described the state of services (Fagan & Delugach, 1984). Wallin (1914) and Van Sickle et al. (1911) provide the most comprehensive descriptions of school conditions, availability of special classes, psychological services, and the nature of service providers. While working for the Connecticut State Board of Education, Arnold Gesell wrote several manuals that became prototypes of materials produced by current state consultants for school psychological services. Many test manuals and compendia of tests appear to have enjoyed widespread popularity (Stern, 1914; Whipple, 1914, 1915).

Organizational developments also were important. After the APA's founding in 1892, the organization's political structure and policy over the first several decades were dominated by scientific rather than professional or applied orientations (Napoli, 1981). The APA failed to respond to the interests of applied psychologists, to provide standards and assistance, provoking the founding of the American Association of Clinical Psychologists (AACP) in 1917. However, responding to overtures from the APA, the AACP disbanded and became the APA Section on Clinical Psychology in 1919. For a variety of reasons, most school psychologists were not affiliated with the APA or any other national group during the early decades of the 20th century. Furthermore, there were few state or local associations for professional affiliation. The organizational developments of the period served to point out the problems of applied psychologists within the APA and the significant role that splinter groups, such as the AACP, would play in the history of psychology, including school psychology (Fagan, 1993).

Informal training efforts, including field experiences, existed at a few institutions, but there were no formal training programs specifically for school psychologists.

During the period 1890–1920 the relatively small number of psychologists practicing in school settings gained their preparation from a variety of backgrounds. Informal training efforts, including field experiences, existed at a few institutions, but there were no formal training programs specifically for school psychologists (Fagan, 1999). Practitioners were teachers who received brief courses in testing, while others had psychological training within master's and doctoral degrees that included supervised field experiences. Witmer had provided instruction in connection with his clinic, and Wallin and Hall also offered instruction along the lines of exceptional children and child study, respectively. Goddard and Gesell provided early training classes on testing and special education in New York City, and Goddard is credited with organizing the earliest internships at the Vineland Training School in New Jersey (Morrow, 1946). One of Goddard's assistants, Norma Cutts, was at Vineland in 1913–1914 and with his help found employment as a psychological examiner with Gesell. That position provided the stage for her own eminent career in school psychology and special education in New Haven, Connecticut (Fagan, 1989a).

Leta Stetter Hollingworth (1886–1939)

Source: Reprinted by permission of the Archives of the History of American Psychology, University of Akron, Akron, Ohio.

Important Contributors

Well-known "school" psychologists of the period included Norma Cutts, Arnold Gesell, Henry Goddard, Gertrude Hildreth, Leta Stetter Hollingworth, Bertha Luckey, Clara Schmitt, Lewis Terman, John Edward Wallace Wallin, Margaret Washburn, Lightner Witmer, and Helen Thompson Wooley. The early representation of women in school psychology practice, and applied psychology generally, can be attributed to discrimination in higher education settings and the lack of career options for women outside of education. During the 19th century, the feminization of elementary and secondary school teaching spread and provided the base from which many would later seek positions in guidance and psychology. Describing the circumstances of "career-minded women in male-dominated America before World War I," Schwarz (1986) states:

> For all their intelligence and ability, these women were expected to forget their ambitions and years of schooling as they reached their twenties. Society's dictates on what was a normal and acceptable life for American women narrowed to marrying a man, raising a family, and settling down to an existence lived mainly as an adjunct to others' lives once they left college. (p. 56)

Arnold L. Gesell (1880–1961)

Source: Studio portrait by Crosby, New Haven, Connecticut. Reprinted by permission of the State Historical Society of Wisconsin.

Of course there are numerous examples of educated women who resisted society's dictates and chose other paths (Rosenberg, 1982). In this regard, the psychological career of Leta Stetter Hollingworth has gained considerable attention (Benjamin & Shields, 1990; Fagan, 1990b). Other notable examples include Norma Cutts (Fagan, 1989a) and Gertrude Hildreth (Fagan, 1988a). Despite society's dictates, many women considered careers in teaching and psychology to be fulfilling and natural extensions of their traditional childrearing role. Women often held administrative positions in school psychological clinics and contributed widely to the spread of school services (French, 1988). In comparison to other psychology fields, women have held strong proportional representation throughout the history of school psychology, perhaps never less than 30% and currently above 70%. A discussion of contributions of women in school psychology appears in Hagin (1993).

Among the most prominent examples of school psychology practitioners in this early period was Arnold Lucius Gesell. Gesell is believed to have held the first position with the title of school psychologist, with the Connecticut State Board of Education, from 1915 to 1919. His position was a mix of direct and indirect services, and archival records vividly describe the conditions of his employment and practice. His experiences were similar in many ways to those of current practitioners: His caseload was often too large, his administrative superiors preferred diagnostic services to others, he traveled considerably from one service setting to another, and he mixed school and nonschool practice (Fagan, 1987a).

Establishment of the Profession (1920–1940)

Though 1890–1920 was a formative period, school psychology lacked many of the primary characteristics of a profession: practitioner autonomy and professional regulation of training, credentialing, and practice. Because psychological practice was largely unregulated and titles such as clinical or consulting psychologist, psychoclinicist, or psychological examiner were employed generically, it is fair to say that all of professional psychology was without much professional status and symbolism at this time. Psychologists in school settings may not have had as much professional status as those in other settings, even though they had acquired more in terms of professional symbols. This lesser status was attributable to the prevalence of nondoctoral practitioners and the fact that many school practitioners were women, factors that have persisted throughout the history of school psychology.

Training and Credentialing

To a limited extent, the professional symbols of autonomy and regulation of training, credentialing, and practice were discernible for school psychology in the period 1920–1940. Whereas some psychologists previously had been trained in conjunction with certain university clinics, it was recognized that psychologists serving schoolchildren were in need of more formal preparation (Fagan, 1999). Witmer had established a training program in clinical psychology at the University of Pennsylvania, and though several of his graduates worked in school systems, the program was not designated school psychology. The first training programs identified as school psychology were at New York University (NYU) in the mid-1920s, where programs existed at the undergraduate and graduate levels. By the late 1930s, Pennsylvania State University was offering doctoral training in school psychology. Other institutions, including Ohio State University, recommended specific courses for individuals seeking preparation for school practice. Thus, during this period there were relevant training courses at some institutions and formal programs at NYU and Penn State (Fagan, 1986b).

New York and Pennsylvania were pioneers in training and credentialing.

In the mid-1920s an examination for employment as a school psychological examiner was in use in New York City schools. To be eligible for the examination, applicants had to have completed a master's degree in psychology from a "university recognized by the Regents of the University of the State of New York" and had to have "one year's experience in mental measurement satisfactory to the Board of Examiners" (Examination for License as Psychologist, 1925). State Department of Education certification for school psychology practice occurred in Pennsylvania and New York in the mid-1930s. That New York and Pennsylvania were pioneers in training and credentialing was no accident. It seems plausible that the NYU program may have been developed in response to the availability of such employment and the New York City examination. French (1984) provides a detailed description of developments in Pennsylvania, which was among the few states actively developing statewide school psychology services even in its rural counties.

Gertrude H. Hildreth (1898–1984)

Source: From the Gertrude Hildreth Papers. Reprinted by permission of the Educational Testing Service Archives.

As of the mid-1920s, no states offered credentials to psychologists in the nonschool and private sectors. Another aspect of professional regulation was the initiation of a short-lived national certification program available to APA members from 1921 to 1927 (Sokal, 1982). The program, though unsuccessful, was an early example of recognition by means of a national-level credential, which reappeared in the late 1940s in APA's American Board of Examiners in Professional Psychology and in the late 1980s as NASP's National Certification in School Psychology. Thus, two primary symbols of professional development, training and credentialing, emerged in the period 1920–1940. More rapid and widespread growth in training and regulation emerged in future periods, especially following World War II.

Literature

The literature available to school psychologists continued to appear in a variety of sources. With no journals specifically devoted to school psychology, most of the field's literature continued to appear in related psychology and education journals, particularly *The Psychological Clinic*, *School and Society*, *Journal of Educational Psychology*, and *Journal of Consulting Psychology*. This literature was devoted to professional and organizational issues, psychoeducational assessment, the problems of children, and the accompanying need for psychological services. There were also numerous books on similar topics. A major literary accomplishment of this period was the first text specifically about school psychology, *Psychological Service for School Problems* (Hildreth, 1930).

Role and Function and Employment Opportunities

In the early 1920s, Gertrude Hildreth worked briefly as a school psychologist in Okmulgee, Oklahoma, before leaving for Columbia University, where she received her doctoral degree and became a faculty member (Fagan, 1988a). Her pioneer book, *Psychological Service for School Problems* (1930), described the historical

Box 2.2 Hildreth's Illustration of a School Psychologist's Day

The following outline illustrates the daily activities on an ordinarily busy day of one psychologist employed in a progressive school.

Morning

Examination with the Binet test of a child applying for admission.

Administration of group tests to a small group of absentees who missed the test during the recent testing survey.

Conference on a problem child in the high school.

Conference on a problem child in the elementary school.

Answering correspondence and making requisitions for the tests to be used in the next survey.

Afternoon

Completion, for the principal, of reports on a group of seventh-grade children whose achievement was found to be deficient on recent tests.

Further work on the construction of reading and arithmetic readiness tests for the primary grades.

Instructions to an assistant for making a set of flash cards for diagnostic work in reading.

Partial diagnosis of the reading difficulties of an upper-elementary-grade pupil.

Study of the reading progress of a French child who had recently entered the school.

Conference with a high school teacher.

This day began at 8:30 a.m. and closed at 5:45 p.m., with a half an hour of recess at noon. The rank order of activities engaged in by the same psychologist, arranged according to the amount of time consumed in their performance during the year, is approximately as follows:

1. Conferences with school staff members, parents, visitors, psychologists in training.
2. Individual testing of pupils.
3. Group testing.
4. Test scoring.
5. Tabulation of results and the construction of graphs and charts.
6. Diagnostic work with individual pupils.
7. Research, including test construction and conferences with staff members conducting research.

Source: *Psychological Service for School Problems*, by G. H. Hildreth, 1930, Yonkers, NY: World Book Co., pp. 246–248.

development of services and vividly portrayed the school psychologist's role and function. Box 2.2 is taken from her text and describes the typical practice of the period (in a progressive school), which bears a remarkable similarity to current practice. Hildreth's book put forth an ideal more than a real model, and her list of services was far more diverse than her previous practice had been in Oklahoma. The book portrayed the possibilities for broader services, even though assessment, often narrowly construed as ability testing, was dominant.

Most school psychologists were enmeshed in a refer–test–report model, with other functions consuming much less of their time.

Psychological testing continued to be the dominant characteristic of role and function for school psychologists throughout this period. Numerous group and individual ability, aptitude, and achievement tests were now available, and the technical adequacy of instrumentation and the variety of tests available were increasing. Among the most prominent was the Stanford Revision of the Binet-Simon Scales introduced in 1916, which was revised in 1937 to include both a Form L and a Form M (the initials stood for the authors' first names, Louis Terman and Maude Merrill). Thus, for the first half of the 20th century, most school psychologists were enmeshed in a refer–test–report model, with other functions consuming much less of their time.

Adequate employment in school psychology had been available throughout the early decades of practice, but the depression years of the 1930s had a substantial impact on employment opportunities for psychologists. Large urban districts such as Chicago and New York City lost several positions and were forced to make adjustments in staffing, including the hiring of Works Progress Administration psychologists to weather this difficult period (City of New York, 1938; Mullen, 1981). Despite the loss of positions in several settings and limited employment opportunities for applied psychologists, the field continued to grow (Napoli, 1981). Services continued to be concentrated in urban areas, but by 1940 school psychology had been accepted nationwide, and the number of practitioners had grown from only a few hundred to probably 500 practitioners employed in schools under various titles.

By the end of this period the clinic model was being complemented by the single-district model, and services were expanding beyond the urban centers to smaller cities and rural areas.

The earlier clinic system model was now widespread, with some rural areas gaining services through traveling clinics. In Massachusetts, the traveling clinics included psychologists, social workers, and psychiatrists operating as a team from a regional mental health facility (Martens, 1939). In Ohio, services were provided from a research bureau affiliated with the College of Education at Ohio State University (Rosebrook, 1942). Although helpful, the traveling clinics were unable to provide the intensity and array of services available to districts employing their own psychologists. Articulating services with local districts was a widespread problem for such clinics in rural areas. The problem can still be observed in areas where services continue to be provided on an indirect basis even when organized within a larger educational agency (e.g., special education cooperative). The growth in school district–based special education increased the demand for district-based psychological examiners. The growing acceptance of school psychology was reflected in an increasing number of districts that found the resources to employ their own school psychologists. By the end of the period of 1920 to 1940, the clinic model was being complemented by the single-district model, and services were expanding beyond the urban centers to smaller cities and rural areas. Despite this expansion of service delivery models and growth of employment opportunities between 1920 and 1940, services continued to be provided by individuals with a variety of training and titles, and a well-defined professional specialty of school psychology was not yet discernible.

Organizational Development

The 1920–1940 period had considerable activity related to professional organizations. Following the establishment of the APA Section on Clinical Psychology in 1919, splinter groups continued to develop. Many consulting psychologists, especially in New York State, continued to maintain a separate association that led to the founding of the Association of Consulting Psychologists (ACP) in 1930 and then to the American Association of Applied Psychologists (AAAP) in 1937. The fact that the AAAP was subdivided into four broadly defined specialties—clinical, consulting, educational, and business and industrial psychology—was a significant symbol of professionalism (English, 1938). School psychology practitioners typically belonged to AAAP's clinical or educational sections, but most school practitioners, and probably most applied psychologists, did not hold membership in either the APA or the AAAP.

These organizations typically granted full membership privileges only to those who held a doctoral degree, with lesser status accorded to nondoctoral practitioners. Because of the growth in the number of nondoctoral school practitioners and their certification, some concessions appear to have been made for them in the AAAP membership requirements (Fagan, 1993). The orientations of these groups also reflected the long-standing differences between academic and applied psychologists. However, relationships between the APA and the AAAP generally were cordial, with many shared members and annual meetings. The two groups remained separate until developments prior to World War II encouraged the unification of psychology groups into one organization. AAAP had several state-level affiliates, which typically held similar names (e.g., Ohio Association of Applied Psychologists). There do not appear to have been separate school psychology state associations in this period.

Growth and Identity of a Profession (1940–1970)

The final three decades of the hybrid years are noteworthy for their role confusion, which shaped organizational identity, and the growth in the number of training programs and practitioners. Education grew enormously as a result of the post–World War II baby boom: the schools were expanding in size and needed additional psychological services. In 1968, special education was serving more than 2 million children, up dramatically from 310,000 in 1940 and 837,000 in 1958 (Dunn, 1973). Between 1940 and 1970, the number of school psychologists grew from about 500 to 5,000, and the number of institutions with formal training programs grew from as few as 2 to more than 100, enrolling a total of perhaps 3,000 students. The ratio of practitioners to schoolchildren improved from 1:36,000 in 1950 to 1:10,500 in 1966 (Fagan, 1988b). Credentialing accomplishments included the growth of school certification—from 13 states in 1946, to 23 states in 1960, to perhaps 40

Between 1940 and 1970, the number of school psychologists grew from about 500 to 5,000.

states by 1970—and the initiation of licensure for psychologists in 1945, with licensure in all states by 1977. The rapid growth and change in school psychology during the period 1940–1970 can be gleaned from Cutts (1955), Farling and Hoedt (1971), and Symonds (1942).

Organizational Development

The merging of the AAAP into a reorganized APA in 1945 gave school psychologists their first national organizational identity in the form of the Division of School Psychologists (APA Division 16). As a separate division, school psychology was a distinct organizational entity from clinical psychology (Division 12) and educational psychology (Division 15). Reflecting APA membership generally, membership in Division 16 grew from 133 in 1948, to 601 in 1956, to 1,229 in 1968. Though the division struggled for many years to gain stability, it provided an organizational identity for a growing number of trainers and practitioners, established a loose network of communication among school psychologists in the existing state psychological associations, and drafted guidelines for training and credentialing (see Magary, 1967a, pp. 722–726, for a copy of Division 16's 1962 certification standards). The division also initiated program accreditation efforts in 1963 and gained approval for the awarding of a school psychology diplomate from APA's American Board of Examiners in Professional Psychology in 1968 (Bent, Packard, & Goldberg, 1999). In 1968 Virginia Bennett, of Rutgers University, became the first person to receive the diploma in school psychology (Fagan. 2004a). The division initiated annual institutes within the APA convention programs, which became widely respected. Though the division failed to capture the membership of most school psychology practitioners nationwide, throughout much of this period it served as a beacon of identity and represented the field to the broader political arena of psychology and education in the United States. During the latter part of the hybrid years, Division 16 was an important factor in giving the field of school psychology national recognition and in making state departments of education aware of the need for improved credentialing and practice standards.

Ohio appears to have had the first separate state association for school psychologists.

Though state and local associations for psychologists dated back to the 1920s, those for school psychologists were more recent. Ohio appears to have had the first separate state association for school psychologists, founded in 1943. The organization was one of probably only three state groups in the 1940s. Five more associations were founded in the 1950s, and by 1969 there were 17 state school psychology associations (Fagan, Hensley, & Delugach, 1986). After the proceedings of several invitational school psychology conferences were disseminated to a loose network of state and local association members, school psychologists in Ohio called an invitational meeting in 1968 to consider establishing a rival national group. That meeting led to the historic St. Louis convention, at which the National Association of School Psychologists (NASP) was officially formed in March 1969. The complex circumstances surrounding the event are described in the *Journal of School Psychology* (Fagan, 1993). It is of some historical interest that Ohio was the state of origin for both the APA Division of School Psychology and NASP.

Literature

The school psychology literature continued to be scattered, although some concentration was provided by the *Journal of Consulting Psychology* (now the *Journal of Consulting and Clinical Psychology*) and the newly founded APA journal, *American Psychologist.* Until the 1960s, the Division 16 newsletter was the only national publication devoted exclusively to school psychology. The 1960s was the most productive literary decade of the hybrid years and included the founding of the *Journal of School Psychology*, *Psychology in the Schools*, and *Professional Psychology* (now *Professional Psychology: Research and Practice*), and the publication of 14 books on school psychology (Fagan, 1986a). Even though the literature reflected problems of role confusion and professional identity, it was the first period in which school psychologists were writing books on topics of their own interest and publishing journals for their own audience. Unique among these books were those presenting philosophies on the training and practice of school psychologists. Gray's (1963b) "data-oriented problem solver" and Reger's (1965) "educational programmer" are orientations with continuing relevance. These reflected the growing interest in school psychology and the struggle for role and function identity. Valett's (1963) *The Practice of School Psychology: Professional Problems* served as a guidebook for professional and ethical dilemmas at a time when only generic codes of ethics were available from the APA. The Gottsegens' three edited volumes on *Professional School Psychology* (see appendix B) reflected the diversity of school psychology late in the hybrid years.

It was the first period in which school psychologists were writing books on topics of their own interest and publishing journals for their own audience.

Conferences

Among the most cited accomplishments of the period 1940–1970 is the Thayer Conference, conducted in 1954 (Cutts, 1955). The conference helped to shape ideas for several decades regarding levels of training, credentialing, and practice. The Thayer Conference proceedings is one of only a few comprehensive surveys of school psychological services undertaken in the first half-century of school psychology, and it is clearly the most comprehensive picture available of the circumstances of school psychology around 1950. During the 1950s and 1960s, other professional school psychology conferences were conducted in several states. For example, the Peabody Conference (Gray, 1963a), held by the Southern Regional Education Board, was part of a series of meetings that drew attention to the need for training programs and internships. State and regional conferences brought practitioners together, which often led to the founding of state organizations. California provides an excellent example of how coordinated efforts of the state department of education and university staff led to substantial development in a short period of time. It is difficult to determine whether this flurry of meetings was stimulated by the Thayer Conference and Division 16, but there appears to have been some connection.

The recommendations made during the 1954 Thayer Conference would have a long-term impact on the future of school psychology.

These conferences furthered the development of a consensus on roles and functions and on training, even though such a consensus was not actually achieved during this period. The Thayer Conference's recommendations would have a long-term impact on the future of school psychology. These included the recommendations for two levels of training and practice with different titles, for credentialing through the state education agency for school practice, and for accreditation of programs through the APA (Fagan, 2005b).

Professional Development

Although the impact of the Thayer Conference on school psychology appears to have been significant, it seems to have been less than that of the 1949 Boulder Conference on clinical psychology. Clinical psychology shared a greater kinship to the APA, nourished by an APA Division of Clinical Psychology dating to 1919, numerous state affiliates, a training and internship system supported by APA accreditation and the Veterans' Administration, struggles with organized medicine and psychiatry, and a rapidly growing network of state licensing boards. Despite organizational strength in a few states, school psychology lacked a national kinship with the group at the time of the Thayer Conference and throughout the hybrid years. Thus when the APA reorganized, school psychology was off to a slower start than the other professional specialties of clinical and counseling psychology (Fagan, 1993).

With the reorganization of the APA, an upward spiral of development in adult clinical psychology was launched. The full effects of that spiral are observed in contemporary licensing, accreditation, reimbursement policies, and other aspects of clinical psychology, some of which Albee (1998) has criticized as a sellout to the medical model. Clinical psychology's focus on adults was so strong that only in the past few decades has a strong child-based clinical subspecialty reemerged. Whereas World War I had demonstrated the value of tests, World War II launched therapeutic interventions as another service domain for psychologists. Prior to that time, clinical psychology services frequently were delivered to children and adults. The state hospital system was largely controlled by psychiatry, and psychologists' services to adults frequently were restricted or supervised by psychiatrists. State department of education certification for school practice preceded licensure by at least a decade and freed school psychologists from supervision by medical personnel (French, 1990). Psychologists had been unsuccessful in gaining legislative recognition for practice in other settings. The first private practice licensure occurred in Connecticut in 1945 at a time when almost a dozen states already had certification for psychologists practicing in schools. Licensure laws were aimed directly at legitimizing practice by doctoral and, to a lesser extent, nondoctoral psychologists. The intent was to free psychological practice from the reins of medical practitioners, with the focus decidedly upon clinical psychologists and, to a lesser degree, counseling and consulting psychologists.

School psychologists were less involved in nonschool licensure because they were largely free of medical supervision in the schools and already were being credentialed by several state departments of education. Because many school psychologists were trained in clinical or educational psychology programs, those seeking nonschool practice already had preparation in a related field and could quickly identify with that field (e.g., clinical psychology). The recommendations of the Thayer Conference had set the stage for school psychology credentialing; it was to be largely outside the scope of state licensing boards and instead was to be the responsibility of state education agencies. School psychology was perceived as highly setting-specific. For all practical purposes, it was conducted almost entirely in school settings, and usually in public schools. Not until the late 1960s was the title of school psychology's APA division changed from school *psychologists* to school *psychology*. The change reflected the quest for a broader identity than practice confined to school settings and for an identity distinct from educational and clinical psychology.

School psychologists gained only indirect benefits from the postwar government sponsorship of clinical psychology. For example, school practitioners with clinical psychology backgrounds could move into nonschool practice in states where such licensing was established. Training programs in applied and professional psychology could place students in the growing number of government-sponsored internships in clinical and counseling psychology, but school-based internships were not part of that movement. In contrast, much of school psychology's postwar growth was tied to developments in education, especially rapidly growing enrollments and special education programs. Nevertheless, the postwar period of the hybrid years was important to school psychology, even though school psychology's professional growth lagged significantly behind that of clinical psychology. It was the first era in which different groups of professional psychologists became recognized and were considered to be professional specialties. Although official recognition of specialties would not occur until the late 1990s (by way of the APA's Commission for the Recognition of Specialties and Proficiencies in Professional Psychology), the distinctions would have much to do with the struggles and growth of school psychology in the thoroughbred years. To a large extent, the initial distinctions of specialties were drawn as a result of conflicts between the professions of clinical psychology and psychiatry, the side effects of which created conflicts between clinical psychology and other psychology specialties.

The expansion of roles that occurred within clinical psychology, toward therapy, was less noticeable in school psychology. Psychological testing continued to dominate the school psychologist's role and function, and broad expansion was thwarted by school administrative restrictions and by overlapping claims to intervention functions made by guidance and special education personnel (Napoli, 1981). Numerous role perception surveys were conducted in the 1960s, along with studies of real versus ideal functions of school psychologists. The studies revealed dissatisfactions with the dominant traditional testing role and preferences for greater involvement in consultation and intervention (Roberts & Solomons, 1970). A national survey by Farling and Hoedt (1971) found that the dominant activities were individual psychoeducational evaluations, report writing, and parent–teacher conferences, and ideal role preferences typically favored reducing the dominant testing activities and increasing other roles, such as consultation, program evaluation, and behavior management.

Role dissatisfactions and preferences evolved from several factors:

1. The growing professional organizations for practitioners provided opportunities to discuss such issues and to propose alternative service delivery systems.

2. The rapid growth of training programs after 1960 put forth a broader philosophy of school psychological services and began to emphasize nontest functions; thus a new wave of school psychologists was being produced to replace those leaving the field. The new wave not only was larger and more broadly oriented to services, but its members also held graduate degrees from programs in school psychology, which fostered greater professional identity.
3. Federal education funds were available to sponsor innovative training practices and school services.
4. The special education arena had undergone a major expansion when it officially recognized learning disability (LD) as a categorical condition in the late 1960s. While the traditional testing model was spurred by this recognition, there was a flurry of activity in the remediation of LD, and some school psychologists perceived this as an opportunity to shift toward intervention roles (e.g., Valett, 1967).
5. Society's concerns for problems in education were reflected in the view of the schools as systems and organizations. Toward the end of the hybrid years and for much of the next decade, there was intense effort to describe school psychologist functions along these lines (e.g., Schmuck & Miles, 1971).
6. The 1960s was a decade of emphasis on prevention and mental health. The Community Mental Health Centers Act and other federal initiatives of the 1960s sensitized the public to mental health, poverty, and social issues requiring intervention. The rapid establishment of mental health centers, community mental health associations, and Head Start programs was reminiscent of an earlier era of clinics and child study clubs.
7. The latter part of the hybrid years was characterized by a shifting intervention orientation from Freudian and dynamic conceptualizations to nondirective Rogerian counseling, brief psychotherapies, sensitivity training, and behavioral therapies. The new approaches were perceived as more compatible with practice in school settings.
8. Finally, surfacing in the 1960s was frustration with the status quo of requiring students to fit into diagnostic categories, ethical concerns about labeling children, and an antitesting mentality.

The period also was historically significant for its civil rights struggles along lines of race, ethnicity, gender, and sexual preference. The unprecedented increase of federal involvement in education was observed in events surrounding the space race, school desegregation, and federally funded educational programs (including Head Start). These were significant departures from the past. Public education for many decades had been viewed as an appropriate arena within which to seek major changes

The founding of NASP in 1969 extended the quest for professionalism . . . and served as the first in a series of events that would characterize the thoroughbred years.

in the social fabric. Now, however, it was federal, instead of state and local, agendas that would be encouraged. With their acceptance of federal laws, regulations, and financial assistance to their schools (seen by some as an intrusion), schools could be urged (required) by the federal government to accomplish goals that state and local authorities had failed or refused to accomplish previously.

The trends and accomplishments of the postwar period created an atmosphere of identity formation for school psychologists, even if the period's identity seemed confused, with its varied orientations of textbook authors and perplexing mix of training, credentialing, and practice titles. It was in response to these conditions, and to the perceived need to bring practitioners nationwide together in a more stable and strengthened identity, that NASP was established. The founding of NASP in 1969 extended the quest for professionalism not only beyond the traditional struggle of academic and applied psychology but also beyond the traditional confines of organized psychology itself, the APA. The event marked the end of the hybrid years and served as the first in a series of events that would characterize the thoroughbred years.

THE THOROUGHBRED YEARS (1970–PRESENT)

By the end of the hybrid years, school psychology was at least a potentially significant political and professional entity in psychology and education, and in several places, it was a potent entity. Most of the symbols of professionalism, such as organization of an association, a unique body of knowledge, a professional code of conduct, specialized training, regulation and credentialing, and so forth, already had appeared in some form (see chapter 7). For example, in the 1930s state education agencies informally identified universities that offered classes appropriate for school psychologists, but formal recognition through accreditation did not appear until the 1960s, from the National Council for Accreditation of Teacher Education (NCATE), and in 1971, from the APA. The use of standards specifically for school psychology did not occur until the 1980s within the NCATE–NASP relationship (Fagan & Wells, 2000). Although recognition of training programs emerged during the hybrid years, the accreditation model observed today is considerably more formal. The earliest model was a prototype of modern-day state department of education (SDE) training program approval. In many states today, both SDE program approval and national accreditation models exist, often interdependently. Similarly, certification procedures today are more sophisticated than at much earlier times, when some school psychologists sought certification by going to their state education agency and demonstrating their skill in giving the Binet. Since World War II, state departments of education increasingly have relied on procedures of transcript review, formal program approvals, and reciprocity in their credentialing practices. Thus, much of what has been accomplished in accreditation, association growth, credentials, levels of training, literature, loci of practice, or professional roles and functions was discernible by the end of the hybrid years. The accomplishments, however, were not equally distributed across the country. Many states and most rural areas still lacked viable psychological services in their schools. Variability in services, especially along rural-urban lines, has persisted throughout the history of school psychology.

Regular and Special Education Legislation and Growth

Table 2.1 identifies the decades of the thoroughbred years as characterized by regulation, association growth, professional division and reorganization, improved professional identity, and broadened arenas of practice. A number of factors since 1970 have strengthened school psychology's identity and promoted more widespread services. One of these factors was a series of legal challenges to special education. Perhaps best known is *Larry P.* v. *Riles* (1984), which focused on minority assessment and placement issues. These challenges, and subsequent court decisions, brought into sharp focus the need for more sensitive multicultural assessment, improved technical adequacy of tests, broader conceptualizations of assessment, and more responsible caseloads. Perhaps the most significant event was the 1975 enactment of landmark civil rights legislation, the Education for All Handicapped Children Act (EAHCA), which sensitized every school district to the need for special education services, including psychological services for all handicapped children.

The legislated right to a free and appropriate public education regardless of the nature of a child's handicap followed a long historical struggle of guaranteeing education to women and to minorities, including Native Americans, Hispanics, and African Americans. The implementation of this legislation, and its reauthorization in 1986, extended the educational rights of the handicapped so that those rights began at birth. Subsequent reauthorizations of this legislation in 1990 and 1997, renamed the Individuals with Disabilities Education Act (IDEA) and the Individuals with Disabilities Education Improvement Act of 2004, contained changes that also influenced training and practice. Other legislation also drew attention to service issues in special and regular education: the 1974 Family Educational Rights and Privacy Act, regarding the collection, maintenance, and dissemination of school records. In addition, Section 504 of the Rehabilitation Act of 1973 laid the groundwork for services to children who may not otherwise have qualified for special education. Most recently, the No Child Left Behind Act (NCLB) was passed in 2001.

Perhaps the most significant event was the enactment in 1975 of the Education for All Handicapped Children Act (EAHCA), which sensitized every school district to the need for special education services, including psychological services for all handicapped children.

The passage of these laws has had widespread effects on the delivery of special education and school psychological services. Prior to the 1970s it was common practice to conduct psychological assessments and recommend special class placements without requiring parents' permission. Beginning in 1973, Section 504, the Family Educational Rights and Privacy Act, the laws leading up to IDEA, and related litigation broadened the rights of individuals with disabilities, enabling them to receive a free and appropriate public education, and reasserted parental and family rights to privacy. Although the legislation and related litigation affected education generally, such laws also drew attention (albeit not always favorable) to psychological services, and this attention served as a catalyst for improved practice guidelines at local, state, and national levels. As in the hybrid years, many of these guidelines were produced by state education agencies or other nonpsychologist groups. One effect of the new

guidelines and regulations was the need to gather and maintain extensive case documentation related to assessment, conferences, educational plans, placement, reevaluations, and due process hearings. This requirement was burdensome for school administrative, instructional, and assessment staff members. The long-term impact of the NCLB, which requires school districts to make adequate annual progress in student achievement, including children in special education, remains to be determined.

Another factor in the thoroughbred years was the decline in regular education enrollments from 1970 to 1990, followed by modest increases to 47.7 million students in 2001–2002 (National Center for Education Statistics, 2003). During the same period, special education enrollments had increased to 4.5 million children by the late 1980s, to more than 5.5 million by the late 1990s, and to 6.3 million in 2001–2002, representing approximately 13 percent of the public school population. The large jump in the population of students with disabilities was an outgrowth of the Education for All Handicapped Children Act and its subsequent reauthorizations. Within a few years following the implementation of EAHCA in 1975, special education services were spreading into previously unserved and underserved regions of the country, with emphasis on serving children for whom many school districts had not previously assumed responsibility. In the decade preceding this law, the field of learning disabilities had gained official recognition, and its rapid growth in the 1970s contributed to the overall impact of EAHCA. Reminiscent of a much earlier period, education was again experiencing problems in serving the needs of selected groups of students, and school psychologists were called upon for assistance. The impact was observed in the increasing number of school psychology practitioners, which grew from 5,000 in 1970 to at least 10,000 by 1980, 20,000 by 1988, 22,000 by the mid-1990s, and perhaps more than 30,000 by 2005. The ratio of practitioners to schoolchildren improved to approximately 1:2,000 or better, where it has remained (Curtis, Hunley, & Grier, 2002; Fagan, 1988b; Hosp & Reschly, 2002; Lund, Reschly, & Connolly Martin, 1998). Smith (1984) and Curtis, Hunley, and Grier identified a relationship between less favorable ratios and greater special education assessment activities.

The number of school psychologists grew from 5,000 in 1970 to perhaps more than 30,000 by 2005.

Services were available nationwide despite continued variability in delivery systems and practitioner qualifications. However, the resurgence and growth of special education made the distinction between special and regular education even greater. By 1980 most districts had two largely separate systems of instruction: regular education and special education. Comprehensive remedial services, long a part of the regular education arena, all but disappeared in the wake of the enormous growth in services for learning-disabled children in the special education arena. The "Regular Education Initiative" and the inclusion movement of the 1980s and 1990s (a trend toward serving children with disabilities in regular educational settings) were responses to problems perceived by the dual systems of schooling created since the 1960s. The reauthorizations of IDEA, increased challenges by parents to have children served under provision of Section 504, and the NCLB have begun to blur the boundaries between regular and special education and to emphasize services based

on need and not just categorical eligibility. School psychology services in several states have spurred or followed this shift in a broadened acceptance of alternative service-delivery models. Mature and well-organized school psychology associations were also able to positively influence these directions and legislation.

Organizational Developments and Conferences

By the onset of the thoroughbred years, most states had enough practitioners to organize state associations for school psychologists. In concert with the rapidly growing National Association of School Psychologists, the state associations fostered the development and implementation of guidelines for improved practice. A fundamental difference between this and the earlier periods was the association leadership's shift from reactive to proactive modes of operation. School psychology was no longer simply responding to what other agencies, especially those of state and federal governments, decided. Instead, school psychology was working to influence the types of decisions these agencies might make. Thus, professional regulation was shifting from external to internal influence, and changes that originated in association activities of the 1970s were seen most clearly after 1980. The APA, APA Division 16, and NASP worked together to influence federal legislation, and often worked in concert with pupil services and child mental health coalitions. This was most evident after 1990, when the NASP established a permanent office in the Washington, DC, area.

A fundamental difference between this and the earlier periods was the association leadership's shift from reactive to proactive modes of operation.

APA Division 16—Division of School Psychology

The APA also took reactive and proactive positions on legislation throughout this period. Its Division of School Psychology influenced these positions through input to its parent organization, but it lacked the resources to have a significant impact on the field. The successful growth of NASP drew attention and membership away from Division 16, which before 1969 had been the only national-level school psychology group. Division 16 membership remained stable during this period at between 2,000 and 2,500. Still, APA and Division 16 made important contributions. After 8 years of planning by Division 16, APA accredited its first school psychology doctoral program in 1971 at the University of Texas–Austin. The school psychology program accreditation was a major symbol of professionalism that helped to establish the field on a par with clinical and counseling psychology. In 1981, APA published its *Specialty Guidelines for the Delivery of Services* which included separate guidelines for school psychology (APA, 1981). In 1997, APA's Commission for the Recognition of Specialties and Proficiencies in Professional Psychology (CRSPPP) approved a specialty definition for school psychology prepared from the input of several key school psychology groups, including Division 16 and NASP. The specialty recognition was reapproved in 2005. The CRSPPP approval further solidified the position of school psychology as an important specialty in professional psychology.

APA–NASP Task Force

In the 1970s, school psychology continued to be practiced primarily by nondoctoral personnel in school settings. When the APA Council passed a 1977 resolution declaring that a doctoral degree would be required for the title of professional psychologist, it fed the growing tension between NASP and the APA over entry levels and titles and led to the creation of an APA–NASP Task Force in 1978 (later renamed the Interorganizational Committee). The tension between the APA and NASP reflected disagreements between state psychology and school psychology associations over matters of credentialing for nonschool practice. The task force influenced several interorganizational decisions, but the joint APA–NASP accreditation process was never given final approval and implemented. The task force also worked with Division 16, NASP, and the University of Minnesota's National School Psychology Inservice Training Network to plan the Spring Hill Symposium in 1980 and the Olympia Conference in 1981. NASP and Division 16 jointly published the proceedings of the conferences in *School Psychology Review* (see Vol. 10, No. 2, and Vol. 11, No. 2). These conferences helped focus attention on the practice of school psychology. The Interorganizational Committee facilitated many activities between the APA and NASP but was unable to resolve the entry-level training issues that spurred its founding in 1978. It was disbanded by the APA in 2002.

Professional Divisions: The APA, APS, and AAAPP

In contrast to its first half-century, the second half-century of APA history was increasingly practice oriented and accompanied by a dramatic shift in practitioner membership. Long-standing tensions between academic and applied psychologists resurfaced. The scientist–practitioner model of the post–World War II APA had served as an acceptable compromise between these forces for decades; however, by the 1980s, that perception had changed. The scales appear to have tipped heavily in favor of practitioner interests. Professional issues such as licensure, practice privileges, liability insurance, managed care, and third-party payments seemed to consume the energy and financial resources of the APA. Internal political issues led to several unsuccessful attempts to reorganize the APA along lines more acceptable to members with scientific interests, and in 1988 the American Psychological Society (APS) was founded as an alternative organization for more academic-scientific psychologists. (In 2005 its name changed to the Association for Psychological Science.) Whereas practitioners had historically established associations as alternatives to academic-scientific dominance within the APA, the academic-scientific constituency now established an association in response to perceived professional dominance.

By 1990 the APS boasted 7,500 members, a newsletter (*APS Observer*), a journal (*Psychological Science*), an employment bulletin, and a separate convention. Another association also had been formed: the American Association of Applied and Preventive Psychology (AAAPP), which by 1991 was offering its own newsletter (*The Scientist Practitioner*), a journal (*Applied and Preventive Psychology: Current Scientific Perspectives*), a convention in tandem with the APS convention, and a program of liability insurance. By 2005 the APS had more than 14,000 members, and the AAAPP had more than 500. The APS had also added three additional journals.

The APA-APS struggles are analogous to those of the APA and AAAP in the late 1930s. The current struggle, however, pits psychologists against psychologists along presumed lines of scientific interests and pits applied psychologists against one another along presumed lines of clinically based practice versus scientifically based practice. The longevity of these recent organizational life-forms, and their impact on school psychology, remain to be seen. At present their impact has been negligible and their membership numbers appear to be decreasing. Nevertheless, the national representation of psychologists is now divided more than it has been for nearly a half-century. Should the trend continue and include the creation of separate state affiliate associations with the APS and AAAPP or program accreditation, it could disrupt the political relationships of professional psychologists at the state level. On the other hand, it may renew state-level academic memberships that waned as state associations took on increasingly professional characteristics. Curiously, the struggles between the APA, APS, and AAAPP have gone almost unnoticed in the official discussions of NASP and APA's Division of School Psychology.

National Association of School Psychologists

From the standpoint of national representation for school psychologists, the thoroughbred years have been dominated by NASP. NASP membership grew from 856 in 1969, to approximately 5,000 in 1979, to 14,000 in 1989, to 21,500 by 1999, and to 22,000 in 2004. Membership dropped to 20,400 in 2005, a figure comparable to its total for 1998. The shifting membership numbers of the past several years likely reflect retirements and the possibility that NASP membership is reaching a plateau after numerous years of growth. NASP began accepting state affiliate associations in the early 1970s. Soon the existing associations were affiliating with NASP, while NASP, in turn, was fostering the establishment of new associations that would later become NASP affiliates. In 1980, of 43 state associations, 33 were NASP affiliates, and by 1998 the number had grown to 52 affiliates representing all 50 states, the District of Columbia, and Puerto Rico. Almost every new state school psychology association was established apart from the existing state psychological association.

Affiliations of state associations and NASP have been symbiotic, with NASP providing a network for action that was not possible through APA Division 16. An example of those benefits can be seen in the 1980 Spring Hill Symposium and its follow-up Olympia Conference in 1981. Division 16 had to achieve its objectives at the 1981 conference because it lacked a network for further action. In contrast, NASP and its affiliates took the framework established at those conferences and carried it back to the state associations for school psychologists for implementation. This network disseminated, implemented, and promoted NASP policies and ideas throughout the states. The policies and ideas of Division 16, on the other hand, had to be promoted through the network of state psychological associations, which represented few school psychologists. Thus differences between NASP- and APA-affiliated associations extended to the national level as well as the state level.

The NASP affiliates were also more likely to follow up on the 2003 Future of School Psychology Conference at Indiana University, although the proceedings were disseminated through special issues of four school psychology journals. In addition, online modules were made available for training and discussion that greatly assisted dissemination of the 2002 Futures Conference outcomes. The 2002 conference information and modules may be accessed at *www.indiana.edu/futures/resources.html.* Discussions of NASP and APA Division 16 history appear in *School Psychology Digest* (Vol. 8, No. 2), *School Psychology Review* (Vol. 18, No. 2), Fagan (1993, 1994), and Fagan, Gorin, and Tharinger (2000).

Related Organizations

Other groups were emerging that represented further professional maturity. University trainers, with a well-established record of leadership in NASP and Division 16, formed two associations in this period, Trainers of School Psychologists (TSP) and the Council of Directors of School Psychology Programs (CDSPP). For historical discussion of TSP and CDSPP, see Phillips (1993). After being loosely affiliated with NASP for several years, Canadian practitioners founded the Canadian Association of School Psychologists in 1985 (see chapter 9). The International School Psychology Association was established in 1982 following a decade of growth as the International School Psychology Committee (see chapter 10). In 1992, APA's Board of Professional Psychology diversified into several specialty boards, including the American Board of School Psychology (ABSP). The ABSP operates under the auspices of the American Academy of School Psychology, founded in 1993. In 1994 the Society for the Study of School Psychology (SSSP) was founded. The SSSP financially supports research and scholarship in the field and is the parent organization of the *Journal of School Psychology.*

Professional Regulation

Nonschool Practice Credentialing

The APA's and NASP's differences of opinion were greatest over policies on the practice of school psychology. At the state level, differences were reflected in conflicts over credentialing, as nondoctoral school psychologists challenged the authority of credentialing agencies to restrict their practice to school settings. Whereas the struggles of clinical psychologists to obtain practice privileges had involved battles with psychiatry and medicine, the battles for nonschool practice by school psychologists were almost exclusively between school and clinical psychology groups. The efforts of state associations were assisted by NASP, but this was not a nationally coordinated effort, nor was APA's general opposition coordinated. These were primarily state-level skirmishes bolstered by national-level technical and financial assistance. Several successes for school psychology were gained (e.g., in California, Connecticut, Illinois, and Ohio), though less so since the mid-1980s.

The struggles and successes did much to spur the identity and morale of school psychologists. In most states, these struggles could not have occurred before the thoroughbred years, when both state psychology and school psychology groups were gaining strength. By the early 1990s much of the tension had dissipated. The relative calm could be related to several factors. The APA Practice Directorate, with a full-time school psychologist employee, was better able to communicate with NASP. More school psychologists were obtaining doctoral degrees than earlier in the period (the percentage had jumped from 3% to at least 20%), making the issue of nondoctoral practice less important. For many nondoctoral school psychologists, nonschool and private practice were not a high priority, nor were many engaged in such work. The number of semester hours required for nondoctoral programs was increasing. The NASP National Certification System conferred a new status on many practitioners, which perhaps allayed the need for greater recognition. Finally, in several states credentialing concerns were shifting to the state education agency, where personnel shortages of school psychologists were encouraging credentialing changes that threatened long-established school-based practices.

Whereas the struggles of clinical psychologists to obtain practice privileges had involved battles with psychiatry and medicine, the battles for nonschool practice by school psychologists were almost exclusively between school and clinical psychology groups.

School Practice Credentialing

In the arena of school practice credentialing, much of the activity was directed at maintaining high standards in states threatening to downgrade requirements and at raising state requirements to the NASP expectation in states undergoing long-needed revisions. In this latter regard, the NCATE partnership agreements with state education agencies regarding program accreditation have fostered higher credentialing standards as well. A good bit of the success in improving certification can be attributed to the efforts of the members of the National Association of State Consultants for School Psychological Services. Even though state consultant positions date to the time of Gesell's practice, only about half the states have a state consultant. Little has been written to recognize the efforts of these state government positions, and perhaps they will soon be obsolete. Whereas they served in a highly administrative role in the hybrid years, in recent times they have also served as liaisons among state departments of education, local school psychologists, university training programs, and state associations. The relationship has been important to the reciprocal conveyance of perceived needs of children between school psychologist and SDE perspectives. In contrast to the hybrid years, almost every state has some form of SDE credentialing for school psychology personnel, and many now have nonschool practice privileges as well, often by way of specialized licensure (Curtis, Hunley, & Prus, 1998). The expectation of the NCLB Act for "highly qualified personnel" may serve in the long run to maintain the gains in credentialing requirements made by state and national school psychology groups.

Program Accreditation

Following the accreditation of its first program in 1971, APA accreditation grew from three programs in 1972 to 20 in 1980. Spurred by growing interest in doctoral training and nonschool credentials, the number grew to 42 in 1990, 59 in 1998, and 67 in 2005–2006, including 10 combined specialty programs (Accredited Doctoral Programs in Professional Psychology, 2005; Fagan & Wells, 2000; Supplement to Listing of Accredited Programs, 2006). Almost from its start, NASP initiated inquiries to NCATE about training guidelines and accreditation. By the end of its first decade, NASP had approved standards for training, field placements, credentialing, and practice, in addition to a code of ethics and several position statements on important issues (Batsche, Knoff, & Peterson, 1989; Curtis & Zins, 1989). These standards documents were revised in 1984, 1994, 1997, and 2000. Those for training were promulgated through NASP's formal relationships with NCATE, including affiliation in 1976 and constituent membership in 1978. A revised NCATE unit accreditation process allowed NASP to perform program evaluations through folio review and to list publicly the programs it approved. This resulted in programs being designated as NASP approved, in addition to or independent of the institution's NCATE accreditation status. This gave NASP a stronger role in school psychology program recognition, even though NASP itself held no accrediting authority. In contrast to the hybrid years, by 1997 all school psychology programs were assumed to hold SDE approval, and 57% of the 294 programs held some form of national accreditation (Thomas, 1998).

National Certification

The revised NASP credentialing standards were prominent in the National School Psychology Certification System (NSPCS) initiated in 1988–1989, which included a national school psychology examination developed by the Educational Testing Service. The involvement of NASP in the creation of this exam is an excellent example of the reactive-proactive involvement of the 1980s. The NSPCS, another symbol of professionalism, enjoyed considerable success, enrolling more than 15,000 school psychologists by 1991 before declining to about 11,000 in 1998 and to about 9,300 in 2005. It improved the identity of the field before state credentialing bodies, some of whom quickly adopted the examination, the credential, or both as part of their own credentialing requirements. Many specialist-level training programs were using the national examination as an exit requirement to receive the degree (Fagan, 2005c).

Whereas Division 16 carried the national banner for school psychology from 1945 to 1970, NASP has carried it since. Both groups helped to enhance the regulation of the profession and to shift such regulation from strictly external to largely internal mechanisms. The two systems of school psychology operating in the United States—one controlled by education, and the other by psychology—have influenced and will continue to influence training and practice (Fagan, 1986c). Conflicts between the APA and NASP dissipated over the past 20 years, although long-standing differences in policies and orientations have persisted. Division 16 has renewed efforts to raise its practitioner membership and to support practitioners by revising its journal format, focusing on broad educational issues, and producing a series of videotaped interviews on practitioner issues. Perhaps in the coming decades the stage will be set for a consolidation of organizational efforts in school psychology, although formal efforts at unification are not observable. At the very least, continued positive collaboration between the APA and NASP and education and psychology could lead to the long-awaited single control system of the profession.

Whereas Division 16 carried the national banner for school psychology from 1945 to 1970, NASP has carried it since. Both groups helped to enhance the regulation of the profession and to shift such regulation from strictly external to largely internal mechanisms.

Training

Since 1970 the number of institutions offering training programs grew from an estimated 100 to more than 200. Program enrollment increased to 7,450 in 1977, decreased to 5,634 in 1987, and then rose to 8,587 by 1997. However, the number of graduates per program (8.4 to 8.9) has been stable since 1987 (Thomas, 1998). Over the past 30 years, program and enrollment growth were most notable at the specialist and doctoral levels, corresponding to a sharp decline in master's programs (Thomas, 1998). A national program survey and directory are no longer available except online through NASP. Based on the participation of programs that have completed the online database, an estimate of the number of programs is in the 230–250 range. Among the more salient changes in training is the emergence of free-standing professional schools offering degrees in school psychology, and the availability of online courses, and in some cases online programs, in school psychology. The expansion of training models no doubt is related to a history of personnel shortages at the practice and training levels that could diminish gains made in broadened roles and functions (Fagan, 2004b). The shift is also in response to technological advancements, Internet access, and the demand for alternative training opportunities by practitioners in nontraditional family and work situations.

Literature

The period 1970–present furthered the literary accomplishments of the 1960s. NASP established a newsletter in 1969 (now the *Communiqué*) and the *School Psychology Digest* in 1972 (now *School Psychology Review*), and published the first directories of training programs and credentialing requirements. The second decade of NASP experienced a shift toward also publishing books and products for profit. Among the more successful have been *Best Practices in School Psychology*, *Children's Needs*, *Home–School Collaboration*, *Children at Risk*, *Interventions for Academic and Behavior Problems*, and an innovative compilation of the handout series included in the *Communiqué* (*Helping Children at Home and School*). For its part, Division 16 published a monograph series between 1973 and 1980, and in 1986 began publishing *Professional School Psychology* (now *School Psychology Quarterly*). The division's newsletter, *The School Psychologist*, changed its format, expanded in length, and changed to a greater practitioner orientation. In addition to the literary accomplishments of Division 16 and NASP, this period included the founding of *School Psychology International*, *Journal of Psychoeducational Assessment*, *Special Services in the Schools* (now *Journal of Applied School Psychology*), and numerous books on school psychology. The *Handbook of School Psychology* and its revisions (Gutkin & Reynolds, 1990; Reynolds & Gutkin, 1982, 1999) reflected the combination of diversity and specialization and provided a resource for the field along the lines of an earlier handbook by Magary (1967b).

The earlier volumes by the Gottsegens were without peer until the *Advances in School Psychology* series of the 1980s. The frequency of authored, position-oriented texts, a trademark of the 1960s, continued to appear, with some espousing particular models of training and practice (e.g., Bardon & Bennett, 1974; Fagan & Wise,

1994; Merrell, Ervin, & Gimpel, 2006; Phillips, 1990a; Plas, 1986; Reynolds, Gutkin, Elliott, & Witt, 1984). The many edited volumes after 1970 reflect the complexity of the field and the emergence of subspecializations. The significant changes in professional regulation and litigation spurred considerable writing in legal and ethical concerns. The demand for comprehensive coverage of legal and ethical issues led to the success of the multiple editions of *Ethics and Law for School Psychologists* (Jacob & Hartshorne, 2007). In November 2006, NASP published its first issue of its online journal, *School Psychology Forum: Research in Practice.*

Analyses of literary content of this period suggested an emphasis on testing and assessment (Fagan, 1986a; Strein, Cramer, & Lawser, 2003) and legal issues and future perspectives (Kraus & Mcloughlin, 1997). A study of publication topics of the faculty in the top 10 APA-accredited school psychology programs found the following order of frequency: professional issues, interventions, assessment, and consultation (Carper & Williams, 2004). Increased pediatric topics seemed "to support school psychologists' widening role definition" (Wodrich & Schmitt, 2003, p. 131). A comparative analysis of literature in the mid-1990s, conducted by Strein et al. (2003), indicated a "substantial congruence between authors' and practitioners' views about what kinds of research needs to be done in school psychology," but also noted a "substantial lack of congruence between these priorities and the kinds of research reported in the USA and international school psychology journal literature" (p. 432). A similar disparity was observed by Miranda and Gutter (2002), between the concern for diversity and the extent to which diversity was addressed in school psychology's literature, and by Greif and Greif (2004), who felt articles including fathers were underrepresented. Occasionally content analyses of a specific journal are provided by some editors at the conclusion of their terms (see, e.g., Harrison, 2000; Oakland, 1986; Shapiro, 1995). These are useful for tracking the history of a specific journal and its themes, topics, and special features.

As discovered in the analyses described above, school psychologists were writing not only for themselves but also for other educational and psychological audiences. Influences beyond school psychology are observable in the areas of test construction, child neuropsychology, special education, and preschool assessment. In the hybrid years, school psychology had finally produced its own literature, but in the thoroughbred years, this literature spread to other fields. Over a 50-year period school psychologists had shifted from learning about their field from others to teaching others about school psychology and contributing to the literature of other fields. The shift lends further emphasis to the field's maturity and professionalization resulting from the purification process of the thoroughbred years. However, this conclusion was challenged by Frisby (1998), who found that school psychology journals tended to store citations from other (nonschool psychology) journals to a greater extent than they fed citations to other journals. The last decade has also seen the inclusion of school psychology entries in published encyclopedias, including encyclopedias specifically about school psychology (Fagan & Warden, 1996; Lee, 2005; Watson & Skinner, 2004). Other school psychology groups, including state associations, Trainers of School Psychologists, and the Council of Directors of School Psychology Programs, provided an array of newsletters and publications. Finally, Roberts, Gerrard-Morris, Zanger, Davis, and Robinson (2006) reviewed the rise of women as authors and editors for major school psychology journals in the period 1991–2004, an achievement corresponding to the increased representation by women in the field. Although school psychology newsletters are typically published by professional associations, *Today's School Psychologist,* published monthly by LRP Publications, has been a private venture since 1997.

School psychologists were writing not only for themselves but also for other educational and psychological audiences.

Roles and Functions of School Psychologists

The thoroughbred years brought about changes in school psychologists roles and functions as social influences and demands changed. As throughout its history, the professional roles and functions developed by responding to the need for services.

Children at Risk

Changes in the American family since the 1960s gained widespread recognition by the 1980s. The model of the two-parent family, where the father worked out of the home and the mother remained at home to focus on childrearing and other homemaking duties, became increasingly rare. Instead, the family of the late 20th century often was headed by a single parent as the result of divorce, forcing mothers into the workplace for economic survival. The rising cost of living also created hardships for married couples and remarried couples, in many cases requiring both spouses to work outside the home to secure and maintain a decent standard of living. Maternal employment was also related to increased education and employment opportunities for women. A widespread effect of these changes was that many children were being raised in comparatively unsupervised circumstances. The subsequent problems of these and other circumstances were eventually observed in the schools, which prompted national studies of the cultural changes and their implications for school psychologists (Fournier & Perry, 1998). By the late 1980s, the intense focus on special education was shifting to another target group: children at risk. These were not traditional special education children being referred to by a new term. Instead, the at-risk category (Barona & Garcia, 1990) included children of divorce, often living in poverty, "latchkey" kids, substance abusers and their children, suicide-prone children, pregnant teens, potential dropouts, and other students who required academic and psychological assistance but probably not traditional special education. These were not necessarily children whose traits were consistently impaired but rather those whose states were temporarily problematic and who were at risk of becoming chronically problematic. Such youngsters required assistance somewhere along a continuum between regular education and special education. Although some at-risk categories showed improvement between 1990 and 2000, there were still large numbers of at-risk children in urban, suburban, and rural settings. An analysis of the categories with state and national data appears in *Children at Risk: State Trends 1990–2000* (Annie E. Casey Foundation, 2002).

In the 1990s, school violence also captured public attention. Several major incidents in which guns led to the killing of children on school grounds drew school psychologists into another social and educational arena. The U.S. Secretary of Education asked NASP to develop a guidebook for districts, a major achievement in the governmental and professional relations arena for NASP (U.S. Department of Education, 1998). Major incidents of school violence appear to have abated somewhat in the past 5 years, but considerable attention has been drawn to bullying in the school and to the importance of finding alternatives to corporal punishment.

Changing Landscapes in Special Education

The traditional roles involving norm-referenced assessment, which dominated school psychological services in earlier periods, persisted throughout the thoroughbred years (Reschly, 1998). The 1970s began with a surge of interest in school consultation and organizational or systems development but seemed to regress to traditional assessment models as a function of the Education for All Handicapped Children Act of 1975. The 1970s was a period of intense special education placement and litigation, although the effect of those trends on the role and function of most school psychologists seemed to contract more than to expand activities, despite a rapidly growing workforce. One study designed to assess the impact of EAHCA found that, although the school psychologist's role had not changed, it continued to be constricted, "with heavy emphasis on assessment, rather than prevention, consultation, or intervention." It also found that too much time was spent with bureaucratic paperwork and with children suspected of having handicapping conditions (Goldwasser, Meyers, Christenson, & Graden, 1983, p. 163). School psychologists reported spending about 70% of their time in assessment activities, 20% in consultation, and 10% in direct intervention with children, and 71% of their time was spent with handicapped children. These activity percentages were supported by Smith (1984). Smith also found that school psychologists desired less time on assessment activities and preferred more time on interventions, consultation, and research. Several of the actual-time versus desired-time discrepancies achieved statistical significance, supporting the contention that role dissatisfaction of the 1960s continued into the 1980s. The trend also was observed in the Reschly and Wilson (1992) and Reschly (1998) studies. The Reschly (1998) data revealed that, although the assessment role remained dominant, the specific functions within that role (e.g., assessment techniques) were shifting, and also that the use of nontraditional assessment approaches was neither more nor less time-consuming than traditional techniques.

By the late 1980s, forces internal and external to the profession were raising concerns regarding the expansion of special education, especially the more than 100% increase in the number of learning-disabled children served. In opposition to the traditional refer–test–report (and place) delivery model, reformers, including school psychologists, rallied around the use of alternative services, the Regular Education Initiative, and varying amounts of inclusion (a modernized, expanded version of an earlier term, *mainstreaming*). The Regular Education Initiative, of the U.S. Department of Education's Office of Special Education and Rehabilitation Services, advocated the integration of general and special education into one educational system for all students. The initiative and its opposition reflected the political instability of traditional special education service models in the wake of persistent efforts to implement the least-restrictive-environment provisions of EAHCA and its reauthorization as IDEA. Discussions in earlier decades about noncategorical services in special education were shifting (at least for the mildly handicapped, and perhaps for others) to discussions of services outside of special education, the possible reduction of special education enrollments, and the use of funds to prevent children from eventually needing to be placed in special education. Prereferral assessment and intervention models rapidly gained attention and became standard procedures of the referral process. No doubt the rising costs of education at a time when government spending was under scrutiny spurred efforts to reduce special education enrollments, since the per pupil cost of special education was more than twice that of regular education (Moore, Strang, Schwartz, & Braddock, 1988). Nevertheless, special education enrollments continued to increase.

A statement by the Office of Special Education and Rehabilitative Services, on the role of school psychology, was a further impetus for positive change (Will, 1989). The NCLB (2001) combined with the increased assessment options under IDEA and the general trend toward more effective use of interventions such as empirically supported or evidence-based interventions and functional-behavioral analysis (FBA) supported this change. Under the 2004 IDEA Reauthorization, the response-to-intervention (RTI) approach for identifying children with learning disability was brought together with evidence-based interventions, functional-behavioral analysis, prereferral assessment and intervention teams, and criterion-referenced and curriculum-based assessment (Fagan, 2008 in press). Although controversial, such practices have found long-term success in some settings (see, e.g., Grimes, Kurns, & Tilley, 2006). Add to these the emphasis being placed on early literacy and reading skills, with many school psychologists planning and implementing programs at the preschool and early elementary school levels. The stability of these approaches to special education and their expansion to other disability areas will likely be determined over the next decade.

Under the 2004 IDEA Reauthorization, the response-to-intervention (RTI) approach for identifying children with learning disability was brought together with evidence-based interventions, functional-behavioral analysis, prereferral assessment and intervention teams, and criterion-referenced and curriculum-based assessment.

Barriers to Change

Whereas the first decade of the era that began in 1975 with EAHCA was assessment- and placement-intensive, the second decade shifted toward instruction and related services, and more recently toward curriculum interventions and functional assessments. The shifts toward prereferral assessment, interventions, and at least secondary prevention for at-risk groups are potential indicators of long-term changes in the roles and functions of school psychologists. Interest and activity in consultation and family assessment and intervention have grown, including home–school collaboration (Christenson & Conoley, 1992). The events of the past 15 years have also signaled the need for mental health interventions, as school psychologists have become more involved in regular education and must respond to concerns about violence and bullying, students' social adjustment, and crisis intervention. However, there is less interest in organizational consultation and development. Is the field truly emerging from the retrenchment of the 1970s and making its first enduring and major changes in roles and functions? Or do Reschly's (1998) data for the period 1985–1996, and those of Curtis, Lopez, Batsche, and Smith (2006), predict continued role stability?

One potential barrier to lasting role changes is the shortage of practitioners, which has gained more attention in the past 15 years. The gap between the supply of and demand for school psychology practitioners is a significant training and service issue. With students facing higher levels of required training, and practitioners entering employment in more diverse settings, the supply problems are anticipated to persist (see, e.g., Curtis, Grier, & Hunley, 2004; and a 2004 special issue of *Psychology in the Schools*, Vol. 41, No. 4). Though the majority of practitioners continue to be employed in school settings, many have found other employment. Training requirements have increased as a function of higher expectations for program accreditation and for practitioner credentialing at both the doctoral and nondoctoral levels. The personnel shortage also extends to faculty of training programs. Other potential barriers to changing roles and functions are well-known: high caseloads, modest salaries, inadequate school budgets, role perceptions held by school administrators, and narrow conceptualizations of psychological services in schools. Additional factors influencing roles and functions are discussed in chapters 4 and 7. The effects of technological advancements such as computers, e-mail discussion lists, software, and so forth have not been studied; however, not surprisingly, this technology has appended itself to the traditional roles of the school psychologist. The advent of computer-generated scoring and report-writing services has received mixed reviews. However, the expanding availability of information and assistance through Internet services may also foster change.

One potential barrier to lasting role change is the shortage of practitioners that has gained more attention in the past 15 years.

Important Contributors

The events of the thoroughbred years helped the profession of school psychology realize its potential as a significant entity within education and psychology. The first decade of the thoroughbred years was characterized by growth and division of associations, growth of a professional identity, and increasing regulation of training and practice. It remained for the school psychology leadership in the second, third, and fourth decades to seek the means to implement such regulation effectively and to consolidate the forces in school psychology. Half or more of the number of training programs, accredited programs, practitioners, available credentials, state associations, and professional literature have developed in the thoroughbred years. School psychology is now a mature, officially recognized specialty of American psychology.

Several individuals who made major contributions to the field of school psychology during the later hybrid years and the earlier thoroughbred years are no longer living. These men and women helped bring school psychology from its uncertain status several decades ago to the profession of today. The specific areas of their contributions are in parentheses.

Jim Agner (leadership)

John Austin (leadership)

Jack I. Bardon (training, leadership, professional identity)

Virginia D. C. Bennett (American Board of Professional Psychology, accreditation, leadership)

Calvin Catterall (international school psychology)

Michael Chrin (leadership, development of school psychology in Ohio)

Norma E. Cutts (development of practice and credentialing in Connecticut)

Muriel Forrest (advocacy for professional standards)

Susan Gray (training, leadership in Head Start)

Liam Grimley (international school psychology)

Irwin Hyman (child advocacy)

John Jackson (minority issues and leadership)

Elizabeth Koppitz (psychoeducational assessment)

Nadine Lambert (training, leadership, assessment)

Frances Mullen (leadership, international school psychology)

T. Ernest Newland (training, development of practice in Pennsylvania, Tennessee, and Illinois)

Rutherford Porter (training, development of practice in Pennsylvania and Indiana)

Marcia Shaffer (leadership in NASP and APA Division 16)

Marie Skodak Crissey (practice, leadership)

Mary Alice White (ABPP approval, accreditation)

Joseph Zins (training, social-emotional development and mental health)

HISTORICAL SUMMARY

The history of school psychology has been interwoven with the development of education and psychology since the latter part of the 19th century. Many of the structural characteristics of contemporary education, psychology, and school psychology could be observed by 1920. However, the 20th century was the first time education, psychological science, and school psychology coexisted at the same time that formal schooling was widely accepted and required.

Study of the history of school psychology shows the chronological sequence, beginning with the need for services in schools and then the emergence of those services, followed by the emergence of training programs and the credentialing of practitioners, followed by accreditation and then external and internal regulation (see Table 2.2). This sequence suggests that new models of training, credentialing, and practice emerged, as opposed to expanding earlier models. For example, in the practice area,

Table 2.2 Growth of the School Psychology Profession*

Area	1890	1920	1940	1970	1990	2000	2005
Practitioners	0	200	500	5,000	22,000	25,000	30,000+
Training Institutions	0	0	2	100	230	218	220
Credentialing by SDE	0	0	3	40	50	50	50
State Associations	0	0	3	17	52	52	52
Primary Journals	0	0	0	2	7	7	8

*The figures are approximations based on data for dates closest to the divisions presented. The number of journals includes the *Canadian Journal of School Psychology* and *School Psychology International.*

many school psychologists function similarly to practitioners in the 1920s, but the dominant form today is much different in terms of employer expectations, available technology, referrals, and practitioner preferences. So, although testing has persisted as a dominant model, its conceptualizations have changed. In the 19th century, phrenology had many advocates, but that method predated the appearance of school psychology. By the late 1800s, Cattell had proposed a battery of mental tests (Cattell, 1890) that reflected anthropometric and other ideas, but those tests failed to achieve broad acceptance, largely because of problems of external validity and the development of rival testing methods. It was the application of Binet's work in the early 1900s that brought mental testing to the study of higher processes and then gained widespread acceptability. These earlier forms of practice continue to influence present practice. However, the dominant ideology of earlier decades was directed at limited-ability testing and direct services, with practically no preventive or accountability functions. Current ideology, having shifted in the direction of interventions and espousing consultation, therapy, prevention, and accountability, could be observed in limited ways at earlier times, but the testing ideology was dominant in the preferences of employers *and* school psychologists. The role of traditional assessment has broadened in scope as additional personal and environmental factors have gained recognition for contributing to the problems of schoolchildren and their schooling (Fagan, 2008, in press). Thus, the focus of psychoeducational assessment is no longer exclusively on the person referred.

Over the course of school psychology's history, several service delivery systems are observed. The models represent the emergence of school psychology's identity as a school-based and school-linked service. Although several models are present, there is a general trend for service models to become more prevalent in the order below.

1. Psychological clinics in institutions of higher learning (university/college, medical school, normal school), or institutional facility
2. School district-based clinic, research bureau
3. Community-based clinic, guidance center
4. State department of education employee serving entire state or region of the state
5. State department of education supervision of regional/county employees
6. School-district contracts with psychologist from nearby city
7. University-based comprehensive clinic serving several districts in its region

8. Regional services or traveling clinics provided by institutional facility
9. Psychologists and examiners in independent practice contracted to provide services to schools
10. Psychologists and examiners employed by community mental health center to serve districts in its region
11. School psychologist in independent practice contracted to provide services to schools
12. School psychologist employed by community mental health center to serve school districts in its region
13. School psychologists employed by several school districts concurrently (with or without formal inter-district contract)
14. School psychologist employed by special education agreement district (e.g., cooperative, Bureau of Cooperative Educational Services (BOCES), Area Education Agency (AEA)
15. School psychologist employed by single school district

The historical study of school psychology reveals three things: that service origins, innovations, and reforms never occur as a result of universal agreement; that change is better appreciated as a well-intended effort at improvement; and that change never occurs uniformly across settings. The profession's history can be viewed as a period of evolution and transition through various available ideologies and practice models, with certain ideologies and models being dominant in different periods. Ideology and practice also are not always synchronous. For example, current professional standards espouse an ideology of training, credentialing, and practice that is far from widespread. Even today, in an era of ideological transition to treatment and prevention in educational settings, some educators and practitioners insist on traditional testing functions. What school psychology has sought for many years is a consensus of its own ideology with that of its employers, which would lead to practice that consists of prevention, consultation, and accountability (research and evaluation), in addition to necessary assessment and intervention functions. The advancements of the thoroughbred years have placed such consensus within reach for the first time. For more than a century, society has looked to its schools and its children as the potential long-range solution to its problems. In that process, society has increasingly turned to various professionals to achieve its long-term goals. The historical model of school psychology served well the limited arena of special education placement. The future of school psychology depends largely on the profession being able to learn from, and improve on, the ideologies and models of its past.

The profession's history can be viewed as a period of evolution and transition through various available ideologies and practice models, with certain ideologies and models being dominant in different periods.

Many events have helped shape the present condition of school psychology. However simple it may seem, the fact that long ago some psychological practitioners chose to provide services as employees *of* boards of education, as opposed to being external service providers *to* boards of education, may be the most significant trend in school psychology in the 20th century. This single factor set into motion a field of practice that would increasingly be influenced and regulated by the forces that shape public education and its employees. School psychologists would thereafter struggle to survive and prosper in the two worlds of education and psychology. They have survived and they have prospered. In the remaining chapters of this book, discussions of contemporary issues and practices build on the historical periods and origins discussed in this chapter. Changes the field is now undergoing will at some time be a part of that history.

Chapter 3

The Employment Context of School Psychologists

Society's needs for regulation and governance, protection, recreation, health, and education are served by a complex interplay of public and private agencies at the federal, state, and local levels. Although some school psychologists work in federal- and state-level agencies, the majority work at the local community level and almost exclusively with health and education agencies. They are most often employed in public educational institutions, including in county and city school systems, under cooperative educational agreements, and in related public agencies with educational programs such as in programs for developmental disabilities, in correctional centers, and in universities. Less frequently, school psychologists are employed in private educational facilities, mental health agencies, medical facilities, and independent private practice. Regardless of their employment setting, school psychologists will be serving children with education-related problems and need to have an understanding of the school setting.

This chapter focuses on the relationship between U.S. public education and school psychology and on organizational issues related to practice, including where school psychologists fit into the public schools and other employment settings. Issues regarding nonschool settings are interwoven into the discussion and also are discussed in other chapters. Although the chapter touches on educational administration, policy, and finance, it is intended only to introduce students to selected topics of education relevant to the preparation and practice of school psychologists.

PURPOSES OF EDUCATION

Although widespread compulsory education did not begin until the 20th century, Americans have taken education seriously since the first settlements were established. The concept of education and schools was present in the early settlements of colonial North America and during every subsequent historical period. The evolution of U.S. society over four centuries created an environment in which compulsory education became the dominant model of schooling. (The first state to enact a compulsory attendance law was Massachusetts in 1852.) The subsequent problems of compulsory education were addressed by other developments, including the rise of the science of psychology and the availability of experts.

Schools are concerned with transmitting knowledge and inculcating proper moral character for citizenship.

Whether dominated by religious or social influences or by the "three Rs," U.S. schools have served the dual purposes of transmitting both the basic academic content necessary for individual economic survival and the cultural values considered necessary to ensure the survival of the nation. Goslin (1965) describes the principal functions of schooling as the maintenance and transmission of culture, the encouragement and implementation of change and the discovery of new knowledge, and the allocation of individuals to positions in society. Spring (1989) describes similar political, social, and economic purposes of education. Other purposes the schools serve include child care, delinquency prevention, courtship and mate selection, cultural and subgroup identity and stability, and social reform (Goslin, 1965; Spring, 1989). To fulfill the early goals of compulsory schooling, interpreted as human capital and structural reinforcement (chapter 2), the U.S. schools have been concerned with transmitting knowledge and inculcating proper moral character for citizenship. Recent crises relate to the perception that scores on nationally standardized tests are declining (content) and that substance abuse, crime, teen pregnancy, and other at-risk conditions suggest a deterioration of national character (values).

The broad purposes of schooling are generally consistent across school settings, in both public and private schools and those serving child populations with or without special needs. However, the interpretation of these purposes in the form of specific curricular objectives and activities may vary considerably among school settings. Developing character and citizenship may lead to a much different curriculum in a parochial school than in a public school. The public school may offer elementary guidance activities to clarify values, whereas the parochial school may prefer religious education stressing obedience to parental authority. In rare instances psychological services may be perceived as counterproductive, as in the case in which counseling might encourage the child to behave counter to parental wishes. In general, however, psychological services are well received in public, private, and parochial school settings.

Varied interpretations of these common purposes also may occur within a school system. For example, all the structural elements of a school system may generally agree with the system's goal of developing good citizenship. However, when this is interpreted by the school board to include sex education, parents and others often express dissent. On the other hand, the goal of providing basic educational skills may be interpreted as requiring segregated remedial education programs instead of grouping students within the regular classroom. Even though districts have fairly strong agreement on goals, the means to achieve those goals vary, and it is in this variation of means and their outcomes that controversy arises.

Implications for School Psychologists' Roles and Training

What does this mean for the school psychologist? School psychologists are employed to help schools develop and achieve their goals. They are aware of the important relationship between academic learning and positive mental health. For school psychologists, students' personal and social learning in addition to academic learning should be considered important goals for the schools. Thus, through a variety of services, school psychologists seek to improve both the academic and the mental health environments of the school.

One conflict school psychologists frequently encounter is the narrow interpretation of school psychological services by some school administrators and teachers. For example, the goal of developing student character, which could capitalize on consultation and intervention skills, may instead simply involve having a school psychologist test students to help the district sort children and assign those judged to have less character into special classes for developing character. Surveys of school psychologists consistently confirm the dominance of their assessment role, which raises serious questions regarding the perceptions held by administrators about the match of psychological services to the goals of education. It is an unfortunate fact that some school districts might not employ school psychologists at all if not for federal and state legislation requiring psychologists to perform assessments. Fortunately, narrow roles such as these appear to be diminishing. Thus, school psychologists can help their field by being concerned with where they fit into the structure and purposes of the educational system and with how they can help the system recognize school psychologists' training and potential contributions.

The conflict between educational goals and the real and potential roles of school psychologists has implications for training as well. Should school psychologists be trained primarily for assessment roles and functions, since that is what most school systems employ them to provide? For as long as training issues have been discussed, the ideology has supported training school psychologists to fulfill not only expected employment roles but also potential roles. Accredited programs offer comprehensive training for assessment, intervention, consultation, research and evaluation, and other functions. Training should equip the school psychologist to provide services that go beyond the status quo to greater role diversity and to leadership for the future.

Professionals in the field of school psychology should not take for granted that this system of education will survive indefinitely in its current form. Nor will it always employ school psychologists to help accomplish its goals.

Incorporation of School Psychologists' Goals in Educational Systems

In an ideal world, the goals and means of all parties to education would be harmonious. That is, the goals of training programs for school psychologists would be consistent with the goals and expectations of school boards and administrators and also with those of parents and teachers. In reality, the constituencies of educational systems come from different training orientations and backgrounds, which influence their methods for selecting and achieving goals. Sarason (1971) discusses conflicts in the cultural perspectives within schools. Though not directed to school psychologists, his book is relevant to their situation. Differences of opinion are a healthy fact of life, resulting in a choice of alternative viewpoints from which goals and the methods for implementing them are chosen. In an arena where the training and backgrounds of the constituencies contribute to the creation of policy and practice, all parties must be prepared to negotiate to create as harmonious implementation as possible. In this environment, school psychologists are in a position of power rather than authority (see discussion later in this chapter), reinforcing the importance of their roles in public relations and collaborative consultation.

Professionals in the field of school psychology should not take for granted that this system of education will survive indefinitely in its current form. Nor will it always employ school psychologists to help accomplish its goals as it presently does. For most of the history of U.S. education, the schools have been without the services of experts such as school psychologists. However, it is unlikely that the original and historical roles (the "sorting" and "repairing" of individual children) alone can effectively and efficiently continue to serve the changing structure and needs of U.S. education. An important task for every prospective school psychologist is to ponder why schools employ school psychologists and to imagine being asked by a potential employer, "What do you think our district is trying to do in this community, and what can you do to help us achieve those goals?" These would be difficult questions for school psychologists who have been narrowly trained for a basic special education testing model and have little understanding of the overall goals and structure of that school system. The answers will provide a better understanding of what the district perceives as the needs of the local schools and where school psychologists are expected to fit into that perception.

SOME BASIC CHARACTERISTICS OF U.S. SCHOOLING

In earlier years, the U.S. public schools consisted primarily of children, teachers, and administrators. Practically no other professional employees, such as supervisors, counselors, or school psychologists, were involved. According to the National Center for Education Statistics (2003), in 2001–2002, U.S. schools had approximately 5.9 million school employees, including 3 million teachers, 224,000 administrative personnel, 54,000 librarians, 100,000 guidance counselors (NCES, 2004a), and at least 29,000 district-based school psychologists (Charvat, 2005). The public schools were educating 47.7 million children in more than 14,500 regular and special school districts with more than 94,000 school buildings. Including private school data for the same year added approximately 5.3 million students and 425,000 full-time-equivalent teachers in 29,279 school buildings (NCES, 2004b). The magnitude continues to support the opinion of Orlosky, McCleary, Shapiro, and Webb (1984) that "one fifth of the total population of the United States is involved in the education industry, either as students or as employees" (p. 209). Although no data are available on school psychologists in private education, almost every public school district in the country has specialized services available, including those of school psychologists and the thousands of mental health workers practicing outside the schools, including counselors, psychologists, psychometrists, family therapists, social workers, and other school psychologists in private practice. The sheer magnitude of the education and mental health industries

Almost every public school district in the country has specialized services available, including those of school psychologists.

draws attention to the complexity of schooling and the significance of finding ways to improve services to children through the collaboration of educators and mental health workers. However, despite the size and diversity of the education system nationwide, structural commonalities exist among the local school districts.

Background—Responsibility of the States

Federal interest in education grew in importance throughout the 20th century, corresponding to the changing status of children and the federal government's interest in their well-being. In the 21st century, children are more important and have greater legal status than at any other period in U.S. history. However, despite the growing influence of federal education agencies, legislation, regulations, and funding, and all the national political rhetoric about the value of education, the U.S. system of education is the constitutional responsibility of state government and is largely regulated and managed at the state and local levels. There is no national school system. Pressure in various forms is brought to bear from the federal level, but the schools are regulated by the states, according to laws enacted by each state legislature and according to regulations established by each state board of education and implemented through the state department of education (SDE).

The federal programs involve a relationship between state and federal governments in which states voluntarily agree to federal incentives, usually financial incentives, through grants and other funds available to those states that demonstrate compliance with federal regulations for education. The widespread growth of special education since the 1975 passage of the Education for All Handicapped Children Act (EAHCA, Public Law 94-142) has been an outgrowth of the state and local educational agencies' response to federal agency initiatives and regulations. Although compliance is voluntary, it is viewed as essential to the civil rights of individuals with disabilities, and federal funding is directly linked to compliance. Because all states participate in these federal programs, every local district must demonstrate to its SDE that it, too, is in compliance with the federal regulations as interpreted and enforced at the state level. The entire compliance process can take several years from the passage of the federal legislation.

Diversity and Commonality of Practices

Although states bear the responsibility for the education of their citizens, they differ in their resources and procedures. The structures and practices in one state, no matter how effective, may not be used in other states. Some states, such as Nevada, have large county-based school systems that result in few districts (17 statewide), whereas other states are highly decentralized (Texas and Illinois have about 890 and 1,040 districts, respectively). Most states have a mixture of county and local systems, resulting in a nationwide total of approximately 14,500 school districts. Even between districts within states, the structure and provision of schooling differ greatly. More affluent school districts often offer higher-quality regular and special education programs than poorer districts. Urban and rural schools may have more financial problems than suburban schools. Agencies other than the public schools may provide special programs that supplement those offered by the district. The result is a labyrinth of diverse systems and practices of schooling. By leaving education to the states, the federal government has in effect created 50 or more ongoing state-level experiments in regulation and more than 14,000 public systems for local implementation.

Despite this diversity, states share several commonalities. They comply with federal regulations to secure additional funds; they have an SDE whose staff oversees the delivery of schooling in the state; they are responsible for ensuring that educational opportunities are available to all children in the state; and they establish funding mechanisms, regulations, and procedures for that purpose. However, with the exception of Hawaii and the District of Columbia, no state has a system of schooling that is directed only from the state government level. Instead, each state provides for schooling by overseeing the activities of local school districts. It is worth noting, however, that the recent crises in education have led several states to consider statewide curricula, objectives, and testing programs. The impact of the No Child Left Behind Act (NCLB) has drawn state and local educational agencies into achievement expectations set by the federal government. Despite these efforts, the delivery of schooling remains at the county and community levels.

Political Influences and Funding

The schools are intensely political places. There is some truth to the cliché that almost everything that goes on in the school has been voted on at some time, by someone, at some level of government. In an era of increasing accountability and oversight, the educational system, in the wake of NCLB, is subject to mandatory competency testing with statewide curricula and to increased local pressure to improve student performance, linked to local government funding. State school boards and many employees of SDEs may be politically appointed by the governor. Local school board members are elected by their constituent citizens, some of whom may be parents of children attending the local schools. These locally elected school boards have the final vote on many activities, including disciplinary procedures, curricula, special programs, textbooks, employment, and the location and maintenance of schools. The schools may employ thousands of professional educators, but the enterprise is intensely influenced by a political process managed by nonprofessionals and noneducators. Professionals such as school psychologists, employed to work with or for the public schools, must understand that this political influence is considerably different from employment in non-public-school settings or nonschool practice. Although such influence is not consistently favorable, it exists in law and holds significant authoritative influence on education and all those employed therein.

Almost everything that goes on in the school has been voted on at some time, by someone, at some level of government . . . All the major sources of funding and the allocation of funds are politically connected.

A closely related aspect of this political influence is the complex process by which local district public education is financed from federal, state, and local sources.

In comparison to state and local funds, federal funds account for a small portion of a district's overall budget. Since 1919–1920, the percentage of total school revenues from federal sources has increased from 0.3% to 6.8% in 1994–1995 and 9% in 2002–2003. For the same periods, state funding increased from 16.5% to 46.8% to 49%, and local funding decreased from 83.2% to 46.4%, to 43% (Snyder, Hoffman, & Geddes, 1997; Hill & Johnson, 2005). In 2002–2003, K–12 revenues were approximately \$440 billion and expenditures were \$455 billion (Hill & Johnson).

Funds come mainly from state and local sources, which include legislative appropriations based on state revenues from a variety of taxes, primarily sales and income taxes, and city and county sources, primarily local property taxes and, secondarily, local sales taxes. Thus, most school district financing is closely related to the wealth of its residents and the value of their property, and to the district's ability to attract commercial businesses. These tax bases are established and regulated by state and local governments. The allocation side of school finance has its political aspects as well. The portion of local property taxes that will go to the schools is politically regulated by local governments, and the state government usually has rules by which its funds are allocated to districts. Finally, the school district's budget is reviewed and approved by the school board and often by city or county governing boards. Thus all the major sources of funding and the allocation of funds are politically connected. It is easy to understand public sensitivity to education issues considering that much of education is supported by taxation and that the only major sources of increased funds for education are through new taxes, increased taxes, or both. This sensitivity is heightened by the fact that citizens may or may not have a direct vote on these tax sources or rates.

State funding may be allocated according to funding formulas that guarantee a minimum per pupil or per classroom expenditure to all districts, or funds may follow a more complicated pattern of differential allocations based on specific employee or educational categories (e.g., different categories of special education). These methods have resulted in a statewide mixture of minimally funded districts and districts of moderate and much more substantial funding as a function of their tax bases. A common national benchmark for comparison has been the per pupil expenditure of districts and states. In 1994–1995 the average per pupil expenditure for the United States was \$5,988 (Snyder et al., 1997). For 2002–2003, one source showed an average per pupil expenditure for the United States of \$8,041 (Hill and Johnson, 2005). The range was from a low of \$4,838 in Utah to a high of \$12,568 in New Jersey. For 2004, a newspaper account cited the average as \$8,287, with a low of \$5,008 in Utah up to a high of \$12,981 in New Jersey (*Commercial Appeal,* August 21, 2006, p. A2). However, the per pupil expenditure is only a rough index of educational quality. A large range of such expenditures usually exists in every state, and numerous other factors should be considered in judging quality (Biddle, 1997; Ceci, Papierno, & Mueller-Johnson, 2002). An analysis of school funding in the United States appears in Jordan and Lyons (1992). The problems associated with funding charter schools and their availability through online programs are discussed in Huerta, d'Entremont, and Gonzalez (2006).

Achieving greater equity in school district funding among poor and wealthy districts, and often among rural and urban districts, has become a major political issue. The struggle has been between the child's right to an equal educational opportunity and the state's responsibility to guarantee at least a minimally adequate education for every child. An obvious and noticeable difference exists between an adequate education and the "most adequate" education one could provide. Although widespread radical reform of school financing has yet to occur, the debate over greater equalization continues. The political controversies and funding schemes have a strong impact on the quantity and quality of the educational services available, including those delivered by school psychologists. The impact may be observed in the program options that are available; the number of school psychologists employed; and their roles and functions, salaries, and benefits.

A state's school foundation program also may guarantee certain levels of funding for various local employee categories. Thus, the state may provide a certain amount of funding for each teacher in the district, with the remainder of the teachers' salaries and benefits provided through local funding. In several states, foundation categories include pupil personnel services. Having school psychology as part of the state's minimum foundation program can spur both increased employment and adequate salaries. However, in most instances the minimum foundation program applies only to employees credentialed through the SDE. Consequently, psychologists who are licensed for private practice but who are not otherwise credentialed by the SDE may cost the district more to employ. Therefore, most school districts employ school psychologists who hold the proper SDE credentials. SDE credentials may also determine the availability of tenure within the school setting (Tenure ... Questions & Answers, 1997; also see chapter 7). Finally, the political nature of public education has its legal side as well. The intermingling of politics and law can be observed in the range of issues, topics, and constituencies the public schools must attempt to manage. For example, the schools must be sensitive to the multicultural character of society. This sensitivity is expressed in its hiring practices, home–school communications, assessment techniques, curricula, and programs. Schools must address gender equality issues in academic areas as well as in their sports programs. In dealing with children with disabilities, school districts must provide a range of programs and related services, including interpreters for the hearing impaired. Physical changes to school buildings must be made to ensure proper access for individuals with disabilities or to ensure a healthier environment by asbestos removal. The necessity to manage so many different perspectives has emerged mainly from legislation and litigation in the past four decades. The greatly increased rights of children to a free and appropriate public education have not occurred without subsequent financial woes to most districts. The management of these political-legal aspects in the context of uncertain and changing sources of school funding is a continuing challenge to the future of public education.

Professional and Business Perspectives

Solutions to school problems often are considered from a private or corporate perspective in contrast to the professional educational perspective. Some school administrative reform proposals have been drawn from the practices of corporate America. Hence, practices such as school-based decision making and total quality management emerge, with their emphases on local input and business concepts about raw materials, motivation, and productivity (Bender, 1991; Glasser, 1990; Valesky, Forsythe, & Hall, 1992). The U.S. education system is unquestionably a big business, and business concepts and practices may be successful in improving some aspects of schooling. According to Pipho (1999), "the K–12 market is a $318 billion market, or 48% of total education expenditures. It is projected to grow 38%, to $440 billion, by 2007" (p. 422). However, the business analogy cannot apply to all aspects of the schools. The schools must strike a balance between business and professional practices and school reform using top-down or bottom-up decision-making practices (Clinchy, 1998). Children will never enter the "business" with equal inputs, and the environment of the school does not have as much control as the typical business environment has over the raw material with which it works. In addition, when the schools complete work on their products, they don't sell them; they give them back to the community. Educators and administrators must be wary of a competitive spirit that makes students' gains in academic achievement the bottom line for decisions. Although aspects of schooling may be improved by such an approach, school psychologists can participate more effectively in local efforts to improve school management by bringing a psychological perspective to bear on the problems of education. The trend of applying a business perspective to the management of schools is closely related to school psychology's increased emphasis on accountability (see chapter 5).

SCHOOL PSYCHOLOGISTS IN THE EDUCATIONAL SYSTEM

Power and Authority

Understanding the relationship of schooling and school psychology in the complex context of this political environment requires an understanding of the relationships of power and authority. *Power* in this discussion means the individual or collective capacity to influence other people and situations. Power may include the use of aggressive, even hostile, physical force. It does not have authority bestowed by law or regulation. A child may have influence over the teacher's methods of instruction or discipline, but the child has no authority to dictate such matters. Parents have the power to resist having their child placed in special education but lack the authority to make the final determination. For a comprehensive discussion of power in school consultation, see Erchul and Raven (1997).

Authority is the legal or regulatory capacity to make decisions and have the responsibility for decision making. In the typical school system, administrative employees have decision-making authority over limited spheres of activity. The superintendent is responsible for activities within the entire system, principals are responsible for all that goes on in their buildings, and teachers are responsible for the activities of their classrooms. Professional pupil personnel (e.g., guidance counselors, school social workers, and school psychologists) have

School psychologists operate from a base of power, but they generally have no authority to make decisions that affect others in their sphere of activity.

practically no decision-making capacity unless it is delegated to them by others in authority. Authority may be direct, as in the case of the relationship between the school board and the superintendent or the superintendent and the school psychologist, or it may be indirect, as in the case of citizens using their elected school board members to carry out their wishes authoritatively.

The concepts of power and authority are important in developing an understanding of the school psychologist's position in the structure of schooling, as well as in the state and national arenas of credentialing and accreditation (see chapter 7). The relationships of power and authority in a typical school system are depicted in Figure 3.1 and include the following characteristics:

1. Authority, which is greatest at the top, lessens with each level from the top downward; power, which is greatest at the bottom, lessens with each level from the bottom upward.
2. Typically, fewer people are in positions of authority than of power.
3. The consumers of the system, including parents and children, have little authority despite considerable power.
4. Power–authority conflicts in the school system are the basis of most interprofessional problems.
5. Professional psychologists employed by the schools never make decisions for others in any authoritative manner except when such authority has been delegated to them by someone in the system with authority.
6. Power and authority may vary as a function of the perceptions regarding a situation. For school psychologists this simply means that their power (influence) will be greater in some situations than in others. For example, the school psychologist may be perceived as having greater influence in team decisions related to children with mental retardation than in decisions related to children with physical disabilities.
7. Perceived authority exists in situations in which an employee with no real authority is believed by others to have authority. Occasionally parents and teachers will ascribe authoritative roles to school psychologists that the school psychologists do not possess. For example, parents may behave as though the school psychologist has the decision-making authority for placing their children in special education. Although perceived authority may appear to be an advantage for the practitioner in some situations, the practitioner should always make clear to the client the limits of his or her authority.

School psychologists operate from a base of power, but they generally have no authority to make decisions that affect others in their sphere of activity. For example, the school psychologist individually does not have the authority to make a final decision regarding a child's eligibility for special education services. Such decision-making authority rests with a multidisciplinary team to which the school psychologist should belong. Of course, school psychologists influence these decisions by exercising their professional judgment of the child's circumstances based on psychological

Figure 3.1. Power and authority relationships in school settings. Although the number of people increases with each level from the top, the relative sizes do not represent specific proportions. School psychologists are included in special services.

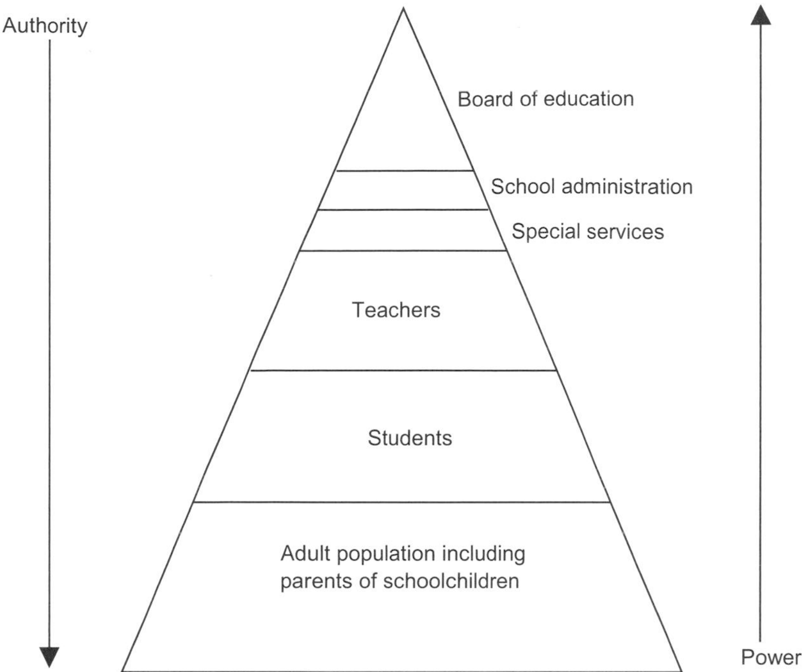

observations and interpretations. School psychologists provide opinions based on their professional expertise; they do not make decisions for others. Parents, as legal guardians of their children, are free to contest the opinions of the psychologist and may seek second opinions or redress through due process hearings provided under the special education regulations. Although the school psychologist may be displeased with or threatened by such prospects, that is the nature of the professional–client relationship.

In recent years, opportunities for school psychologists to advance to district-level administrative positions have improved. Thus the former school psychologist, operating from a base of power, may now hold an administrative position such as school principal, pupil personnel director, director of special education, or even district superintendent. In such instances, the trained school psychologist has been allocated a position of considerable authority. That person is now serving the district as an administrator and not as a school psychologist, which could bring about an effective blend of authority and power. The change of position is an opportunity to sensitize other administrators to the value of school psychological services. Perhaps as more school psychologists aspire to such positions, greater opportunities for broadening the role of psychological services will be achieved (see e.g., Blagg, Durbin, Kelly, McHugh, & Safranski, 1997).

School psychologists customarily operate from bases of power that include *referent power* and *expert power* (Erchul, 1992; Martin, 1978). Referent power exists when school psychologists are perceived to be helpful people with values and goals similar to those of their clients. Referent power is a process of identification that usually develops over a long time in the working relationship between school psychologists and their clients. Expert power exists when the school psychologist is perceived to have valuable information regardless of the level of referent power. Expert power may be developed on a short-term basis and may relate more to credentials and perceived professional knowledge. Developing a balance of referent and expert power is important to overall success in the day-to-day practice of the school psychologist.

Structure and Organization of Services

Psychological services occur within the basic structure of schooling at the state and local levels. Figure 3.2 represents the structural organization of educational services in the state. The principal agencies include the legislature; state department of education; subordinate educational agencies, including city, county, urban, and cooperative educational systems; and the subparts of those systems, from governing board to individual pupil. In the examples provided, authority flows from the state legislature's constitutional responsibility for the education of its citizens to the state board

Figure 3.2. Flow chart of responsibility for education.

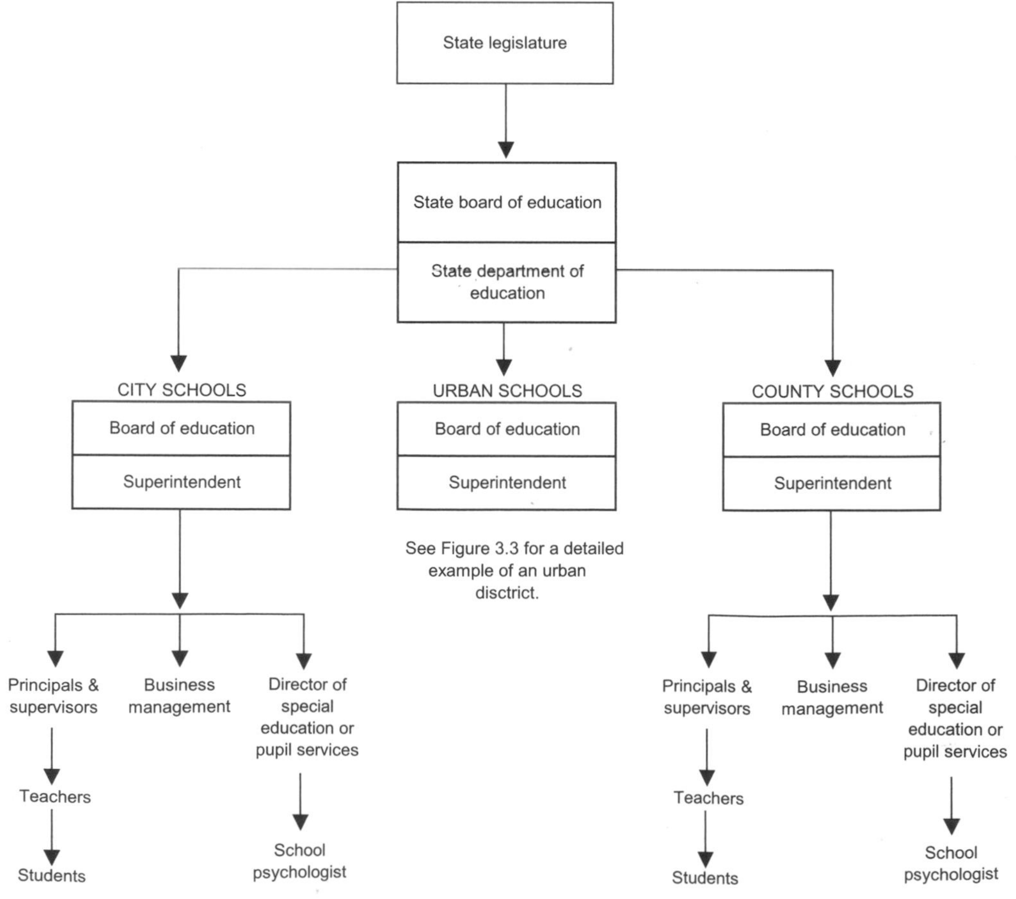

of education and its state department of education, which prepare and implement regulations to carry out the legislature's decisions. Authority then flows to the local board of education responsible for implementing the state's regulations, which also represents its constituents' desires regarding the style of local schooling. From there authority flows to the superintendent and administrative structure responsible for carrying out the local board's decisions and to the principals responsible to the superintendent for the implementation of policies in their buildings. Finally, authority flows to teachers responsible for the classroom interpretation and curricular delivery of the many state and local decisions. Undergirding the entire structure is the power of parents and guardians, whose children are the recipients of all of the above.

Figure 3.2 shows the common position of school psychologists in this structure for city and county school systems. The model is representative of most small school systems, including those in rural areas. The school psychologist often is directly responsible to the school superintendent or to a director of special education or pupil personnel services. In the small city and county system, the school psychologist often is linked directly with special education, may be immediately responsible to the director of special education, and may even have an office in physical proximity to the district's top administrators.

Organization of Urban School Systems

In contrast to smaller school systems, in urban school systems, the school psychologist is one of many service providers within an administrative structure for a comprehensive array of special services. The structure may be within a larger administrative unit for special education, mental health, or pupil personnel services. The school psychologist may be in relative proximity to other mental health and pupil service professionals but not very close to administrative lines of authoritative influence. Figures 3.3 and 3.4 identify the position of school psychologists in the Memphis City Schools, a district that in 2005 served 119,000 students in 191 K–12 schools and ranked 21st in size among districts in the United States. Figure 3.3 locates Memphis school psychologists in the Division of Exceptional Children and Health Services. The array of psychological, social work, nursing, and other services provided by this division is depicted in Figure 3.4. School psychologists may be assigned to assessment, consultation, and intervention roles, as well as to alcohol and drug abuse and sex abuse counseling or to other district service areas. The division has an overall executive director and assistant executive director, with several supervisors to assist in coordinating services across the entire district (Figure 3.4). The division is structurally related to other major school divisions and is directly under the authority of the school superintendent. This division is authoritatively separated from the other divisions, an arrangement that may have considerable impact on the overall orientation of services. School psychologists are part of the Mental Health Center, a major area within the Division of Exceptional Children and Health Services, and have their own coordinator.

The 60 or more school psychologists in the Memphis school system are assigned across the school district's areas serving elementary, middle, and high schools and specialized programs (e.g., alcohol and drug programs). Each area has a supervising psychologist who works closely with the area's special education coordinator and oversees the school psychologists' services in their assigned area schools. Thus, school psychologists are linked to traditional special education services (e.g., eligibility assessments), but they also provide an array of consultation and intervention services to both regular and special education within their area school assignments. In the district's overall structure (Figure 3.3), the Department of Pupil Services is removed from school psychologists, counselors, and social workers and is instead linked to attendance and management information services. Furthermore, the services of school psychologists are structurally disconnected from research and evaluation and from several school reform efforts under other departments and divisions.

Nevertheless, the title given to the psychological services unit, the Mental Health Center, signals the breadth of its orientation and services as well as its availability to the regular education sector. The Mental Health Center is supported by local district funds with supportive contracts with state agencies. All school psychological services for the Memphis City Schools are delivered through this center, which employs appropriately credentialed school, counseling, and clinical psychologists in addition to social workers and substance abuse counselors. Each school has its own support team, whose services are coordinated by the building-based school counselor. Although the overall organizational structure of the Memphis City Schools is typical of large urban districts, the mental health center concept is a unique service delivery scheme that was established in 1970 and in 1982 received an APA Division of School Psychology/National Association of School Psychologists joint award for service delivery excellence.

Organization of Other Service Structures

Additional organizational structure arrangements are represented in Figure 3.5, which depicts three alternative types of service delivery to one or more school settings, public or private. In the first, the local educational agency is a *cooperative agreement district.* Several arrangements of joint or cooperative agreements are in operation in the United States (Benson, 1985). For example, in rural areas several school districts may combine resources to provide services for children with disabilities. Even in suburban areas districts may combine resources to provide more efficient services for children with low-incidence disabilities (e.g., blindness) or to provide a comprehensive system of special education (e.g., North Suburban Special Education District in the Chicago area). Although typically found in rural areas, such agreement districts may be distributed throughout the entire state to serve special populations of children. These arrangements attempt to maximize the provision of services while minimizing the costs of service provision through sharing. In most instances, these agreements are created among local and county school districts, and the overall agreement is managed by one or more member districts or by a superordinate district. The special educational services typically are provided in the existing facilities of participating districts. The cooperative agreement district has its own board and director and employs a variety of special teachers and pupil service workers, including school psychologists. The cooperative may contract for, or employ, specialized services such as physical therapists. The cooperative provides school psychological services in ways that are compatible with or enhance those provided by school psychologists in the local districts.

Figure 3.3. Example chart of responsibilities and administrative relationships in urban school settings. Reproduced by permission of the Memphis City Schools, Memphis, Tennessee.

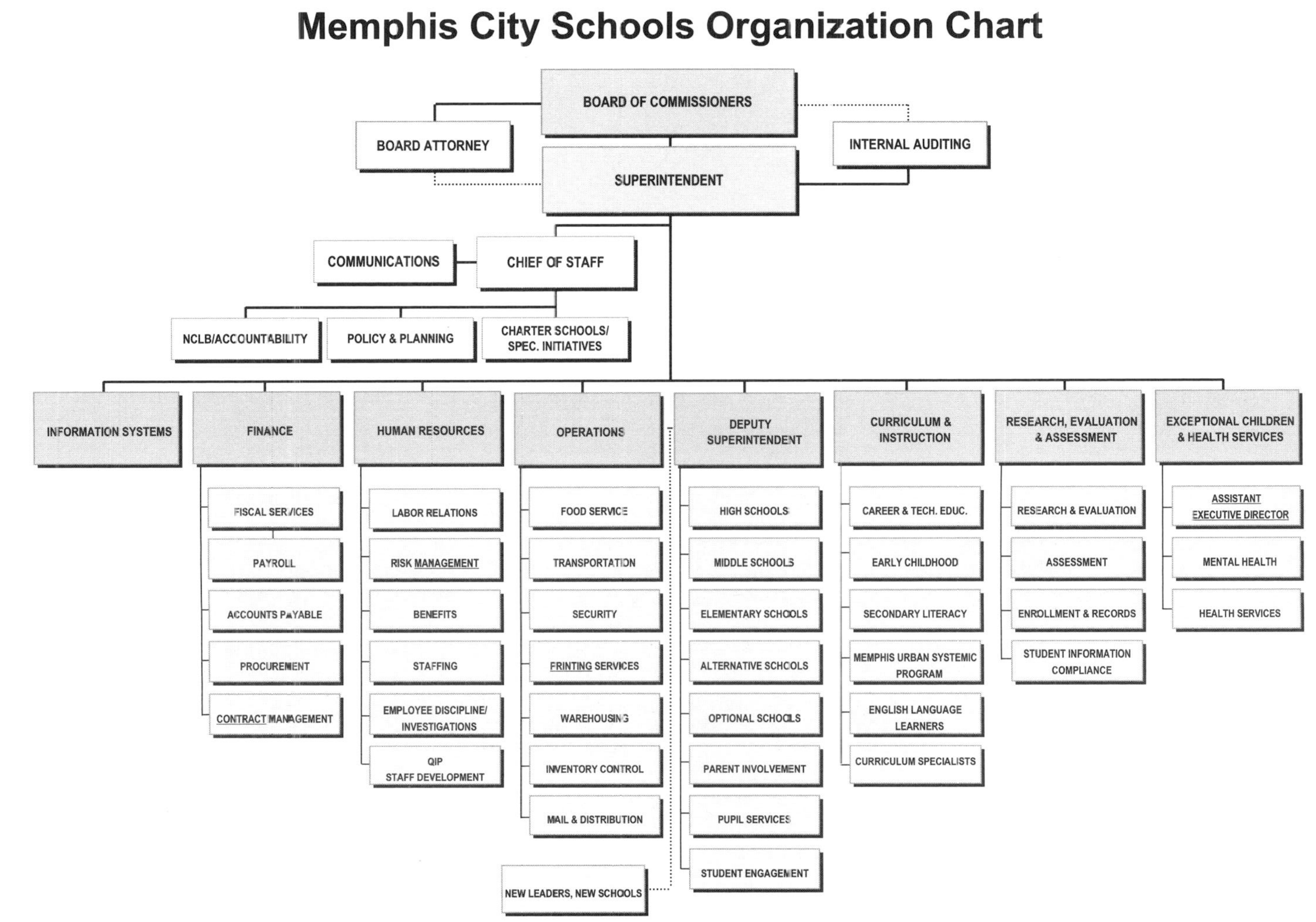

Figure 3.4. Example chart of responsibilities and administrative relationships in urban school psychological services. Reproduced by permission of the Memphis City Schools, Memphis, Tennessee.

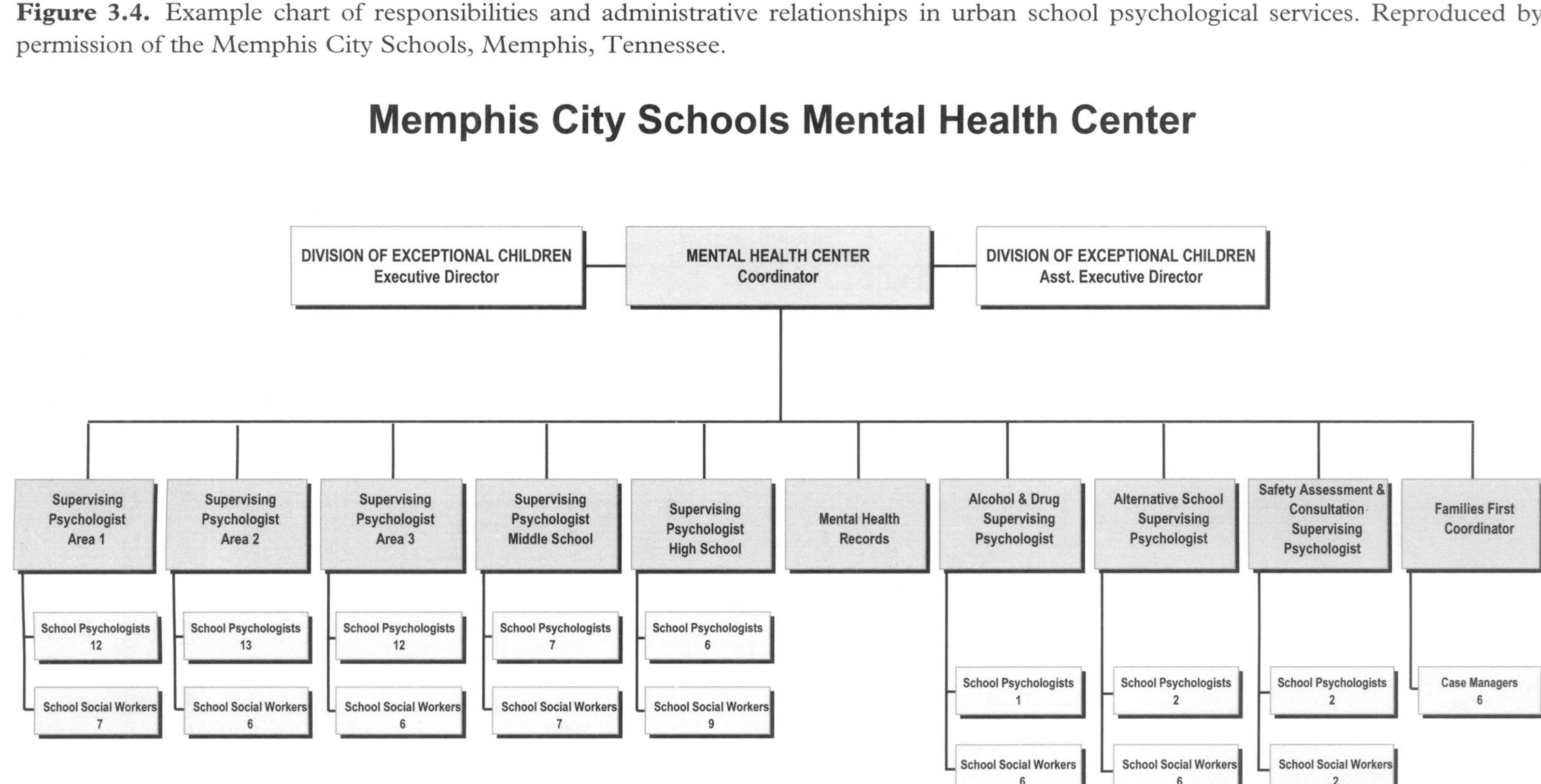

In a second arrangement, the school psychologist is hired by a *noneducational agency*, such as a rural mental health center, specifically to serve the needs of several school settings that have agreed to share the cost of such services. In this instance, the school psychologist usually is an employee of the mental health agency and not of the participating school districts. Services could be delivered from the center to the school settings with the school psychologist's office located at the mental health center. In other arrangements, the services are provided at the center with children being brought to the center by parents. In this arrangement, the school psychologist often works side by side with clinical or counseling psychologists who are not serving the schools, and perhaps with social workers and a psychiatrist who is on-call to the mental health center. The size and diversity of the staff often are a function of the center's location and funding, and the availability of other service agencies. In rural areas, the staff may be small, and the mental health center may be linked to other community services.

The future of school psychology will witness increasing diversity in the options available for the delivery of school psychological services.

In a third arrangement the school psychologist is self-employed and working with several school settings concurrently, serving perhaps 1 day per week in each. This practice, often referred to as *contractual services*, generally is frowned upon by district-based school psychologists because the contracted provider's duties tend to be limited to special-education testing. In addition, the local district can be perceived as shirking its responsibility to provide comprehensive psychological services. In response to some contractual practices, associations have tended to provide guidelines for such services rather than shun them entirely (American Psychological Association, 1995; NASP, 2000b). In general, districts wishing to employ private contractors should consider the specific services needed and how they blend into the district's comprehensive services to all schoolchildren, the credentials to be sought in contractual employees, and the use of a contractual agreement. Contractual services are not intended to be a less expensive substitute for offering more comprehensive services using district-employed school psychologists. Nevertheless, contractual services are common in some rural settings, particularly when a full-time school psychologist cannot be recruited, and this arrangement may be used for selected services such as reevaluations in combination with other services provided by district-based school psychologists. Examples show the positive aspects of contractual services (Allen, 1993; Wonderly & Mcloughlin, 1984). A nationwide network of contractual services (PsyEdsSolutions) also links local service providers with requests for specific contractual services and vice versa. A similar service has been advertised in Arizona (*www.School-Psychologist.com*). Although the dominant models of service delivery are depicted in Figure 3.2, the examples in Figure 3.5 suggest the diversity of delivery options to schools that are appropriate in some circumstances.

Emerging Models for School Psychology Services

The options available for the delivery of school psychological services continue to increase in diversity (see chapter 11). Among these are comprehensive school-based health clinics (Pfeiffer & Reddy, 1998; Tyson, 1999; Vance & Pumariega, 1999).

Figure 3.5. Other organizational arrangements for delivering school psychological services.

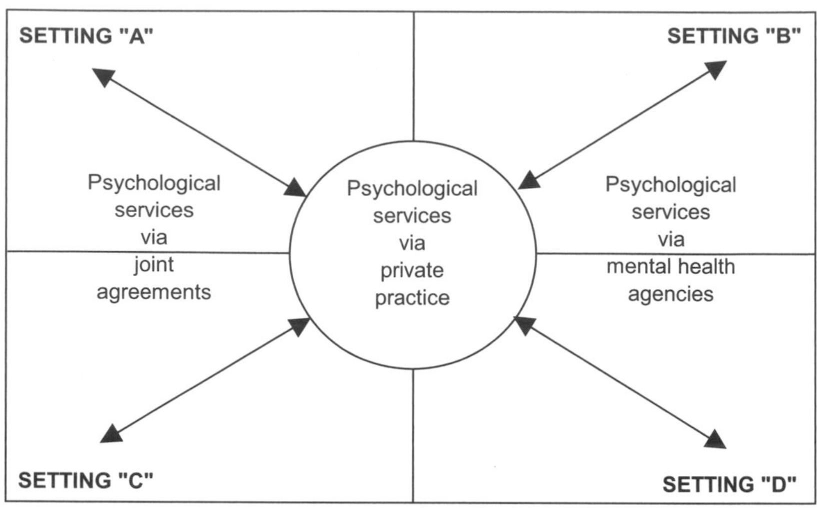

According to Martin (2005), the number of such centers has increased from 120 sites in 1988 to more than 1,500 U.S. sites in 2005. Although the increase is significant, it represented less than 2 percent of the 90,000 public schools in 2005. These centers offer comprehensive health and mental health care. Centers are distributed across school settings but are most commonly found in urban and secondary settings. More information can be obtained from the National Assembly on School-Based Health Care (*www.nasbhc.org*). Information on the school psychologist's role in this effort to integrate public health and mental health models into education also can be found in Bucy, Meyers, and Swerdlik (2002) and Nastasi (2004). Another example is the

Figure 3.6. Relationship of pupil personnel services to regular and special education.

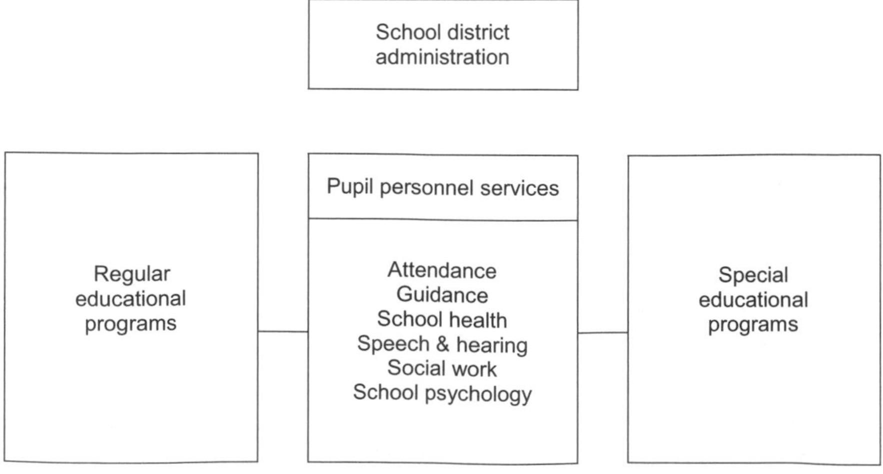

School Mental Health Project's Center for Mental Health in Schools, at the University of California, Los Angeles, which is a major source of information on comprehensive student support services. Its newsletter, *Addressing Barriers to Learning*, is available at no charge (e-mail *smhp@ucla.edu*).

Contractual school psychologists also provide psychological services to charter schools. Because these are public schools with a certain amount of oversight by local and state authorities, school psychologists can be expected to be responsible for providing services to charter school students. Little has been published about school psychologists' services to these settings, but they will likely be similar to other public schools within the geographic area of the local district.

Aspects of Service Location

Where the school psychologist is positioned in the organizational structure also influences service delivery. System factors have been discussed in many sources, and conflicts with school administrators and organizational policies have been discussed throughout the history of the profession (Symonds, 1933; Wallin, 1920). Organizational influences on school psychology practice are described by Curtis and Zins (1986), Illback (1992), and Maher, Illback, and Zins (1984). Organizational factors and the topic of school reform appear in a 1996 miniseries in *School Psychology Review* (Vol. 25, No. 4). All of these discussions view the school system and other employment settings from a dynamic systems perspective in which changes in one aspect of the system influence greater or lesser changes in other parts. Thus, aspects of the system's goals, administrative structure, policies, funding, or collegial relationships influence the manner in which psychological services will be organized and delivered within the system. Curtis and Zins (1986) also discuss the factors influencing the delivery of services within the school psychology administrative unit, such as orientation and philosophy of service providers and supervision of services. Little is known empirically about the impact of these different factors on the effectiveness of services. The available discussions, however, provide informative and practical investigations of the intuitive relationships that exist. This topic is discussed again in chapters 4, 7, and 8. Early discussions in Cutts (1955), Gottsegen and Gottsegen (1960), and Magary (1967b) on school psychology in various school and community settings have continued relevance for practitioners.

At the local level, public education is composed of two major instructional sectors: regular education, serving about 85–90% of the school population, and special education, serving about 10 15%, which includes children identified as disabled according to federal and state guidelines (e.g., mentally retarded and learning disabled) and additional categories according to state or local guidelines (e.g., gifted, teen pregnancies). The rapid growth of special education since the 1960s has been accompanied by a decline in generally available academic remedial services in regular education. In effect, public education has become divided into students within the regular educational sector and those within the special educational sector. For too many students this means special assistance is unavailable unless their circumstances are serious enough to warrant eligibility for special education. Exceptions to this decline have been the widespread availability of Chapter 1 instructional services for

Public education is composed of two major instructional sectors: regular education, serving about 85–90% of the school population, and special education, serving about 10–15%.

millions of disadvantaged children (Stringfield, 1991) and accommodations provided to students under Section 504 of the 1973 Rehabilitation Act (Pub. L. 93-112). Yet many districts continue to have limited remedial services available for students in the domain of regular education even if they are not qualified for Chapter 1. The recent interest in direct assessment and intervention for pupils' academic and behavioral problems grew out of the realization that many students in need of assistance are not eligible for special education.

A variety of service options exist within the special education sector. The general model for these options was presented by Deno (1970) and discussed in Dunn (1973) and often is referred to as the "cascade plan of services." Regardless of the categorical nature of the child's disability, the options serve as a guide for intervention and placement decisions, and the options are related to the concepts of mainstreaming, normalization, inclusion, and the least-restrictive-environment provisions of federal and state regulations. Many of the options overlap the regular and special education sectors. Within the special education sector, the school psychologist often is administratively responsible to a director of special education (most often a trained special educator with a master's degree and administrative certification). Almost the entire business of referral management—assessment, placement decisions, interventions, follow-up, and reevaluations—routinely flows through this administrator's department. At the local school-building level, school-based support teams review requests for service, conduct prereferral assessments, and engage school psychologists in various roles. The service options also include an array of instructional and related services for eligible children, such as multidisciplinary assessment teams and teams that develop individual educational plans (IEPs) and family service plans (FSPs). The school psychologist should be organizationally positioned to work on behalf of children in the regular and the special education sectors and to be involved with the entire array of these service options.

Pupil Personnel Services

School psychologists are part of an array of pupil personnel services (PPS) situated between regular and special education. These services may be administered from different district departments or contracts and are depicted together in Figure 3.6 only for convenience of illustration. The concept of PPS historically has included individuals working in the fields of school psychology, school social worker, guidance counseling, speech and hearing specialists, school health workers, and attendance officers (Ferguson, 1963; Hummel & Humes, 1984). The PPS staff may be large and diverse, as in urban districts (see Figures 3.3 and 3.4), or very small by comparison, as in many rural districts.

Pupil personnel services, though available for the educational improvement of students in regular and special educational sectors, often help to regulate the flow of students from one sector to the other, or within sectors. This relationship has led to the use of the term *gatekeeper* in referring to school psychologists and others involved in this activity. Different combinations of PPS staff spend varying amounts of time working on behalf of each sector. The flow between regular education and special educational services often involves school psychologists, speech and language clinicians, and social workers. These professionals also spend time working with children in the regular sector, but traditionally they have been more heavily involved with special education. School health, guidance and counseling, and attendance workers spend most of their time on behalf of children and programs in the regular sector.

When administratively located within a department of pupil personnel services, school psychologists may be identified to a greater extent with the entire school system and not just with special education. In this arrangement, psychological services on behalf of children suspected of having disabilities are coordinated through the pupil personnel services and the special education units. A natural tension often exists between these units as their respective administrators strive to serve the needs of the district's regular and special education sectors. When the respective directors have parity in administrative authority and have influence with upper-level administrators, comprehensive service delivery should result. When parity is lacking, school psychological services may be drawn too heavily toward or away from regular or special education. In some instances, special education and pupil personnel services may be under one or another's administrative authority, as when PPS is organizationally subservient to a department of special education and its director. In this arrangement school psychological services are likely to be drawn more toward the needs of children suspected of having disabilities than to the needs of other at-risk children in the regular setting. The trend toward serving eligible special education students in regular educational settings (sometimes referred to as *mainstreaming* or *inclusion*) may be more difficult when school psychologists' organizational location is inconsistent with the desired practices. It also is unclear what long-term impact the movement toward inclusion will have on the organizational location of special education and psychological services.

Proximity to Administration

An important point with regard to the above organizational arrangements (Figures 3.1 to 3.5) is that school psychologists are consistently disconnected from the line of authority extending from administrators to students and are instead organizationally appended to the lines of power. The physical proximity of the school psychologist to the school administration is an important consideration in these arrangements, and trade-offs are involved. Whereas the school psychologist in a larger school setting has the advantage of having an administrative supervisor who is a professional psychologist, considerable distance may separate the practitioner and the central administration, and it is doubtful that he or she can obtain a working knowledge of the entire district. Smaller districts permit greater access to the administration. The school psychologist often serves every school in the district but may be provided administrative supervision by a nonpsychologist. Thus, the trade-offs that are inherent in the organizational placement of school psychologists affect how much influence, or power, school psychologists may be able to exert on system policies and programs.

Centralized Versus Decentralized Services

The physical location of the school psychologist's office—whether in the local school building or in a more centralized office—has advantages and disadvantages.

Building-based (or *in-house*) school psychologists in one study "reported higher rates of satisfaction and perceived effectiveness and lower rates of burnout" than traditional school psychologists assigned to several buildings (Proctor & Steadman, 2003, p. 237). Another study, although conducted with 9th- and 12th-grade students in Estonia, found that student evaluations of services were more favorable in schools having a psychologist than in schools served by center-based psychologists (see Kikas, 2003). These studies support efforts to provide building-based psychological services and to continue developing comprehensive school-based health centers.

Among the factors working against building-based services is the lack of office space with sufficient privacy to conduct school psychological services. Bose (2003) found that most of the school psychologists studied were satisfied with their environments for conducting testing, although another study in Georgia, Maryland, and Ohio suggested that the adequacy of general work space was a problem (C. Wise, Li, & Smith, 2000). The Georgia Association of School Psychologists has a position paper on workspace standards for the school psychologist (GASP, 1999). An offshoot of the building-based school psychologist is the model found in the Charlotte-Mecklenburg (North Carolina) school district, where many of the buildings have a school psychologist who also serves in the roles of school counselor and school social worker. Although this model has been in existence for many years, it has not been systematically studied for its effectiveness and acceptability.

A practitioner with an office in the local building would have the advantages of proximity to teachers and students, especially for consultation and crises. However, a disadvantage is that being in a local building might lead to an overload of referrals. Also, because much of the school psychologist's time is often devoted to consultation and administrative tasks, which are not as visible to others in the building, teachers and administrators might complain that the school psychologist is not spending enough time on assessments. The school psychologist's objectivity also might suffer. Among the services a school psychologist brings to the schools is an objective professional viewpoint from beyond the context, and possible biases, of the school. Nevertheless, where school psychologists are available, the advantages of placement in the local school building would outweigh the disadvantages, as long as school psychologists continued to have opportunities to provide input on districtwide policies and concerns. Needless to say, contractors who provide school psychological services are even less connected to the system. Centralized and decentralized services are discussed in Elliott and Witt (1986a).

State Department of Education

School psychological services usually are coordinated at the state level by the state department of education (see Figure 3.2) through a department of special education, special services, or pupil personnel services. The state-level department has the dual role of developing and disseminating credentialing requirements, training and employment opportunities, and practice guidelines. Although the person responsible for coordinating these services often has little or no school psychology training, the ideal person would be trained and experienced in school psychology. However, almost half the states have no credentialed school psychologist working for the SDE to whom districts and school psychologists may turn for assistance.

Thus power versus authority conflicts and organizational issues experienced at the local district level often pervade the delivery of services statewide.

Supervision—Administrative Versus Professional

The administrative location of services brings school psychologists under the supervision of individuals who may not be trained in psychology. The issue of administrative versus professional supervision is very important. *Administrative* supervision is the interpretation and implementation of district policies and regulations affecting school psychologists in their capacity as employees (Strein, 1996a). For example, the superintendent approves school psychologists' requests for reimbursement for expenses at professional meetings according to a specific per diem schedule of payment. *Professional* supervision refers to the interpretation and implementation of actions taken by school psychologists in their capacity as professional psychologists (Strein, 1996b). For instance, the director of psychological services assists school psychologists in their interpretation of case study information and their recommendations for intervention. In many instances, school psychologists are organizationally subordinate to nonpsychologists, such as the director of special education, principal, or superintendent.

In a 1992 survey, the most frequently identified backgrounds for the practitioners' supervisors were special education (35%), school psychology (37%), clinical psychology (4%), and regular education (16%) (D. Smith, Clifford, Hesley, & Leifgren, 1992). More than 60% of the supervisors had no background in school psychology. School psychologists are responsible for choosing their methods of assessment and intervention, though in some unfortunate instances this power is usurped by administrators who have authority but not expertise. Psychologists may not have the capacity to make choices within their domain of expertise (e.g., selection and interpretation of tests, counseling strategies, and program evaluation methodologies) when administratively supervised by nonpsychological personnel. In larger school systems, professional and administrative supervision are more often available from individuals trained in psychology or a closely related field. This arrangement ensures that the administrative supervision will be sensitive to the school psychologists' concerns and that professional supervision will be available from another trained psychologist. Such arrangements conform more closely with the standards of national organizations for school psychologists (APA, 1981; NASP, 2000b).

The most frequently identified backgrounds for the practitioners' supervisors were special education (35%), school psychology (37%), clinical psychology (4%), and regular education (16%) (D. Smith et al., 1992).

A 1999 survey of practicing school psychologists indicated that clinical (professional) supervision fell below the levels recommended by the APA and NASP. Only 10% of responding practitioners were involved in clinical supervision, although most school psychologists said they want to be involved in such supervision (Fischetti & Crespi, 1999). A study of school psychologists in West Virginia suggested that the supervisor's level and area of training were related to the overall job satisfaction of school psychologists (Solly & Hohenshil, 1986). This was supported in a review by M. Brown and Hohenshil (2005) and in a meta-analysis by VanVoorhis and Levinson (2006). In the Fischetti and Crespi study, the practitioners involved in supervision were generally being supervised by qualified personnel. A study by Hunley et al. (2000) found that school psychologists in supervisory capacities often lacked training in supervision and were themselves often supervised by nonpsychologist personnel in the school district. Although a mixed benefit, the school district's administrative structure almost always places school psychologists under the supervision of someone in the district's administration. This can provide protection in instances in which clients dissatisfied with psychological services choose to litigate.

Employee Benefits

Employee benefits are another factor that influences practice. Employment by a public school district or agency has distinct advantages that often are not available with other arrangements. These include the possibilities for tenure, collective bargaining, employment and salary stability, travel expenses and mileage, continuing education, sick leave, health and life insurance programs, retirement programs, credit unions, office space, secretarial assistance, equipment, computers and technology, phones, and mail. Furthermore, districts and agencies often provide their own assessment policies and procedures, testing equipment, intervention materials, and supplies at no cost to the employee. Finally, some districts provide funds for attending professional meetings, on-the-job mileage reimbursement, and professional membership fees. Few of these benefits are available to school psychologists in independent private practice, and some, such as tenure, are not available to those employed in any nonpublic school settings.

Collective Bargaining

The issue of collective bargaining is perhaps of greater significance to teachers than to most school psychologists. However, because teachers constitute the largest employee group in a public school district, their bargaining unit often seeks to represent and bargain on behalf of many other employee groups, including school psychologists. The implications of this include power–authority conflicts that can affect services to children and families. School psychologists, especially those in urban settings, became concerned with such matters in the 1960s and 1970s, when greater militancy on the part of teachers often placed school psychologists between the administration and teachers in the event of strikes. Some associations of school psychologists adopted the position that school psychologists were neither administrators nor teachers and that they should not be forced "to support actively one side or the other" or be assigned "to duties other than those regularly pursued by the psychologist in normal circumstances" (NASP Adopts Position on Testing and Strikes, 1973). More recent policy statements make references to relationships with other professionals but do not directly discuss collective bargaining and work stoppages (APA, 1981; NASP, 2000b). In some larger districts, school psychologists have established their own bargaining unit, whereas in others, typically small and rural settings, school psychologists negotiate individually with the administration. An earlier survey of NASP membership indicated that 37% belonged to the National Education Association (NEA), 9% to the American Federation of Teachers (AFT), and 35% to a local teacher union (Graden & Curtis, 1991). The relative stability of such membership is observed in the findings of Curtis, Lopez, Batsche, and Smith (2006), with 34.4% in NEA, 9.7% in AFT, and 29.5% in local unions. Local membership in a teacher union may be contingent on belonging to its state and national affiliate. In the previous example of the Memphis City Schools, the school psychologists have a representative in the teacher union, the Memphis Education Association, which bargains for them. Local membership fees include dues for state and national membership.

Collective bargaining is related to the "guest" analogy (see the later section "The Guest in the School") and the question of whether school psychologists also should hold teacher licensure (see chapter 6). In some states, the school psychology credential issued by the SDE is considered a teaching credential with an endorsement in school psychology, as though it were a teaching field. In other states, the SDE may issue a separate credential for PPS specialists or a similar title. The regulations and policies in education typically are oriented to SDE-credentialed instructional personnel. Practitioners who are not credentialed may be excluded from some benefits of the school setting. In other instances, school psychologists who hold teacher certification have been concerned that during teaching strikes they might be pressed into classroom service. The issues involved reflect the long history of psychological services personnel seeking parity and status with others in the school setting while also seeking a separate identity as psychologists. A discussion of the issues and positions surrounding collective bargaining in school psychology can be found in Agin (1979) and Hyman, Friel, and Parsons (1975). The absence of recent research and discussion suggests that collective bargaining is a lower-priority concern among school psychologists.

School psychologists . . . are generally satisfied with their employment.

Job Satisfaction

Job satisfaction is a frequently surveyed aspect of the employment setting. Studies of job satisfaction have shown that school psychologists, especially those with several years of experience, are generally satisfied with their employment and that they have a positive outlook on the future of school psychology (M. Brown, Hohenshil, & Brown, 1998; M. Brown & Hohenshil, 2005; D. Smith, 1984; D. Smith et al., 1992; VanVoorhis & Levinson, 2006). Another study suggested that the percentage of practitioners planning to remain in the field until retirement had increased from 31% to 41% since the mid-1980s, and 77% said they would choose school psychology again as a career (Reschly & Wilson, 1992).

Affiliation with professional school psychology associations seems positively related to satisfaction (Levinson, Fetchkan, & Hohenshil, 1988; VanVoorhis & Levinson, 2006). The ratio of school psychologists to students seems related to satisfaction as well (Anderson, Hohenshil, & Brown, 1984; Fagan, 1988b), and this relationship may be partially explained by the broader functioning of school psychologists who serve with better service ratios (Curtis, Hunley, & Grier, 2002; D. Smith, 1984; D. Smith et al., 1992). There is also some evidence that job satisfaction may be related to gender issues in the workplace (Conoley & Henning-Stout, 1990; Henning-Stout, 1992). An earlier study of school psychologists in West Virginia suggested that satisfaction was greater when the supervisor's training and expertise approximated that of the school psychologist (Solly & Hohenshil, 1986). Proctor and Steadman (2003) suggested that building-based practitioners have higher rates of satisfaction than those assigned to several buildings.

Factors that appear most closely related to dissatisfaction were school system policies and practices and perceived lack of opportunities for advancement (Anderson et al., 1984; M. Brown & Hohenshil, 2005; Levinson et al., 1988; VanVoorhis & Levinson, 2006). No doubt, the perception of dissatisfaction caused by policies and practices is related to supervisory and organizational issues. Despite showing some dissatisfactions, a meta-analysis by VanVoorhis and Levinson (2006) indicated considerable job satisfaction among school psychologists over the period 1982–1999, and their conclusions were supported by a 2004 survey of NASP members (Worrell, Skaggs, & Brown, 2006). Finally, job dissatisfaction, including employment conditions related to caseloads, supervision, and the desire to leave the profession, appears to be implicated in practitioner burnout. The extent of burnout has been judged to be a serious concern (Huebner, 1992), and several aspects of school psychologist employment have been identified as stressful (P. Wise, 1985). (See chapter 8.)

The limitations in career advancement within the school system are inherent in the preparation of school psychologists. As shown in the next section, the school psychologist is to some extent treated as a guest in the public school system. Because school psychologists' training and credentials are unlike those of other members of the system (that is, they typically lack a teaching credential and experience), there are few avenues for advancement within the schools. Typical avenues of advancement for school psychologists are administrative positions in psychology or pupil personnel services (e.g., director of psychological services). For school psychologists who hold a teaching certificate and sufficient experience, advancement to other administrative positions is available (e.g., director of special education or principal). In several states, school psychologists are able to use years of experience as a school psychologist as a substitute for the teaching experience requirement to obtain administrative credentials. However, administrative credentials also require appropriate graduate-level instruction in addition to experience.

The Guest in the School

The educational system is populated primarily by teachers and others trained in education and is primarily devoted to the teaching of children. It is perceived by many members of the school and the broader community as a place for the delivery of instructional services, not necessarily psychological services. With all the previously discussed factors influencing the schools and the character of its organizational structure, it is easy to understand how noninstructional and nonadministrative personnel such as school psychologists are perceived as outsiders, or guests, in the house of education (Elliott & Witt, 1986b).

In a recent survey of school personnel, more than half viewed the school psychologist as a guest in the building rather than as a member of the school staff (Hagemeier, Bischoff, Jacobs, & Osmon, 1998). School psychologists may lament these perceptions but they are part of the reality of many school systems. Even staff members in maintenance, cafeteria, and office positions may be perceived as more connected to the operation of the school than is the school psychologist. The following list uses the guest analogy to posit several ways in which school psychologists are perceived. All PPS workers share these problems of perception to greater or lesser degrees.

The fact that most school psychologists are not building-based may be positive, because their presence brings an alternative perspective to that of the school-based team.

1. ***Each house has its own rules.*** Every school building, and to some extent each of its classrooms, has its own written and unwritten rules for many things, including dress, conduct, communication, scheduling, or protocol. Because school psychologists are neither instructional nor typically building-based personnel, they may not be perceived as fitting easily into the established rules of the local building or classroom. Instead, school psychologists often are perceived as belonging to a different house with a different set of rules. The school psychologist's orientation is more akin to the issues and values of psychologists than to those of classroom teachers.
2. ***Guests typically are invited to one's house.*** Frequently, school psychologists are invited to the school building through referrals from teachers. The referral process ordinarily involves a third party, such as the director of special education, who assigns the teacher's referral to an assessment team, which includes a school psychologist. The teacher initiates the invitation, though the referral does not pass directly from the teacher to the school psychologist. Sometimes, however, the school psychologist may be an uninvited guest who appears at the classroom door unannounced after being referred by someone other than the teacher. Furthermore, in most school districts teachers are not participants in the decision regarding the selection of a school psychologist. In many joint agreement districts, even school administrators may have little or no input in such decisions.
3. ***Guests typically are not perceived as members of the family.*** School psychologists do not have an office, nor do they have to dine in the school building. Many school psychologists have no prior teaching preparation, and about half have no formal teaching experience (Graden & Curtis, 1991; D. Smith et al., 1992). Regardless of studies demonstrating that teaching experience is not essential to the practice of school psychology, the perception of many educators is that such experience is important (see chapter 6). Some educators also do not perceive special education as an indispensable aspect of the school district and hence do not think of school psychologists as indispensable to the district either. This is less of a problem for guidance counselors, who typically are required to be credentialed teachers with a few years of teaching experience and are less identified with the special education

sector of the school district. Discussions of secondary-level school psychological services can be found in Nagle and Medway (1982) and Steil (1994).

4. ***Guests are perceived as temporary.*** School psychologists often are available in buildings only for short periods. In most instances they are not building-based employees but are district-based employees. This is especially true for psychologists who come to the school building from nondistrict agencies such as mental health centers, intermediate units, or private practice. However, despite the disadvantage of the centrally based practitioner being perceived as an outsider, the fact that most school psychologists are not building-based may be positive, because their presence brings an alternative perspective to that of the school-based team.

5. ***Guests usually have similar background and status to house members, so school psychologists are seen as different and therefore not even likely guests.*** Guests are usually people with whom their hosts have much in common. Despite similarities in gender and age, in many cases school psychologists often are seen as having little in common with other educators. School psychologists may be perceived as having specialized knowledge, greater privileges, and higher salary (even in those settings where they are paid the same as teachers at the same degree level). Such perceived inequality works against the perception of school psychologists as welcome guests, much less members of the family. Of course, school psychologists are less likely to be perceived as outsiders in their relationships with other PPS staff such as guidance counselors or social workers.

Implications of Being a Guest

The guest analogies are important in relation to changing roles and functions, especially in consultation services. Because the delivery of school psychological services relates to the culture of the school and the community (Sarason, 1971), even the traditional role of psychological testing is delivered in the context of assumptions. The importance of certain types of ability and achievement is viewed differently, along with the process of schooling and the outcomes of schooling in that society. Consultation is built on that cultural context, and its success depends heavily on the relationships between the individuals involved and their expectations. Thus, perceiving school psychologists as guests can present serious barriers to consultation, especially in its entry stage (see chapter 4). However, the more recent collaborative consultation approach views teachers and school psychologists as professional peers and partners rather than as a relationship between teachers and outside experts (Curtis & Meyers, 1985; Graden, 1989; Gutkin & Curtis, 1990; Zins & Ponti, 1990). The success of this relationship could lead to a healthy erosion of the guest analogy and provide the long-sought-after status for school psychologists in the house of education.

Identification of the Client

In every profession, services are rendered on behalf of clients. Given that school psychologists serve in several available employment settings and constituencies, the question of who the school psychologist's client is has no simple answer. The answer will depend on the employment setting or the service request. The term *client* may refer to the person in need of professional help, the person who employs a professional, the person paying for the help, the person who is under the protection of another, the person receiving the services of a professional, or the person benefiting from such services. Consequently, in the work of the school psychologist, the client may include one or more of the following: child, parent or parents, teacher, principal, special education director, school superintendent, school board, or an agency administrator or governing board.

In perhaps the most direct employment context, that of independent private practice, the parents of a dependent, minor-age child request psychological services directly from the school psychologist. As the child's guardians, the parents have considerable legal influence in the case study and can be logically considered the psychologist's client. But what about the child, who not only receives the services but also ultimately benefits from the services and who has the individual power to refuse to participate cooperatively in such services? It is for these often conflicting circumstances that school psychologists commonly view the child *and* the parents as their most immediate clients. This attitude is held by school psychologists in most settings, although often school psychologists see the child as the most important client. Despite the emphasis on the parent and child, a case can be made for considering others as clients also. For example, school administrators are responsible for the school psychologist's employment. They pay for such services, and they may be held legally responsible for the outcomes of the services delivered. Teachers have direct influence on children and usually will be involved in the referral and the intervention process. From a power standpoint, providers of school psychological services would be seriously hampered if teachers were to choose to protest psychological services by simply not making referrals. Finally, other professionals with whom school psychologists work, such as pediatricians, may perceive themselves as indirect clients since they, too, are involved in the case study and may have served as a conduit for the referral.

In some circumstances, the school psychologist may provide services that directly benefit school employees while only indirectly benefiting parents and children. For example, the school psychologist may seek to improve referral procedures through in-service education of teachers. Another example is when a school district or community agency employs a school psychologist to conduct stress or crisis management sessions for its employees. The client issue is complicated in any employment setting because of the legitimate interests of parents, teachers, and others in authority and the importance of the child as a direct or indirect service recipient. Even though parents and children are near the bottom of the power–authority pyramid (Figure 3.1), school psychologists most often work at the request and approval of parents and children and provide services for their benefit.

The power–authority context of client issues is sometimes referred to as a dilemma of divided or mixed loyalties. The dilemma pits the school psychologist's loyalty to one client against loyalty to another client. The dilemma is relevant to all professional psychologists who work with children. Discussions of client–professional relationships as a function of employment parameters and roles are provided by May

(1976) and Stewart (1986). These discussions help school psychologists understand the frustrations of their circumstances as well as those of their employer and clients. The issue of divided loyalties is most acute in circumstances in which one or more of the potential clients behave as though they are the school psychologist's exclusive client. This may occur, for example, when administrators demand that case study recommendations be made from their perspective but the school psychologist prefers taking a position advocating for the child; when parents remind the psychologist that their taxes pay the psychologist's salary and they vehemently disagree with the psychologist's judgment that their child does or does not qualify for a particular program; when teachers question the psychologist's value to the school district because the psychologist fails to recommend that a problem child be removed from their class; or when a director of special education requires the psychologist to test more children per week than the psychologist feels is ethically responsible to the children being served.

With experience, the school psychologist comes to understand that almost all referrals of children involve several clients. To minimize client conflicts, the school psychologist persists in keeping the interests of the child as the main focus of the assessment and intervention process. Each of the potential clients presumably is most concerned with doing what will have the greatest benefit for the child. If school psychologists can keep that as the focus and reasonably assure all clients that they have only the best interests of the child as the focus of their work, serious conflicts should be avoided. Minimizing conflict also involves preventive groundwork: the school psychologist strives to involve all relevant parties and treat them as valued, significant collaborators throughout the referral process. School psychologists, who have the power of influence but not of authority, assure all clients that their job is not to make decisions for the clients or the child, but rather to provide objective professional judgments on behalf of the child, whose welfare is theoretically the focus of everyone's concern. School psychologists, and other professionals, should recognize that clients are not dependent on them, but rather psychologists are dependent on their clients; that clients are not an interruption of the school psychologist's work but are the purpose of their work; and that clients are doing school psychologists a favor by letting them serve their needs and are an important part of the business of school psychology (*Our Voice*, 1983).

Almost all referrals of children involve several clients.

The traditional practice of focusing services on the individual child, with assistance from the parents, has been changing in the direction of focusing on the entire family. The shift is seen not only in school psychology but in several professional fields, and it is commonplace to hear references to family assessment or family therapy. The family service plan of federal legislation for the handicapped is an expression of this shift in focus. It seems reasonable, therefore, to consider the family as an emerging client of the school psychologist, which embraces the above aspects of the child and parents as client. In recent years, several publications have focused on services to families of exceptional children (Barbarin, 1992; Christenson & Conoley, 1992; Fine, 1991; Gallagher & Vietze, 1986; Gargiulo, 1985; Seligman, 1991; Seligman & Darling, 2007). Family systems assessment and intervention were the theme of a 1987 issue of the *School Psychology Review* (Vol. 16, No. 4). As noted in that issue, although school psychological practice continued to focus on the individual child, growing interest in a family perspective was anticipated (Carlson & Sincavage, 1987). The 2002 Futures Conference also focused on the importance of family perspectives in practice (Christenson, 2004), and several resources are included in volume I of *Best Practices in School Psychology IV* (Thomas & Grimes, 2002).

SCHOOL PSYCHOLOGISTS IN COMMUNITY AND NONSCHOOL SETTINGS

All school psychologists work in and with the community, including a community's families, public and private schools, mental health service agencies, and government. They are strategically located in service delivery models based on social ecology (Bronfenbrenner, 1979; Elliott & Witt, 1986a; Seligman & Darling, 2007; Woody, LaVoie, & Epps, 1992). Although most school psychologists work in the public schools, some have taken employment in other settings, including denominational and independent schools, nonschool agencies, and independent private practice (D'Amato & Dean, 1989; Gilman & Teague, 2005; Graden & Curtis, 1991; Reschly, 1998; Reschly & Wilson, 1992). These settings are indirectly linked to the public schools because they often work with children for whom the public schools are responsible. Thus the phrases *school-based* and *school-linked* services represent these two sectors of practice (Reeder et al., 1997).

School psychologists in community, or school-linked, settings may be employed for similar reasons as those in public school (school-based) settings but under different contractual agreements, role and function expectations, and supervision. In denominational and independent schools, psychological personnel are often employed part-time and are more likely to be administratively responsible to the principal or director of the facility. Because the student population usually is smaller and more select, the school psychologist may be asked to provide a narrower range of services, such as learning disability evaluations and individual and group counseling. Some community facilities serve only children with disabilities and employ school psychologists to provide specific services (D'Amato & Dean, 1989; Mordock, 1988). If the psychologist is a full-time employee, then conditions of employment and benefits similar to those of public school settings may exist.

School psychologists also may be employed in community and regional mental health centers. In the structure of these agencies, the school psychologist may be part of the psychological services department, serving under a director or a supervising psychologist who in turn is responsible to the director of the mental health center and the center's governing board. Here, administrative and professional supervisors are typically trained in mental health services, though the supervisor usually will not be another trained school psychologist.

In non-public-school settings, school psychologists still are under the authority of others and must continue to operate from a base of power. Referrals for service typically are directed to the school psychologist from others in the agency following a contact with the agency made by a parent or other professional. In independent or group private practice, the school psychologist often acquires referrals directly from parents on behalf of their minor children. Although several earlier resources gathered information about independent private practice (Iowa School Psychologists Association, 1983; Rosenberg, 1995; and Rosenberg and McNamara, 1988), little has appeared in more recent school psychology literature. Considerably more recent information on related clinical and counseling psychology is available from APA Books (see *www.apa.org*), the journal *Professional Psychology: Research and Practice*, and the newsletters *Monitor on Psychology* and *The National Psychologist*. The APA also has a division for psychologists in independent practice (Division 42).

Employment in non-public-school settings may increase psychologists' proximity to children and families while decreasing their proximity to public school settings and services. Because most community services for children with disabilities are provided through the public schools, the power–authority trade-offs of service settings are an important consideration. For example, case study recommendations from an outside psychologist may be given less credibility (or occasionally more) by the district administration than those provided by a district-employed psychologist. Also, parents may seek the advice of a nondistrict school psychologist (school-linked) because they perceive the district school psychologist (school-based) as aligned with the school administration. In any employment setting, however, psychologists do not make decisions for clients; rather, they act as resources for a comprehensive array of psychological services when requested by their clients. The school psychologist is an important source of professional opinion but is not a decision-making authority.

Employment in non-public-school settings may increase psychologists' proximity to children and families while decreasing their proximity to public school settings and services.

By law, decisions regarding special educational placements and services are the responsibility of school-based teams and not the responsibility of individual practitioners, whether they are school based or school linked. In school settings, the school psychologist is a recognized member of a team that makes important decisions about the education of children. The teams in which the school psychologist participates may be called child study teams, school-based assessment or support teams, pupil services, placement teams, or multidisciplinary teams. School psychologists in nonschool settings must recognize that their efforts are but one piece of the complex puzzle of child assessment and intervention. This can be a serious source of conflict between school-based and school-linked practitioners based in the community. A practitioner in private practice may choose to diagnose a child as having a learning disability; however, the school district may disagree based on its multidisciplinary team's assessment and comprehensive case review. Issues of power and authority, and the setting from which the school psychologist enters teamwork, are important to team functioning. The discussion of school psychology in nontraditional settings is revisited in several chapters of this book because of its relevance to role and function, preparation, credentialing, and employment.

It is readily apparent that school psychologists, regardless of employment setting, need to understand the dynamics of the school system, its policies and procedures, and the place of school psychology in the context of teamwork. Several studies of team functioning have been conducted that demonstrate the varying power of the school psychologist in team decisions (Butler & Maher, 1981; Crossland, Fox, & Baker, 1982; Pfeiffer, 1980; Yoshida, Fenton, Maxwell, & Kaufman, 1978). Also helpful is a 1983 special issue of the *School Psychology Review* that was devoted to the topic of multidisciplinary teams (Vol. 12, No. 2) and a chapter by Rosenfield and Gravois (1999). The 1998 *School Psychology Review* miniseries on mental health programming in schools and communities (Vol. 27, No. 2) is also pertinent to this topic. In New Jersey, a coalition of pupil services groups developed a "Position Statement on Roles and Functions of Child Study Team Members" to provide clarification to parents and educators engaging their services (New Jersey Coalition, 2002).

COMMUNITY RESOURCES

Whether school psychological services are provided from within the public schools or from other settings, it is unlikely that the setting is able to serve the needs of its clients completely. School psychologists should be highly familiar with resources available to assist with certain client needs. These resources may be available in the local community, through county and state offices, and through national associations and government agencies. Happe (1990) includes a format for acquiring information on community resources and a listing of many state and national agencies and associations. Unfortunately, Happe's resource listings have not been updated in more recent editions of *Best Practices in School Psychology* (Thomas & Grimes, 1995, 2002). Several courses and field experiences for school psychologists may include methods for developing a community resource file of agencies contacted or visited.

The school psychologist's role as a liaison between the school and other agencies is important.

The importance of the school psychologist's involvement with community resources often is overlooked in discussions of roles and functions, which usually emphasize assessment and consultation. The school psychologist's role as a liaison between the school and other agencies is important. The school psychologist often "provides the best link among the schools, the family, and various agencies because of his or her association with the institution in which the child spends several hours a day and because of his or her training and experience in human relations, professional jargon, and educational matters" (Plas & Williams, 1985, p. 332). As part of the interdependent network of helping services and agencies, school psychologists serve as community resources to others while serving as liaisons for their own clients.

Chapter 4

Roles and Functions of School Psychologists

The book thus far has described what a school psychologist *is*. This chapter describes what a school psychologist *does*, including the most common roles for school psychologists and the specific day-to-day functions of the psychologist in the schools. It also presents and discusses the notions of roles and functions from an indirect or direct service delivery model. Much of the information in this chapter will undoubtedly be discussed and elaborated on in other classes (e.g., assessment, consultation, and intervention) as well as in practica and internships. An effort has been made to include up-to-date and relevant readings for students wishing to follow up on specific topics of interest.

Perhaps never in the history of the profession have the roles and functions of school psychologists been so diverse and so much in flux. Entire states in the United States (e.g., Iowa) have adopted practices, known as *flexible service delivery,* that are based on a problem-solving model and involve minimal traditional assessment. On the other hand, many school psychologists are still functioning in much the same way that school psychologists have worked for decades. This chapter attempts to cover the multitude of possible roles and functions while presenting a realistic picture of what current students can expect to find as they prepare to practice the profession of school psychology.

HISTORICAL BACKGROUND

The current roles and functions of school psychologists are described and understood much better now than they were in the early part of the 20th century. Almost every year new data become available describing the typical practice of school psychologists. The earliest such study appears to have been a survey of the training and testing practices of practitioners conducted by Wallin (1914). Wallin found that most practitioners were not particularly well trained, nor were they providing a broad range of services. The role of psychometrician was considered not only appropriate but also essential, and practice often was limited to the administration of the few techniques for measuring ability and achievement that were available at that time. In this role, the school psychologist facilitated the "sorting" of children into different educational programs. The role soon expanded to include interventions, often remedial instruction or counseling, as reflected in the description in chapter 2 by Hildreth (1930). Role expansion also was observed in the discussions of school psychology in a special issue of the *Journal of Consulting Psychology* (Symonds, 1942). Nevertheless, the role of sorter persisted as the primary role, whereas other roles and functions could be considered to fall within the framework of "repairer." Lesser roles were in research, consultation with teachers and parents, administration, and teaching.

Discussions at the 1954 Thayer Conference focused heavily on roles and functions, especially as related to doctoral and nondoctoral training and credentialing (Cutts, 1955). The proceedings, which reported results of surveys of the early 1950s, indicated that testing and assessment functions continued to account for more than two thirds of the practitioners' time. Cutts also reported on administrators' and others' perceptions of the work of the school psychologist.

The literature of the 1960s and 1970s was replete with opinions and surveys regarding the most appropriate roles and functions of the school psychologist (see e.g., Fagan, Delugach, Mellon, & Schlitt, 1985). The era was characterized by a persistent dissatisfaction with the psychometric testing role (sorter) and the accompanying limited testing functions. The preference was for interventions, especially counseling and consultation (repairer) roles, during an era of growth in training programs and curricula. For example, in her 1963 book, Gray suggested two roles for the psychologist in the schools: (a) the data-oriented problem solver who brings research competencies to bear on the problems of the schools, and (b) the transmitter of psychological knowledge and skills who helps to disseminate current research into the applied setting of the schools (1963b). Unfortunately from the perspective of this profession, the traditional sorter role has been resistant to change, with practitioners continuing to report that more than half of their professional time is spent in such activities, although they would prefer devoting more time to other activities (Reschly, 1998; Reschly & Wilson, 1995).

The 1980s and 1990s continued in much the same way. A good deal of discontent was aimed at the traditional roles, but little movement was seen toward any kind of large-scale change. The comprehensive roles and functions portrayed by the National School Psychology Inservice Training Network in 1984 and refined in 1997 (Ysseldyke et al.) have been slow to be put into practice in any widespread manner. Ysseldyke (2005) noted that although he and others have repeatedly called for change and have pointed out the lack of empirical evidence to support the traditional manner of identifying students with disabilities (particularly learning disabilities), he remains "troubled by the virtual absence of change over time in predominant assessment practices" (p. 126). The most recent data (Curtis, Lopez, Batsche, & Smith, 2006) note that school psychologists are spending considerably more time in special education–related activities overall compared with 1989–1990 but that the number of initial special education evaluations and reevaluations has declined and there are fewer 504 plans, fewer in-service programs, and fewer student groups. As discussed in chapter 1, these changes may reflect a change in roles and functions or the addition of other duties plus an increasing shortage of school psychologists. Merrell, Ervin, and Gimpel (2006) note that a struggle continues within the profession between the many things school psychologists are able to do and the few things that they are expected to do. Whether the sorter and repairer roles will remain dominant or will change in the near future remains to be seen.

Roles and functions of school psychologists have been shaped by many forces throughout the history of the profession, and these forces continue to shape new roles and functions while preserving traditional ones. In addition, just as children are influenced by many factors in their environments, the current roles and functions of individual school psychologists are influenced by numerous personal, professional, and external variables. Chapter 1 provided data on the average percentage of time school psychologists engage in various professional activities. Although such data are helpful as summaries, they do not describe the activities of any one practicing school psychologist, and it is probably safe to say that no two school psychologists spend their time in exactly the same way.

DETERMINANTS OF ROLES AND FUNCTIONS

As shown in Figure 4.1, the role of each individual school psychologist can be viewed as a combination of what the person brings to the job (e.g., personal characteristics and professional skills), job-site characteristics (e.g., job descriptions and school system expectations), and various external forces (e.g., legislative developments, social changes, and research findings). Additional discussion of determinants occurs in chapter 7. A discussion of desirable characteristics of students and practitioners can be found in chapter 6.

What the School Psychologist Brings to the Job

The school psychologist does not come to the job as a blank slate but rather with a background of personal characteristics, life experiences, and training. Although at times in the book it may seem as though school psychologists are lumped together, keep in mind that each school psychologist is a unique individual.

Figure 4.1. Variables influencing school psychologists' professional roles and functions.

Brought to the Job		Found on the Job
Personal characteristics		Job-site characteristics
Personal background		Job description
Professional training		Needs
Reasons for choosing school psychology		Available resources
Professional interests		
Expectations		
	External Forces	
	Legal and legislative changes	
	Societal problems	
	Research findings	
	World events	

Personal Factors

Students consider school psychology as a career option for any number of reasons. They may have taken an undergraduate course coincidentally taught by a school psychology faculty member who sparked their interest in the field. They may have worked with a school psychologist at some time during their own childhood or adolescence, or perhaps they have a child or a sibling who required the services of a school psychologist. They might be a teacher who worked with a particularly effective school psychologist. They may have stumbled across school psychology by accident or had a school psychologist as a family member or neighbor. Whichever of these possibilities applies, the reason they were attracted to school psychology training may influence their eventual on-the-job performance. Variables such as age, gender, race, marital status, socioeconomic status, the type of community in which they were raised (e.g., urban, suburban, or rural), and the type of schooling they received (e.g., public versus private schooling, enrichment programs versus regular education) also may influence a potential practitioner's professional role. Personality characteristics likewise influence their professional role (Itkin, 1966). For example, outgoing, assertive, and gregarious individuals may be more apt to enjoy consultation, staff development, and public speaking activities. School psychologists perceived to be warm, friendly, and nonjudgmental may be more sought after by teachers for advice about classroom management, crisis intervention, or other work-related problems.

The reason they were attracted to school psychology training may influence their eventual on-the-job performance.

Professional Training Factors

Professional training also has a major impact on the way school psychologists function on the job. Even when two school psychologists possess identical academic transcripts, they may have vastly different orientations, depending on when their training occurred, the theoretical orientation of the faculty with whom they studied, and the experiences they had at the particular schools they attended. In addition, even within a given training program, faculty members may move on, go on sabbatical, or retire, creating a very different program for the next group of students. In the same way, the other students going through school at the same time may influence the thoughts and feelings of their peers. A group with one or more slightly older, nontraditional students who have taught or have children of their own creates a different learning atmosphere than does a group of students who are all 22 years old and right out of college. Likewise, the diversity of students in terms of gender, professional experience, and cultural background provides a unique blend with a strong impact on the individuals in the program.

The type of graduate degree obtained also may influence professional functioning. As described in chapter 6, currently the specialist level of training (a minimum of 60 graduate semester hours spread over a 3-year period and including practica and internship experiences)

The specialist level of training (a minimum of 60 graduate semester hours spread over a 3-year period and including practica and internship experiences) is nationally acknowledged as the appropriate minimum entry level for school psychologists.

is nationally acknowledged as the appropriate minimum entry level for school psychologists. Beyond that entry level, practicing school psychologists are expected to continue to upgrade their knowledge and skills through a variety of continuing education options and opportunities.

School psychology training programs, particularly doctoral programs, often emphasize one area of specialization over others (e.g., behavioral consultation, individual and group counseling, or psychoeducational assessment). Graduates of such programs are well prepared for positions emphasizing these specialized skills in addition to possessing basic practitioner competencies. Other programs (including most specialist-level programs) attempt to provide more generalized training so that students can adapt to a variety of professional environments. Chapter 6 provides an in-depth look into differences between doctoral and specialist-level training.

The geographic location (state, province, or country) in which a practitioner's training is received, the practicum and internship requirements fulfilled, the research interests of faculty members involved in training, and even (or perhaps especially) the interpersonal dynamics of the faculty members contribute to the practitioner's role. The administrative issue of whether the program is in a department or college of education, a department of psychology within a college of arts and sciences, or a department of educational psychology administered jointly by education and psychology may influence the type of training and the trainee's eventual role as a school psychologist (see chapter 6 for a discussion of this topic). The balance of psychology courses and education courses in the training program, and the balance of other students—whether from other psychology graduate programs or in education-related areas including special education or school counseling—also have an effect.

Some graduate programs, particularly those in larger metropolitan areas, may attract a large number of part-time students who work on their school psychology degrees while concurrently holding jobs or taking care of families. Other programs are composed primarily of full-time students who complete all academic requirements in 2 years and go immediately into internship positions. The latter types of programs may have nearly all of their classes during the day, and all of the students admitted in any particular year may take all of their coursework together. Programs in large urban areas may offer more night and weekend classes, and students may be taking only one or two classes each semester over an extended number of years. Increasingly, prospective students are inquiring about opportunities to meet some or all of their academic requirements through nontraditional means, such as distance learning.

Many training-related issues are settled more by chance than by plan. Students choose to apply to specific graduate programs for a variety of reasons, not necessarily because of the quality or reputation of the program. Their spouse may have been accepted to a graduate program there. They plan to live with their parents to keep expenses down. Maybe they continued at a school because they went there as an undergraduate and already know their way around.

Other students may not have much choice as to the program they attend. "Place-bound" students, for example, are those who are unable to move somewhere to attend graduate school, usually because of family or financial circumstances, and they must choose between attending a local program or not attending graduate school at all. Also, with increasing numbers of applicants and a constant number of slots, the choice of program may be based mainly on where or if the prospective student gets admitted.

The availability of financial assistance is another important determinant. All other factors being equal (e.g., quality, length, and reputation of the program), most students will choose the program that offers them the best deal financially in terms of tuition waivers, additional stipends, and duties or hours of work required to earn assistantship funding.

Typically, the decision-making process about graduate schools is different for students contemplating a master's or specialist-level training than for those contemplating doctoral training. Doctoral training traditionally is more specialized than predoctoral training, and prospective students (particularly those who have already completed a master's or specialist training program) generally are more aware of the need to match their own professional interests with the emphasis of a given doctoral program (Erchul, Scott, Dombalis, & Schulte, 1989). Although geographic, financial, and personal variables still may influence the prospective student's choices of doctoral institutions, other factors, such as the reputation of the program, the research interests of faculty members at an institution, and the accreditation status of the program, take on added importance for many candidates. Doctoral programs generally have more stringent entrance requirements than predoctoral programs; therefore, a prospective student's choice of a doctoral-level institution may be dictated more by whether or not the student is accepted into a particular program.

Job-Site Characteristics

Just as no two school psychologists are alike, no two job sites are identical. Job sites may vary on numerous characteristics from the supportiveness of coworkers and administrators to the community's awareness of the school psychologist's role.

Number of Pupils Served

The more students that school psychologists are expected to serve, the more time they will need to spend in assessment-related activities dealing with the identification, diagnosis, and placement of children with disabilities. Some school psychologists find it difficult to meet the demands of their assessment responsibilities and to participate in decisions on appropriate educational interventions for children with disabilities. School psychologists who work with fewer children may choose to, and may be expected to, expand into one or more additional roles, such as teacher consultant, individual or group counselor, staff development planner, group testing coordinator, or educational researcher.

Other Job-Related Factors

Many other job-related factors influence a school psychologist's professional practice. Some school psychologists work only in elementary schools, some only in secondary schools, and others in a combination of elementary and secondary schools. Secondary schools differ from elementary schools not only in the ages of the students but also in structure (e.g., different teachers for each subject and standardized instructional periods). The role of the school psychologist in each setting reflects these age and structural differences.

School psychologists' roles and functions also may vary depending on whether the school or schools are in an urban, suburban, or rural district. Some of these differences were discussed in chapter 3 and include the number of students served, the amount of time spent driving between schools, whether the office is located in an administrative building or in one of the schools, and who the practitioner's immediate supervisor is and what that person's professional training is. A supervisor with training in school psychology or in special education may have different expectations than a supervisor without that training or background. Sometimes a school psychologist's job is largely related to his or her predecessor's role. If the predecessor was perceived as competent and was well liked, then the newly hired school psychologist will be expected to function in much the same way. If the predecessor was perceived as incompetent, unpopular, or both, the newly hired school psychologist may be able to do almost anything as long as it is considered an improvement.

Oakland and Cunningham (1999) conceptualize the forces that affect the role of the school psychologist as being dependent upon the amount of external control the profession exercises. For example, variables such as licensure and certification, professional associations, and training are controlled largely by those in the field of school psychology. Variables such as financial support for the schools, state and federal statutes, and technology are influenced, at least to some extent, by school psychology practitioners and organizations. Other variables such as the political climate, the changes in society, and the history of certain situations are out of the control of the field of school psychology. Oakland and Cunningham suggest further that sources of tension that exist may need to be resolved before the profession of school psychology can move forward. The tensions discussed include unity versus plurality in school psychology, brevity versus completeness of professional preparation, thoroughness versus economy, services needed versus ability to deliver them, remediation versus prevention programs, special education versus general education, and traditional versus emerging assessment practices.

Shortages of School Psychology Practitioners

Shortages among school psychologists have a tremendous impact on professional practice. What happens when a school district or cooperative cannot find enough school psychologists to meet its needs despite all of its best search efforts? Obviously schools have some needs that must be met, such as students needing services for academic or behavioral difficulties and teachers requiring consultation about a problem with a student in the classroom. If no school psychologist can be found, what do school districts do? Among the strategies employed are increasing the load of the school psychologists on staff, hiring other staff members to perform some of the duties of the school psychologist, hiring retired school psychologists or those not wishing to work full-time on a contractual basis to work a certain number of days or complete a set number of case studies, hiring school psychologists who work full-time for

Shortages among school psychologists have a tremendous impact on professional practice.

another district to work evenings and weekends, paying someone to attend graduate school in school psychology with the understanding that the individual will come back to the district as a school psychologist for a given number of years (or repay the district for the training), and offering bonuses to interns if they agree to continue working in the district following the internship.

The Presence of Related Personnel

School psychologists' day-to-day functions may be influenced by the presence or absence of other related professionals. Some school districts, for example, hire school social workers who are responsible for obtaining social and developmental information about children from parents or for conducting individual and group counseling in the schools, or to do both jobs. Some school districts employ paraprofessionals or other personnel to perform some of the assessment duties often expected of school psychologists. Paraprofessionals are individuals who are not actually members of a given profession (in this case school psychology) but who receive sufficient training to be able to assist professionals with some tasks. Still other districts may employ school counselors, speech and language clinicians, occupational and physical therapists, psychiatrists, and other psychologists. The presence or absence of such professionals in the schools may dramatically influence the role of the school psychologist.

External Forces

School psychologists do not operate in isolation from society in general. Anyone who believes that public schools operate autonomously has not seen the impact of the No Child Left Behind legislation. Legislative and sociocultural changes have a huge influence on the practice of school psychology.

Societal Changes

Today's school psychologists do not operate in the same way as the school psychologists of the 1990s, 1980s, or before. Society has changed, and these changes have had a dramatic effect on children in the schools and consequently on the professional role of the school psychologist. In most classrooms nationwide, the children who live in intact two-parent homes are in the minority. More than 70% of mothers of school-age children work outside the home. Most of these women are employed at least partly out of economic necessity. Because few households have at least one stay-at-home parent, many children, even elementary school–age children, are left at home, unsupervised, for long periods. These so-called latchkey kids are of great concern to educators as well as to parents who feel that there are no available or affordable alternatives. Parents of junior high and high school students often worry about leaving their teenagers home without supervision in an era of substance abuse and sexual experimentation. Some school districts provide before-school and after-school programs, but recently, governmental budget cuts have put such programs at risk.

Most children in kindergarten today have been enrolled in preschool or day care either within the public school system or in privately run programs. This in itself represents a vast change from children starting school 25 or 30 years ago. In addition, critical events such as unemployment, poverty, or substance abuse in families and in society generally may influence school psychologists' professional practice. The societal context of schooling has changed, which in turn has influenced the need for school psychology services and the types of services required in the changing educational system.

Legal Cases, Legislative Acts, and Ethical Issues

Two of the most influential factors that have shaped school psychology over the years have been legal and ethical issues. Although students will become thoroughly familiar with these issues in their classes and in their readings, for example, of books such as *Ethics and Law for School Psychologists* (Jacob & Hartshorne, 2007), the following brief discussion covers some of the legal cases, legislative acts, and ethical issues that have most directly influenced the roles and functions of school psychologists.

In terms of legal issues, school psychologists often are involved in many facets of the legal system, particularly in court cases surrounding assessment-related issues. Legal issues that are most relevant to school psychologists can be divided into two major categories: (a) legal cases that result from the application of psychological assessment (i.e., cases in which assessment practices themselves are being challenged), and (b) legal cases that introduce psychological assessment as evidence or support (i.e., cases in which psychological assessment results are used to substantiate or refute a claim).

Cultural bias in testing. The court cases that have focused on the relationship between educational tests and cultural biases have had the greatest influence on the roles and functions of school psychologists (Bersoff, 1981). The fundamental question posed by legal challenges in such cases is, Are traditional psychological tests in educational settings fair for all students regardless of race, ethnic background, and gender? A second and more subtle question is, What happens to children as a result of testing in the schools? (Reschly, 1979).

The first case was *Hobson* v. *Hansen* (1967), in which a disproportionate number of African American children in the Washington, DC, public schools were placed in lower-level classes on the basis of their scores on group-administered tests. The primary issue in *Hobson* v. *Hansen* revolved around the question of whether the results of such group tests actually reflect a student's "innate abilities." In that case, the court found that the group tests that were used were not sufficient to justify placement in low-ability level classes.

Since *Hobson* v. *Hansen,* a number of other cases have been adjudicated that focused on individual intelligence testing and the resulting overrepresentation of minority group members in special education classes, especially classes for the mildly or "educably" mentally retarded. Such cases include *Diana* v. *California State Board of Education* (1970); *Guadalupe Organization, Inc.* v. *Tempe Elementary School District No. 3* (1972); *Larry P.* v. *Riles* (1984); and *PASE* v. *Hannon* (1980). (Additional information on specific cases can be found in Bersoff, 1982a, 1982b; Jacob & Hartshorne, 2007; Reschly, 1983; and Reschly, Kicklighter, & McKee, 1988a, 1988b, 1988c.) One difficulty that has transcended all of these court cases involves defining and measuring the construct *intelligence*. Traditional definitions of intelligence may in reality be more closely related to a person's ability to function within a predominantly white, middle-class, public school system than to any innate general cognitive ability. Reschly (1979) suggested that every time IQ test results are included in a report or in a student's file, such results should be accompanied by a warning like the surgeon general's warning for cigarettes:

> IQ tests measure only a portion of the competencies involved with human intelligence. The IQ results are best seen as predicting performance in school, and reflecting the degree to which children have mastered middle class cultural symbols and values. This is useful information, but it is also limited. Further cautions: IQ tests do not measure innate-genetic capacity and the scores are not fixed. Some persons do exhibit significant increases or decreases in their measured IQ. (p. 224)

More recent legal cases in which assessment practices have been challenged have switched the focus from the ambiguous notion of a student's innate intelligence to the more straightforward evidence of a student's actual level of achievement in the classroom setting (Reschly et al., 1988c). In one such case cited by Reschly et al. (*Marshall et al. v. Georgia*, 1984, 1985), students had been divided into instructional groups based on their mastery of specific skills within an established curriculum, not on their IQ score. The students' progress was closely monitored in each subject. Students were not simply placed into a certain level and left there without regard to their successes or failures. Even though a disproportionate number of black students were in the lowest classroom group in the *Marshall* case, the judge found in favor of the schools. As noted by Reschly et al., this probably was because the type of curricular-relevant assessment used, called curriculum-based assessment (CBA) or curriculum-based measurement (CBM) in the literature, was found to be directly related to positive learning outcomes. For more information about curriculum-based assessment and curriculum-based measurement, see Gickling & Rosenfield, 1995, and Shinn, 1995. Such cases have a direct impact on the everyday assessment and intervention practices of school psychologists.

How test results are used as evidence. The second group of legal cases includes those in which psychological tests have been introduced as evidence to substantiate or refute a claim. Cases in this group have not received the attention given to the cases cited in the first group; however, many school psychologists over the years have been summoned to testify about psychological tests. Some of the more controversial cases are those involving special education versus regular education placement decisions. For example, a child's test scores, classroom performance, and other data are used to determine if the child would be better off in a residential program, in a regular classroom, or in a special education classroom. Child custody decisions concerning children who have been evaluated by a school psychologist are also controversial.

Some of the more controversial cases are those involving special education versus regular education placement decisions.

School psychologists also may become involved in other types of legal issues or cases. They may be asked to work with students who have been victims of or witnesses to crimes. Likewise, they may be asked to work with students who have committed crimes. As addressed later in this chapter in the discussion of crisis consultation, school psychologists may be asked to perform a more indirect role in some instances by working with teachers whose students are facing crises.

Legislative influences. The influence of legislation on school psychology can be seen most clearly in the Education for All Handicapped Children Act of 1975 (EAHCA; Pub. L. 94-142), the Education of the Handicapped Act (EHA) Amendments of 1990 (Pub. L. 101-476), which became known as the Individuals with Disabilities Education Act (IDEA), and the Individuals with Disabilities Education Act Amendments of 1997 (Pub. L. 105-117). Although originally slated to be updated in 2002, amended IDEA regulations were finally published in August 2006.

As noted in chapters 2 and 7, the original EAHCA legislation in 1975 mandated that all handicapped children be identified, diagnosed, and placed in the least restrictive educational environment. That is, *all* children are entitled to an education at public expense and in the most "normal" program possible. Although school psychologists often are involved in the identification, diagnosis, and placement of handicapped children, the diagnostic responsibilities set out in EAHCA are often the most time-consuming for the psychologist in the schools. The EHA and IDEA have reinforced and expanded on EAHCA by extending the principles to infants and young children, including expanding provisions for assistive technology, and emphasizing the need for family involvement in educational planning.

Ethical issues facing school psychologists. As described in some detail in chapter 7, school psychologists operate under a variety of ethical guidelines through their national and state associations. (The APA and NASP ethical codes appear in appendixes C and D.) Although many ethical issues are clear-cut, others are more ambiguous and can be decided only after careful consideration of all the facts in a given situation. Throughout this chapter, information about legal and ethical issues is provided as it applies to the various roles and functions of the school psychologist. (Jacob & Hartshorne, 2007, provide a comprehensive discussion of legal, legislative, and ethical issues that have an impact on school psychologists.)

BASIC SKILLS USED BY SCHOOL PSYCHOLOGISTS

Although many factors influence the precise roles and functions of individual school psychologists, there are commonalities of training and practice. Most school psychologists have been trained in certain basic skills, which they will use to a greater or lesser extent depending on the factors described above. There are a number of different ways of conceptualizing these basic skills. Current students are probably most familiar with the following list of domains from the National Association of School Psychologists standards for school psychology training programs (NASP, 2000c). These 11 domains are commonly regarded as the basis for training and practice of school psychologists.

1. Data-based decision making and accountability
2. Consultation and collaboration
3. Learning and instruction
4. Socialization and development of life skills
5. Student diversity in development and learning
6. School and systems organization, policy development, and climate
7. Prevention, crisis intervention, and mental health
8. Home/school/community collaborations
9. Research and program evaluation
10. School psychology practice and development
11. Technology standards

What specific skills do school psychologists need to address each of the 11 domains and how do they acquire those skills? Each training program uses a unique combination of coursework and field experiences to make certain that students are competent in each domain. They may not have a course that corresponds with each domain name, but they will be expected to have addressed each one in some depth prior to certification. For example, the Introduction to School Psychology class is directly related to school psychology practice and development (Domain 10), although the course will probably cover material regarding data-based decision making and accountability (Domain 1), school and systems organization, policy development, and climate (Domain 6), and so forth. Likewise coursework in research and statistics, as well as a final research project or thesis, will provide many of the skills needed under Domain 9 on research and program evaluation. Technology standards (Domain 11) are probably infused through a number of classes that require students to be familiar with PowerPoint presentations, Internet searches, e-mail, word processing, computer scoring of standardized tests, and more.

The remaining pages of this chapter present information on the actual roles and functions of school psychologists. Unlike the previous two editions of this text, this edition presents an overview of the traditional roles of the school psychologist and that of the new or emerging roles of the school psychologist. It begins with descriptions of some of the most common functions of psychologists in the schools. After these descriptions, scenarios are presented to demonstrate how school psychologists may combine these functions into a typical day's schedule.

A school psychologist's ultimate professional goal is to help children. There are many ways to attain this goal but not all ways are appropriate in all situations with all children. Some authors (e.g., Elliott & Witt, 1986b) have conceptualized the roles and functions of school psychologists in terms of the services school psychologists possess in their professional repertoires and the ways they deliver these services. In this *service delivery* model, roles are viewed as helping students directly (e.g., counseling), indirectly

A school psychologist's ultimate professional goal is to help children.

(e.g., consultation with teachers), or somewhere in between, on a continuum of services (e.g., assessment of an individual student, design of interventions that teachers or parents will implement).

The roles and functions described in this chapter are not necessarily unique to the practicing school psychologist working within a public school system. These roles may also be applied to nontraditional settings (see chapter 8). Some of the roles and functions of school psychologists are similar to the activities of clinical and counseling psychologists (e.g., counseling and some types of assessment), whereas other roles and functions seem more unique to the profession (e.g., planning school-based interventions or participating in multidisciplinary staffings). Overall, in order to help children, school psychologists must be able to conceptualize problems, support their ideas with data about the problems, work with others to help solve the problems, and evaluate outcomes.

Overall, in order to help children, school psychologists must be able to conceptualize problems, support their ideas with data about the problems, work with others to help solve the problems, and evaluate outcomes.

TRADITIONAL ROLES AND FUNCTIONS OF THE SCHOOL PSYCHOLOGIST—ASSESSMENT

The traditional practice of the school psychologist involves three basic roles: assessment, intervention, and consultation. The three roles are described here as if they were mutually exclusive, but the truth is that they are always combined to some extent. It would be difficult to imagine the purpose of an assessment in which results were not conveyed to those asking for the assessment (consultation) or in which the assessment was not linked by the psychologist, the teacher, and the parent to some sort of action for improvement (intervention).

The traditional role of the psychologist in the schools revolves around the assessment of individual children. This *child study* role remains a major one for the school psychologist. A brief review of the assessment process is presented here as an introduction to the later in-depth discussions of assessment and practicum (field experience) courses.

First some definitions are necessary to distinguish between the terms *assessment* and *testing*. These terms should not be used interchangeably. As defined by Cohen, Swerdlik, and Phillips (1996), psychological assessment can be seen as "the gathering and integration of psychology-related data for the purpose of making a psychological evaluation, accomplished through the use of tools such as tests, interviews, case studies, behavioral observation, and specially designed apparatuses and measurement procedures" (p. 6). Psychological testing, according to the same authors, refers to "the process of measuring psychology-related variables by means of devices or procedures designed to obtain a sample of behavior" (p. 6). In this book, the term *assessment* is used to refer to a complex problem-solving or information-gathering process. The reason that school psychologists assess individual students is to understand the difficulties a child is experiencing in order to intervene and ultimately help the child. Although administering psychological tests may be a part of this

assessment process, such tests should be administered only when necessary to understand a child's difficulties and should not be automatically administered in every case to every child.

The Referral Process

Assessment occurs in the context of a referral process. The assessment of an individual child begins with a referral form, which is usually completed by the child's teacher and signed by a parent or guardian. A sample referral form is shown in Figure 4.2. The types of children referred and the difficulties they experience were explored in a national survey of school psychologists who serve elementary and secondary school settings (Harris, Gray, Rees-McGee, Carroll, & Zaremba, 1987). Harris et al. suggest that nearly two thirds (62%) of referrals are for students in kindergarten through fifth grade. The researchers found that referrals most often were the result of a teacher's concerns (57%), although sometimes referrals are made by parents or are self-referrals. Boys were 3.5 times as likely to be referred for services as girls; elementary school students (i.e., kindergarten through fifth graders) were more likely to be referred than older students; and students with poor academic performance or with social–emotional difficulties constituted more than 80% of the referrals.

A more recent study found that 57% of total referrals to school psychologists in the study's sample were for reading difficulties (Bramlett, Murphy, Johnson, Wallingsford, & Hall, 2002). Other frequent reasons for referrals in the Bramlett et al. study were for written expression (43% of referrals), task completion (39%), mathematics (27%), conduct (26%), and motivation (24%), with some referrals for more than one category. Reasons cited as receiving between 10% and 20% were defiance, peer relationships, listening comprehension, oral expression, and mental retardation. Reasons given that represented between 2% and 9% of the total included truancy, violence, depression, anxiety, shyness or withdrawal, and suicidal thoughts, as well as low-incidence behaviors such as autism and traumatic brain injury. Racial differences have also been found in referrals by teachers (Andrews, Wisniewski, & Mulick, 1997). What this means is just as boys are referred more often than girls, students of one race may be referred more often than students of another race.

The range of referrals found in the studies suggests that children in schools often need instructional as well as psychological assistance. A Canadian study produced similar findings (Cole, 1992). One study examined differences between high referring and low referring teachers (Waldron, McLeskey, Skiba, Jancaus, & Schulmeyer, 1998). Results indicated that some teachers tend to use referral to the school psychologist as a last resort after trying a large number of interventions (*low referring*). High-referring teachers, on the other hand, use referral to the school psychologist as a first step in solving a problem a student is experiencing. Increasingly schools are using a process known as *prereferral assessment*, which arose from a desire to reduce or at least to focus the large number of referrals received by school psychologists. The process involves a team problem-solving approach to diagnose difficulties that are occurring in the classroom and to intervene early, if possible, bypassing the more traditional referral process (Brandt, 1996).

Figure 4.2. Sample referral form.

I. Personal Information

Name of child Date of request
Home address Date of birth
Home telephone Age Grade

II. Family Information

Name Education Occupation
Father
Mother
Ages of siblings
Is this child ___adopted or stepchild? ___foster child?
___living with only one parent? ___living with both parents?
Primary language of home: ___English ___Other (specify)

III. School Information

Name of school
Address Phone
Principal's name Teacher's name
Grades repeated Years in present school
Services presently offered to the child
Attendance record
Previous schools attended

IV. Health Information

Date of last physical examination
Doctor's name
Results of last physical examination
Is the child on medication? If so, what?
Date and results of last vision screening
Date and results of last hearing screening
General physical health
During the last two years has the child experienced any medical problems?
If yes, please explain.

V. Reason for Referral

Why are you referring this child for psychological evaluation at this time?

What questions would you like to have answered?

Is there anything about the child's home or family environment that you believe might have a bearing on the child's attitude and behavior? If so, please explain.

What types of interventions have already been tried to address the child's difficulties?

Informed Consent

Once a referral is initiated, parents or guardians must give signed consent for an assessment. In fact, EAHCA and its reauthorizations as IDEA take parental consent a step further and address the issue of *informed consent*. Not only must the school give parents the opportunity to consent to assessment, but it also must make a reasonable effort to notify parents that an assessment is being recommended and to ensure that they understand what an assessment is, why it is being suggested, and what might result from the assessment. This requirement is usually straightforward. Occasionally, though, securing informed consent requires finding an interpreter, when the parents' primary language is not English, or tailoring an explanation to parents with limited education or ability so that they understand it.

Referral Questions

When the referral form has been completed and informed parental consent has been obtained, school psychologists often translate the request for assessment into one or more referral questions. For example, what does the teacher, parent, or student want to know? What is the nature of the problem? The clarification of referral questions helps to define the problem and is an important part of the assessment process. Elliott and Witt (1986b, p. 21) observed that, "Behavior and learning problems of children are functionally related to the setting in which they are manifest." In other words, the child exists within particular school and home contexts. What one teacher or parent perceives as a problem may not necessarily be perceived as a problem by another teacher or parent. Also, conditions in certain classrooms or homes may cause or intensify a child's problem behavior. Such environmental factors deserve careful consideration throughout the assessment process.

Data Collection Procedures

Referral questions can be addressed using a number of data collection or assessment procedures. School psychologists use a *multifactored* approach to assessment, which often includes testing, although not automatically. No single source of data addresses all aspects of a referral question so multiple sources must be used.

Questions for Collection of Data

Assessment should be done with a purpose in mind, and Salvia and Ysseldyke (2007) suggest that, within school settings, assessments be conducted to help make four types of decisions about students using the following questions.

1. Prereferral classroom decisions: Does the student need some sort of help beyond what is currently being done in the classroom? Should the child's difficulty be discussed by a teacher assistance team or an intervention assistance team? Is there something the teacher can do within the classroom to help the student? What other intervention options are available?

2. Entitlement decisions: Are the student's problems serious and persistent enough to warrant a referral to the school psychologist and other child study team members? Assessment procedures enhance the abilities of school personnel to identify students who are significantly above or below average in general abilities, in academic achievement, or in social or behavioral skills. In addition, assessment results are used by multidisciplinary teams in deciding whether an individual child qualifies for and might benefit from special instructional services.
3. Postentitlement classroom decisions: Assessments are conducted to provide information about an individual child's or a group of children's academic strengths and weaknesses. Such information should be applied within the classroom environment and be helpful in developing an individualized instructional plan for a child or in making curricular modifications across the classroom, building, or district.
4. Accountability and outcome decisions: Assessments provide additional information to teachers, parents, and children themselves regarding how much benefit individual children are deriving from their classroom placements. On a broader scale, assessments can help provide information as to how well educational programs in general are achieving their goals.

Initial Contact With the Referral Source

The school psychologist's first step in the assessment process often involves meeting with the individual who made the referral to determine specific referral questions. Even at this early stage, the psychologist begins to formulate initial hypotheses about the child's difficulties. This process of hypothesis formation is one of the most difficult steps for school psychology students, because such hypotheses tend to be hunches based on professional experience and training.

Although the teacher most often is the person responsible for filling out the referral form, it is critical to meet with the parents as well as the teacher to gain an understanding of the problems the child is experiencing. The parents may have additional concerns or insights to share prior to testing. The parents also have information about the child's health history, educational progress, and developmental milestones that may not be available from other sources. On the other hand, if the parents have made the referral, meeting with the teacher provides much additional information about the child's academic, social, and behavioral progress. Teachers also have the advantage of seeing how the child compares with others of the same age within the classroom. If the parents initiate a referral and the school psychologist is working outside of the school setting (e.g., in private practice or a mental health center), then parental permission is needed before the teacher or anyone else may be contacted concerning the child.

Teachers also have the advantage of seeing how the child compares with others of the same age within the classroom.

Classroom Observations

Following discussions with teachers and parents regarding the clarification of the referral question, many school psychologists begin to gather firsthand information about the referred child by completing one or more direct observations. Several standardized systems and computerized systems exist for completing such observations (e.g., Sattler, 2002), although some school psychologists report that their classroom observations center on a number of rather specific questions:

1. What was the child doing? What were other children doing?
2. What was the child supposed to be doing?
3. Where did the observation occur: classroom, playground, or elsewhere?
4. When and for how long did you observe?

According to Sattler, classroom observations give the examiner the opportunity to observe and to systematically record the child's behavior in a natural setting. Data collected from observations can be compared with reports from the child's teachers and parents. Data from naturalistic observations (i.e., observations in settings familiar to the child) also can be helpful when compared with observations of the child's behavior during the more structured and less familiar standardized testing setting if such testing is conducted. Along the same lines, Elliott and Witt (1986) note that "a primary goal of psychoeducational assessment is to determine what a child does and does not know, and how the child learns best so successful interventions can be designed" (p. 21). Seeing the child in the natural habitat of the classroom can provide a perspective on the child that would not be gained in the one-to-one setting in which most psychological testing occurs. In addition, Hintze and Shapiro (1995) state that in cases of problematic classroom behavior, systematic classroom observations allow us to observe "the behavior of interest in the settings where the problem actually has been happening. As such, the data are empirically verifiable and do not require inferences from observations of other behaviors" (p. 651).

Increasingly, school psychologists are trained not to limit their observations to the individual child in question and to observe and assess instructional environments. As Ysseldyke and Elliott (1999) note, there has long been an interest in instructional environments, but only recently has technology advanced to the point that such environments can be described using standardized measurement procedures. The variables considered in assessments of instructional environments include use of classroom time, motivation techniques, and opportunities provided for practice of skills, among others.

Examination of School Records

A great deal of information can be gleaned from school records, although school personnel should first be asked about their policies and about who has access to what records. The school psychologist will want to determine the child's current grade placement, previous schools attended, school history (i.e., has the child ever been retained, accelerated, or received any kind of special services?), group test results, attendance record, and previous assessments, if any. Information about health history and results of vision and hearing screenings also may be found in school records. Such information is critical in understanding the difficulties the child is experiencing. Checking the child's date of birth and age is often advisable as well, because individuals filling out referral forms have been known to make mistakes and because results of testing are often based on the child's chronological age.

Testing

Throughout the interviews with teachers and parents, the classroom observations, and the examination of school records, the school psychologist attempts to gain a clearer picture of the child and his or her difficulties. The use of a variety of test instruments is often helpful at this point to gather more information about the child. Testing, although sometimes portrayed as the albatross around the neck of the school psychologist, actually has many direct and indirect benefits. Not only do tests provide quantifiable data about an individual child, but they also give the school psychologist the opportunity to work with the child on a one-to-one basis. Skilled examiners often learn as much or more about a child through their observations during testing as they do through the computation of test scores. In addition, children often enjoy the opportunity to work one-to-one with an adult at school. In keeping with the notion of a multifactored assessment, some or all of the following types of tests may be administered as part of a test battery:

1. Cognitive ability tests: Tests that traditionally have been called intelligence tests or aptitude tests.
2. Academic achievement measures: Tests that assess a child's performance in one or more academic areas (e.g., reading comprehension, spelling, or math).
3. Perceptual tests (visual, auditory): Tests that examine a child's perceptual abilities (e.g., hearing differences between words with similar sounds or seeing hidden figures).
4. Tests of fine and gross motor abilities: Tests that look at a child's coordination, including everything from drawing and handwriting (fine motor abilities) to tossing a beanbag or walking a balance beam (gross motor abilities).
5. Behavioral, personality, and adaptive behavior measures: Such measures typically are outside the realm of academic tasks. Instead, they address children's behavior in various settings, their overall level of adjustment, and their non-school-related skills (often called self-help skills).
6. Curriculum-based assessment techniques. As mentioned earlier with respect to recent legal cases, curriculum-based assessment (CBA) is specifically geared to the academic tasks the child is expected to master. Such assessments usually look at tasks the child has already mastered, tasks the child is on the verge of mastering, and tasks that are beyond mastery at the time of testing. Such assessments may also allow comparison with the performance of the student's peers.

Interviews

Parents, teachers, and others (e.g., physicians, reading specialists, speech and language therapists, social workers, and extended family members) often are quite aware of the difficulties a child is experiencing. Talking to these individuals early in the assessment process helps to provide a more complete picture of the child. In many cases, children themselves are quite aware of their own difficulties, and even young children can be fairly candid about the reasons for these difficulties. Maintaining confidentiality under such circumstances can raise ethical questions. Sattler (1998) has devoted an entire book of more than 1,000 pages to the important skill of interviewing children and families.

Compilation of Assessment Results

Once all of the assessment procedures have been completed, the results are compiled, organized in relation to the referral questions, and shared with others. Presentation of the results usually takes two forms: (a) a written report designed to be read by school personnel and placed in the student's permanent record, and (b) an oral recounting of the results in conferences with parents or teachers or in multidisciplinary staffing sessions, or both.

Report Writing

Psychological or psychoeducational reports can have many formats (e.g., Ross-Reynolds, 1990; Sattler, 2002; Tallent, 1993). Ideally the psychological report should take the reader logically and chronologically through the process of assessment. Reports should be written clearly, be as free of technical jargon as possible, and reflect the consumers of the report by presenting the information that would be most helpful to them. The goal of explaining the test results so that someone with little background in psychological assessment will understand them is vital to the assessment process. Every effort should be made to relate the information in the report to the referral questions. There is no need to include in the report everything that is known about the youngster. All of the data accumulated during the assessment process cannot possibly be contained in a single report. Rather, the psychologist must find the most effective ways to synthesize all of the data and to communicate effectively the most important points and how they lead to recommendations for intervention. Ownby (1991) emphasizes that the psychologist's report should shape the thinking and the beliefs of those reading the report and perhaps even modify the behavior of the reader.

If a test battery has been administered to the child, then the report should describe the individual test results as well as describe how the various tests and subtests relate to each other. Integrating test results will point out any apparent inconsistencies in the child's performance.

The report should address qualitative or behavioral aspects in addition to quantitative test results. Did the child initiate conversation or merely answer questions? How did the child respond to praise or frustration? Were there particular behaviors exhibited on all of the tests that seemed to indicate low self-esteem? Comments about the child's behavior should include specific examples. Instead of saying "Leta was very anxious during the testing," the report should include a description such as

Ownby (1991) emphasizes that the psychologist's report should shape the thinking and the beliefs of those reading the report and perhaps even modify the behavior of the reader.

"She bit her nails throughout, rarely made eye contact with the examiner, and never initiated conversation."

There is a growing controversy about computer-generated psychological report writing. Although many school psychologists will gratefully use computer programs to score results of psychological tests, they are usually less comfortable or confident in allowing computer programs to interpret the test results and write reports. Several different types of computer reports are available (Cohen et al., 1996). *Simple scoring* reports provide test scores. *Extended scoring* reports expand the data by providing more complex statistical analyses, such as noting significant differences between subtest scores. Neither of these scoring report programs, however, attempt to interpret test scores.

According to Cohen et al., interpretive reports can be broken down further into descriptive reports, screening reports, and consultative reports. Descriptive reports provide brief comments about the various test scales. Screening reports highlight certain more unusual test results, bringing them to the attention of clinicians as areas on which to follow up. Consultative reports are designed to provide technical information to be shared among professionals. Finally, and of most concern to professionals, are integrative reports. As the name implies, integrative reports attempt to integrate information about the person being assessed, pulling together information from a wide variety of instruments and observations, summarizing that information, drawing conclusions, and even suggesting interventions or strategies.

Although the use of computer-assisted software with testing instruments has many advantages, test scoring and test interpretation of most psychoeducational assessment instruments are, in part, subjective processes for which extensive training is needed. The interpretation of assessment data by a program designed by an individual is no better or worse than the interpretation done by any other individual. Practitioners just starting out in the field may choose to view computer-generated reports and to select portions of the reports that seem accurate and valuable. One should never assume, however, that the report is accurate just because of its appearance or because it is marketed. Tallent (1993) notes that "computerized testing is a still-emerging technology ... with the potential to have influence on many lives" (p. 206). Tallent cites the *Guidelines for Computer-Based Tests and Interpretations* (American Psychological Association, 1986) as establishing critical rules for those using such report-writing systems. Psychology students and practicing psychologists are responsible for everything in their reports. If reports contain errors in scoring or interpretation, even if the computer program was in error, the psychologist is accountable for the content of the report.

Parent Conferences

The best approach for a school psychologist to take in a parent conference is to imagine the parents' position, how they would want to be informed of their child's results, and what they would want to know (Wise, 1986, 1995). Most parents identify strongly with their children. They want to hear strengths as well as weaknesses. They want to know that anyone working with their child thinks of their child as an individual, not as just another case study. Even parents who are quite aware of their child's limitations may become emotional in the course of parent conferences. Tears as well as denial are not uncommon reactions of parents.

Parents of children with disabilities may experience feelings of guilt and grief (Murray, 1985). The guilt may arise from the notion, founded or unfounded, that something the parents did caused the disability. The feelings of grief may arise from the knowledge that certain dreams parents have for their children may not come true with this particular child. It is sad for parents to realize that a child with limited intelligence may not go to college or that a child with a physical disability may never become a great athlete. Many resources exist on the topic of parent conferences. Some of those most relevant to school psychologists include Featherstone (1980), Fine (1991), Fish (2002), Gallagher (1980), Gargiulo (1985), Hubbard and Adams (2002), Murray (1985), Seligman and Darling (1997), and Wise (1986, 1995).

Teacher Conferences

Teacher conferences present their own unique challenges. Some experienced teachers can be particularly intimidating to new school psychologists. Teachers and school psychologists sometimes seem to think of themselves as adversaries, each knowing what is best for a child. Teachers may be suspicious of a school psychologist who has never been a teacher and "wants to tell me what to do," whereas school psychologists may view teachers as being intolerant of children who are different from the norm in any way. Of course, both positions are counterproductive to helping the child. As described below, the consultation role for school psychologists encourages collaborative problem solving between teachers and psychologists and is probably the best strategy in meeting the needs of children.

Multidisciplinary Staffings

Since the passage of EAHCA in 1975 and subsequent IDEA legislation, school psychologists and school systems generally have moved away from individual parent and teacher conferences in favor of sharing assessment results with all involved parties at the same time. The advantages of using a multidisciplinary team of school psychologists, educators, and other professionals are that each person in attendance will be able to hear all of the information presented and then will be able to participate as an equal partner in the decision-making process. The model of multidisciplinary staffing evolved as an effort to limit any one individual's influence and to protect against decisions that may be biased against minority children (Huebner & Hahn, 1990). The disadvantages of such teams include the notions that parents may find it intimidating to face so many educators at once, that parents and others may be reluctant to disagree with recommendations supported by several trained professionals, and that parents may need time to absorb the results of testing before they are ready to think about what is best for the child (Wise, 1995).

Much of the work that school psychologists do takes place within teams of other professionals.

Much of the work that school psychologists do takes place within teams of other professionals. In decades past, school psychologists were often considered the gatekeepers of special education; that is, the data that the school psychologist presented decided whether or not a student qualified for certain programs. Now, most of these decisions are made by a group, with each member holding a particular piece of the puzzle that, when put together correctly, should reveal the best educational placement for that student. Of course, anyone who has worked on a group project of any sort knows that sometimes groups work together in productive ways and sometimes they do not. Shaw and Swerdlik (1995) provide a discussion of topics related to team functioning. This topic is discussed in greater detail later in this chapter in the section on the emerging roles of school psychologists.

General Considerations Involved in Traditional Assessment

For the school psychologist to fulfill the responsibilities of the traditional child study role, the professional must address the issues listed below.

1. What is the established referral process?
   a. Who decides on the referral form to be used?
   b. Who completes the referral form?
   c. Who secures parental consent?
   d. What if parents refuse consent?
   e. Should students be given a chance to refuse testing?
   f. Who decides which children should be seen first?
   g. Where are completed referral forms kept?
2. Who should be referred?
   a. Are the school psychologist's services limited to children who may qualify for special education services?
   b. Are the school psychologist's services available to any child experiencing difficulty at school or at home?
   c. Are the school psychologist's services available to children who may be gifted or talented?
3. What are the alternatives to the "refer–assess" cycle?
   a. Is prereferral intervention available?
   b. Are other services available through the school (e.g., counselor, social worker)?
   c. What community services could be used (e.g., mental health center)?
4. Should a classroom observation be conducted?
   a. When should the observation be done?
   b. How long should the observation last?
   c. What observational method(s) should be used?
   d. What might be learned from an observation?
   e. How might the school psychologist's presence influence the observation?
5. Where and how are school records maintained?
   a. Are records kept for life or disposed of periodically?
   b. Who has access to student files?

6. What testing procedures should be used?

   a. What are the reasons for testing this child?
   b. Which tests are most appropriate based on the child's age, race, sex, native language, and presenting problem?
   c. Are these tests readily available to the school psychologist?
   d. What qualifications are needed to administer, score, and interpret the tests?
   e. Will the tests help to answer the referral question(s)?

7. Who should be interviewed about the child's difficulties?

   a. The classroom teacher?
   b. The parent(s) or other family members?
   c. The child?
   d. Other school personnel (reading teachers, speech and language therapists, counselors, social workers)?
   e. Nonschool personnel (e.g., physicians)?

8. What is the purpose of these interviews?

   a. To gain information about the child's strengths and weaknesses?
   b. To obtain a social, developmental, and medical history?
   c. To find out more about the people in the child's environment?
   d. To share information and findings?

9. When should these individuals be interviewed?

   a. Before testing?
   b. After testing?
   c. Instead of testing?
   d. Before and after testing?

10. How should these individuals be interviewed?

   a. Separately or collectively?
   b. At school or at the child's home?
   c. In person or over the phone?

11. How should the assessment results be conveyed?

   a. Orally in a parent conference?
   b. Orally in a multidisciplinary staffing?
   c. In the form of a written report?
   d. Orally as well as in written form?

Legal and Ethical Issues

Specific legal and ethical issues are relevant to each of the roles and functions of school psychologists. For the assessment portion of the traditional role, the major legal issues include the following:

1. Parents and older students have a right to allow or deny consent for the assessment process based on the information they have been provided.

2. Parents, students, and school personnel have the right to assume confidentiality in all of their dealings with the school psychologist except in situations involving danger to one or more individuals. The limits of confidentiality should be explained clearly in initial interviews with all parties.
3. Students and parents have a right to their privacy and a right to not have their privacy invaded.
4. Students and parents have the right to expect competent and current assessments. School psychologists are expected to keep up with developments in the field and to provide appropriate services to their clients. At the same time, school psychologists should recognize their limitations (in terms of professional training, professional experience, and time management).
5. Students and parents have the right to expect assessments that do not discriminate on the basis of race, religion, nationality, primary language, cultural background, gender, or socioeconomic status.

A much lengthier discussion of these issues is contained in Jacob and Hartshorne (2007).

Training Needs

To be prepared for traditional assessment activities, the school psychologist needs training and practice in behavioral observation techniques, interviewing methods, a variety of assessment skills (e.g., skills for selecting, administering, scoring, and interpreting results of individually administered tests, and skills for assessing classroom environments), skills in conducting conferences and meetings, and report-writing skills. It also is imperative for the school psychologist to be aware of the administration and organization of schools, normal versus exceptional child development, and general psychological testing and measurement principles. Likewise, training in legal and ethical issues is mandatory to ensure adherence to the highest professional standards. Finally, the school psychologist needs good critical thinking skills to integrate all of this information and understand all of the forces responsible for creating the existing problem.

Advantages and Disadvantages

The advantages of traditional assessment activities are that, in many circumstances, they can help educators, parents, and others understand the behavior of a particular child. They also provide direct contact with the student. Traditional assessment is comfortable and has been mandated in legislation. Many people choose the profession of school psychology because they like the idea of working on a one-to-one basis with children, and traditional assessment provides opportunities to do so. In addition, the assessments school psychologists perform as part of their child study role are data based.

Salvia and Ysseldyke (2007) describe norm-referenced assessment, in which each child's performance is compared with that of other children, as follows.

> Commercially prepared norm-referenced tests are standardized on groups of individuals representative of all children, and typical performances for

> students of certain ages or in certain grades are obtained. The raw score that an individual student earns on a test, which is the number of questions answered correctly, is compared with the raw scores earned by other students. A *transformed score*, such as a percentile rank, is used to express the given student's standing in the group of all children of that age or grade. (p. 30)

Criterion-referenced assessments allow the school psychologist to monitor a child's progress. They "measure a person's mastery of particular information and skills in terms of absolute standards" (Salvia & Ysseldyke, p. 30). Criterion-referenced tests provide answers to questions such as, How many lowercase letters of the alphabet can Kelly identify? Ideally, criterion-referenced assessments and norm-referenced assessments complement one another by providing two important measures of a child's progress. In addition, data gathered from both types of assessments can lead directly to research, a function that is too often viewed as the lowest priority for school psychology practitioners. The use of data-based assessment can lead to increased accountability among school psychologists.

The disadvantages of traditional data-based assessment include the notion that because there are many children with problems, spending several hours with some of them will hardly make a dent in the needs of a school system. A study by Lichtenstein and Fischetti (1998) found that time spent on evaluations ranged from just under 4 hours to more than 24 hours, with a median of nearly 12 hours per case. Therefore, conducting lengthy evaluations is probably not the best way to have a major impact on the schools. Also, performing assessment activities day after day may be the quickest road to professional burnout. Every time a school psychologist finishes with one child, two more referrals may appear.

Finally, once the data have been collected and interpreted, then what? The child still has not been helped. In fact, when the child study role involves labeling children, there may even be negative consequences for the child. A discussion by Hynd, Cannon, and Haussmann (1983) summarized arguments for and against labeling children. The most critical negative factors appear to be that labeling a child as disabled may prejudice the way others respond to that child, many people may focus on the negative facets of the child, and the label may lower everyone's expectations for the child. On the other hand, labeling a child as disabled has traditionally been the only way the child has been able to receive special services because of various state and federal regulations.

TRADITIONAL ROLES AND FUNCTIONS OF THE SCHOOL PSYCHOLOGIST—INTERVENTION

Following assessment, in the traditional role the school psychologist works with others involved in the case to come up with some remedial techniques that will alleviate the problem and help the child. Although the ultimate goal of assessment is to help children by identifying intervention strategies, a comprehensive assessment such as that described above does not automatically precede the intervention. Many school psychologists currently advocate, and many states require, a prereferral approach in which intervention assistance teams (often called teacher assistance teams, or TATs) meet with teachers individually or in small groups to discuss students who might be experiencing a variety of difficulties. Such teams plan strategies collaboratively, which in turn may eliminate the need for a formal comprehensive case study evaluation. The prereferral intervention or intervention assistance approach is described in Graden, Casey, and Bonstrom (1985); Graden, Casey, and Christenson (1985); Zins, Curtis, Graden, and Ponti (1988); and Ross (1995). This approach is a vital part of the emerging role that is discussed later.

Selection of an Intervention Strategy

Recommending and developing interventions involve creativity and common sense, as well as familiarity with current research. Witt and Elliott (1985) provide guidelines to use when considering various interventions. They suggest examining the *effectiveness* of the intervention and the *acceptability* of the intervention, that is, how well it works and how positively it is perceived by consumers. Some factors that are considered when determining an intervention's effectiveness and acceptability include the anticipated duration of the implementation to results, the type of intervention (whether the activity fits easily into the daily routine), the time and other resources needed for the intervention to be successful, the theoretical orientation of the intervention (e.g., behavioral), and the person responsible for implementing the intervention (e.g., a teacher or parent). Witt and Elliott suggest that the child's perceptions of the acceptability of the intervention strategy also be considered.

Acceptable intervention strategies are those that consider the available resources as well as the dynamics of the individual situation. Phillips and McCullough (1990) present the following list of eight "feasibility considerations" for deciding what interventions to implement:

1. How disruptive the intervention will be for the teacher, the classroom, and the school
2. How various individuals and systems will be affected (e.g., student, teacher, and family)
3. The availability of required support services
4. The degree of competence of the person(s) expected to carry out the intervention
5. The chance of the intervention's success
6. The length of time before results are obtained
7. The probable prognosis if the intervention is not implemented
8. The chance that the intervention will lead to a permanent change in the student's behavior

Students and interns often wonder how to determine what interventions to consider. Courses or field experiences discuss interventions and provide ideas. Some books also link particular problem areas with intervention ideas (e.g., McCarney, Wunderlich, & Bauer, 1993; Marzano, 2003; Rathvon, 1999). School psychologists

Figure 4.3. Catterall's model of strategies for prescriptive interventions.

Intervention Technique	Indirect Approach	Direct Approach
Environmental	Environmental	Installed
	Activities done *around* the student	Activities done *to* the student
Personal	Assigned	Transactional
	Activities done *by* the student	Activities done *with* the student

research interventions in books, in journals, and on the Internet. They also attend workshops and conferences to help expand their resourcefulness. The NASP newsletter, the *Communiqué*, contains pullout pages on particular issues, which are suitable for handing out to parents and teachers. Canter, Paige, Roth, Romero, and Carroll (2004) compiled many of these pullout pages and added others in a book titled *Helping Children at Home and School: Handouts for Families and Educators.*

To select an intervention, the practitioner or team organizes the optional interventions, which include all those that are directed toward the target difficulty. Models are available that can then be used to sort and compare the interventions. For example, to classify the types of interventions available, Catterall (1967) suggested a four-part model of intervention activities. He categorized intervention techniques according to two dimensions: first, whether the activity's focus is direct or indirect, and, second, whether the intervention technique focuses on the environment of the student or on the student himself or herself. Figure 4.3 shows Catterall's model of intervention activities.

Catterall described *environmental* interventions as those activities implemented *around* the student, such as selecting a particular classroom or establishing classroom rules. *Installed* interventions are strategies in which something is done *to* the student, such as positive reinforcements, punishments, or peer tutoring. *Assigned* interventions are activities done *by* the student, such as honors assignments or homework. *Transactional* interventions are those activities done *with* the student, such as individual or group counseling or classroom contracts. Catterall's model may be especially useful in ensuring that all possible types of intervention strategies are considered.

Maher and Zins (1987) presented a different approach to the organization of school-based intervention strategies. They identified six intervention domains: cognitive development, affective functioning, socialization, academic achievement, physical fitness, and vocational preparation. They also identified three intervention modes: one-to-one, group, and consultation. For example, to help a child improve his or her academic achievement, options include individual tutoring (one-to-one), small-group remedial reading (group), or working with the classroom teacher to enhance the child's learning within the classroom (consultation).

Procedures for recommending intervention strategies are different for children identified as having disabilities and for children who are not disabled. Since the passage of EAHCA in 1975, decisions made concerning children with disabilities (particularly decisions involving inclusion or part-time or full-time special education class placement) must be joint decisions agreed upon in multidisciplinary conferences with documentation placed in the child's individualized educational plan (IEP). Prior to the passage of

EAHCA, school psychologists often decided single-handedly which students qualified for special education services, which students did not qualify, and which students, if any, should be taken out of special education placements. Currently, though school psychologists often wield a fair amount of influence in placement decisions, the final decision is made by a team composed of professionals and the child's parent or guardian.

Individual and Group Counseling Interventions

Most school psychologists are prepared to provide some individual and group counseling services, and many enjoy this role. Catterall's model mentioned individual and group counseling as examples of transactional interventions, that is, interventions done with students. The amount of time school psychologists spend doing individual or group counseling is greatly influenced by the setting in which they work; their training, experience, and interest in counseling; their time and scheduling flexibility; and the presence or absence of other qualified professionals within the school and community. Some school districts employ school counselors, school social workers, or other professionals specifically to perform counseling services for students in all grades. Other districts employ counselors who are available only in the high schools and who may spend much of their time coordinating class schedules, arranging group testing, and advising vocational and college students.

The amount of time school psychologists spend in individual or group counseling is greatly influenced by the setting in which they work.

Some school districts expect school psychologists to perform crisis intervention activities, a type of counseling that is short-term and addresses a student's immediate need to talk to someone about a particular problem or event, such as the death of a family member or parental divorce. Other school districts may expect the school psychologist to counsel secondary school students only. Still others may encourage school psychologists to refer nearly all potential counseling cases to local mental health centers or other facilities and individuals in the vicinity. In such cases, when the psychologist is involved in referring students for counseling outside of the school district, the psychologist functions as a liaison with service providers in the community.

In some states a school district may be required to provide all necessary psychological services, including counseling, to students with disabilities or even to all students. In some cases, school psychologists may be expected to spend a large amount of time providing individual and group counseling to these students. In fact, school psychologists may be the professionals most qualified to provide counseling to students with disabilities. Examples of group interventions in which school psychologists may be involved include groups that work with children of divorce, children having difficulties with anger management, and children dealing with grief, along with more general groups to help students improve their social and problem-solving skills.

Training Needs

School psychologists involved in planning and implementing recommendations for interventions must possess competencies in a number of areas. They should have good interpersonal skills, such as the ability to establish and maintain rapport, listen, and work collaboratively. They also should be able to generate realistic solutions to problems using knowledge of intervention research, available resources, and Internet research. Skills in evaluating outcomes include evaluating programs and deciding what changes need to be made for an intervention to be successful. Patience is also needed if, as found by Waguespack, Stewart, and Dupre (1992), teachers recall fewer than half of the steps involved in an intervention after a week, even when they have been provided with written instructions for implementation. Some of these skills are acquired during training (e.g., research skills), whereas others are acquired over time during the internship and later on the job. Students should not expect to have all the answers when they complete their training. Instead, it is hoped that students will acquire an interest in continuing their education throughout their careers so that they can keep up with research-based trends and innovations.

Legal and Ethical Considerations

The major legal and ethical considerations associated with the traditional intervention role concern the appropriateness of particular interventions. Two of the most controversial intervention techniques in the schools have been the use of corporal punishment (spanking or paddling) and the use of "time-out," in which a student is removed from classroom activities and isolated from peers for a period of time. Each of these is discussed at length in Jacob and Hartshorne (2007). Another body of literature surrounding legal and ethical issues in interventions addresses problems unique to counseling, such as confidentiality when a student in counseling suggests that he or she is going to harm someone or commit suicide. Is the psychologist obligated, legally or ethically, to reveal information in such cases, or if the student is being abused by a parent, or is pregnant, or if the student is taking or selling drugs? Again, school psychologists must be aware of current ethical and legal thinking on such dilemmas. The place to start is to become familiar with the ethical principles of NASP, the APA, and any state associations to which they belong. Jacob and Hartshorne's (2007) book is an excellent source of down-to-earth discussion of these issues. Training programs are themselves ethically obligated to provide students and interns with the opportunity to consider all aspects of these matters.

A final ethical question with respect to interventions is more general and examines the right of any professional to change another person's behavior without that person's expressed permission. It is one thing for someone who wishes to quit smoking to make an appointment with a psychologist or counselor to learn behavior modification techniques to reach that goal. It is another matter for a teacher to ask a school psychologist for help in modifying the behavior of a child who has difficulty completing assignments, who asks questions without raising his or her hand first, or who talks too frequently to classmates. Jacob and Hartshorne (2007) advise that the school psychologist has a responsibility to set reasonable goals that will be in the best interest of the child over the long run. (However, it would be nearly impossible for a school psychologist to ascertain whether it is a reasonable goal to teach a 6-year-old child to raise his or her hand before asking a question.)

Advantages and Disadvantages

The school psychologist's traditional intervention roles provide the opportunity to help children by making suggestions to teachers, parents, and others. When suggestions work, the intervention role provides feelings of professional accomplishment and success. These are the kinds of rewards most school psychologists are hoping for—the knowledge of making a difference in one child's life.

Some of the disadvantages of the intervention role are similar to the disadvantages of assessment. Even if one child is helped, many other needy children are out there who are not being helped. Working with one child at a time is rewarding, but is there something that could be done that would help more teachers to help more children in the same amount of time? Some of the intervention activities (e.g., behavior modification plans or social skills training) require the expenditure of large amounts of time, often by the school psychologist, who explains the program, sets it up, and evaluates its effectiveness. Unlike the well-established reliability and validity of many instruments used in assessment activities, many if not most intervention methods have little research to support their validity, although efforts are under way to remedy this problem (e.g., see Elliott, Witt, & Kratochwill, 1991). In addition, the person implementing an intervention hears only about the strategies that did not work. ("I tried that behavior modification plan like you said for one day but Billy still wouldn't listen, so I gave up. Any other ideas?") When this happens the school psychologist may end up in a losing battle to combat the "yes-but" response discussed by Berne (1964): "Yes, but that won't work because he doesn't do any of his work." "Yes, but his parents won't go along with that." "Yes, but I have 30 other students who will want rewards, too."

Finally, in the traditional role of the school psychologist over the past 25 or 30 years most of the intervention activities have been directed only toward students who are determined to be in need of special education services. Students with disabilities have been considered the primary purview of the school psychologist. If a student experiencing difficulty in the classroom does not qualify for special education, the school psychologist could suggest interventions to classroom teachers or parents, but no special education services could be offered. School psychologists often refer to the youngsters who did not qualify for special education but were not succeeding in the regular classroom as the "kids who fell through the cracks" of the educational system. This heartbreaking situation has been another large reason that the field is moving toward the emerging model of service delivery.

TRADITIONAL ROLES AND FUNCTIONS OF THE SCHOOL PSYCHOLOGIST—CONSULTATION

To avoid the "yes-but" response discussed above and to have an effect on a greater number of students, many school psychologists have embraced consultation. Whereas assessment allows practitioners to determine the kind of services a student needs, consultation strengthens the chances that the appropriate services will be delivered. The term *consultation* is used to mean a great many things. More than a dozen types of consultation are discussed in Fagan and Warden (1996). At times consulting has been used synonymously with advising, counseling, suggesting, and problem solving. When used by school psychologists, *consultation* generally refers to a mutual problem-solving process between two or more professionals. One of the professionals, the consultant, is viewed as an expert in some area. The other professional, the consultee, is experiencing a work-related problem and seeks the consultant's help to solve the problem. This definition comes from the mental health literature, most notably the work of Caplan (1970).

Other issues that arise in discussions about consultation include the notion of consultation as an *indirect* role. That is, school psychologists work with consultees, often teachers, to solve work-related problems the teachers are having, usually with their students. School psychologists, then, are helping students indirectly by working directly with teachers. The consultee actually has direct responsibility for the students and may choose to accept or reject the consultant's assistance. Martin (1983) also emphasized the idea of consultation as focusing on prevention rather than intervention. Consultation must be voluntary; that is, no one should be forced to consult about a work-related problem. When people come to a consultant for help because they have been told they must (e.g., a parent is told, "If you and your child don't cooperate with the school psychologist, your child will be suspended from school"), the chances of establishing a positive working relationship conducive to mutual problem solving are just about nil.

It is particularly important for school psychologists to view consultation as a collaborative relationship between two or more professionals.

It is particularly important for school psychologists to view consultation as a collaborative relationship between two or more professionals. Curtis and Meyers (1985) noted that "one of the most fundamental principles underlying [consultation] is that a genuinely collaborative professional relationship among those engaged in the problem solving process is essential to success" (p. 81). Zins and Ponti (1990) are more specific about the collaborative nature of consultation: "Consultants and consultees work together to solve problems, and it is highly desirable for them to do so in the context of a partnership that emphasizes trust, openness, and cooperation" (p. 675).

Consultation encompasses many different skills. An effective consultant possesses a strong knowledge base and good interpersonal and communication skills. In addition, the effective consultant develops the consultee's ability to use inner resources. The consultant will not always be present when a problem arises. Therefore, the consultee should not be encouraged to depend on the presence and advice of the consultant. Conoley and Conoley (1992), among others, provide an elaborated version of this consultation model.

Certain steps or stages are characteristic of consultative relationships. These steps can be summarized as follows:

1. Enter into the consultation relationship
2. Diagnose the nature of the work-related problem
3. Collect data
4. Create and maintain a workable relationship
5. Define boundaries of the consultation relationship

6. Identify and develop possible resources
7. Make decisions
8. Terminate the consultation relationship

Forms of Consultation

Consultation can involve working with individuals or with whole groups or systems. The most common forms of consultation practiced by school psychologists are mental health consultation, behavioral consultation, crisis consultation, and organizational consultation. Other types of consultation relevant to school psychologists include advocacy consultation, case consultation, collaborative consultation, ecological consultation, parent consultation, and problem-solving consultation. Fagan and Warden (1996) have written about these additional types of consultation.

Mental Health Consultation

Mental health consultation has been described as the "prototypic consultation approach" (Conoley & Conoley, 1992, p. 6). Caplan's (1970) volume, *The Theory and Practice of Mental Health Consultation,* was a milestone work in defining consultation, particularly as it applied to the mental health field. Meyers, Alpert, and Fleisher (1983) define mental health consultation as being based on the notion that, for problem solving to occur, the feelings of the consultee must be addressed. The reasoning is as follows: When a teacher consults with a school psychologist regarding a student in the teacher's classroom, the teacher's relationship with, and feelings toward, the student should be considered. If the consultant can alter the teacher's feelings about the student, then the teacher's behavior toward the student might change; and if the teacher's behavior toward the student changes, then it will likely cause a change in the student's behavior. It is further believed that if the teacher is aware that a change in his or her behavior toward the student has brought about a change in the student, then the teacher will generalize what she or he has learned to similar situations in the future.

If the definition of mental health consultation is extended, it seems logical that school psychologists might consult with other school personnel in promoting positive mental health in the schools and preventing or addressing mental health–related difficulties. Johnson, Malone, and Hightower (1997) cite research "which demonstrates that competence, mental health, and achievement are inseparable in schools" (p. 81). Building on the work of previous researchers, they further suggest that school psychologists use their consultation skills to work with teachers and thereby to improve the climate of the schools and foster the positive mental health of large numbers of students.

Behavioral Consultation

Behavioral consultation involves applying the principles and procedures of behavior modification and social learning theory to the work-related problems of the consultee. Typically a teacher comes to the school psychologist with a specific child or group of children who are exhibiting some type of unacceptable behavior. For example, a teacher might mention his or her concern about a child who picks fights with other children on the playground. With this initial contact by the teacher, the school psychologist has entered into a consultative relationship. The next step would be working with the teacher to define and clarify the problem. The school psychologist might ask some questions: Does the child fight only on the playground? How about in the classroom? Does the child fight only with one particular child or with several children? How often do these fights occur? How long has this fighting behavior been going on? Is the child experiencing any other kind of difficulty in the classroom or at home? Does the child have any friends in the classroom? Do the fights occur only during a specific type of activity (e.g., competitive games)? The school psychologist's role in this initial interview is similar to his or her role in the prereferral stage of a comprehensive assessment, discussed earlier in this chapter.

In the data-gathering step, the practitioner would observe the child on the playground and perhaps in other settings, keeping track of the number of fighting episodes as well as the antecedents and consequences of the fighting. Once the consultant has worked with the consultee to define the inappropriate or problem behavior (fighting or pushing), an appropriate behavior that would be incompatible with the undesirable behavior can be identified, that is, an acceptable behavior that cannot be done at the same time as fighting. Running laps around the playground, for example, would be incompatible with pushing or fighting. Also during the observations of the inappropriate behavior, along with antecedents and consequences, the consultant would look for teacher behaviors, peer behaviors, classroom or playground events, and the child's own behaviors that might be maintaining the inappropriate behavior.

Throughout the consultation, the consultant should be monitoring his or her working relationship with the teacher, as well as checking in and asking how things are going and making certain the teacher knows what to expect next. The teacher should have realistic notions of the boundaries of the working relationship. The consultant might say, "I'll be observing Jennie on the playground, in the cafeteria, and in the classroom on several occasions this week. Then I'll get back to you when I'm here next week so we can set up a plan for you to use with Jennie to decrease her pushing behavior and increase her cooperative behavior." At the meeting the next week, the consultant would share the observations and work with the teacher to set up a system that reinforces Jennie's efforts at cooperation and decreases her aggressive behavior. Perhaps Jennie could earn points for running a certain number of laps per week and lose a given number of points for every fight in which she is involved. The important point to remember is that the teacher, having been given the necessary information, should be at least an equal, if not greater, partner in suggesting the possible resources, deciding which program to follow, and implementing the program. Jennie is the teacher's responsibility; therefore, the teacher can accept or reject the consultant's assistance. Common sense suggests that the more involved the teacher is in setting up a program, the stronger his or her commitment will be and, therefore, the greater the chances that the program will succeed.

Consultation involves a relationship-building process. It is not merely a task to be completed by the school psychologist.

Terminating the consultation relationship is different for school psychologists than for consultants in other fields. School psychologists often are viewed as neither insiders nor outsiders in a given school. As discussed in chapter 3, school psychologists may be viewed as guests who make frequent visits to the schools. In the case of Jennie, after her teacher has a plan in place, the consultant will probably want to maintain a working or collaborative relationship with her in case other problems develop or other children in her classroom need direct or indirect services in the future. The notion of follow-up is particularly important for school psychologists for this reason. The consultant will need to check in with teachers to find out whether the recommended plan is succeeding. Such checking in may be brief and informal; often it occurs in the hallway or in the teachers' lounge. Because consultation is a relationship-building process, it is not a task that is simply completed by the school psychologist. Rather, it is a way of functioning as a partner with teachers, parents, and others that transcends many of the other roles and functions of the psychologist in the schools. Rosenfield (2002) provides an excellent overview of instructional consultation, including a variety of useful forms and references. Likewise, Zins and Erchul (2002) identify many of the issues, steps, and types of consultation.

Crisis Consultation

Crisis consultation takes an indirect approach to crisis intervention by helping teachers or others in the school to deal with students who are undergoing a crisis. The school psychologist discusses strategies with the teacher so that the teacher can work more effectively with one or more students facing a particular crisis. Students who have not worked previously with the school psychologist may be uncomfortable talking to a stranger about a private issue. They may be more comfortable talking to a favorite teacher. This teacher, however, may be uncertain as to how to deal with the student and may request some suggestions or ideas from the school psychologist.

In one study (Wise, Smead, & Huebner, 1987), school psychologists were given a list of 32 critical events and asked to mark those that they had been approached about during the previous semester. More than half of the psychologists were asked to deal either directly (crisis intervention) or indirectly (crisis consultation) when students were failing a subject, when students were being abused, when students' parents were divorcing or separating, and when students were experiencing problems with one or more teachers, repeating a grade, having difficulty with parents, and moving.

The valuable contributions that school psychologists make in helping school personnel respond to crises were emphasized during the 1997–1998 school year, after a series of unfortunate incidents in which students were involved in in-school shootings. Scott Poland, a leader in the area of responding to school crises and coauthor of *Crisis Intervention in the Schools* (Pitcher & Poland, 1992), serves as a team leader of the National Organization for Victim Assistance and is a member of the National Emergency Assistance Teams (NEAT). Poland's NEAT member team, consisting of two school psychologists and five other helping professionals, was invited to Jonesboro, Arkansas, after two students shot and killed a teacher and four students at a middle school. The team's role was to identify those most in need of services, to provide professional support and training to the caregivers already in the community, and to conduct a public forum to facilitate the processing of emotions within the community. (Poland's account of his team's work in Jonesboro appears in the 1998 NASP *Communiqué*.) As an outgrowth of the attention focused on school-based violence during the 1997–1998 school year, NASP played an active role in developing *Early Warning, Timely Response: A Guide to Safe Schools* (Dwyer, Osher, & Warger, 1998), published by the U.S. Department of Education and disseminated to more than 100,000 public and private schools in September 1998. Likewise, school psychologists were involved in the aftermath of the September 11, 2001, attack on the World Trade Center in New York and the devastating hurricane season of 2005.

Organizational Consultation

Organizational consultation applies the principles and practices of consultation to the larger framework of a school building or an entire school system in an attempt to improve the functioning of the entire organization or to implement planned changes. Any skilled observer who spends time in the schools can see areas in need of change. Centra and Potter (1980) developed a model of school-related variables, any or all of which may affect student learning. These variables include school or school district conditions, within-school conditions, teacher characteristics, teaching behavior, student characteristics, student behavior, and student learning outcomes.

Any skilled observer who spends time in the schools can see areas in need of change.

Usually when someone talks about organizational consultation in the schools, she/he are talking about making changes relating to some or all of these seven variables. Harrington (1985) suggests that organizational problems within schools typically concern ambiguous, changing, or nonmeasurable goals; poor communication within the system; or attempts to implement changes without enough forethought. Harrington further suggests that school psychologists interested in organizational development and consultation adopt one or more of the following four roles:

- Planning leader: Helps to organize and coordinate change.
- Information and communications link: Collects organizational data and clarifies, synthesizes, and interprets the data for others.
- Learning specialist: Applies knowledge about learning and educational theory to the problems at hand.
- Consultant to management: Clarifies the problems and solutions for administration and acts as a liaison among the various groups involved.

School psychologists may be in ideal positions to engage in organizational consultation for a variety of reasons. First, the school psychologist is neither an insider nor an outsider in the school. Because school psychologists rarely work in just one school, they are not considered regular staff members in a given building, yet over time they usually work with enough individuals within a given school that they are not strangers either. Many school psychologists also have the advantage that, because they work in a number of different schools, they have the opportunity to observe what works and what does not work in other schools. Finally, school psychologists' backgrounds in research design, consultation, and assessment skills should prove useful for the practice of organizational consultation.

Illback, Zins, and Maher (1999) suggest that "viewing schools from a systems perspective enables the evaluator to gain a broader understanding of factors that potentially influence the operation of the school" (p. 922). They note that systems are made up of subsystems. In schools, such subsystems may be the individual school buildings, the school administration, the board of education, the special education personnel, or even the school psychologists. Subsystems are all interconnected, and a change in one subsystem causes changes in the other subsystems. Illback et al. note that one important organizational role for school psychologists relates to evaluation of programs. As schools move toward more outcome-based assessment of students for purposes of accountability, the program evaluation role may escalate in importance.

Training Needs

As noted above, to be effective consultants, individuals need good interpersonal skills, an awareness of the parameters of consultation, and knowledge about the subject under consideration. Conoley and Conoley (1992) label the skills needed for consultation "relationship-enhancing skills," skills in "problem formulation and resolution," and "personal and group process skills." School psychologists new to the profession or even new to a particular school may not be immediately sought out as consultants. They may have to prove themselves first as competent professionals in more traditional roles (e.g., child study and intervention). At the same time, newly trained school psychologists may not possess the knowledge and experience needed for effective consultation. They may have effective interpersonal skills and feel comfortable with brainstorming and problem-solving strategies, but they may lack the wealth of resources and techniques that teachers or parents are looking for. A great deal has been written about consultation in the school psychology literature, for example, Christenson (1995), Conoley and Conoley (1992), Gutkin and Curtis (1999), Kratochwill, Elliott, and Callan-Stoiber (2002), Rosenfield (2002), and Zins and Erchul (2002). One thought-provoking article about training needs suggests not only that school psychologists need to be trained as consultants but also that teachers should be trained as consultees. Such training would enable teachers to formulate better questions and to become more active participants in the consultative relationship (Duis, Rothlisberg, & Hargrove, 1995).

Legal and Ethical Issues

Hughes (1986) suggested that certain ethical issues apply to all types or models of consultation. For example, regardless of the type of consultation, school psychologists need to be concerned with students' rights, parents' rights, the rights of consultees, and the rights of the school system that employs them. With regard to students' rights, Hughes noted that school psychologists' actions "should (a) not abridge children's rights and (b) promote values of human dignity and respect for individuals' rights" (p. 490). If school psychologists become aware, either through consultation or other roles, of practices that are unethical or go against a child's rights, they have a responsibility to the child to work to change these practices.

According to Hughes (1986), parents have a right to privacy and confidentiality and a right to give or withhold informed consent to any plan or program in which "a child is singled out for special treatment in a manner that permits classmates to perceive the child as different in a negative way" (p. 492). Consultees also have a right to privacy, confidentiality, and informed consent. Because the consultative relationship is voluntary, consultees have a right to accept or reject any suggestions or advice that evolves from the consultation. Employing school districts also have rights. Hughes suggests that school districts have the right to know how successful their school psychologists have been in achieving the objectives of consultation. In other words, school districts have a right to accountability data from the school psychologist; that is, they should be told how the school psychologist spends his or her time and how effective the school psychologist is (see chapter 5).

As with everything they do, school psychologists acting as consultants have a responsibility to students, parents, and school personnel to carry out all duties in a professional, competent, fair, and confidential manner.

Jacob and Hartshorne (2003) raise similar ethical issues regarding the consultation role for school psychologists. They note that "in the course of the consultative process, it may become apparent to the psychologist that he or she is unable to assist the consultee. If so, he or she is obligated ethically to refer the consultee to another professional. ... It may also become apparent during the consultative process that another professional is better able to assist the consultee" (p. 223). As with everything they do, school psychologists acting as consultants have a responsibility to students, parents, and school personnel to carry out all duties in a professional, competent, fair, and confidential manner.

Advantages and Disadvantages

Consultation in all of its various forms can be an extremely valuable and satisfying role for the school psychologist. Consultation activities provide school psychologists with the opportunity to have an indirect impact on a large number of students. Consultation may be viewed by school personnel as a particularly valuable resource when difficult problems arise. In addition, it may be a useful tool in preventing problems. Consulting with a new teacher about behavioral strategies, for example, may help that teacher develop the confidence and skills needed to face problems as they arise or even to prevent problems. On the other hand, many school psychologists enjoy one-to-one contact with children. Since the consultant works only indirectly with students, the psychologist acting as consultant may spend more time with adults and less time with children. The idea that the consultee, usually the teacher, is free to accept or reject the suggestions of the consultant can be another frustrating aspect of consultation. A great deal of time and energy may be spent in collaborative problem solving only to have the results ignored completely or inconsistently applied.

THE EMERGING ROLES OF THE SCHOOL PSYCHOLOGIST

Over the years many articles and books have been written by authors proclaiming a changing role for school psychologists. At various times in the profession's history academics have announced that change is on the way and that school psychology students would no longer be doing the traditional assessment-related activities that are so familiar. It may be true that in some locations such change has occurred, but the majority of school psychologists have continued to function in the traditional roles described above. However, it now appears that a more far-reaching change really may be imminent.

Many forces seem to be contributing to the changing roles of school psychologists: the current political climate, the IDEA reauthorization, impetus from within the profession to expand the roles, and the public's dissatisfaction with the schools. First, in the current political climate, the pressures to meet the stipulations of the No Child Left Behind Act have forced schools to focus on quantifiable outcome results for all students. All students have to be making gains in order for a school to meet the standards of "adequate yearly progress" in the legislation. "All students" includes students with disabilities, students functioning well in regular classrooms, and the students mentioned above who have typically slipped through the cracks of the educational system. Schools need help with these efforts, and no one can better assist than school psychologists with knowledge of assessment, statistics, research methodology, and learning and instruction.

The second impetus has been the 2004 reauthorizations of the IDEA legislation and the 2006 regulations to implement it, which emphasize the model of response to intervention (RTI) over more traditional assessment techniques. Many scholars over the years have suggested that the traditional way of identifying such students has major flaws, particularly for students with learning disabilities. The traditional model of identifying a student with a learning disability has been to administer an intelligence test and an achievement test and look for a discrepancy between the two. Then if a student is not working up to his or her potential as measured on the intelligence test, a learning disability is suspected. Critics of the traditional techniques theorized that the same sort of discrepancy could occur for other reasons, such as a motivational problem, a poor instructional match between the student and the teacher, or emotional difficulties. The latest thinking, supported by the August 2006 regulations to implement IDEA, is that there may be better ways to identify and assist students with learning difficulties and learning disabilities. One such way is the RTI model, in which the school psychologist systematically observes how a student responds to one or more evidence-based interventions. The method may reveal more about the student's difficulties than searching for a discrepancy that may not show up until a student is in the third or fourth grade.

There has also been a third impetus to change from within the profession. Many practitioners and university trainers have been looking for a way to expand the role from the traditional one to the emerging role. However, the responsibilities of simply completing the routine assessments, reassessments, staffings, and so forth have left little time or energy for anything else. School administrators have typically been agreeable to some changes in the school psychologist's role as long as they get all of their other duties accomplished. Although data are not available, anecdotal evidence from interns is that they are surprised to be working almost exclusively with the special education population and not meeting the needs of other students who are struggling academically or emotionally. Seasoned school psychologists also voice frustration at not feeling as though they are making real changes in their schools. The administration at one intern's school keeps track of how many case studies each psychologist conducts. If they go below a certain number in a year (80 in one case), the administrator adds another school to that individual's load. Thus, opportunities for role expansion are undermined. This kind of administrative pressure and other frustrations have increased school psychologists' desire to change.

The fourth impetus, which is similar to school psychologists' frustration with their limited roles, is the frustration of the public in general about the state of U.S. public schools. Parents complain that their students are not being challenged academically; many also feel their children are not safe at school. Teachers complain that because of the pressure to "teach to the tests" and to make sure that students are meeting state and national standards, they are losing control of what they are permitted to teach in their classrooms. Teachers also note that students have many more behavioral and emotional difficulties than did students in the past and that parents generally cooperate less with the schools and are less involved in their students' education than they need to be. Even the popular media have become involved, with a 2006 series titled *America's Schools in Crisis*. The series, which was completed by a partnership between the *Oprah Winfrey Show* and *Time* magazine, featured schools in which students were dropping out at an alarming rate (30% or more). Urban and rural schools seem to be especially hard hit. Both have diminishing resources but are expected to meet the same standards as wealthier suburban schools. One example given on the show was of a class of more than 30 students in a classroom with only about 20 desks.

These and other forces combine to make this an excellent time for school psychologists to use all of their skills and knowledge in ways that can benefit the whole school system. The prototype for this role was suggested by Susan Gray as early as 1963 in her description of a data-oriented problem-solving role for the school psychologist. It was reinforced in 1997 by Ysseldyke et al. in their document *School Psychology: A Blueprint for Training and Practice II* (1997), known as the NASP *Blueprint*. A more recent version of the *Blueprint* was published in 2006 (Ysseldyke et al., 2006). The 2006 *Blueprint* begins with the notion of working toward two outcomes, in that "school psychologists should work to: (a) improve competencies for all students, and (b) build and maintain the capacities of systems to meet the needs of all students as they traverse the path to successful adulthood" (p. 12). The traditional role, focused as it has been on students with disabilities, has been much less focused on *all* students.

The emerging role builds on the data-based problem-solving skills of the school psychologist but relies on all of the skills and knowledge that school psychologists have acquired through education and experience. It is built around a basic problem-solving model of identifying the problem, defining the problem, designing an intervention, implementing the intervention, and then reevaluating to determine if the problem has been addressed adequately or if additional intervention is needed.

Identifying the Problem

Often the process of problem identification begins in a school-based meeting, similar to what may happen in the traditional role described above. Such meetings are called different things in different parts of the country, but some of the terms include *general education initiative*, *prereferral intervention*, *flexible service delivery*, *teacher assistance teams*, and *student assistance teams*. At such meetings someone, usually a teacher, brings a concern to the team members' attention. The following example is probably one of the more typical problems faced at such meetings. A first-grade teacher discusses Andy, one of her students, who is struggling with learning to read, cannot sit still for more than a few moments at a time, does not complete homework assignments, and has difficulty paying attention. Under the traditional model Andy would likely have been referred to the school psychologist for an assessment to determine the cause of the problem. In the emerging model, additional information about Andy would also be requested, but probably not using a formal assessment conducted by the school psychologist. Instead, the participants would most likely request some curriculum-based testing to see how Andy compares with other students in his class and perhaps a functional–behavioral analysis (FBA) to determine the causes of his out-of-seat behavior and his low-homework-completion rate.

Defining the Problem

In the traditional model, Andy would have been assessed by the school psychologist using informal measures (e.g., teacher and parent interviews, classroom observation, and review of school records) and formal measures (e.g., intelligence tests, achievement tests, and standardized behavior rating scales). A multidisciplinary staffing or eligibility determination meeting would then have been held with all parties involved (teacher, parents, school principal, school psychologist, and school social worker) to determine the basis for his learning problems.

In the emerging model of school psychology, some sort of curriculum-based measure (CBM) would be used to see how Andy is performing and how his performance compares with that of his peers. Andy would probably be measured on reading fluency, reading accuracy, phonetic awareness, and so forth. Brown-Chidsey and Steege (2005) note that during this phase, "Some problems may be very small and likely to resolve on their own over time. Alternatively, other problems may be of immediate concern. If the difference between a student's current performance and what is expected is large, that student is likely to have a serious school problem that needs to be resolved" (p. 7). In the emerging model, the school psychologist would likely continue to use interviews, reviews of school records, classroom observations, and other data collection procedures associated with the traditional model.

Designing an Intervention

In the traditional model, if Andy were found to have a learning disability the multidisciplinary team would determine what and how much service he would need from special education, whether he would come to the special education room or receive those services through inclusion in the regular classroom, and what long-term and short-term goals should be established. In the emerging model, evidence-based interventions would be discussed to determine the best interventions for Andy. Andy might be provided with a peer tutor within the classroom to help him stay on task and to take turns reading with him. A chart might be developed to monitor his homework completion rate. A given length of time would be set to give the intervention a chance to remediate Andy's difficulty.

Implementing the Intervention

In the traditional model and the emerging model, this step is basically the same: to implement the intervention. The concept of intervention integrity is important regardless of the model and refers to the intervention being carried out as planned. A good deal of frustration on the part of school psychologists over the years has revolved around the improper implementation or lack of implementation of carefully planned interventions by teachers, parents, or others involved. This problem can be circumvented by working carefully with the people who will be implementing the strategy to make sure that they feel comfortable with the intervention and believe that they have the skills to carry it off. Rathvon (1999) emphasized the importance of supporting those doing the implementation, understanding the teacher's or parent's perspective, and checking in frequently to see how the intervention is working. It is far better to fine-tune a strategy along the way than to find out there was a problem that caused the teacher or parent to become frustrated and just give up. This checking-in process is called *progress monitoring* and involves not only informal contacts and updates but also data collection and analysis (Brown-Chidsey & Steege, 2005). The process of monitoring progress is important in any intervention, but it is a vital link in determining the student's response to the intervention.

Reevaluating the Implementation and Results

In the traditional model of school psychology, reevaluations are written into the IDEA legislation. Youngsters identified as eligible for special education must be reevaluated at least every 3 years to determine if they are making progress in meeting their IEP goals. There are also end-of-year meetings in which the progress of all students with IEPs is discussed. Other than that, it is up to the teacher to keep track of each student's progress unless additional concerns are raised.

The emerging role emphasizes continuous progress monitoring, and decisions about the next step for a student are based on data. If the student is responding to the evidence-based intervention, that intervention is continued. If the student is not responding, a new intervention may be in order. This process continues until an effective match between the student and an intervention is found. If the repertoire of interventions has been tried and the student continues to have difficulty, it may be time to consider having the school psychologist administer a traditional assessment battery. In Andy's case, if the teacher has tried peer-assisted learning, homework-completion monitoring, and a behavior modification plan to increase his in-seat behavior, and Andy is starting to catch up to his classmates in reading and behavior, the intervention will continue. If he is making little progress despite everyone's best efforts, then more information might be needed about Andy, and more intensive interventions

The emerging role emphasizes continuous progress monitoring, and decisions about the next step for a student are based on data.

may be appropriate. The emerging role can be used for behavioral and social–emotional difficulties as well as for academic problems.

ADDITIONAL ROLES AND FUNCTIONS OF SCHOOL PSYCHOLOGISTS

Most school psychologists working in school systems spend the majority of their days involved in helping students through the activities described above. Whether functioning in a traditional manner or making the move to the emerging role, school psychologists use a combination of the basic skills in data-based problem solving, intervention planning, and consultation. Still many school psychologists are involved in one or more less traditional roles and functions to some degree. Usually these roles (e.g., research, training, and administration) do not help students in a direct manner but rather help students through providing data, training, supervision, and support to others who do work directly with students. A few less traditional roles, however, benefit children directly but expand services to somewhat less traditional clients or are offered in less traditional settings (e.g., providing support for postsecondary students with disabilities, expanding services to infants, or providing services to those in charter schools). Sometimes these additional roles and functions are taken on by a school psychologist already working full-time in the schools. For example, a school psychologist might be assigned to a committee to look at group testing in the school and/or the interpretation of group testing results. Another school psychologist might be involved in developing a program for gifted students or helping to train school bus drivers to use behavior modification techniques to control their passengers.

Research

Some school psychologists become involved in short-term or long-term research projects, such as in the following examples:

- Evaluate the effectiveness of a behavior modification plan for an aggressive fifth-grade boy
- Examine past records to determine gender differences in the reason-for-referral section of the referral form
- Evaluate the effectiveness of special class placement versus mainstreaming for junior high students with learning disabilities
- Compare the behavior of second-grade students undergoing social skills training with second-grade students not undergoing such training.

School psychologists' involvement in research endeavors traditionally has been conducted in large part by university-based trainers of school psychologists. As described in chapter 6, trainers typically acquire additional skills in research and statistics in pursuit of their doctoral degrees. Some trainers may have become trainers because they enjoy the research aspect of the job. In addition, universities generally expect faculty to conduct and publish research in order to be promoted and tenured, the so-called publish-or-perish syndrome. Finally, university settings generally have facilities that support research efforts, such as computers, libraries, and even graduate students to serve as research assistants.

School psychologists employed by the public schools have not traditionally received much encouragement from their employers to conduct research. Those wishing to conduct research may have to make time for such projects in addition to all of their other job demands. Some school psychologists have ideas for research projects they would like to undertake, but they lack the technical expertise or collegial support to do so on their own. In recent years, efforts have been made to link practitioners in the field who are interested in certain areas of research with individuals at universities who have the resources to assist in relevant projects. Such "professional matchmaking" efforts should be encouraged on a larger scale. A similar practice is evolving in teacher training, in which an attempt is made to develop close collaborative relationships between education department faculty and school-based teachers and administrators. Such a practice provides better field experiences for students, cooperative teaching arrangements on and off campus, and increased opportunities for education research projects.

Occasionally school psychologists become involved in research projects somewhat involuntarily. Because school psychologists may be the members of the school staff with the most background in research design and statistics, they may be sought out by administrators, teachers, or school board members to plan studies, gather data, and disseminate results.

Phillips (1999) proposed a system in which research is incorporated more effectively and less painfully during training (e.g., faculty members need to be models of research skills and students should be included in research projects early in their training) and in which research is viewed more broadly in practice. In other words, research should be seen as a necessary part of any problem-solving process, as a means of defining important issues in the profession, and as a way of keeping in touch with the professional literature. Phillips made a distinction between school psychologists who are "knowledge brokers," that is, the evaluators and disseminators of research, and school psychologists who are "melders," those who are actually conducting research projects.

Research should be seen as a necessary part of any problem-solving process, a means of defining important issues in the profession.

Staff Development and In-Service Training

An additional task undertaken by many school psychologists involves staff development or in-service training. As school psychologists travel from school to school and consult with teachers and other school personnel, they may be able to identify training needs common to a school or even an entire district. For example, as news of the RTI movement spreads, school psychologists may hear from teachers who want help understanding response to intervention, who want to know how to do curriculum-based measurement, who want more information about evidence-based interventions, and so forth. Such requests may provide excellent opportunities for in-service workshops for teachers in which information on these topics is shared and discussed. In many ways the planning of in-service workshops can be viewed as a sort of grand-scale or organizational consultation. At times the school psychologist may be the presenter at such in-service workshops. At other times, the school psychologist may be involved in planning the workshops and locating speakers from outside the district. School psychology students who overcome their fear of public speaking will find opportunities to reach large audiences, either at in-service workshops or in other forums, and to indirectly influence more children's lives, along with changing the school psychologist's role and functions.

University Training

Many school psychologists are involved in training prospective school psychologists. Some of these trainers work for universities and spend all or most of their time in teaching, conducting research, and becoming involved in professional service activities. Other school psychologists are employed as practitioners in the schools but spend some time supervising practicum students and school psychology interns and teaching university classes as part-time adjuncts to training programs. Full-time faculty members who are on the tenure track at a university are almost always expected to have doctoral degrees, and most commonly PhD degrees. Adjunct faculty, however, may be able to teach undergraduate classes with a master's or specialist degree.

Supervision and Administration

Some large school districts or special education cooperatives hire one school psychologist to supervise the other school psychologists and to perform the various administrative functions necessary to run a psychological services unit. Such an individual usually has a doctoral degree in school psychology, educational administration, or a related field. A school psychologist functioning in such a supervisory capacity usually has a reduced caseload relative to other school psychologists on staff to compensate for time spent in administrative and supervisory duties. Although every school psychologist has some administrative responsibilities, such as paperwork and meetings, supervising school psychologists may spend the majority of their time involved in these and other administrative activities.

EVOLUTION OF PROFESSIONAL ROLES AND FUNCTIONS

Professional roles and functions are not static. They grow and change based on many factors including political and social climate, educational developments, and psychological research findings.

Research to Guide Emerging Roles

A substantial body of professional literature addresses what school psychologists do on the job (actual role), what they would like to do (preferred role), and what others—parents, teachers, and students—think they actually do or would like to do (perceived role).

Researchers studying actual roles have asked school psychologists to maintain logs of their activities for a certain period of time or to estimate how much of their time is spent engaged in particular roles and functions (e.g., LaCayo, Sherwood, & Morris, 1981; Smith, 1984). A recent study (Bramlett et al., 2002) sent surveys to a random sample of 800 NASP members, asking them to estimate how much time they spent on various professional activities, among other questions. Of the 370 usable surveys returned, it was determined that nearly half (47%) of the respondents' time was spent in assessment. Beyond assessment, of the respondents' time, roughly 16% was spent in consultation, 13% interventions, 8% counseling, 7% conferencing, 3% supervision, 2% in-services, 1% research, 1% parent training, and 3% other.

Occasionally studies on roles and functions focus on one particular activity. For example, Fish and Massey (1991) were interested in how much time school psychologists spend with the various systems in students' lives (i.e., family, school, and community members). They asked their subjects to record the contacts they had with family members, school personnel, and various members of the community. Their findings suggest that school psychologists spend an average of 18% of the day in contact with school personnel, 8% of the day in contact with family members, and 2% of the day in contact with other members of the community. (Presumably the remainder of their time was spent with students or engaged in other activities such as completing paperwork, reading professional literature, or driving between schools.)

Another study (Watkins, Tipton, Manus, & Hunton-Shoup, 1991) examined the role relevance and role engagement of school psychologists' various professional activities. *Role relevance* was defined as "the degree to which various roles are seen as relevant to (or important defining features of)" the field of school psychology (p. 328). *Role engagement* includes the roles in which school psychologists are involved in their professional practice. The study found common ground between role relevance and role engagement. School psychologists responding to the study were engaged in assessment, consultation, counseling, and interventions and also considered these roles relevant to the practice of school psychology. In addition to the more traditional roles, school psychologists in the study were engaged in several other activities that they considered relevant to the profession, namely, program development and accountability, continuing education, training and supervision, and educational and vocational counseling.

Bahr's study suggests that school psychologists support some role changes ... but that generally school psychologists are unwilling to completely overhaul their traditional roles.

Reschly (1998) discovered that school psychologists continue to spend more than 50% of their work time in tasks related to psychoeducational assessment, most often in determining children's eligibility, new or continued, for special education programs and services. He found that between 1992 and 1997 "there have been no discernible changes in either current or preferred roles" (p. 4). In the 5-year period, school psychologists continued to express preferences for a combination of the traditional roles of assessment, intervention, and consultation. Few of the practitioners expressed interest in expanding their roles in the direction of systems and organizational consultation or research and evaluation. Bahr (1996) presents data supporting Reschly's (1998) work. Bahr's study suggests that school psychologists support some role changes (e.g., increased use of curriculum-based assessment, increased consultant follow-up with teachers) but that generally school psychologists are unwilling to completely overhaul their traditional roles.

Some studies have examined others' perceptions of the roles of the school psychologist. Roberts (1970) found similarities between school psychologists' own perceptions of their actual and desired roles and teachers' perceptions of the actual and desired roles of school psychologists. In the Roberts study the area of greatest difference involved teachers' desire for school psychologists to be more involved in counseling individual students. Hughes (1979) asked school psychologists, pupil personnel directors, and school superintendents for their actual and ideal perceptions of the role of the school psychologist. All three groups supported a move away from the traditional diagnostic assessment role. However, the three groups differed in the direction they wanted to see school psychologists go. School psychologists in the sample wanted to expand their roles in consultation (mental health and organizational development) and research. Pupil personnel directors wanted the time saved from the assessment role to be evenly distributed to all of the other roles (e.g., counseling, parent education, and consultation). The superintendents in the study wanted school psychologists to spend their time doing more counseling.

More recently, Peterson, Waldron, and Paulson (1998) asked a group of Midwestern teachers about their interactions with school psychologists. Results indicated that although most of the teachers (89%) had at least talked to a school psychologist, they had little contact, because the school psychologists were rarely around. The teachers in the study preferred the psychometrician and the problem-solver roles for school psychologists, and they believed that school psychologists could offer valuable suggestions about teaching practices. Unfortunately, the teachers believed that the school psychologists were unavailable because of heavy caseloads and multiple building or district assignments.

In an effort to determine what students would like from school psychologists, Culbertson (1975) asked a group of college undergraduates two questions: (1) If you were to plan an ideal elementary, middle or junior high, or high school, would you include a psychologist as a member of the school team? (2) If yes to the above, what would you like the role and duties of the psychologist to be? Please describe (p. 192).

> Of the students surveyed, 92% indicated that they would include a psychologist as a team member. As to what such an individual would do, the top five responses, in order, were helper (i.e., someone to talk to), assessor of students' abilities, counseling adviser, ombudsman, and information communicator.

Examples of Balanced Roles and Functions

Most school psychologists perform a combination of the roles and functions discussed above. Although assessment, intervention, and consultation are presented here as though they are mutually exclusive activities, in practice the distinctions among them become blurred. Interviewing a teacher about a particular child, for instance, may be part assessment, part intervention, and part consultation. Chapter 1 provides survey information about the relative portion of time school psychologists spend on these roles. The scenarios in Boxes 4.1, 4.2, and 4.3 portray the overlap among the roles and functions in the practice of school psychology. The three daily logs illustrate the variety of activities in which the school psychologists are involved, the differences in activities depending on the ages of children served, and the differences and similarities in activities depending on whether the district has adopted a traditional or an emerging role for school psychologists.

Trainers' Contribution to Preparation for Changing Roles

University professors engaged in training students to enter the field of school psychology are in a unique and sometimes uncomfortable position. Most have worked in the schools as practicing school psychologists at some point in their careers and recognize the realities of the field (e.g., too many students with difficulties, too much paperwork, and too much pressure to place students in special education classrooms). On the other hand, they know that school psychologists have the training and skills to do more than serve as the gatekeepers to special education. Thus, trainers of school psychologists are caught between emphasizing the traditional role and not preparing students adequately for the emerging role, or emphasizing the emerging role and not preparing students adequately for more traditional positions. Therefore, most try to achieve a balance. They teach students a variety of skills, including assessment (traditional and nontraditional), consultation, and intervention, and they hope that graduates not only are employable but also will be able to help improve the educational climate of any setting in which they find themselves employed.

Box 4.1 School Psychologist 1: Daily Log

Background: School Psychologist 1 is employed by a small-town district. She works in three elementary schools and a junior high with students in grades Pre-K–8. She serves a total of 1,800 students. She spends 1 day per week in each of her four schools. Fridays are spent at her office catching up with e-mails, phone calls, paperwork, and report writing. Fridays are also the one day in the week that she tries to go out to lunch with the only other psychologist employed by the district, to stay in touch, to share what is going on in the various schools, and to discuss professional issues. School Psychologist 1 follows a fairly traditional role.

continued

Box 4.1 *Continued*

Monday, October 2

7:30 a.m.	Stopped at office for e-mail messages, phone messages, and supplies.
8:00 a.m.	Arrived at Grace School.
8:00–9:30 a.m.	Participated in Teacher Assistance Team (TAT) meeting.
9:30–10:00 a.m.	Checked with principal regarding new referrals and follow-up to TAT meeting.
10:00–10:30 a.m.	Observed boy with attention problems in first-grade classroom.
10:30–11:00 a.m.	Talked to first-grade teacher about my observations; teacher decided to move child to front of room and to check with parents about whether he needs glasses. Promised to check back with her next week.
11:00–11:45 a.m.	Began testing a fourth-grade girl who is having learning and behavior difficulties in the classroom.
11:45 a.m.–12:45 p.m.	Had lunch in teachers' lounge and talked with teachers about their needs for in-service programs. Topics suggested included autism, working with children of low average intelligence who cannot keep up in regular classrooms, and working with children experiencing crises (parental divorce, sexual abuse, death of a sibling); no decision yet. A more formal needs assessment will be developed.
12:45–1:00 p.m.	Checked e-mail and phone messages. Did quick Internet search on in-service workshops.
1:00–1:30 p.m.	Counseled a sixth-grade student who has just moved into the district and is having trouble adjusting.
1:30–2:20 p.m.	Administered achievement tests and sentence completion test to fifth-grade boy referred for academic difficulties and low self-esteem.
2:30–4:00 p.m.	Met with districtwide NCLB committee to discuss testing results and school report card.
4:00–4:30 p.m.	Scored and interpreted tests; caught up on paperwork; made phone calls.

Box 4.2 School Psychologist 2: Daily Log

Background: School Psychologist 2 is one of two school psychologists assigned to work full-time in a large urban high school. His office is in the high school and he spends all of his time there. The school has 3,000 students in grades 9–12. School psychologists working exclusively in high schools seem to be, by necessity, in the center on the continuum spanning traditional role to emerging role. Generally they are more involved in providing counseling, crisis intervention, and support services to students in special education than they are with initial assessments of students.

continued

Monday, October 2

8:00 a.m.	Arrived at Hillcrest High School.
8:00–9:00 a.m.	Met with ninth-grade teachers concerned about students' attitudes toward school and poor study habits. Planned a PTA program for later in the month on the topic of how parents can help students succeed; also discussed the possibility of a peer counseling program.
9:00–10:00 a.m.	Held group counseling session with six 10th-grade girls identified as having low self-esteem and poor social skills. In the session last week, four of the six admitted having been abused by their boyfriends and most had been either abused or neglected by parents or other family members.
10:00–10:30 a.m.	Participated in a conference call with the assistant principal to the leader of a community task force aimed at stopping gang activities. Discussed ways in which school and community personnel could work as a team.
10:30–11:30 a.m.	Administered achievement tests and talked with an 11th-grade boy who is failing all of his courses and is thinking about dropping out.
11:30 a.m.–12:30 p.m.	Had lunch in the teachers' lounge. Two teachers voiced concern about a 12th-grade girl whom they suspect is pregnant. Another teacher asked for help with a hearing-impaired student who has been mainstreamed into her class but does not seem to be keeping up with assignments.
12:30–1:30 p.m.	Held individual counseling session with a ninth-grade boy who referred himself for help in dealing with serious family problems and feelings of anxiety.
1:30–2:15 p.m.	Met with two school psychology graduate students; gave them a tour of the building, discussed the role of the school psychologist in the secondary school, and answered some of their questions.
2:15–3:15 p.m.	Observed in a cross-categorical special education resource room at teacher's request. Students are not getting along with each other and these problems are interfering with getting work completed.
3:15–4:00 p.m.	Did paperwork, e-mail messages, phone calls, etc.
7:00–9:30 p.m.	Attended class at local university on vocational assessment and transition services for high school students with disabilities.

Box 4.3 School Psychologist 3: Daily Log

Background: School Psychologist 3 works for a large middle- to upper-middle-class suburban district. Her district has six elementary schools, each serving about 600 students each in grades pre-K–5; three middle schools, each serving 800 students in grades 6 through 8; and one large senior high school with 3,000 students in grades 9–12. The district employs eight school

continued

Box 4.3 *Continued*

psychologists, with each one serving anywhere from 1,000 to 1,200 students. The total number of students served by School Psychologist 3 is 1,000. She serves one elementary school, and she shares one of the middle schools with another school psychologist. School psychologist 3's district has moved to a model they call *flexible service delivery*, or FLEX. This represents the emerging role model of school psychology.

Monday, October 2

7:30 a.m. Arrived at Fairland Elementary School (considered to be the main office). Checked e-mails, voice mail, etc.

7:45–8:30 a.m. Attended Teacher Assistance Team meeting. Arranged to observe a kindergarten child and a first grader later in the day to gather more information. The principal wants to set up a volunteer program to help with reading. Two teachers, the school counselor, and I offered to help with this (brainstorming ideas about how to recruit volunteers, how to support volunteers, how to monitor the program, etc.). Heard about a child who has just moved into the district (fourth grade) and is reading at a pre-first-grade level. The student's mother is coming in after school to talk to his teacher. I agreed to attend this meeting to introduce myself and ask some questions about previous schooling.

8:30–8:45 a.m. School day begins; welcome students as they enter. (This is a new policy from the principal. All staff members are expected to greet students in the hall every morning.)

8:45–9:15 a.m. Taught social skills to a group of students in a self-contained special education classroom.

9:30–10:00 a.m. Observed kindergarten student in the classroom and on the playground. The student seems to have difficulty controlling his impulses; he shoves, pushes, and grabs everything and everyone in his path and pays little if any attention to directions, warnings, or consequences.

10:00–10:30 a.m. Talked to kindergarten teacher about my observations; she would like me to talk with him about his behavior at some point but she also wanted some ideas for helping him behave appropriately in the meantime. I suggested placing him somewhere in the room (front row?) with the fewest distractions and the best opportunities for teacher intervention. Also, developing a reward system for compliant behavior with frequent reinforcement. We decided to focus first on increasing in-seat behavior, since he would be less likely to push and shove others from his chair. I agreed to stay and begin taking baseline data for his in-seat behavior.

continued

10:30–11:00 a.m.	Observed in-seat behavior of this student every 10 seconds. The student was in his seat for less than 5 minutes out of 30 minutes. All of the other students used as comparisons in the class were in their seats at least 20 minutes during the same time period.
11:00 a.m.–12:00 noon	Individual counseling with two students (30 minutes each). One student, a fourth grader, is working on difficulties with anger management. The other student, a fifth grader, has parents who are going through a very bitter divorce.
12:00 noon–12:15 p.m.	Drove to middle school.
12:15–1:00 p.m.	Lunch in middle school teachers' lunchroom. Talked with the sixth-grade teacher team concerned with the large number of students who cannot read or write beyond the most basic level. I agreed to coordinate a curriculum-based measurement of some sort to gather data about the problem. In the meantime, we considered an after-school remedial program 2 days a week. The program would be voluntary but "strongly recommended" to some students if they want to pass their courses this year. We also discussed writing a grant proposal for next year for assistance with this problem.
1:00–2:30 p.m.	Attended a middle school team meeting. Several problems were discussed along with the sixth-grade reading difficulties mentioned above.
2:30–3:15 p.m.	Conducted Internet search regarding curriculum-based measures for sixth-grade reading skills. Also looked for some evidence-based interventions to try with these students. Checked e-mail and voice mail messages; returned phone calls, etc.
3:30–4:00 p.m.	Met with the other school psychologist and the school counselors in the middle school. Talked about a possible joint presentation on service delivery in a middle school for an upcoming state school psychology conference.

CONCLUSION

The roles of the school psychologist are multifaceted. School psychologists are engaged in numerous activities that are all ultimately aimed at helping children. Although each role demands unique training and skills, all of the roles, from child study to intervention and from consultation to research are based upon data-based problem-solving skills and positive consultation and collaboration skills. Without data-based problem-solving skills to identify a child's strengths and weaknesses, to determine whether our intervention strategies work, to support the efficacy of our consultative skills, and to support or refute our research hypotheses, we are at best do-gooders, that is, individuals with good intentions but without empirical substantiation for our work. Without positive consultative and collaborative skills, our best efforts may not be attended to or carried out.

Chapter 5

Evaluation and Accountability of School Psychologists

So far, this book has described the history of school psychology, examined the relationship of school psychology to employment settings, and elaborated on the actual and ideal roles and functions of school psychologists. This chapter addresses the various processes involved in the evaluation and accountability of school psychologists as a group and as individuals. Few issues are as important to the profession of school psychology, or as potentially anxiety-producing, as the issues of professional evaluation and accountability. In a study of stressful events in the professional lives of school psychologists (see chapter 8), "notification of unsatisfactory job performance" was ranked as the most stressful event, more so than even "potential suicide cases," "threat of a due process hearing," or "working in physically dangerous situations" (Wise, 1985).

Although most school psychologists agree with the general principle that the overall practice of school psychology should be examined periodically to determine its effectiveness and its relevance, when it comes to evaluating individual members of the profession to determine their professional effectiveness, the response is a bit more cautious and a good deal less enthusiastic. After all, school psychologists are only human. Yet, by agreeing that the evaluation of others is useful, as most school psychologists seem to do on a daily basis, they also commit themselves to being evaluated. Recent discussions among school psychologists, specifically and in education circles generally, are concerned with the effect of educators on learning outcomes for students. However, is it useful or even possible for school psychologists to go beyond an accountability model that documents only professional activities and actually demonstrate how those activities have resulted in positive learning outcomes for children?

The issues of professional evaluation and accountability have become increasingly critical in the current era of No Child Left Behind. Schools and school systems are required to demonstrate adequate yearly progress to such an extent that some have even dubbed this the era of "No Child Left Untested." School psychologists now also may be asked to play an important role in helping school systems address larger and higher-stakes issues of educational accountability

HISTORICAL BACKGROUND

Evaluation and accountability are continuing phenomena rather than new to the profession of school psychology. Witmer had to make his case for the clinic at the University of Pennsylvania and maintain records of cases and services delivered

(Brotemarkle, 1931). Gesell frequently was held accountable to the State of Connecticut for his caseload and practice (Fagan, 1987a). The notion of an annual report was quite popular in large urban schools. For example, the *Bureau of Child Guidance Five Year Report, 1932–1937* (City of New York, 1938) is a hardbound book of more than 150 pages that includes descriptions of services, enumerative data, and results of treatment. *The Bureau of Child Study and the Chicago Adjustment Service Plan* (City of Chicago, 1941) is another example of an annual report containing accountability data.

Some urban school clinics were founded using private funds in all likelihood because the district and state administration were unwilling to risk public funds for such ventures prior to substantiation of the clinics' value or outcomes. This was the case for the Vocational Bureau of the Cincinnati Public Schools founded in 1910 (Veatch, 1978). Veatch's dissertation provides a historical account of the bureau's development into its psychological services and of its accountability struggles over several decades. Annual reports were also filed that were part of the Cincinnati district's annual report to the board of education. The reports include considerable details about services (e.g., Cincinnati Public Schools, 1912).

Although most of these historical reports are largely only accountings of how many students were seen, they do contain some results of the school psychologists' activities. Therefore, documents such as those mentioned above show that, although accountability has become more prevalent during the past 30 or so years, it has been an important concept within school psychology throughout the history of the profession. Undoubtedly records such as those cited above helped to convince school personnel and school boards to maintain such services even during the depression of the 1930s (Mullen, 1981).

CURRENT PRACTICES

School psychologists are evaluated at various points in their careers, beginning with their application to training or degree programs and continuing with ongoing credentialing reviews.

Program Application Reviews

To be admitted to a school psychology training program, prospective school psychologists must meet or exceed certain criteria. These criteria usually include an examination of a student's undergraduate academic record, scores on the Graduate Record Examination or another standardized test (e.g., Miller Analogies Test), three or more letters of recommendation, and perhaps an autobiographical sketch or a personal interview. Such criteria provide university trainers with the opportunity to accept applicants into their programs who have a reasonable chance of successfully completing the training program and becoming competent and productive school psychologists. At the same time, an effort is made to screen out applicants who for one reason or another appear to be unacceptable candidates for training and practice.

Student Evaluations

Once a student has been admitted to a graduate program, certain standard academic evaluation requirements (e.g., term papers, course exams, and research projects) help faculty members monitor the student's progress. At the nondoctoral level, students often are required to complete a master's thesis or other research project, a portfolio, or a comprehensive examination before receiving a degree. Students in doctoral programs must meet additional entrance and exit requirements, such as qualifying examinations and dissertation defenses.

In addition to meeting academic requirements, school psychology trainees are subject to an evaluation of their personal and professional characteristics. Several authors have identified desirable personal characteristics for school psychology students and practitioners (Bardon, 1986; Bardon & Bennett, 1974; Fireoved & Cancerelli, 1985; Magary, 1967a). The most recent edition of the credentialing standards of NASP (NASP, 2000d) also includes a list of such professional work characteristics. Characteristics listed in the standards include "respect for human diversity, communication skills, effective interpersonal relations, ethical responsibility, adaptability, as well as initiative and dependability" (p. 45). Ysseldyke et al. (1997) suggest that school psychologists "be prepared to listen, adapt, deal with ambiguity, and be patient in difficult situations" (p. 11). Certainly these are characteristics that school psychology students must possess as well.

Although most school psychology faculty members acknowledge the importance of such characteristics or attributes in professional success, the challenge for training programs is to define the characteristics in sufficiently specific and meaningful terms such that they are measurable as well as valid predictors of success. Reaching a consensus among school psychology faculty members or practitioners regarding these issues is difficult, but it is likely that during the course of training, and particularly in practicum courses, students will be evaluated in some or all of the following professional skills and characteristics:

1. Listening skills
2. Oral and written communication skills
3. Respect for others
4. Ability to accept constructive criticism
5. Overall emotional maturity
6. Ability to work with children
7. Ability to work with parents and school personnel in a positive, nonthreatening way
8. Willingness to go beyond course requirements
9. Flexibility in adapting to change
10. Observance of school protocol and school rules (e.g., checking in at office, dressing appropriately, securing parental permission)

11. Observance of professional ethics (e.g., maintaining confidentiality, not overstepping boundaries of training, presenting data honestly)

Once a characteristic is defined in specific and measurable terms, program faculty members also must decide whether an individual who is deemed deficient in that characteristic is willing and able to remediate the deficiency and also whether an enduring deficiency in that characteristic is sufficient grounds to terminate a student from a training program or an internship. As noted by Ysseldyke et al. (1997), "Absence of prerequisite interpersonal and social skills may be an insurmountable barrier to development of a high level of expertise" in such areas as consultation and collaboration (p. 12).

Credentialing Reviews

Upon completion of graduate studies and prior to state certification, students may be required to take a state-mandated minimum competency examination. Such a test may assess basic skills (i.e., language and math) as well as knowledge of the field of school psychology. Since 1988, school psychologists interested in national certification have been required to submit to a national board evidence of their professional training, knowledge, and experience, including their scores on a national certification test. The national certification exam also may be taken independently of the national certification process and is, in fact, used for certification by many states. Many training programs also require a passing score on the national Praxis exam as an additional program requirement before graduation.

The internship year is designed to be a time of careful evaluation as well (see chapter 8). For many school psychologists, the internship year is the last time they will be so closely and totally supervised by a practicing school psychologist, someone who is qualified, through training and experience, to comment on the intern's technical expertise as well as on general progress and skills. Upon completion of an internship, trainees move from student status to professional status, and evaluations by appropriately trained and knowledgeable supervisors may no longer be possible. Therefore, during the internship, university trainers and field supervisors want to make certain that their students meet the highest professional standards before those students receive an official seal of approval. In fact, the NASP credentialing standards (2000d) require that new practicing school psychologists have 1 year of supervision following their initial certification and before permanent certification is granted. This postgraduate supervision should consist of "a minimum of two hours per week, in a face-to-face format" (p. 47). Practical considerations, however, render this requirement difficult in many settings, particularly for those employed in rural and small school districts where the school psychologist often works alone.

For many school psychologists, the internship year is the last time they will be so closely and totally supervised by a practicing school psychologist.

Once the graduate has completed the internship plus any additional training program requirements and state-mandated credentialing requirements, his or her first test of professional competence is finding a job. Of course, finding a job often depends on factors other than professional competence, such as the status of the job market, the applicant's ability to relocate, and how well the applicant's skills and interests match those in existing job openings. (These factors are discussed in chapter 8.)

Employment Reviews

Upon obtaining employment, school psychologists undoubtedly will undergo periodic professional evaluations. School systems generally require annual evaluation of members of their professional staffs, particularly before granting tenure to those persons. Such evaluations are conducted to help individuals improve their skills as well as to weed out the occasional staff member who is not performing adequately. Educators often speak of *formative* and *summative* evaluation procedures. Formative evaluations are those carried out during the course of an intervention or program. Summative evaluations are those carried out at the conclusion of a program. In the case of a first-year school psychologist, a formative evaluation might include on-the-job observations during assessments or multidisciplinary team staffings, progress reports, feedback from those who have had direct experience working with the school psychologist, and so forth. A summative evaluation for a first-year school psychologist likely would be an end-of-year report detailing activities and accomplishments. Strengths and weaknesses may be noted as well.

In his book *Handbook of Teacher Evaluation*, Millman (1981) distinguishes in a more pragmatic way between the formative and summative roles of evaluation as these evaluations apply to teachers. "Formative teacher evaluation helps teachers improve their performance by providing data, judgments, and suggestions that have implications for what to teach and how. On the other hand, summative teacher evaluation serves administrative decision making with respect to hiring and firing, promotion and tenure, assignments, and salary" (p. 13).

Although most school psychologists probably would agree that evaluations can be beneficial, many would be less than agreeable to such evaluations if their salaries, their assignments, or even their jobs were riding on the results of evaluations. In reality, however, jobs *may* depend on the results of evaluations. One difficulty that often arises for school psychologists, particularly those employed in small school districts or rural areas, is that of finding someone qualified to evaluate their skills. There may not be anyone in the school system, including the school psychologist's immediate supervisor, with training or background in school psychology. Thus, an evaluation of professional skills may pose something of a dilemma. Local districts could address this issue by hiring external reviewers to conduct periodic evaluations. The problem of having school psychologists evaluated by nonpsychologists again raises the issue of administrative versus professional supervision (discussed in chapter 3).

EVALUATION OF SCHOOL PSYCHOLOGY TRAINING PROGRAMS

University training programs also undergo formative and summative evaluations. Universities generally have offices of institutional research and planning that are responsible for maintaining data regarding the number of students enrolled in each program on campus, the number graduating from each program, student demographic data (e.g., age, gender, and race), the number of faculty members assigned to each program, and so forth. In tough economic times, these numbers may be carefully scrutinized by administrators and by the various boards that govern the university (and to whom the university as a whole is accountable) to determine a program's cost-effectiveness relative to the number of graduates produced.

In addition to completing university-maintained records, school psychology program directors may be asked to complete annual reports focusing upon the number of program inquiries and applicants, the number of students admitted to the program, the quantity and quality of students currently enrolled, the major accomplishments for the year, job placement record of graduates, and so on. Such reports may be read by the department chairperson, the college dean, the university provost and academic vice president, the president, and perhaps even the higher board that oversees the governance of the university. Program directors may also be asked to set goals for the training program on an annual basis and to demonstrate how the program met (or failed to meet) the previous year's goals. In addition, universities may require all programs to conduct self-studies periodically and to undergo reviews by internal or external reviewers in order to confirm the self-study report. Faculty members in school psychology programs also are evaluated, typically once each year prior to receiving tenure (usually during their sixth year of employment). After being tenured, faculty members are evaluated periodically as determined by department or university policy. These evaluations are usually conducted first by department personnel committees and department chairs and then by the college dean, the university provost and academic vice president, and the president of the university. Of course, in many universities, students also have the opportunity to evaluate their faculty members after every course.

Faculty members in school psychology programs also are evaluated.

Depending on a program's state and national approval status, periodic reviews are conducted by state departments of education, regional accreditors, NASP in conjunction with NCATE, and the APA. Such reviews generally are conducted on a multiyear cycle—for example, every 5, 7, or 10 years—to examine whether the training program is continuing to maintain high professional standards. Many students enrolled in school psychology training programs may be asked to participate in such reviews. Usually such participation entails an individual or group being asked to meet with one or more reviewers from off campus. For the most part, meetings between students and evaluation or accreditation teams are intended to determine if the faculty's information about the program is accurate. For example, if the written information states that faculty members hold monthly meetings for all program faculty, students, and staff, students may be asked about the frequency and content of these meetings. Students may also be asked for information about the skills they have acquired in order to determine if the training is producing desired outcomes. Chapter 7 presents more information about the accreditation process for training programs.

PROFESSIONAL ACCOUNTABILITY AND SCHOOL PSYCHOLOGY

For practicing school psychologists, evaluations have been closely related to, if not synonymous with, the concept of professional accountability, that is, a professional's documentation of or accounting for his or her professional activities. School psychologists who work for others, particularly those who receive local, state, or federal monies, are answerable to their employers and to the public. Ysseldyke et al. (1997) noted that data-based decision making and accountability should be the organizing theme of school psychology. In that context, the following five reasons show why accountability is important to the profession of school psychology and to those who practice it.

Accountability as a Way to Help Children

First, accountability may help psychologists help children more effectively (Zins, 1990). By maintaining records and evaluating what has been done, to find out what does and does not work well, professionals are able to make increasingly accurate decisions to meet children's needs. For instance, if the records indicate that children who have difficulty learning to read make greater academic gains when they receive help from their peers, compared with students who do not receive peer tutoring, then the school psychologist would probably be more likely to suggest peer tutoring in future cases. This notion of basing recommendations on data is the crux of the evidence-based intervention model.

Canter (1991b) described how an accountability system implemented by the school psychologists in the Minneapolis public schools directly and indirectly influenced professional practice.

> For example, when data over 10 years consistently indicated that boys are referred two to three times as often as girls, discussion and reviews of the research literature generated concerns regarding the under referral of girls for problems such as anxiety and depression. Further literature review, internal staff development, inservice programs for schools, and consultation with community professionals helped heighten awareness of less visible problems that could be addressed by early prevention and intervention activities. (p. 61)

Accountability as a Means of Professional Enhancement and Renewal

A second reason that accountability is important relates to improving professional effectiveness (Zins, 1990). In another example, a school psychologist develops a survey to evaluate his conference skills and distributes the survey to teachers and parents with whom he has worked. The completed surveys indicate that, although the conferences were positive overall, a few of the parents believed the school psychologist used too much technical jargon to explain their children's strengths and weaknesses, and a few of the teachers noted that the psychologist seemed to talk down to them. The psychologist can use that feedback to change how he relates to parents and teachers in conference settings. By improving his own professional effectiveness he can indirectly improve services to children.

Feedback about personal effectiveness can also lead to professional renewal. However, many school psychologists voice feelings of frustration at not receiving sufficient feedback when their efforts have been successful. The only feedback might be that received from teachers when an intervention plan fails to work. When an intervention succeeds, few people make a special effort to seek out the school psychologist. Accountability efforts such as evaluations and reviews can provide occasional pats on the back for a job well done.

Accountability as a Means of Organizational Improvement

A third reason for accountability efforts is that they may indicate when changes are needed (Zins, 1990). For example, a school administrator keeping track of the daily activities of a district's school psychologists may find that they spend an average of 15% of their time driving from various schools back to their main office. When asked why they spend so much time on the road, they indicate that they share test kits and therefore must pick up the test kits they need every morning and drop them off every afternoon. The administrator might then decide to purchase additional test kits, or at least find a more efficient way of sharing materials, thus cutting back on driving time and increasing time spent productively.

Accountability data can reinforce the organization's use of school psychologists by showing the effectiveness of their contribution (e.g., through public relations) and then using feedback from their consumers to tell the district that their services are needed. Phillips (1990b) suggested that a sample group of school psychologists could carry timers to periodically document their day-to-day functions. Each time the timer went off, the school psychologists would note what they were doing, who they were with, and so forth. This type of recording could raise awareness of school psychologists' activities, which could then be used by training programs to determine what to emphasize, and by accrediting bodies to determine what to require (Williams & Williams, 1992).

Accountability as a Means to Improve Public Relations

A fourth reason for generating accountability data is that such efforts are tools for public relations, consumer satisfaction (Medway, 1996), and marketing (Tharinger, 1996), for both the individual and the organization. Having accountability data is an advantage for an individual who is seeking employment or undergoing a professional evaluation. What better way to prove one's capabilities than to present data from consumers documenting successful efforts and programs? Evaluations also show the school district that school psychologists are productive and essential members of a school staff. Rosenfield (1996) provides one example of accountability data leading directly to a school board's expansion of psychological services. Particularly in the face of gloomy economic conditions for education, school boards may be looking for ways to trim their budgets without cutting academic programs or increasing class size. School psychologists and other noninstructional personnel in the schools (e.g., counselors, social workers, and speech and language therapists) may be viewed as frills—nice to have around when money is plentiful but not essential when schools are faced with cutbacks. As Trachtman (1996) noted, from the viewpoint of a school administrator, "[If I] had a few additional dollars to spend, I'm not really sure how I would choose between maintaining a gym, a science lab, a library, a music or art room, a uniformed marching band or a school nurse, guidance counselor, or psychologist" (p. 9).

Fortunately, since 1975 federal laws have protected school psychologists by mandating that schools identify, diagnose, and place all children with disabilities or forfeit their share of federal funding. If these laws were to be significantly modified, however, school psychologists would need extensive documentation of their own effectiveness merely to justify their presence in the schools.

Having professional accountability is simply the proper and the ethical thing to do.

Accountability as a Means to Achieve Ethical Practice

A fifth reason for accountability is important, albeit less concrete and less frequently mentioned than the other reasons. Having professional accountability is simply the proper and the ethical thing to do. Trachtman (1981, p. 153) differentiated between two types of accountability: imposed accountability and offered accountability. *Imposed accountability* refers to the accounting of professional activities at the request of someone with authority over the professionals (e.g., a supervisor or a district superintendent). *Offered accountability* refers to efforts to document professional activities, not because the documentation is required but because the school psychologist feels a professional and ethical responsibility to do so. School psychologists who contribute to so many critical decisions about young people based on assessment data would be hypocritical and unethical not to subject themselves and their own activities to assessment.

Pros and Cons of Accountability Efforts

Some readers may ask why any school psychologist would *not* be involved in accountability efforts. Arguments against accountability efforts tend to be based on a short-term rather than long-term view of the profession. Some professionals in the field argue that accountability efforts are too time-consuming, taking time away from more important activities, or that "no one ever reads annual reports anyway, so why bother?" However, accountability provides school psychologists with a somewhat rare opportunity to reflect on their professional activities and to consider how they might improve the ways they function. Particularly if education is viewed from an outcome-based perspective, accountability is a critical process for demonstrating professional outcomes. Data collected annually can be used to show changes in services over time.

In view of the arguments made above, three assumptions should be made regarding how professional accountability efforts can be accomplished: (1)

professional accountability is possible; (2) professional accountability is essential; and (3) no single system of accountability can properly evaluate the variety of roles and functions of school psychologists.

TYPES OF ACCOUNTABILITY

This section describes various types of accountability and sources of accountability data, and examines actual efforts to achieve accountability that are documented in the school psychology literature. An imaginary scenario presents Ms. Goalworthy, who is the director of school psychological services in a large school district. She was informed on May 1 that her annual administrative report is due in the superintendent's office on June 30. She has been asked to include the following sections in that report: (1) goals set during the previous school year for the current school year; (2) the budget for the current school year; and (3) staff activities for the current school year.

The first section involves a discussion of the goals for the current school year that were established in the previous year. Ms. Goalworthy's report probably will include a few statements about how the goals were met. If some of the goals were not met, she would discuss impediments to meeting the goals, such as insufficient money, staff shortages, or an excessive number of referrals. She also would be likely to describe other accomplishments that were not included in the original goal statement but that were carried out during the period in question.

Section 2, regarding her budget for the previous year, is also fairly straightforward. As director, Ms. Goalworthy was allocated a certain amount of money. The largest single expenditure typically would have been assigned to personnel services or salaries. The expenditures in this category included her salary, the salaries of the school psychologists who work in her unit, and the salaries of the secretaries employed to work for the staff, along with employee benefits (health insurance, dental insurance, and retirement plan, etc.). Other items in the budget for school psychological services included computers and relevant software, assessment instruments (new, replacement, or additional copies), test protocols, travel expenses (mileage between schools; conference registration fees, transportation, and hotel costs; and meals for professional meetings), books and journals, photocopying, telecommunication, and miscellaneous office supplies.

With inflation and some of the other costs mentioned above (such as mileage, equipment, photocopying, and telecommunications), the cost of employing school psychologists is an expensive endeavor. With this much money at stake, Ms. Goalworthy is aware of how important accountability is. In fact, she can see why administrators might be tempted to compute the cost of school psychologists on a per case basis and why they see the caseload as a useful criterion to measure costs per accomplishments.

In section 3 of the report, on staff activities, the task becomes harder. She has a general idea of what the individual school psychologists in her administrative unit have been involved in, but how should she summarize their activities over the past year in a brief but meaningful way?

Descriptive Approaches

As a director, Ms. Goalworthy is familiar with the *descriptive* and *evaluative* approaches to accountability (Monroe, 1979). A descriptive approach describes what took place, whereas an evaluative approach studies the impact of the events that occurred (see Figure 5.1). Usually in a report like the one Ms. Goalworthy must write, the first approach to be considered would be a descriptive one, involving what might be called an *activity log*, or a list of the various activities in which staff members were engaged. Thus, Ms. Goalworthy might write the following:

> During the current school year school psychologists on our staff were able to complete, in a timely fashion, all assessments referred to them. In addition, the psychologists were engaged in the following activities:
>
> 1. Introduced the concept of "response to intervention" (RTI) to district personnel through a series of in-service workshops.
> 2. Cofounded (with school social workers) a counseling group for high school students with children.
> 3. Applied for and received a grant of $25,000 to study new ways of teaching social studies and science to students with reading difficulties.
> 4. Acted as liaisons to local health professionals in identifying and treating children with attention deficit hyperactivity disorder (ADHD) and autism.
> 5. Started a group for parents of children with low-incidence disabilities.

The second type of descriptive approach to accountability is enumerative, which entails a list of activities and a frequency count for each of several activities. To prepare an enumerative report, Ms. Goalworthy must ask each school psychologist on her staff to complete a number of tables similar to Figure 5.2.

From these tables she might compile a set of master tables that list the following:

1. The number of children referred to teacher assistance teams (TATs)

Figure 5.1. Sources and types of accountability data.

Types	Sources				
	School Psychologists	Teachers	Administrators	Parents	Students
Descriptive					
Activity log	⋆				
Enumerative	⋆		⋆		
Evaluative					
Process	⋆	⋆		⋆	⋆
Outcome	⋆	⋆		⋆	⋆

2. The number of children referred for assessment following TAT intervention attempts
3. The number of children assessed who have been placed in various types of special classes
4. The number of children assessed according to various age groups
5. The number of teacher consultations in which school psychologists have participated
6. The number of children counseled on an individual basis by school psychologists
7. The number of children counseled in groups by school psychologists
8. The number of parent conferences held
9. The number of multidisciplinary staffings in which school psychologists have participated
10. The number of research and evaluation activities engaged in by staff members

Figure 5.2. Sample yearly activity sheet for school psychologists.

Directions: Mark the number of hours you spent engaged in each of the activities during the current school year.

		Grade Level of Youngster		
Activity	**Preschoolers**	**K–6**	**7–9**	**10–12**
Classroom observation				
Review of school records				
Teacher interview				
Parent interview				
Intellectual assessment				
Assessment of achievement				
Social/behavioral assessment				
Personality assessment				
Parent conferences				
Multidisciplinary staffings				
Psychological reports				
Individual counseling				
Group counseling				
Teacher consultation				
Staff development				
In-service workshops				
Contact with outside agency				
Continuing/professional development of the school psychologist				

Evaluating the effectiveness of the school psychologist's job is not nearly so easy, and yet this seems to be the accountability wave of the future.

While Ms. Goalworthy is compiling her master tables, a conclusion of enumerative data is presented, along with an introduction, definition, and discussion of evaluative data. Enumerative data also may include information regarding the average amount of time spent in professional activities. Thus, it would not be unusual for school psychologists to be asked how much time, or what percentage of their time, they spend per week in teacher consultations, in parent conferences, or in assessment activities. For example, LaCayo, Sherwood, and Morris (1981) asked a national sample of 750 randomly selected school psychologists to record their daily activities. They found that school psychologists in their sample spent 39% of their time in assessment, 33% in consultation, 6% in counseling, and the remainder in other activities. A more recent study (Reschly, 1998) found that school psychologists in 1997 "devote slightly over half of their time to psychoeducational assessment, about 20% of their time to direct intervention, about 17% to problem-solving consultation, 7% to systems and organizational consultation, and 2% to research evaluation" (p. 4).

Descriptive Data Versus Evaluative Data

The difference between descriptive data (the activity log or enumerative data) and evaluative data (a measure of process or outcome) can be thought of as a difference between *accounting* and *true accountability*. Accounting, though important for purposes of record keeping, does not examine the quality or effectiveness of services provided. Process and outcome accountability, on the other hand, focus on the non-quantitative aspects of service delivery, such as the quality of the services, the satisfaction of the parents and teachers, and the benefits to the children served.

Evaluative Data

Counting the number of case studies completed or the number of children placed in special education programs, or estimating the amount of time spent in teacher consultation is relatively easy, albeit somewhat bothersome to complete. Evaluating the effectiveness of the school psychologist's job is not nearly so easy, and yet this seems to be the accountability wave of the future. How can a school psychologist's skills as a consultant be measured? Was counseling successful? Did special class placement help? How satisfied are parents and teachers with the psychologist's conferencing or report-writing skills? How much has a child's life in school improved because of the school psychologist's expertise? Is the amount of time spent engaged in certain activities warranted? Answering these questions requires the school psychologist to collect evaluative information, which is often broken down into two components: *process* data and *outcome* data.

Collection of Process Data

Collecting process data involves gathering information regarding others' perceptions of how effective school psychologists were in reaching objectives and delivering services. For example, Cornwall (1990) conducted a study in which teachers, parents, and physicians were asked to rate psychoeducational reports in terms of (a) their clarity, (b) whether or not they addressed and answered the referral questions, (c) how well they described the youngster's difficulties, and (d) how useful the recommendations were. Knoff, McKenna, and Riser (1991) conducted an exploratory study of school psychologists and trainers of school psychologists as a first step in the development of a Consultant Effectiveness Scale. Their scale lists factors most important to effective consultation (i.e., knowledge of the consultation process, expert skill, personal characteristics, interpersonal skills, and professional respect). Process data provide school psychologists with useful information about how they function. For example, Ms. Carver, a school psychologist who works primarily with junior high and high school students, wanted to know how the students perceive her role and her competence in that role. She developed a form (Figure 5.2), which she distributed to all of the students she has worked with during the current school year. The form was mailed to all of the students at their homes. They were asked to complete the form anonymously and drop it off in her mailbox at school by the end of the week. Results were then tabulated. Ms. Carver learned that of the 20 students who completed the form, all agreed that the time spent with her was worthwhile. Most of the students agreed that she listened to them and that she cared about them. All of them said they would send their friends to her if they had problems in school or at home.

The collection and the interpretation of process data may be more complicated than it appears at first glance. A form such as the one in Figure 5.2 is far from perfect in terms of technical adequacy (e.g., reliability). In Ms. Carver's case, most of the students had voluntarily sought out the school psychologist for help with a particular problem they were having. Those students who did not think Ms. Carver would be helpful probably did not ask for her assistance in the first place. In addition, the students may have been equally positive in rating anyone willing to listen to their problems and to act in a caring manner. What about the students who did not return the survey? Can it be assumed that they had equally positive feelings about the counseling? Of course not!

A related example is that of the evaluation of college and university faculty members. Universities as a whole, or departments or colleges within universities, often have policies regarding teacher evaluations. Students may be asked to complete evaluations of their professors in some or all of their classes each semester. Faculty members have found these evaluations to be helpful and informative in many cases. However, complicating factors may exist. For example, do professors who give higher grades receive higher marks than professors who are tough graders? If so, what does this say about the validity of teacher ratings as a measure of teacher effectiveness? Do professors of elective courses receive higher marks than professors of required courses? Do professors of graduate courses with small numbers of students receive higher marks than professors of large, undergraduate survey courses? Such questions make it difficult if not impossible to compare professors' ratings in an academic department or area.

Similar questions arise in the collection of process data for accountability among school psychologists. Do parents who hear bad news or criticisms rate the school psychologist as highly as parents who hear good news? (For example: Your child is in the educable mentally retarded range of intelligence. Your child's problems seem mostly influenced by factors in the home. Your child has done so well in the learning disabilities resource room this year that we are suggesting she be placed in the regular classroom full-time next year.) Does a teacher who wants a troublesome child out of his classroom give the school psychologist high ratings when the intervention plan involves leaving the child in his class? What kind of ratings will a school psychologist who opposes retention get from a principal who views retention as an ideal remedial strategy for immature youngsters?

Collection of Outcome Data

Back to the example of Ms. Goalworthy, the director of psychological services who was preparing to turn in an annual evaluation, it is time to start collecting outcome data. By this time she has filled out tables of enumerative data based on the information furnished by the school psychologists on her staff. She may also have glanced at evaluation forms completed by parents and teachers to assess the psychologists' consultation skills. The next step, collecting outcome data, involves taking a look at intervention strategies and asking the questions: How many intervention strategies have been implemented as agreed to in meetings between school

Figure 5.3. Sample evaluation process form.

Directions: Please answer the questions below as they apply to your work with Ms. Carver during the current school year.

1. How many times during this school year have you worked with Ms. Carver?
2. What have you done during your time with Ms. Carver? (check all that apply)

   ___a. taken tests
   ___b. talked about school
   ___c. talked about relationships with others
   ___d. talked about my family
   ___e. talked about a specific problem
   ___f. talked about my goals

3. Do you think that the time you spent with Ms. Carver was worthwhile?
   ___Yes ___Sometimes ___ No
4. Check all of the following statements that you agree with.

   ___a. Ms. Carver helped me to understand my school problems better.
   ___b. Ms. Carver helped me to understand my own strengths and weaknesses.
   ___c. Ms. Carver taught me problem-solving techniques.
   ___d. Ms. Carver listened to me.
   ___e. Ms. Carver cares about me.
   ___f. Ms. Carver helped me to do better at school.
   ___g. I would recommend that other kids see Ms. Carver if they're having trouble with school.

5. I wish Ms. Carver had spent more time ______________________.
6. I think Ms. Carver is (check all that apply)
   ___nice ___mean ___friendly ___a good listener ___dumb ___helpful
7. I will probably come back to see Ms. Carver if ______________________.

psychologists and teachers or school psychologists and parents? How many of the intervention strategies that were implemented have been effective? To what extent was the child's referral problem resolved or alleviated?

Sources of Accountability Data

Implicit in discussions regarding types of accountability is the assumption that someone must be responsible for keeping track of the school psychologist's professional activities and evaluating the process and outcome of the services. Usually in the case of descriptive data such as activity logs or enumerative data, school psychologists are asked to maintain records of their professional activities and turn in the records periodically to a school administrator (e.g., director of psychological services or special education director). Forms such as those in Figure 5.1 may be furnished to the school psychologists at the beginning of the year to improve the chances of accurate record keeping. The evaluative accountability data described above (i.e., process and outcome) rely on consumers of psychological services as sources of information. Certainly with process data, students, parents, teachers, and administrators are the most likely parties to evaluate the level of satisfaction with the school psychological services provided. All of these people also are sources of outcome data, but outcome data also have another source. Paraprofessionals, graduate students, or other impartial individuals may gather outcome data in a much more scientific manner. For example, if a behavior modification plan is introduced as an intervention, a trained student or paraprofessional could observe the child and record data during all phases of the project. One way of seeing whether a social skills training program is working is to have someone observe the children in the program in a naturalistic setting (i.e., real life, nonlaboratory), either on the playground, in the lunchroom, in the hallways, or in the classroom.

CHALLENGES OF PROFESSIONAL EVALUATION AND ACCOUNTABILITY

School psychologists may all agree that professional evaluation and accountability are important. Why then are some school psychologists reluctant to be more involved in such endeavors?

Obstacles of Time and Perceptions

The obstacles to the practices of professional evaluation and accountability have been mentioned or alluded to above and are as follows:

1. Accountability efforts take time away from other activities.
2. Accountability efforts can be perceived as burdensome. Busy people, asked to keep track of the time spent on each activity in which they were engaged for an entire month, are required to have either extraordinary organizational skills to keep continuous records or extraordinary memories to mark down all that they did at the end of a week or a month. Fairchild and Seeley (1996) note that accountability efforts "become unmanageable when efforts

are made to evaluate all services and involve all consumers without adequate resources to accomplish such a task" (p. 46).

3. Accountability efforts are often expected but rarely rewarded.
4. Accountability efforts are sometimes seen as exercises in futility, for example, wondering if anyone really reads the reports.

These four obstacles apply to all types of accountability efforts, but additional obstacles often exist that are specific to the collection of evaluative accountability data. For instance, how much time should be allowed for an intervention to take effect before evaluating its success? Should the evaluation look at short-term effects, long-term effects, or both? What constitutes success? If a third grader was reading at the early first-grade level in October and had progressed to the late first-grade level by March, was the intervention successful? If a seventh grader was involved in 10 fights during the first 2 months of the school year and only 5 fights in January through March, is the group counseling strategy effective? If an intervention strategy was not implemented as designed, is it appropriate to count that against the school psychologist? Difficulties such as those described above in defining successful outcomes and eliminating extraneous variables are among the obstacles inherent in the process of accountability. These issues often perplex those involved in data collection and interpretation.

Another obstacle to the collection of outcome data relates to *clientage*. As described in chapter 3, the client of the school psychologist may be a child, a parent, a teacher, a school administrator, an entire school board, or a combination of these parties. Ambiguity with regard to clientage complicates the issue of accountability to the extent that one person's perception of the outcome may be different from another person's perception of the same outcome. For example, a school psychologist consults with a first-grade teacher about a child who has difficulty paying attention in class, sitting still, and completing work independently. The teacher and principal believe that the child is immature and would benefit from another year in first grade. The parents are not in favor of retention, believing the child will grow out of it and succeed in second grade next year. After talking to the teacher and the parents and observing the child in the classroom, the psychologist's recommendation is to place the child in second grade. It is further recommended that the child be placed in the most structured second-grade classroom available. Finally, it is suggested that the child's behavior be carefully monitored to determine whether a full case study would be appropriate sometime during the coming year if difficulties continue. If the principal, the teacher, and the parents are questioned, their level of satisfaction with the outcome of the school psychologist's decision likely will vary.

Measures of Professional Competence and Professional Excellence

Other obstacles confront the processes of professional accountability and evaluation. For example, even if successful outcomes could be defined, there is still the problem of defining competence and excellence in the practice of school psychology. How is competence defined within the profession of school psychology? What constitutes professional excellence? In other professions, for example, a competent medical doctor may be one who is cautious, makes few mistakes in

How is competence defined within the profession of school psychology? What constitutes professional excellence?

diagnosis or treatment, and treats patients with respect. An excellent medical doctor may be one who saves the most lives, makes the fewest mistakes, faces the fewest malpractice suits, is consulted most frequently by his or her medical colleagues, or perfects a particular operation. A competent attorney may be one who is familiar with the laws and does a good job representing his or her clients. An excellent attorney may be one who wins the most cases, brings in the highest settlements, or sways the greatest number of jurors. It is reasonable to think of doctors and lawyers in terms of products, that is, as people cured and cases won.

What qualities define a teacher as competent or as excellent? Again, teachers can be thought of in terms of products. A competent teacher is one whose students progress at an appropriate pace. An excellent teacher may have students who make great gains academically. Perhaps one teacher's students score higher on standardized tests than do other students in the school. Perhaps a particular teacher seems to inspire students to produce excellent reports, artwork, or musical compositions. Perhaps the teachers in the next grade report that students who had one particular teacher are better prepared to continue their studies. Perhaps parents report that their children are more enthusiastic about learning and have made greater gains than they made in previous years.

What are the products of the competent school psychologist compared to the excellent school psychologist? The answers are much more difficult to pinpoint. Doctors, lawyers, and teachers all work directly with individuals or groups for extended periods of time. School psychologists often play a more indirect role with children. They may work with children mainly through parents or teachers. Trachtman (1981) suggests that school psychologists often work as "enablers"—their efforts enable parents or teachers to help children. How can the efforts of the enabler, that is, the school psychologist, be separated from the efforts of the enactor, that is, the parents or teachers?

School psychologists rarely save children's lives, fix children's difficulties single-handedly, or consistently sway participants at multidisciplinary staffings. The changes brought about usually are more difficult to define and more dependent upon the efforts of others in the child's environment. Is it reasonable to hold school psychologists accountable for interventions that other people are responsible for implementing? If an intervention is successful, can a school psychologist take credit for the success? If an intervention does not succeed, is the school psychologist to blame?

Another difficulty in evaluating school psychologists relates to the physical context of much of their work. The functions of assessment, counseling, parent conferencing, and teacher consultations are generally conducted in one-on-one settings behind closed doors, with no one except the client around to watch and evaluate the psychologist's performance. Can a child evaluate assessment or counseling skills objectively? Can parents be objective in evaluating conferencing skills when they are emotionally involved in the process of sharing information? Can psychologists be at all objective in evaluating their own activities and skills?

Alternatives in Evaluation

School psychologists might wish to consider what has been termed a *collaborative model of professional evaluation*, or collaborative consultation, in which teams of psychologists help each other set annual goals, discuss how the achievement of the goals might be attained, collect data to support the attainment of goals, periodically meet to discuss progress toward goal attainment, and share documentation of goal attainment. This is adapted from a model for teachers set forth by McLaughlin et al. (1998). One member of the team might examine skills in working with parents of preschoolers, a second member might examine counseling skills with middle school students, and a third team member might examine skills in classroom environmental analysis. Each individual would establish unique goals for the year. Within the team, however, ideas for skill development, evaluation, and documentation could be shared and discussed at the start of the year. Progress toward goal attainment could be discussed at midyear, and ideas to overcome barriers to goal attainment could be generated. At the end of the year, the team could share the data collected by members and consider goals for the following year. Advantages of such a model include the support and suggestions received from other team members, the notion that evaluation does not have to include every part of the job every year, and the presentation of a finished evaluation product without a tremendous expenditure of time.

CURRENT PRACTICES IN ACCOUNTABILITY

The question of how many school psychologists are actually involved in accountability efforts was one topic of a study by Fairchild and Zins (1992). In their polling of a random sample of NASP members, more than half (57.8%) of respondents reported that they were involved in the collection of accountability data. Of those collecting accountability data, almost all (96.8%) were involved in collecting enumerative data. More than one third (36.6%) collected process data, and 44.1% reported collecting outcome data. More than half of the respondents (52.7%) who were involved in the collection of accountability data reported collecting two or more types. In an earlier article, Fairchild (1975) described six accountability tools that he thought might be beneficial to school psychologists. The six tools included the following:

- *The daily log*. Fairchild identified five activities in which school psychologists were involved: assessment, intervention, evaluation, consultation, and administration. He then developed a coding system for recording this information into a daily log format. From these he tallied weekly, then monthly, and finally yearly summaries of his activities.
- *Time-elapsed information*. In this technique, a log is kept of the date a child was referred for services, the initial contact date, and the date of the conference with the individual referring the child.
- *Accountability interview*. Fairchild viewed this technique as enabling the school psychologist to obtain feedback and prevent potential problems. In the article,

Fairchild noted that he elicited teacher feedback indirectly through building principals.

- *Follow-up questionnaire.* Teachers and parents whose children were seen by the school psychologist completed anonymous surveys containing three questions:

  a. "Did you have a better understanding of the child as a result of your discussion with the school psychologist?"
  b. "Were recommendations realistic and/or practical?"
  c. "Were the recommendations of the psychologist effective?" (p. 157)

- *Telephone follow-up.* Fairchild made at least one phone call to parents of all children he had evaluated.
- *Behavioral consultation.* When a referral was received from a teacher, the school psychologist met with the teacher to identify a particular target behavior. The teacher and psychologist then decided on a criterion of success (e.g., Andy remains in his seat 90% of each 50-minute class period). Baseline behavior was measured, as was behavior throughout and following the implementation of the intervention plan. Success could thus be plotted. This example is quite similar to the current trend toward functional behavioral assessment.

Fairchild's description of the six tools for school psychologists was an early effort to show school psychologists how they could document their professional activities.

Other accountability efforts also can be found in the school psychology literature. A NASP publication, *Accountability for School Psychologists: Developing Trends* (Zins, 1982), was a compilation of accountability instruments developed by school psychologists across the country. The first part of the publication was divided into three sections that corresponded to the three types of accountability: enumerative data ("Descriptive Approaches"), process data ("Effectiveness as Perceived by Others"), and outcome data ("Measures of Behavior Change"). Following these three sections, an annotated bibliography was organized by six topics: program documentation, quality assurance, personnel evaluation, program planning, program dissemination, and self-monitoring and self-change.

Efforts toward professional accountability have become much more vital within the past two decades. Reschly (1983) noted that accountability was gaining momentum throughout the field of education partly because of legal decisions:

> The due-process procedures and other legal guidelines establish the potential for close scrutiny of nearly all aspects of the work of the school psychologist. Psychological reports, regarded a decade ago as confidential documents which were not shown to parents, are now among the educational records which parents can examine. Information in the reports can be challenged by parents.... Classification decisions, interpretations of behavior, and recommendations are now open to question. The validity

> and fairness of tests and other assessment devices can be challenged on the basis of due-process protections and on other legal grounds. (p. 87)

School psychologists in a variety of settings are involved in accountability efforts. Trainers are particularly apt to find themselves immersed in evaluations of their programs. Information such as credit-hour production, program enrollment, graduation rates, and success and placement of graduates is frequently requested within the university by department chairs and deans who must write their own annual evaluations to submit to those individuals or groups assigned to oversee them (e.g., higher administration, state boards of higher education). In addition, training program faculty must prepare periodic reports of the program's activities and accomplishments to remain in compliance with state and national accreditation agencies (discussed in chapter 7). Even professional organizations are accountable to their members and at times to other governing bodies as well. Officers of such associations may be asked to furnish information regarding membership, money spent, publications produced, and other activities in order to prepare an annual report to the membership. NASP, for example, does this annually by surveying its leadership about the NASP office and the performance of the executive director.

Aside from their own self-evaluation in schools and other settings, school psychologists also may be involved in accountability and professional evaluation. Armed with graduate-level training in psychological research methods and statistics, the school psychologist may be asked to become involved in districtwide accountability efforts. Such efforts may involve anything from teacher evaluation to curriculum evaluation. In fact, with the current outcome-oriented movement within education, many school districts nationally are attempting to identify learning objectives and assess whether those objectives are being met. As assessment specialists, school psychologists may be involved in identifying these learning objectives, developing or selecting assessment instruments to measure the level of attainment of the objectives, and interpreting and evaluating the results of the assessment efforts. Involvement in such endeavors extends school psychologists' problem-solving approach to the system level.

NEW CHALLENGES IN ACCOUNTABILITY

Two issues in school psychology today seem particularly relevant to a discussion of professional evaluation and accountability: use of the response-to-intervention (RTI) model and the related topic of evidence-based intervention. RTI is a concept from the reauthorization of IDEA, which states that whether or not a child responds to interventions may be more important in determining the child's needs for special education than the results of more formal testing. In previous years, in order to qualify a student as having a learning disability, the school psychologist, in consultation with other education professionals, had to document that a discrepancy existed between the student's ability levels and his or her achievement levels. So a fourth-grade student with an IQ of about 100 who was working at the second-grade level probably would qualify for such services, whereas a similar student working at the fourth-grade level probably would not qualify. (Note that this is a simplification of the earlier model; other factors were taken into consideration as well.) Under RTI a student might not show such a discrepancy, but if the student did not respond favorably to repeated attempts to improve his or her academic performance, the student probably would still qualify for additional services. Much confusion currently exists across the country about RTI and its implementation, and it is a major topic of conversation when school psychologists get together formally or informally. The importance of accountability in an era of RTI is clear. The RTI model is based on record keeping and careful documentation of what works and what does not work for an individual student, a classroom, a school building, and a school district. School psychologists with training and experience as data-based decision makers should prove invaluable in helping schools implement RTI.

The second trend, the use of evidence-based intervention, relates to RTI. School psychologists have always been asked by teachers, parents, and others how to handle problems that arise: What can I do about a child who doesn't pay attention, who doesn't turn in his homework, who doesn't read well, etc.? Over the years, school psychologists have developed strategies to answer such questions based on their own experience, their knowledge of child development, their training in scientific research, and their own common sense. The question over the last few years, though, has become, How can school psychologists, and educators in general, bridge the gap between common sense, professional experience, and scientific research? In other words, can school psychologists become—and encourage students to become—scientist practitioners and not just practitioners? Can science and practice inform each other? Is this something school psychologists can and should aspire to?

Much of the growth in evidence-based interventions is linked to the growth over the last 15 or so years in meta-analytic research, a technique that allows researchers to take all of the studies on a given intervention and examine them to see whether the research actually supports the use of a given technique. For example, an extensive review by Hoagwood and Erwin (1997) found evidence to support the use of three interventions with children: cognitive–behavioral therapy, social skills training, and teacher consultation.

In 1999 a Task Force on Empirically Supported Interventions in Schools was established by Division 16 of the APA and the Society for the Study of School Psychology. The huge task of this committee was to "focus on reviewing the empirical literature and addressing the conceptual, methodological, and cultural diversity issues on prevention programs, classroom intervention programs, interventions for social behavioral problems, interventions for academic problems, family/parent interventions, and comprehensive school health care programs" (Stoiber & Kratochwill, 2000, p. 78). The group was also asked to focus on the usefulness of assessment approaches to problem solving and to develop a manual documenting their observations.

The relationship between evidence-based intervention and accountability should be clear. As more interventions are documented as effective, practicing school psychologists can be confident that the strategies and techniques they recommend or implement have a good chance of changing a student's achievement or behavior.

Such positive changes can then be documented by the school psychologist and used for accountability purposes.

CONCLUSION

Accountability is a vital part of the school psychologist's professional role. In the short run, it provides feedback about professional performance and suggests ways in which to improve. In the long run, accountability may be the most important part of a school psychologist's job, for it may justify the professional's being in the schools and thus ensure the profession's continued existence.

Chapter 6

The Preparation of School Psychologists

Most texts on school psychology limit the discussion of how school psychologists are trained, or treat the topic briefly in conjunction with discussions of credentialing. This book discusses credentialing in the context of professional regulation (see chapter 7) and discusses training in a separate chapter. An understanding of how school psychologists are prepared for practice is important to students preparing for a career in the field. Chapter 1 introduced the most common levels of training obtained by individuals seeking to be credentialed as school psychologists. This chapter describes the preparation of school psychologists in greater detail, discusses topics important to preparation, considers how preparation relates to standards for program accreditation and credentialing, and explores expectations for the continuing professional development of school psychologists in the future. This information will help readers understand the potential training and credentialing problems encountered when moving from one state to another, and the relationship between basic and advanced graduate preparation in school psychology. Readers also should be able to make some comparisons between national-level trends and guidelines for preparation and the program in which they are enrolled.

GROWTH OF TRAINING PROGRAMS

As discussed in chapter 2, early practitioners functioned as generalists responding to a variety of referrals and problems. Practice largely involved individual psychometric evaluation of children and adolescents suspected of being mentally, physically, or morally defective. The purpose of psychological services in most settings was to help school personnel sort children into more appropriate classroom placements, including the relatively small but increasing number of special education classes. Most practitioners had only limited involvement with direct interventions, often along the lines of academic remediation, counseling, and parent–teacher consultation.

Reflecting the limited role and function of school psychologists, early training of practitioners was a mix of concepts, from the child study movement following

---

Note: Portions of this chapter first appeared in Fagan (1990a) and are reproduced here by permission of the National Association of School Psychologists.

G. Stanley Hall and clinical psychology that grew out of the orientation of Lightner Witmer. The Hall orientation evolved into developmental and educational psychology, whereas the Witmer orientation evolved into several clinical fields. It has been posited that the training and practice of school psychologists have been influenced by these two orientations and their transformations in practice brought about by disciples of Hall and Witmer (Fagan, 1992). Training usually was in a psychology or philosophy department, often in the education college, and emphasized experimental studies with few applied courses, except for those in clinical psychology (Fagan, 1999).

The lack of available training meant the demand for school psychological personnel was met by professionals with training in a variety of education- and psychology-related fields. Training emphasized the use of recently developed tests of intelligence, school achievement, and motor skills. Early practitioners held various titles and degrees: some held the bachelor's degree, more held the master's degree, and a few held the doctoral degree. University course sequences appropriate for students planning to work in the schools were available in the 1920s. However, the first preparation programs labeled school psychology were in the undergraduate and graduate program offerings at New York University in the late 1920s (Fagan, 1999). Graduates of training programs specifically in school psychology were rare. Until the 1930s no state education agency certification requirements existed, nor were there national training standards espoused by the APA or other national groups to influence the direction of training. In some instances, practitioner training was simply teacher training augmented by a brief course in intelligence testing.

Several factors broadened the range of preparation after 1940: increased demand for practitioners, greater acceptance of nontesting roles for psychologists, increasing numbers of states having state department of education (SDE) certification requirements, training guidelines developed by APA's Division 16, improved testing technology, widespread interest in school and community mental health, and the level of theory development during this period (e.g., psychodynamic, behavioral, Gestalt, and nondirective).

With the development of associations for applied psychologists, the study of school psychology training gained in importance. A committee report on training in New York State put forth recommendations for professional courses, field experiences, lengths of programs, and desirable personal characteristics of students (New York State Association for Applied Psychology, 1943). The similarity between the committee's recommendations and contemporary program descriptions is notable (e.g., 2½ years of graduate study, practica, and a minimum of a 6 months of internship). Broader preparation that was more specific to school psychology was increasingly available after 1935. The Pennsylvania State University doctoral program was founded in the late 1930s and the University of Illinois program in 1953. Although the Illinois program established by T. E. Newland was not the first doctoral program in school psychology, it was among the first well-organized programs (Cutts, 1955). Early descriptions of the Illinois program reveal its sensitivity to educational as well as psychological foundations; the need for broad,

The lack of available training meant the demand for school psychological personnel was met by professionals with training in a variety of education- and psychology-related fields.

generalist preparation; and other aspects still included in professional training standards.

By the time of the Thayer Conference in 1954, only 28 institutions offered programs specifically in school psychology, with 10 granting the doctoral degree.... The NASP database of programs suggests that as of 2006, 213 institutions have school psychology programs.

By the time of the Thayer Conference in 1954, only 28 institutions offered programs specifically in school psychology, with 10 granting the doctoral degree (Fagan, 1986b). The institutions were not well distributed geographically. Leadership roles in training were taken by New York University, Pennsylvania State University, Columbia University, the University of Michigan, and the University of Illinois. Many people contributed to the early training of school psychology professionals and later to actual program development: Charles Benson, H. H. Goddard, Gertrude Hildreth, Leta Hollingworth, Francis Maxfield, T. E. Newland, Percival Symonds, J. E. W. Wallin, Lightner Witmer, and countless more recent figures. Contemporary trainers owe much to the planning and thinking of these people.

The Thayer Conference, in 1954, was the first comprehensive national meeting to deal with issues of training in school psychology. The proceedings of the conference were distributed widely for several years following the conference and identified the need for more master's and doctoral programs (Cutts, 1955; Fagan, 1993). By the 1960s, training programs offered courses on the foundations of psychology and education, special education, intelligence and personality testing, academic remediation, and psychological interventions (e.g., counseling, psychotherapy, and consultation). Nevertheless, most programs continued to have traditional experimental psychology requirements. The Thayer Conference recommendations not only set the stage for future training, but also created a framework within which many of the future conflicts in training, accreditation, credentialing, and practice would evolve (Fagan, 2005b).

The historical growth of training programs, most dramatic between 1960 and 1980, has been the subject of several studies summarized in Fagan (1986b). As of 2006, there are about seven times as many training institutions as existed in 1960. The 1998 NASP *Directory of Graduate Programs* identified 218 institutions that provided information on their programs (Thomas, 1998), and the NASP database of programs suggests there are 230 to 250 institutions as of 2006. The number of institutions offering training in school psychology appears to have stabilized since the 1990s. Greater similarity in the content of programs also has developed, along with discernible distinctions between doctoral and nondoctoral preparation (M. Brown, Hohenshil, & Brown, 1998; Reschly & Wilson, 1997).

STUDENT AND PRACTITIONER CHARACTERISTICS

Motivations and Backgrounds

School psychology attracts students for many reasons and from many backgrounds. Among the reasons given for entering the field are excellent job opportunities and stability, employee benefits, an interest in education, the desire to work with children and families, and a generally strong humanitarian attitude. Because many of these motivations overlap with those for entering other helping fields, it is common to find that some school psychology trainees have had previous experience in teaching, guidance and counseling, or mental health. In addition, students may have varied undergraduate backgrounds, including sociology and social work, elementary and secondary education, special education, and psychology. Psychology and education fields account for most of the students' backgrounds, with a diversity of undergraduate teaching majors. For example, students have entered training programs from art education, counselor education, educational administration, physical education, social studies, and special education. Some students have turned to school psychology from the seemingly unrelated fields of business and technology.

Desirable Personal Characteristics

In addition to the varied motivations students have for entering the field, several personal characteristics also are desirable among future practitioners. Perhaps foremost is the academic ability and aptitude to successfully complete graduate-level education. A strong sense of personal responsibility and an appreciation of moral and ethical responsibilities to the profession and its clients also are important. A statement of desired characteristics given by the New York State Association for Applied Psychology (1943) included "maturity in manner and outlook, ease in inter-professional relationships, responsiveness to the effects of rapidly changing educational and social conditions, and above all emotional security and objectivity" (p. 239). Discussing the importance of learning to think like a psychologist in real-life situations, Bardon and Bennett (1974) described the character of the school psychologist:

> [He] must care about what happens to people. He must be capable of genuine identification with different kinds of people and their modes of behavior, including those whose cultural backgrounds, ethnic origins, and basic beliefs may be different from his. He must have a sincere and positive attitude toward humanity that will enable him to try new approaches and to persist even in the face of discouragement, lack of results, and frustration. (p. 176)

Bardon (1986) summarized several other opinions of successful attributes in addition to those cited in 1974. These include interpersonal warmth, flexibility, sensitivity, stress resistance, circumspection, eagerness to learn, dedication, reflective judgment, and "an attitude of positive skepticism" (pp. 65–66). Bardon's thinking is consistent with the characteristics specified in the Rutgers University program where he taught in the 1960s (see, Magary, 1967a, pp. 741–742). Other desirable employee characteristics include being well organized, prompt, adaptable, and able to profit from supervision; able to get along with parents, educators, and students; and able to work productively with individuals, groups, and systems. One survey of school psychology supervisors indicated that after basic competency, what most interested the supervisors were the candidate's ability to work closely with others, along with "facility in verbal and written communication, diplomacy, consideration for others' viewpoints, empathy for the client, and a dedication or commitment to the field of school psychology" (Fireoved & Cancelleri, 1985, p. 4). Magary (1967a) identified desirable characteristics based on brochures from training programs and state departments of education and on the thinking of Carl Rogers. Magary, a past president of APA's Division of School Psychology, noted that "the school psychologist should be characterized first and foremost by an interest in wishing to help children" (p. 740). Others have also identified being able to work effectively with a variety of teachers, having desirable personality characteristics, being sensitive to others, and having communication skills.

No list of characteristics has achieved consensus among trainers and employers; however, national-level sanction is implied in the list of professional work characteristics given in NASP's credentialing standards (NASP, 2000d, p. 45). This list includes respect for human diversity, communication skills, effective interpersonal relations, ethical responsibility, adaptability, initiative, and dependability. Personal stability was removed from the 1994 edition. The 1985 edition also included conscientiousness, cooperation, independence, motivation, productivity, and professional image. All of these continue to be important even if difficult to enforce in the credentialing process. Although the lists contain no definitions of these characteristics, the current list at least ensures that these characteristics were reviewed by many groups and the NASP school psychology leadership prior to being adopted.

Throughout training, students are closely observed for evidence of appropriate personal characteristics, especially during their field experiences.

Even in the absence of definitions or consensus, personal characteristics are considered to be important. Cournoyer (2004) recommends the scrutiny of school psychology trainees according to the NASP list of professional work characteristics and provides examples supporting her position. Throughout training, students are closely observed for evidence of appropriate personal characteristics, especially during their field experiences. Trainers of school psychologists have been as concerned about their students' personal characteristics as they have been about their academic progress. Bardon (1986) properly acknowledged that "it is possible the effectiveness of school psychologists is determined as much, if not more, by the way they function and interact than by what they know and what duties they perform" (p. 65). A study of program directors in clinical and counseling psychology programs indicated strong concern for character and fitness information in both the admission and postadmission phases of training. The directors assigned high importance to personality psychopathology, psychological health, appropriate substance use, integrity (honesty), prudence (good judgment), and caring (respect and sensitivity; Johnson & Campbell, 2004, p. 408). The importance of training students in leadership skills was discussed by Kruger, Bennett, and Farkis (2006) and related to broader concerns for role expansion, including prevention activities.

CHARACTERISTICS OF PREPARATION PROGRAMS

Diversity Representation

For a variety of reasons, professional fields of psychology lack proportionally representative cultural diversity. School psychology as a field includes less than 8%

minorities, far below percentages of minorities in the general population, and that representation has improved only a few percentage points over the past 25 years (Curtis, Lopez, Batsche, & Smith, 2006). The modest increases at least allay earlier fears of declining representation (Hunley & Curtis, 1998). More encouraging levels of ethnic diversity are observed among graduate students (17%) and program faculty (15%; Thomas, 1998). More recent training program data are unavailable. A national *Directory of Bilingual School Psychologists* (NASP, Multicultural Affairs Committee, 1998) included only about 400 listings across 35 language proficiency types (including sign language and visual impairment). Since 45% of the directory entries were Spanish speaking and some entries were practitioners outside the United States, the directory further reflects school psychology's need for greater diversity. The lack of preparation school psychologists have in conducting assessments with Hispanic students was observed in a study by Ochoa, Rivera, and Ford (1997). The continued improvement of minority representation in school psychology requires a long-term professional effort that will not be easily accomplished (Fagan, 1988b, 2004b; Jackson, 1992; Zins & Halsell, 1986). The NASP Education and Research Trust offers minority scholarships, but they are limited to ethnic minorities.

Women represent almost 80% of the school psychology graduate student population, 45% of program faculty, and more than 70% of practitioners.

A few training programs have grants or special expertise for training school psychologists to work with diverse populations. A framework for diversity training is presented by Gopaul-McNicol (1997) and the Division 16 (APA) newsletter, *The School Psychologist*, which published two series on the topic of multicultural training and specific programs (1994, Vol. 49, No. 4, and 1995, Vol. 50, No. 1). A special section of *Professional Psychology: Research and Practice* (2004, Vol. 35, No. 1) looked at practical suggestions for achieving multicultural competence and the delivery of mental health services to Native American, African American, and Spanish-speaking populations, mainly adults. Matines (2004) described a method using coding sessions to evaluate the effects of multicultural training on consultation with teachers. The topic of multicultural issues in school psychology is treated comprehensively in the *Journal of Applied School Psychology* (2006, Vol. 22, No. 2), including assessment, interventions, home–school partnerships, and cultural factors in systems-level interventions. Additional sources specific to school psychology are the *Comprehensive Handbook of Multicultural School Psychology* (Frisby & Reynolds, 2005) and the *Handbook of Multicultural School Psychology: An Interdisciplinary Perspective* (Esquivel, Lopez, & Nahari, 2006).

In contrast to minority representation, representation by women has increased consistently in the past three decades. Women make up almost 80% of the school psychology graduate student population, 45% of program faculty, and more than 70% of practitioners. This increase, which was predicted (see e.g., APA, Committee on Employment and Human Resources, 1986), is consistent with women's increased publication in school psychology journals (Skinner, Robinson, Brown, & Cates, 1999). Their representation in editorial and association leadership positions and academic settings has increased as well (see, e.g., Roberts, Gerrard-Morris, Zanger,

Davis, & Robinson, 2006). A survey by Akin-Little, Little, and Eckert (2006) found several differences between men and women faculty members in terms of tenure, rank, and job perceptions, but it seemed likely that some of these differences could be explained by the fact that men had more years of experience. A related review found that women in academia perceived their academic climate as favorable and were generally satisfied (Akin-Little, Bray, Eckert, & Kehle, 2006).

As more individuals with disabilities enter the workforce with the assistance of the Americans with Disabilities Act (Pub. L. 101-336), their representation in the field of school psychology is anticipated to grow. Little is known of current numbers or of efforts to include them in training and practice. Making accommodations for students with self-acknowledged learning disabilities or ADHD in their training and practice is fairly uncomplicated. Training individuals with more severe disabilities, however, could require technology for accommodations matched with employer expectations for on-the-job performance. To encourage appropriate representation of individuals with disabilities in the field, training programs could team with professional associations to develop a list of job skills and behaviors applicants must have or be reasonably expected to develop or compensate for in order to perform effectively as practitioners.

Teacher Certification and Experience

Discussions about school psychologists' preparation generally consider prior certification or experience as teachers desirable; however, empirical studies have not found a significant relationship between teaching experience and a school psychologist's success (Gerner, 1981, 1983). From 1940 to 1980, the number of state departments of education requiring teacher certification or experience for credentialing in school psychology fell dramatically. Currently, very few states require school psychologists to have teacher certification without providing some alternative avenues for those lacking such certification (for specific state requirements see Curtis, Hunley, & Prus, 1998, or links provided at the NASP website). Still, as noted in chapter 3, many school psychologists hold teaching credentials and have prior teaching experience, perhaps reflecting the ongoing recruitment of school psychologists from the ranks of experienced teachers and students in undergraduate teacher education programs. None of the state psychology licensing boards require teaching credentials for the title of school psychologist. What is considered important is to ensure, through training and field experiences, that future school psychologists gain a comprehensive understanding of the educational system in which they will be directly or indirectly employed, as well as an appreciation for the role of the classroom teacher. Finally, as school psychologists expand their range of practice settings, it will be important for such individuals to gain an understanding and appreciation of relevant nonschool settings as well. Supervised field experiences and continuing education may be the most constructive avenues for such preparation.

Currently, very few states require school psychologists to have teacher certification without providing some alternative avenues for those lacking such certification.

Common Levels of Preparation

Chapter 1 provided a synopsis of the typical levels of training attained by school psychologists, including data from D. Smith (1984), Wilson and Reschly (1995), and recent NASP membership data. Table 6.1 summarizes the levels of training held by respondents to these and an earlier survey. The data from Smith and from Reschly and Wilson emphasize practitioner data, although the latter and the NASP data include trainers. Despite the different methodologies in these surveys, it is obvious that most school psychologists do not hold doctoral degrees. The recent NASP survey revealed that 80.5% held a specialist or higher level of preparation. The percentage of NASP members holding the doctoral degree is up 6% from the previous member survey of 1998. Because the percentage holding the doctorate is higher when trainers are included in the sample (Graden & Curtis, 1991), the current NASP survey data reflect a higher overall percentage of doctoral degree holders than exists among the practitioners-only cohort. Over the past 30 years, there has been a distinct trend toward increased numbers of practitioners who have training at the specialist and doctoral levels, with declines in the number who have training only at the master's level and the virtual disappearance of those with only bachelor's-level training.

Enrollment Patterns

Enrollment patterns provide another means of judging the typical training of school psychologists. The survey data of D. Brown and Minke (1984); McMaster, Reschly, and Peters (1989); and Thomas (1998) suggest that total enrollment in school psychology programs decreased in the 1980s (from 7,293 to 5,634), and then increased to 8,587. The increases were only at the specialist and doctoral levels, with a substantial decrease at the master's level. Between 1984 and 1998 the proportion of graduate students who were at the master's level declined from 20.1% to 2.6%, those at the specialist level increased from 48.3% to 68.5%, and those at the doctoral level declined slightly, from 31.6% to 28.9%. A comparison of the McMaster et al. (1989) survey with that of Thomas (1998) reveals a decline in the number of master's programs from 42 to 13, a gain in specialist programs from 164 to 193, and a gain in doctoral programs from 67 to 82. These data and the analyses by Reschly and McMaster-Beyer (1991) and Reschly and Wilson (1997) suggest that the specialist degree level has gained in popularity and that growth at the doctoral level has been less pronounced than was predicted by D. Brown and Minke (1986) and Fagan (1986c). The directories during the period 1977–1998 reveal that the number of institutions offering training was fairly stable (mean = 209, range 203–218 of reporting institutions), but the average number of graduates per program declined slightly between 1975–1976 and 1981–1982 (12.2 to 11.1) and was stable between 1986–1987 and 1996–1997 (8.4 to 8.9). The total number of graduates declined about 20 percent, from 2,350 in 1981–1982 to 1,897 in 1996–1997 (Thomas, 1998). More recent program data from NASP's database indicate increased enrollments and graduates in 2006 (Miller, 2007).

A continued increase in the proportion of specialist and doctoral programs is predicted, as well as fewer 2-year programs and the elimination of 1-year master's programs. Surveys of practitioners will increasingly reveal 6th-year, specialist, or

Table 6.1 Summary of School Psychology Training Levels of Study Respondents (percentage distribution)

	NASP Member Data[a]	Reschly and Wilson[b]	Smith[c]	Farling and Hoedt[d]
Bachelor's	–	–	0	1
Master's (1 yr)	–	–	17	28
Master's (2 yr)	32.6	23	45	63
Master's (3 yr) or Specialist	34.9	56	22	1
Doctorate	32.4	21	16	3

[a] Based on membership survey data for the National Association of School Psychologists 2004–2005 (reported in Curtis, Lopez, Batsche, & Smith, 2006).
[b] "School Psychology Practitioners and Faculty: 1986 to 1991–92 Trends in Demographics, Roles, Satisfaction, and System Reform," by D. J. Reschly and M. S. Wilson, 1995, *School Psychology Review, 24*, 62–80. This study employed only three categories: master's (30–59 semester hours), specialist (60 or more semester hours), and doctoral.
[c] "Practicing School Psychologists: Their Characteristics, Activities, and Populations Served," by D. K. Smith, 1984, *Professional Psychology: Research and Practice, 15*, 798–810.
[d] *National Survey of School Psychologists*, by W. H. Farling and K. C. Hoedt, 1971, Washington, DC: Author.

doctoral training, with lesser-trained personnel fading entirely within the next 2 decades, unless a technician-type credential in school psychology practice emerges that would provide a demand for less than specialist-level training. The growing opportunities for online and freestanding professional school training may also encourage larger numbers of people to enter the field, especially at the doctoral level.

Length of Training Programs

The length of training programs provides another perspective on the typical training of school psychologists. The 1989 NASP *Directory of Graduate Programs* (McMaster et al., 1989) indicated that the average number of semester hours required for master's, specialist, and doctoral degrees in 1986–1987 were 42, 66, and 100, respectively. The 1998 directory (Thomas, 1998) reported 40, 66, and 103.5, respectively. Typical course requirements by degree level are discussed later in this chapter. Although more recent training program data are not available from NASP, it is unlikely that the length of programs has changed.

SELECTION OF PROGRAM, DEGREE, AND LEVEL OF TRAINING

Students should consider the following objectives when exploring their preparation for the practice of school psychology:

1. Work with school-age children, including those with disabilities?
2. Work primarily in public school settings?

3. Work as an employee in a public school environment?
4. Pursue a nondoctoral or doctoral degree?
5. Seek generalist or specialized training?
6. Pursue long-term interest of working in a practice or in an academic setting?
7. Work in a particular state or region?

The answers to these questions may help students select a training program, choose among program electives, and decide whether to seek doctoral preparation.

Resources for Selecting a Program

NASP maintains an online directory that can be used to gather information on school psychology graduate programs. The listings provide curriculum and semester-hour requirements for each training institution and other specific program information useful in selecting a program and judging its content. An annual publication by the APA, *Graduate Programs in Psychology*, provides similar information about school psychology and other psychology programs and complements the NASP listings. Students also find useful information on websites of specific institutions and graduate programs. Because doctoral and nondoctoral programs are increasingly complying with the standards promulgated by NASP and APA, their published program standards also are useful references. Prospective and incoming students also should plan to make an on-the-job visit with one or more practicing school psychologists to observe firsthand what school psychology is about.

For students considering a particular program, the program administrator is the most reliable source of information. Recently published directories and university bulletin descriptions may not keep pace with changes. Inquiries to the institution will allow students to make more informed decisions regarding the appropriateness of the program for their needs and interests. Students can determine what prerequisite coursework is desired or required but when possible, they should visit the program and talk directly with faculty and currently enrolled students. Information on the historical development and philosophy of certain doctoral programs can be found in former issues of *Professional School Psychology* (now *School Psychology Quarterly*). Some programs have an unpublished written history available for distribution.

A document that continues to be useful is Gerner and Genshaft's *Selecting a School Psychology Training Program* (1981), which addresses such issues as degrees, field experiences, credentialing requirements, program orientations, and interviewing questions. They also refer to the relationship between a training program and the credentialing requirements of the state in which the program is located. This is a major consideration at the nondoctoral level. Because most programs are organized to meet requirements of a particular state department of education (SDE) or state board of examiners in psychology (SBEP), nondoctoral programs often conform closely to state agency requirements. Thus NASP's *Credentialing Requirements for School Psychologists* (Curtis et al., 1998) and NASP's online links to credentialing agencies are helpful for choosing a program and determining school-based and independent credentialing requirements. Additional resources for use in internship selection are discussed later in this chapter and in chapter 8. Another useful guide is Morgan (1998). Students interested in research-oriented programs might find Little's (1997) survey helpful.

Level of Training Needed

School psychologists trained at the specialist degree level are competent to provide a broad range of services (M. Brown et al., 1998; Reschly & Wilson, 1997; Woody & Davenport, 1998), even though some have questions about specialist-level preparation for nonschool settings (Reschly & McMaster-Beyer, 1991). Individuals seeking training in school psychology should pursue nothing less than a specialist degree, or an equivalent level of preparation with a minimum of 60 graduate semester hours, in a training program approved through NASP or through a state education agency that acknowledges NASP standards, perhaps through a partnership with the National Council for Accreditation of Teacher Education (NCATE). Entering a program with such approvals will enhance the student's later eligibility for the NASP National School Psychology Certification System. Various arrangements may be used to meet the NASP guidelines for training and for national certification. Many programs offer the master's degree and the educational specialist degree (EdS) in tandem for a total minimum of 60 semester hours. In some instances, the hourly requirements are met through a lengthy master's degree or through the EdS degree only. The content of the program and its accreditation status are more important than the title of the degree offered. However, in some states the educational specialist degree is required for credentialing.

The question of whether a practitioner should hold the doctoral degree has existed throughout the history of school psychology, especially since the reorganization of the American Psychological Association (APA) in 1945. In the case of independent practitioners, every national organization from which school psychologists have sought professional identity has considered the doctorate as the proper entry level of training, with the exception of NASP (Fagan, 1993). The intensity of the debate increased following the APA Council of Representatives' decision, in 1977, to recognize only the doctoral level for the title professional psychologist. The doctoral–nondoctoral issue is too complex for in-depth coverage in this book; summary viewpoints are available in Fagan (1986c, 1993) and *School Psychology Review* (Vol. 16, No. 1, and Vol. 18, No. 1). Even though the majority of school psychologists have been trained at the nondoctoral level (see, e.g., chapter 1), the demand for doctoral-level personnel can be observed in the growth of APA-accredited doctoral programs since 1971 (Fagan & Wells, 2000).

However, because the doctoral degree is seldom required for practice in the schools, and the schools will continue to be the primary employment setting, one important consideration is the relative cost of doctoral study compared with the income that could be gained from continued employment. In 1996–1997, the average tuition for resident school psychology students was $4,308 per year, and the average cost per credit hour was $219 (Thomas, 1998). These figures are more than double those reported for 1986–1987 (McMaster et al., 1989). More recent data are unavailable but it seems fair to assume that these figures have risen by at least another 50% since 1998. Assuming a practitioner already holds the specialist degree and is credentialed for school practice, pursuing doctoral work on a full-time basis would involve giving up a salary for perhaps 3 years before entering or returning to employment. Salary loss for 3 years might total $110,000 to $180,000 and tuition would cost at least $18,000. A conservative estimated cost of $130,000 could not be matched by graduate student stipends, tuition waivers, and a paid internship, the total of which might be only around $55,000. Add the costs of living expenses, transportation, out-of-state tuition, books, and materials, and it becomes obvious that, under any circumstances, doctoral preparation is a long-term investment and not a short-term financial advantage.

Students often take out loans, and growing student indebtedness is worrisome. In 2003 the median debt of doctoral-level practitioners was $67,000, and among school psychology graduates, 56% reported debt of $41,000 or more (Wicherski & Kohout, 2005). Unless the practitioner anticipates returning to a significantly greater salary level in his or her former employment or additional sources of revenue such as from private practice or an administrative position, students may find little financial advantage to pursuing a doctoral degree. Nor does pursuing the doctorate to enter a university position guarantee a financial advantage; some academic positions do not pay as well as doctoral- or even specialist-level practitioner positions. Reschly and Wilson (1995) reported an average primary employer income of $37,587 for practitioners and $46,657 for faculty, but the average age of faculty was 6.5 years older than that of practitioners (47.9 versus 41.4). Although incomes have grown since the 1990s, it is unlikely this gap has been reduced. More recent comparative salary data are not available. However, a recent survey of graduate students in doctoral programs suggested that pay and benefits are important considerations for later employment, and that only 10% held aspirations for teaching in a graduate-level school psychology program (Baker, 2006).

Because the doctoral degree is seldom required for practice in the schools, and the schools will continue to be the primary employment setting, one important consideration is the relative cost of doctoral study compared with the income that could be gained from continued employment.

From a financial standpoint, it may be better for the student to pursue a doctoral program immediately after completing the specialist degree than to return for such training after a period of employment. The length of additional academic preparation is at least 1 year, plus doctoral programs usually require completion of an internship. Returning to school after beginning employment also involves lifestyle considerations, such as family responsibilities and expenses or the ability to get employment leave. These can make returning to graduate work more difficult than pursuing it originally. Prospective doctoral students should weigh the advantages and disadvantages of advanced training against their long-term career goals. Although doctoral programs often prefer full-time students, many offer part-time studies that allow students to maintain employment and defray the cost of their education. Graduate-student stipends and tuition waivers, however, are seldom available to part-time students.

For some students, money may not be the most important issue involved in a decision. Foremost may be the opportunities to obtain greater knowledge, competence, and status and to expand professional options. Some contend that the doctoral degree is not necessary for school-based practice and adds little or no competence. The specialist degree appears to be sufficient for school practice; additional competencies developed through doctoral training may be more significant to effective practice in nonschool settings (Phillips, 1985; Reschly & McMaster-Beyer, 1991). However, breadth of training, opportunities for advancement in school settings, and employment in the private sector with full professional privileges are worthy incentives in making long-term career choices. In a field where an increasing percentage of practitioners hold the doctoral degree, seeking the doctorate for its own sake will also be an incentive.

Regardless of whether a student seeks doctoral or nondoctoral preparation, one note of warning is needed: Students should apply only to programs that hold appropriate state and national approval or accreditation. The changing demographics of school psychology and the persistently favorable job market may encourage future students to pursue graduate work through nontraditional programs and online courses, but students should approach such options with caution.

Administrative Location of Preparation Programs

Compared with some areas of psychology, school psychology has had a confusing history of training, credentialing, and accreditation. Throughout this history, training programs have been located in both psychology and nonpsychology departments in colleges of education and colleges of arts and sciences. If readers review the entries in training directories, they will be surprised by the diversity of department and college titles in which school psychology preparation occurs. The diversity has resulted from historical trends in the development of school psychology, including graduate admission of students from diverse backgrounds in education and psychology, conflicts between psychology and education departments, accreditation influences from different agencies, and, until recent years, lack of clear professional identity. Departmental diversity is the norm, not the exception, in school psychology training. An analysis of data in the former NASP directory (Thomas, 1998) and from the Council of Directors of School Psychology Programs resulted in the distributions shown in Table 6.2.

Approximately two thirds of specialist-level and three fourths of doctoral-level programs are in education units, such as colleges of education. The distributions in Table 6.2 are consistent with earlier analyses (D. Brown and Lindstrom, 1977; Goh, 1977), and it is unlikely they have changed. The diversity also can be observed in the numerous degree titles granted, with the most common being MS, MA, EdS, PhD, EdD, and PsyD. In some states, programs tend to be in education units (which occasionally includes the psychology department), whereas in others they tend to be located in psychology departments in colleges of arts and sciences.

The content of the program is more important than its administrative location or the title of the degree it may confer.

Table 6.2 Location of School Psychology Training Programs, by Academic Unit

	Number	Percent
Doctoral degree programs ($N = 87$)		
Education	64	74
Psychology	21	24
Unable to determine	2	2
Specialist-level programs ($N = 196$)		
Education	126	64
Psychology	55	28
Unable to determine	15	8

Source: Adapted from Thomas (1998) and CDSPP.

Frequently, programs are in a department of educational psychology, counseling and guidance, or other academic unit that is clearly psychology based. The content of the program is more important than its administrative location or the title of the degree it may confer. This principle is reflected in the diversity of administrative units observed for program accreditation. Programs in education and in psychology departments are accredited at the doctoral and nondoctoral levels. In 2005–2006, two thirds of the 67 APA-accredited doctoral programs in school psychology (including 10 combined programs) were located in departments other than psychology, and mostly in education college units. Nondoctoral accreditation is well dispersed across education and psychology units.

Does academic location of a program make a difference in the quality of preparation? No studies have been done on the job effectiveness of school psychologists related to the location of their academic preparation. An earlier analysis based on data from the 1989 NASP directory found no significant differences in programs based on academic location or accreditation (Reschly & McMaster-Beyer, 1991). A much earlier study suggested that the importance of content areas did not differ significantly as a function of academic administrative unit (Goh, 1977). Ross, Holzman, Handal, and Gilner (1991) cautiously suggest that, at least among APA-accredited doctoral programs, academic unit may be related to performance on the Examination for the Professional Practice of Psychology given by state licensing boards.

Location could help prepare school psychologists to work more effectively with teams made up of other educators and psychologists. For example, a program located in an education unit could train students who are preparing to work in pupil personnel services or a program located in a psychology department could train students who are preparing to work as health services providers to learn and work together as teams. Even with many school psychology programs strategically located in education units and in accredited combined psychology programs, the authors know of no program that specifically purports to train school psychologists concurrently with other specialists in a team format. Greater efforts in this regard may occur once the student begins an internship or a job. There is also a growing number of APA-accredited professional psychology programs that combine clinical (including child-clinical) and counseling psychology. A summary of the 2003 Consensus Conference on Combined and Integrated Doctoral Training in Psychology appears in the *Journal of Clinical Psychology* (Vol. 60, No. 9), and an example of a combined program appears in Givner and Furlong (2003; see also Beutler & Fisher, 1994; Minke & Brown, 1996). Although some people may believe that psychology department–based programs are superior, in a 1995 ranking of the six best school psychology programs, five were identified as being in education units (*U.S. News and World Report*, 1995 America's Best Graduate Schools, March 20, p. 109.).

Although no reason is known for judging a program as superior if it is in the education unit or the psychology unit, regardless of degree level, pragmatic concerns may encourage students to seek one academic unit or another. Programs located within education units are often more flexible in admissions criteria and scheduling of classes. In an education-based program, a student may be more likely to be admitted on a part-time basis, with a selection of daytime and evening courses. Some psychology-based school psychology programs are located in colleges of education where a "spread effect" may have influenced greater flexibility than is the case in psychology units in arts and sciences. Because of student employment opportunities and the influence of adult education, urban programs may also be more flexible in these respects than rural programs.

In addition, for licensing psychologists, the state's board of examiners in psychology (SBEP) may recognize only courses completed in a psychology unit and may prefer the PhD and doctor of psychology (PsyD) over the EdD. State departments of education (SDE) usually grant approvals through mechanisms coordinated with colleges of education (see chapter 7) and may prefer that training be completed in an education unit. Problems with degrees and units are more common when applications are for private practice licensure than when a school psychology credential is sought through the SDE. Thus, although students should feel confident that training programs administered from within either education or psychology units will provide appropriate preparation, they should be aware of potential credentialing implications. Graduates from a program that has proper accreditation in school psychology, especially at the doctoral level, will encounter fewer difficulties with any credentialing authority.

Alternative Degrees and Training

In recent years, professional degrees such as the doctor of psychology (PsyD) have emerged and offered advanced training in nontraditional formats available to school psychologists. Among academic school psychologists in the early 1990s, 3% held the PsyD, 76% held the PhD, 17% held the doctor of education (EdD or DEd), and 3% held other degrees (Daniel Reschly, personal communication, 1999). However, in 1998–1999, Wells (1999) found that among a sample of new doctoral graduates in school psychology (faculty and practitioners) 24% held the PsyD, 70% the PhD, and 6% the EdD. The 1989 NASP directory of training programs identified only four programs offering the PsyD, but the 1998 directory identified nine such programs. Data from the NASP listings are not yet available, but it is likely that several additional training programs are now offering the PsyD. An earlier study of the acceptability of the PsyD suggested it was not as widely accepted for academic employment as the traditional PhD or EdD (Prout, Meyers, & Greggo, 1989). Such problems seem less prevalent among recipients of the PsyD in clinical psychology (Hershey, Kopplin, & Cornell, 1991). The PsyD seems to have greatest appeal to students seeking practitioner positions. Training programs that wish to offer doctoral status but are unable to get authorization for the PhD may confer the PsyD instead. Holding the PsyD degree does not appear to be a hindrance in seeking SDE or SBEP credentialing, but the PsyD in school psychology is observed much less often among training program faculty (Akin-Little, Little, & Eckert, 2006, March). The number of freestanding professional schools with training in school psychology is expected to increase. Programs have emerged at Walden, Argosy, and Capella universities, and several others that may also offer online, nontraditional training opportunities. These entities may have campuses available in several cities and offer preparation at the doctoral and nondoctoral levels. As of 2005, none of the freestanding programs had achieved NASP approval, although some were working to gain such status.

In the coming decade, nontraditional programs are expected to be accepted by credentialing and accreditation agencies, and Web-based and other training options are expected to expand.

Another aspect of nontraditional training opportunities is the growing availability of Web-based courses in established, "land-based" university training programs (Harvey, 2005). A recent survey indicated that 24% of the responding NASP-approved programs offered at least one Web-based school psychology course (Bradley-Klug & Powell-Smith, 2001). A discussion of Internet courses on the Trainers of School Psychologists Listserv (*sptrain@lsv.uky.edu*) revealed considerable concern about such courses, especially those that are clinical (e.g., assessment and interventions). There also was a sense that personnel shortages in school psychology could increase the demand for alternatives to traditional campus-based courses; for example, enrollment limits could force worthy students to seek alternative training. Online courses and graduate degree programs in the field of education are widespread and will influence the growth of such activity in school psychology. Web-based programs already helped meet the training needs of school psychology students displaced from their programs in the aftermath of the 2005 Hurricane Katrina. In the coming decade, nontraditional programs are expected to be accepted by credentialing and accreditation agencies, and Web-based and other training options are expected to expand. These changes not only are in response to student demand; they also are the result of universities' quests to find less expensive means to provide courses that draw considerable revenue.

Relationship of Training to Accreditation and Credentialing

Levels of training and types of degrees have complex relationships to accreditation and credentialing, dictating the type of professional title and practice permitted. The complexity of these relationships is discussed in chapter 7 and suggested by Figure 7.1. The organizations, committees, agencies, and programs represented in Figure 7.1 illustrate the complex nature of accrediting and credentialing in school psychology (see also Fagan, 1986c, 1990a). Students selecting a training program will want to pay attention to standards for accreditation and credentialing and to the requirements of the SDE and the SBEP for the state in which the program is offered and where the trainee plans to practice.

PROGRAM CHARACTERISTICS

Programs can be considered on the basis of the models used for training, the content of the curriculum, field experiences, and accreditation.

Models of Training

The term *model* has several meanings when used in discussions of training, practice, credentialing, and accreditation. For example, one hears about the behavioral model of training, the consultation model of practice, the NASP model of credentialing, or the APA model of accreditation. In these contexts, *model* may connote a preference, an ideal to emulate, a theoretical orientation, or an exemplary practice. The outcome of the different usages has resulted in a litany of so-called training models. Add to those a consultation model, a scientist–practitioner model, an ecological model, a behavioral model, or a medical model (see, for example, Conoley & Gutkin, 1986). The term gets more confusing when the names are blended, such as the behavioral consultation model. Such blends may lend precision to the orientation of a particular model; however, when they are used to define training models, they fail to recognize the many forces that combine to create the specific program encountered by a student in training. For that reason, this book uses the term *model* to represent only the salient characteristics of a particular program of preparation. Every program is unique and has its own specific model, although it may resemble one or more of the master models identified below. Programs are like fingerprints that provide individual identification while conforming to general principles of anatomical design.

Master Models: Scientist–Practitioner, Professional, and Pragmatic

Various forms of three broad, or "master," training models permeate ideas about the preparation of school psychologists. The following explanations accompany Figure 6.1 and Table 6.3. Professional psychology training programs often identify themselves with either the scientist–practitioner (S–P) model or the professional model. This is especially true of doctoral programs in the development of their rationales and curricula within the accreditation parameters at the national level.

Scientist–Practitioner (S-P) Model

The S–P model was adopted for clinical psychology training at the Boulder Conference, held in Boulder, Colorado, in 1949 (Raimy, 1950). The model has been applied to the training of all professional psychologists and linked to the process of accreditation in clinical, counseling, and school psychology. The S–P model

Figure 6.1. Program-specific model of preparation.

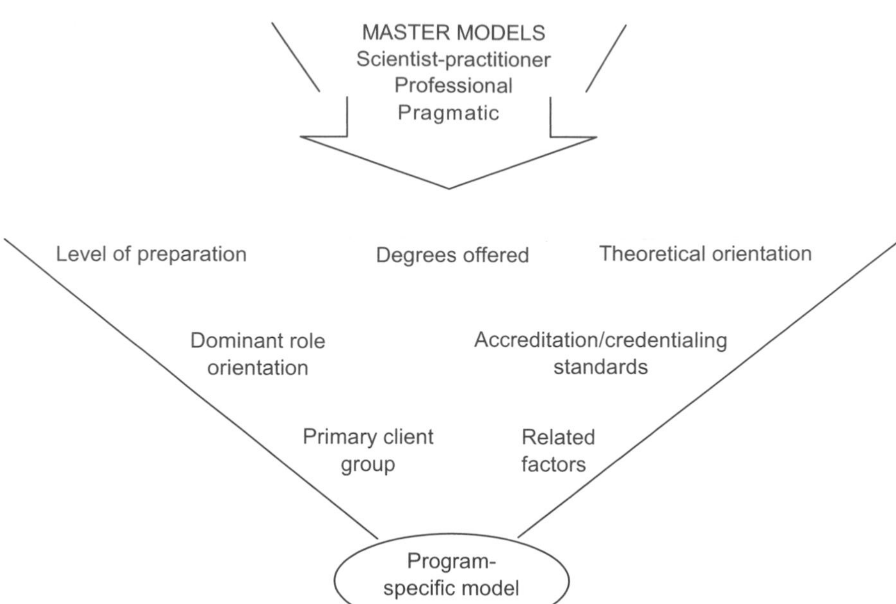

advocated that preparation "should be grounded *on* and *in* research in general and experimental psychology" and that professional psychologists should be expected to do research (Frank, 1984, p. 427). Training should include a blend of psychology's research and practice orientations so that trainees would be prepared to conduct and understand research, as well as practice effectively with clients. In this respect, the school psychologist would be expected to be, first of all, a psychologist in the traditional sense of the term, and second, a practitioner. As the model has evolved in practice, programs have identified themselves along a continuum; some emphasize training with more of a basis in science and research and others emphasize practice. The proper positioning of a program's rationale, and the demonstration of its implementation, became important to its accreditation. Programs slanted toward the scientist end of the continuum emphasize statistics, research design and experience, and theses and dissertations, and they generally view training as preparation for conducting school psychology research. On the practitioner end, requirements are greater in the areas of assessment and intervention, ethics, professional development issues, supervised practica, and other field experiences. The continuum thus balances the world of science and the world of practice.

Most programs position themselves between the two ends of the continuum. There is also the notion that the model did not intend the use of a continuum; rather, all professional psychology programs should adhere to some balance of research and practice preparation within the S–P concept.

The S–P model has been criticized on the grounds that professional psychologists do not need to be trained to perform research (few practitioners trained under the model later engage in research), that research and clinical skills may be

Table 6.3 Factors Influencing Specific Training Program Models

Level of Preparation	Degrees Offered	Theoretical Orientation
Paraprofessional	BA/BS	Psychodynamic
Entry level	MA/MS	Behavioral
	EdS	Ecological
Advanced	PsyD	Social learning
	EdD	Eclectic
	PhD	Empirical

Accreditation/Credentialing Standards	Related Factors
APA, NCATE/NASP	Faculty characteristics
State department of education	Available courses
Regional accreditation system	Institutional support
State psychology licensing board	Physical facilities
NASP national certification	Student characteristics

Dominant Role Orientation	Primary Client Group
Assessment	Infant/toddler/preschool
Consultation	Elementary
Research and evaluation	Middle/junior high
Prevention	Secondary
Interventions	Postsecondary
Systems/organizational development	Parents
Mixed	Teachers
Other	Administration/system
	Nonschool
	Urban/suburban/rural
	Mixed
	Other

incompatible, and that scientists and practitioners differ along several personal dimensions (Frank, 1984). Despite such criticisms, the model has survived. A historical discussion of the model appears in Lambert (1993).

Professional Model

With the growth of professional psychology, other training program models were put forth, including the professional model, which emerged from the Vail Conference in 1973. The Vail Conference deliberated a broad range of issues, including admissions to training programs; minority and female representation; faculty involvement in practice; understanding of social, political, and community ramifications of practice; understanding of employment settings and the range of clients served; and the need for continuing professional development (Korman, 1974). In the professional model, training to conduct research is deemphasized in favor of training for program evaluation and understanding of research. In addition, greater emphasis is placed on preparation for practice, emphasizing the professional identity of the psychologist and the world of practice. As described by Korman, the original intent of the model was not to abandon comprehensive psychological science or to depreciate the value of the S–P type of training program. Instead, it was to provide "one type of heuristic model to guide those programs defining themselves by a basic service orientation" (p. 442).

The model reflects more than just an emphasis on the practitioner end of the S–P model's continuum, though overlaps are apparent. The acceptance of the professional model is associated with the rapid growth of freestanding schools of professional psychology (not traditional university-affiliated ones) that grant the doctor of psychology degree and that prepare a large percentage of recent graduates in clinical psychology. These schools are represented by the National Council of Schools and Programs of Professional Psychology (NCSPPP), which celebrated its 30th year in 2006. The NCSPPP represents 57 APA-accredited member programs that "award more doctorates in clinical psychology than nonmembers—about 90% of them PsyDs" (DeAngelis, 2006, p. 30; for a discussion of the group's educational model see R. L. Peterson, Peterson, Abrams, & Stricker, 1997). The PsyD was proposed as far back as 1918 (Hollingworth, 1918), well before accreditation of programs or credentialing of practitioners existed. A comparison of clinical psychology PsyD programs in different types of training settings and traditional PhD programs revealed important differences in terms of admissions, length of time to completion, and student indebtedness (Norcross, Castle, Sayette, & Mayne, 2004). A comparable study in school psychology is needed.

The strong presence of the S–P model in school psychology training may be related to several factors: (a) the presence of relatively few freestanding professional schools offering the PsyD in school psychology, (b) the historic influence of educational psychology and its research orientation, (c) the slower professional development of the field compared with clinical psychology, (d) the importance of evaluation and accountability to successful practice in school settings, (e) the diversity of traditional academic units in which school psychology programs are housed, and (f) the influence of empirical orientations on the practice of school psychology, such as Gray's (1963b) data-oriented problem solver. The research aspect of the S–P model as applied to school psychology has several benefits for conceptualizations of practice, service delivery, and evaluation of both (Bardon, 1987; Martens & Keller, 1987; Stoner & Green, 1992). Widespread doctoral training is a relative newcomer to school psychology, and the attendant training ideologies have been promulgated by professionals who have long-term association with the S–P model. For example, the model fits appropriately into Phillips' (1985) distinctions between the terms *training* and *education* and into Bardon and Bennett's (1974) discussion about learning to think like a psychologist.

As school psychology has gained in professional stature, it has adopted alternative models for practitioner preparation, as already observed in clinical and counseling psychology. This shift of models recalls Cook's cautionary statement that "difficult as it may be to train the scientist–professional and then to enable him to maintain this role in his work, it offers our best hope of avoiding a commonplace profession and a disembodied science" (Cook, 1958, cited in Gray, 1963b, p. 394).

Because doctoral programs in school psychology often are intermingled with nondoctoral programs at the same institutions, the tendency is to consider the S–P model as permeating all levels of preparation. Knoff, Curtis, and Batsche (1997) believe the scientist–practitioner model should be extended to specialist-level as well as doctoral-level preparation. However, although an MS or EdS degree may be part of a doctoral program identified as scientist–practitioner, lesser training cannot be expected to fulfill the model's comprehensive preparation. The typical semester hours devoted to various aspects of study at each degree level support this position. Consequently, the S–P model can refer only to the entire preparation sequence that culminates in the doctoral degree (see Table 6.4).

Pragmatic Model

To what model, then, do nondoctoral degree programs adhere? In a third model, called the *pragmatic model*, the preparation of school psychologists is directed primarily toward the credentialing requirements of the state in which the program is located. The pragmatic model is highly prescriptive, with required courses that correspond to courses and competencies specified in state education agency regulations.

The pragmatic model overlaps both the scientist–practitioner and professional models and suggests that all professional preparation programs experience some external control. Because credentialing is important to psychologists at all levels of preparation, every program is somewhat prescriptive. However, nondoctoral programs, limited by university hourly requirements that must be aligned with state credentialing expectations, can become almost entirely prescriptive and result in a high degree of similarity among programs. Accreditation standards, which also have a prescriptive influence, may encourage similarity at the entry level while allowing advanced generalist training or subspecialization at the doctoral level. Because NASP accreditation guidelines specify competencies in many areas that also apply to nondoctoral programs, they are more prescriptive in comparison to the APA guidelines.

The pragmatic model also is appropriate and necessary for ensuring the later entry-level credentialing of trainees. Nothing in its pragmatic orientation precludes students from being educated as opposed to trained or from becoming professionals as opposed to mere technicians (Ysseldyke, 1986).

Table 6.4 Average Number of Semester Hours by Areas and Degree

Areas	Master's	Specialist	Doctorate
Core psychology	15	18	31
Assessment	10	12	13
Intervention	9	12	13
Educational foundations	6	8	8
Professional school psychology	9	16	20
Total averages (hours)	42	66	100

Source: Based on data from McMaster, Reschly, and Peters (1989).

The technician level of preparation is more likely in states where the nondoctoral credentialing standards are directed at only practice issues and prescribe virtually all of a program's coursework, and where the curriculum is oriented toward narrow, traditional psychometric tasks. However, such inflexibility among state regulations and programs is diminishing as a result of broader training and accreditation, and because school districts now recognize the need for comprehensive services.

Influences of Master Models on Program Models

The three master models influence a program's broad conceptualization of training and its subsequent development of a specific training program model. The specific model of a preparation program is influenced by factors identified in the seven categories of Table 6.3: level of preparation, degrees offered, theoretical orientation, accreditation and credentialing standards, related factors, dominant role orientation, and primary client group. Several alternatives are given for each category, but the items included are only examples and are not inclusive. The interaction of these factors culminates in the model of training observed in a specific program, and the model may be different for each program (e.g., EdS or PhD) at a single institution. For example, one program's model might be characterized as offering the specialist degree for entry-level preparation to provide services primarily in elementary school settings, and employing a behavioral orientation in a pragmatic curriculum developed to meet state certification. Another program could be characterized as being at the advanced level, culminating in the PhD to prepare school psychology academicians, and employing an ecological orientation in a curriculum slanted toward the scientific aspects of APA's scientist–practitioner model.

With so many possible combinations, it is not surprising that analyses of training models have failed to discern any single dominant or generally accepted model or the effectiveness of one specific model of training over another (see, for example, Pfeiffer & Marmo, 1981). Bardon and Bennett's (1974) comment, "Characteristic of school psychology training programs is their lack of a single, identifiable model" (p. 177), is still appropriate. Nevertheless, the diversity of program models has been judged a healthy trend that has existed for decades (Bardon, 1986; Bardon & Bennett). Even though training programs will continue to be identified with the scientist–practitioner, professional, or pragmatic master models, a more specific overall description of a program's training model will involve the interaction of several factors.

Content of Programs

The content of entry-level programs has considerable uniformity despite increased course offerings, growth in the number of training programs, and their diverse administrative locations. This uniformity reflects the influences of professional and political forces, perceptions of the realities of daily practice, and enforcement of accreditation standards at the entry level. Table 6.4 presents a summary of content-area emphases at each degree level based on the 1989 NASP *Directory of School Psychology Graduate Programs* (McMaster et al., 1989; more recent data summaries are not available). On average, entry-level training consists of a balanced menu of core psychology, assessment, intervention, and professional coursework. Doctoral training, on average, emphasizes the core psychology and professional areas while retaining almost the same emphasis on assessment, intervention, and educational foundations.

The differing emphases at the doctoral and nondoctoral levels reflect long-standing analyses of program data (Goh, 1977; Pfeiffer & Marmo, 1981; Reschly & McMaster-Beyer, 1991). In Goh's study, nine areas of emphasis were found to account for 73% of the total variance: (a) school-based consultation, (b) educational assessment and remediation, (c) behavior modification technology, (d) psychological evaluation, (e) psychotherapeutic procedures, (f) quantitative methods, (g) community involvement and consultation, (h) professional roles and issues, and (i) psychological foundations, including child development and learning. These factors were present in both doctoral and nondoctoral programs, with factors a, b, and c accounting for 49% of the variance at all levels. More recent content analyses have not been published. It is probable that content emphases have remained similar but with additional content related to multiculturalism, crisis management, and problem-solving approaches to assessment and intervention.

In the past decade, legislation has had a strong focus on the teaching and practice of interventions with research support, often referred to as empirically supported, evidence-based, or empirically validated interventions. However, a survey of school psychology training directors by Shernoff, Kratochwill, and Stoiber (2003) revealed that directors had low familiarity with many of the evidence-based interventions listed, and such interventions were less observable in courses than in practical training experiences. Evidence-based intervention in training is controversial, but is growing in acceptance. In school psychology it is part of the increasing implementation of more direct assessment and intervention procedures, including functional–behavioral assessments, and the gradual decline of projective assessment, a type of personality assessment test. A special 2005 issue of *School Psychology Quarterly* (Vol. 20, No. 4) is devoted to evidence-based parent and family interventions.

The content of entry-level programs has considerable uniformity.

Entry-Level Programs

Surveys of course content and an earlier NASP training directory (D. Brown & Lindstrom, 1977) have found the following courses and experiences to be most often present in nondoctoral, entry-level programs:

1. Advanced statistics
2. Research methods and design
3. Child and adolescent development
4. Psychology of learning
5. Intellectual assessment
6. Personality assessment
7. Educational assessment

8. Educational foundations (e.g., administration, curriculum)
9. Child study practicum
10. Seminar on school psychology
11. Counseling and psychotherapy
12. Consultation
13. Educational remediation
14. Characteristics of exceptional children
15. Behavior management
16. Practicum
17. Internship

More recent directories of training programs have not included specific analyses of curricular content. However, the specificity of SDE credentialing requirements and the nondoctoral training standards of NASP appear to have influenced a commonly observed set of nondoctoral program courses and experiences. A survey of training for projective assessment appears in Hermann and Kush (1995). Supervisory practices appear in Romans, Boswell, Carlozzi, and Ferguson (1995).

The NASP Standards for Entry-Level Training

The current NASP entry-level training program standards (NASP, 2000c) are considerably more rigorous than those first published by NASP (NASP, 1972). Even though APA Division 16 promoted training standards well before NASP did, the standards were not widely adopted by education groups. The NASP standards, promoted by way of its relationship with the National Council for Accreditation of Teacher Education (NCATE), have gained acceptance by SDEs since the 1980s. Because of their widespread acceptance, the NASP standards provide one of the best means of anticipating entry-level program content. Accreditable programs are expected to demonstrate that they have 60 or more semester hours of academic credit in didactic and field experiences. The curriculum guidelines of the NASP standards indicate areas of competency rather than specific course requirements, and they are based on the 1997 edition of *School Psychology: A Blueprint for Training and Practice II* (Ysseldyke et al., 1997). The domains are a substantial departure from the traditional requirements, which were based more on courses in the areas of psychological foundations, educational foundations, intervention and problem solving, statistics and research methodologies, and professional school psychology. The 11 domains of school psychology training and practice include the following:

1. Data-Based Decision Making and Accountability
2. Consultation and Collaboration
3. Effective Instruction and Development of Cognitive/Academic Skills
4. Socialization and Development of Life Skills

5. Student Diversity in Development and Learning
6. School and Systems Organization, Policy Development, and Climate
7. Prevention, Crisis Intervention, and Mental Health
8. Home/School/Community Collaboration
9. Research and Program Evaluation
10. School Psychology Practice and Development
11. Information Technology

The *Blueprint III* (Ysseldyke et al., 2006) will guide the content requirements of NASP's next revision of its training standards, perhaps by 2010.

The NASP standards require a minimum of 60 graduate semester hours of preparation, culminating in the granting of the specialist degree or its equivalent.

The NASP training program standards include expectations for field experiences, including practica and internship, with practica occurring prior to the supervised internship. The internship must include a minimum of 1,200 clock hours, at least half of which must be in a public school setting. Related internship standards define the nature of supervision, setting, and other experiences desired of a quality internship. The internship may be completed on a full-time basis for 1 academic year or part-time over 2 years (see chapter 8).

The NASP standards require trainees to receive a minimum of 60 graduate semester hours of preparation that meets all competency and field experiences as well as other desirable characteristics of a school psychology program (as many as 6 hours may be granted for the internship). The preparation should culminate in the granting of the education specialist degree or its equivalent. This level of preparation is usually achieved by offering the master's degree in tandem with the specialist degree (e.g., 36 and 30 hours, respectively), the specialist degree only (minimum of 60 hours), or a lengthy master's degree of 60 hours. The terms *specialist* and *sixth-year* programs represent similar levels of training, that is, 4 years of undergraduate and 2 years of graduate training, not including internship. The specialist program culminates in the awarding of the specialist degree, whereas the sixth-year program usually does not terminate with a degree, though a certificate of completion may be awarded (a sixth-year certificate or certificate of advanced graduate study). The NASP reference to specialist level can be met by any of these approaches. Specialist degree programs may have more terminal requirements (e.g., written and oral exams, research papers) than sixth-year programs. The specialist degree often requires a "culminating experience" in addition to an internship. A 1997 survey of NASP-approved nondoctoral programs revealed that the most frequently required culminating experiences were oral examination (28%), written comprehensive examination (59%), research thesis (43%), and major paper but not a thesis (21%). Other culminating experiences that were sometimes required included student portfolios and internship. Programs typically had more than one required culminating experience (Fagan, 1997). Many of these programs use the Praxis examination in school psychology as a substitute for the culminating written examination. Students must pass the examination at the level for credentialing in their state or the NCSP level from NASP (Fagan, 2005c).The curriculum and degree configuration used to comply with NASP standards depends on what graduate degrees an institution is authorized to confer. State higher education governing boards allow only certain institutions to offer post–master's degrees, including the specialist degree. With proper planning, appropriate preparation of entry-level school psychologists can be accomplished by any of the above examples. Students pursuing specialist-level training on a full-time basis should expect it to require a minimum of 3 years of full-time study, including the internship. By pursuing studies in the summer, this may be reduced somewhat, depending on the frequency and sequencing of required coursework. Part-time students should expect their training to last at least 4 years. Part-time students also should be aware that institutions maintain time limits on degrees so that after a set number of years (e.g., 6) earlier work may have to be revalidated or repeated. Every academic degree has a window within which it must be completed.

Doctoral Programs

Many doctoral programs are offered in academic departments that also offer nondoctoral school psychology programs. In some departments, a career ladder approach may be available in which students might progress from one degree to another without loss of credits. However, in most instances the doctoral degree is more than an extension of the nondoctoral level, and the doctoral track may have moderate overlap with the nondoctoral track. In some instances in the first few years of training, doctoral students may pursue a different curriculum than nondoctoral students. In other instances, the differences are minimal in the first few years, and doctoral students may even be drawn from applicants already in the nondoctoral track or from among graduates already credentialed or practicing as school psychologists. Students considering doctoral training should explore these program differences, because some may require considerably more time to complete a doctoral degree when students have followed the nondoctoral track in their early years of graduate study. As a general rule, full-time students pursuing doctoral degrees can expect a minimum of 4 years of study, which usually does not include the predoctoral internship year. Part-time study, which would take considerably longer, is available in some doctoral programs, although financial assistance is seldom available to part-time students. Part-time students should be aware that institutions maintain time limits on degrees so that after a set number of years (e.g., 10) earlier work may have to be revalidated or repeated.

Full-time students pursuing doctoral degrees can expect a minimum of 4 years of study, which usually does not include the predoctoral internship year.

NASP Standards for Doctoral-Level Training

The curriculum portion of the NASP training standards differentiates between the doctoral and nondoctoral levels by requiring that doctoral-level program provide greater depth in the multiple domains of school psychology. Thus, all of the NASP domains listed earlier apply to the content of all program levels, ensuring that both entry-level and doctoral school psychologists have a comprehensive level of preparation for the world of practice. Typically, doctoral programs place greater emphasis on research and subspecializations, structural aspects of the program, and the internship. For example, the 2000 NASP standards require a minimum of 90 graduate semester hours and a 1,500-hour internship, at least 600 hours of which are in a school setting (unless a previous school-based internship was completed). The NASP standards have outcome-based expectations in addition to the traditional process-based training standards, a trend of the past 20 years.

APA Standards for Doctoral-Level Training

In contrast to NASP, APA considers the doctoral degree as the appropriate entry level for the position of school psychologist and for independent practice in any employment setting. The APA's training expectations are directed only to the doctoral level. The APA specialty guidelines for school psychology (APA, 1981) provide a statement about the curriculum expected in the preparation of professional school psychologists:

> The education of school psychologists encompasses the equivalent of at least 3 years of full-time graduate academic study. While instructional formats and course titles may vary from program to program, each program has didactic and experiential instruction (a) in scientific and professional areas common to all professional psychology programs, such as ethics and standards, research design and methodology, statistics, and psychometric methods, and (b) in such substantive areas as the biological bases of behavior, the cognitive and affective bases of behavior, the social, cultural, ethnic, and sex role bases of behavior, and individual differences. Course work includes social and philosophical bases of education, curriculum theory and practice, etiology of learning and behavior disorders, exceptional children, and special education. Organization theory and administrative practice should also be included in the program. (p. 43)

The APA guidelines also identify the field placement expectations, which are virtually identical to those stipulated for NASP. These expectations are reflected in the specialty definition document for school psychology (*Petition for Reaffirmation of the Specialty of School Psychology,* 2005, originally approved in 1997). The APA's accreditation domain B, Program Philosophy, Objectives, and Curriculum, describes the importance of sequential training based on the science and professional practice of psychology and stipulates the following curriculum areas:

a. The breadth of scientific psychology, its history of thought and development, its research methods, and its applications.
b. The scientific, methodological, and theoretical foundations of practice in the substantive area(s) of professional psychology in which the program has its training emphasis, to include individual differences in behavior, human

development, dysfunctional behavior or psychopathology, and professional standards and ethics.

c. Diagnosing or defining problems through psychological assessment and measurement and formulating and implementing intervention strategies (including empirically supported procedures).
d. Issues of cultural and individual diversity that are relevant to all of the above.
e. Attitudes essential for lifelong learning, scholarly inquiry, and professional problem solving as psychologists in the context of an evolving body of scientific and professional knowledge.

Field experiences including practica and internships are also expected (APA, 2005, pp. 12–13). APA accreditation guidelines are applied to programs in the United States and Canada.

International School Psychology Association Standards

The International School Psychology Association (ISPA) *Guidelines for the Preparation of School Psychologists* are useful because they are cross-cultural, reflecting the guidelines of several countries (Cunningham & Oakland, 1998). The guidelines emphasize core knowledge in psychology; professional practice preparation; professional skills in decision making, reflection, and enquiry; interpersonal skills; research and statistical skills; and knowledge of ethics and establishment of professional values. Although the ISPA guidelines do not specify degree-level expectations, the general model curriculum overlaps to a large extent with the expectations of the APA, NASP, and no doubt several other countries. At present, these standards appear to have little bearing on the organization of programs in the United States and Canada. However, they will likely increase the awareness of trainees to international issues and practices. They could also have an impact on the development of programs in countries where programs do not already exist. The ISPA training guidelines and other international perspectives are discussed in chapter 10.

Nondoctoral and Doctoral Differences

Goh (1977) reported factor results on combined doctoral–subdoctoral programs and analyzed emphases that trainers rated significant to the doctoral level. The only areas consistently cited at the doctoral level were school-based consultation and quantitative methods. These results were supported by D. Brown and Minke (1986), who found that advanced graduate training in school psychology differed most from specialist training by providing areas of subspecialization and additional research information and skills. The results also were supported by Reschly and Wilson (1997) and Woody and Davenport (1998). Such differences reflect traditional conceptualizations of the doctoral degree and the significance placed on the scientist–practitioner model in professional psychology (Martens & Keller, 1987). As a general rule, the doctoral student can expect to encounter additional statistics and research courses (Little, Lee, & Akin-Little, 2003), a major research requirement such as a dissertation, related requirements such as a major area paper, additional written and oral examinations, and an internship. Some institutions accept previous internships completed at the entry level. The analyses of entry-level and doctoral programs by Reschly and McMaster-Beyer (1991) found that "the broader scope of doctoral training provides better preparation for practice in diverse settings such as private practice, mental health clinics, and medical settings and may, as well, establish a better background for understanding learning and behavior problems in school settings" (p. 373). They concluded that the different emphases in program levels support the distinction of credentials for school and nonschool practice. Thus, their analyses support the long-standing APA policies on credentialing and do not support the NASP policy that considers the specialist level as sufficient for credentialing for school and nonschool practice.

Portfolio Assessments

Irrespective of the level of training, many programs employ a portfolio assessment process. Following guidelines provided by the faculty, students develop a portfolio throughout their training that can be used as part of their overall assessment process (see e.g., Hass & Osborn, 2002). For example, students may be reviewed annually and submit their portfolios for review as part of that process. The portfolio could include transcripts of courses and grades, logs of field experiences, community service activities, research productivity, assistantship duties, letters of commendation, and other activities that speak well for the students' levels of competency or that indicate areas that need further development. Faculty and student self-ratings on competencies can be compared as part of the review process. The portfolio content areas could be designed to be compatible with accreditation training expectations, for example, to match the NASP content standards.

Internship as a Training Experience

The internship, like other field experiences, is essentially a training experience. It is a direct extension of the training program and gives students supervised opportunities within which to demonstrate knowledge and skills acquired from didactic experiences and to acquire new knowledge and skills in the field. The standards therefore require close supervision of the internship through the cooperation of the training program, the intern, and the field supervisor.

Several resources will help students who are seeking a doctoral-level internship and help them understand accreditation of those internships. (For a concise discussion of internships and their accreditation see Pryzwansky and Wendt, 1987.) Each December the *American Psychologist* lists APA-approved doctoral internship centers but does not identify them by specialization. The magnitude of this enterprise is reflected in the December 2005 listing of more than 500 pre- and postdoctoral internship sites in 46 states, the District of Columbia, Puerto Rico, and Canada (Accredited Internship and Postdoctoral Programs for Training in Psychology: 2005, 2005). The Association of Psychology Postdoctoral and Internship Programs (APPIC) publishes an annual directory of its members who meet specific doctoral internship criteria, and APA-accredited internships are automatically included. Each of the internship entries identifies which psychology specialties (clinical, counseling, and school) are sought and whether only APA-accredited program applicants are selected or if they are preferred or acceptable. Non-APA-accredited applicants are rated accordingly. The 2005–2006 *APPIC Directory* listed 595 agencies accepting one or more specialties (APPIC, 2005). Only six of these agencies were identified as school districts, four of which were APA approved.

The APPIC initiated a computer matching program for internships and applicants in 1998–1999. The rationale and matching program are described in Keilin (1998). According to APPIC online data (*www.appic.org*), the match rate in school psychology was 83% in 1999 and 2003 and did not differ significantly from other areas of professional psychology. The 2003 match rates for students pursuing the PhD were significantly higher than those for PsyD students (85% vs. 77%). There is also an annual guide to full-time and half-time internship sites that either specifically seek or will accept school psychology trainees. The 2006 edition listings (APA and NASP, 2006) included 420 full-time and 36 half-time predoctoral internships at 92 sites, 78 of which reported paying stipends; the 2006–2007 median stipend was $18,187. Seven full-time postdoctoral positions were listed, with median stipends of $29,000. This directory incorporates the APPIC listings and is among the best sources for doctoral students in school psychology.

The relative scarcity of doctoral-level school psychology internship sites and their limited geographic distribution are serious barriers to the development of school psychology programs at the doctoral level. Another barrier is that some of APPIC's requirements for getting internships listed in its directory are perceived as incompatible with the delivery of school psychological services in many settings (e.g., availability of additional professional psychologists and interns). As a result, few of the internships listed are in school districts; most are in medical facilities, mental health centers, or residential schools. The Council of Directors of School Psychology Programs (CDSPP), a doctoral program faculty group, is an advocate for the creation of additional school-based and school-psychology-related internships and approved internship guidelines (CDSPP, 1998).

Because NASP internship requirements are part of its training standards, and because those standards are directed at entry-level school practice, it is not surprising that the NASP standards are inconsistent with those of APPIC. With increased student interest in obtaining doctoral degrees, there is a strong need for NASP to develop separate doctoral standards for training and to assist in developing a greater number of nationally accredited doctoral internship sites. The selection and evaluation of doctoral-level internships typically are controlled by the program, the student, and the internship site. M. Brown, Kissell, and Bolen (2003) reviewed doctoral-level internships in nonschool settings. School psychology interns were found to have strengths in traditional practice areas (e.g., assessment and consultation) and weaknesses in counseling and psychotherapy, an area that was commonly practiced in those settings.

The relative scarcity of doctoral-level school psychology internship sites and their limited geographic distribution are serious barriers to the development of school psychology programs at the doctoral level.

Brown et al. suggested that doctoral students seeking nonschool internships seek additional preparation in these areas.

Many internships are available at the nondoctoral level, but there is no national directory of sites. Some states have well-organized internship systems coordinated among the training programs, state departments of education, and internship sites, which are usually local school districts. Ohio and Illinois are excellent examples of this level of organization, and each state may offer as many as 100 sites each year. Unfortunately, most states are not well organized, and internships are found or created on an ad hoc basis and controlled only by the training program and the internship site. In these states, internships often are simply informal arrangements between the training program and selected local school districts.

Subspecializations

The term *specialty* refers to the professional fields of clinical psychology, counseling, school psychology, and others approved by the APA Commission for the Recognition of Specialties and Proficiencies in Professional Psychology (CRSPPP; B. Murray, 1995). In February 1998, under the Petition for Reaffirmation of the Specialty of School Psychology, school psychology was among the first specialties to receive approval (*Petition for Reaffirmation of the Specialty of School Psychology*, 2005; originally approved in 1997; Phelps, 1998). Although most specialist-level programs are prescriptive, thus precluding students from concentrating their studies in a particular area of expertise, doctoral-level programs usually provide opportunities for subspecialization or for more in-depth coverage of different topics through elective courses. Subspecialties are areas of special proficiency or competency within the specialty of school psychology. Because many school psychology doctoral programs combine courses from academic units in psychology and education, a variety of advanced generalist and subspecialty concentrations are available. In some programs, the subspecialization permeates several aspects of the program, including its field experiences. For example, a doctoral program preparing school psychologists with a subspecialization in neuropsychology may expect students to complete a dissertation on a neuropsychological topic and to seek an internship in a medical facility with supervised neuropsychological training.

In a previous survey of doctoral programs, almost two thirds of U.S. doctoral programs had an advanced generalist orientation, with most of these allowing the student to develop a subspecialty. More than 30 subspecialties were identified as associated with particular doctoral programs, with the most frequent being behavioral assessment and intervention, consultation, neuropsychology, preschool and early childhood, and prevention (see Fagan & Wise, 2000, pp. 213–217). The results were comparable to a survey conducted 10 years earlier (see Fagan & Wise, 1994, pp. 183–186). An unusual subspecialty, school psychology and sport psychology, was the focus in 2005 of a special issue of the *Journal of Applied School Psychology* (Vol. 21, No. 2).

More than 30 subspecialties were identified, with the most frequent being behavioral assessment and intervention, consultation, neuropsychology, preschool and early childhood, and prevention.

In rare instances, subspecialization is provided at the specialist entry level. For example, Gallaudet University in Washington, DC, offers nondoctoral subspecialization with the deaf and hard of hearing. Because many subspecializations are related as much or more to faculty expertise as to a commitment of the administrative unit, subspecializations may wax or wane as a function of faculty mobility and interests. For instance, rural subspecialization is not always related to the geographic location of the program (Cummings, Huebner, & McLeskey, 1985). Some students attend urban universities but obtain rural subspecialization as a function of selected courses, faculty expertise, and field experiences. In short, when faculty members leave, the subspecialization often goes with them.

Generalist and Subspecialty Preparation

Throughout the history of school psychology, most practitioners have performed a variety of functions while adapting to the range of problems presented to them. The necessity for practitioners to have broad training to meet these conditions has long been recognized. Thus, most entry-level training programs embraced a generalist orientation that drew upon knowledge and skills from educational foundations, experimental and clinical psychology, special education, and related fields. The generalist model has prevailed in training despite the common reference to school psychologists as being specialists or members of specialized services teams or as holding a specialist degree.

With the rapid development of the profession since the 1970s, the issue of whether practitioners should be trained as generalists or specialists has gained increasing attention. Studies have suggested that rural or urban practitioners benefit from specialized training experiences related to the sociocultural characteristics of their settings; that subspecialty training is more likely to occur in doctoral programs than in nondoctoral programs; and that there is a need for, and growing interest in, several areas of subspecialization, including consultation, early childhood and family services, bilingual and bicultural services, neuropsychology, and vocational school psychology.

Several factors interact to encourage greater subspecialization, including an increasing number of students selecting doctoral programs, the continuing-education requirements of the NASP National Certification System, a strong employment market for doctoral generalists and subspecialists both in and out of school settings, and the implementation of state and federal regulations. For example, the Education of the Handicapped Act Amendments of 1986 (Pub. L. 99-457) may have increased job opportunities for school psychologists who have subspecializations in the infant–toddler and preschool levels. This demand is enhanced by the No Child Left Behind Act (Pub. L. 107-110), with its academic achievement expectations and the growing emphasis on early literacy and reading skills.

In the past, most psychologists with areas of subspecialization were clinical psychologists. It was fairly common for referrals to be exchanged between school psychologists in school settings and clinical psychologists in nonschool agencies or private practice. An offshoot of the increased number of doctoral practitioners and those with subspecialties is the trend of school psychologists moving into nonschool practice in hospitals, clinics, professional groups, and self-employment (D'Amato & Dean, 1989). Although the trend is observable, it has not been strong, nor has it reduced the size of the school-based workforce. However, as the trend continues and school psychologists enter private practice or nonschool agencies, competition will build between them and clinical or counseling psychologists. It will be more common in the future to see school-based school psychologists making referrals to non-school-based school psychologists. It also is likely that the schools will commonly employ generalists and that school psychologists in the nonschool sector will compete with one another for referrals from the schools. Some of that competition will be among school psychologists with recognized subspecialties. Finally, developments in clinical and counseling psychology indicate that school psychologists in nonschool settings will be self-employed or employed in community agencies and will seek collective employment with other health services providers, which will encourage greater subspecialization. Students or practitioners who are planning doctoral-level preparation should consider their desire and need for either advanced generalist or subspecialty training.

Of course, through experience, continuing education, and personal interests, many school psychologists specialize without obtaining a doctoral degree. For example, recognizing a need in their employment settings, school psychologists may obtain additional expertise in the assessment of low-incidence handicaps, preschool assessment, or parent training. Educators' concerns about violence in the schools have encouraged many school psychologists to develop additional skills in prevention, risk assessment, and crisis intervention. As practitioners become more experienced, they commonly develop areas of special expertise. Such subspecialization does not always involve returning to graduate school for formal preparation. Frequently the necessary expertise is gained through conventions, workshops, in-depth reading, and supervised apprenticeships.

The interest in subspecializations can be observed in the growth in popularity and number of special interest groups in NASP. Initiated in the late 1970s, these groups have become a vehicle for promoting communication among members who share expertise in selected areas. In 1992 NASP had 14 interest groups and in 1998–1999 it had 10. In 2006–2007 the 19 subspecialty areas included autism and pervasive developmental disorders, behavioral school psychology, character education and social–emotional learning, computer and technological applications in school psychology, consultee-centered consultation, crisis management in the schools, early childhood education, military families, multiculturalism, neuropsychology in the schools, positive psychology, prevention, reading, retirement, rural school psychology, school psychologists working with students who are deaf or hard of hearing, state school psychology consultants, students of school psychology, and supervision. The changes reflect the growth in numbers of practitioners and their shifting interests over time. School psychologists who have subspecialties and belong to interest groups are active in policy development and in preparing manuscripts for journals.

CONTINUING PROFESSIONAL DEVELOPMENT

Formal preparation should provide the basic skills, theories, concepts, and supervised experiences needed to successfully initiate a professional career. Regardless of an individual's entry level in the profession, even at the doctoral level, there is an expectation of continued professional development (CPD). The range of settings, clients, presenting problems, and professional issues are simply too great to be accounted for in formal academic preparation. Formal preparation attempts to bring the future professional to a broad understanding of psychology and education, and to inculcate a sense of professional responsibility that includes recognizing when one's skills and professional judgments are insufficient to deal with certain situations.

Throughout the history of school psychology, various informal means have existed for achieving CPD, such as journals and convention programs. More formal opportunities have developed in the past several decades, especially after the 1950s, when the Division of School Psychology (Division 16) initiated professional institutes for school psychologists (Fagan, 1993). With the unprecedented growth of state-level school psychology associations since 1970, every state has offered CPD opportunities to varying degrees. Workshops and skill development programs have become very popular. The annual conventions of the APA and NASP provide excellent opportunities for developing and improving skills. Division 16 offers school psychology presentations in the context of the APA convention. Several associations and publishers, including APA and NASP, offer audiotapes, videotapes, and CDs for rent or sale on numerous topics, including conference presentations. The Internet offers another potential source for CPD, and practitioners have access to PowerPoint and Web-based programs. For example, NASP offers online CPD modules to members. A guide to Internet sources for school psychologists is provided by Steingart (2005). The APA website also offers online CPD modules that help practitioners meet requirements for continued licensure and could be used for the NCSP (*www.apa.org/ce*).

Regardless of an individual's entry level in the profession, even at the doctoral level, there is an expectation of continued professional development (CPD).

National Certification Requirement for CPD

The most organized CPD effort in school psychology is that included in NASP's National School Psychology Certification System. In addition to its membership requirements, the system requires that the school psychologist complete at least 75 contact hours of CPD within each 3-year renewal period. Certificate holders are expected to obtain CPD in a variety of job-related activity areas. The choices of activities are flexible and include nine categories, each with credit allowances, ceiling limits, and required documentation: workshops, conferences, and in-service training; college or university courses; teaching and training activities; research and publications; supervision of interns; postgraduate supervised experiences; program planning and evaluation; sequenced or informal self-study programs; and leadership in professional organizations. Some states' departments of education, psychology licensing boards, and state associations for school psychologists also have CPD requirements. Though not specific to school psychology, APA-sanctioned continuing education programs are frequently listed in its newsletter, the *Monitor on Psychology.*

Respecialization

Students occasionally wonder what to expect if they decide to switch from one professional psychology specialty to another (e.g., from school to clinical psychology) or to change from a nonprofessional to a professional field (e.g., from a developmental psychology concentration major to school psychology). Few institutions offer formal retread programs; however, some will admit students who have already completed a doctoral degree in a psychology field. The retraining process involves the completion of all requirements, often including an internship, or a second internship, for respecialization. Although allowances will usually be made for some common requirements, such as certain courses and research experiences, retraining can be expected to require at least 1 year of academic preparation and an additional year of internship. Two examples include Crespi (1999), who describes the program of respecialization at Hartford University, and Haggan and Dunham (2002), who provide an analysis of what might be required for nondoctoral clinical psychologists seeking respecialization in school psychology.

Postdoctoral Study

Postdoctoral study in psychology has been available for many decades but has only recently been considered by doctoral recipients in school psychology. Its general absence is a function of the lack of postdoctoral opportunities specifically in school psychology and the strong employment market for doctoral recipients. In some fields of psychology, the employment market has been less attractive and doctoral recipients have sought postdoctoral studies to make themselves more competitive for future, usually academic, positions. With increased subspecialization in school psychology doctoral programs, postdoctoral study is a natural extension of graduate work. It is also possible that the increasing professionalization of the field will eventually require postdoctoral study for full practice privileges in the private sector, especially in medical-related facilities. Many states require a year of postdoctoral supervised experience for psychology licensure by the SBEP. Furthermore, there is ongoing discussion of guidelines for postdoctoral education and training in school psychology and of APA accreditation of postdoctoral residency study (Pryzwansky, 1998; Shaw, 2002).

A study by Logsdon-Conradsen et al. (2001) described postdoctoral fellowship practices and suggested that only a small percentage of school psychology doctoral recipients pursued such activities. As of December 2005, the APA accredited only nine postdoctoral sites, and none appeared specific to school psychology. Nevertheless, some supervised postdoctoral opportunities for school psychologists are available, and guidelines for such advanced preparation are supported by the APA Division of School Psychology and the overarching multigroup representation of the School

Psychology Synarchy Group. With limited but important legislative gains in the area of pharmaceutical privileges for licensed doctoral psychologists, increased doctoral and postdoctoral opportunities for training in psychopharmacology are anticipated. J. Carlson, Demaray, and Oehmke (2006) found that although one fourth of practitioners surveyed had clients who were being treated with psychotropic medications, the practitioners' training had come most frequently from workshops and reading. The importance of this training to school and other professional psychologists is discussed in Phelps, Brown, and Power (2002); in J. Carlson, Thaler, and Hirsch (2005); and in a special 2005 issue of *School Psychology Quarterly* (Vol. 20, No. 2).

NONCURRICULAR PROGRAM CHARACTERISTICS AND ACCREDITATION

Many aspects of a program's overall quality are not necessarily obvious from an inspection of its curriculum. The NASP online Career Center offers students assistance in selecting a training program by providing information about the field and specific training programs, as well as employment information. Gerner and Genshaft (1981) advised students to examine several factors when making program selections and included hints for interviewing when applying to programs and internships. They suggest how to judge a program's orientation, its involvement with students, balance of content, and relationships with other academic units. Accreditation guidelines of APA and NCATE/NASP also cover many areas in addition to program content.

National Accreditation

School psychology program accreditation is conducted by both the APA and the National Council for Accreditation of Teacher Education. In the NCATE process, programs are evaluated against the NASP standards (hence, NCATE/NASP is used in reference to school psychology accreditation). However, NASP is not an accrediting body but an affiliate of NCATE. In the NCATE accreditation process, NASP evaluates programs through a review process in which a program must document that it meets each of the NASP standards. The program review process was introduced with the revised NCATE accreditation process of the mid-1980s. NASP forwards its recommendations to NCATE as part of that broader accreditation review. NCATE performs a similar but broader review of the institution's education unit of which the school psychology program is a part (e.g., the college of education). The NASP standards used in the NCATE process include the areas of program context and structure, domains of school psychology training and practice, field experiences and internship, performance-based program assessment and accountability, and program support and resources.

The APA accreditation standards apply to professional psychology generally and are not specific to school psychology programs. As of 2006, APA continued to offer accreditation only to programs in clinical, counseling, and school psychology and to combinations of these specialties. Other specialties or subspecialties are not yet recognized for accreditation. The APA process focuses on a program's identification with psychology regardless of its institutional location. APA accreditation reviews several domains, including a program's general eligibility; philosophy, objectives, and curriculum; program resources; cultural and individual differences and diversity; student–faculty relations; program self-assessment and quality enhancement; public disclosure; and relationship with the accrediting body (APA, 2005). A noticeable difference between the standards of APA and those of NCATE/NASP is APA's focus on the psychological character of the program and its clear curricular and noncurricular identification with professional psychology and either the scientist–practitioner or professional model.

Despite the favorable evaluation of a pilot project in 1982–1983, a joint APA–NCATE accreditation process has never been implemented (Fagan & Wells, 2000). At present, parallel reviews may be conducted by both agencies, but a truly joint process that blends the standards of each agency does not exist. Although it is possible that NASP will attain greater autonomy for program reviews through the NCATE process, which could open avenues for further collaboration with APA at the doctoral level, this collaboration is unlikely.

The most recent comprehensive NASP *Directory of School Psychology Graduate Programs* (Thomas, 1998) indicated that NCATE accredited 180 (61%) of the 294 reporting programs, including 102 (53%) of the 194 specialist-level programs. At the doctoral level, NCATE/NASP or NCATE/NASP and APA accredited 78 (90%) of the 87 programs. APA-only accredited programs accounted for 44 (51%). In the same analysis, virtually all programs held SDE approval. However, 128 of the 294 programs (44%) are identified as having only SDE approval, suggesting that only about 56% of all programs hold some form of national accreditation (see also Fagan & Wells, 2000). In 2005–2006, there were 67 APA-accredited doctoral programs in school psychology (including 10 combined programs), which constituted about 75% of available programs in the United States and Canada (Accredited Doctoral Programs in Professional Psychology, 2005, and Supplement, 2006).

The decisions of NCATE and APA accrediting bodies provide an excellent source of information about school psychology programs. Each year the APA publishes a list of accredited doctoral programs in its December issue of *American Psychologist.* NCATE publishes its *Annual List of NCATE Accredited Institutions*, which includes programs in school psychology at the doctoral and nondoctoral levels in the accredited education units. Because NCATE officially accredits the education unit and not specific programs within the unit, a school psychology program's listing in NCATE's annual list does not in itself guarantee that the program met NASP guidelines. A list of those programs that were granted conditional or full approval by NASP in its review process is available from NASP's website and is periodically published in the *Communiqué.* Lists of accredited programs and copies of the accreditation standards may be obtained by writing to the following organizations or visiting their websites:

1. American Psychological Association, Education Directorate, Office of Program Consultation and Accreditation, 750 First St. NE, Washington, DC 20002-4242 (*www.apa.org/ed/accred.html*).

2. National Council for Accreditation of Teacher Education, 2010 Massachusetts Ave. NW, Suite 500, Washington, DC 20036-1023 (*ncate@ncate.org*).
3. National Association of School Psychologists, 4340 East West Highway, Suite 402, Bethesda, MD 20814-9457 (*www.nasponline.org*).

State and Regional Accreditation

Several states have their own process of program approval whereby the SDE reviews school psychology programs either independently or concurrently with others' reviews (e.g., through NCATE partnerships). A list of states employing program approval or partnership agreements can be requested from NCATE or from the National Association of State Consultants for School Psychological Services. NASP's interest group on State School Psychology Consultants also has a list. In almost all instances, the institution in which a school psychology program is located participates in regional accreditation. National accreditation is predicated on the institution holding proper regional accreditation. The names and addresses of the six regional accrediting bodies are available through most libraries or from NCATE. A historical overview of school psychology accreditation appears in Fagan and Wells (2000).

Paraprofessional Training

Issues of training and accreditation are directed only at sanctioned levels of preparation in school psychology. These include the master's, specialist, and doctoral programs. Because master's programs of less than 60 hours are diminishing in availability, the question is occasionally raised as to whether there is a role for school psychological personnel with less training. An individual with this level of preparation, often referred to as a paraprofessional, "undergoes training involving certain limited aspects of a discipline and works alongside the professional under direction and supervision" (McManus, 1986, p. 10). Paraprofessionals perform a range of very specific skill-oriented tasks and may be trained at the master's or bachelor's level; in some instances school psychologists may even train students at the local district level as assistants. Gerken (1981) noted the early interest of NASP in paraprofessionals through its competency continuum, which consisted of seven levels (NASP, 1973). She also noted that the practice has failed to gain widespread acceptability because of fears that paraprofessionals would reduce potential positions for better qualified school psychologists and perhaps erode the quality of services. McManus (1986) described the use of student paraprofessionals in the areas of peer tutoring and counseling, record keeping, and assessment, and she reviewed literature suggesting the consumer benefits of expanding the role of the school psychologist to other activities.

The paraprofessional concept attracted more attention in the early 1980s than in recent years. The reviews of Gerken (1981) and McManus (1986) continue to be the most comprehensive available in the school psychology literature. Together they provide strong support for the concept and use of paraprofessionals to complement and improve the delivery of school psychological services. They provided examples of successful models in several settings and guidelines for the use of paraprofessionals for those interested in establishing such practices in their own settings. Additional opinions are expressed in the NASP *Communiqué* (Vol. 9, No. 6, and Vol. 10, No. 6). A more recent discussion of using testing technicians to support traditional services does not recommend the practice based on training, credentialing, ethical, and testing standards (J. E. Hall et al., 2005). The use of paraprofessionals in building-level instructional activities is fairly widespread (e.g., teacher aides), but in response to the expectations of the NCLB, several states now require paraprofessionals to be certified (Christie, 2005). The NASP Listserv often discusses the work of less-trained testing professionals in and out of the school system. Although viewpoints vary, it seems clear that most entry-level school psychologists are dissatisfied with the quality of such services. It is doubtful that the field of school psychology will support paraprofessional training and credentialing in school psychological services, although the use of paraprofessionals in various instructional roles would be supported.

Paraprofessionals perform a range of very specific skill-oriented tasks and may be trained at the master's or bachelor's level.

PROGRAM COMPLETION

Every program in every academic department exists within a bureaucratic institution of higher education. The experienced graduate student can tell the entering graduate student that there is more to graduating than just completing the courses and field experiences. The program's regimen of courses and experiences is the content of one's training, but students face many rules and regulations for actually completing the degree. These very important requirements are usually spelled out in the institution's graduate bulletin or in a departmental graduate student handbook. These publications are the student's guide to degree completion and should be read carefully. The faculty is not responsible for making sure students have reviewed and followed them. For example, it is the student's responsibility to know how and when the thesis or dissertation is to be filed with the graduate school. Thus, it is important for students to know the requirements and procedures for the following:

1. Selecting an adviser and major professor
2. Preparing a degree plan
3. Registering for courses, including changes of program
4. Taking leaves of absence
5. Transferring credits, taking experiential credits, and getting credits by examination
6. Getting annual student evaluations
7. Securing financial support
8. Fulfilling expectations for students granted fellowships or research or graduate assistantships

9. Securing field experiences
10. Choosing a thesis and dissertation committee
11. Taking specialty examinations
12. Conducting and defending one's research, including getting clearance from departmental and institutional research review committees
13. Filing for graduation
14. Seeking employment

In addition to graduation requirements, there are hurdles in the filing of materials for credentialing. Early in their training, new students should inquire about the process of filing for certification and licensure. This will avoid considerable difficulty at the end of the formal training period. This process is discussed in chapter 7.

Chapter 7

The Regulation of School Psychology

The professional control and regulation of school psychology is conceptualized in three spheres: accreditation, credentialing, and practice. Chapter 6 discussed the nature of training and identified its relationships with accreditation and credentialing. This chapter reviews the many factors that influence and regulate the field of school psychology, including the preparation of students, how school psychologists are credentialed for practice, and the factors that influence their day-to-day roles and functions. The variables involved in the three spheres are interrelated but have considerable independence.

Unlike most other books about school psychology, this book does not have a separate chapter on legal and ethical aspects of the field. Legal and ethical issues are best understood in the context of regulation and daily practice. Combining them in this chapter provides a more integrated, realistic, and comprehensible treatment of school psychology's regulation and brings such matters to bear on important issues of practice. Although all school psychologists will encounter legal and ethical aspects of their practice, few will be involved in practice litigation. At the same time, all school psychologists face training and credentialing controls and are confronted by a complex array of variables that influence their practice, including legal and ethical variables. Furthermore, many introductory school psychology courses require students to study comprehensive treatments of legal and ethical considerations, which are more readily available than in the past.

All school psychologists face training and credentialing controls and are confronted by a complex array of variables that influence their practice, including legal and ethical variables.

Before beginning this chapter, students could consider and list the factors they believe influence or control (a) their school psychologist training program, (b) their credentialing requirements, and (c) anticipated roles and functions in the field of school psychology. After reading this chapter, students can compare their list to the factors discussed.

BACKGROUND AND INTRODUCTION

The mature status of a profession is indicated by its internal and external regulation. Among the most salient symbols of maturity that help to define a profession are its recognition and regulation through accreditation and credentialing.

Note: Portions of this chapter appeared in Fagan (1990a) and are reproduced here by permission of the National Association of School Psychologists.

Professionalism

A *profession* is typically defined along the lines of practitioners' specialized knowledge, advanced training, independence and autonomy, and moral commitment. The professional "does not work in order to be paid, but is paid in order to work" (Hatch, 1988, p. 2). That psychology is a profession is no longer a matter of debate (Bevan, 1981; Fox, Barclay, & Rodgers, 1982; Petersen, 1976). Psychology's professional status has been achieved through its unique academic origins and field experiences and also has involved the acquisition of the major symbols of professionalism, including (a) the organization of the members of the profession into an association, (b) an identifiable body of knowledge unique to the profession, (c) restricted access to this body of knowledge, (d) a code of professional conduct and ethics, (e) specialized training, (f) credentialing, (g) regulation of training practices, (h) professional autonomy in practice, (i) employment opportunities for professionals, and (j) a body of literature specific to the profession. School psychology, as a specialty area within psychology, also has acquired most of the major symbols of professionalism. Some in the field contend that it should be considered a separate profession; however, the same could be said of other specialty areas of psychology. It is generally accepted that the major professional psychology specialties (e.g., clinical, counseling, and school psychology) have long shared considerable knowledge and practice (Bardon, 1979; McKinley & Hayes, 1987) and, therefore, are not separate professions. Thus, they are customarily referred to as the profession of psychology and the specialty of school psychology.

Increased professionalization is accompanied by increased regulation. Such regulation usually accords the profession greater prestige and respect, because regulation implies that the field has advanced to a point at which the public and the profession require protection from unqualified practitioners. The forms of professional regulation may be internal, such as a code of ethics, as well as external to the field, such as legislation and licensing laws. Even though the concept of professional regulation may have negative connotations, such as increased regimentation and decreased flexibility, none of the established professions are without regulation. According to Schudson (1980), "What is distinctive about the professions is nothing intrinsic to the work of professionals but is simply the status-honor they somehow accrue. ... Social recognition is the crucial feature in defining a profession" (p. 218). This chapter discusses several factors that help to define school psychology as a major professional specialty of psychology while at the same time controlling the field in various ways.

Emergence of Regulation

The present structure of factors influencing the regulation of school psychology evolved over several decades. As observed in chapter 2, the earliest national credential for psychologists was that granted through the short-lived American Psychological Association's certification program of the 1920s. State-level regulation of school psychology originated in the 1930s with state department of education (SDE) certification standards in New York and Pennsylvania. These were the earliest state-level attempts to regulate how individuals became credentialed to practice school psychology. The certification standards were no doubt influenced by existing training in those states and by laws regulating the examination of children under the provision of special educational programs for the mentally retarded. The SDE certification standards were intended for, and limited to, psychological service providers within the jurisdiction of the SDE, typically the public schools. Following World War II, psychologists began to be licensed for private practice by a separate state board of examiners in psychology (SBEP), whose statewide jurisdiction had broad practice exemptions for government agencies, including the public school systems. The separate credentialing models by SDE and SBEP were employed in other states, and by the late 1970s both avenues of credentialing were available in almost every state. Each model was aligned with state and national education groups or psychology groups, thus resulting in two separate networks of credentialing standards and practices for school psychologists.

Somewhat later, primarily in the 1960s and 1970s, national accreditation was initiated to regulate school psychology training programs. In some states, official SDE program approval, linked to its own certification regulations, preceded national-level accreditation. For example, the SDE would review a training program for school psychological examiners or school psychologists and would officially designate the program as having met its requirements for certification. Graduates of an approved program would thereby be "entitled" to certification for practice in the settings under the jurisdiction of the SDE. Because public education was regulated and represented through state-level organizations and agencies that were aligned with national-level groups, national accreditation of training programs in the arena of education, including school psychology, was brought under the jurisdiction of education accreditors. Currently the major education accreditor is the National Council for Accreditation of Teacher Education (NCATE), which was formed from a merger of other education groups in 1954 and began reviewing school psychology programs in the 1960s (Fagan & Wells, 2000).

The psychology arena developed as a separate entity with its own state-level regulatory and representative groups and agencies. These state-level groups and agencies also had national-level counterparts, such as the APA, that developed a system of accreditation for professional psychology. The major psychology sector accreditor is the APA, which has accredited doctoral programs in professional psychology since the late 1940s. SBEP has never conducted state-level program approval (like that of the SDE) in the psychology sector. That is, state psychology boards have never been in the business of reviewing training programs and formally approving them. Instead, state psychology boards have relied on the accreditation and recognition processes of the APA, regional accreditors, or other groups. The accreditation of school psychology programs by NCATE or the APA became better defined during the 1970s. The APA accredited its first school psychology program in 1971. Although the relationship between NCATE and NASP dates to the early 1970s, NCATE's accreditation of school psychology programs employing NASP standards did not occur until the early 1980s. Today almost all school psychology training programs hold SDE program approval or national-level accreditation or both (Thomas, 1998). Discussions of historical aspects of credentialing and accreditation appear in Fagan and Wells (2000) and Pryzwansky (1993).

The duality of control is evident in so many aspects of the field of school psychology that have been created out of the "two worlds" of school psychology: education and psychology.

The history of the regulation of day-to-day practice is less clear. Although guidelines for school psychology practice have been in existence for just the past few decades, the APA published its first statement of professional ethics in 1953 (APA, 1953). Several revisions have been published, and the most recent edition appears in appendix C (APA, 2002). The NASP ethical principles were first published in 1974 and were revised in 1984, 1992, 1997, and, most recently, in 2000 (see appendix D and NASP, 2000a). Many other factors influence day-to-day practice, including local employment circumstances, legislation, litigation, and funding.

In summary, the regulation of school psychology is a mixture of factors in the arenas of education and psychology for credentialing, accreditation, and practice.

Structure of Accreditation and Credentialing

The complexity of the historical links between accreditation and credentialing is shown in Figure 7.1. The structure of these relationships is presented in the summary analysis in Figure 7.2. When Figure 7.2 is superimposed on Figure 7.1, what emerges are two major areas of quality control in the profession: (a) accreditation, the procedure for evaluating the preparation of potential school psychologists, and (b) credentialing, the procedure for granting titles and functions to students who have completed their professional preparation. In recent years, SDEs have further confused the credentialing arena by increasingly using the term *licensure* instead of *certification* as the credential they grant. To simplify, this discussion uses the term *SDE license* to refer to practice credentials granted by the state department of education and the term *SBEP license* to refer to practice credentials granted by the state board of examiners in psychology. In some states the SDE or the SBEP credential is still referred to as a certificate. The range of titles employed by the SDE or SBEP appears in Curtis, Hunley, and Prus (1998).

A few guidelines will help to clarify the relationships described by Figures 7.1 and 7.2.

1. *Power and authority relationships.* In Figure 7.1 dotted lines represent power relationships and solid lines represent authority relationships, regardless of the extent of power that may coexist (see chapter 3). Inspection of Figure 7.1 reveals a considerably greater number of power relationships than authority relationships involved in accreditation and credentialing. Although it often seems to be a necessity, decisions to get involved in accreditation or credentialing are in fact strictly voluntary for training programs, agencies, associations, and individuals. There may be serious consequences for nonparticipation, but the process is voluntary.
2. *Accreditation and credentialing.* Organization, committee, and agency relationships in the top portion of the chart (north) relate to accreditation; those in the bottom portion of the chart (south) relate to credentialing. Relationships in the north portion of the chart are typically conducted at the national level, whereas those in the south portion are typically conducted at the state level. No authoritative link exists between the north and the south; that is, the regulation of credentialing is largely independent of the regulation

of training. Nevertheless, powerful and influential relationships exist between the sectors. These relationships appear in Figure 7.2.

3. *Structures and policies in relation to education and psychology.* Organization, committee, and agency relationships in the left portion (west) of the chart relate to established structures and policies of education. Those on the right portion (east) of the chart relate to psychology. Few authoritative links exist between the east and the west; that is, the regulation of psychology is largely independent of the regulation of education. Within both the education and

Figure 7.1. Power and authority for accreditation and credentialing in school psychology.

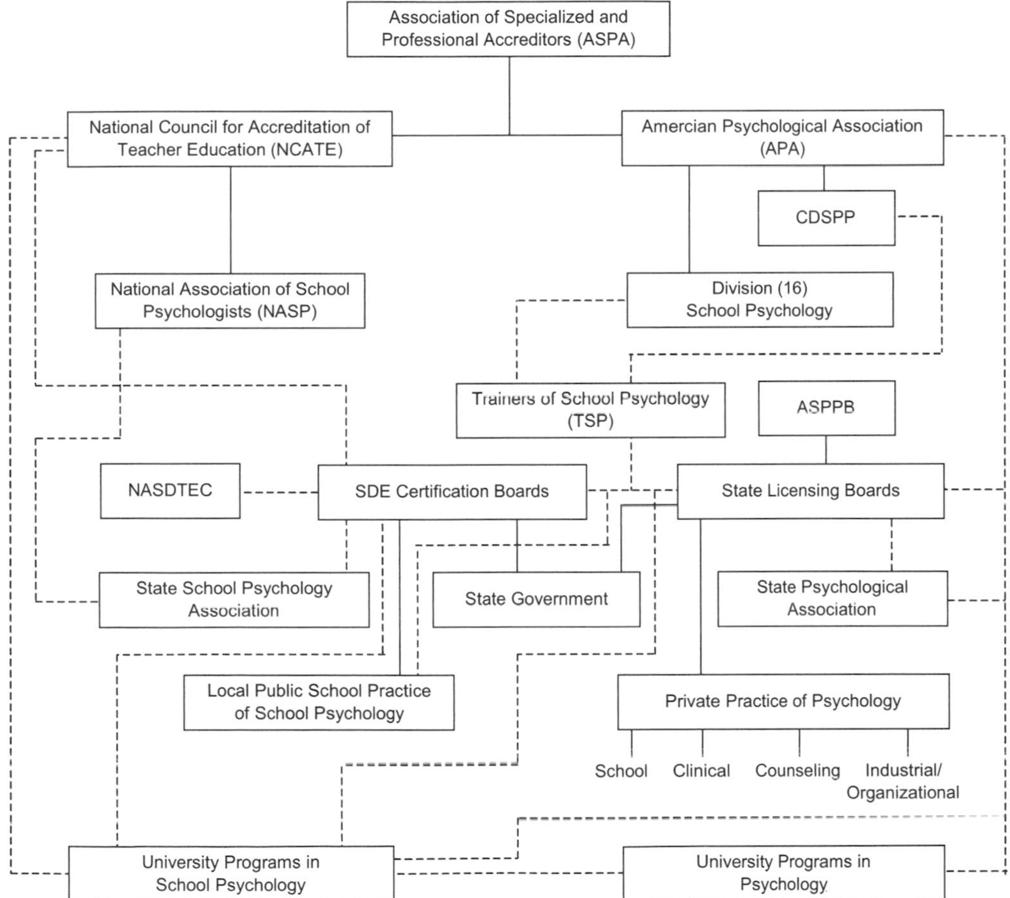

ASPPB is the Association of State and Provincial Psychology Boards
CDSPP is the Council of Directors of School Psychology Programs
NASDTEC is the National Association of State Directors of Teacher Education and Certification
SDE is state departments of education
Source: "School Psychology's Dilemma: Reappraising Solutions and Directing Attention to the Future," by T. K. Fagan, 1986c, *American Psychologist, 41*, pp. 851–861. Copyright 1986 by the American Psychological Association. Reprinted with permission.

Figure 7.2. Power and authority relationships among the four major areas of control in the accreditation and credentialing process.

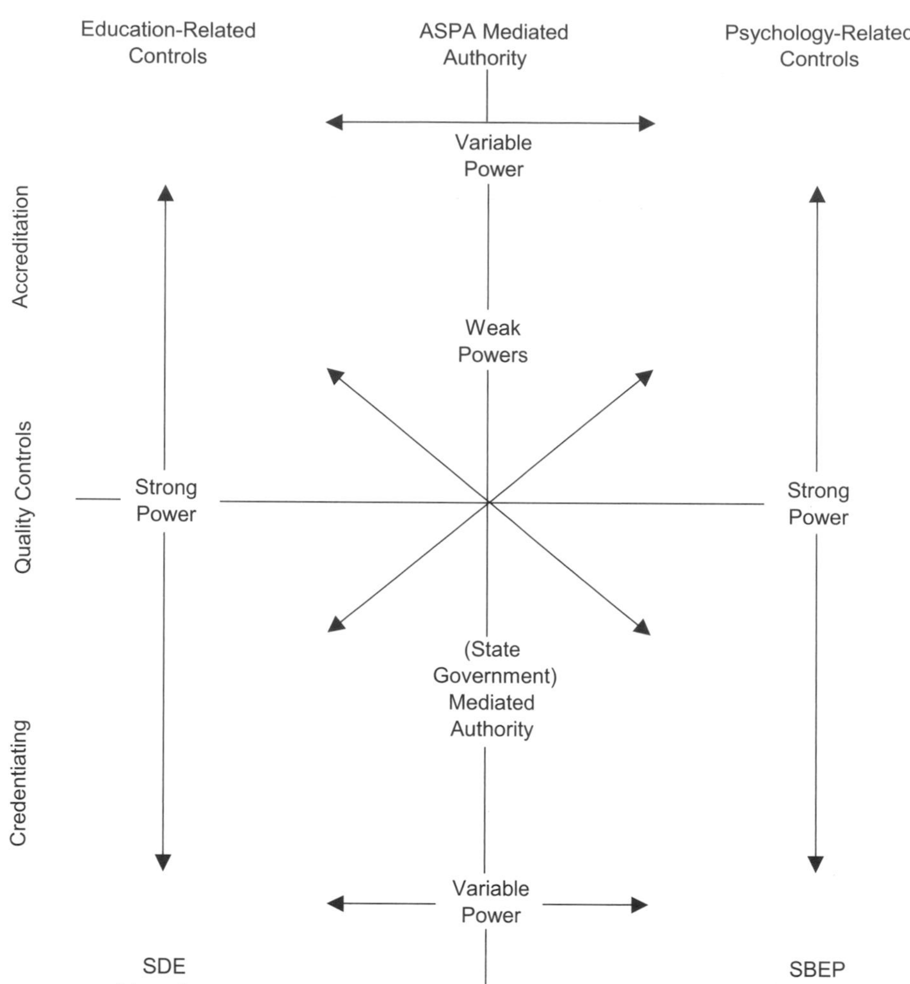

Source: "School Psychology's Dilemma: Reappraising Solutions and Directing Attention to the Future," by T. K. Fagan, 1986c, *American Psychologist, 41*, pp. 851–861. Copyright 1986 by the American Psychological Association. Reprinted with permission.

the psychology sectors, there are much stronger cross-regional relationships running north and south than east and west. In other words, state-level education and psychology groups tend to have closest ties to national-level education and psychology groups, and generally weak east–west relationships exist at both levels.

4. *Mediating forces.* Few agencies are positioned to mediate effectively across education and psychology arenas, for either accreditation or credentialing. At the national level, the Association of Specialized and Professional Accreditors (ASPA, founded in 1993) can serve this purpose for

accreditation. At the state level, the legislature may serve a mediating function for matters of credentialing. For example, conflicts between SDE and SBEP licensing laws or regulations may have to be mediated by legislative action or by the efforts of other government agencies.

THE PROCESS OF ACCREDITATION

It is through the process of accreditation that doctoral and nondoctoral training programs achieve recognition as having met national quality standards. The common characteristics of programs and their areas of evaluation were identified in chapter 6. As shown in Figure 7.1, with the exception of the training programs themselves, the major forces influencing accreditation operate at the national level (the northern portion). At present, the primary national-level agencies involved in the accreditation of school psychology programs include NCATE and the APA. Both NCATE and the APA are members of the Association of Specialized and Professional Accreditors (ASPA). The U.S. Department of Education's National Advisory Committee on Institutional Quality and Integrity and the Council for Higher Education Accreditation are the oversight bodies that extend accreditation privileges to NCATE and the APA.

It is through the process of accreditation that doctoral and nondoctoral training programs achieve recognition as having met national quality standards.

Association of Specialized and Professional Accreditors (ASPA)

Originally founded in 1949 as the National Commission on Accrediting, the Council on Postsecondary Accreditation (COPA) was founded in 1975 to identify qualified accreditors in numerous fields. COPA recognized and monitored "dozens of organizations across the country that, in turn, set standards for colleges and universities or prescribed criteria for programs in a wide range of disciplines" (Jacobsen, 1980, p. 10). Generally, COPA designated one organization to have exclusive accrediting authority within a field, and through periodic review ensured that the accreditor was performing appropriately. COPA was dissolved in 1993, and the Association of Specialized and Professional Accreditors (ASPA) was formed to continue these responsibilities. ASPA oversees and approves the activities of accrediting agencies in more than 50 fields, including teacher education and psychology (*www.aspa-usa.org*).

For their part, NCATE and the APA require institutions or programs to conduct self-studies and be reviewed by the accreditor at regular intervals. This includes the submission of detailed reports for review, and on-site review by a team of evaluators representing the accrediting organization. Recognition by ASPA means the accreditor has developed quality standards, adheres to the ASPA Code of Good Practice, represents professionals in its field, has the resources and motivation to conduct accreditation activities, and does not allow its accreditation decisions to seriously conflict with any existing accreditor recognized by ASPA. Although the accrediting agencies are part of a voluntary, nongovernmental process, their decisions influence government funding agencies, scholarship commissions, employers, and potential students.

Overlapping Authority of the APA and NCATE

Some fields appear to lend themselves to the simple designation of exclusive accrediting authority. Psychology is more complex. Though the APA has exclusive authority to accredit programs in the professional fields of clinical, counseling, and school psychology, other organizations have authority to accredit practitioners in related areas of practice. For example, the Council for Accreditation of Counseling and Related Educational Programs (CACREP), in part related to the American Counseling Association, accredits programs in the field of counseling, and the Council on Rehabilitation Education (CRE) accredits rehabilitation counselors. Thus, overlaps exist in accreditation for fields related to counseling.

The NCATE/NASP accreditation relationship is an example of accrediting authority that overlaps with that of the APA in the field of school psychology. The APA's authority to accredit clinical and counseling psychology programs has existed since the late 1940s. NCATE was formed in 1954 and granted authority to accredit in all fields of teacher education. Conflicts arose in the late 1960s when NCATE was already reviewing programs in school psychology and when the APA was seeking to extend its authority to school psychology. NCATE was broadening its authority to include all programs leading to SDE credentials (in both instructional and noninstructional fields), regardless of the administrative location of the program on campus. Thus its reviews were no longer confined to colleges of education but could include school psychology programs in a college of education or in a psychology department in a separate college. The intensity of the conflicting authority for accreditation in school psychology heightened in the late 1970s, leading to the formation of the APA-NASP Task Force in 1978 (the name was changed several years later to the APA/NASP Interorganizational Committee, or IOC). It was the task of this group to seek an acceptable means of managing the conflicts in doctoral-level accreditation. The IOC served an important function of mediating differences between NASP and the APA on matters of credentialing as well as accreditation standards. It had no accreditation authority, nor did it directly regulate such matters. The type of conflict experienced between the APA and NCATE/NASP has not been as problematic between the APA and CACREP or CRE because they are not purporting to accredit in a field whose professional programs and titles include the term *psychologist*. Historical information about the IOC may be found in Fagan (1993) and Fagan and Wells (2000). The IOC was discontinued in 2002. The conflict, though presently unresolved, is far less intense.

Diversity of Influence and Representation

Other groups that may influence the process of accreditation include the APA Division 16 (the Division of School Psychology), NASP, and organizations of trainers, including the Council of Directors of School Psychology Programs (CDSPP), and Trainers of School Psychologists (TSP). The means by which these groups influence the accreditation process are many and varied. Typically they influence the development and revision of accreditation standards and the policies and procedures for their implementation and enforcement. The most important indirect groups are Division 16 and NASP, which have direct power relationships to the APA and NCATE, respectively. However, the authority to accredit rests exclusively with the APA, through its Commission on Accreditation, and NCATE. All others in the arena, excluding ASPA (and its relationship with the U.S. Department of Education and the Council for Higher Education Accreditation), have only power relationships to these accreditors. The CDSPP, representing doctoral programs only, has close power alliances with the APA and Division 16 and supports APA policies regarding the doctoral degree as the appropriate entry level for credentialing with the title of professional psychologist. TSP, representing both doctoral and nondoctoral programs, is an unaligned organization. Whereas CDSPP has direct access to Division 16 and APA accreditation networks, TSP does not have access to the accreditation networks of NCATE/NASP. For the most part, TSP has had only minor influence on accreditation policy. Historical discussion of CDSPP and TSP can be found in Phillips (1993).

Authority to accredit rests exclusively with the APA and NCATE.

Where accreditation is concerned, few organizations are directly involved in either the education sector or psychology sector (northwest and northeast, respectively, in Figure 7.2). Presumably, those involved represent a broad constituency in school psychology. However, the major accreditors themselves (APA and NCATE), representing a wide variety of psychologists and educator groups, give those groups substantial influence on school psychology accreditation. For example, APA accreditation criteria and procedures (APA, 2005) are determined by the APA's governing body upon recommendation of the APA Commission on Accreditation and the Office of Program Consultation and Accreditation in the APA Education Directorate. The commission's membership represents five domains: graduate departments of psychology (4 members), professional schools and training programs (10 members), professional practice (4 members), the general public (2 members), and consumers of education and training (1 graduate student). In 2006 the APA expanded its membership to include internship and postdoctoral residency programs, diversity, and open seats. All NCATE criteria and procedures (NCATE, 2002) are approved by the NCATE council representing teacher educator organizations, teacher organizations, child-centered organizations, educational leadership organizations, policy-maker organizations, specialist organizations (e.g., NASP), subject-specific organizations, technology organizations, and others (e.g., the National Board for Professional Teaching Standards). Despite considerable compatibility of the APA and NASP accreditation standards at the doctoral level, significant differences between the APA and NCATE include the controlling influence of nonpsychologists on the enforcement of NASP standards through NCATE, and the lack of educator influence on school psychology accreditation through the APA. School psychology's direct influence is limited to CDSPP representation to APA's Commission on Accreditation, and one NASP representative to the NCATE Council.

Accreditation Conflicts and Issues

The following aspects of school psychology accreditation help to clarify the nature of conflicts and issues involved in that process.

APA School Psychology Program Accreditation

The APA develops its accreditation standards for professional psychology generically (APA, 2005). It does not have specific school psychology standards, but rather applies its generic standards to specific specialties of professional psychology through on-site program reviews. A three-member team reviews program materials, makes an on-site visit, and reports its findings and recommendations to APA's Commission on Accreditation for final action. APA does not accredit nonprofessional programs such as those in experimental psychology. APA accredits in the fields of clinical, counseling, and school psychology, but only at the doctoral level; it has no authority to accredit programs at subdoctoral levels. Thus, accreditation conflicts between APA and NCATE/NASP apply only to the doctoral level. In recent years, the number of accredited combined specialty programs has grown (e.g., counseling and school psychology) and additional growth is encouraged (Beutler & Fisher, 1994; Minke & Brown, 1996; see the 2004 special issue of *Journal of Clinical Psychology*, Vol. 60, No. 9). Finally, APA is a multipurpose professional association of which accreditation is but one activity.

NCATE Accreditation and NASP Approval

In contrast to the APA, NCATE is a single-purpose organization that exists exclusively to conduct accrediting activities on behalf of the many groups represented on its governing council. NCATE accredits teacher education institutions and programs at both the undergraduate and graduate levels, including doctoral preparation. NCATE standards are applicable to an entire education unit (e.g., college of education) and employ the guidelines of several specialty groups or state partnerships to review specific program areas. Although NASP has training standards for doctoral and specialist school psychology, it has no authority to independently accredit school psychology programs. As a constituent member of NCATE, NASP is permitted to have its training guidelines promoted and enforced through the authority of the NCATE accreditation process.

As mentioned in chapter 6, NASP employs a review process for approval of school psychology programs. Although this process is an important part of NCATE's overall accreditation review of an institution, in most instances this process does not include a specific on-site review of the school psychology program by trained NASP evaluators. However, through NCATE partnerships with states, specific program reviews may be conducted by a team of state-level evaluators selected by the SDE, and this team would be more likely to include a school psychologist. There are trade-offs in being reviewed for accreditation by APA and NCATE/NASP. The APA uses generic standards and a site review, whereas NCATE/NASP uses specific standards but does not require an on-site visit. At the nondoctoral level, NCATE/NASP is the only accreditation available in school psychology. It remains, however, that NASP's official designation represents primarily a "paper review." The pros and cons of these reviews are discussed in Fagan and Wells (2000).

NASP Sole Approval

An agreement between NCATE and NASP allows NASP to separately approve programs at NCATE institutions and those that do not participate in the NCATE accreditation process or that have been denied NCATE unit accreditation. With the large number of nondoctoral specialist-level programs in school psychology, NASP's ability to identify NASP-approved programs separately marked an important shift in the recognition of NASP standards. The agreement with NCATE was an approval and not an accrediting agreement, and NASP has no authority to accredit. It is uncertain if additional changes allowing NASP greater influence, and perhaps even authority in the accreditation of programs, will occur in the future.

Prior APA Accreditation

In 1991 NCATE/NASP agreed that if a program already held APA accreditation, it could receive a streamlined process of NASP review within the NCATE process. If the APA-accredited program is graduating students whose internships meet NASP standards for school experience, NCATE/NASP approval is reasonably assured. However, APA does not offer reciprocal approval for NCATE/NASP-accredited doctoral programs.

Internship Accreditation

APA also has authority for separately accrediting psychology internships but NASP does not. NASP internship standards are incorporated into the training standards that are promoted through NCATE. Training programs are responsible for ensuring that the internships of its students meet NASP internship standards. Separate approval of internships is not part of the NCATE/NASP accreditation process.

Accreditation Processes

The following gives a simplified chronological sequence for obtaining accreditation. First, a program is established with identifiable philosophy and goals, curriculum, faculty, facilities, policies, and student body. After graduating several students, the program voluntarily applies for accreditation. Sometimes a prereview visit is made by a consultant to determine the feasibility of going forward with accreditation. If the program is considered ready for formal review, a period of self-study leads to the preparation of a program report, which is submitted to the accreditor (APA or NCATE/NASP). In the APA process, the program's materials are evaluated and a site visit is made. Following the visit, the visiting team makes recommendations to the APA. After further review, including opportunities for a rejoinder to the accreditor's report, the program is granted or denied accreditation. In the NCATE process, NASP program approval is only one part of the overall education unit accreditation process of

NCATE. The program report is submitted directly to NASP for review. The results of the review are conveyed to NCATE and the program. The program is given an opportunity to respond to NASP's decisions regarding program weaknesses before a final decision is reached about the program's approval status. In both processes, the length of time from initial request to a final decision could be 1–2 years. Reaccreditation reviews, including site visits, are conducted periodically (e.g., 5–10 years).

Pros and Cons of Accreditation

Programs that identify themselves as being accredited by APA or NCATE/NASP or both have passed a rigorous review, and the supposition is that they can be relied upon to provide preparation that meets standards of quality. Accreditation allows the institution and program to advertise itself accordingly, and its students to boast that they have graduated from an accredited program. Of course, such a stamp of approval is no guarantee that accredited programs prepare better school psychologists than those prepared through unaccredited programs. A study by Wells (1999) compared recent APA-accredited and non-APA-accredited doctoral program graduates. The findings raise questions about the value of accreditation for doctoral program graduates. For example, no statistically significant differences were reported for obtaining APA-accredited internship sites, practice credentials, employment settings, and salaries. With accreditors shifting to requiring outcome data on graduates, these results suggest that at least some outcomes have unclear relationships to the training process or that nonaccredited programs align their curricula with state licensure standards that in turn are aligned with APA accreditation expectations. Nevertheless, on average, accreditation seems to be a valued assurance that at least a required pattern of studies is provided.

Most school psychology programs hold some form of national accreditation, and virtually all hold SDE approval.

In the field as a whole, the use of accreditation is a clear indication that a field has progressed to a point at which its practitioners require various forms of regulation. Accreditation is among the more powerful symbols of professionalism. Accreditation may also assist programs in pleading their case for more faculty, improved facilities, and additional course requirements.

Although accreditation gives training programs several privileges, the sacrifice is sometimes considered too great. Achieving program accreditation can be expensive, requires extensive faculty time in preparation and review, and necessitates the arranging of curriculum to others' expectations. For these reasons, some institutions have chosen not to participate in national accreditation. The penalties for nonparticipation vary. Some students may be deterred from applying to the program because the absence of accreditation suggests lower quality or because of concern that it will make their later efforts to get credentialed more difficult. The program and institution also face a potential loss of prestige. The program also might not qualify for SDE approval or its graduates might not be acceptable for state certification or licensure. For these and other reasons, most school psychology programs hold some form of national accreditation, and virtually all hold SDE approval.

Other Influences

Formal accreditation is not the only aspect of control or regulation of training. A less formal review process is that of designation (Pryzwansky & Wendt, 1987). Conducted jointly by the Association of State and Provincial Psychology Boards (ASPPB) and the Council for the National Register of Health Service Providers in Psychology (National Register), voluntary reviews of doctoral programs in professional psychology permit programs to be included in an annual publication, *Doctoral Psychology Programs Meeting Designation Criteria*. The National Register uses several criteria for designation, many of which correspond closely to those for APA accreditation. The purpose of designation is to provide assurance that a doctoral program is basically psychological in nature, a concept that corresponds closely to the language of many state licensing laws. Designation facilitates the work of state licensing boards, all of whom are members of the ASPPB.

Of course, other factors also influence the manner in which students are prepared. The internship experience is very important (see chapter 8). The nature of this influence is expressed in the accreditation or approval criteria for internships promoted by APA (2005), the Association of Psychology Postdoctoral and Internship Centers (2001), and NASP (2000c). However, national accreditation, designation, and SDE program approval are paramount among the direct, controlling variables of preparation for employment. Another important direct factor is the orientation of the student's training program and its faculty (discussed in chapter 6). Among the indirect factors influencing preparation for employment are SDE credentialing requirements; the position statements, policies, and standards of APA, NASP, ASPPB, and state associations of school psychologists; the SDE rules and regulations for the approval of training programs; and the regulation of practice. In combination, these forces strongly influence, and in some instances dictate, the types of curricula, faculty, facilities, and policies of graduate training in school psychology. The influence can result in a highly prescriptive training program (such as the pragmatic model, described in chapter 6) designed to meet the nondoctoral accreditation criteria of NCATE/NASP and the approval criteria of the SDE. Finally, accreditation and approval are important because of their close relationship to another major area of regulation, credentialing.

CREDENTIALING

The current widespread practice of SDE and SBEP licensure in school psychology is a clear recognition of the professional accomplishments of the field. Three types of credentials are available to school psychologists: practice credentials for the school sector through SDE licensure, practice credentials for the nonschool sector through SBEP licensure, and nonpractice credentials, including the diploma from the American Board of School Psychology (ABSP) and National Certification in School Psychology (NCSP).

Practice Credentials

Practice credentials legally authorize an individual to use particular titles or to render particular services; thus, the credentialing agencies control titles and practice. Discussions of the variety of credentials offered in school psychology are found in Merrell, Ervin, and Gimpel (2006), Prasse (1988), Pryzwansky (1993, 1999), and Pryzwansky and Wendt (1987).

State Department of Education

Almost all states offer an SDE credential to perform school psychological services. The requirements for SDE licensure vary, with titles and practice responsibilities often aligned with degrees and field experience. Though many states license at one title and degree level only, several have multiple levels and other titles. A few states provide SDE licensing in conjunction with, or dependent upon, SBEP licensing. Most SDE rules and regulations for the schools include comprehensive descriptions of services to be provided by school psychology personnel (e.g., assessment, consultation, or counseling). In states with multiple levels of licensing, the lower levels may correspond to limited service provision, such as assessment only. A few states operate a career ladder approach, with one title but different levels of licensing related to peer reviews and experience. For example, a state might provide a temporary, provisional, and permanent credential in school psychology. In the 1990s, Tennessee school psychologists, licensed by the SDE at the nondoctoral level, participated in a career ladder of three levels, based on experience and peer reviews and accompanied by higher salaries. The title of school psychologist and the functions permitted were the same at each level. School psychologists were required to use the career ladder program when the legislature mandated it for all teacher personnel in the public schools. The overall cost of the program led to its demise several years ago.

State Board of Examiners in Psychology

SBEP licensing is generally at one level, psychologist, or two levels, psychologist plus psychological examiner or associate, aligned with the doctoral and master's degrees, respectively. Some states also license with specialty designations (e.g., clinical or school psychologist) at one or more levels. The influence of managed medical care has accompanied the increasing use of the designation of health service provider (HSP) for qualified professional psychologists. In general, the HSP holds the doctoral-level license from the SBEP and any additional qualifications to be granted that title (Pryzwansky, 1999). An HSP designation may be necessary for insurance program reimbursement as a professional psychologist.

As a general rule, single-level licensure, such as a doctoral with the title of psychologist, is accompanied by broad definitions of practice, even when specialty designations are included in the license. In theory, professional psychologists are expected to confine their practice to their areas of competency in accord with their professional ethics. In effect, the credential brings together the psychologist's individual training and competencies with the profession's code of behavior. In states having more than one level of licensure, the limits of practice for psychological examiners or associates are typically spelled out in the law or in its regulations. Some states also have practice descriptions and limitations for the doctoral level.

Specialty Licenses

A few states have specialty licenses for school psychologists at nondoctoral levels to practice in the nonschool sector, but limits of practice are usually included. A detailed analysis of licensing as it pertains to school psychology appears in Prasse (1988), and state-by-state requirements appear in Curtis et al. (1998). Internet links are available through the NASP website. Because most school psychologists hold nondoctoral degrees, an SDE practice credential is most common. Though rare exceptions can be found, generally speaking, none of the available credentials require postdoctoral academic training, and paraprofessional credentials are unavailable. However, a postdoctoral year of supervised experience is often required for SBEP licensing. In the future, SBEP licensed school psychologists may potentially receive postdoctoral training and credentialing in psychopharmacology, leading to prescription privileges in practice. Although this practice is currently available in only a few states, widespread growth of the practice is anticipated in clinical psychology over the coming two decades. The extent of school psychologist participation will likely be small but noteworthy. A prescription privileges law became effective in 2005 in New Mexico, but it does not appear that any school psychologists are providing such services.

Conflicting Positions of the APA and NASP

Despite numerous variations in state-level certification and licensing, the basic controversy surrounding school psychology credentialing is related to the title and practice of the doctoral and nondoctoral levels, positions that are aligned with the APA and NASP, respectively. The APA reserves the title of school psychologist for practitioners who hold the doctoral degree and meet the licensing requirements of the SBEP. The APA's position is intended to apply to the school sector as well, that is, APA advocates the doctoral level for the title of school psychologist, with SDE licensing. Nondoctoral practitioners should be allowed to practice only with other titles (e.g., school psychological examiner) and under the supervision of doctoral-level psychologists. On the other hand, NASP advocates that, for the entry-level credential, the title of school psychologist should be granted, in the school and the nonschool sectors, to individuals holding the specialist degree or its equivalent (60 semester hours), including an internship. To attain the independent practice level, the entry-level school psychologist should be supervised for 1 year of postdegree practice and complete continuing professional development consistent with NASP credentialing standards (NASP, 2000d).

The basic controversy surrounding school psychology credentialing is related to the title and practice of the doctoral and nondoctoral levels, positions that are aligned with the APA and NASP, respectively.

The standards of the APA and NASP represent their ideologies more than the state of the art. Few states in the school and nonschool sectors credential according to the NASP position, although the nondoctoral level is practically universal for school practice and is recognized for nonschool practice in several states. In the SBEP licensing arena, APA guidelines are followed in most states, though variations are common. No state adheres rigidly to the APA position for school-based practice. The close alignment of the APA standards and state psychology licensing laws demonstrates the importance of power relationships between the national and state levels for both accreditation and credentialing. Eventually NASP would like to command similar influence in the SDE and the SBEP credentialing arenas. NASP's influence in the SDE arena has been steady and impressive, but in the SBEP arena its influence has been very limited. The APA–SBEP accreditation and credentialing relationship has led to efforts to alleviate inconsistencies between changing accreditation and licensing requirements. In the past 40 years, changes in these areas have occurred that make it difficult for licensing boards to evaluate the preparation of practitioners who obtained their degrees many years before. In 1992, the APA Council of Representatives approved guidelines for the evaluation of those whose preparation was prior to 1979 (APA Education Directorate, personal communication, 1992). The guidelines emphasize the importance of attending a regionally accredited training institution, preparing a dissertation that is primarily psychological, and doing the equivalent of a 1-year supervised internship.

The controversy between NASP and the APA, often referred to as the "doctoral issue," is as related to professional titles as it is to degrees. Titles appear in laws and regulations related to third-party insurance reimbursements for services. In most states, such privileges are reserved for those with the title of psychologist. When the term *psychologist* appears in the titles of practitioners with different levels of preparation, debates over service provision and privileges gain in intensity. Also involved are issues of status and identity as a professional psychologist. According to Engin (1983), these conflicts in credentialing "may be the most emotionally laden aspect of APA's position on non-doctoral school psychologists" (p. 38). Discussions of the doctoral issue appear in Bardon (1983); Fagan (1986c, 1993); Fagan, Gorin, and Tharinger (2000); Trachtman (1981); and *School Psychology Review* (1987, Vol. 16, No. 1, and 1989, Vol. 18, No. 1). For background discussions of the training and credentialing perspectives of the APA, see Pryzwansky (1982); for NASP, see Engin and Johnson (1983). These sources are of continuing relevance to grasping the long-standing differences of the APA and NASP.

The overlapping authority between education and psychology agencies in the accreditation arena is observed in the credentialing arena as well (see bottom half of Figure 7.1). Unlike accreditation entanglements, the overlap in credentialing has been managed in most states by restricting credentials to certain locales of practice. Thus the SDE credential applies only to settings under its jurisdiction, usually public school agencies. Recognition of the SDE's authority to credential its own personnel is evident in the exemptions for SDE-credentialed school psychologists and counselors in state SBEP licensing laws and in the APA's model licensure act (APA, 1987a). The exemptions allow school psychology personnel to use their titles and perform their functions as long as such actions are confined to the jurisdiction of the SDE. In some states, the SDE's authority also extends to private schools.

The differing SDE and SBEP credentialing requirements have created conflicts for school psychologists in most states. Although exemptions allow school psychologists to practice in the schools, many desire to extend their practice to the nonschool sector without having to obtain a doctoral degree and pursue the separate credential through the SBEP. This has led to several confrontations among state psychology and school psychology associations, state departments of education, and state licensing boards. One of the most combative credentialing controversies in recent years occurred in Texas in 1995–1996. The Texas controversy involved issues of titles and degrees as well as jurisdictional authority of different boards at different times. Published discussions of this case are instructive on the complicated issue of credentialing (Clay, 1996; Curtis, Batsche, & Tanous, 1996; Hughes, 1996). A similar struggle is reflected in Arkansas's use of the term *specialist in school psychology* instead of *school psychologist* for school-based practice with the SDE credential. This and other confrontations have resulted in amended SDE and SBEP credentialing laws, broader exemptions, and other "creative credentialing" pursuits to allow limited nonschool practice privileges. Although such efforts have resulted in the desired practice extensions in several states, these practitioners have not been given the same privileges as doctoral licensed psychologists (e.g., third-party insurance reimbursement).

Another avenue to nonschool practice has been through credentials created for nondoctoral practitioners in fields related to school psychology, notably mental health and counseling. For example, the North American Association of Masters in Psychology (NAMP, founded in 1994) offers its Nationally Certified Psychologist credential. The NAMP certificate, initiated in 1998, is not a practice credential but rather a recognition credential similar to NASP's NCSP. The American Counseling Association (ACA) has supported the creation of nondoctoral credentials such as the Licensed Professional Counselor and the Licensed Marriage and Family Therapist. The ACA and its state affiliates have been successful in their efforts in many states. The American Mental Health Counselors Association (AMHCA) advocates on behalf of nondoctoral counselors but does not offer a specific credential. The options for counselor licensure among school psychologists are discussed by Crespi and Fischetti (1997).

Students should be knowledgeable about the states in which they plan to practice because the credentialing for school-based and private practice are regulated at the state level.

Links Between Training and Credentialing

The relationships between training and credentialing can dictate the type of professional title and practice school psychologists will have. It is as important to understand these relationships as it is to grasp other aspects of professional preparation. Students should be knowledgeable about the states in which they plan to practice, because most of the relationships in the education sector lead to SDE credentialing (whereas those in the psychology sector lead to non-school-based and private credentialing) and because these credentialing mechanisms are authoritatively regulated at the state level. Although commonalities exist among SDE and SBEP credentialing authorities, easy reciprocity of credentials or equivalence of credentialing requirements in school psychology is the exception, not the norm. Two examples demonstrate the importance of the decisions involved and the relationships (Figure 7.1).

In the first example, student A is interested in employment as a school psychologist in his home state, has no interest in practicing in a nonschool setting, and is not committed at this time to pursuing a lengthy program of graduate preparation leading to a doctoral degree. Familiar with the nondoctoral nature of SDE credentialing in his home state and the fact that the SDE closely scrutinizes the programs of preparation, A selects an institution that holds both NCATE/NASP accreditation at the specialist level and SDE program approval. Upon completing the program, A is automatically endorsed for SDE credentialing by his institution, and the SDE subsequently grants him its practice credential. A is now authorized to practice as a school psychologist in the public school systems of that state. Depending on how similar his home state's requirements are to those of other states, A may or may not be eligible to obtain similar credentials elsewhere. Nor is A authorized, or eligible, for nonschool practice as a school psychologist, because SBEP credentialing in his state requires a doctoral credential. Should A move to another state with different SDE credentialing requirements, no reciprocity with his current SDE, and a doctoral-level-only SBEP licensure requirement, A could be without any credential to continue independently delivering psychological services.

In the second example, student B is interested in maximizing flexibility in the marketplace and seeks preparation for school and non-school-based practice while retaining the title of school psychologist in both sectors. B wants to practice in the same state as A, but she is interested in subspecializing in a particular area of school psychology. B selects an out-of-state institution that holds NCATE/NASP accreditation at the doctoral and nondoctoral levels, APA accreditation in school psychology at the doctoral level, and an advanced graduate concentration in the desired subspecialty. B also notes that the program requirements readily match those for credentialing of her home state's SDE. Upon completing the doctoral degree, which included an approved 1-year internship, B returns to her home state and makes application for both SDE and SBEP credentialing. After completing additional written and oral examination requirements of the SBEP, B is credentialed to practice independently as a school psychologist in school and nonschool settings and privately. Should B choose to move to another state, it is very likely that additional credentials for both school and nonschool practice could be obtained with a minimum of additional examination or other requirements. However, a year of postdoctoral supervised practice might be required for an SBEP credential. Credentialing to practice in the schools would be virtually guaranteed in every state.

The examples demonstrate the manner in which two persons, defining their goals differently, achieve appropriate training. Many variations of these patterns could be used to show the intricate relationships among training, accreditation, and credentialing. For instance, if the home state had provided nondoctoral credentialing for school psychologists to practice in the nonschool sector, or if all credentialing of school psychologists had been under the control of the SBEP, each person might have made different choices for training. Thus, it is important for prospective entry-level and advanced students to consider the credentialing requirements of their chosen states and the accreditation status of the training program. Even before entering training, students should consider the states in which they will later seek practice, and whether they desire to work primarily in the school or nonschool sector.

Acquisition of Credentials

The process for acquiring practice credentials is something even beginning students should investigate. Credentialing agencies for school and nonschool practice have different procedures and requirements. The typical patterns are summarized in this section.

State Department of Education

In the case of the SDE credential, two routes are most common. In states without SDE program approval, or for students entering from out-of-state, they may submit an application—including transcripts, evidence of internship, and program completion statement—directly to the credentialing office in the SDE. This process, sometimes called *transcript review*, matches application materials to the SDE's requirements. A credential is then issued, deferred pending clarifications, or denied. In states with program approval, applicants submit materials through the credentialing office of the college of education at the institution in which they completed their approved training program. Out-of-state applicants may have to do the same through one of the approved programs in the state to which they have moved. In these instances, the student's application materials are matched against the requirements of the approved program through which he or she seeks certification. The dean of the college of education or the dean's representative serves as the institution's credentialing officer to the SDE. The college of education gathers the applicant's materials and, after reviewing them, forwards the submitted materials with a recommendation for credentialing to the SDE. In the approved program process, the applicant's materials are not forwarded to the SDE until every requirement of the approved program appears to have been met. The SDE works out any problems directly with the college of education, which in turn works them out with the applicant.

Securing SDE credentialing can take 1 to 3 months after the completion of training. Students are encouraged to contact the college of education about its procedures well in advance of completing the program. In either the transcript review process or program approval, out-of-state applicants often encounter some deficiencies in their training compared with the new SDE requirements. In some cases, additional coursework must be completed prior to being approved for credentialing in the new state. It is important for students to match their training program to the SDE requirements of the states in which they intend to seek employment, including the state in which they'll complete their internship. The SDE credential is periodically renewed according to state requirements. Most states require applicants to undergo a criminal history background check through the state's bureau of investigation, including fingerprinting.

State Board of Examiners in Psychology

Securing an SBEP credential is almost always a completely separate procedure from that for securing an SDE credential. Application materials are sent directly to the state board of examiners in psychology, which are usually located in the state capital. Requirements for SBEP credentialing involve specific degrees in the specialty, field experiences, letters of recommendation, and a passing score on the Examination for Professional Practice in Psychology (EPPP). The EPPP is geared to the generic standards for psychology credentialing and includes broad coverage of experimental as well as professional psychology. Preparatory courses for the EPPP are offered across the country throughout the year. For the initial credential, the SBEP reviews the applicant's degree and field experiences and makes a determination about eligibility to take the EPPP. The EPPP is given throughout the year at approved sites in each state. The SBEP may also require an oral examination of each candidate who has passed the EPPP. Once these hurdles are crossed, the applicant is issued a credential, which must be renewed on a regular basis. Generally speaking, SBEP credentialing fees are much higher than SDE credentialing fees. Cutoff scores for the EPPP vary by state, and an applicant can usually acquire reciprocity in another state if he or she already has an acceptable EPPP score and a valid credential.

The Association of State and Provincial Psychology Boards (ASPPB), the most important source of SBEP licensing across the United States and Canada, has been working to increase reciprocity for credentials by offering a Certificate of Professional Qualification in Psychology (CPQ; McGuire, 1998). The program has outpaced other reciprocity efforts, and by 2005 about three dozen states or provinces had accepted the CPQ (Bradshaw, 2005). Several publications related to SBEP credentialing and the EPPP are available from ASPPB, including *Certificate of Professional Qualification in Psychology, Entry Requirements for the Professional Practice of Psychology, The Handbook of Licensing and Certification Requirements for Psychologists in the United States and Canada,* and *Items from Previous Examinations* (for the EPPP). Other publications are related to doctoral candidates' past performance on the EPPP and information about the examination's construction, content, and administration. ASPPB offers a practice version of the EPPP on the Internet (*www.asppb.org*). There also is an effort to devise a national model for the oral licensing examination. The ASPPB was previously the American Association of State Psychology Boards. Its early history is discussed in H. S. Carlson (1978).

The issue of mobility is discussed in a special section of *Professional Psychology: Research and Practice* (2003, Vol. 34, No. 5). Psychologists interested in working in other countries will be interested in efforts to increase global mobility described in Hall and Lunt (2005).

Pros and Cons of Credentialing

Credentialing is a major symbol of professional status, and practitioners' credentials ensure the right to use certain titles and practices. They also offer advantages to the agencies and consumers who employ psychologists. However, the contributions of credentialing, though well known, are not uniformly appreciated. As with accreditation, the history of the credentialing process has involved sacrifices. In discussing the history of licensing, Hogan (1983) indicated that licensing practices had the following shortcomings: (a) they did not necessarily protect the public from incompetent practitioners; (b) they may exacerbate shortages in the supply of practitioners and in their distribution; (c) they may increase the cost of professional services; (d) they may prevent the use of paraprofessionals; (e) they may inhibit the change of training processes; and (f) they may discriminate against minorities, women, the aged, and the poor. The historical strengths of credentialing and codes of ethics are given in Sinclair, Simon, and Pettifor (1996). A comparison of credentialing requirements across 13 professions revealed that psychologist preparation was lengthy in comparison to income, and that credentialing requirements needed reexamination (De Vaney Olvey, Hogg, & Counts, 2002). On balance, the advantages appear to outweigh the disadvantages, and the credentialing of psychologists continues to become more stringent and popular. Surveys continue to indicate that SDE credentials are held by almost 90% of school psychologists, and SBEP or other agency credentials are held by at least one third. Nearly two thirds of school psychology faculty members hold an SBEP license (Curtis, Lopez, Batsche, & Smith, 2006; Graden & Curtis, 1991; Hyman, Flynn, Kowalcyk, & Marcus, 1998).

Practitioners' credentials ensure the right to use certain titles and practices.

Nonpractice Credentials

In addition to SDE and SBEP credentials, national credentials are sought by many school psychologists. These credentials include the diploma from the American Board of Professional Psychology (ABPP) and the certificate from the NASP National School Psychology Certification System. Both credentials are recognition of quality preparation or practice, but they do not directly authorize individuals to render services. That is, they are not substitutes for SDE or SBEP practice credentials. Another option is to be listed with the National Register of Health Service Providers in Psychology, a widely recognized registry of more than 14,000 licensed psychologists. This registry may influence a practitioner's private practice especially in the arena of managed care (*www.nationalregister.org*).

American Board of School Psychology

The diploma in psychology was initiated by the APA in 1947 for clinical psychology and extended to school psychology in the late 1960s (Fagan, 1993; Pryzwansky & Wendt, 1987). Those holding the diploma are called diplomates or board-certified psychologists. As with all credentialing procedures, candidates wishing to obtain this recognition agree to be rigorously examined. The process is limited to doctoral-level psychologists and involves interviews and extensive evaluation of the candidate's practice. The credential is awarded only once and need not be renewed.

In 1992, the American Board of Professional Psychology expanded its influence by forming a federation of specialty boards, including an American Board of School Psychology (ABSP). The ABSP provides the only competency-based doctoral-level school psychology credential. Board-certified school psychologists are fellows in the American Academy of School Psychology (Pryzwansky, 1999). Relatively few doctoral-level school psychologists are ABPP diplomates. A survey of trainers (Hyman et al., 1998) found that only 7% (nine trainers) of respondents held a diplomate (five in school, three in clinical, one other). Though not published in the final report, Reschly and Wilson (1995) found that about 1% of the field overall held the diplomate, according to a 1992 survey. Wells (1999) found that, of recent doctoral recipients, 2% held the diplomate, 2% were in the process of getting it, and 10%

planned to pursue it. This suggests that even among newer doctoral members of the field, only a small proportion pursue the diploma. A history of the ABPP appears in Bent, Packard, and Goldberg (1999). A practitioner might also be a diplomate in more than one field (e.g., clinical or neuropsychology).

National School Psychology Certification System

In 1988, NASP initiated its National Certificate in School Psychology (NCSP), a certification program premised on its standards for training and credentialing. The requirements for the certificate include a degree in school psychology from a program that meets NASP training standards, including those for the internship, a state certificate or license to practice school psychology, and a passing score on the school psychology exam (using the cutoff established by the National School Psychology Certification Board). The school psychology exam is a specialty test of the National Teacher Examination (NTE), which students should take at or near the completion of the internship. The examination is geared to the training and practice standards of NASP and is applied at a greater scope than the EPPP. Examination data presented for 2002–2003 revealed an overall average of 693 (range was 650–740) for 1,819 examinees, with substantial differences between some of the cultural groups represented (Vazquez & Dunham, 2004). Although no courses are geared specifically to the NTE school psychology exam, the Educational Testing Service publishes a study guide for the school psychology test (ETS, 2003), and a test guide has been prepared by Thompson (2004). NCSP renewal occurs every 3 years and requires the completion of 75 contact hours of continuing professional development (CPD). The requirement for CPD is stringent and unique among credentials in school psychology. The entire NCSP program and CPD requirements are outlined in a brochure available from NASP (or at *www.nasponline.org*). According to the NASP website, as of February 2006, more than 9,500 school psychologists held the NCSP, and it was recognized in 26 states as part of their SDE credentialing standards.

One of the long-term objectives of the national certification program is improved state-to-state credentialing reciprocity. The NTE school psychology examination has already been adopted by several states as part of their credentialing requirements. Because the NTE exam is a part of the NASP National School Psychology Certification System (NSPCS), the same test results may be used in different states. However, cutoffs may vary. Ideally, reciprocity would improve to the point that holding a NASP certificate would be sufficient to automatically reestablish credentials when moving. The NSPCS provides the framework within which NASP guidelines for training and credentialing, the APA and NCATE/NASP accrediting guidelines, and the diverse state credentialing requirements could evolve into greater homogeneity. In that instance, the NSPCS could emerge as the major mediating factor between the national and state levels for school psychology credentialing, at least in the education arena of Figure 7.1. (Batsche [1996] offers a discussion of the development of the NCSP and its requirements.) In addition to reciprocity, some states pay NCSP school psychologists a higher salary. For example, in Louisiana, school psychologists

As of February 2006, more than 9,500 school psychologists held the NCSP, and it was recognized in 26 states as part of their certification standards.

holding the NCSP receive several thousand dollars in extra compensation. In states that have not approved this privilege, it is possible for individual districts to reward NCSP holders as equivalent to nationally certified teachers (York, 2001). Another indication of the growing acceptance of the NTE exam in school psychology is its use by about half of the NASP-approved programs as a graduation requirement (Fagan, 2005c).

Credentialing Summary

Two practice credentials exist in almost every state—SDE and SBEP licenses—and two national-level, nonpractice credentials are also available: the American Board of Professional Psychology's ABSP and the NASP National Certificate in School Psychology. The credentials are closely aligned with the organizations and policies that influence school psychology from the education and the psychology arenas. Students progressing through their training from the nondoctoral to the doctoral levels and beyond could secure all these credentials. However, most school psychologists will attain an SDE credential and the NCSP; few will ever need to obtain all the available credentials.

The primary agencies influencing credentialing are the SDE and the SBEP, whose authority is mediated by the state legislature. SDE and SBEP laws and regulations have direct influence on credentialing. Indirect influences emanate from other documents (e.g., NASP and APA standards). The accreditation standards of NASP and the APA are often closely aligned with the credentialing standards of the SDE and SBEP, respectively. Other indirect influences on credentialing standards and procedures include official position statements of the APA, NASP, or the state associations (e.g., statements of comprehensive services); the policies of the ASPPB or the National Association of State Directors of Teacher Certification; and the orientation of the state's training programs and faculty. The primary organizational documents influencing credentialing include the *Specialty Guidelines for the Practice of School Psychology* (APA, 1981), the APA's model licensure act (APA, 1987a), and the *Standards for the Credentialing of School Psychologists* (NASP, 2000d). The ASPPB also approved a model licensing act that could further enhance reciprocity in licensing (Association of State and Provincial Psychology Boards, 1998). Revisions to the APA's model licensing act are being considered in 2007.

Multiple Credentials

School psychologists often hold other credentials in addition to their SDE credential for school psychology practice. Some may also be licensed as psychological examiners or psychological associates. At the doctoral level the school psychologist may be SDE credentialed and separately credentialed as a health service provider in school, clinical, or counseling psychology for nonschool practice. The school psychologist may be eligible for a certified professional counselor or marriage and family therapist license through a board separate from the SBEP. Finally, some may be credentialed in several areas by the SDE. For example, they may be credentialed as teachers, guidance counselors, or educational diagnosticians, as well as school psychologists. A small number also hold school administrator credentials.

Academic Credentials

The credentials needed to be considered for a position as an academic school psychologist or to be employed as a faculty member in a school psychology training program include, for entry level, the doctoral degree in school psychology, including an appropriate internship experience, letters of recommendation, and a résumé describing education and experience. Depending on the type of academic position desired, the PhD may be preferred over the EdD or the PsyD degree. Although school-based experience as a school psychologist is very desirable, the reality is that research experience and publications will likely be more heavily weighted in considering the application because of the need for those to achieve tenure. In institutions not granting doctoral degrees, and programs offering the PsyD degree, field experience as a school psychologist may be preferred. For purposes of program accreditation, holding practice credentials or being eligible for practice credentialing is often necessary. Reschly and Wilson (1995) found that among program faculty, the following degrees were represented: PhD (76%), EdD/DEd (17%), PsyD (3%), and other (3%), although these figures do not appear in the published version of the research. Graden and Curtis (1991) suggest that faculty make up only about 4.6% of the total number of persons in school psychology. Prorated against a figure of 22,000 school psychologists at that time, their data suggest a total of perhaps 1,000 academic school psychologists in the United States. Given the personnel shortages in programs, it is doubtful that the number exceeds that amount, and a figure of between 800 and 1,000 seems more likely.

The proportion of women in academic positions increased from about 33% in 1989 to 46% in 1998. Minority representation in faculty positions increased from 11% in 1989 to 15% in 1998, about equally balanced between male and female minorities. Overall, 85% of the faculty members in school psychology programs were nonminorities. Seventy percent of the 874 faculty were identified as SDE certified, and 58% were licensed as psychologists or school psychologists (Thomas, 1998). A useful guide for women and minority faculty is produced by the APA (1998).

In a survey by Hyman et al. (1998), 65% of responding trainers indicated they were licensed as psychologists in their states, and 38% believed the license enhanced their academic standing. Among credentialing concerns of trainers is the widespread licensing requirement for postdoctoral supervised experience. It is difficult to acquire this experience in the context of academia, where tenure is judged on teaching, research, and service, and supervised experience could detract from those pursuits. The APA is working on a resolution to this matter, which may accept the equivalent of a postdoctoral year through the extensive experience obtained in the predoctoral program. Crespi (1998) discussed the types of credentials that supervisors should possess for postdoctoral to school-based specialist-level supervision (see also Fischetti & Crespi, 1997). Demaray, Carlson, and Hodgson (2003) describe program directors' ratings of important factors in hiring new faculty for training programs by degree levels and accreditation status. Their results suggest that students seeking academic positions in doctoral-level programs ought to possess strong research skills and have evidence of research productivity.

Miscellaneous Credentials

Considered broadly, credentials include almost any evidence of accomplishments relevant to an individual's career as a school psychologist. Credentials are obviously enhanced by higher degrees, more experience, and recognitions such as the ABSP or the NCSP. Other school psychology recognitions also add to credentials: awards from professional associations such as School Psychologist of the Year, continuing professional development certificates, and distinguished service awards from professional organizations. Awards and citations from local groups (e.g., PTA and the Council for Exceptional Children chapters) are also important. In some states special recognitions and credentials exist for specific practices, such as New Hampshire's Specialist in the Assessment of Intellectual Functioning, or California's certification of advanced training and specialization for school psychologists (e.g., in functional analysis and behavioral intervention), which is offered by its state association's committee for continuing and professional development.

REGULATION OF SCHOOL PSYCHOLOGY PRACTICE

Psychological services in school settings are influenced by several systemic factors (see chapter 3 and Curtis & Zins, 1986; Maher, Illback, & Zins, 1984). In addition, several factors influence the roles and functions of the school psychologist (see chapter 4). For example, Tindall (1964) and Monroe (1979) identified the potential influence of the psychologist–pupil ratio, litigation and legislation, and ethics. Even though the APA and NASP formulate ethics and standards for practice and SDEs regulate the delivery of services, practice also is regulated to a large extent by very local factors enmeshed in the employment context. The following direct factors hold the greatest influence over what school psychologists do on a daily basis.

Practice also is regulated to a large extent by very local factors enmeshed in the employment context.

Direct Influences

The determinants affecting school psychology practice include district demands and expectations, the district's perceptions of its needs, consumer responses to services, the desired functions of school psychologists, and their personal competencies.

District Demands and Expectations

What school administrators perceive as the school psychologist's role and function determine to a large extent what the school psychologist will do. In too many settings, administrators, especially directors of special education and superintendents, know only the traditional roles of administering and interpreting tests and conducting case studies of children suspected of being eligible for special education. Because school administrators have authority over the school psychologist, this is perhaps the strongest direct influence on the psychologist's role and function. Thus, although school psychologists may have competence in a broad range of services, they lack the authority to determine what services they will provide, or when and where they will provide them. These decisions are made by the officials in authority. It is the rare school psychologist who can say without exaggeration that he or she totally defines his or her role and function and the parameters of service delivery.

In their roles as consultants, school psychologists should employ public relations and information-giving skills that better inform their consumers about the entire range of possible services and how they match the needs of the district. Effective use of such public relations strategies will improve the employment conditions of school psychologists. Ineffective use of the school psychologist results in restricted roles and functions. School districts could facilitate such information-sharing efforts by having a readily available job description for its school psychologist personnel. Aspiring school psychologists should ask to see a job description when seeking employment. If one is not available, he or she should prepare one.

The School District's Perceptions of Its Needs

Ordinarily the district's demands would be expected to follow closely from the district's perceptions of its needs. However, districts frequently have not adequately assessed their needs in areas that relate to the deployment of psychological services, or, regardless of a needs assessment, districts continue to relate to psychological services in a traditional way (see the discussion of goal conflicts in chapter 3). For decades, research on roles and functions has shown that school psychologists spend 60% to 70% of their time in activities that make up only about 25% of their training. That is, much of their training is underused in areas such as consultation, interventions, research, and evaluation. For all the changes that U.S. education has undertaken, it is surprising that the traditional roles and functions of school psychologists have persisted. Because school psychologists are assessment specialists, they need to be involved in assessing district needs, and they should speak up about how more diverse roles and functions can better meet district needs. For example, a school psychologist's needs assessment might determine that many children in the school district need help in dealing with their anger and developing more appropriate social skills. Instead of providing traditional one-on-one assessment and intervention services, the school psychologist could establish group services, perhaps with the assistance of the school-based guidance counselor or social worker. The important point is that perceptions of district needs influence district demands. A district should involve as many constituencies as necessary to properly assess its needs and to consider more broadly the ways school psychologists can help to meet them.

Consumer Response to Services

The kind of feedback a district receives about its psychological services, or about the services that other districts' psychologists are providing, can also shape the roles and functions of the school psychologist. Feedback, positive or negative, may come from parents, educators, or students. Consumer satisfaction with services is very important to the maintenance of services, and consumer dissatisfaction can be a significant source of change. Feedback is necessarily after the fact (reactive), and thus consumers' feedback about services presumes that such services were offered. The accountability strategies discussed in chapter 5 are helpful in conveying to the school administration the importance of broadly conceived psychological services. Consumer response can also be proactive. Consumers may pressure the administration to offer different types of psychological services that they may have learned of elsewhere or to increase certain existing district services with which they have been highly satisfied. School psychologists can even nurture this process by helping consumer groups advocate improved psychological services, or changes in special education or the referral process, and so on.

Consumer response can be an effective reactive and proactive influence for change. Although this fact is widely recognized, this determinant of school psychologists' roles and functions is not widely used to improve services. Publications that may be useful to practitioners are *Making Psychologists in Schools Indispensable* (Talley, Kubiszyn, Brassard, & Short, 1996), the *Professional Advocacy Resource Manual* (Canter & Crandall, 1994), and the NASP handouts series (Canter & Carroll, 1998). There are also suggestions in the various editions of Thomas and Grimes's *Best Practices in School Psychology* (1985, 1990, 1995, 2002, 2008).

School psychologists also need to offer concrete expectations for outcomes, in the form of reinforcers, to encourage change in administrators' attitudes and behaviors. Existing outcome studies can be used to demonstrate results; for example, consultation and prereferral assessment procedures have been shown to reduce formal referrals and therefore costs. Consumer response can be among the most influential factors because it can wield power either at the ballot box or in the media. School administrators listen to consumers because they perceive the consequences of failing to do so. Consumers can also emphasize the importance of practices observed elsewhere without appearing to be self-serving in seeking role changes among school psychologists.

Thus, a combination of information, expectations, and contingencies may be more effective than other efforts in changing district demands for school psychological services. Too often, the district is concerned about losing funds because of noncompliance, and thus the dominant demand is for more traditional casework to achieve compliance. School psychology professionals can alter districts' demands by demonstrating that compliance can be achieved more effectively and in the long run by reducing formal referrals. The result would be broader service delivery and presumably stronger consumer satisfaction. In short, simply informing school authorities about school psychologists' broad training and potential services is not enough to influence daily practice. However, in this scenario, the determinants of district demands and needs would still be ahead of consumer response, but this determinant can have an important impact on perceptions of needs and subsequent district demands.

Desired Functions of the School Psychologist

This determinant refers to the kinds of roles and functions the individual school psychologist wishes to perform. Studies of school psychologists' actual and preferred services have consistently shown discrepancies and attest to the distinction between this determinant and that of district expectations and demands (see, e.g., Curtis, Graden, & Reschly, 1992; D. K. Smith, 1984; D. K. Smith, Clifford, Hesley, & Leifgren, 1992). A survey of Ohio school administrators suggested that some services that are highly valued by practitioners may not be so valued by administrators (Thomas & Pinciotti, 1992). These discrepancies may relate to accounts of job-related burnout among school psychologists (Huebner, 1992; Miller, Witt, & Finley, 1981; P. S. Wise, 1985). This direct determinant—what school psychologists desire to do—probably has less influence in the system than the determinant of what others in authority expect them to do.

Personal Competencies of the School Psychologist

Every school psychologist brings to the workplace a body of knowledge and skills acquired through formal training, experience, and continuing education. In theory, at least, school psychologists confine their activities and practice to the body of knowledge and skills in which they are competent. Discrepancies in roles and functions can easily result when the district's expectations and demands call for services that the school psychologist is not competent to provide. They also can occur when the school psychologist's available skills are underused because of restrictive expectations. School psychologists can play an important part by assessing the service needs of their consumers and striving to acquire the necessary skills through additional formal education, supervised experience, and continuing education. As school psychologists broaden their skills, the potential for comprehensive service delivery increases.

Indirect Influences

Several indirect factors also help to determine the roles and functions of school psychologists in daily practice. These include the orientation of the training program, credentialing requirements for school psychologists, state laws and regulations, state and local professional associations, and NASP and APA positions.

Orientation of the Training Program

Each training program is organized around some type of model, with both didactic and experiential training. The orientation of the training program, which is partially dependent upon the competencies and orientations of its faculty, influences the day-to-day practice of the school psychologist. If the faculty holds strong behavioral psychology orientations, such strategies are likely to be expressed in their students' approach to service delivery. Thus orientation of the training program, personal competencies, and desired functions are closely related determinants of roles and functions. Because the program's orientation does not guarantee personal competencies, and because that orientation and set of competencies may not be in accord with consumer or district perceptions of their needs, role and function expectations and demands are not directly influenced. A related aspect of this influence is that the internship is usually considered a training experience and a part of the overall training program. The orientations of the supervisors and colleagues involved in the internship experience may differ from that of the academic faculty. It is frequently acknowledged by trainers that the orientation they imparted to their students is modified or enhanced, perhaps even eroded, by internships in which the students were encouraged to practice differently. It is also likely that as school psychologists gain experience, they alter their orientations. Thus a program's orientation may not be a consistent predictor of its students' short-term or long-term orientations.

Credentialing Requirements for School Psychologists

A state's SDE and SBEP credentialing requirements indirectly influence day-to-day practice by defining the areas in which a school psychologist is to be trained or judged competent. This determinant is closely related to the training program orientation and to accreditation. Changes in credentialing standards might not be observed in practice for several years. That is, such changes in requirements are seldom retroactive to those already credentialed. Nevertheless, changes in credentialing requirements can have long-term impact on roles and functions. The most immediate impact of changes in credentialing requirements would be observed in training program requirements, especially those of nondoctoral programs that tend to follow the pragmatic model. The influence of credentialing requirements on the strongest direct determinants of roles and functions (that is, district demands and expectations and a district's perceptions of its needs) is considered weak and therefore indirect.

State Laws and Regulations

Most states have statutes or SDE rules and regulations that generally describe the roles and functions of school psychologists. However, such statements are typically guidelines about service provision and not enforceable statements about what the school psychologist must be doing. For example, they might stipulate that assessment, consultation, and in-service education are important services, but they fail to prioritize those services or to stipulate what portion of a school psychologist's time should be applied to each area. In fact, the rules and regulations might only require the district to have psychological services available and not have its own school psychologist. More definitive statements may appear in federal legislation for the disabled and the SDE rules and regulations for the laws' implementation. In some states, these statements may be so specific as to indicate what tests the school psychologist is expected to administer for certain types of referrals. However, all SDEs have statements about the expectations for assessment and related services, due process procedures, confidentiality, team meetings, and so on that directly influence the school psychologist's daily practice.

Unlike credentialing requirements, laws and rules and regulations are often immediately enforceable and apply to all those in practice regardless of when they were credentialed. This can be considered an indirect determinant because laws and regulations seldom address school psychologists specifically, and they do not stipulate priorities. Nevertheless, because such influences have authoritative backing, if such laws and regulations have proper wording they could have a direct and dramatic effect on roles and functions. For example, an SDE description of services could require school psychologists to spend no less than 30% of their time in consultation activities or stipulate a caseload of no more than 75 cases per year based on an average of no more than two case studies per week. Of course, local district guidelines or collective bargaining agreements that stipulate such expectations would have direct impact, but those would be included in the first two direct determinants (district demands and expectations and a district's perception of its needs).

State and Local Professional Associations

Though state and local professional groups have no authority for making changes, they can be effective indirect determinants of school psychologists' daily practice. Perhaps their strongest indirect influence is on training programs, credentialing requirements, and SDE rules and regulations. Through their SDE and legislative lobbying efforts, these organizations can influence state laws, rules and regulations, and their implementation. To the extent such associations could have direct impact on daily practice, it would most likely be by changing the response of consumers, the perceptions of the district's needs, and subsequently the expectations and demands for services.

NASP and APA Positions

Though more removed from the sphere of daily practice than state associations, national groups are also indirect influences. The training, credentialing, and practice standards of the APA and NASP are actually formal position statements of these groups. The APA's *General Guidelines for Providers of Psychological Services* (1987b) and *Specialty Guidelines for the Delivery of Services by School Psychologists* (1981) and NASP's *Guidelines for the Provision of School Psychological Services* (2000b) are especially related to daily practice or roles and functions. The latter two documents identify the proper role of the school psychologist in accordance with training and ethical guidelines, and they specify a preferred service ratio. NASP position statements on such topics as mental health services in the schools, school violence, early childhood care and education, grade retention, reevaluations, or corporal punishment may also influence practice. Many of the chapters in *Best Practices in School Psychology* (Thomas & Grimes, 1985, 1990, 1995, 2002, 2008), though not formal position statements, reflect the interests of NASP. The series of videotapes on consultation and current issues produced by the APA's Division 16 also reflect the interests of this national group. These unofficial, yet obviously sanctioned, books and products may indirectly influence daily practice. Certainly the national organizations would like to think they have some influence. Finally, other organization-sponsored standards or guidelines exist that do not get the visibility that those above have received but are nonetheless very important (e.g., *Standards for Educational and Psychological Testing*, prepared by AERA, the APA, & NCME, 1999; see also Turner, DeMers, Fox, & Reed, 2001).

Although the influence of formal standards documents can be observed in accreditation and credentialing practices, the mechanisms for national-level influence on daily practice are complicated and unclear. In a few instances, NASP and APA Division 16 have become involved in local practice and professional issues such as the *Larry P. v. Riles* case in California (1972, 1984) and the Muriel Forrest case in New York (*Forrest v. Ambach*, 1980). Also, in other incidents NASP made direct contact with a district superintendent expressing concern for the problems identified by that district's school psychologists. The expression of support by a national organization for the school psychologists in these cases has been more noteworthy than the outcomes. The cases help the national group to scrutinize its policies and their impact and to better articulate its positions. However, such interventions have not led to direct changes in daily practice. Any subsequent changes in the field have been the result of local forces using state or national association guidelines or positions to influence changes. The improvements were more a result of changes in district perceptions and expectations than the result of national group intervention. Often the uninvited intervention by a national group is not appreciated by the school district and can heighten tensions between administrators and psychologists. Nevertheless, important changes can be made by proper coordination of national and state group intervention with the influence of local determinants.

The primary determinants of the school psychologist's daily practice are in the school district and its community.

Changing Roles and Functions

The strongest mechanisms for role and function change are local. The primary determinants of the school psychologist's daily practice are in the school district and its community. Efforts to change school psychologists' roles and functions will be ineffective if the first three determinants—district demands and expectations, districts' perceptions of their needs, and consumer responses—are not changed. Indirect efforts, such as changing training and credentialing requirements, improving legislative recognition of school psychological services, taking formal positions on practice, or revising standards and ethics, are important but less influential.

Meaningful changes in roles and functions require shifts in the top three direct determinants, concurrent with shifts in school psychologists' desired functions and personal competencies, that have presumably been influenced by the indirect variables in Table 7.1 (e.g., training and credentialing). In this analysis, role and function change requires coordinated efforts at the local, state, and national levels by practitioners, trainers, and the leadership of groups that have power and authority in school psychology. Lasting change also must be accepted as a gradual process rather than the result of revolution or school reform delivered from the state or national levels.

Ethical and Legal Influences

A few of the above determinants deserve extra comment. These include professional ethics, legal matters related to federal legislation, and litigation.

Everyone has opinions of what constitutes ethical behavior, what is right, or what one ought to do in certain circumstances. That is, everyone has a personal code of behavior. When people choose to join a profession, they voluntarily modify or expand their personal beliefs by accepting the code of practice of that profession. This allegiance to a prescribed set of professional guidelines for behavior symbolizes the profession's ideal of placing the client's interests before all others. It is this aspect of professionalism that is sometimes referred to as a calling to one's profession. When people join a professional association, they agree to

When people choose to join a profession, they voluntarily modify or expand their personal beliefs by accepting the code of practice of that profession.

adhere to its code of ethics and can expect to be held accountable accordingly by their peers in that association. Thus, in making professional decisions, school psychologists modify their "intuitive level" of decision making in favor of a "critical–evaluative level" (Jacob & Hartshorne, 2007). They make decisions based on the observations and research findings related to the practice. This is the essence of Gray's (1963b) concept of the data-oriented problem solver and of the scientist–practitioner model. School psychologists also make decisions based on current legal decisions and ethical considerations.

General Concepts of Ethical Practice

The day-to-day practice of school psychology does not require frequent review of the APA or NASP codes (see appendixes C and D, respectively), although familiarity with, and adherence to, the codes is expected. School psychologists have had instruction in ethics during their academic preparation, including reviews of the codes, and have demonstrated an appropriate sense of professional responsibility during training and internship. In addition, continued professional development (CPD) fosters ethical knowledge and practice. Nevertheless, situations arise that require practitioners and academic school psychologists to review what course of action would be most proper. In so doing, school psychologists are guided by general concepts embraced by their ethical codes.

(1) Codes of ethics refer to the overt behavior of the professional. They relate to what the professional ought to do (rather than feel or think) about situations. Thus, codes guide overt behaviors. (2) Client welfare and the welfare of the community are paramount considerations in guiding professional behavior. This general concept is related to ethical principles that deal with competence; the rights, dignity, and welfare of others; and responsibility to the broader community. These propositions are identified in the APA code's preamble and general principles and in the NASP code's sections II (Professional Competency) and III (Professional Relationships).

(3) Peer review is helpful and its use is encouraged in resolving difficult situations. This approach presumes that professionals keep abreast of developments in their field and have a reasonable sense of what their peers do or would do in similar situations. Practitioners who are unclear about how to resolve a situation can discuss it with other school psychologists before reaching conclusions and taking action. (4) The use of ethics to guide professional behavior is central to the regulation of practice and credentialing. Although the advice of "Let your conscience be your guide" would seem to lend itself to abuse, review mechanisms exist in each SBEP for handling suspected violations of the credentialing law, including violations of the profession's code of ethics. Similar mechanisms exist within SDE credentialing processes. Violations of ethics may also be reviewed by the state psychology and school psychology associations and by the APA and NASP, and ethical codes may be used by the courts as guidelines for determining proper behavior.

(5) Professionals respect the work of their colleagues and that of practitioners in other professions. The school psychologist avoids belittling the work of other school psychologists or making recommendations only to certain other professionals in the community. For example, what should a school psychologist do if some elementary teachers tell him or her that they are opening a tutoring service in the

community and would appreciate having some referrals sent their way? Dealing with such situations is not always easy. Practitioners can avoid these dilemmas by maintaining lists of available referral resources in several service categories. School psychologists inevitably come to evaluate the work of some professionals more highly than others. Nevertheless, professionals should avoid showing preferences. If they believe that the services of some practitioners are improper, the alleged violations should be handled in the same manner as other ethical violations, and not by systematically steering referrals to favored colleagues in school psychology or other fields. 6. In the management of alleged ethical violations, the overriding goals are to correct the present situation and prevent its recurrence. The process is more corrective and educative than punitive, though in some instances punitive actions may result, including dismissal from graduate training, expulsion from association membership, or revocation of an individual's credentials. In court proceedings, the process can be far more adversarial, with very serious punitive consequences in cases of malpractice. In most instances, professionals seek to resolve suspected ethical violations privately and informally with the parties involved. The APA and NASP have developed procedures for adjudicating ethical complaints, and guidelines are available from these organizations. Because professionals are expected to report and properly adjudicate such complaints, failure to do so may constitute a violation of the codes. Jacob and Hartshorne (2007) discuss an eight-step problem-solving model for considering ethical complaints, based on the work of Koocher and Keith-Spiegel (1998). The model emphasizes first identifying the problem and ethical issues involved and then considering various options for action and their implications.

The above are general considerations with which to review codes of ethics. Other configurations exist, including Jacob and Hartshorne (2007), who consolidate their considerations of ethical codes around four broad principles: "(a) respect for the dignity of persons, (b) responsible caring (professional competence and responsibility), (c) integrity in professional relationships, and (d) responsibility to community and society" (p. 10). Their configuration captures the essence of the guiding principles of the APA and the NASP codes.

APA and NASP Codes

The APA *Ethical Principles of Psychologists and Code of Conduct* consists of a preamble, five general principles (A through E), and specific ethical standards (1.01 through 10.10) that are broad enough to apply to psychologists in varied professional and scientific roles (APA, 2002). The code applies to psychologists in all practice settings. However, because they apply to clinical and counseling psychologists who typically do not work in school settings, the APA code may be especially relevant to school psychologists practicing outside the schools. For example, the code addresses therapy more specifically than the NASP code. SBEP credentialing examinations assume familiarity with the APA code. Both codes address assessment, relationships, including sexual misconduct, consent, and confidentiality. The 2002 APA code appears in appendix C.

The NASP code applies to school-based and non-school-based practitioners as well as to university trainers, state consultants, administrators, and supervisors in their respective roles and places of employment.

The 2000 edition of the NASP *Principles for Professional Ethics* (2000a) is specific to the specialty of school psychology and applies to all school psychologists regardless of setting. Thus the code applies to school-based and non-school-based practitioners as well as to university trainers, state consultants, administrators, and supervisors in their respective roles and places of employment. The principles are organized around several broad areas: professional competency, professional relationships, general principles of professional practices, and professional practice settings including independent practice. The NASP code is especially helpful to school-based practitioners. It addresses conflicts that may occur in the context of school practice and in school-based practitioners' relationships with nonschool practitioners and the private practice of school psychology. The 2000 edition appears in appendix D. The ethics presented in the NASP principles complement NASP's *Guidelines for the Provision of School Psychological Services* (NASP, 2000b) and reinforce them in several ways. For example, both documents provide guidelines for school psychologists in private practice and specifically forbid private practice by district school psychologists with clients for whom they are responsible in their school setting. This is an important issue because an increasing number of school psychologists are seeking dual employment, which may give rise to conflicts of interest. Familiarity with both documents is assumed in the examination process for the NCSP. The distinctions between the intent of the NASP code and that of the NASP standards are addressed by Reinhardt and Martin (1991).

Examples of Ethical Problems

Among the few nationally representative studies of the ethical dilemmas of school psychologists is that of Jacob-Timm (1999), in which 226 responding NASP members identified 222 ethically challenging incidents that were assigned to 19 categories. The more prevalent categories were administrative pressure to act unethically, especially incidents related to special education eligibility, placement, and services (49 dilemmas); assessment, such as questionable findings and diagnoses, inadequate interpretations, and poor-quality reports (32 dilemmas); confidentiality, such as duty to protect a child from harm and breach of confidentiality (30 dilemmas); and unsound educational practices, for example, detrimental teaching practices, ineffective programs, and discipline (28 dilemmas). Other categories included failure to address student needs, job competence and job performance, psychologist–parent dilemmas, psychological records, conflictual relationships, client self-determination and informed consent, therapeutic interventions, academic settings, supervision, sexual issues, payment, taking credit for other's work, confrontation of unethical conduct, credentials, research and publishing, plus a 20th category, miscellaneous (e.g., the psychologist was a poor role model). Despite not achieving a nationally representative sample of respondents, the survey's identification of specific incidents encountered by many school psychologists makes this research useful for instruction.

An earlier national survey of APA members and fellows identified 23 categories of 703 "ethically troubling incidents," with the top three categories related to confidentiality, conflictual relationships, and methods of collecting fees (Pope & Vetter, 1992). Fifteen incidents (2% of the total) were mentioned in the category "school psychology," and the examples given suggest administrator–practitioner conflicts in role and function. Examples included, "My school district administrator would like me to distort test data to show improvement" and "As a school psychologist there is often pressure from administrators to place children in programs based on the availability of services rather than the needs of the individual student" (Pope & Vetter, p. 406). Despite a lack of representativeness in sampling, the problems cited by the school psychologists in this study suggest serious ethical conflicts related to some employer–employee relationships. Often the relationship in which school psychologists are supervised by nonschool psychologists contributes to these dilemmas; such problems may be more widespread than is recognized. Survey data reported in Jann (1991) suggest that supervisory pressures are fairly common, though less problematic, when the supervisor is a school psychologist. However, regardless of the circumstances, the alteration of assessment information or the placement of children in programs on bases other than their needs constitutes serious ethical and legal misconduct.

Competency. A related ethical dilemma occurs when school psychologists' supervisors ask them to perform services for which they are not competently prepared. This issue illustrates the need for continuing education and is relevant to ethical principles that deal with practitioner competency and client welfare. This particular dilemma was addressed in a *Communiqué* article as part of a series on ethical issues (Grossman, 1992). In other instances, school psychologists may engage in activities for which they think they are competent but are not. For example, aspects of the SDE's comprehensive job description for school psychologists may not apply to all individuals who hold the credential. Some practitioners may not be adequately prepared for consultation or group counseling, for example, and should not provide such services until they have received preparation. A more blatant ethical violation is that of practicing outside the bounds of what is typically considered the field of school psychology. For example, making diagnoses or recommendations about sensory functioning and physical health are considered to be the domain of other professions. Information relevant to school psychology training and practice is provided in *Petition for Reaffirmation of the Specialty of School Psychology* (2005) and in Ysseldyke et al. (1997). Among the more egregious historical examples of practitioner incompetence was the case of Dr. Gestalt. "When a school board member asked his school psychologist about the nature of the Bender–Gestalt test used in his practice, the psychologist, with incredible and undeniable naiveté, replied, 'Oh, that's a test made up by Dr. Bender and Dr. Gestalt'" (Rosenfeld & Blanco, 1974, p. 263).

Respecting the client's right to privacy is a paramount ethical and legal aspect of practice.

Privileges and Special Categories. Additional dilemmas arise when services are required for special categories of children. For example, in some states school psychologists may be prohibited from providing services to children identified as having traumatic brain injury (TBI) until the practitioner has acquired additional training. Continuing efforts at the national level to secure prescription privileges for professional psychologists could also cause a dilemma. The APA's Division 16 issued a report on the implications of prescription privileges in school psychology (Kubiszyn, Brown, Landau, DeMers, & Reynolds, 1992). Prescription privileges and other special practice applications will have different implications for doctoral and nondoctoral practitioners, and continuing professional development will be essential to the expansion of roles and functions and to ethical practice in the future (Fowler & Harrison, 2001).

Confidentiality and the Right to Privacy. Respecting the client's right to privacy is a paramount ethical and legal aspect of practice. Professionals who work in a public school setting with colleagues who have varying interest in their work can create problems of confidentiality. These concerns are closely related to the dilemmas of clientage discussed in chapter 3, in which parents, teachers, administrators, and others might want to be involved in the practitioner's case and have access to information that is considered confidential. The accessibility of assessment records and reports, conversations about a case, written communications, phone conversations, and so on all pose threats to confidentiality that are less probable in the isolation of individual private practice.

As seen in some litigation, maintaining confidentiality is not a simple matter when the client is a minor and the school psychologist does not have the security of "privileged communication." That is, under certain and not necessarily rare circumstances, school psychologists and other pupil personnel service staff can be expected, even forced, to divulge information that the child may have thought was being discussed confidentially. The concepts of confidentiality, privileged communication, and respect for the privacy of others are essential to the ethical practice of psychologists.

Ethics in Training. Although specific to students in clinical and counseling psychology, the findings of Fly, van Bark, Weinman, Kitchener, and Lang (1997) provide a perspective on the ethical transgressions of students in training. Using a "critical incident" technique employed by previous studies, they found that the categorical proportion of transgressions were confidentiality (25%), professional boundaries (both sexual and nonsexual; 20%), plagiarism or falsification of data (15%), welfare (10%), procedural breach with ethical implications (10%), competency (9%), integrity–dishonesty (8%), and misrepresentation of credentials (3%). Outcomes of the transgressions included remedial action in 44% of cases and dismissal from the program in 22% of cases. The study pointed to the importance of managing ethical incidents in professional training; only 54% of the students involved had taken an ethics course. A discussion on managing problematic students from the standpoint of training, supervision, and student peers appears in a special section of *Professional Psychology: Research and Practice*, 2004, Vol. 35, No. 2).

Ethics and the Law. School psychologists must be familiar with legal aspects of ethical actions. Disregard for confidentiality can result in defamation of character, including *libel* (written defamation) and *slander* (spoken defamation). Another complicated area of confidentiality is the balance between making tests accessible to professionals with a legitimate interest in their contents and the need to protect the copyright privileges of test publishers (see e.g., APA, Committee on Psychological Tests and Assessment, 1996a; Canter, 1990b; Woody, 1998).

Confidentiality and the Law. The arena of confidentiality probably poses the most intense dilemmas for pupil personnel workers. In some instances, dilemmas of ethical behavior, such as issues of confidentiality, have both ethical and legal ramifications. Jacob and Hartshorne (2007) discuss the conflicting ethical and legal aspects of *Pesce v. J. Sterling Morton High School District* (1986), a case in which the school psychologist's decision to maintain confidentiality was judged to be inconsistent with the state's child abuse reporting laws (see pp. 199–201). The school psychologist's claim to confidentiality was insufficient to ignore the reporting requirements of abuse laws. It is generally conceded that legal requirements supersede ethical considerations.

Other Legal Pitfalls. Almost nothing is known about the frequency of sexual misconduct and abuse between school psychologists and their clients despite more open discussion of these issues. Occasionally such matters make their way into the local papers, and such behavior almost certainly results in the revocation of all practice privileges and credentials of the practitioners involved.

Finally, with the increasing interest in private practice and the availability of "third-party reimbursement" for school psychological services, school psychologists must be familiar with the ethical issues and legal aspects of private practice. For example, fraudulent practices in billing for services have attended the recent expansion of professional psychology into the private sector (Pope & Vetter, 1992). The issues surrounding third-party insurer payments for school psychological services are discussed by Canter (1990a, 1991a). Discussions of areas in which ethics and law overlap and often conflict can be found in Cardon, Kuriloff, and Phillips (1975); Jacob and Hartshorne (2007); Phillips (1990a); Prasse (1995); Reschly and Bersoff (1999); and Sales, Krauss, Sacken, and Overcast (1999).

Other Resources

The Canadian Psychological Association has a code of ethics (CPA, 2000), which with some modification has been adopted by the Canadian Association of School Psychologists (CASP). CASP also provides *Standards for Professional Practice in School Psychology* (CASP, n.d.). The International School Psychology Association has a code of ethics that corresponds closely to the main provisions of the APA and NASP codes (Oakland, Goldman, & Bischoff, 1997). A related set of ethical standards is that of the American Counseling Association (ACA, 2005). Though not directly applicable to school psychologists who are not ACA members, these standards are unique in providing sections specifically on counseling relationships, consulting, and private practice. The ASPPB publishes its own *Code of Conduct* (2005) and a related instructional videotape, *Ethical Dilemmas Facing Psychologists*. The Canadian Psychological Association website (*www.cpa.ca*) compares the Canadian code with those of the APA and the ASPPB. Some states have a code of ethics for educators that may supersede the codes of the APA or NASP. For example, Georgia's code of ethics for educators applies to all professionals who hold a certificate from the state's Professional Standards Commission (see *www.gapsc.com/Professionalpractices/Nethics.asp*).

Few texts on ethics and law specifically address school psychologists (Gredler, 1972; Jacob & Hartshorne, 2007; Valett, 1963). The Jacob and Hartshorne text draws together legal decisions and ethical codes to help clarify professional actions in most situations. The book is a comprehensive treatment of legal and ethical issues in school psychology and includes numerous examples from case studies to illustrate specific principles. An earlier work by Valett is also relevant to contemporary school psychological practice. Valett presents an interesting discussion of professional issues and dilemmas related to several areas of practice. The book discusses many aspects of the field of school psychology, and each chapter poses practical problems for discussion. The many vignettes in the book provide practice problems relevant to ethical, legal, and just plain practical concerns. Valett gives the following example related to administrative problems at a hypothetical school:

> A group of parents have questioned the continued use of personality tests in the counseling and school psychology program. They have requested that the school psychologist make a presentation at the next PTA meeting of all tests presently used and the way in which they contribute to the educational program and work with individual students. (p. 269)

Technological advancements have raised additional ethical concerns, including the use of computer-generated report-writing and test-scoring programs (Carlson & Martin, 1997; Sutkiewicz, 1997), fax machines (Batts & Grossman, 1997), and pagers (DiVerde-Nushawg & Walls, 1998; Tracy, 1998). A survey of the use of technology by practitioners in private practice, and related ethical concerns, supports the need for additional guidelines (McMinn, Buchanan, Ellens, & Ryan, 1999). A summary of guidelines for using technology in school psychology practice appears in Harvey and Carlson (2003), who also caution that technology should be used to enhance practice rather than replace traditional practice, and that responsibility continues to rest with the practitioner. A discussion of the types of technology available for use, and related ethical concerns, appears in Pfohl and Pfohl (2002). Ethical concerns and responsibilities related to participation in Internet groups (e.g., e-mail discussion lists) are examined in Humphreys, Winzelberg, and Klaw (2000).

Finally, it is important to rely on recent research and opinion related to ethical behavior. Although earlier reviews provide perspectives on professional behavior, expectations of professionals change over the years, reflecting the broader societal context in which services are delivered. Guidelines have been established for specific situations and clients, such as for gay, lesbian and bisexual groups (see Division 44 Commission, 2000). Some state association newsletters carry regular columns on ethics, and a series of ethics articles have appeared in the Division 16 newsletter, *The School Psychologist*, and in the NASP *Communiqué* (see, e.g., the index in Vol. 19, No. 7). Case studies occasionally appear in the *American Psychologist*. Reviews of ethical issues in training and practice have also appeared in the journal *Professional Psychology: Research and Practice*. Because ethics and best practices guidelines are closely related, *Best Practices in School Psychology* (Thomas & Grimes, 1985, 1990,

1995, 2002, 2008) is a very useful guide. Graduate education in ethical principles is discussed in a 1992 special section of *Professional Psychology: Research and Practice* (Vol. 23, No. 3), and ethics training in school psychology programs is discussed in Daley, Nagle, and Onwuegbuzie (1998) and Swenson (1998). Additional information on legal and ethical issues is provided by the school psychology literature related to child maltreatment and children's rights. Historical perspective is provided by Hart (1991), and comprehensive discussions appear in special issues of the *School Psychology Review*, such as on psychological maltreatment of children (1987, Vol. 16, No. 2, 1987), on children's rights (1991, Vol. 20, No. 3), and on children, research, and public policy (1996, Vol. 25, No. 2).

In addition to the ethical aspects of conducting research, the matter of publication authorship has recently been addressed (Murray, 1998), as have concerns for copyright laws in the use of test and instructional materials (Woody, 1998). A recent article identified the most common questions posed to the APA's Practice Directorate (Committee on Professional Practice and Standards, 2003). The article discussed differences between ethical and legal violations, common practice concerns in professional relationships, confidentiality and privileged communication, management of records, termination of services, and issues related to psychology as a business. The article contains numerous resources for additional clarification and is most helpful for psychologists in private practice. A survey by Helton and Ray (2005) suggests different ways in which school psychologists and special educators predicted they would respond to dilemmas associated with implementation of the IEP, assessment data, related services, and the adequacy of instructional materials. The strategies, including prevention, suggest ways practitioners could resist local pressure to behave unethically. A discussion of how the 2002 APA code of conduct applies to school psychology practice and the management of dilemmas appears in Flanagan, Miller, and Jacob (2005).

The Jacob and Hartshorne book is a comprehensive treatment of legal and ethical issues in school psychology and includes numerous examples from case studies to illustrate specific principles.

Legislation

As mentioned in chapter 3, public education is an intensely regulated business. Part of that regulation is related to legislation, constitutional provisions, and court rulings delineating the scope of the state's responsibility to educate its citizens, the rights of students, the needs of exceptional students, provision of professional services, professional malpractice, and research. In-depth discussions of the background and implications of these influences appear in Fischer and Sorenson (1991), Jacob and Hartshorne (2007), Phillips (1990a), Reschly and Bersoff (1999), Reynolds, Gutkin, Elliott, and Witt (1984), and Sales et al. (1999).

FERPA, Section 504, and IDEA

Two laws were passed in the 1970s that were among the most important legislation for the daily practice of school psychologists. The first was the Family Educational Rights and Privacy Act of 1974 (FERPA, Pub. L. 93-380). Influenced by the Russell Sage Foundation Conference Guidelines (Goslin, 1969), FERPA clarified the rights of parents and of students 18 and older to inspect, challenge, and correct records and required written permission for the gathering and dissemination of records. The second was the Education for All Handicapped Children Act of 1975 (EAHCA, Pub. L. 94-142), which was influenced by Section 504 of the Rehabilitation Act of 1973. EAHCA was reauthorized in 1997 as the Individuals with Disabilities Education Act (IDEA, Pub. L. 105-117) and most recently as the Individuals with Disabilities Education Improvement Act, 2004 (Pub. L. 108-446). These laws have been a virtual civil rights act for the disabled, entitling them to a free and appropriate public education, nondiscriminatory assessment practices, due process procedures, and an individualized educational plan (IEP) for services to be delivered under the least restrictive environment (LRE) concept. An extension of EAHCA in 1986 granted aspects of the previous law to infants and toddlers through an individualized family service plan (FSP; Pub. L. 99-457).

These laws essentially ended an era in which student records were liberally shared among school personnel and community agencies, when students were evaluated for special educational placement without parental permission, and when special education was often delivered in highly segregated facilities. The laws established what have become routine requirements for providing special educational programs for all eligible children, regardless of the nature of their disabilities, and for providing related services, including psychological services. Parental consent is now an integral part of the assessment process, as well as of the gathering and dissemination of child study information. Among the more controversial aspects of the legislation for the handicapped have been the provisions for nonbiased assessment, due process and informed consent, and educational placement in the least restrictive environment, sometimes implemented by such practices as mainstreaming and inclusion. The impact of the legislation on school psychology was the topic of a special issue of the *Journal of School Psychology* in 1975 (Vol. 13, No. 4). The issue included articles on school psychologists as witnesses in due process hearings, legal–ethical conflicts, and training.

The literature of the mid-1970s was replete with discussions of FERPA and EAHCA. That literature and more recent discussions are highly relevant to practice. For example, Telzrow (1999) questioned the extent to which schools and professionals were prepared to implement the major provisions of the 1997 amendments to IDEA and offered suggestions for better implementation. Havey (1999) found that 38% of reporting school psychologists had been involved in one or more due process hearings and on average spent 1 hour testifying and 7.5 hours in preparation. The most common issues in their hearings were assessment and appropriateness of placement. Tips on serving in due process hearings or as an expert witness are in Elias (1999), Kimball and Bansilal (1998), Stumme (1995), and Zirkel (2001).

The 2004 reauthorization intensified the long-running debate on eligibility criteria, especially in the area of learning disabilities. Adding to the growing insistence on empirically supported interventions in psychology and validated instructional practices in education, the new eligibility criteria for learning disabilities allow response to intervention (RTI) to be substituted for significant discrepancy between normative ability and achievement. Collectively, these add strength to the historical movement to establish practices more in line with psychoeducational science, to take more preventive approaches, and to increasingly deliver services in the regular education sector.

These laws ended an era in which student records were liberally shared among school personnel and community agencies, when students were evaluated for special educational placement without parental permission, and when special education was often delivered in highly segregated facilities.

Discussions have also centered on inclusion (see, e.g., Pfeiffer & Reddy, 1999). Recent trends toward greater inclusion of special education students within regular education programs, and the provision of services to at-risk children, have drawn attention to the differences between the provisions of Section 504 and those of IDEA. The former is more inclusive and requires services for some children who may not be eligible according to IDEA (e.g., children with attention deficit disorders). It seems probable that in the future more families will turn to the provisions of Section 504 to justify accommodations of instructional and related services for their children. This could speed up a shift in special education toward more noncategorical services and a greater emphasis on interventions and outcomes. Both Section 504 and IDEA have overlapping protections for children and families related to due process, assessment, educational plans, and so on.

To examine some important differences in the two laws, comparisons of the laws are published in a *Communiqué* series initiated in September 1992, and resources are available from the Council of Administrators of Special Education (*www.casecec.org*). The Jacob and Hartshorne (2007) text is a major source for such comparisons. The diagnostic decisions of school psychologists are heavily influenced by the disability classifications as defined by these laws and their regulations. Most school districts adhere to these definitions in the implementation of special education programs.

Another classification system is the American Psychiatric Association's *Diagnostic and Statistical Manual of Mental Disorders: 4th Edition* (DSM-IV-TR, American Psychiatric Association, 2000). Together these classification systems drive the diagnostic categorization of the practice of school psychology. The application of DSM-IV to school psychology was discussed in a 1996 special issue of the *School Psychology Review* (Vol. 25, No. 3) and the application of DSM-IV-TR in a book by House (2002).

The No Child Left Behind Act (NCLB)

Perhaps nothing has stressed the importance of providing school psychology services to regular education as much as the implementation in 2001 of the No Child Left Behind Act (NCLB, Pub. L. 107-110). Although the law has expectations for special needs students, it is predominantly aimed at regular educational practices. With its emphasis on student academic proficiency, adequate yearly progress, reduction of dropout rates, improved attendance, and highly qualified educators, including school psychologists, this law has created as much debate in general education circles as did the implementation of EAHCA in the 1970s. Armed with competencies in statistics, research design, test interpretation, and consultation techniques, in addition to traditional practice competencies, school psychologists may be drawn into regular education to a greater extent, thus loosening the strong historical ties to special education. However, as with the Goals 2000 program during the 1990s, the future of the NCLB ideals beyond the current federal government administration remains to be seen.

HIPAA

The Health Insurance Portability and Accountability Act (HIPAA), implemented in 2003, set rules for how records are transmitted electronically and how privacy of personal health care information is maintained. Although the impact of this law on school-based practice appears modest, it is an important law for any health service professional in the private sector. A discussion of the school-based implications appears in Icove and Palomares (2003), and implications in the private sector appear in the APA's *Monitor on Psychology* (2003, Vol. 34, No. 1). Several resources are provided in the September/October 2002 issue of *The National Psychologist*. The fifth edition of Jacob and Hartshorne (2007) also carries information on HIPAA.

Litigation

Several major court decisions related to federal legislation have influenced the delivery of special education and the practice of school psychology, especially in the area of assessment (Reschly & Bersoff, 1999; Salvia & Ysseldyke, 2007). Some of these decisions preceded and influenced the wording and enactment of FERPA in 1974 and EAHCA in 1975. The rulings affected the following aspects of special education and school psychology practice:

- The rights of disabled children to receive a free and appropriate education (*Mills v. Board of Education of the District of Columbia*, 1972; *PARC v. Commonwealth of Pennsylvania*, 1971, 1972);
- The assessment of minority children (*Hobson v. Hansen*, 1967; *Guadalupe Organization, Inc. v. Tempe Elementary School District No. 3*, 1972; *Larry P. v. Riles*, 1972, 1984; *Parents in Action on Special Education [PASE] v. Hannon*, 1980)
- The confidentiality of professional–client communications (*Pesce v. J. Morton Sterling High School District*, 1986; *Tarasoff v. Regents of California*, 1974, 1976; Zirkel, 1992)
- The importance of professional ethics in practice (*Forrest v. Ambach*, 1980, 1983)
- The necessity to follow the provisions of special education laws (*Mattie T. v. Holladay*, 1979)

Many other cases also have influenced the practice of school psychology and special education. These are often discussed in graduate courses related to special education, psychoeducational assessment, and legal and ethical aspects of practice. The work of Reschly, Kicklighter, and McKee (1988a, 1988b, 1988c) describe the impact of selected cases on school psychology practice. Assistance in conducting research on litigation is available in Knapp, Vandecreek, and Zirkel (1985). The relative absence of landmark litigation in the past decade suggests a growing acceptance of special education legislation and increased effectiveness of school districts' implementation. Although reauthorizations of IDEA and the recent NCLB are significant events, they are adjustments to the educational processes initiated in the 1970s to provide better special education and to diminish the gaps in achievement across cultural groups.

School psychologists have become much more active in the legislative process at the state and national levels. The activity is both reactive (responding to legislative efforts already in progress) and proactive (initiating legislative efforts) on issues important to children and families, education, psychology, and school psychology. Several state associations have active legislative networks or lobbyists. NASP has been highly visible in its School Psychologists Action Network (SPAN). In this process, school psychologists often provide testimony to legislative bodies and promote legislation through legislative contacts. The importance of such efforts was learned in the 1970s when school psychology struggled with the mandates of FERPA and EAHCA. Although NASP and the APA had input into the legislative process at that time, it was very modest compared with their present positions. A guide to providing testimony appears in Sorenson, Masson, Clark, and Morin (1998) and in materials available from NASP and the APA. The legislative area of professional school psychology groups is among the most visible of association activities.

Influence of Government Funding on Practice

The widespread regulation of practice in the past 40 years has created potentially uncomfortable circumstances in several areas of service delivery. Permission from parents and guardians for initiating services is now routine, sharing of records among professionals and agencies is more cumbersome, and clients ineligible for traditional special education services are often eligible under Section 504. All of these conditions are well known to practicing school psychologists. In the 1990s two additional areas of concern emerged. First was the requirement that families have a diagnosis to receive compensation from the government through its Supplemental Security Income (SSI) Program. This is different from the Medicaid reimbursements school districts receive for school psychologists' services. The SSI compensation is paid directly to the person or the parent or guardian and not to the school district. To be eligible for SSI, a person must be age 65 or older, blind or disabled, have limited resources and income, and meet certain other requirements (Social Security Administration, 2000). The SSI program applies to adults and children with physical or mental impairments. The monthly compensation may be at least $500 for each disabled child in the family. School psychologists have been approved in many states to assess children for SSI income benefits. Some school psychologists feel pressured by parents to identify their child as disabled in order to receive these funds. It is not known how widespread a legal or ethical problem this has become, but the controversial program has come under scrutiny (Stanhope, 1995). Little has been published regarding abuse of the assessment process in the school psychology literature, although many school psychologists have privately acknowledged that parents of some indigent children have pressured them to label their children so they can receive SSI.

A second concern is the rapid growth in the number of college students seeking a disability label, usually a learning disability or attention deficit hyperactivity disorder (ADHD), to obtain special considerations in the admission process, supportive services, or other accommodations (e.g., course substitutions, extended time for exams, preferential seating, readers, and transcribers). This situation requires professionals to become investigative practitioners instead of advocates, as they were previously.

The issue in both these situations is not the legitimacy of the programs or the need for services; rather, it is that the client stands to gain something from being labeled. School psychologists, especially those working in secondary and postsecondary educational settings, may find themselves in somewhat adversarial roles with their clients, not unlike the role attorneys may play when they're defending a client they suspect to be guilty. The problems and dilemmas surrounding these cases are detailed in a paper about students who sought accommodations for the Law School Admissions Test (LSAT; Ranseen, 1998). Reviewing 50 cases in which individual adults were diagnosed as ADD or ADHD and received accommodations on the LSAT, Ranseen found that only 8% had any previous diagnosis during childhood or adolescence, and 48% were diagnosed following *completion* of law school. The paper should be required reading for anyone involved with postsecondary assessments for accommodations. The paper is also worthy for its discussion of the problems of adult ADD and ADHD diagnosis. At the very least it will raise the level of consciousness for practitioners.

School psychologists or those in training will want to be alert to the issues surrounding practices with Section 504 and the 1990 Americans with Disabilities Act (ADA; Pub. L. 101-336). Many postsecondary institutions have adopted specific documentation requirements and procedures predicated on national guidelines from the Association on Higher Education and Disability (see resources at *www.ahead.org*).

Liability Insurance

The complex relationships of ethics, legislation, and litigation underscore the importance of carrying professional liability insurance. Only a few agencies and major carriers offer professional liability insurance plans. Typically school psychologists purchase liability insurance through their membership in NASP or the APA. Rates vary depending on the state, coverage and deductibles, and practice setting. For NASP members, coverage is available through the American Professional Agency (*www.americanprofessional.com*) and through Forrest T. Jones and Company (*www.ftj.com*). The cost of coverage through these agencies is quite reasonable, and coverage is provided for students as well as school-based and private practitioners. The American Professional Agency's website has a section on shopping the market that helps consumers decide on coverage and carriers. Higher costs might be anticipated from other carriers, including plans available for doctoral psychologists from the APA Insurance Trust, which is affiliated with the American Psychological Association (*www.apait.org*). Liability insurance protects practitioners from the excessive cost of defending themselves in litigation brought by clients, and provides compensation to clients if harm is shown to have been done by practitioners. Other organizations offering insurance programs include the American Counseling Association and the American Mental Health Counselors Association.

The complex relationships of ethics, legislation, and litigation underscore the importance of carrying professional liability insurance.

Sources of Funding

Another variable influencing school psychology practice is the source of funding for school psychological services. Few studies have attempted to connect the sources of funding with the types of services provided by school psychologists. Eberst (1984) found that the most common funding for school psychological services emanated from sources related to special education and then general education, and finally funding came from local sources. Summarizing her findings, Eberst concluded:

> The type of funding appears to have little effect on the role and function of school psychologists. The comments of the respondents suggested that school psychologists spend most of their time conducting individual psychoeducational assessments of handicapped children, writing reports, and serving on multidisciplinary and/or evaluation teams. These activities are mandated in most states, regardless of the primary source of funding used. (p. 15)

The Eberst study seemingly supports the authors' contention that administrators' perceptions of needs and their role expectations and demands determine what school psychologists do on a daily basis. Funding itself does not appear to be a strong determinant but seems to help shape the perceptions and subsequent expectations for services. It does not appear to be critical from the perspective of the practitioner, since at least half of the practitioners surveyed in the Eberst study reported being uncertain about the source of funding for their positions (Curtis, Hunley, Walker, & Baker, 1999; Graden & Curtis, 1991).

In the past decade, states have drawn on Medicaid funding to reimburse school psychologists' services in school settings. A recent survey revealed that in 41 states, mental health services provided in school systems were reimbursed by Medicaid. The most commonly reimbursed services included individual and group therapy and psychological evaluations. The credentials required of the service provider varied from state to state, but it was clear that school-based school psychologists were often able to have their services reimbursed. The amount of statewide Medicaid funding expended to school systems at the time of the survey varied, from under $1 million to more than $83 million (Wrobel & Krieg, 1998). The extent of influence that Medicaid or other third-party reimbursement plans might have on school psychology practice is unclear.

A Brief Look at Canadian School Psychology

Canadian and U.S. history have many commonalties. Though European influences are noticeable, Canada's educational system and its practice of school psychology are similar in many respects to those of the United States. Whereas the U.S. system of education is developed around state and federal influence, that of Canada is developed around 10 independent provincial systems of elementary and secondary education with direct federal influence; however, Canada does not have a national department of education. Regulatory influences can be observed, with provincial legislation analogous to the provisions of EAHCA and its IDEA reauthorizations. Many parallels exist within the field of school psychology. Practice concerns such as role and function restrictions, supervision, or the issue of doctoral versus nondoctoral practice are also observed in Canadian literature and conferences. Provincial authorities regulate the practice of psychology, and struggles between provincial psychology boards and education boards for the credentialing of educational (school) psychologists are often parallel to those observed in the United States. In several provinces psychologists and school psychologists are in separate associations (e.g., in Alberta, British Columbia, Manitoba, and Quebec), and they hold separate affiliations with the Canadian Psychological Association or the Canadian Association of School Psychologists.

With modest changes, the direct and indirect forces identified for professional regulation of school psychology in the United States could be applied to Canada as well.

Figures 7.1 and 7.2 and Table 7.1 in this chapter could be readily implemented to describe the professional regulation of school psychology in Canada. With modest changes, the direct and indirect forces identified for professional regulation of school psychology in the United States could be applied to Canada as well. The rich cultural influences of its bilingual (English and French) and native heritage make the practice of Canadian school psychology as complex and challenging as practice in the United States (Fagan, 1987b). The importance of Canadian school psychology is reflected in the decision to include a chapter on the topic in this book.

CONCLUSION

The factors controlling the preparation, credentialing, and daily roles and functions of school psychology professionals are summarized in Table 7.1. The scheme of determinants in Table 7.1 represents the opinions of the authors; others might view the relative strength of the determinants differently. The controlling variables are divided into direct and indirect variables for each area of regulation. For example, of the variables involved in controlling preparation and credentialing for practice, the direct variables for preparation serve as the indirect variables for credentialing, and vice versa. The direct variables in each domain are largely independent and become the indirect variables in the other's domain. Thus, the factors directly controlling practice are distinct from those for training and credentialing. At least in part, the distinction may explain the persistence of traditional school psychology practice, even after many years of increased training and credentialing requirements.

Table 7.1 Sources of Professional Control

Preparation for Employment	Credentialing for Employment	Roles and Functions During Employment
Direct Influence	***Direct Influence***	***Direct Influence***
APA accreditation standards	SDE licensing requirements	District demands and expectations
NCATE/NASP accreditation standards	SBEP licensing requirements	District perception of needs
SDE program approval requirements		Consumer response to services
Designation (National Register & ASPPB) criteria		Desired functions of school psychologist
		Competencies of school psychologist
Indirect Influence	***Indirect Influence***	***Indirect Influence***
ASPA	NCATE/NASP accreditation standards	Orientation of the training program
CDSPP	APA accreditation standards	Credentialing requirements
SDE certification requirements	SDE program approval requirements	State laws and regulations
SBEP licensing requirements	Designation criteria	State and local professional associations
APA/NASP IOC	ASPPB position statements	NASP and APA position statements
APA position statements	APA position statements	Ethics
NASP position statements	NASP position statements	Legislation and litigation
State association positions	State association positions	
SDE rules and regulations	NASDTEC positions	
APA Division 16 positions	APA Division 16 positions	
Training program and faculty orientations	NCSP requirements	
	Training program and faculty orientations	

As Figures 7.1 and 7.2 and Table 7.1 make clear, two broad domains of influence exist in school psychology. Major changes in the education arena or in the psychology arena have subsequent impact on school psychology. Accreditation changes by the APA or NCATE will influence standards for school psychology training; changes in certification or licensing agencies will influence credentialing standards. Legislation and litigation in education or psychology can influence the daily practice of school psychologists.

The influence of the determinants may vary as a function of school and nonschool employment. Educational influences on employment conditions are expected to be more evident in school settings, whereas psychological influences are expected to be more evident in nonschool settings. Practice determinants of school-based settings would require adjustment to apply them to nonschool settings. Whether school psychology is seen as trapped between the fields of education and psychology or adroitly straddling them, the dual influences are dramatic. Despite the dual influences, school psychology has acquired the major symbols of professionalism, as well as the attendant regulations.

Chapter 8

Practica, Internships, and Job Considerations

For students just beginning school psychology training, the prospects of internships and jobs may seem too remote to consider. Just getting through the current term—not to mention comprehensive exams, research projects, portfolios, and whatever other long-range academic obstacles lie in wait—may appear to be an impossible dream. Still, it is important for students to start thinking about short-term and long-term professional goals early in training, for it will motivate them to prepare appropriately to meet their professional goals. This chapter examines a number of vital issues, including practicum experiences, internships, first jobs, and career options beyond the first year, such as alternative job settings that are available to those with degrees and experience in school psychology.

FIELD EXPERIENCES: HISTORICAL BACKGROUND

The notion of field experience, including internships, as an essential part of practitioner training is nearly as old as the field of school psychology itself. Witmer provided practical demonstrations as part of his instruction to practitioners during the early years of the psychological clinic at the University of Pennsylvania. Morrow (1946) contended that the earliest formal internships were those offered at the Vineland Training School in New Jersey as early as 1908, saying that these were essentially school psychology internships. Norma Cutts was among the interns trained at Vineland. Training school publications of that era suggest the nature of the paid experience (Goddard, 1914). Wallin (1919) had called for such experience in the training of psychologists, but few programs appear to have complied immediately.

Although practica, or field experiences, in university clinics and community agencies were part of school psychology training and credentialing requirements by the mid-1930s (Fagan, 1999), the practice of requiring field experiences increased in popularity, and detailed proposals for a 1-year internship as part of doctoral training were put forth in 1945 (APA & AAAP, 1945). The first state department of education (SDE)–sponsored internship program appears to have been the one initiated in Ohio in the 1950s (Bonham & Grover, 1961). The Thayer Conference proceedings (Cutts, 1955) provide considerable discussion of practicum and internship conceptualizations, practices, and recommendations.

In 1963, a conference was held at George Peabody College for Teachers in Nashville, Tennessee, to discuss the internship in school psychology. In the proceedings from the so-called Peabody Conference, Susan Gray (1963a) noted that "since the internship is usually taken in an area geographically and administratively separate from the training institution, it deserves particular attention, for the inevitably wide variability in such non-university settings carries within it the danger of diffusion of purpose and of standards for training" (p. 1).

Although the Peabody Conference was specifically aimed at doctoral-level internships, many of the ideas and principles established at that conference remain in practice today. For example, the proceedings maintain that the internship should be part of the continuous training process leading to preparation in school psychology, and that the internship should be a transitional phase between being a student and being a professional. Another issue addressed at the Peabody Conference and still highly relevant is that, ideally, the internship should offer a balance between service and training. Interns should be expected to work hard for and provide service to their employers. On the other hand, the training aspects of the internship should not be neglected. Interns should not be considered merely inexpensive school psychologists. Rather, the internship should be a year filled with new experiences, complete with ample opportunities to discuss issues, ask questions, observe procedures, acquire skills and knowledge, and try out a variety of professional roles and functions.

The widespread formalization of field experience through practicum and internship requirements is much more recent and is directly related to increases in credentialing requirements by SDEs and licensing boards, reciprocally connected to increased numbers of training standards, especially by the American Psychological Association (APA) and the National Association of School Psychologists (NASP). Early SDE credentialing requirements often included a practicum and less often an internship. At the present time, all SDEs and licensing boards have some form of field experience requirement for credentialing (Curtis, Hunley, & Prus, 1998).

CURRENT PRACTICES IN FIELD EXPERIENCES

Discussions of field experiences for students in school psychology training programs refer to two quite different types or levels of professional preparation. A clear distinction should be made between field experiences completed in conjunction with academic requirements, often called *practica*, and field experiences that serve as the final step in training, known as *internships*.

Practica

According to the *Standards for Training and Field Placement Programs in School Psychology* (NASP, 2000c), *practica* are defined as

> [c]losely supervised on-campus or field-based activities designed to develop and evaluate a school psychology candidate's mastery of distinct professional skills consistent with program and/or course goals. Practica activities may be completed as part of separate courses focusing on distinct skills or as part of a more extensive experience that covers a range of skills. (p 36)

Practicum experiences are expected to be completed for academic credit. They are to be closely supervised; to help students integrate and apply their academic knowledge and skills; to correspond directly to the training program's training objectives in terms of content, supervision, and evaluation; and to precede the internship experience. Students often are required to complete specific assignments, and grades are assigned based on the quality of these completed assignments. Practicum experiences also provide students with hands-on opportunities to find out if the field of school psychology is for them. At the same time, practica provide faculty members and on-site supervisors with opportunities to see students in action and to assess their professional and interpersonal skills.

Training programs vary dramatically in their practicum requirements. Thomas (1998) noted that master's-level training programs require a median number of 225 "clock hours" (i.e., actual hours spent) of practicum experience, with a range of 40 to 1,200 hours. Specialist-level programs require a median number of 360 clock hours (range of 25 to 1,278 hours), whereas doctoral-level programs require a median number of 600 clock hours of practicum work (range of 30 to 2,000 hours). Some training programs require practicum work in nonschool settings, such as on-campus clinics, as well as in school settings, whereas other training programs require experience only in one type of setting.

Practicum experiences ideally should be developmental or graduated.

Practicum experiences ideally should be developmental or graduated. As students learn various professional techniques in their classes, they begin to apply those techniques under close faculty supervision while working with actual clients. In this way, it is hoped that a strong relationship will be forged between academic training and practical skills. Students generally receive academic credit for their practicum experiences, although the amount of credit varies from one training institution to another.

Practicum training might be thought of as an introduction to the practice of school psychology. Through practica, students gain an initial awareness of some of the rewards and also some of the frustrations inherent in being a human service professional. Students begin to notice that in addition to skills and training, professional success is tied to interpersonal skills such as diplomacy, initiative, and cooperation. It is during the practica that students often gain firsthand knowledge of the complexity of many of the issues encountered by school psychologists. They learn that in working with an individual child, the school psychologist also must work with a family, a classroom, a school building, a school system, state and federal legislation and mandates, and professional guidelines. In addition, students learn firsthand the importance of conducting all of their work in a socially responsible and ethical manner.

A major difference between practica and internship experiences involves the role of the university in each of the settings. In practica, a university faculty member is generally the person directly responsible for supervising and evaluating the students' experiences. The faculty member arranges settings for the experiences, makes the assignments, and assigns the grades. Although a field-based person, such as a school psychologist or school principal, may play an active role in ensuring that a practicum is a positive learning experience, and that person may be involved in consulting with the faculty member regarding a given student's performance, it is the faculty member who is ultimately responsible for the experience.

There is some discussion among trainers of school psychologists as to whether practicum requirements should be completed in an on-campus clinic setting, a public school setting, a combination of these settings, or some alternative setting (e.g., a parochial school). Some of the advantages of the on-campus clinic setting are that students receive more intensive supervision, that faculty members can control the students' experiences better, and that students and faculty may have less travel time. Also, within clinic settings, if the clinics are in the school psychology department or program, the faculty or administrators may spend less time trying to secure sufficient and adequate practicum sites. The advantages of working within the public school setting include a wider range of issues, earlier exposure to the workings of schools, possible contact with actual school psychologists, and the potential for a wider variety of roles and functions. Some schools have opted for a combination of clinics and schools, for example, with the first practicum being conducted under the closer supervision of the clinic setting and the second practicum being conducted off-campus in the public schools.

Internships

The school-based internship experience in school psychology is a professional apprenticeship. According to the *Standards for Training and Field Placement Programs in School Psychology* (NASP, 2000c), *internship* is defined as

> [a] supervised culminating, comprehensive, pre-degree field experience through which school psychology candidates have the opportunity to integrate and apply professional knowledge and skills acquired in prior courses and practica, as well as to acquire new competencies consistent with training program goals. (p. 36)

Most commonly, for students in sixth-year or specialist-level training programs, the internship follows 2 years of full-time graduate-level academic training including practicum and field experiences. For students in doctoral programs, the internship typically follows all required coursework but is still completed prior to receiving the doctoral degree. In either case, the internship is often the final requirement for the terminal degree. It is a halfway house that provides the opportunity for a smooth transition between the academic environment and the full-time job of the practicing school psychologist. Although most, if not all, training programs provide practical opportunities for students to work in the schools and develop their professional skills while completing their coursework, these practicum requirements are not equivalent to a full-time, year-long supervised internship in the schools. To obtain nonschool licensure in most states, students are required to do at least one postdoctoral year of supervised experience in addition to the predoctoral internship.

In all field experiences—practica as well as internships—three parties generally are involved: the student, the university supervisor, and the site supervisor. Although all three parties play important roles, the degree of influence over and professional responsibility for the student tend to shift from the university supervisor to the site supervisor in the transition from practicum to internship. During the internship, the site supervisor has much more responsibility than do university personnel for the day-to-day supervision and evaluation of the intern's activities. The site supervisor and the intern work closely together in developing a comprehensive internship plan and in ensuring that items on the plan are accomplished and evaluated. University faculty members observe interns from a more distant perspective, visiting the intern occasionally during the year, hosting the intern's return visits to the university, and acting as consultants when questions or problems arise. Although the university supervisor usually assigns the final grade and gives official university approval for the intern, the site supervisor generally advises the university faculty member as to the intern's professional performance and recommends that the intern be approved or not be approved for credentialing.

Interns often report that they learned more during the internship year than in all their years of undergraduate and graduate coursework and practicum experiences combined. Interns also have reported that the knowledge they acquire in their graduate classes became clearer and more meaningful during the internship. One student remarked to the authors that, much to her surprise, by the end of her internship she had used information from every class she had taken in graduate school, including research and statistics.

Interns often report that they learned more during the internship year than in all of their years of undergraduate and graduate coursework and practicum experiences combined.

Despite extensive practicum experiences, students entering their internship often feel unsure of their professional abilities. Even those who have excelled in their undergraduate and graduate studies may experience self-doubts. Moving from graduate student status to intern status can involve a number of stressors: moving away from a familiar environment, leaving friends and colleagues, meeting new people, starting a new job, and changing one's status from student to professional (Phillips, 1990b; Solway, 1985). By the completion of the internship, however, most students seem to develop not only enhanced professional skills but also enhanced self-confidence overall. Gray (1963a) stated that during the internship, students learn about their own strengths and weaknesses, and how to accentuate their strengths while correcting or at least minimizing their weaknesses.

A formal discussion of current practices in internships might logically begin with a look at internship requirements. In the NASP *Standards* (2000c), the following guidelines apply to the internship experience:

3.2 The internship is a collaboration between the training program and field site that assures the completion of activities consistent with the goals of the training program. A written plan specifies the responsibilities of the training program and internship site in providing supervision, support, and both formative and summative performance-based evaluation of intern performance.

3.3 The internship is completed on a full-time basis over one year or on a half-time basis over two consecutive years. At least 600 hours of the internship are completed in a school setting. (Note: Doctoral candidates who have met the school-based internship requirement through a specialist-level internship or equivalent experience may complete the doctoral internship in a non-school setting if consistent with program values and goals. Program policy shall specifically define equivalent experiences and explain their acceptance with regard to doctoral internship requirements.)

3.4 Interns receive an average of at least two hours of field-based supervision per full-time week from an appropriately credentialed school psychologist or, for nonschool settings, a psychologist appropriately credentialed for the internship setting.

3.5 The internship placement agency provides appropriate support for the internship experience including: (a) a written agreement specifying the period of appointment and any terms of compensation; (b) a schedule of appointments, expense reimbursement, a safe and secure work environment, adequate office space, and support services consistent with that afforded agency school psychologists; (c) provision for participation in continuing professional development activities; (d) release time for internship supervision; and (e) a commitment to the internship as a diversified training experience. (pp. 18–19)

In addition to the NASP requirements for internships, individual states and training programs often have requirements of their own. In the document *Standards for the Credentialing of School Psychologists* (NASP, 2000c), the following description of the internship is provided:

> The internship experience will consist of a full-time experience over one year, or half-time over two consecutive years, with a minimum of 1200 clock hours, of which at least 600 must be in a school setting. A comprehensive internship experience is required for candidates to demonstrate under supervision, the ability to integrate knowledge and skills in the professional-practice domains and to provide a broad range of outcome-based school psychological services. Internship experiences are provided at or near the end of the formal training period, are designed according to a written plan that provides a broad range of experiences, occur in a setting appropriate to the specific training objectives of the program, are provided appropriate recognition through the awarding of academic credit, occur under conditions of appropriate supervision, are systematically evaluated in a manner consistent with the specific training objectives of the program, and are conducted in accordance with current legal and ethical standards for the profession. (p. 45)

A set of questions relative to the internship experience required by different states and training programs is provided at the conclusion of this chapter. Guidelines from each state department of education, as well as discussions with training program faculty members, should provide answers to these questions.

Other Internship Considerations

Information on some of the less formal aspects of the internship year is included in this section: deciding on an internship site, applying for an internship, and choosing between sites. The section also includes additional information on what happens if something goes wrong during the internship.

Deciding on an Internship Site

When it comes to the consideration of internship and job sites, individual differences are readily apparent. All individuals bring their own priorities, values, professional and personal likes and dislikes, and strengths and weaknesses to their search for the perfect internship or job site. Many of these variables may change as life circumstances change, such as marriage or children. Many prospective interns begin their search by focusing on geographical, social, and financial factors or considerations. The following questions guide students through this decision-making process.

Students should ask the following questions:

1. Are there internships available close to where I currently live?
2. Do I want to stay in the area where I currently live?
3. Can I afford to live in a particular area on an internship salary?
4. If not, can I live with my parents, other relatives, or friends for the duration of the internship?
5. What factors limit my mobility (e.g., family, romantic attachments)?
6. How do I feel about various locations in terms of climate, personal safety, cleanliness of the environment, proximity to loved ones, educational opportunities, and so on?
7. How far am I willing to drive to work each day? What are the roads like on which I would be driving? How is the traffic? Is public transportation an option?
8. If I am married, is my spouse willing and/or able to relocate?
9. Are there opportunities for my spouse to find a job, take classes, work toward a degree, and/or make friends?
10. Does moving now make sense for my spouse and for me?
11. If I have children, how good are the local schools?
12. Is there high-quality, reasonably priced day care available?
13. Will there be a problem if I am the school psychologist in the school my children attend?
14. What kinds of opportunities for a social life will I have in a given location?
15. How is the overall cost of living (e.g., housing, taxes, food, health care) in the area?

16. Is housing available?
17. If I am ill or disabled, is there access to medical care?
18. How large is the community?
19. What do I like to do in my spare time (e.g., hobbies, religious affiliation, shopping, recreational activities, cultural events, etc.)? Will I be able to pursue these activities in my new location?
20. Are there opportunities to complete any additional graduate coursework nearby?
21. If I move somewhere for an internship, what are the chances that a school psychologist's job would be open at the same school, district, or location during the following school year?

Once possible locations are determined, the next step is to find out whether an internship placement is available near the preferred location. Internship openings are generally publicized through a variety of channels: state school psychological associations, training programs, state departments of education, and the NASP Career Center (*www.nasponline.org/careers*). In Illinois, for example, the annual convention of the Illinois School Psychologists Association, held in early spring, has a large room set up specifically for site supervisors and administrators (often a chief school psychologist or a special education director) to interview prospective interns and job seekers. In Ohio, the Inter-University Council has internships allocated to it by the SDE and then distributes the internship slots according to program needs. The Illinois method allows more freedom of mobility among prospective interns, whereas the Ohio method allows better regionalization of the interns, along with their continued proximity to their training programs. Illinois and Ohio offer paid internships. This may not be the case in all other states. Jobs for school psychologists are often posted over the Internet as well. Another comprehensive source of job information online can be accessed by subscribing to *www.schpsy-jobs-subscribe@yahoogroups.com*.

Applying for an Internship

When an internship becomes available, applicants are usually encouraged to submit a résumé (also called a *curriculum vitae*), academic transcripts, letters of recommendation, and other materials. Universities generally have placement offices designed to facilitate this process. Personnel in these placement offices maintain files for job applicants. Such files are called *placement files* or *placement papers* and are sent to prospective employers at the student's request. The benefit of using the services of a placement office is that it saves students the inconvenience of collecting and sending out the various required papers—particularly the letters of reference—each time they apply for a job. In addition to having an initially easier procedure, a placement office aids with updating and maintaining files for future use. Placement offices also keep track of a limited number of job openings, and listings of appropriate available jobs may be sent out periodically to those using their services. They may also provide services to help with résumé writing and interviewing skills. School psychology faculty members may be invaluable sources of information as well. Faculty members, especially those who have been around for awhile, often know of various internship sites and can point out the strengths and weaknesses of particular sites. Faculty members also may be willing to review résumés and offer suggestions for items to include and items to delete. Students also are advised, if not required, to ask *at least one* of their school psychology faculty members to serve as a reference. Only in rare cases would a student be justified in not having such a recommendation. Whether or not a school psychology faculty member's name is listed as a reference, site supervisors frequently seek out trainers' opinions of the applicants before making decisions.

Preparing for the Internship Interview

The format of internship interviews varies considerably from place to place, depending on the educational agency's experience with interns and the number of applications they receive. Some school districts invite all applicants to come for interviews on the same day. School personnel move the prospective interns through various stations of the interview process throughout the day and often make their decisions within a short period of time. Other educational agencies are much less structured. They merely schedule an interview at a mutually convenient time.

The person or persons conducting the interview will have specific questions, such as, What instruments would you use if you were asked to assess a developmentally delayed 3-year-old with a hearing impairment? or How would you handle an irate parent who disagrees with the results of your assessment? Some interviewers ask difficult questions to determine how an applicant reacts to stressful situations. Other interviewers may simply talk about what the job would entail and then take the candidate around to meet a few staff members. Still others may ask questions that seem more appropriate for prospective teachers than school psychologists, such as, What would you do if a student in your class misbehaved? In the latter case, the candidate should answer from a school psychologist's perspective (e.g., As a school psychologist, it would be more likely that a teacher with this problem would consult with me about the problems he or she is having. If that were to happen, I would probably suggest . . .).

In most interviews the candidate is asked if he or she has any questions. Candidates should *not* start by immediately asking about salary, fringe benefits, and the long-term job outlook. Instead, general questions about the community and school district show the candidate's interest in the position. A lack of questions might indicate to the interviewer the candidate's lack of interest.

The first of the two lists that follow contains community- and school-related questions that a candidate for an internship or job might ask. The second contains questions about the job. Not all of these questions would be asked during the interview. On the other hand, a candidate would want answers to most if not all of these questions before making a final decision about an internship site, particularly if he or she is in the enviable position of choosing between two or more internship offers.

Questions about community and school include the following:

1. What is the overall socioeconomic level of the population in the community?
2. What is the educational level of the people in this area? How committed is the community to education?
3. How many schools are in the district (or cooperative or education agency, etc.)?
4. What are the district's greatest needs?
5. How do students in the schools perform academically compared with state or national norms? How is the district doing in meeting state and national benchmarks for the No Child Left Behind Act?
6. How big are the schools?
7. How are the schools divided in terms of grades?
8. What is the average class size?
9. Is there some sort of districtwide handbook?
10. What are the rules in general regarding punishment and rewards?
11. What kinds of special education classes or other services are available?
12. How much inclusion is occurring, and how do the teachers respond to having children with disabilities in their classrooms?
13. What are some of the problems causing concern in the district (such as gangs, drugs, theft, or violence)?
14. How safe are the schools?
15. What kind of turnover rate is there for teachers and other school personnel?
16. What is the financial status of the school district?
17. How enthusiastic are staff members about new ideas, new programs, and so forth?
18. How familiar are administrators, teachers, and other staff members with the various roles and functions of the school psychologist?
19. How involved is the community in school activities?
20. What kinds of resources are available nearby in terms of medical care, counseling, and so on for purposes of referral?

Questions about the job may include the following:

1. What would be the length of my contract (e.g., 185 days, 200 days, 11 months)?
2. How many schools is the school psychologist responsible for, and what would the intern do?

3. How far apart are these schools?
4. What resources and materials are available (e.g., up-to-date testing materials, secretarial services, computers, test-scoring software, word processing, and dictating machines)?
5. What type of computers does the office use, and would I have access to the Internet and e-mail?
6. Where would the school psychologist's (and the intern's) office be, and would it be near the offices of other school psychologists?
7. Is there adequate space for the intern to work in the various schools?
8. How many school psychologists are employed in the school or district?
9. Who is the internship supervisor?
10. What is my supervisor's philosophy of school psychology?
11. About how much supervisory time does an intern receive?
12. What are the expected time allocations for various roles (e.g., assessment, consultation)? Is there much opportunity for nontraditional assessment and interventions?
13. Will I have the opportunity to work with more than one school psychologist?
14. How much turnover has there been among the school psychologists?
15. How well do the school psychologists get along with one another?
16. How many case studies is the intern expected to complete?
17. How much responsibility would the intern have for these cases?
18. What is the approximate salary offered to interns?
19. What kinds of fringe benefits are available (e.g., medical insurance, dental insurance, sick days, retirement plan)?
20. If I do a good job during the internship, what are the chances that there would be a permanent position open for me next year?

The Job Offer: The Principle of Supply and Demand

For many years the school psychology profession has had insufficient numbers of trained personnel to fill all of the available internships and jobs. Educational agencies need school psychologists to comply with federal and state legislation, and prospective interns with even a moderate degree of geographical mobility have had their choice of internship sites. According to a recent online publication from NASP (Charvat & Feinberg, 2003), the current shortage of school psychologists is expected to persist and perhaps even increase in the future. Although this bodes well for students looking for internships and jobs, it also may affect school psychology professionals' roles and functions. For example, Thomas (2000) noted that in 2000 only about a third of school psychology positions were meeting the suggested NASP ratio of one school psychologist to 1000 students. At the same time, Reschly (2000) found that the median age of school psychologists had increased, and many were starting to consider retirement. If a substantial number of school psychologists retire in the next few years, and if the number of students in school psychology training programs stabilizes, and finally, if the number of students enrolled in public schools remains constant or increases, then the ratio of school psychologists to students will continue to decline. Serving a larger number of students may limit the role of school psychologists, keeping them in the more traditional assessment role. The ratio of school psychologists to students nationally ranged from 1:700 in Connecticut to 1:3,625 in Mississippi, as reported by Thomas in 2000, and the national mean ratio was 1:1,816. In 2006, Curtis, Lopez, Batsche, and Smith reported a mean ratio of 1:1,500.

Even with such shortages, students seem to worry about getting offers for internship positions.

Candidates who are neatly dressed, speak well, arrive on time, ask appropriate questions, and appear polite yet friendly will generally have a better chance at being offered a job over someone who looks messy, mumbles, arrives late, has no questions, and appears rude or hostile.

Few if any internship sites consider academic grade point average as the single most critical factor in the decision-making process. Letters of recommendation from program faculty are important, however, and may make the difference as to who gets a desired internship.

Impressions made during the interview are also important. Candidates who are neatly dressed, speak well, arrive on time, ask appropriate questions, and appear polite yet friendly will generally have a better chance at being offered a job over someone who looks messy, mumbles, arrives late, has no questions, and appears rude or hostile. The people doing the interview are not only looking for someone with academic credentials, they also want someone with whom they think that they and others can get along. In an informal survey conducted of intern supervisors in Illinois a few years back, the supervisors noted that they were looking for interns who would be a good match personally and professionally with them and with their district or cooperative.

Students are encouraged to prepare a professional portfolio of material to take with them on their internship interviews. The portfolio can include a variety of things but should always contain a copy of the student transcript, catalog descriptions of the courses completed, copies of sample psychological reports written (with all identifying information deleted), notes from interventions and counseling sessions, and some information about the philosophy and objectives of the student's training program. Compiling all of the information into a convenient, readable format is to the candidate's advantage. The portfolio also is convenient for applying for postinternship job interviews or graduate work.

A professional portfolio should contain the following information:

1. A current résumé
2. A one-page statement of your philosophy of education and school psychology, and your professional goals
3. A copy of your internship plan

4. Letters of reference
5. Any reviews or evaluations you received during training
6. A list of your experiences in teaching, counseling, and intervention
7. A summary of your research project or thesis (or the proposal for the project if it is not complete)
8. A list of assessment instruments administered
9. A sample behavioral consultation plan
10. The number of actual hours you spent in the schools during practicum
11. One (or more) psychoeducational report that you consider your best work *with all identifying information removed*
12. A summary of any group work you have done
13. A summary of any individual counseling you have done
14. A summary of your duties in any assistantship
15. Any certifications (teacher certifications, etc.)
16. Transcripts from all postsecondary coursework
17. Syllabi from all of your graduate classes and possibly photocopies of text covers and tables of contents (this will save you time when seeking certification or admission to other graduate programs in the future)
18. List and description of any committees you have served on
19. Memberships in professional associations and organizations
20. Certificates from workshops or conferences you have attended
21. A copy of your program's graduate guidelines

Many students with good technology skills will meet program portfolio requirements with an online (paperless) portfolio. These are becoming increasingly popular among colleges of education generally and in school psychology programs specifically in order to meet requirements in a uniform and convenient manner. For interviews, however, it is advisable to take hard copies of the information.

Although much of the preceding discussion about internship application and interviewing is appropriate for both doctoral and nondoctoral internships, doctoral internships are managed in a more formal way and through a national-level selection process (see the chapter 6 section on internship as a training experience).

THE INTERNSHIP YEAR—OPPORTUNITIES AND DIFFICULTIES

Once students have been offered and accepted an internship, they usually sit down with the person supervising the internship to develop an internship plan. The plan is a list of activities and competencies they must meet according to national (NASP), state, and training program requirements. For example, a state may require that at least 20 school days be spent with each of four populations (e.g., preschool, elementary school, secondary school, and low incidence handicapped), so time must be set aside to accomplish this. Similarly, training programs may require an intern to assess at least four preschoolers, consult with at least 10 teachers, observe in every special education program, and document these activities.

Aside from sharpening existing skills, the internship period gives students an opportunity to expand their repertoire of skills. If most of a student's field experience has involved children ages 5–12, they should make it a point during the internship to work with infants, preschoolers, and adolescents. Interns should take this time to attend workshops, read up on professional topics, and discuss legal and ethical questions and concerns with their supervisor and colleagues. Although many topics and questions were discussed hypothetically during training, the real situations that occur during internship give those professional, legal, and ethical questions added importance.

Interns should take this time to attend workshops, read up on professional topics, and discuss legal and ethical questions and concerns with their supervisor and colleagues.

Many interns report that their internships start off slowly. They are not sure what to do, and their supervisors, especially those who have not supervised interns before, are not certain what to do with their interns. It is not uncommon for interns to spend much of the first month or so visiting local agencies, being introduced to personnel at their supervisors' schools, observing their supervisors performing a variety of tasks, attending workshops, and just generally becoming oriented to the site. Although such activities contribute to a certain amount of restlessness on the intern's part, the slow pace generally picks up after a month or 6 weeks, and by the end of the year interns may look back with some regret at the good old days, before they had calendars full of meetings, appointments, and other responsibilities.

Intern supervisors vary in the amount of supervision they are willing and able to provide, although they are required to provide at least 2 hours of supervision per week. Some supervisors spend several weeks observing the intern's skills in assessment and consultation before allowing the intern to work independently. Other supervisors assume that, because an intern has earned the university's seal of approval, the intern's skills are adequate and close observation is not needed. Likewise, some supervisors will read and correct interns' psychoeducational reports all year. Others will read the first few reports, make suggestions, and feel sufficiently comfortable with the intern's report-writing skills to read only the most difficult reports or those involving potentially delicate situations.

Things That Can Go Wrong During the Internship

Although most internships progress smoothly, trouble sometimes arises. Such troubles can occur at any time during the internship and usually take one of the following forms.

Intern–Supervisor Conflicts

After going through the application, interview, and selection processes, interns and supervisors are usually fairly compatible with one another. However, as in any working relationship in which two individuals must work closely together, there are occasional disagreements and conflicts. For example, an intern may want more supervision than the supervisor is providing, a supervisor may find that the intern does not meet what he or she considers the minimum level of competence in assessment or counseling, an intern may feel the supervisor is using out-of-date assessment techniques, or the supervisor may be overwhelmed with job demands and find the intern to be overly dependent or demanding.

When such conflicts arise, interns often confide in their fellow interns at other sites or with the faculty from their training programs; supervisors may also call the university to complain or to consider their alternatives. Some of these conflicts may be worked out by mutual agreement or through common-sense arrangements; for example, if the intern wants more supervision, voicing the concern to the supervisor might result in scheduling a 2-hour meeting at the same time each week or arranging to have lunch together twice a week. Other conflicts may not be as easy to resolve (e.g., sexual harassment or extreme philosophical differences), and only another supervisor or another site are feasible alternatives. As with most interpersonal conflicts, keeping communication lines open, considering alternatives, and seeking outside advice are all important ways to work through such conflicts. An intern's university supervisor can be an important sounding board and should not be underestimated.

Computers, specifically e-mail, can be used to promote communication between interns and university supervisors to make sure that all is going well with the internship. With e-mail, interns from a training program may communicate with each other and with their trainers, asking questions, seeking advice, and making suggestions on a more immediate basis than is possible with the twice yearly site visits by the trainer. Using e-mail also prevents the so-called telephone tag that often occurs when busy people try to get in touch with each other by telephone. E-mail exchanges also can be shared so that others have a better understanding of the day-to-day world of the intern, although confidentiality must be considered. Finally, many training programs and intern consortiums have guidelines for what to do in intern–supervisor conflicts. All parties are urged to document the progress of the internship, especially if the intern (or supervisor) has concerns.

Personal Crises

Occasionally during the internship year, either the intern or the supervisor experiences a personal crisis, such as a serious illness or the death of a family member, that brings the internship to a standstill. If the intern is unable to complete the year under such circumstances, arrangements generally can be made to postpone all or part of the internship until the following school year. Most universities have rules regarding the number of years in which all coursework and requirements must be completed. If the intern's supervisor is unable to fulfill his or her supervisory duties, other arrangements can usually be made as well. For example, in a district with several school psychologists, the intern may simply be assigned to another supervisor. In other cases, the intern may have to secure another internship placement for the duration of the experience. In all cases, training program faculty should be consulted and kept informed as circumstances change.

Intern Impairment

Several articles have addressed the notion of trainee and/or intern impairment (Bernard, 1975; Boxley, Drew, & Rangel, 1986; Knoff & Prout, 1985; Lamb, Cochran, & Jackson, 1991). In their 1991 paper, Lamb et al. defined impairment as something that interferes with the performance of professional duties. Such interference may take the following forms:

1. An inability or unwillingness to acquire and integrate professional standards into one's repertoire of professional behavior.
2. An inability to acquire professional skills and reach an accepted level of competency.
3. An inability to control personal stress, psychological dysfunction, or emotional reactions that may affect professional functioning. (p. 292)

This discussion emphasizes the continued importance of accountability and evaluation, coupled with professional ethical responsibilities, throughout school psychology training and practice. Faculty members and internship supervisors are responsible for closely and consistently monitoring and documenting students' skills and progress to ensure quality control within the school psychology profession. In addition to the ethical guidelines for professional behavior prepared by NASP and the APA, many state associations also have their own ethical guidelines. Interns should spend time throughout their training becoming familiar with these principles.

BEYOND THE INTERNSHIP

Most new graduates of school psychology programs want to find jobs initially as school psychologists and to begin practicing the skills acquired over the past 3 or so years of training. Most state departments of education have specific procedures that students must follow to obtain certification in school psychology, such as certain paperwork or state-mandated competency tests. Students' school psychology training programs will outline certification requirements and may also require the NCSP Praxis examination. A list of questions can be found at the end of this chapter regarding state certification requirements.

Other students may decide to return to school for additional training, either to gain skills in a particular area of school psychology, such as counseling, early childhood assessment and intervention, or neuropsychological assessment, or to prepare for other school psychology–related career options, such as school psychology faculty positions.

The Job Search

Moving from student status to professional status is often considered a major turning point in life. Many graduates are amazed and even overwhelmed at the respect they are given as professionals. Although such respect is flattering, it carries with it an additional responsibility for ethical and mature practice and greater accountability for professional actions.

The same issues and questions faced when seeking internships apply to the job search. Geographical, family, and financial factors are influences. The job description, salary, and fringe benefits are important in job seeking. Nancy Sherer, the Human Resources Benefits Manager at Western Illinois University, suggests asking the following questions about benefits and workplace conditions, in addition to asking the human resources department about benefits and requesting brochures:

1. What options will I have for health insurance, health maintenance organizations, long-term disability, life insurance, dental insurance, and vision insurance?
2. On what date would my coverage begin under these plans?
3. What is my cost for coverage under these plans?
4. What is the cost for my spouse and children to be covered?
5. Will I be covered through the summer months even if I don't work during the summer?
6. If I have a health insurance claim, what will my portion of the cost be?
7. What are the exclusions or limitations of the coverage?
8. If I am ill or injured, what insurance premium would I be required to pay?
9. Am I restricted to certain health care providers?
10. Do I have any coverage if I go outside of the network providers?
11. How are claims filed?
12. If I do not choose additional life insurance now, what would be required to add life insurance at a later date?
13. What retirement plans are available? What amount do I contribute? What amount is contributed by my employer?
14. If I terminate employment, what amount of my retirement may I withdraw?
15. What is the workplace policy for sick days, personal days, and family leave?

In addition, other questions may include whether or not the staff is unionized, and if so, whether nonmembers are required to pay union dues. Sherer emphasizes the importance of taking the time to study all employment options.

School psychologists looking for their first position should try to work in close proximity to a more experienced colleague, that is, a mentor, who will provide support and advice when difficulties arise and who will help in establishing a professional role. NASP credentialing standards signal the importance the profession places on such close working relationships by calling for 1 year of supervised postinternship experience before permanent credentials can be granted through an SDE or elsewhere. Of course, compliance is difficult given that many school psychologists are in settings alone or with only one other practitioner. To combat this professional isolation, many new school psychologists also find it helpful to keep in touch with their graduate school faculty members, their internship supervisors, or their graduate student peers in order to form a network of professional support. The advent of e-mail has aided this process greatly. E-mail discussion lists, such as the NASP Listserv, where NASP members can get ideas and advice, can be a source of quick consultations on particular issues. NASP Listserv topics have involved a discussion on what to do about a youngster with selective mutism and whether to indicate a specific program for a student in a psychological report, and a request for ideas about helping schools develop crisis intervention plans. Occasionally a school psychologist will share specific test scores and request that colleagues help with interpretation. Although e-mail does not take the place of face-to-face contact with a colleague, it may help ease feelings of professional isolation.

Beyond Finding the First Job

Although many school psychologists are content to simply practice their profession from the time they become certified until the time of their retirement, others choose to expand their professional horizons. Practicing school psychologists who wish to stay current with professional advances and topics have various ways of accomplishing this. Continuing education, or continuing professional development (CPD), is one possibility. CPD is currently mandated for maintaining national certification status. It may take many forms, such as attendance at professional conferences and workshops, independent readings, teleconferences, university coursework, and independent research efforts. Developing new skills, keeping up with professional developments, and trying out a variety of intervention techniques are all ways to maintain a high level of interest and involvement in the field of school psychology.

Another way to get a foot in the door of professional associations is to contribute time and talents to the newsletter.

Another avenue that some school psychologists pursue is that of active participation in professional organizations and associations. Organizations such as state school psychology associations and NASP welcome the involvement of students, interns, and school psychologists. There is always work to be done on the various organizational committees and subcommittees, and professional associations welcome contributions of members' time and talent for their newsletter.

Job Stress and Burnout

Job stress and burnout among school psychologists have been a topic of investigation for over 20 years (Huebner, 1992; Proctor & Steadman, 2003; Wise, 1985). Chapter 3 reported the results of several studies on job satisfaction among practicing school psychologists (Conoley & Henning-Stout, 1990; Fagan, 1988b; Henning-Stout, 1992; Levinson, Fetchkan, & Hohenshil, 1988; and Solly & Hohenshil, 1986). Such studies suggest that many factors relate to job satisfaction, including age, affiliation with school psychology associations, gender, psychologist-to-student ratio, and quality of professional supervision. Wise (1985) formulated a list of professional stressors, the School Psychologists and Stress Inventory, and asked a national sample of practicing school psychologists to rate the relative stressfulness of each of the stressors. Figure 8.1 presents the rankings of the relative stressfulness of events listed in the inventory.

Figure 8.1. Relative rankings of stressful events by 534 school psychologists. (1 = most stressful; 35 = least stressful).

1. Notification of unsatisfactory job performance
2. Not enough time to perform job adequately
3. Potential suicide cases
4. Working with uncooperative principals and other administrators
5. Feeling caught between a child's needs and administrative constraints (i.e., trying to fit a child into an existing program)

5.* Threat of a due process hearing
7. Lack of appropriate services for children
8.* Child abuse cases
8.* Incompetent and/or inflexible "superiors"
8.* A backlog of more than five reports to be written
11. Working in physically dangerous situations (e.g., gang-ruled high schools)
11.* A backlog of more than 10 referrals
13. Pressure to complete a set number of cases (e.g., being required to test at least 100 children a year)
14. Conferences or staffings with resistant teachers
15. Conferences or staffings with resistant parents
16. Teacher dissatisfaction with recommendations
17. Report writing
18. Conducting in-service workshops
19. Keeping the district "legal" (i.e., in compliance with federal, state, and local regulations)
20. Public speaking engagements (e.g., PTA)
20.* Insufficient recognition of work performed
20.* Telling parents their child is handicapped
23. Lack of consensus in a staffing
24. Inadequate secretarial help
25. Being told that you have it easy by classroom teachers
26. Having to change schools or districts
26.* Lack of contact with professional colleagues
26.* Screening bilingual children
26.* Conducting parent groups
30. Lack of availability of appropriate assessment materials
31. Impending teachers' strike
32. Supervising an intern or school psychology graduate student
33. Keeping up with current professional literature
34. Carrying testing equipment around in unfavorable weather conditions
35. Spending time driving between schools

* Duplicate numbers indicate a tie in rankings.

Huebner (1992) administered the School Psychologists and Stress Inventory along with the Maslach Burnout Inventory (Maslach & Jackson, 1986) and a questionnaire regarding demographic data as well as job satisfaction. The MBI has three scales: emotional exhaustion, depersonalization, and personal accomplishment. Huebner's findings suggested that burnout was a serious problem for many school psychologists. In fact, more than one third of his respondents met the criteria for emotional exhaustion, more than one fourth met the criteria for reduced personal accomplishment, and nearly one tenth met the criteria for depersonalization. Huebner further reported that specific stressors seem to contribute to burnout among school psychologists. Stressors relating to lack of adequate support or resources, such as incompetent or inflexible supervisors, inadequate secretarial help, and lack of contact with colleagues, seemed to be the most important contributors to emotional exhaustion and depersonalization. Stressors related to time management (e.g., backlogs of referrals and reports), high risk to self and others (e.g., potential suicide cases or threat of a due process hearing), and interpersonal conflict (e.g., having conferences with resistant teachers or working with uncooperative administrators) also contributed to emotional exhaustion.

A more recent study (Huebner & Mills, 1998) investigated the link between occupational stressors, burnout, and personality characteristics among school psychologists. Higher scores on the neuroticism scale related to higher degrees of emotional exhaustion and reduced personal accomplishment and to lower levels of depersonalization. Extraversion and conscientiousness were negatively correlated with emotional exhaustion and positively correlated with reduced personal accomplishment. Agreeableness was negatively correlated with emotional exhaustion and depersonalization.

Proctor and Steadman (2003) looked at one particular stressor in the professional lives of school psychologists. They questioned whether school psychologists who serve only one school had different levels of job satisfaction, burnout, and perceived effectiveness than those who serve multiple schools. Their results suggest that those who serve a single school do seem to be more satisfied, are less inclined to experience professional burnout, and see themselves as more effective than their colleagues in multiple settings.

Reducing Professional Stress

School psychologists can learn how to cope with the high degree of stress often encountered on the job. The Proctor and Steadman (2003) study suggests that being assigned to just one school may help. In addition, Huebner and Mills (1998) suggested that school psychologists pay attention to their own well-being as well as the well-being of their colleagues. Maslach (1976) suggested the use of professional time-outs, in which an individual substitutes alternative professional activities for his or her primary professional activity. For example, school psychologists whose primary functions involve conducting assessments and planning interventions for children with disabilities may wish to become involved in other functions, such as helping to develop a gifted program in a school, working with a group of parents of children

Peer support groups may alleviate some of the feelings of professional isolation.

with disabilities, participating in the district's preschool screening program, or talking to a high school psychology class about what a school psychologist does. Involvement in state school psychology committees and other leadership activities, and conference attendance, are other coping strategies.

Huebner (1992) noted that strategies aimed at changing the organization itself might be especially effective for school psychologists whose stressors are related to the organizational aspects of the school system. If the system lacks testing materials or has insufficient secretarial help, for example, the school psychologist might work to secure additional funding by documenting such needs for school administrators or by applying for state or federal grants.

Zins, Maher, Murphy, and Wess (1988) suggested the establishment of professional peer support groups as a strategy for dealing with stress and burnout. In addition to providing support for group members, such support groups may serve professionals by providing a network of colleagues to share ideas, obtain feedback, and discuss problems and issues. School psychologists often work in settings in which they are the only members of their profession in a given school building or even in one or more school districts. Peer support groups may alleviate some of the feelings of professional isolation created in such situations.

Considering a Change in Jobs

An additional strategy for coping with professional burnout is to consider changing jobs. A book titled *Stay or Leave* (Gale & Gale, 1989), regarding job selection generally (i.e., not specifically geared to helping professionals), cites five reasons why the majority of high performers move to new positions. The five include "Limited personal growth opportunities; restrictions that inhibit their ability to do their best work; personality conflicts with superiors or coworkers; insufficient recognition or compensation; and economic realignments, mergers and acquisitions" (p. 13).

Although the language of some of these reasons sounds more appropriate for someone in the business world than for those in the helping professions, the underlying reasons that people in various settings move on to new jobs are fairly standard. Although most school psychologists work in supportive settings with friendly colleagues, some are unhappy with their jobs for a variety of reasons. Some school psychologists complain about the lack of opportunities for role expansion or personal growth. Such complaints generally include the following kinds of statements: "I feel as though all I do is test." "My supervisor told me if I want to do counseling that's fine, provided I still complete 120 case studies a year." "I'd like to do more consultation but I'm snowed under with referrals and reevaluations."

Similar to these complaints are those relating to restrictions that limit one's work: "I can't do counseling because the social worker counsels." "My supervisor, who is not a school psychologist, thinks that all I can or should do is test." "Most of the teachers I work with don't even want to hear the word 'inclusion;' they just want me to get children with difficulties out of their classrooms so they can teach those who can learn most easily." "I feel overtrained for the job I'm expected to perform."

More recently, in light of new legislation and trends in education in general and in school psychology in particular, dissatisfaction has been related to the lack of clarity on the job: "No one seems to know how to tell if a child is learning disabled." "We're supposed to look at response to intervention (RTI) but the implementation of interventions in the classroom is inconsistent and the teachers still want the child out of their classrooms." "Everything is changing and we don't really know what we're supposed to be doing if we don't do assessment."

Dealing With Personality Conflicts

Personality conflicts with superiors or coworkers can be among the most stressful occurrences in life. Professionals often spend nearly as much or more time with their coworkers than with spouses or friends (and at least spouses and friends are chosen). Coworkers can have annoying personal habits (too much perfume or too little deodorant); they can talk too loudly or too much, interrupt, criticize, hoist work off onto others and not carry their fair share of the workload, try to tell others what they should be doing, and so on. Even though psychologists may believe that they can modify the behavior of even the most cantankerous coworker, they may fail, or may give up and look for a new job.

As if difficult coworkers are not enough of a problem for school psychologists, difficult supervisors can be much worse. Supervisors of school psychologists often are not trained as school psychologists. Supervisors may be assistant superintendents, directors of special education, pupil personnel directors, or principals, or they may hold a variety of other educational administrative positions. Some may have quite different ideas, philosophies, and priorities when dealing with children with difficulties and disabilities. School psychologists often have a difficult enough job without having to defend their actions to an unsympathetic supervisor. In Wise's (1985) study of stressful events for school psychologists (Figure 8.1), 4 of the 10 most stressful events related to administration and supervision: notification of unsatisfactory job performance (no. 1), working with uncooperative principals and other administrators (no. 4), feeling caught between a child's needs and administrative constraints (no. 5), and incompetent and/or inflexible superiors (no. 8). Chapter 3 identifies similar job stresses and dissatisfactions.

The fifth reason Gale and Gale (1989) gave for switching jobs—economic realignments, mergers, and acquisitions—may be the least relevant to school psychologists. Yet school systems may undergo frequent realignments, such as having school psychologists, school social workers, speech and communication therapists, and guidance counselors work out of a centralized office, or changing a district from a group of neighborhood schools to a series of centers that serve all children in the district in one or more grades. Such realignments can cause much grumbling among school personnel, parents, and children, particularly during transitional periods. Mergers, also called *school consolidations*, frequently occur in rural areas that are no longer able to support independent local schools because of decreased funds or populations. These consolidations are usually born of necessity rather than choice and, as with realignments, often foster heated emotions and difficult transitional periods.

When school psychologists decide to leave a job for the above reasons or for personal, family, or financial reasons, they usually give some thought to available alternatives or options, such as the following: Move to another school psychologist position or to a position that may expand options within the field, go back to school, move into a related field, move into an unrelated field, and use school psychology–related skills in a nonschool setting.

No job will be perfect, but certain factors can make one position more appealing than others to the job seeker. Opportunities for role expansion, reasonable supervision, congenial coworkers, or an improved physical environment may make a large difference in the level of job satisfaction. School psychologists may choose a new position because it represents professional advancement. Over the past few years, members of the NASP Listserv have raised questions regarding the possibility of telecommuting or of part-time work for practitioners with young children at home. If office space is at a premium, schools or districts may allow school psychologists to work with children and teachers in the schools while performing administrative duties such as report writing and record keeping at home. Such arrangements may encourage individuals to accept positions at greater distances with the understanding that they will not have to commute 5 days a week.

Looking at Other Strategies to Reduce Professional Stress

Going back to school in a school psychology–related field is discussed at length in chapter 6. After working in a field for several years, most people become aware of things that they are interested in and wish they knew more about. Students returning to school to pursue a doctoral degree may decide to specialize in another area such as neuropsychology, organizational development, or the psychology of reading. Other individuals may decide to return to school part-time or full-time to take courses in educational administration or supervision to become supervisors of other school psychologists or district administrators of special education or pupil personnel services. School psychologists who have returned to school have obtained law or medical degrees instead of the more traditional doctorate in school psychology, often specializing in areas related to school psychology, such as school law or pediatric medicine.

Research has consistently revealed that most school psychologists are satisfied with their jobs.

Many school psychologists decide at some point in their careers that they would like to have a larger impact on the school system itself by becoming school administrators or supervisors of school psychologists. The NASP *Communiqué* ran an article about five school psychologists who changed to jobs in administration (Blagg, Durbin, Kelly, McHugh, & Safranski, 1997). Most of these individuals had worked more than 10 years as school psychologists before making the switch. Other individuals may take positions with state departments of education, applying their school psychology training to statewide issues.

Research has consistently revealed that most school psychologists are satisfied with their jobs. This discussion is not intended to give readers a bleak picture of school psychology or to imply that every school psychologist eventually burns out and decides to pursue alternative educational or employment options. However, all of the so-called helping professions, including school psychology, have their rewards and frustrations, and their strengths and weaknesses. Finally, most people change jobs and even careers at some point. Several options have been presented in this section to help school psychologists cope with stressful job situations. Yet another option might include pursuing employment in an alternative setting, as discussed next.

Roles for School Psychologists in Alternative Settings

School psychologists who choose not to work for a school system or are unable to find an acceptable position within the schools have other options. Alternatives are limited by personal factors such as personality, the community, and proximity to various kinds of facilities and services. Studies have not been done that show the numbers of trained school psychologists working in alternative or nontraditional settings. One publication noted that between 5% and 31% of school psychologists work outside of the schools (frequently those with doctoral degrees; Gilman & Teague, 2005). A 2005 exchange on the Trainers of School Psychologists e-mail discussion list found that anywhere from 10% to 60% of doctoral-level graduates are employed in the schools; the rest are employed in private practice, university settings, mental health centers, and so forth. Nevertheless, chapter 1 describes how a large majority of practicing school psychologists are employed in school settings.

Teachers in Higher Education Institutions

The most familiar role of school psychologists in higher education is that of the trainer of school psychologists. Individuals who choose such a position may be involved in varying degrees of graduate training while also teaching undergraduate or graduate classes in related fields of psychology, education, special education, or guidance and counseling. Working as a university faculty member offers many advantages. In most universities, faculty members have more flexibility than in the public schools, and less paperwork. A drawback of university teaching is the lack of opportunity to spend time helping children directly. Faculty members may have more of an impact on the field of school psychology in general through their students and their research efforts but less of a direct impact on individual children. To compensate for this lack of contact with children, many school psychology faculty members supervise students in practica and internships, hire themselves out as consultants to nearby school districts, or maintain private practices on a part-time basis. Also, to be hired as faculty on a tenure track requires a doctoral degree.

A drawback of university teaching is the lack of opportunity to spend time helping children directly.

Other higher education opportunities include teaching in a local community college or in a 4-year institution in a program other than school psychology. For example, many doctoral and some nondoctoral practitioners are competent to teach courses in educational psychology, special education, or general psychology. The part-time teaching positions in these areas are often convenient supplements to the school psychologist's regular school-based duties.

Another less familiar role for the school psychologist within the realm of higher education is that of working with college-age students. Sandoval (1988) suggested several possibilities for school psychologists. Many of the students school psychologists work with in elementary and secondary schools attend college and often have the same needs for special services. School psychologists may act as consultants to help those students by, for example, consulting with faculty about classroom accommodations, acting as advocates for students with disabilities, working with the admissions office to interpret the school records of students with disabilities, and providing additional assessment services, if needed. Once accepted into a college, a student with disabilities may need additional support services, such as group or individual counseling or assistance with vocational assessment and guidance, some or all of which could be provided by a school psychologist employed in a counseling center, health center, or center for students with disabilities. School psychologists employed by junior colleges or 4-year colleges and universities may also be involved in preventive activities (e.g., substance abuse), promotion of positive mental health, career planning, stress management (e.g., test anxiety), and crisis intervention activities (e.g., for victims of sexual assault).

Medical, Day Program, and Residential Settings

An additional alternative for the school psychologist seeking nontraditional employment might be a position with a medical school or with medical personnel in the area. Shellenberger (1988) suggested that school psychologists could be most beneficial to family physicians by acting as psychological, educational, and research consultants. Although such a role may require additional training for the school psychologist, opportunities exist to work cooperatively with family physicians. Related to the field of medicine is the possibility for qualified personnel to work with families of chronically ill children on social, psychological, behavioral, and educational development. A school psychologist could act as a liaison between physicians, families, and schools in meeting the needs of children with such chronic conditions as asthma, juvenile diabetes, cancer, AIDS, and so on. One publication suggested that 5–15% of school-age children in the United States suffer from chronic health conditions (Johnson, Lubker, & Fowler, 1988). Power, DuPaul, Shapiro, and Parrish (1998) noted that "the neighborhood school is the logical setting to base health programs, given that schools are highly accessible to families and already have a mechanism to coordinate the efforts of parents and professionals. . . . Psychologists and other school-based professionals increasingly are viewed as serving an important role" in addressing a wide range of student health problems in the schools (p. 15). In addition, school psychologists with some specialized training in the area of pediatric neuropsychology may be hired to help with neuropsychological assessments of young people with traumatic brain injuries.

Among the promising ways for pediatricians and school psychologists to work cooperatively is in the assessment, diagnosis, and treatment of children with attention deficit hyperactivity disorder (ADHD) and other learning and developmental disabilities.

Wodrich (1988) discussed the contribution that school psychologists might make to the practice of pediatric medicine. He noted that pediatricians today are often asked questions about school readiness, behavior problems, and learning problems, in addition to the usual array of medical questions. School psychologists with training and experience in answering such questions could certainly make a contribution, either indirectly by consulting with pediatricians or directly by working with the children, their families, and their schools. Among the promising ways for pediatricians and school psychologists to work cooperatively is in the assessment, diagnosis, and treatment of children with attention deficit hyperactivity disorder (ADHD) and other learning and developmental disabilities. Surely the treatment of such prevalent problems would benefit from a multidisciplinary approach to research as well as treatment.

Along this same line, some school psychologists have found employment within residential and day treatment facilities. Mordock (1988) noted that school psychologists employed in such facilities might be involved in the traditional roles of assessment, intervention, consultation, education, and evaluation as well as the nontraditional roles of managerial and administrative functions. Generally, residential and day treatment facilities address the needs of children who are emotionally disturbed or developmentally delayed or who have been in trouble with law enforcement authorities. According to Morris and Morris (1989), a school psychologist might be part of a team of professionals involved in the diagnosis, program design, and program evaluation of children in such facilities. Many of these roles and functions are those for which school psychologists are well prepared, and little additional formal training would be necessary.

Mental Health Centers

An additional possibility for school psychologists seeking alternative settings involves practice in community mental health centers. Conoley (1989) suggested the role of community or family service provider as an appropriate role for school psychologists. Working within a community mental health center, the school psychologist could engage in family consultation, parent training, and family therapy using many of the assessment techniques and intervention strategies that are part of the school psychologist's usual repertoire. Conoley emphasized the use of behavior change strategies and assessment of individuals and families as particularly relevant to community mental health practice. Moreover, there is a need for increased home–school collaboration for which the school psychologist is specially trained.

Davis (1988) addressed the training needs for those moving from school to community mental health center settings. He suggested that individuals trained with skills in assessment, therapy, and consultation would probably have the easiest time applying school psychology skills within mental health centers. Davis also mentioned that community mental health centers may offer more opportunities to become involved with preventive activities than those offered within traditional school settings.

Private Practice

Many of the roles and functions practiced in the schools can be adapted to practice in the private sector, for example, assessment of individual children, counseling, or the planning of behavior management strategies. Pryzwansky (1989) noted that, as yet, few school psychologists are involved in private practice on a full-time basis. In fact, he reported that in a study by Pion, Bramblett, and Wicherski (1987), only 5% of doctoral-level school psychologists were engaged in full-time private practice. The percentage of master's- or specialist-level school psychologists in full-time private practice is also small.

Pryzwansky (1989) suggested that the number and percentage of school psychologists in private practice may increase in the future. He attributed that potential increase to several factors. First, if public education were ever faced with cutbacks in federal funds, particularly for students with disabilities, it might lead to widespread unemployment among school psychologists. Private practice is one option for such individuals. Second, an increase in professional programs leading to the PsyD degree might increase the number of school psychologists who would be eligible for licensure by state boards of examiners in various states. However, these predictions have yet to be borne out.

Finally, private practice is attractive because it may represent higher income possibilities than practice within the schools. The incomes of those in private practice are to a large extent controlled by how many hours they are willing to work, the fees they charge and are able to collect, and their ability to attract clients. They have additional overhead expenses such as office space, assessment instruments, billing, and secretarial help that school practitioners do not have. In addition to the potential financial rewards, private practice offers more professional independence. Private practitioners are not bound by all of the rules and regulations of a local board of education or school administration, and they can set their own hours and establish their own procedures. They may even be able to specialize in a particular type of case, such as child custody cases or cases involving abuse and neglect.

The incomes of those in private practice are to a large extent controlled by how many hours they are willing to work, the fees they charge and are able to collect, and their ability to attract clients.

The drawbacks of private practice include the financial risk involved in having to attract sufficient numbers of clients. Private practice is a business and must be run like a business. Although private practitioners are not accountable to a supervisor or a board of education, they are accountable to their clients and other certification boards, and thus may be more vulnerable to client influences on diagnoses and interventions. In addition, activities such as going to conventions (public relations) and continuing professional development take time away from business and thus have a direct impact on income. Insurance companies' restrictions on reimbursable services also affect income.

Business and Industry

Outside of the more traditional service models are opportunities for individuals trained as school psychologists to work in business and industrial settings. Maher and Greenberg (1988) suggested that businesses have increasing needs for individuals interested in human resource development. Human resource development includes motivating employees, improving the quality of the work environment, and increasing the level of satisfaction that employees derive from their jobs, among other things. One of the differences between the traditional roles of the school psychologist in the school setting and the nontraditional role of the school psychologist in business and industry involves the ages of the clients. To be better prepared for such a role, school psychologists would need training in human development and education across the life span (Harrison & McCloskey, 1989). Some of the specific activities suggested by Harrison and McCloskey for the school psychologist in business and industry include services for handicapped employees, general business services (including personnel assessment, personnel education and training, organizational interventions, and counseling), research, and publishing.

Retirement Planning

Planning for retirement should begin as soon as an individual starts working. Years go by quickly, and it is important to have the resources to enjoy a comfortable and relatively worry-free retirement. School districts and universities have retirement funds to which the employer and the employee each contribute a portion of the employee's salary. For example, the district and the employee may contribute 7% of the worker's salary toward retirement.

Those working in private practice will have different retirement plan options, such as a 401(k) and various types of Individual Retirement Accounts (IRAs). As with questions about insurance and other fringe benefits, employees should talk about retirement plan options with their human resources staff or with a professional financial adviser.

CONCLUSION

This chapter addressed some of the more practical aspects of internships, first jobs, long-range career planning, and alternative or nontraditional settings for school psychologists. As such, information from several previous chapters was applied to help readers examine and contemplate their own professional goals, and to ensure that their preparation and training in school psychology are more meaningful.

Chapter 9

School Psychology in Canada: Past, Present, and Future Perspectives

Donald H. Saklofske, University of Calgary
Vicki L. Schwean, University of Calgary
Riva Bartell, University of Manitoba
Juanita M. K. Mureika, School District 18, New Brunswick
Jac Andrews, University of Calgary
Jeffrey Derevensky, McGill University
Henry L. Janzen, University of Alberta

School psychologists in Canada have struggled to achieve a unique professional identity in Canadian schools and other educational contexts, as well as within psychology associations and regulatory bodies. School psychology, as a specialty area of professional psychology, has found itself embedded in a system in which it is sometimes similar or complementary and other times unique and even misunderstood. School psychologists' roles in relation to those of other educational professionals have led to competition for discrete territory. However, the past few years have witnessed some positive and optimistic changes that bode well for the future of school psychology in Canada. The increasing complexities of schools and educational environments, and the huge demands placed on educational institutions, have shifted the emphasis from "silos" of expertise to interdisciplinary collaboration. The contributions that psychology, and particularly the practice of school psychology, can make to children, teachers, and schools as social and learning environments, and to education in general, are increasingly being recognized by educators, administrators, government officials, and the public.

Only very recently has the Canadian Psychological Association (CPA), the national association and accrediting body for psychology programs in Canada, given formal recognition to the specialty of school psychology. The CPA has implemented criteria for accrediting doctoral-level school psychology training programs to complement the accreditation of clinical and counseling psychology programs. A growing interest in school psychology was witnessed at the 2006 CPA conference. The Psychologists in Education section at the conference had a very large presence of papers and posters, a growth trend that has been observed over the past few years. There was also full attendance at symposia and discussion sessions related to the training of school psychologists and practice issues. In those sessions, university faculty and trainers commented that the number of applications to graduate programs

The contributions that psychology, and particularly the practice of school psychology, can make to children, teachers, and schools as social and learning environments, and to education in general, are increasingly being recognized by educators, administrators, government officials, and the public.

in school psychology was growing and that school boards are very actively recruiting school psychologists. Thus, there is every indication that school psychology is undergoing a rapid and progressive transformation in Canada.

This chapter provides a contemporary overview of school psychology in Canada, updating the previous edition to bring it in line with current developments and issues in Canadian school psychology. The chapter begins with a review of the historical antecedents leading up to the current developments. It then describes current university programs in school psychology, credentialing issues, and the roles and functions of school psychologists. The chapter ends with an overview of the professional associations and publications for school psychologists and some projections for the future.

HISTORY OF SCHOOL PSYCHOLOGY ACROSS CANADA

The course of school psychology is traced as an independent discipline, notwithstanding the recognition that it has been influenced by other professional designations. Canada's federal government, unlike the United States', has little direct input into education, educational practices, and psychological services, with such powers being left to the appropriate provincial bodies. As such, school psychology's history is difficult to describe from a national standpoint.

Prior to 1950

Though some have argued that the 1950s signal the real origins of school psychology in Canada (Janzen, 1980; Perkins, 1990; Saklofske et al., 2000; Saklofske & Grainger, 1990), others have suggested a much earlier beginning (Janzen & Massey, 1990). The *attendance officers* of the early 1900s were, with somewhat of a stretch, the equivalent of today's psychological service personnel working in schools. These attendance officers most likely provided some psychological intervention in schools with an emphasis on guidance counseling and testing.

The earliest direct mental health services in schools can be traced to the Toronto Department of Public Health in the first half of the 1900s (Perkins, 1990). As typified by the work of Binet, the primary role of the service was to help identify so-called mentally defective children for placement in special auxiliary classes. As it became clear that not all children exhibiting learning problems had intellectual handicaps, greater emphasis was placed on working more closely with school personnel to identify and intervene in the problems underlying school failure. Thus, the beginnings and evolution of school psychological services in Canada, as in the United States, likely date back to the early 1920s and are rooted in public recognition of the need to provide mental health services to children and adolescents in public school settings. Initially, these services were provided by existing personnel, such as teachers, visiting teachers, guidance staff, and those trained in educational and clinical psychology (Fagan, 1996b).

Canada's federal government, unlike the United States', has little direct input into education, educational practices, and psychological services, with such powers being left to the appropriate provincial bodies. As such, school psychology's history is difficult to describe from a national standpoint.

1950s and 1960s

In the report *Psychology in Canadian Universities and Colleges*, MacLeod noted that psychologists could be found working in some Canadian schools (MacLeod, 1955). Others had made a similar observation but had not elaborated on the responsibilities of those psychologists (Dorken, 1958; Dorken, Walker, & Wake, 1960; Keating, 1962). In the early 1960s, Bowers (1962) commented on the growing demand for trained psychologists in applied settings and hoped "that the staffs of university departments of psychology will keep the training of school psychologists 'continually under review'" (p. 52). In the same year, Stein, having identified 95 school psychologists across Canada, undertook a study of their status and roles (1964). He concluded that the existing school psychology personnel had no specific university preparation or psychological experience. All had some teaching experience, and they did appear to have qualifications and experience that are "related somewhat to school psychology" (Stein, 1964, p. 12).

A few years later, McMurray (1967) noted that no Canadian psychology departments had graduated students with a specific specialty in school psychology. However, at that time, a PhD school psychology component had just been introduced within the Division of Applied Psychology, Ontario Institute for Studies in Education. This was to change with the development of school and educational psychology graduate programs at the University of Alberta, University of Calgary, University of British Columbia, and McGill University.

1970s and 1980s

Though school psychology began to emerge as a professional specialty in Canada only in the 1950s, by the early 1970s most areas of Canada had professionals working in the role of school psychologists (Janzen, 1976). The 1970s and 1980s witnessed considerable growth and development despite ongoing debate over the title and role definition of school psychologists. School systems throughout the country no longer wanted merely to segregate a segment of the school population that was experiencing significant learning, behavior and emotional problems. Similarly, there was a growing interest in intellectually gifted and talented individuals, each with their own special needs. School boards, such as the public system in Calgary, not only continued to increase its number of school psychologists, it also hired some with specialization in areas such as intellectual giftedness and neuropsychological assessment. Graduate students also began to avail themselves of the opportunities for school-based field placements and extensive practicum opportunities.

Though school psychology began to emerge as a professional specialty in Canada only in the 1950s, by the early 1970s most areas of Canada had professionals working in the role of school psychologists (Janzen, 1976).

With greater school needs came expanded functions for school psychologists. Weininger (1971) made an impassioned plea against the prevailing tendency to see the school psychologist as an "omnipotent, computer-like Superman, all seeing, all knowing, and ever ready to function at maximum efficiency twenty-five hours a day" (p. 125). While the numbers and roles of school psychologists were expanding, there remained a paucity of school psychology training programs in Canada, resulting in an increased reliance on American universities to train future school psychologists (Schmidt, 1976). One aspect of this solution diminished the distinction between psychology and educational psychology, with the latter viewed as an application of general psychology to the particular field of education. This distinction also had its roots in the United Kingdom, which at that time was a great source of many professors of educational psychology in Canada.

The 1980s also witnessed debates over the roles and title of school psychologists (Holmes, 1986). At the same time, the impetus for affiliation with professional organizations was evolving at provincial, regional, and national levels. During this period Canada witnessed the development of school psychology associations. A special issue of the *Canadian Journal of School Psychology* (1990) noted that provincial organizations had been established in British Columbia, Alberta, Saskatchewan, Manitoba, Ontario, and Quebec.

During this period of rapid growth at the provincial level, Canadian school psychologists maintained a loose affiliation with the National Association of School Psychologists (NASP) in the United States. Representation consisted of one member of the NASP Board of Directors (the Canadian–Mexican Director) and two delegates, representing eastern and western Canada. Don Dawson (1980, 1981, 1982) chronicled the relationship with NASP and, together with Marjorie Perkins from Ontario, urged expanded Canadian involvement in NASP. However, NASP soon after discontinued the Canadian/Mexican regional status and replaced it with an international affiliate membership option for Canadian school psychologists, in large part because of the formation of a national school psychology organization in Canada, the Canadian Association of School Psychologists (CASP). CASP remains a collegial rather than a regulatory association and retains a loose affiliation with the provincial school psychology organizations as well as the CPA. CASP also began publishing the only national journal devoted exclusively to school psychology, the *Canadian Journal of School Psychology*.

The rapid growth in applied training programs that had begun in the late 1960s (Arthur, 1971) and the hiring of school psychologists were reflected in Dawson's 1982 paper, "The Future of School Psychology in Canada," which became a rallying call for school psychologists seeking a professional identity. It also predicted that the decades of the 1980s and 1990s would be a critical period for school psychology. Estimates of the number of school psychologists practicing in Canada changed from Dawson's figure of more than 1,000 at the start of 1980 to Fagan's (1989b) view that the number of school psychologists had grown to 4,000 by the end of the decade.

While noting the phenomenal growth in the profession in the United States since the late 1960s, Fagan similarly predicted commensurate growth in Canada.

1990s

Saklofske and Janzen (1993) noted the increased prominence that school psychology had achieved in the past 10 years in Canada. They pointed to the now well-established university training programs; the significant activity, both provincially and nationally, to develop professional school psychology associations, especially in the western Canadian provinces; and the growing body of Canadian research focusing on school and educational psychology that was being published in Canadian, American, and international journals. In 1993, Holmes said "It is worth reiterating that school psychology is now experiencing its adolescent growth spurt and the attendant maturation dilemmas of that developmental period. ... To call it exciting is an understatement. Guessing the outcome in the next decade or two is impossible, except that it will be in the direction of continued expansion and change" (p. 143).

The 1990s saw a proliferation of universities offering master's and doctoral training programs with either a specialty or subspecialty in school psychology, although none of these was accredited. This movement paralleled a shift in the roles of the school psychologist, with somewhat less emphasis on traditional psychometric functions and an enhanced role in consultative and therapeutic services. However, provinces such as Manitoba, through its Department of Education, Citizenship, and Youth, developed the school clinician (psychologist) certificate for school psychologists holding a master's degree. McGill University's school/applied child psychology doctoral program became the first Canadian university program to be accredited by the American Psychological Association (APA). This was followed by the APA accrediting the Ontario Institute for Studies in Education's (OISE) combined school psychology and child clinical psychology program with an emphasis on children, youth, and families. Institutions that have adopted this scientist–scholar–practitioner model were McGill, OISE, and the other major training programs, including those located at Mt. St. Vincent University, and the universities of Manitoba, Alberta, Calgary, and British Columbia.

The New Millennium: 2000s

To meet the growing needs of accreditation and licensure, the Canadian Psychological Association in 2005 established national criteria for the accreditation of doctoral-level training programs in school psychology. Although no programs are currently accredited by CPA (the OISE and McGill University school psychology programs are APA accredited), it is expected that this will change in the next few years. School and educational psychologists currently play a meaningful role within the CPA and the provincial associations and regulatory bodies. The Psychologists in Education section of CPA is one of the larger and

The specialty of school psychology will become more visible, more valued, and better funded in the future.

more active groups and will certainly be a driving force in relation to both training and the practice of school psychologists in Canada.

Although there is continued optimism for the field, the last few years have yielded some realities of budget limitations and cutbacks, as well as the search for alternatives to time-consuming psychoeducational testing. The assessment of children with special needs will and must remain a part of the school psychologist's function. At the same time, the roles and responsibilities of school psychologists in Canada are evolving. The field of school psychology will continue to address its professional status and relationships with other psychological and educational professions, along with its capability to thrive within a uniquely structured service delivery model in the schools and larger educational contexts. As a result, it will become more visible, more valued, and better funded. A recent report indicated that in western Canada, 12% of psychologists are active in the specialty of school psychology (Watkins, Dobson, & Berube, 2006). That figure is expected to grow with the increasing demands placed on schools to meet an ever-widening range of student needs. The establishment of national criteria for accreditation of doctoral-level programs in school psychology will clarify the training standards and attract more students to specialize in school psychology. In addition, as the government allocates funds to other areas of service delivery, such as medical health authorities, to pay for school psychology services, the quality and visibility of school psychology will be enhanced.

SCHOOL PSYCHOLOGY: CURRENT ISSUES

In a 2001 special edition of the *Canadian Journal of School Psychology*, authors from across the country reviewed the status of school psychology in their respective province or territory. A number of common themes were identified to describe the status of school psychology in Canada, including professional identity, supply and demand, roles and functions, training and preparation, and credentialing and portability. The following section addresses each of these important areas.

Professional Identity of School Psychologists

The professional identity of school psychologists in Canada is shaped by a combination of factors, including university training programs, training standards established by accrediting agencies such as APA and NASP, legislation, provincial licensing requirements, policy documents, and districts' expectations about school psychologists and the needs of students. Also, because special education in Canada is *not* regulated and funded by federal mandates, as is the case in the United States, substantial differences can be seen in special education policies, programs, and service delivery across the provinces and Canada's northern regions (Andrews & Saklofske, 2007).

In many Canadian schools and school boards, the title of school psychologist is still seen as synonymous with "the tester." Although this view has a strong element of truth, school psychologists also perform other practices, such as consultation, individualized educational programming, counseling, and direct and indirect intervention. Thus, the professional identity of school psychologists appears to be expanding and is more in line with a specialty area of professional psychology. Interestingly, this mirrors what studies have shown about the roles and functions of school psychologists in the United States (Fagan, 2002; Reschly & Wilson, 1995). Some discontent has been expressed among school psychologists in Canada and the United States about their roles and functions, although survey studies have consistently shown that psychologists are generally satisfied with their jobs (Hosp & Reschly, 2002). What school psychologists do or are expected to do invariably describes and defines them, and their individual and collective identities as school psychologists.

Although school psychologists are generally well regarded, their capacity to serve the needs of students, teachers, and the educational system in general is not always fully appreciated in some provincial and educational jurisdictions. For example, in some areas of Canada, school psychologists are less well recognized because of the profession's relatively small size and because professional associations, which can play a strong advocacy role, are less well developed. Furthermore, some school boards and schools expect school psychologists to assume a much broader role (for example, collaborative consultation) that is not currently being fulfilled. However, this is a double-edged sword, with many school psychologists capable of and wanting to participate in much more comprehensive service delivery than is supported by the schools.

What school psychologists do or are expected to do invariably describes and defines them, and their individual and collective identities as school psychologists.

In addition, factors such as budget cutbacks, reduced resources, and outsourcing of some school psychology functions to other educational and allied professionals (e.g., occupational therapists) present a potential threat to school psychologists' functions. A current debate in several areas in Canada focuses on the hiring of psychological assistants and psychometrists to carry out many of the functions of fully trained school psychologists. In several provinces, some school boards are preferring or even requiring that school psychologists have a teaching degree and some teaching background. On the other side of the coin, it is not likely that students applying with only a BEd degree would have the necessary psychology prerequisites required for acceptance into a number of school psychology graduate programs. This is an area of concern for university school psychology training programs, and it is critical to role definition, job security, and professional identity of school psychologists.

Andrews (2002) addressed the issue of professional identity by stating that school psychologists should accept what they do and get better at it. He argued that school psychologists have contributed positively in the areas of assessment, consultation, and intervention over the years and that they have been generally positively viewed by those who have received their services (e.g., students, teachers, parents). In fact, it is these areas of expertise that distinguish school psychologists from other helping professions with a focus on student learning and development. Andrews suggested that in some places, school psychologists need to demonstrate to the public that their skills enhance the quality of learning and development in children and youth and that they are integral to promoting student success and well-being. One way of supporting this process is to strengthen the identity of school psychologists provincially and nationally. At the provincial level, faculty involved with university training programs must work more closely with the provincial school psychology associations as well as the school divisions to promote the work of school psychologists. At the national level, the Canadian Association of School Psychologists (CASP) must develop a closer and more effective relationship with the provincial school psychology associations and university training programs to promote a provincial as well as national identity for school psychology.

So far, CASP has not been sufficiently involved with provincial (school) psychology associations or universities to promote school psychology practices and training. Alternatively, the CPA Section of Psychologists in Education (SPE) has participated in the development of training recommendations and guidelines as well as supported CPA in the adopting of a profile of training requirements or standards, following the lead of APA and NASP. At the June 2006 CPA conference, university faculty from across the country who are involved with training programs in school psychology interacted in a presentation that focused on identity issues. There was a consensus that the various university programs need to work closely with each other as well as with CPA and CASP to promote the development of school psychology at the provincial and national levels.

Supply of and Demand for School Psychologists

In the 2001 special edition of the *Canadian Journal of School Psychology* (CJSP), articles frequently mentioned the heavy workload of many school psychologists, particularly in the larger school boards within more populated provinces. The underrepresentation of school psychologists, particularly in northern Canada, was also noted. In terms of the workload, the dramatic increase of special education referrals for assessment and programming, in addition to the many other school psychology functions, has significantly affected the ratio of school psychologists to students who require immediate and longer-term direct and indirect services. Also, from the perspective of a system in which school psychologists serve as an integral part of the school team to address matters of prevention and wellness and resiliency for all students, the number of school psychologists falls even further from the ideal.

The dramatic increase of special education referrals for assessment and programming, in addition to the many other school psychology functions, has significantly affected the ratio of school psychologists to students who require immediate and long-term direct and indirect services.

For example, school psychology caseloads in most Nova Scotia school districts are excessive. It is not uncommon for one school psychologist to serve 3,000–4,000 students distributed over approximately 12 schools (Hann, 2001). Similarly, Carney (2001) reported that ratios of psychology staff to students in large Ontario school boards typically ranged from 1:100 to 1:12,000. Carney noted that "based on data from 17 boards ... the overall ratio was one registered psychology practitioner for every 5,600 students" (p. 54). Janzen and Carter (2001) stated that large urban school systems in Alberta have full-time school psychologists on a ratio of 1:10,000 students. Saklofske and Grainger (2001) reported that the public school system in Saskatoon, Saskatchewan, had a ratio of about 1:4,400, and the Catholic system, which employed just one school psychologist at that time, had a ratio of 1:14,000.

The provincial estimate in New Brunswick in 2006 was a psychologist-to-student ratio of 1:3,800 for the Anglophone sector of the New Brunswick school system, though this also varied by district. The ratio for the Francophone school system was approximately 1:1,000. This difference reflects the fact that the Anglophone school system employs about 29 school psychologists, whereas the Francophone sector employs twice that for half the number of students. Such variability across Canada can be further illustrated in Manitoba using 2005–2006 school population data and December 2003 figures for full-time-equivalent (FTE) psychologists. Here, the K–12 student population of Greater Winnipeg is 99,000, with 57 FTE certified school psychologists, yielding a ratio of 1:1,737. In contrast, the K–12 student population of rural Manitoba is 87,600, served by 36 certified school psychologists, yielding a ratio of 1:2,417. This ratio may be misleading, because several rural school divisions do not employ school psychologists at all and, instead, use psychological services by contract or use social workers. Still, the disparity between urban and rural service ratios is noteworthy, although not surprising. These data contrast sharply with the ratio of about 1:1,000 usually recommended by NASP and other school psychology advocates. Hence, it appears that school psychologists will struggle to keep up with the demands of assessment, program planning, consultation, and so forth for the foreseeable future.

In terms of the representation or distribution of school psychologists across Canada, it is generally well known that rural areas within all provinces are typically underserved. It is difficult for rural school divisions to attract school psychologists because of quality of life issues and the professional encumbrances found within most rural settings (e.g., travel time and limited access to other support services, materials, and resources). Coincidentally, some urban centers also have difficulty acquiring school psychologists because of the greater appeal of other larger cities. For example, Martin (2001) reported that the practice of school psychology has experienced recruitment problems in rural and urban Newfoundland because graduates of nearby university training programs are not seeking employment as educational psychologists. He suggested that this is partially explained by low salaries and high costs associated with the profession in that region relative to other associated professions (e.g., teachers).

In addition, it is difficult to supply school psychology services to Canada's northern regions and territories. For example, the Northwest Territories and Nunavut (the newest territory, established in 1999) have no training programs for psychologists. The departments responsible for education in the Northwest Territories do not regularly employ school psychologists, although these services may be contracted with private practitioners from the south as required. According to Blakely and Wells (2001), school divisions wanting access to full-time school psychologists must hire their own. Hence, because most divisions do not employ school psychologists, few teachers and students in Canada's far north have the specialized support of school psychology.

Many studies have reported that the profession of school psychology is finding it increasingly difficult to fill the academic position for trainers of school psychologists (e.g., Miller, 2001; Miller & Masten, 2000; Miller & Palomares, 2000; Tingstrom, 2000). A recent edition of the *School Psychology Quarterly* (2004, Vol. 19, No. 4) focused on the state of development of university faculty in school psychology across the United States and Canada. The articles underscored that school psychology is facing a serious shortage of faculty, which is compromising training and research (Kratochwill, Elliot, & Carrington-Rotto, 1995; Little, Akin-Little, & Tingstrom, 2004; Nagle, Suldo, Christenson, & Hansen, 2004; Rosenfield, 2004). A survey analyzing school psychology faculty by doctoral graduate programs found that accredited programs embedded within the scientist–practitioner model produced the majority of individuals in academic positions (Little et al., 2004).

Because there are only two accredited doctoral programs in school psychology in Canada (i.e., McGill and OISE), Canadian universities seeking to establish and maintain school psychology programs experience significant problems recruiting and retaining doctoral-level school psychology faculty. For example, Canadian universities typically receive only a handful of applicants for a tenure-track position in school psychology, and in many cases, candidates present with doctoral degrees in specialty areas of psychology other than school psychology (e.g., clinical or developmental). To fill positions, it is not uncommon for Canadian graduate programs in school psychology to "grow their own" faculty, a practice that may be fraught with problems. The major shortage of faculty in graduate training and research programs in school psychology in Canada has created a pressing need to focus on critical components within school psychology graduate programs that can affect students' decisions to pursue an academic career. Foremost among these is accreditation. Other components include the incorporation of mentoring and modeling, such as participation in research groups, undergraduate teaching and supervision, and collaborative research with faculty.

It is difficult to supply school psychology services to Canada's northern regions and territories because most divisions do not employ school psychologists, so few teachers and students in Canada's far north have the specialized support of school psychology.

The shortage of doctoral-level school psychologists seeking academic positions in Canada is, as expected, directly linked to the fact that only a half dozen or so Canadian university programs grant a PhD in school psychology and only two of these have been accredited. It is difficult to report on the number of school psychology students who are admitted into, or graduate from, existing Canadian PhD programs in school psychology; however, there is little question but that the numbers of students are insufficient to meet the needs of academic institutions. Thus, the demand for school psychology is generally high across Canada, but the supply is limited. In light of this, it is important that the need for school psychologists be placed high on the agenda of critical issues to be addressed at the provincial and territorial levels as well as at the national level.

ROLES AND PRACTICES OF SCHOOL PSYCHOLOGISTS

Background Issues

An examination of the evolution of school psychology in Canada points to two important factors that have significantly affected the roles and functions of school psychologists and, consequently, defined their clientele: (1) the historical time lag between the earlier provision of psychoeducational services in schools and the eventual professionalization of the providers of psychological services in schools; and (2) the fact that external societal and consumer forces—such as demands and expectations by school district administrators, parents, and most significantly, legislative and court decisions—primarily determined the nature and conditions of delivery of school psychological services (Bartell, 2006). The impetus for the development of school psychology as a professional specialty within Canadian schools came primarily from without rather than from within the field of psychology, and it came from a multiplicity of local, provincial, and national forces. This tended to impede and blur the development of a coherent professional core and identity. On the other hand, these very same forces gave school psychologists the sense of purpose and broader scope of practice that brought them into the mainstream of schools and schooling (Bartell, 2006).

The demand for school psychology is generally high across Canada, but the supply is limited.

The unique history of school psychology in North America, and the recognition that the profession continues to be driven, shaped, and controlled, at least in part, by key external forces, is actually beneficial, because it helps rejuvenate role definition and practice as circumstances change. However, the challenge to the profession's practitioners, trainers, and researchers remains. To counterbalance external influences and its identification with mainly assessment functions, the profession needs to establish an identity that reflects the changing realities: one, the context of the school as an ecological system; and two, the advances in research and knowledge in the developmental, social–psychological, learning, and clinical areas.

The development of empirically supported prevention initiatives and programs is an important case in point. There is a growing emphasis on a coordinated system of primary (universal), secondary (identified), and tertiary (targeted) preventions and interventions. In turn, this compels practitioners to adopt broader systemic, ecological, and developmental perspectives in their roles and delivery systems so they may understand, anticipate, prevent, address, and ameliorate the developmental and learning needs of all children and their families in broader supportive school and community contexts (Bartell, 1995, 1996a, 1996b, 2003, 2006; Finn, Heath, Petrakos, & McLean-Heywood, 2002; Schwean, 2006). The growth of school psychology during the past 50 years has been unparalleled. However, changes in the traditional roles and models that define the practices of school psychologists have been slow by comparison.

The education of children in Canada is a provincial/territorial mandate. As a result, wide discrepancies in terms of job descriptions, funding, and priorities exist. Canada is a vast and diverse country geographically, culturally, and linguistically. Irrespective of this jurisdictional diversity, the primary role of school psychologists has been, and continues to be, focused on the problems faced by children, educators, and parents in the context of the schools. Among the factors that continue to dictate the roles and functions of school psychologists and the delivery of psychological services are the number of psychologists employed in a particular district, the size of their caseloads, the psychologist-to-student ratio, the psychologists' training and professional orientation, rural versus urban work settings, the priorities established at local levels, and the overall perceived credibility of the psychological team and the profession within each of the provinces (Saklofske & Janzen, 1993).

The growth of school psychology during the past 50 years has been unparalleled. However, changes in the traditional roles and models that define the practices of school psychologists have been slow by comparison.

Nevertheless, the literature portrays a considerable commonality in school psychologists' practices. For example, surveys conducted by Dumont (1989) and Neudorf (1989), the 1990 and 2001 special issues of the *Canadian Journal of School Psychology*, and data from a national study (Kaufman & Smith, 1998) reveal that the more traditional roles of school psychologists are still widely practiced. These include psychological and psychoeducational assessments, direct service delivery models, and the development and implementation of clinical and educational prescriptive programs. However, the more traditional roles are increasingly being modified or replaced in some jurisdictions. Alternatives to direct services to individual children have been gaining momentum in recent years. Cole and Siegel (1990, 2003) and Sladeczek and Heath (1997) address consultation, and Cole (1995) and Mykota and Schwean (2006) address prevention and intervention programs. Parent and teacher training is addressed by Greenough, Schwean, and Saklofske (1993) and Philips, Schwean, and Saklofske (1997). Multimodal school-based interventions are covered by Da Silva (2003) and Stirtzinger, Campbell, Green, DeSouza, and Dawe (2001). Canadian school psychologists are realizing that alternative roles and functions and new approaches such as systems of care (Schwean, 2006), which involve active support and participation, may be more effective and appropriate in meeting the needs of students, parents, and teachers.

Cole and Siegel (1990) portrayed the current and projected roles of Canadian school psychologists in a two-dimensional grid system. They described the goals of service delivery (primary, secondary, and tertiary) and the various recipients of school psychological services (e.g., school systems, teachers, parents, and students). Bartell (1995) recommended that to better meet the developmental and learning needs of all students, school psychologists need to transform their roles and functions and adopt a systemic ecological and developmental perspective on the broader contexts within which children live, learn, and grow. Furthermore, Canadian schools, families, and communities continue to require school psychologists to provide support in meeting the educational demands of a rapidly changing world. If Canadian school psychologists are to remain in control of their own destinies, they must continue to evolve, that is, to transform their roles and functions. Roles may continue to evolve haphazardly as circumstances and needs change, or they may be guided by a shift in the delivery paradigm that makes the school psychologist an agent of change (Bartell, 1996a, 1996b, 2006). This topic is discussed below.

A growing trend in several provinces is for school psychologists to work in alternative settings, such as hospitals, clinics, community service agencies, or private practice, depending on their training and licensing. Their roles may vary compared with those of a psychologist employed by a school district. In other cases, school psychologists may work in nonschool settings but provide services that are consistent with the traditional practices of school psychologists. Concomitantly, this trend to expand the training paradigm is also found in some Canadian universities. One such example is the school/applied child psychology program at McGill University, housed within the Department of Educational and Counselling Psychology. This APA-approved program emphasizes the doctoral-level training of school psychologists in the traditional school psychology role as well as in the mental health role in the wider community.

It may be argued that the diversified training of school psychologists will benefit the profession of psychology as a whole, as well as promote the specialty of school psychology. Canadian school psychologists with expertise in more than one practice setting will not only secure their own job prospects, but also promote an awareness of school psychology in settings other than schools. On the other hand, there is grounds to argue that splitting one's professional expertise could dilute, blur, or even jeopardize the unique role of the school psychologist. Bartell (1996b) argued for an ecological, contextualized, and systemic conception of the role and service delivery of the school psychologist and for the infusion of mental health influences throughout the school as a whole. This theme continues to be discussed at recent APA and NASP conferences as well as at the 2006 CPA conference in Calgary.

A growing trend in several provinces is for school psychologists to work in alternative settings, such as hospitals, clinics, community service agencies, or private practice, depending on their training and licensing.

The recent interest in new ideas and perspectives is encouraging and is reflected in the school psychology literature, for example, on the ecology of school psychology (Sheridan & Gutkin, 2000), on decontextualized programs (Elias, Zins, Graczyk, & Weissberg, 2003), and on systems of care (Schwean, 2006).

Changing Roles and Functions of School Psychologists

The changing roles of school psychologists in Canada can be illustrated in the Atlantic province of New Brunswick, one of the smallest in Canada. The province further highlights the importance of external provincial influences on the roles and functions of school psychologists in Canada. In 2002 the New Brunswick Department of Education released a landmark document, *Guidelines for Professional Practice of School Psychologists* (New Brunswick Department of Education & CPA, 2001). This document and the 2004 *Guidelines for Referrals for School Psychological Consultation* (New Brunswick Department of Education & CPA, 2004) were based largely on research emerging from the National Association of School Psychologists that suggested that traditional testing (the "refer–test–place" model of practice) was less reliable and useful than curriculum-based assessment and classroom interventions. Following the IDEA reauthorizations of 2004, these documents noted the lack of reliability of the ability–achievement discrepancy model of diagnosing learning disabilities, the appropriateness of response-to-intervention (RTI) approaches to programming for students with learning differences, and the need for school psychologists to be more prevention-oriented in their service delivery.

New Brunswick is in a unique position in that the inclusive education policy frees school psychologists from the mandate to test for placement. Instead, school psychologists are able to spend their time in schoolwide prevention initiatives, solving problems within schools for students with difficulties and assisting with RTI approaches, and also to use their assessment skills when the more ecologically based interventions have not provided sufficient insight into the student's problems.

The New Brunswick documents were recently adopted by the Canadian Psychological Association as policy documents. They are currently being rewritten, with the permission of the New Brunswick government, to reflect and influence Canadian practice nationally. The CPA has also taken an active interest in the development of school psychology as an important domain of the profession of psychology. In 2002, the CPA released two documents describing the role of the school psychologist as well as a position paper advocating the enhanced participation of psychologists in schools (*http://www.cpa.ca/documents/school%5F2.pdf*; Mureika, French, & Service, 2002a, 2002b). The Canadian perspective on the practice of school psychology was also presented at the 2003 NASP convention and is detailed in the Trainers of School Psychologists newsletter (Mureika, Falconer, & Howard, 2004) as well as in the CASP newsletter and publications of the CPA Section of Psychologists in Education in 2004.

Direct Student Services

Under most circumstances, school psychologists in Canada are not likely to regularly provide direct educational and psychological assistance for students. This type of activity is usually designated to teachers, learning specialists, and special educators. However, a growing number of school psychologists report that they are more often asked to provide some direct clinical services, usually in the form of therapeutic intervention and counseling. In most cases, this support is short term, with students who are being referred to outside agencies for long-term treatment. School psychologists play a central role in the development of individualized educational programs (IEPs) and individual behavior support plans (IBSPs), and they may be called on to monitor a child's academic and behavioral progress and the success of the implemented IEPs or IBSPs.

A growing number of school psychologists report that they are more often asked to provide some direct clinical services, usually in the form of therapeutic intervention and counseling.

The most obvious direct service role provided by school psychologists is psychological and psychoeducational assessment. In fact, this is a professional role that school psychologists should embrace, as it is a defining strength of the profession. This role is not testing for the sake of testing or overly simple ability–achievement discrepancy testing; rather, it is an empirically driven process of describing the psychological strengths and needs of children, which will in turn better serve their needs and interests (Prifitera, Saklofske, & Weiss, 2005; Weiss, Saklofske, Prifitera, & Holdnack, 2006).

Psychological and Psychoeducational Assessments

School psychologists continue to work in close collaboration with educators to assess student learning and academic progress and other factors that may contribute to or detract from successful school experiences. Assessments by Canadian school psychologists often vary depending on the presenting problem and the reason for the referral (e.g., to develop a program for a particular child, or for placement or retention decisions). These assessments often include standardized instruments, some of which have been developed in Canada and others that have been adapted with Canadian norms (e.g., WISC-IV) to assess intellectual, educational, social, emotional, personality, or neuropsychological development (Saklofske & Janzen, 1990). More recently, other types of assessment procedures have been implemented and are gaining in popularity, including curriculum-based instructional assessment, dynamic assessment, bilingual assessment, functional–behavioral assessment, and continuous performance appraisal. Psychological assessment is not merely relegated to standardized tests but can also include informal assessment, interviews, as well as observations of classroom behavior following Sattler's (2001) four pillars of assessment (Saklofske, Schwean, Harrison, & Mureika, 2006).

Placement, referral, and retention decisions should be made on the basis of the comprehensive assessment findings that are designed to provide an in-depth understanding of the child's ability, achievement, and behavior. Specific recommendations for the child, teacher, and family will emanate from the assessment. Parent, child, and teacher meetings to discuss the findings, recommendations, and a plan of action are also part of the typical assessment process (e.g., Lawrence & Heller, 2001). However, there is some evidence that Canadian school psychologists may not be using a comprehensive assessment protocol in certain instances, such as the diagnosis of mental retardation (Lecavalier, Tassé, & Lévesque, 2001). This may compromise the integrity and effectiveness of the intervention and prevention processes, which rely on complete and accurate information. In 2004 the CPA developed a position paper, the "Ethical Use and Reporting of Psychological Assessment Results for Student Placement" (CPA, 2004), linking the appropriate use of psychological test results with the CPA Code of Ethics and stressing the importance of using more than one source of information to make placement decisions about students.

Referral, Interdisciplinary Collaboration, and Consultation

School psychologists play a key role as agents referring individuals to community services (Carney, 1995a, 1995b). They are also linked into a multidisciplinary service delivery system for children and adolescents more often than educators. Collaboration between physicians, including psychiatrists, pediatricians, and neurologists, is common practice for many Canadian school psychologists. Additional service to children is often supplemented by publicly funded professionals allied with the medical field, including physiotherapists, occupational therapists, social workers, and nurses. Government cutbacks and fiscal restraint can affect the level of these services, but the principle of universality aims at ensuring medical treatment for all

Canadians. This multidisciplinary and interdisciplinary approach is particularly helpful in situations where children are experiencing considerable educational, psychological, and physical health difficulties and require the assistance of many partners to enhance their success in school and in their everyday lives.

Consultation has become a widely used approach for providing services to children and adolescents, although in the late 20th century, these models were slow to be implemented in certain parts of Canada (Sladeczek & Heath, 1997). Although differences exist across models of consultation (e.g., Cole & Siegel, 2003), the adoption of consultation by many school psychologists and educators has far-reaching implications. The challenge of Canada's vast geography and external forces has provided the foundation for greater availability of consultation services. For example, Greenough et al. (1993) described the relevance of collaborative consultation in more sparsely populated and remote regions of northern Saskatchewan where the population is predominantly aboriginal. These regions of Canada pose unique social, cultural, economic, linguistic, and educational demands that require a very different approach to school psychology service delivery.

Consultation allows for greater collaboration between the student's home and the school. ... More and more, it appears that consultation is the first service offered by school psychologists.

Consultation models represent an important educational role for teachers and parents, increasing their skills in analysis and resolution of problems. As discussed in chapter 4, consultation not only represents a more cost-effective service, it also promotes several additional benefits that are not usually associated with more traditional school psychology roles such as assessment. Consultation allows for greater collaboration between the student's home and the school, and increased home and school collaboration has been shown to increase student achievement and learning (Christenson, Rounds, & Gorney, 1992). Collaborative consultation is also more likely to be effective when students with behavioral disorders are treated in the interactive context of the school, rather than in isolation (Bartell, 1995; Finn et al., 2002; Schwean, Saklofske, Shatz, & Folk, 1996). Successful behavioral consultants must have expertise both in coordinating and facilitating the problem-solving process and in modifying behavior (Kratochwill, Elliott, & Carrington-Rotto, 1995).

Canadian school psychologists have shown considerable progress in the development of consultation skills. Continued application of consultation methods, supported by Canadian-based research, will undoubtedly increase the prevalence of this important role for school psychologists. More and more, it appears that consultation is the first service offered by school psychologists. Through this process, the psychologist is able to assess the totality of the student's situation, including the student's and others' response to that situation, and engage in problem solving with the school and family to quickly begin the intervention process. Teachers report that this approach is very supportive and enables them to intervene immediately on behalf of a student without having to wait for formal test results. From the perspective of classroom practice, the problem-solving approach seems to offer more timely information than the formal test results, which are understandably belated.

The recent and increasing role of consultation in school psychology practice can be nicely illustrated using the framework of positive behavior interventions and supports (*http://www.pbis.org*). That framework is being promoted in New Brunswick as a model of schoolwide discipline through the Department of Education document *Meeting Behavioural Challenges* (New Brunswick Department of Education, 2004). In the framework, psychologists intervene at three levels in different ways, the first two of which are very much grounded in the consultation role. At level 1, school psychologists engage in school-wide support, teaching and in service, and screening. At level 2, school psychologists support school-based problem-solving teams in identifying, developing, and monitoring short-term, targeted interventions for students at risk of either behavioral or learning difficulties. At level 3, school psychologists employ direct student interventions (e.g., psychological assessment or functional–behavioral assessments) to support either special education plans or individual behavior support plans.

Crisis Intervention and Crisis Team Management

Canadian school psychologists have become much more visible in the role of crisis intervention and crisis team management. Increasing school violence, school bullying and aggression, substance abuse, catastrophic accidents, critical events within a community (e.g., mass unemployment), and natural disasters require swift, immediate action and intervention. For example, Beran and Tutty (2002) reported that 27% of children in grades 4–6 experienced both verbal and physical bullying, with similar figures noted for children in grades 1–3. In many ways, the skills of the school psychologist must be relied on to deal with community-based disasters, such as the death of a student or teacher in a car accident, and the stress responses that can follow such tragic events. These events may also serve as "teachable moments," in which adults can help students learn from the realities that life unexpectedly hands them instead of, as used to be the case, not talking about or addressing the effects of traumatic events.

The unfortunate reality is that no school is immune or exempt from the kinds of crises that can significantly and negatively affect all members of a school community. Even successful schools in affluent areas are at risk for some type of crisis (Jay, 1989). Recent events of fatal school shootings in both Canada and the United States clearly demonstrate this sobering fact. Canada is considered a safe haven for many refugees from around the world. As a result, many Canadian schools receive children who have witnessed or experienced tragic circumstances. Estimates indicate that approximately 31% of Canadian immigrant children have lived in some form of unstable and poor conditions (Cole, 1998). Children exposed to violence in their school and community are at risk for immediate psychological stress responses and for posttraumatic stress disorder (PTSD). Through crisis intervention, students who are at risk for developing PTSD can be monitored and, if required, referred for mental health services by the school psychologist. School psychologists can also play a key role in supporting school staff who see these children on a daily basis.

The unfortunate reality is that no school is immune or exempt from the kinds of crises that can significantly and negatively affect all members of a school community.

Prevention and intervention are also necessary components of any crisis intervention team (Poland, Pitcher, & Lazarus, 1995). Cole (1995) contends that primary intervention programs can focus on all students in a school and encourage prosocial behaviors and antiviolence beliefs. Secondary programs target at-risk students who are experiencing academic, social, and emotional difficulties that could lead to violence. Tertiary prevention programs focus on students who have a history of difficulty and may require specialized programs such as anger management. In most jurisdictions in Canada, school psychologists occupy an important role in crisis intervention and crisis team management. As a case in point, New Brunswick developed a protocol for *Keeping Our Schools Safe: Violence Prevention and Crisis Response in New Brunswick Schools* (New Brunswick Department of Education, 2001). This document outlines prevention, intervention, and postvention practices and procedures for schools. Ongoing Canadian research has also examined the effectiveness of school-based programs for reducing and preventing bullying in schools (Beran, Tutty, & Steinwrath, 2004). There is a clear role for school psychologists in this process at all levels of implementation.

Program Development and Evaluation

The expanding roles of Canadian school psychologists include program development and the evaluation of existing programs. The new emphasis on outcomes requires school psychologists to occupy a more active role in program evaluation, with the associated ability to design, implement, and evaluate curriculum programs and social intervention programs (e.g., substance abuse, antiviolence, HIV/AIDS prevention, and suicide prevention). Some Canadian school psychologists are more active than others in this role, depending on caseloads and district policy. Increased responsibilities and accountability in this area represent an exciting opportunity for Canadian school psychologists by diversifying their roles and allowing them to implement evidence-based programs to increase student learning and well-being (Greenspoon, 1998).

Parent Training

From a pedagogical perspective, educators have long sought to build a partnership between the school and home. Within rural communities, the school often has assumed a leadership role in community events. Psychologists in smaller towns are well integrated within the community, and they could fill the need for educational workshops on a multitude of issues. Where available, these workshops are well attended. Also, parenting courses, designed to improve parenting skills and decrease child-rearing problems, are thriving.

Recent Examples of the Changing Roles of School Psychologists in Canada

The Canadian mosaic has changed rapidly during the past decade as Canadian society has become more ethnically and culturally diverse. The need for psychological services in Canada's two official languages, French and English, has been increasing. The pressure to provide services in French and to offer French immersion classes inside and outside Quebec and New Brunswick continues to grow. The demand for teachers of English as a second language has also increased dramatically to meet the needs of a large number of immigrants. This influx of new Canadians is in addition to the large number of children of aboriginal and First Nation Indian ancestry, and schools emphasize a sensitivity to cross-cultural differences (Ormrod, Saklofske, Schwean, Harrison, & Andrews, 2006; Saklofske et al., 2006). Parents and communities want opportunities for their children to learn in both official languages as well as to preserve languages from a family's cultural heritage (e.g., Chinese, Cree).

Canada's Two Official Languages: The Case of Quebec and New Brunswick

This sensitivity to cross-cultural differences of language and culture, including religion, in relation to school psychology services, may be described most clearly in terms of historical and contemporary changes in the province of Quebec. Unlike other provinces, the public education system in Quebec was predicated on religious lines. Although the province has a number of private secular and religious schools (e.g., Jewish, Greek, and Muslim), the vast majority of students within the province attend public, provincially supported schools. Throughout the province, two separate school systems exist, the Catholic and Protestant school boards. The Catholic school system has a strong religious program of instruction as well as the traditional educational component. The Protestant school boards were created for all individuals who were not Catholic, and the schools have no religious program, with the exception of a course in moral and nondenominational religious education. This is further complicated by the fact that the language of instruction could be either French, for the majority population, or English. While children throughout the province are francophone, a considerable number are English-speaking pupils (anglophone). As a result, many Quebec school boards have both English- and French-speaking populations, so that a large city such as Montreal, for example, could have four elementary schools that reflect four combinations of student populations: Catholic-French, Catholic-English, Protestant-French, and Protestant-English.

Given a significantly declining population and the provincial government's desire to maintain its linguistic heritage, Quebec passed legislation mandating that children whose mother tongue was not English were no longer eligible for an English education and were required to attend French schools. Thus, psychological services had to be provided in French and English. With a further decrease in the school population and a need to consolidate services in 1998, school boards were realigned based upon linguistic and geographical lines. Now that the schools and school boards are designated as either English or French, French is a required subject for all elementary and secondary school students. In French immersion programs (English-speaking children attending English schools where most of the curriculum is presented in French) school psychologists must have a working knowledge of French to be familiar with the curriculum. They are frequently required to complete educational assessments using French versions of standardized instruments, such as the WISC-IV. Psychological reports can be written in English, but parent meetings often are held in French; thus, although being bilingual is not necessarily a

As a result, many Quebec school boards have both English- and French-speaking populations, so that a large city such as Montreal, for example, could have four elementary schools that reflect four combinations of student populations: Catholic-French, Catholic-English, Protestant-French, and Protestant-English.

requirement, it is extremely advantageous, especially in the public school system. The need for bilingual proficiency in some private English schools is not as compelling.

In New Brunswick, language also has had an impact on school psychology. Two distinct and separate departments of education exist, defined by language. There are nine English and three francophone school districts, and psychologists are hired to work in both settings. However, there is no crossover of psychologists, and very little collaboration exists between the departments and districts. Anglophone school psychologists formed an association in the late 1980s, the New Brunswick Association of Psychologists and Psychometrists in the Schools. The group has about 30 members who maintain active and ongoing communication through an e-mail discussion list and biannual meetings. The francophone school psychologists have not had such an association for a number of years; however, they recently developed guidelines for practice in conjunction with the Department of Education, with practice guidelines similar to those in the anglophone association document. Issues related to language, culture, and other sociopolitical factors continue to influence the roles and services assigned to, and provided by, school psychologists; however, the hope is that children's and teachers' needs will be the primary focus of the kind and extent of these services.

Extension of School Psychology Services to Preschool Children and Adults

The involvement of school psychologists as service providers to children in kindergarten and early childhood programs, and in adult education, has been slow to develop in many Canadian communities. Clearly, the involvement of school psychologists will have to increase if early identification and prevention programs are to be implemented comprehensively and effectively. With many adults also returning to colleges for continuing education, school psychologists have an opportunity to participate at all levels of educational service delivery. It is now recognized that many incarcerated adolescents and adults had learning disabilities, ADHD, and other conditions that may have contributed to school failure and early school leaving, and those conditions must be confronted if rehabilitation programs are to be effective. School psychologists will also continue to play a significant role in special education services delivered across the full spectrum of age and grade ranges.

Concluding Comments on School Psychologists' Roles and Functions

As the 21st century gets under way, the roles of school psychologists in Canada are becoming more diverse. The performance of psychoeducational assessment will not decrease because such tests are essential to identifying and addressing the psychological and educational problems of individual students, whether children or adults. Certainly, school psychologists rightly view psychological testing for diagnosis and program planning as their unique expertise in school settings. However, there is also a greater movement toward interprofessional collaboration, consultation, and program development, plus a growing need to provide services in both official languages, to be responsive to community and cultural groups, and to provide prevention service programs. Given these trends, it is fairly evident that a much larger number of school psychologists will be needed to work collaboratively with administrators, teachers, allied professionals, and parents in multicultural, bilingual, or even multilingual environments.

Canadian districts will follow the experiences of school districts in the United States, which have moved to a problem-solving, consultative model from a model that involves only testing for placement. That change has resulted in an increased demand for psychological services in schools, and the number of school psychologist positions has, in turn, increased. School psychologists also will need the relevant training to position themselves in leadership and liaison roles that will enable them to help raise social policy issues and promote effective educational and psychological programs in the broader community of the school.

TRAINING OF SCHOOL PSYCHOLOGISTS

The levels and kinds of university training and entry-level qualifications for employment as a school psychologist vary across Canada (Saklofske, 1996). Until more Canadian school psychology training programs endorse specific accreditation standards (e.g., those developed by the APA or CPA for doctoral-level training or by NASP for specialist-level training), training programs found across Canadian universities will continue to vary. Fortunately this now seems to be the direction for the future. School psychology programs such as those found at the University of British Columbia and the University of Calgary have continued to evolve and to be guided, in part, by the recommendations and standards proposed by the Trainers of School Psychologists, the National Association of School Psychologists, the Canadian Psychological Association, and the International School Psychology Association. Furthermore, according to reports at the 2006 CPA conference, the doctoral training programs at the universities of Calgary, Alberta, and British Columbia are preparing for CPA accreditation within the next few years.

Until more Canadian school psychology training programs endorse specific accreditation standards (for example, those developed by the APA or CPA for doctoral-level training or by NASP for specialist-level training), training programs found across Canadian universities will continue to vary.

At this time, relatively few programs in Canada specifically prepare school psychologists (see Table 9.1). Only five programs grant a PhD in school psychology, and only two of those programs, McGill University and the Ontario Institute for Studies in Education, University of Toronto (OISE), have sought and been awarded accreditation from the American Psychological Association. Although the CPA has now endorsed accreditation standards for PhD programs in school

Table 9.1 Graduate School Psychology Programs in Canada

Program	Degrees Granted	Accred-ited	Admission Criteria	Academic Preparation	Professional Preparation	Length of Program
Department of Education, Mount Saint Vincent University, Halifax, Nova Scotia	MA, School Psychology	No	Undergraduate degree in psychology. Prefer that students also hold a degree in education. In addition, students require related work or volunteer experience; three letters of reference; and an individual interview (see *www.msvu.ca/calendar/Graduate/Programs/MasterArtsSchoolPsychology.asp*).	Required courses (11 ½ units), which include coursework in the core academic areas of psychology, assessment and intervention services, interpersonal and consultation skills, ethics, and research methodology and statistics.	3 ½ units are directed toward internship and practicum courses.	Two-year, full-time program
Department of Educational and Counselling Psychology, Faculty of Education, McGill University, Montreal, Quebec	PhD and post-PhD, MA Graduate Diploma in School/Applied Child Psychology	APA	For the PhD, generally, an MA or MEd in educational psychology, two letters of recommendation, summary proposal of intended thesis research, statement of experience, career plans, and program appropriateness, copy of research project, results of the Graduate Record Examination, and undergraduate major or honors degree in psychology (see *www.coursecalendar.mcgill.ca/gps2005-06/GPSO-5-26.html*).	There are 60 credit units of required courses in areas such as psychological assessment, ethics, professional practice, the core academic areas of psychology (e.g., development, cognition, biological bases of behavior), professional practice, and interventions.	Of the 60 credit units, 12 credit units are practicum courses. In addition, students must select an additional 12 credit units of practicum complementary courses that are situated within school and community contexts. A 24-credit unit internship is also required.	Unspecified

Human Development and Applied Psychology, Ontario Institute for Studies in Education, University of Toronto, Toronto, Ontario	MA and PhD in School and Clinical Psychology	APA	Admission to the MA program requires a 4-year bachelor's degree in psychology, or its equivalent. Admission to the PhD program normally requires a 4-year bachelor's degree in psychology or its equivalent and an MA in SCCP or its equivalent (see *www.oise.utoronto.ca/depts/hdap/sccp.html*).	MA comprises 11 half-courses, a practicum, and a thesis. Coursework focuses on psychological and psychoeducational assessment, ethics, core areas of psychology, intervention, and research. The PhD program comprises eight half-courses, a practicum, a comprehensive examination, a doctoral dissertation, and an internship. Students are required to take courses in research, statistics, biological bases of behavior, social bases of behavior, psychological assessment, psychoeducational intervention, and psychosocial intervention.	MA students are required to undertake a 250-hour practicum. All PhD students are required to undertake a 2-day per week practicum (approximately 500 hours of experience) and to complete at least 1,500 hours of supervised internship in an approved training center.	MA 2-year, full-time program. There is a residency requirement of at least 2 years of full-time study for the PhD.
Department of Psychology, University of Manitoba, Winnipeg, Manitoba	MA, School Psychology	No	Applicants are expected to have completed a 4-year honors degree in psychology. Students lacking sufficient background in psychology may be eligible for admission to a pre-master's program. Other components taken into consideration include undergraduate grade-point average, scores on the Graduate Record Examination, and letters of reference (see *www.umanitoba.ca/faculties/arts/psychology/school_psychology/program.php*).	This is a 60 credit hour program that includes coursework focusing on ethics and professional standards, assessment, intervention, the core areas of psychology, consultation and collaboration, decision making, program evaluation, and research methodology and statistics.	An initial three-credit-hour practicum (150 hours) is scheduled for the winter semester of the candidate's first year and focuses primarily on assessment activities. The second six-credit-hour practicum (300 hours) takes place in the winter semester of the second year and is intervention-based.	Two years of full-time study.

psychology, to date, no Canadian program has received CPA accreditation. In addition to these five programs (which also grant master's degrees), three additional programs offer a master's degree in school psychology. It is difficult to report on the number of school psychology students who are admitted into, or graduate from, existing Canadian school psychology programs each year, because almost all of these programs vary their admittance rates annually. Readers are encouraged to consult the websites of these and other Canadian universities to ensure up-to-date information.

CREDENTIALING AND REGULATION OF SCHOOL PSYCHOLOGISTS IN CANADA

The agencies involved in the credentialing of school psychologists are many and varied. Credentials may be issued by different agencies in the varied provinces and territories, and the graduate level degrees and experiences are inconsistent across the country. As observed in the United States, the variations are associated with historical alliances to educational and psychological associations, training programs, and government agencies.

Credentialing Agencies

The title of psychologist may only be used by persons who hold certificates of registration from the provincial or territorial psychology regulatory boards. The registration of psychologists occurs at the provincial and territorial levels, and variability is reflected in the entry-level qualifications: academic entry requirements, supervised experience, examinations, and exemptions. These eligibility criteria have been summarized by the Canadian Psychological Association (see Table 9.2). Current descriptions and criteria for registration for the 10 provinces and two territories are posted on to the CPA website (*http://www.cpa.ca*), under provincial and territorial regulatory bodies. Unless the jurisdiction's laws allow other agencies, such as school boards and education departments, to hire and title individuals as school psychologists, school psychologists must also be registered psychologists.

Although a teaching degree or teaching background is not required for provincial certification and licensure as a psychologist, some departments of education and school districts within the provinces have stipulated or shown a preference for valid teaching certification for school psychologists.

Although a teaching degree or teaching background is not required for provincial certification and licensure as a psychologist, some departments of education and school districts within the provinces have stipulated or shown a preference for valid teaching certification for school psychologists (e.g., Newfoundland and Labrador). Moreover, provincial certification and licensing requirements have changed significantly in the past few years. Hence, those interested in school psychology positions in Canada should review information in the recent policy manuals of provincial departments of education and school districts, as well as consult with provincial psychology regulatory associations.

Table 9.2 Provincial Certification and Licensing Requirements for Psychologists

	Academic Entry Requirements	Supervised Experience	Examinations	Exemptions
British Columbia	**Doctoral** • Independent practice **Master's** • Psychological Associate Independent practice	**Doctoral** • 1 year predoctoral **Master's** • 1 year postmaster's internship and 3 years supervised practice	• EPPP 70% • Written jurisprudence • Ethics exam	University, government, schools
Alberta	**Master's** • Independent practice	**Master's** • 1 year (1,600 hours) postmaster's	• EPPP 70% • Oral • Ethics exam	University (unless teaching in professional practices areas)
Saskatchewan	**Doctoral** • Independent practice **Master's** • Independent practice	**Master's** • 1 year (1,500 hours) postmaster's	• EPPP 70% • Oral • Ethics exam	None with respect to counseling and clinical psychology or psychological assessment
Manitoba	**Doctoral** • Independent practice **Master's** • Psychological Associate independent practice	**Doctoral** • 1 pre- and 1 postyear **Master's** • 2 years post	• EPPP doctoral 70%; master's 65% • Oral (both)	University, government, schools, hospitals

Table 9.2 (*Continued*)

	Academic Entry Requirements	Supervised Experience	Examinations	Exemptions
Ontario	**Doctoral** • Independent practice **Master's** • Psychological Associate – Independent practice	**Doctoral** • 1 pre- and 1 postyear **Master's** • 4 years post plus 1 year on supervision register	• EPPP 70% • Oral • Ethics included in written jurisprudence exam	University
Quebec	**Doctoral (proclaimed 2006)** **Master's (prior to 2006)** • Independent practice	• None (supervised experience is consistent with graduate program requirements)	• No EPPP • Written or oral ethics exam as part of French language proficiency exam, if required	None
Newfoundland & Labrador	**Master's** • Independent practice	**Doctoral** • 1 pre- and 1 postyear **Master's** • 2 years post	• EPPP 70% • No oral • No ethics exam	University

Table 9.2 *(Continued)*

	Academic Entry Requirements	Supervised Experience	Examinations	Exemptions
Northwest Territories	**Master's** Psychology, from a Canadian university	1 year (1,600 hours) while on an intern's registry. Previous supervised experience from another jurisdiction may be considered.	• Exam may be required • No ethics exam	None
Nova Scotia	**Master's** • Independent practice	**Doctoral** • 1 pre- and 1 postyear **Master's** • 4 years post	• EPPP 70% • Oral • Ethics exam	EPPP requirements waived if qualified for transfer under MRA
Prince Edward Island	**Doctoral** • Independent practice **Master's** • Independent practice in institute/agency only	**Doctoral** • 1 pre- and 1 postyear **Master's** • 2 years post	• EPPP 70% • Oral • Ethics exam	University
New Brunswick	**Master's** • Independent practice Note: CPNB recently voted to move to a doctoral entry level for licensing, effective 2011.	**Doctoral** • 1 pre- and 1 postyear **Master's** • 3 years post	• EPPP 70% • Oral or interview • Ethics exam	University

Updated August 27, 2002 (CPA) and 2004 Amendments to the Mutual Recognition Agreement of the Regulatory Bodies for Professional Psychologists in Canada, June 2004. Further updated by authors (2006).

Manitoba and British Columbia have unique, long-standing approaches to the regulation of school psychologists. Both systems are external to the provincial psychology regulatory bodies. School psychologists in Manitoba are hired by school divisions and the Child Guidance Clinic. To be hired as school psychologists, candidates must first obtain a clinician certificate issued by the Manitoba Provincial Department of Education, Citizenship, and Youth, which has clearly articulated education and training criteria. In turn, to be certified as a school psychologist, practitioners must be full members of the Manitoba Association of School Psychologists (MASP). MASP is an independent body, separate from the Psychological Association of Manitoba (PAM), which is the regulatory body for granting certification as a psychologist. Should a new Psychologists' Act be proclaimed that results in the removal of current registration exemptions (e.g., being able to practice school psychology within schools) and the clinical certificate, the status and practice of school psychology in the province could change in undetermined ways. For example, would master's-level school psychologists become psychological associates (as is the case in Ontario)? Would Manitoba follow the Saskatchewan model, or would it maintain a one-level registration with entry at the master's level, as is the situation in Alberta? In this regard, changes in provincial credentialing requirements for psychologists in Manitoba could affect the university training programs students' preparation to meet these requirements. This could be particularly problematic if having a PhD remained a requirement for certification and there are no exemptions for master's-level clinicians to practice school psychology in schools.

The British Columbia Psychological Association (BCPA) now registers psychologists at the master's and PhD levels. Prior to this, there was a considerable strain in the relationship between BCPA and the British Columbia Association of School Psychologists (BCASP). This led BCASP to set standards independently for school psychologists, which have been widely accepted by employers of school psychologists. These standards follow standards outlined by NASP and require the candidate to successfully pass the school psychology Praxis examination offered by the Educational Testing Service (ETS). Of course, this credential is only applicable and valid in the school setting because of the exemptions in the Psychologist's Act, which also includes colleges, universities, and government institutions. Since the exemption clause to the act is quite specific in defining the employment situation in which a person can be called a school psychologist, BCASP can exclude a person from membership if he or she is not employed in a school setting or a publicly funded and operated education setting.

Canada's provinces and territories vary considerably with respect to the registration of school psychologists and the regulation of school psychology practice. Additional changes can be expected in several provinces over the next few years. (Readers can consult the CPA website, *http://www.cpa.ca*, for links to the provinces' and territories' regulatory bodies and current descriptions of their licensing requirements.)

Portability of School Psychology Credentials

For many years, it was very difficult for school psychologists to move their practices from one province or territory to another because of the variability of entry standards for the independent practice of psychology. For example, in the late 1990s, British Columbia maintained a doctoral-level entry requirement for psychologists, Ontario opted for a two-tiered entry standard (master's and PhD) for independent practice, Alberta maintained the master's degree entry level, and Saskatchewan was exploring a change from an exclusively doctoral-level entry to also recognize a master's-level entry for independent practice. Quebec was also actively debating a change to a doctoral standard for entry practice. Moreover, the provincial regulatory boards also varied in the specific skills and knowledge required and the assessment of these areas with respect to the registration of applicants. In many cases, school psychologists from one province or territory who wanted to reside and practice in another province or territory had to go through a lengthy, and sometimes costly, recertification process within their new province or territory. In other cases, it was just not possible to make such a professional move.

Canada's provinces and territories vary considerably with respect to the registration of school psychologists and the regulation of school psychology practice.

In 1998, representatives from each of the regulatory boards in Canada began meeting to develop an agreement that would allow psychologists registered in one Canadian jurisdiction to have their registration for another jurisdiction fast-tracked by psychology boards. In 2001, the Regulatory Bodies for Professional Psychologists in Canada signed the Mutual Recognition Agreement articulating the conditions under which a psychologist who is licensed and registered to practice without supervision in one Canadian jurisdiction will have his or her qualifications recognized in another jurisdiction (see e.g., *http://www.cap.ab.ca*).

Under the provisions of the Mutual Recognition Agreement, psychologists already registered in one province or territory will be able to achieve registration in another jurisdiction much more quickly if they possess the entry-level qualifications required by that regulatory body. In this regard, qualified applicants will not have to undertake a period of supervised practice in the new jurisdiction or retake oral or written examinations if they have already met those requirements in another jurisdiction in Canada. However, regulatory boards may still require additional information or examinations on issues specific to practice in that particular jurisdiction. Among other things, the Mutual Recognition Agreement identified an agreed-upon core of competencies and assessment methods for several areas, including interpersonal relationships, assessment and evaluation, intervention and consultation, research, ethics and standards, and general knowledge in psychology. This agreement was last amended in June 2004 (see *www.cpa.ca*).

PROFESSIONAL ASSOCIATIONS

The emergence and founding of professional associations for school psychologists and psychologists parallels the complicated history of such organizations in the United States. As discussed below, there are competing national-level organizations, and in many provinces and territories there are separate associations for psychologists and school psychologists. The variations have had a significant impact on the professional identity of the field.

Identity Issues Revisited: Psychology Versus Education Professional Associations

School psychologists in Canada tend to identify more or less with the professions of psychology and education. This identity is partly influenced by their university training programs. Those who initially completed BEd degrees and who may have teaching experience are more likely to maintain their connections with the provincial teachers' associations. This link with the teaching profession is also related to the requirement, in some provinces and school districts, that school psychologists and other support staff hold teacher certification in order to be hired to work in the schools. This also makes it considerably easier for school boards to link their psychology positions to teacher salary grids, pension programs, and other benefit packages. School psychologists who have been more aligned with the discipline and practice of psychology are more likely to identify with the provincial and national psychology associations. However, issues of professional identity and affiliation have created a kind of schism in what should be a unified profession. For example, many more school psychologists are practicing than is reflected in the membership of the school psychology associations, either provincially or nationally. CASP has attracted only a very small percentage of practicing school psychologists into its membership, even though it has been in existence since the mid-1980s. Thus, no one national association lays claim to representing school psychology and school psychologists; however, at the provincial level, associations such as BCASP and MASP can be viewed as such.

Organization of School Psychology Associations

The relationships among the various associations that represent psychologists have not always been positive. The creation of provincial school psychology associations, which are independent of the provincial psychology regulatory bodies, has produced some direct conflicts. This unfortunate tug-of-war most often relates to the use of the title *psychologist* as a professionally regulated title or as part of the name of a provincial association. This conflict has been somewhat conspicuous in British Columbia (McKee, 1996) but also can be seen in other provinces such as Manitoba. Sweet (1990) documented the series of events that led to the formation of BCASP. After several years of injunctions, court hearings, and legislative changes, BCASP was granted the status of a registered society, independent of both the British Columbia Psychological Association and the British Columbia Teachers' Federation. At that time, Sweet clearly saw the need to explore the regulation of school psychologists:

> The profession remains largely fragmented, lacks an identity, and most serious of all, is unregulated; since the lifting of restrictions on the use of title within school districts, anyone can be hired by a district and called a psychologist. ... We have moved from a situation replete with Type 1 errors, where *bona fide* school psychologists were denied title, to one which is fraught with the danger of Type 2 errors, the granting of title (and

> function) to unqualified persons. There is no doubt that a major task for the profession in the near future is to police its own ranks. . . . To fail to do so would be to invite those who opposed the amendment to seek its revocation. (p. 5)

The creation of provincial school psychology associations, which are independent of the provincial psychology regulatory bodies, has produced some direct conflicts.

A fairly recent event in Ontario provided a reassuring example of the pulling together of various organizations in support of school psychologists. In 1996 the *Canadian Journal of School Psychology* published a special edition with a collection of papers from depositions made on behalf of a number of psychological associations. The submissions responded to the Toronto school board's 1995 threats to reduce psychological services by two thirds (Carney & Cole, 1995). Several of the submissions were received from representatives of CASP (Carney, 1995b), the CPA (Beal & Service, 1995), the Ontario Psychological Association (Hamovitch, 1995), and the Section on Psychology in Education of the Ontario Psychological Association (Jobin, 1995). The initial recommendation to significantly reduce school psychologists and their services was reversed, and the Toronto Board of Education continues to provide quality psychological services.

Provincial Psychology Associations

Table 9.3 lists the associations and contact information for the provincial and territorial psychology associations. Links to the provincial regulatory bodies can be found through the provincial psychology associations' websites and through the CPA website.

Provincial School Psychology Associations

Historically, in instances in which school psychologists were not eligible for registration because of doctoral or other requirements, they were much more likely to either form their own associations, as occurred in western Canada, or to maintain closer connections with provincial departments of education. Manitoba presents an interesting mosaic of professional connections. Though many school psychologists have joined MASP, and a large number are registered psychologists with the Psychological Association of Manitoba, all are required to hold a clinician's certificate from the Manitoba Provincial Department of Education, Citizenship, and Youth. In instances in which school psychologists, at either the master's or the PhD level, are required to be registered as psychologists (e.g., Saskatchewan and Ontario), there is a much stronger affiliation with the provincial psychology associations. However, in Saskatchewan, where the act regulating all psychologists was only enacted several years ago, the provincial association for school psychologists also remains very strong.

It was possibly because of this split identity, along with the increased recognition of school psychology as a specialty area of training and practice, that school

Table 9.3 Provincial and National Psychology Associations

Association des psychologues du Québec (APQ) Tel: (514)738-1881, 1-(800)363-2644 *www.ordrepsych.qc.ca* *info@apq.psycholog.qc.ca* Quebec, *www.aqps.gc.ca*	Association of Newfoundland Psychologists Tel: (709)739-5405 *www.nfpsych.com*
Association of Psychologists of Nova Scotia Tel: (902)422-9183 *apns@apns.ca* *www.apns.ca*	Association of Psychologists of the Northwest Territories *omegathree@theedge.ca*
British Columbia Psychological Association Tel: (604)730-0501 Toll-Free: 1(800)730-0522 *www.psychologists.bc.ca* *bcpa@telus.net* British Columbia Association of School Psychologists *www.bcasp.ca*	College of Psychologists of New Brunswick Tel: (506)382-1994 *cpnb@nbnet.nb.ca* *www.cpnb.ca*
Manitoba Psychological Society Inc. Tel/Fax: (204)488-7398 *www.mps.mb.ca* Manitoba. *www.masp.mb.ca*	Ontario Psychological Association Tel: (416)961-5552 *info@psych.on.ca* *www.psych.on.ca*
Prince Edward Island Psychological Association Tel: (902)888-8371 *www.cpa.ca/peiprov/html* *tadixon@edu.pe.ca*	Psychologists Association of Alberta Tel: (780)424-0294 Toll-Free: 1(888)424-0297 *www.psychologistsassociation.ab.ca* *paa@psycholgistsassociation.ab.ca*
Psychological Society of Saskatchewan *pss@psychsocietysk.org* *www.psychsocietysk.org* Saskatchewan Educational Psychology Association *www.saskedpsych.ca*	Registration of Psychologists in the Nunavut Territory Government of Nunavut Box 390, Kugluktuk, NU, X0B 0E0 Tel.: (867)982-7668
Canadian Psychological Association 151 rue Slater Street, Suite 205 Ottawa ON K1P 5H3 Tel: (613)237-2144 Toll-Free: 1(888)472-0657 Fax: (613)237-1674 *www.cpa.ca*	Canadian Association of School Psychologists CASP Executive Director 10660 Trepassey Drive, Richmond, B.C. V7E 4k7 *www.cpa.ca/casp*

psychology associations began to appear during the 1980s. The increasing numbers of school psychologists employed by school systems produced the critical mass necessary for the creation of these new associations. The formation of provincial school psychology associations arose from common needs: a sense of professional identity, a communication network, continuing professional education, and a body that could lobby and act as advocates for a profession that felt somewhat disconnected from psychology associations but also not fully connected with the teaching profession.

The creation of school psychology associations, which was primarily a phenomenon of the 1980s, was especially conspicuous in western Canada, where they still continue to thrive. Unfortunately, the Alberta Association of School Psychologists, which was a driving force in creating the national school psychology association CASP, has essentially ceased to exist. In the Atlantic provinces, smaller associations representing school psychologists have also been formed to provide continuing education and meet other professional needs (e.g., New Brunswick Association of Psychologists and Psychometrists in the Schools). However, many of Newfoundland's school psychologists, whether or not registered as psychologists within the Newfoundland Psychologists Association, have joined other associations, such as the School Counsellors' Association of Newfoundland.

Historically, in instances in which school psychologists were not eligible for registration because of doctoral or other requirements, they were much more likely to either form their own associations . . . or to maintain closer connections with provincial departments of education.

The greatest number of psychologists who represent all specialty areas and work in all areas—health, social services, corrections, public and private corporations, private practice, and educational settings—are found in Quebec and Ontario. In 1988, Quebec school psychologists working primarily in the elementary schools formed an interest group called the Groupe d'interet en Psychologie Scolaire with the support of the provincial regulatory association. This specialty interest group is now known as the Association Québecoise des Psychologues Scolaires. However, L'Ordre des Psychologues du Quebec (OPQ) is the regulatory body, with about 7,500 members, and all psychologists working in schools must be registered by the OPQ. Until this year, a master's degree in psychology was the entry-level requirement for registration as a psychologist in Quebec. This has now changed so that the PhD is the entry-level degree for registration. As noted in Table 9.2, Ontario employs a two-tier registration system. During the period that the doctoral degree was the required academic qualification for registration (prior to 1978), the interests of nondoctoral psychologists, including a number of psychologists employed by education boards in Ontario, led to the creation of the Ontario Association of Consultants, Psychometrists, and Psychotherapists. However, changes to the Psychologist's Act increased the prominence of psychologists employed in educational settings as a special interest group within the Ontario Psychological Association.

Because many school psychology associations are relatively small, the mailing addresses and contact persons (i.e., president, secretary) tend to change with annual elections. Though several of the more established associations have websites (e.g., British Columbia, *www.bcasp.ca*; Saskatchewan, *www.saskedpsych.ca*; Manitoba, *www.masp.mb.ca*; Quebec, *www.aqps.gc.ca*), the best way to contact provincial school psychology associations is through the provincial psychology associations (see Table 9.3).

National Psychology Associations

Canadian school psychologists have demonstrated a strong desire to extend their professional networks to include national and international associations. They were active in NASP prior to the formation of many of the provincial school psychology associations. NASP continues to be an attractive association for Canadian school psychologists, as does Division 16 for those who are members of the APA. A smaller number of Canadians have also joined the International School Psychology Association.

Canadian Association of School Psychologists

While the provincial school psychology associations were gathering momentum, the seeds of the Canadian Association of School Psychologists (CASP) were planted by Dr. Barry Frost in the early 1980s. Following the establishment of the four western provincial school psychology associations, an informal working group composed of Dr. Carl Anserello (British Columbia), Drs. Barry and Ruth Frost (Alberta), Dr. Don Saklofske (Saskatchewan), Retha Finch-Carriere (Manitoba), and Dr. Marjorie Perkins (Ontario) developed the framework for what became known as CASP. Shortly after, CASP was incorporated as a professional association of school psychologists across Canada. The following objectives of CASP are included in its bylaws:

- To promote professional educational and social accountability among school psychologists across Canada
- To provide professional development for school psychologists nationwide
- To develop and promote national standards and ethical principles for school psychologists
- To represent the concerns and interests of school psychologists in a variety of settings
- To facilitate communication between and among professionals working in the area of school psychology

CASP has three levels of membership and maintains an informal and loose connection with Canadian provincial school psychology associations, the International School Psychology Association, and the CPA. CASP has developed standards for professional practice in school psychology (Bartell & Saklofske, 1998) as well as a code of ethics. CASP also publishes the *Canadian Journal of School Psychology* (CJSP) and, until recently, a joint newsletter with CPA. Although annual conferences were previously held in partnership with one of the provincial school psychology associations, this has not occurred for some time. However, CASP has cosponsored several recent workshops that have been well attended.

The future of CASP is currently being debated, and the next year or two will determine if CASP continues to exist as a professional organization.

Unfortunately, the membership in CASP has declined markedly over the past several years, from about 400 to approximately 140 members. The drop in interest could be due to several factors, including the general inactivity of CASP in providing a strong voice for school psychologists, the lack of regular conferences, difficulties publishing the CJSP, and changes to provincial regulatory standards. For example, Saskatchewan once had the largest CASP membership, but several years ago psychologists with master's degrees became eligible to be registered with the Saskatchewan Psychological Association. Furthermore, Saskatchewan school psychologists continue to maintain strong professional connections through the Saskatchewan Educational Psychology Association. The CASP membership from Ontario and Quebec was never large, and unfortunately the impact of CASP has not been great in Atlantic Canada, even though there are smaller numbers of psychologists in these provinces. The future of CASP is currently being debated, and the next year or two will determine if CASP continues to exist as a professional organization.

The Canadian Psychological Association

The Canadian Psychological Association was organized in 1939 and incorporated in 1950. The CPA is the national professional association and in most ways parallels the American Psychological Association. More than 6,000 members make this a relatively strong national association, although the provincial psychology group in Quebec has about as many members as CPA. At the same time, CPA has become an effective organization through the development of professional standards and codes of ethics, and through the promotion of training and educational opportunities for psychologists. As is the case with the APA, the CPA has created a number of special interest divisions.

The CPA is the national professional association and in most ways parallels the American Psychological Association.

The CPA's Section on Psychologists in Education (SPE), with a membership of more than 230, has a much more diverse membership than APA Division 16, NASP, and CASP. The membership of the CPA section includes university trainers, researchers, school psychologists in direct practice and in administrative roles, psychologists in the public and private sector addressing issues relevant to education and mental health, and graduate students in school psychology and the more general area of educational psychology. The following is excerpted from the section's mission statement (see *http://www.cpa.ca/psyedu.html*):

> The CPA Section on Psychologists in Education includes members across Canada who are front-line school psychologists, psychologists in hospitals, agencies, and private practice addressing issues pertinent to education and mental health for infants to elderly; university academics in education psychology and psychology departments who conduct applied research and/or act as clinical trainers; and graduate students from all the above areas. Section goals included urging communication between members over this wide country so that common issues can be addressed between and among

Provinces; indeed, so that issues can be confronted with support from [the] CPA head office in Ottawa. The section has merged its newsletter recently with CASP's to increase circulation and, thus, communication among Psychologists in Education in Canada.

A recent revision to the SPE mission statement includes the following goals:

- To promote communication among Canadian psychologists interested in education issues
- To facilitate the application of research outcomes in educational psychology to instructional settings
- To increase public awareness of the activities and contributions of Canadian psychology to the whole area of education
- To enhance the quality of education at all levels, from preschool to university

One example of the collaboration between the CPA-SPE and CASP is the publication of the research-based booklets in the CANSTART series. These program booklets are authored by Dr. Marvin Simner from the University of Western Ontario (retired) and are available from the CPA (*http://www.cpa.ca/publist.html*). Titles include *Predicting and Preventing Early School Failure: Classroom Activities for the Preschool Child*; *Promoting Reading Success: Phonological Awareness Activities for the Kindergarten Child*; and *Promoting Skilled Handwriting: The Kindergarten Path to Meaningful Written Communication.*

Other Professional Groups

Some school psychologists also have received some of their training through teacher education and special education programs and thus may identify more with organizations such as the Canadian Council for Exceptional Children and the Canadian Society for the Study of Education, as well as the provincial and national teachers federations. Some school psychologists have come from graduate programs with a strong emphasis in counseling and therefore are more likely to maintain memberships in the Canadian Counselling Association and its provincial counterparts. For example, in Newfoundland, school psychologists do not have an association. They are registered with the board of examiners of the Newfoundland Psychological Association, and their professional identity is linked to that group; however, school psychologists are also found in the membership of the School Counsellors Association of Newfoundland.

RESEARCH AND PUBLICATIONS BY AND FOR SCHOOL PSYCHOLOGISTS

Saklofske and Janzen (1990) stated that a journal signals that a profession or discipline has a history and future and an identity and status, and that it is important for the dissemination of knowledge and applications. The publications in school psychology represent an exchange of information and ideas about basic and applied research, clinical applications, and professional issues. Although the United States has several well-established school psychology journals and numerous other publications of direct relevance to school psychologists, far fewer are published in Canada.

The primary Canadian journal focusing on research and applied or practice issues in the field of school psychology is the *Canadian Journal of School Psychology*. The first issue of this journal appeared in 1985 and provided a national forum for practitioners and researchers in school psychology and education to publish the results of their investigations, especially those that are particularly relevant to the Canadian context. Although the journal continues to publish mainly refereed research and applied papers, new sections have been included that focus on research in progress and on reviews of tests and books, both in English and in French. The editorial board consists of prominent Canadian and American researchers, trainers, and practitioners. Three of the authors of this chapter (Derevensky, Janzen, and Saklofske) have served as CJSP editors.

The primary Canadian journal focusing on research and applied or practice issues in the field of school psychology is the *Canadian Journal of School Psychology*.

The journal is published twice a year and continues to produce a number of special issues (e.g., "Behavior Disorders of Children and Adolescents," "Advocacy Issues and Events in School Psychology," and "Challenges and Issues for School Psychologists in the 21st Century"), along with regular issues. Two special issues merit mention: the 1990 special issue, "The State of the Art of School Psychology in Canada," represented a collection of papers portraying school psychology training, practices, and professional issues in each of the Canadian provinces and the Yukon. A similar special issue, *School Psychology in Canada*, was published in 2001.

The Canadian Psychological Association publishes the *Canadian Journal of Behavioural Science* and *Canadian Psychology*, two bilingual journals that frequently include articles of relevance to school psychologists (e.g., ethics, assessment, intervention, consultation, and addiction). The CPA also publishes monographs (see *http://www.cpa.ca/publist.html*) that have been well received by school psychologists. Other Canadian journals that are frequently read by school psychologists include the *Alberta Journal of Educational Research* and the *McGill Journal of Education*. Several special education journals, including the *Canadian Journal of Special Education*, *Exceptionality Canada*, and the *Developmental Disabilities Bulletin* are also important references for school psychologists.

All of the provincial psychology and school psychology associations publish newsletters, which usually include a mix of business, professional announcements, and short articles of an applied nature. Similarly, the various specialty areas within the CPA (e.g., clinical psychology, counseling psychology, school and educational psychology) publish newsletters. CASP and the SPE have a joint newsletter, which is published by the SPE, thus reaching a wider readership of interested researchers and practitioners. Furthermore, a growing number of school psychology researchers in Canada publish in a wide range of national and international publications.

Canadian psychologists also publish in and edit journals, journal articles, books, and book chapters. For example, Saklofske recently became the editor of the *Journal of Psychoeducational Assessment*, and Snyder and Saklofske continue to coedit the *Canadian Journal of School Psychology*. Some recent books with contributions from Canadian school and educational psychologists include *Effective Consultation in School Psychology* (Cole & Siegel, 2003); *Handbook of Psychoeducational Assessment* (Andrews, Saklofske, & Janzen, 2001); *Clinical Interpretation of the WAIS-III and WMS-III* (Tulsky et al., 2003); *WISC-IV Clinical Use and Interpretation* (Prifitera et al., 2005); *Culture and Children's Intelligence* (Georgas, Weiss, van de Vijver, & Saklofske, 2003); *WISC-IV Advanced Clinical Interpretation* (Weiss et al., 2006); *The WISC-IV Companion: A Guide to Interpretation and Educational Intervention* (Truch, 2006); *Educational Psychology, Third Canadian Edition* (Woolfolk, Winnie, & Perry, 2006); and *Principles of Educational Psychology, Canadian Edition* (Ormrod et al., 2005).

Finally, these publications demonstrate the links, forged through research, between science and the practice of school psychology. In Canada, most psychology researchers are doctoral-level academics employed by university psychology departments. Continuing basic research is needed in areas such as the psychological constructs of attention, perception, memory, and language; language and literacy; developmental psychopathology; and cognitive neuroscience. Equally important is applied research that addresses the need for evidence-based prevention and intervention practices to address student learning, social–emotional development, behavioral performance, instructional methodology, school practices, classroom management, and other areas salient to school-based services and improved student outcomes. The range of questions posed by research in real-life settings requires concerted efforts to conceptualize and advance research as a process that incorporates design, implementation, evaluation, and analysis in ways that are sensitive to specific contexts of practice.

THE CHANGING FACE OF SCHOOL PSYCHOLOGY IN CANADA: PROJECTIONS FOR THE FUTURE

Many of the traditional roles and practices of school psychologists will continue well into the 21st century. Significant advances in understanding of the conditions (both exogenous and endogenous) that can affect a child's educational as well as psychosocial and emotional development, together with the increasing emphasis on the development of effective educational programs, will certainly ensure that diagnostic assessment remains a major contribution from school psychologists. At the same time, the skills and knowledge that school psychologists bring to educational settings have been restricted by the almost exclusive role of testing. The role of school psychologists must expand to meet the changing needs and expectations of schools in Canada (Saklofske et al., 2006). There is an increased recognition that school psychologists must vary the way they use their professional knowledge and,

The skills and knowledge that school psychologists bring to educational settings have been restricted by the almost exclusive role of testing. The role of school psychologists must expand to meet the changing needs and expectations of schools in Canada.

in turn, the way they participate in the delivery of services in school and educational settings. This last section portrays and encourages a paradigm shift and the changing roles of school psychologists in Canada.

The number of Canadian children at risk for school-related problems because of genetic, prenatal and natal, or infectious disease, or experiential factors, including poverty, is significant and disconcerting. For example, recent data reveal that close to half a million Canadian children ages 5 to 14 years present with a diagnosable disability (Statistics Canada, 2001). Depending on their severity and clinical characteristics, these risk factors represent a developmental threat to adaptation that has a lifelong impact; they can place children onto life trajectories that significantly affect health and well-being. Unfortunately, Canada has a severe shortage of school psychologists. As a result, student waiting times for assessment and intervention are far beyond acceptable limits (Lupart, Goddard, Hebert, Jacobsen, & Timmons, 2001). In an era in which society recognizes the rights of children to receive appropriate and timely developmental and educational experiences, it is critical that the helping professions understand and assess the nature of vulnerability and protective factors experienced by children at risk for poor school outcomes, and that practitioners use the results as a basis for developing effective intervention strategies (Mash & Dozois, 1999).

Particular attention has been drawn toward the high level of mental health needs of Canadian children. Mental health problems are currently the leading health issues Canadian children face. Recent surveys have demonstrated that despite prevention and intervention efforts, anywhere from 14% to 20% of children ages 4 to 17 years exhibit clinically significant mental disorders at any given time. Within this context, it is disconcerting to note that only a minority of these children receive intervention services. For example, in a recent position paper, the CPA (2002) reported that only 5% of children with a diagnosable mental health condition receive any form of intervention, and only 1% to 2% are treated by specialists. Even more catastrophic are findings that the diagnosis and treatment of mental health problems follow a pattern of economic inequity; services are frequently not available in minority and low-income communities, which have a higher prevalence of child mental health problems. Relative to other Canadian children and youth, children of First Nations are more likely to be born into poverty and are among those at greatest risk for mental health problems. Recent epidemiological studies have demonstrated a prevalence rate almost three times that of the national rate in this group. This high prevalence often occurs within a context of fragmented or nonexistent services (Mussell, Cardiff, & White, 2004).

For the majority of children who have mental health problems or disabilities, or who are at risk for these conditions, the school is the sole provider of primary support and services. Though schools can play a strong equalizing role in delivering a wide range of assessment and intervention services, several factors impede their ability to meet this challenge. The shortage of school psychologists, together with a prevailing service delivery model that focuses primarily on the delivery of specialist services, results in children with the most severe and apparent conditions being the only ones who receive appropriate psychological support and services within educational settings. The vast majority of children at risk for mental health and learning problems are not identified at an early and critical point, and early intervention is virtually nonexistent. The lack of investment at a critical stage in the development of these children will be reflected in their long-term disadvantages and economic and social dependency. The ability of schools to address the diverse needs of children presenting with or at risk for varying conditions is further compromised by significant fragmentation of child services among various federal and provincial jurisdictions, sectors, and disciplines. Several ministries and agencies, including education, social services, justice, and health, typically deliver services to children and families, with little coordination among them. Contributing further to the fragmentation, many institutions, agencies, and professionals function within disciplinary "silos," which further impairs professionals' ability to use the existing services and resources effectively and efficiently, including those available within schools.

Given the degree of unmet need, the significant shortage of school and applied child psychologists, and the fragmentation of existing services, continued investment in a specialist service delivery model is unlikely to adequately address the needs of at-risk children, resulting in a variety of poor outcomes. Rather, what is needed is a universal paradigm shift toward a comprehensive service delivery system that emphasizes the promotion of healthy development for all children, the prevention of disorders in children at risk, and the provision of treatment for children with disorders (Waddell, McEwan, Shepherd, Offord, & Hua, 2005). Many child advocates have argued that the logical place to situate this system is within schools, as they are accessible community settings that are comfortable and nonstigmatizing for most children and their families, and they house well-trained personnel, access to supportive services, and mandated service delivery mechanisms.

> The value of providing ... services within the school setting is intuitively apparent. Schools offer familiar environments to intervene with children and adolescents ... and in many jurisdictions are recognized as key players in the provision of ... services and supports. ... The Committee was advised that when appropriate, services should be delivered in places where children, adolescents, and their families spend most of their time (schools and homes) and at appropriately flexible times of the day. (Kirby & Keon, 2004, p. 12).

Realization of comprehensive services within schools can best be implemented by adopting a "systems of care" approach. In systems of care, all agencies work together to ensure that children with needs and their families have access within their home, school, and community to the services and supports they need to succeed. Generally, systems of care are developed around the principles of having child-centered, family-driven, strengths-based, culturally competent, community-based, cost-effective, interdisciplinary, collaborative, and multimodal or integrative services. They are driven by objective, clinical research and program evaluation data, while also being responsive to the unique needs and perspectives of the child and family. Of critical importance is the creation of a separate, single funding envelope that combines various funding streams for delivery of services. Many systems of care adopt an implementation vehicle known as *wraparound*. In essence, *wraparound* is a definable planning process involving the child and family that results in a unique set of community services and natural supports individualized for that child and family to achieve a positive set of outcomes. Although many argue that achievement of this vision within Canadian schools and communities is a pipe dream, there are already numerous examples of systems of care that have been successfully implemented within school divisions throughout Canada.

Several practices are integral to the success of systems of care in schools, including psychologists' need to take on expanding roles. In contrast to the current situation in Canada, where most school psychologists spend a disproportionate amount of their workdays involved in student-focused direct and indirect assessment and intervention (i.e., delivery of specialized services), the school psychologist within a systems of care would broaden his or her role to include roles such as the following:

- Frontline provider of educational and mental health services
- Developer and provider of strengths-based promotion and prevention strategies
- Advocate for the child, family, and system
- Interprofessional team participant or leader
- Consultant to other professionals
- Administrative leader in the delivery organization or system
- Quality assurance and quality improvement consultant
- Outcome evaluator and researcher in systems of care
- Provider of in-service training
- Case manager
- Developer of educational and mental health services policy and planning within communities, regions, and provinces

These evolving roles have significant implications for the training of school psychologists. A paradigm shift toward delivering services through a systems of care approach requires that the psychology community and academia must also shift their training, their practices, their perception of the role of research, and their approach to policy in this area (Tolan & Dodge, 2005). Training models must be developed that emphasize (a) organizing services using evidence-based practice; (b) working with other professionals in prevention, consultation, education, and other areas in addition to direct treatment; (c) developing models that enable midcareer incorporation of new approaches; (d) focusing studies on epidemiology, developmental psychopathology, preventive and mental health approaches, interprofessional collaboration, community capacity building, and evaluation procedures; and (e) placing more emphasis on research as the tool for developing the field. Most important, training programs should emphasize preparing psychologists to serve as advocates for effective treatment, prevention, and promotion of efforts by demonstrating the value of scientific research and scientific method in guiding public policy (Tolan & Dodge, 2005).

This chapter is a call for the profession of school psychology in Canada to take up the challenge—to promote systemic change in child care policies and service delivery systems in order to ensure that the burden of suffering experienced by children at risk for poor life outcomes can be significantly reduced.

This chapter is a call for the profession of school psychology in Canada to take up the challenge—to promote systemic change in child care policies and service delivery systems in order to ensure that the burden of suffering experienced by children at risk for poor life outcomes can be significantly reduced. School psychologists in Canada can bring about this change by uniting under a national umbrella that gives a strong, unified voice to the issues at hand. As Mureika (2007) notes, linking school psychologists through the CPA Section of Psychologists in Education provides a venue for a national network that can ultimately press for a responsive, accessible, effective, coordinated, and comprehensive system of care for children.

Chapter 10

International School Psychology

Thomas Oakland, University of Florida

When people first travel abroad, differences in language, religion, dress, food, clothing, attitudes, driving styles, and other features that help define a culture are often very apparent. However, as travelers become more familiar with this new culture, similarities between it and their native culture also become more apparent. In a similar fashion, impressions of the differences in how school psychologists are prepared and practice in other countries often change to include more mature beliefs that recognize both similarities and differences. As shown in this chapter, differences often reflect social, economic, geographic, and cultural conditions within a country. Despite these differences, considerable similarities exist in the more important areas that define the specialty of school psychology.

People who are flexible in their thinking and do not assume automatically that their ways are superior are likely to appreciate the richness of the specialty of school psychology when it is viewed internationally. The diversity found within school psychology internationally reflects its strengths and demonstrates its capacity to adapt to important local conditions. Moreover, the school psychology profession in Canada and the United States can benefit from learning about the various methods employed by their international colleagues to meet the educational and psychological needs of students, parents, and teachers. Those who believe school psychology is an American tradition may be surprised to learn that many school psychology milestones occurred first in other countries. For example, school psychology emerged first in Europe, and the Venezuela Society of School Psychology was the world's first freestanding national society of school psychology, formed in 1968 (Oakland, Feldman, & Leon DeViloria, 1995).

Those who believe school psychology is an American tradition may be surprised to learn that many school psychology milestones occurred first in other countries.

This chapter describes some important and defining qualities of the international dimensions of school psychology and examines similarities and differences commonly found within this specialty of professional psychology. Issues that pertain directly to Canada and the United States are not emphasized. Topics include the history of school psychology, including eight contributions that had a material influence on forming, shaping, and defining international school psychology; school psychologists' demographic qualities; and their roles and functions, preparation, and external and internal qualities that influence them. Three internationally approved standards are described in some detail. The status of education and school psychology in Mexico is summarized. A discussion of possible futures for the profession at the international level is followed by information on ways to seek employment internationally.

HISTORY OF INTERNATIONAL SCHOOL PSYCHOLOGY

School psychology's origins lie in the disciplines of philosophy and biology and later in psychology and education. A country's cultural and social conditions constitute the soil and nutrients that give birth to and sustain its school psychology practices (Oakland, 1993).

Early Roots

Significant social changes in Western Europe and the United States during the latter half of the 19th century gave rise to the origins of psychology and the need for applied psychologists in public education (see Table 10.1). For centuries, lifestyles generally were characterized by personalized, rural, family-centered environments dependent on agriculture and small family-run businesses. Members of the immediate and extended family generally took care of one another's needs as best they could. Children were raised to follow in their parents' footsteps, boys to assume responsibility for the farm or small business, and girls to marry, raise children, and assume other important domestic duties. Children were expected to work at an early age. Education generally was restricted to teaching basic reading and number facts,

Table 10.1 Milestones in International School Psychology

1879 First psychology laboratory established in Germany by Wundt
1896 First psychological clinic established at the University of Pennsylvania by Lightner Witmer
1898 First appearance of the term *school psychologist* in print by Munsterberg
1899 First school-based child study departments established in Antwerp, Belgium, and Chicago, Illinois
1905 A reliable measure of mental ability published by Binet
1948 UNESCO-sponsored international conference on school psychology
1954 Thayer Conference on school psychology in the United States
1956 UNESCO-sponsored European conference on school psychology
1968 Formation of the first national association of school psychology: Venezuelan Society of School Psychology
1972 Formation of the International School Psychology Committee (ISPC)
1975 First ISPC-sponsored international colloquium on school psychology
1979 International Year of the Child
1982 International School Psychology Association's constitution and bylaws adopted
1990 ISPA's Code of Ethics adopted
1996 ISPA's Definition of School Psychology adopted
1996 ISPA's International Guidelines for the Preparation of School Psychologists adopted

typically within the home. Families required the services of few professionals, even physicians, as family members and close friends assumed responsibility for their common and special needs. Life generally was stable.

However, during the late 1800s, many lifestyles changed. People often were thrust into depersonalized, urban, industrially centered environments. Life changes associated with these conditions were exacerbated when families migrated to a new country. Boys were less able to follow in their fathers' vocational footsteps. Child labor laws restricted their work, thus creating time for, and in some locations requiring, at least an elementary education. Both boys and girls were to be educated. Education began to replace lineage and physical endurance as important pathways to personal success and social stability.

Emergence of Social and Educational Issues Within Schools

In school settings, children's behaviors that were overlooked in homes often became evident. Some children displayed remarkable levels of achievement and cognitive abilities. Some children learned slowly, others had sensory or physical problems, and still others attended school irregularly, were unruly, or displayed other qualities that made them different from their peers or that were unacceptable to teachers. Teachers needed assistance to help address students' educational needs.

With increasing urbanization, other problems emerged that may have been overlooked or simply were not evident in smaller and more personalized settings, or, if identified, were attended to by families and friends. For example, more children were orphaned, were brought before the law for repeated misdemeanors or even felonies, ran away from home, or exhibited other social, emotional, or mental problems that suddenly warranted public attention. New public and private agencies and institutions were established to care for their needs, including juvenile courts, almshouses, settlement homes, and state-run institutions for the mentally retarded and emotionally disturbed. Professionals with expertise in the social sciences were needed to assist agency personnel in accurately assessing children's needs, diagnosing their problems, and suggesting primary, secondary, and tertiary prevention methods to address their needs and those of society. The professions of psychology and social work emerged, in part, from these conditions.

Need for a Discipline of Psychology

Preparing professionals in a social science first requires the presence of a social science. One began to emerge in the mid-1800s following the pioneering efforts of psychologists in Western Europe and the United States. Efforts of some early pioneers are most evident. Wilhelm Wundt established the first laboratory of psychology in Leipzig, Germany in 1879. Francis Galton later opened a laboratory in London and collected psychological data on a cross-section of Londoners. Jean-Marc Gaspard Itard and Edouard Seguin developed methods to work with children with developmental disabilities. Sigmund Freud's work captured the attention of many influential persons, helped legitimize psychological theory and practice, and had a large influence on institutions, in particular social service agencies and courts.

These and other pioneers who laid the foundations of psychology typically had degrees in biology or its companion profession, medicine. Many were influenced by Charles Darwin's 1859 publication, *On the Origin of Species*, which advanced a coherent theory of organic evolution.

Four Common School Psychological Services Systems

School psychology emerged first within Western Europe and North America. While four forms of school psychological services were evolving in Western Europe during the first half of the 20th century (Wall, 1955), similar services took root in Canada and the United States. The various forms of services reflect the dynamic nature of school psychology and the need of the field to tailor services in light of a country's needs, resources, and other conditions. Under one system, school psychologists were assigned to one large school or a group of schools. They often were members of a team that also included a school social worker and a medical officer. Their object was to promote primary prevention programs to prevent the occurrence of academic, social, emotional, and related problems. School psychologists typically were responsible for improving the mental health of the school community, improving teaching skills, and providing guidance and adjustment services to normal students.

A second system, found mainly in the United Kingdom, emphasized the coordination of services between the school and the community. Services were attached to and required funding from local education agencies. Activities included the coordination of prevention, research, and guidance activities; provision of remedial interventions and psychotherapy; and diagnosis. The goals of this second system were to prevent the occurrence of problems or, once identified, to address them directly. Elementary, secondary, and technical school students were the intended beneficiaries of their services.

A third system relied principally on community-based child guidance clinics for the provision of services. These clinics typically were headed by psychiatrists who, together with psychologists and social workers, formed a team to assess and diagnose childhood disorders and recommend interventions that typically were implemented in schools, homes, and other institutions.

A fourth system, founded in the United Kingdom in 1893, emphasized research on issues important to child growth and development. Work by Alfred Binet in Paris, Galton in London, and G. Stanley Hall and the Child Study Movement in the United States exemplifies this system.

Growth of School Psychology Between the Early and Middle 20th Century

A profession is expected to base its practices on well-defined theory, research, and technology developed by a mature discipline. During the first third of the 20th century, many people believed the emerging discipline of psychology lacked sufficient maturity and knowledge to warrant status as an emerging profession. School psychology grew little during this period.

The discipline and the profession of psychology, including school psychology, developed in parallel fashion. Each benefited from the other. For example, the early work by Binet and others led to the development of tests useful in the practice of school psychology through the assessment of achievement, intelligence, and other qualities vital for academic success. The availability of tests also supported research on issues important to the emerging discipline of psychology, including its specialties in child development and educational psychology.

As noted in chapter 2, the term *school psychologist* first appeared in English in 1898, in the writings of Hugo Munsterberg (it is not known if it appeared earlier in another language). He advocated that school psychologists serve as consultants between research psychologists and teachers (Fagan, 2005a). The term appeared again in 1910, when William Stern, a German psychologist, suggested that assessment services provided by psychologists were needed in schools (Fagan & Delugach, 1984). Stern (1910) drew parallels between schools employing physicians to attend to students' medical needs and employing psychologists to attend to students' psychological needs, especially those who display abnormal characteristics.

School psychology displayed few signs of evolving into a profession with international dimensions during the first half of the 20th century. However, events associated with nations' recovery from World War II had a major influence on the profession's character and international dimensions. Some of the most important are summarized below.

INCREASED INTERNATIONAL PROFESSIONALISM

The growth and expansion of school psychology in Western Europe, together with international bodies' interest in school psychology, began to emerge following World War II. Eight important events contributed to forming, shaping, and defining international school psychology: Two United Nations Educational, Scientific, and Cultural Organization (UNESCO) conferences took place in Europe, one in 1948 and the other in 1956. In the United States, the American Psychological Association held the Thayer Conference on school psychology in 1954. Calvin Catterall and others laid the foundation for international school psychology in the early 1970s, followed by the International Year of the Child in 1979. The work of Catterall and others culminated in the formation of the International School Psychology Association in 1982. Finally, two international surveys of school psychology were undertaken, the first in 1948 by UNESCO, and the second in 1990. Three later events also helped shape and define international school psychology: the approval of a definition of school psychology, guidelines for academic and professional preparation, and a code of ethics. These are discussed in more detail below.

1948 UNESCO Conference

World War II had profound effects across all of Europe. Financial, industrial, and human resources had been severely depleted and were insufficient for rebuilding the infrastructure for a modern and civilized society. Furthermore, resources needed to provide educational and social services were in short supply. In 1948, the UN Educational, Scientific, and Cultural Organization convened an international conference of representatives from 43 nations to discuss methods that ministries of education could use to promote needed school psychological services (UNESCO, 1948). The conference resulted in three recommendations: Establish research institutes to improve the quality of teaching and school achievement, establish guidance programs based on sound psychological practices, and improve the preparation of large numbers of school psychologists.

1956 UNESCO Conference

A second UNESCO conference 8 years later explored ways that the science of child study and educational psychology could be used more effectively in European schools. The conference report reaffirmed the need to improve guidance services, educational methodology, and teaching practices, and to increase the number of school psychologists (Wall, 1956). Improved services for children with handicapping conditions also were recommended.

The conference report emphasized the need for services that were pervasive and integrated into all important components of schooling, were tailored to students from preschool through technical and vocational schools, assisted students in making transitions from school to work, provided counseling, assisted in teacher preparation, and used consultation. European countries that became leaders in school psychology (e.g., Denmark, France, Sweden, and the United Kingdom) took an active role in these meetings, and their services were influenced by the conference's recommendations.

Thayer Conference in 1954

The Thayer Conference on Functions, Qualifications, and Training of School Psychologists (Cutts, 1955), held in the United States in 1954, also had an important influence on school psychology abroad, because of the growing influence of the United States in international affairs. The conference was instrumental in defining the profession of school psychology within the United States, identifying two levels of preparation, delineating the primary functions of practice, and suggesting desired personal and professional qualities. Recommendations from the conference have had far-reaching consequences on the practice of school psychology within the United States and have provided standards somewhat different from those found in Europe.

Foundations Laid for International School Psychology

Calvin Catterall helped establish the foundation for international school psychology during the 1970s and early 1980s (Fagan & Bischoff, 1984). He brought to light the international dimensions of school psychology through his correspondence, study tours, scholarship, and leadership in forming the International School Psychology Association (ISPA) in 1982. He maintained a personal correspondence with leaders of school psychology in many countries, and he often traveled abroad to visit with them and had them as guests in his Columbus, Ohio, home. Catterall organized study tours of school psychology services to most continents. His books on international school psychology included descriptions of school psychology services in 34 countries and three broader geographic regions (Catterall, 1976, 1977,

1979a), introducing the international scope of the specialty to a larger number of school psychologists.

Frances Mullen also was instrumental in laying the foundation for international school psychology (Fagan & Wells, 1999). She believed American psychologists could benefit from knowledge of psychological practice in other countries. In 1972 she proposed and was instrumental in forming an international committee within the American Psychological Association's Division of School Psychology (Division 16). The following year she and Catterall drew up a statement of purpose for the committee and distributed it to colleagues around the world. She later served as editor of *World*Go*Round*, the committee's newsletter.

International Year of the Child, 1979

The International Year of the Child, spearheaded by a 1979 United Nations declaration, highlighted the importance of reviewing children's psychological, social, and educational needs; the nature of existing services; and the provision of new programs consistent with each country's conditions, needs, and priorities. This international focus on children served as a magnet, drawing leaders of school psychology within their respective countries to a common table to discuss common issues and to work together to achieve common goals. A 1979 meeting of the International School Psychology Committee in York, England, featured issues important to the International Year of the Child. This conference set the stage for the 1983 International Conference on the Psychological Abuse of Children and Youth, held in the United States. Materials and proceedings of this international conference are contained in the personal archives of Thomas Fagan at the University of Memphis. These two international meetings provided a successful test of school psychologists' ability and commitment to work constructively on important issues that transcend geographic boundaries.

The ISPA evolved from the International School Psychology Committee, first formed in 1972 within the American Psychological Association's Division of School Psychology and in 1973 within the National Association of School Psychologists (NASP).

Formation of the International School Psychology Association

Efforts to sustain professional activities require a viable professional association. The International School Psychology Association (ISPA) emerged from efforts by national leaders in school psychology within the United States (e.g., Catterall and Mullen) and Europe (e.g., Anders Poulsen in Denmark) to promote professionalism in school psychology at an international level. The ISPA evolved from the International School Psychology Committee, which was first formed in 1972 within the American Psychological Association's Division of School Psychology and within the National Association of School Psychologists (NASP) in 1973. Calvin Catterall and Frances Mullen were most instrumental in these efforts. The ISPA's constitution and bylaws initially were approved in 1982. Anders Poulsen described some of the difficulties encountered during ISPA's formative period and later development, such as a lack of financial resources, divided leadership, and the illness and later death of Catterall (ISPA, 2004, 2005). Poulsen has served as ISPA's guiding light for more than 30 years.

ISPA has four major objectives: (1) to foster communication between psychologists in educational settings, (2) to encourage the implementation of promising practices in school psychology, (3) to raise the effectiveness of education, and (4) to promote the maximum contribution of psychology to education. ISPA sponsors yearly meetings, called *annual colloquia*, frequently holding them in countries in which school psychology is young and developing. Recent annual meetings were held in Portugal, Turkey, Slovakia, Brazil, Hungary, Latvia, and the People's Republic of China. ISPA began publishing its newsletter, *World*Go*Round*, in 1973. It also sponsors a scholarly journal, *School Psychology International* (*http://www.ispaweb.org/t3.html*).

In 2006 ISPA's membership was about 500, with members in about 50 countries. Twenty-three national associations of school psychologists are affiliated with ISPA. Members of the ISPA executive committee in 2006 resided in Hungary, the Netherlands, the United Kingdom, Australia, and the United States. Its international office was in Denmark for many years but has moved to the United States.

Twenty-three national associations of school psychologists are affiliated with ISPA.

International Surveys

In 1948, UNESCO conducted a survey of 43 ministries of education to determine the availability of school psychology personnel and the nature of their services and to obtain information pertinent to salaries and professional preparation (UNESCO, 1948). Respondents indicated that work was provided mainly in three areas: detection of mentally retarded children, educational guidance, and prevocational guidance. Services generally were provided in larger cities and often through institutes, laboratories, and other centers providing educational consultation. Although many educators expressed an interest in the practice of school psychology, school psychology services typically were not available in schools. This 1948 survey provided information important to the 1948 UNESCO conference and described above in this section.

In 1990, a second and more comprehensive international survey of school psychology was conducted in 54 developed and developing countries (Oakland & Cunningham, 1992). Information from this survey provided a more current and expanded picture of school psychology internationally and formed the basis for developing a definition of school psychology, together with guidelines for the academic and professional preparation of school psychologists.

STATUS OF SCHOOL PSYCHOLOGY INTERNATIONALLY

In 1990, an estimated 57,000 school psychologists worked in the 53 reporting countries other than the United States. Given the growth of school psychology within the past decade, this figure now is estimated to be at least 66,000. Thus, including school psychologists from the United States, the number of school psychologists in the world has reached 100,000. The information in the following review of international school psychology practice is drawn from the 1990 survey, augmented by more recent surveys (Jimerson et al., 2004) and by information found in the *Handbook of International School Psychology* (Jimerson, Oakland, & Farrell, 2006).

The average number of school psychologists is strongly associated with a country's gross national product (GNP), a measure of a country's wealth arising from its production of goods and services. In the 1990 survey, countries with a high GNP averaged about 2,000 school psychologists per country, whereas those with a low GNP averaged about 300. Some countries with large populations had few school psychologists. The then-Soviet Union had about 1,000, and China had about 250. Some countries with small populations had fewer than 10 school psychologists. Internationally, the average ratio of school psychologists to students was 1:11,000. However, ratios vary in relation to a country's GNP. The median ratios were 1:3,500 in high-GNP nations and 1:26,000 in low-GNP nations (Oakland & Cunningham, 1992). China had the largest ratio of 1:680,000, given its student population of 170 million. This ratio is expected to improve, given current efforts by leaders in education and psychology to increase the number of school psychologists working in Chinese schools (Jimerson, Oakland, & Farrell, 2006).

In 1990, an estimated 57,000 school psychologists worked in the 53 reporting countries other than the United States. Given the growth of school psychology within the past decade, this figure now is estimated to be at least 66,000.

The development of school psychology practice strongly reflects a country's domestic conditions. In most developing countries, fewer psychologists are prepared in clinical, counseling, and other areas of professional psychology, and the practice of psychology, including school psychology, is less specialized. Thus, there are fewer psychologists to provide clinical services. Services often are not found in rural areas. A school psychologist working in a rural area within a developing country may be the only psychologist within a large geographic region who is professionally prepared to work with children. His or her practice will be broader (e.g., it may include counseling services to children, youth, and families; vocational guidance; assessment; consultation; and systems intervention within the community and schools). In contrast, in most developed countries, the ratio of psychologists in private practice to the population is better, and the practice of psychology, including school psychology, is more specialized.

School psychologists typically are women in their 30s, who have been in the profession an average of 10 years. Median incomes differ considerably, with those working in high-GNP nations receiving pay that is approximately 600% more than those working in low-GNP nations. Those working in low-GNP nations generally are younger, have fewer years of service, and have an undergraduate degree in psychology as their highest degree. Titles used to describe those who provide school psychological services differ. The most common titles are psychologist, school psychologist, educational psychologist (a commonly used title in countries associated

Among the faculty who teach in school psychology programs internationally, 35% have doctoral degrees, 50% have master's degrees, and the degrees of the remaining 15% are unknown. Seventy percent teach full-time and 30% teach part-time.

with the British Commonwealth), or counselor. In some countries titles do not include the term *psychologist* because this term is neither widely accepted nor acceptable.

The preparation of school psychologists has a decisive influence on the nature of school psychology services (Wilson & Reschly, 1996). Understanding the varied preparation of school psychologists internationally provides important insights as to the nature of their services. Many countries offer both undergraduate and graduate school psychology programs. High-GNP countries typically offer more programs at the master's level, whereas low-GNP countries typically have fewer master's programs and more undergraduate programs. Almost all students first obtain a 4- to 5-year undergraduate degree in psychology, and few major in education. Master's degrees typically require an additional 2 years of preparation. Until somewhat recently, the only doctoral-level school psychology programs were in the United States and Canada. Brazil, Mexico, and the United Kingdom recently established doctoral programs in school psychology. Conflicts between doctoral and nondoctoral school psychologists generally are unknown outside of North America because almost no doctoral-level school psychologists work full-time in schools in other countries.

School psychology programs are subject to external review by professional associations in about half of the reporting countries. In contrast to school psychology programs in low-GNP countries, those in high-GNP countries are more likely to be subject to external reviews, especially by psychological associations. These reviews are provided by psychological associations in 39% of countries and by educational associations in 16% of countries. Thus, when viewed internationally, the psychology profession tends to have a stronger influence on the preparation of school psychologists than does education. The somewhat common request that all psychologists, including school psychologists, be members of the national psychological association also reflects school psychology's stronger ties with psychology than education.

Among the faculty who teach in school psychology programs internationally, 35% have doctoral degrees, 50% have master's degrees, and the degrees of the remaining 15% are unknown. Seventy percent teach full-time and 30% teach part-time. Faculty typically work 21 hours weekly at a university and an additional 5 hours in other locations. Most have two or more jobs. Twenty percent reportedly have scholarly reputations nationally and 2% have scholarly reputations internationally. Salaries received by faculty vary considerably. Salaries are higher for faculty who have taught longer and who have worked in high-GNP countries. In 1990, faculty salaries for those who have taught between 5 and 10 years averaged US$33,000 in high-GNP countries and US$4,000 in low-GNP countries.

THE INFLUENCE OF REGULATIONS

The degree to which school psychology is regulated also reflects its development. Regulation includes various restraints imposed either externally (e.g., who may use the titles psychologist and school psychologist) or internally (e.g., the presence of a professional association with high standards for membership and an association-sponsored ethics code). Regulations in school psychology are found principally in legal and ethical standards. Professional psychology, including school psychology, generally is stronger in countries that impose external and internal standards on service.

External Conditions That Influence School Psychology's Growth

Professional psychology, including school psychology, generally is stronger in countries that impose external and internal standards on service.

The influence of external regulations on practice within the 53 countries that participated in the 1990 survey, excluding the United States, was found to be considerable (Cunningham, 1994, 2006). In the analysis of results, the 53 countries were clustered into one of six groups based on the degree of external regulation.

School psychology was unregulated in the eight countries in cluster 1 (Burkina Faso, Ethiopia, Greece, Iran, Niger, Papua New Guinea, the Republic of South Korea, and Yemen). The degrees of regulation increased incrementally for those in clusters 2 through 5 (in 2: Chile, Costa Rica, Ecuador, Egypt, Ghana, India, Japan, and Sudan; in 3: Austria, Dominican Republic, Italy, Kuwait, Lebanon, the Netherlands, People's Republic of China, Poland, Russia, Saudi Arabia, and Thailand; in 4: Australia, Brazil, Colombia, Germany, Hong Kong [China], Hungary, Iceland, Ireland, Nigeria, Spain, Czechoslovakia, Turkey, and Venezuela; and in 5: Canada, Finland, France, Norway, Scotland, South Africa, Sweden, and Switzerland). School psychologists working in countries in cluster 6 had the highest degree of regulation (Denmark, England, Israel, and New Zealand). The practices of school psychology in this sixth cluster are similar to those in the United States.

The nature of services often was similar within each cluster and differed somewhat from services performed by school psychologists working in other clusters. For example, school psychologists working in cluster 1 focused more heavily on biologically based conditions (e.g., providing basic care to children with severe mental retardation). Those in clusters 2 and 3 devoted greater effort to socializing younger students and providing vocational guidance to older students. For example, the socialization of young children was a high priority to families in Central and South American countries. Furthermore, countries heavily influenced by communism or socialism (e.g., China, Italy, Poland, and Russia) used school psychologists to help promote socialist values. School psychologists working in the countries in clusters 4 and 5 typically conducted educational and psychological appraisals and worked on special education issues within public school settings. In cluster 6 countries, school psychologists performed many of the activities found in clusters 4 and 5; in addition, their work often emphasized systems interventions, that is, consultation, organizational development, research, and evaluation.

Changes that have taken place since 1990 may alter the composition of the country clusters. For example, school psychology has grown considerably in China, in many formerly Eastern European countries, and in the Baltic countries. There also has been some decrease in school psychology practice in Sweden and a considerable decrease in Venezuela. Nevertheless, the degree to which school psychology services are regulated is strongly associated with various domestic conditions. For example, compared with countries in the lower numbered clusters, countries in the higher clusters tended to be wealthier and have lower birth rates, have more physicians per person, have higher levels of education, and spend more federal tax revenues on housing, social security, and welfare.

Overall, school psychology is strongest in countries that are wealthier, devote a higher percentage of their tax revenue to elementary and secondary education, have and enforce universal education, have well-established regular education programs, offer well-established special education services, and have low dropout rates. School psychology is weakest in countries with weak elementary and secondary education systems and those in which educational programs in rural areas are inferior to those found in urban areas.

Internal Conditions That Have Influenced School Psychology's Growth

Although various conditions outside of psychology and education strongly influence school psychology, various conditions within its control also influence its future. School psychology has considerable influence over the following conditions: formation of professional associations; recruitment and maintenance of professional membership; creation of professional literature, history, and certification and licensure provisions; use of models for professional preparation; establishment of professional and political relationships with others (Oakland & Cunningham, 1999).

One example of the growth and development that can come from effective national leadership, as described above, is the case of Brazil. In 1988, professional school psychology in Brazil was in its infancy and was cared for through a national psychological association; however, school psychology was not the highest priority for the association. Recognizing this, two directors of school psychology programs, Solange Wechsler, at the University of Brasilia, and Raquel Guzzo, at the Pontifica Catholic University in Campinas, united forces to help create the Brazilian Association of School and Educational Psychologists (ABRAPP). The association's first national meeting, held in 1992, attracted more than 400 conference delegates. It then cosponsored an international meeting of school psychologists in 1994, which attracted more than 800 delegates, the largest international meeting of school psychologists.

ABRAPP continues to recruit and maintain membership. It published the first scholarly journal in school psychology in Brazil in 1997 and has been instrumental in publishing books needed by school psychology programs. ABRAPP's lobbying efforts to mandate school psychology services throughout Brazil were fulfilled when the president of Brazil signed a decree requiring these services. ABRAPP's efforts to improve the quality of services to Brazilian children include encouraging Brazil's most able students to become school psychologists, improving students' academic and professional preparation, creating other resources needed for effective service, and continuing to secure and maintain funding for school psychology services. This is but one example of how effective national leadership by members of the school psychology profession can raise the status of school psychology among psychologists and officials in education and improve political relationships.

Use of Testing

Assessment is a universal enterprise (Oakland & Hambleton, 1995), and school psychologists are expected to be experts in assessment. The practices of school psychologists working in the United States and other industrialized nations are enhanced by the availability of various tests and other assessment methods to assist them in their work. However, tests are not universally available. School psychologists in many countries have few if any locally developed standardized tests to use and must rely on tests developed elsewhere, including those that lack locally appropriate norms, reliability, and validity estimates.

An international survey of tests used with children and youth in 44 countries, not including the United States, identified 455 tests used somewhat frequently (Hu & Oakland, 1991; Oakland & Hu, 1989, 1991, 1992). Measures of intelligence, personality, and achievement were most readily available. About 50% of the tests were developed in other countries and imported for use. Foreign-developed tests tended to be used more commonly than locally developed tests within the 44 reporting countries. Validity studies were available on between 50% and 70% of the tests and reliability estimates were available on 50% to 60% of tests. Local or national norms were available on 80% of achievement tests and about 60% of intelligence and personality tests.

School psychologists in many countries have few if any locally developed standardized tests to use and must rely on tests developed elsewhere, including those that lack locally appropriate norms, reliability, and validity estimates.

The use of tests is not uniform throughout the world. Highest test use occurs in highly industrialized nations; lowest test use occurs in the least developed countries. The Middle East and least developed nations typically rely on tests developed in other countries. The survey on testing showed that the 10 most commonly used tests included, in descending order of use, (a) Wechsler Intelligence Scales for Children, (b) Ravens Progressive Matrices, (c) Bender-Gestalt, (d) Rorschach, (e) Stanford-Binet, (f) Wechsler Adult Intelligence Scales, (g) Thematic Apperception Test, (h) Differential Aptitude Test, (i) Minnesota Multiphasic Personality Inventory, and (j) Frostig Developmental Test of Visual Perception (Oakland & Hu, 1992). These tests assess a narrow range of abilities, and some are adult measures. Eight were developed in the United States. Tests maligned in the United States as being culturally biased often are used outside the United States. Such tests frequently lack adequate norms, validity, and reliability estimates for use in these countries. At least two tests, the Thematic Apperception Test and the Frostig, are known to have low reliability and are not widely used in the United States. The International Test Commission is concerned about the widespread use of tests developed in one country, and used in others which may lead to test misuse. Therefore, the commission has developed guidelines to help countries adapt tests to develop more valid measures (*www.intestcom.org*).

School psychologists and others who use tests report a critical need for both group and individual tests of achievement, intelligence, vocational interests and aptitudes, social development, and personality. They also report moderate needs for entrance measures for primary, secondary, and tertiary schooling. Virtually all responding countries reported the need for tests that assess qualities important for those who are mentally retarded, blind, deaf, slower learners, emotionally and socially disturbed, physically impaired, and gifted. The need for measures to identify students with learning disabilities is most critical. An estimated 150 million children internationally have a learning disability (Oakland & Phillips, 1997). Thus, children with learning disabilities exceed those with all other mentally handicapping conditions combined and constitute the largest number of underserved or unserved students (Oakland, Mpofu, Gregoire, & Faulkner, in press).

LAWS AND ETHICS THAT GUIDE PRACTICE

As described earlier, school psychology services tend to differ between countries, reflecting in part the degree to which countries regulate services and practices. Laws governing professional entry, as well as types and authorization of services, generally signify more advanced stages in a profession's development. The demonstration of suitable ethical behaviors and the availability of an ethics code also signify more advanced development. The following sections review information about different countries' laws and ethics regarding school psychology.

Laws Governing School Psychology

Countries differ considerably in the types of laws governing who may declare themselves to be school psychologists. In developing countries, school psychologists typically are required to have an undergraduate degree in psychology. They also may be required to hold membership in the national psychological association. In countries with higher professional standards, such as Israel and many countries in Western Europe, a graduate degree commonly is required (e.g., a master's degree in education or psychology). No country requires a doctoral degree for entry into the profession of psychology or the specialty of school psychology.

Laws that govern school psychology practice also differ. Most countries have no laws governing psychology or school psychology practice. In some countries, federal laws and statutes govern psychological services (e.g., Scandinavian countries), and state laws prevail in others (e.g., Germany). Laws that regulate school psychology services within special education exist only in the most highly developed countries and often are similar. For example, laws governing special education services often resemble those implemented under the Individuals with Disabilities Education Act and reauthorizations in the United States (e.g., Oakland, Cunningham, Poulsen, & Meazzini, 1991).

Most countries have no laws governing psychology or school psychology practice.

In some countries, such as Brazil, the federal government has delegated considerable control of professional psychology to its national psychological society. In these countries, all psychologists typically must be members of national psychological societies and abide by their rules and regulations. Although a country may have laws that authorize the provision of school psychology services, the laws may not be enforced. For example, a head of state may decree that all schools must have one or more school psychologists. However, the financial resources needed to implement the decree may be unavailable. The country also may not have sufficient numbers of qualified personnel to fully implement the laws.

Ethics Governing School Psychology

Advanced professions are expected to have self-imposed standards that reflect their moral and ethical values. These standards are offered as part of an implicit social contract between a profession and society. The contract gives a profession considerable freedom for self-governance, and in turn, the profession places the interests of its clients and those of society above more self-serving interests of the profession and its members.

Professionals are expected to display suitable ethical behaviors. Codes of ethics common to many professions include the following five features: nonmalfeasance (i.e., doing no harm), beneficence (i.e., helping others derive benefit from one's services), autonomy (i.e., promoting clients' freedom to think, choose, and act, albeit within legal boundaries), loyalty, and justice.

Professional associations typically are expected to assume leadership for the formation and enforcement of ethics codes. Ethics codes often have five purposes: to educate the profession and public as to suitable behaviors, to acknowledge the profession's obligation to provide services at a high level, to create enforceable standards of conduct, to create criteria important to certification and licensure, and to advocate high levels of service when lower levels may be promulgated by others (e.g., when a school principal mandates conditions incompatible with professional ethics). Among an estimated 23 national associations of school psychology, few have developed ethics statements.

ISPA LEADERSHIP IN DEVELOPING STANDARDS

Well-established professional associations can be expected to assume leadership for the development and enforcement of statements that help define the parameters of professional practice, professional preparation, and ethics codes. The ISPA leadership recognized that these essential provisions did not exist in most countries. Thus, members developed and approved statements addressing these three areas to acknowledge the international nature of the specialty and to aid national associations' development. These statements are summarized below. The development and approval of these statements were facilitated by data from a prior survey (Oakland & Cunningham, 1992) and from other sources that indicate that similarities among school psychologists, and the services they perform, outnumber differences.

Definition of School Psychology and Provision of Services

The following draws heavily from *A Definition of School Psychology*, a position statement approved by the ISPA General Assembly in 1996 (Oakland & Cunningham, 1997). School psychologists are prepared in a core curriculum that contains academic content in basic areas of psychology and education, professional content important to the practice of school psychology, and information relevant to work in culturally diverse settings. Professional content provides preparation in assessment, intervention, consultation, organizational and program development, supervision, and research. School psychologists acquire knowledge and experiences by working in various settings in which services may be delivered, including schools, homes, clinics, agencies, hospitals, and other institutions. Practices may include individual, group, and organizational work in publicly and privately supported settings.

School psychologists are knowledgeable about various assessment models and methods. The primary goals of assessment are to describe a person's abilities and qualities accurately, determine the etiology of disorders, plan and evaluate interventions, and prevent the onset of disabling conditions.

School psychologists learn to design, or identify, and implement various interventions intended to help promote development; acquire and optimize personal, social, family, and community resources; and minimize difficulties and disorders. Interventions involve school psychologists working directly with individuals, groups, and systems, or working indirectly, such as through consultation and testing, with teachers, principals, and other educational personnel, parents and other family members, as well as other professionals and paraprofessionals. Interventions may be directed toward promoting well-being and preventing the onset of problems (*primary prevention*), minimizing difficulties once they occur (*secondary prevention*), and stabilizing disabilities and working to ensure that basic and needed services are provided to those who are expected to manifest one or more disabling conditions over some years (*tertiary prevention*). Direct services include counseling and other forms of therapeutic services, teaching, tutoring, and other interventions in which a school psychologist works with one or more individuals in need of services. Indirect services include assessment and program planning, preservice and in-service professional preparation, supervision, consultation, collaboration, research and evaluation, and other methods by which needed services are delivered by others with the assistance of school psychologists.

Consultation services typically recognize and emphasize the importance of using cooperative and collaborative methods to address problems. They encourage participation in ways that promote knowledge of psychology and education and that ensure proper applications to enhance growth and development.

School psychologists are committed to a service delivery model in which research and theory form a primary basis for practice.

Organizational and program development services are provided to schools, school districts, agencies, and other organizations and administrative units at local, regional, national, and international levels. Services may include assessment and evaluation, interventions, coordination, program planning, curriculum and instructional development and evaluation, and consultation. Typical goals include promoting and strengthening the coordination, administration, planning, and evaluation of services within one unit or between two or more units responsible for serving infants, children, youth, or adults.

Supervision refers to services provided by professionals with advanced preparation and experience who are able to assume responsibility and accountability for the provision of school psychology services. The administrative unit responsible for providing school psychology services would be directed by a school psychologist who also is responsible for supervising the activities of school psychologists working within the unit.

School psychologists are committed to a service delivery model in which research and theory form a primary basis for practice. They can be expected to be knowledgeable about research relevant to practice and to guide their services accordingly. In addition, school psychologists are expected to contribute to research and theory by actively engaging in research, evaluation, professional writing, and other scholarly activities intended to advance knowledge and its applications relevant to school psychology. School psychologists also are knowledgeable about, and provide services that are consistent with, legislation, public policy, administrative rulings, and ethical principles and codes that govern services. School psychologists continue their professional development in ways that help ensure that their practices are consistent with current knowledge, legislation, and codes of professional practice and conduct.

Academic and Professional Preparation of School Psychologists

ISPA's leadership recognized that guidelines were needed for the preparation of school psychologists in order to ensure quality control in school psychology programs and to reflect curricula found in countries with well-established programs. In many countries, a school psychologist can obtain a degree and certificate to practice upon completing a 4- or 5-year degree, one equivalent in length to many undergraduate degrees in the United States or Canada. However, students graduating from these programs typically have been required to take all their courses in psychology, school psychology, and education. They often have few electives. Their coursework in these three areas resembles that of many specialist-level school psychologists in the United States. Thus, although academic degrees needed by school psychologists differ from country to country, the coursework and other preparation may be remarkably similar (Oakland & Cunningham, 1992; Cunningham, 1994; Cunningham & Oakland, 1998). Knowledge of these similarities enabled ISPA to develop the *International Guidelines for the Preparation of School Psychologists*, which were approved by the ISPA General Assembly in 1996 (Cunningham & Oakland). Under those guidelines, the preparation of school psychologists typically includes academic preparation and professional practice, which are described below.

Core Academic Knowledge of Psychology. Students typically take courses in the following academic areas: developmental psychology, psychology of learning and cognition, educational psychology, personality psychology, social psychology, statistics and research design, experimental psychology, and biological psychology.

Assessment and Intervention Services. All school psychology students receive preparation in assessment and intervention. Preparation typically emphasizes intellectual, academic, emotional, and social assessment. In addition, programs prepare students for behavioral, affective, educational, and social-systems interventions. The primary prevention of academic and social problems is a common and important goal. The school psychologist's main focus on children and youth within the context of classrooms, schools, families, communities, and other systems is universal.

Interpersonal Skills. Effective collaboration, consultation, and leadership require well-developed interpersonal skills. Trust and faith, qualities enhanced by well-developed interpersonal skills, form the foundation of all professional relationships. In addition, listening and communication skills, respect for the views and expertise of others, recognition of the assets and limitations of other professionals, and a mature understanding of issues and effective methods to address them are other interpersonal skills that influence a school psychologist's ability to work with others.

Professional Skills in Decision Making. Professional judgments require more than a cookbook approach to practice. Professional judgment should consider the important qualities that characterize the child and the contexts within which the child is being raised. Decision making should be informed by theory and research and be motivated by problem-solving orientations that consider the viability of alternative courses of actions. The importance of developing and employing reflective problem-solving methods is emphasized.

Purposes of Statistical Methods and Research Design. Many programs in Canada and the United States prepare school psychologists to be scientists as well as practitioners. A goal of these programs is to prepare professionals who have solid knowledge of current theory and science, whose practices are based on research, and who themselves contribute to the literature. For such programs, courses in research design and statistics enhance students' roles as practitioners and scientists. Although the preparation of school psychologists in some countries also has this scientific emphasis (e.g., Denmark and Israel), most psychologists are prepared to be consumers of literature, which they incorporate based on their knowledge of current theory and research, but they are neither prepared nor expected to contribute to this literature. Such school psychology programs are more likely to require courses in quantitative and qualitative methods of assessment, descriptive and inferential statistics, and research design, which enable school psychologists to become reflective consumers of literature. Most research in psychology is conducted by persons with doctoral degrees. Since few school psychologists receive doctoral degrees, expectations that school psychologists will contribute to literature through scholarly activities are not common.

Knowledge of the Legal and Ethical Basis for Services. Students in school psychology programs also receive information on the legal basis governing practice—the laws, administrative rulings, and regulations, if such exist in their country.

However, legal provisions often do not strongly influence the work of school psychologists.

Model School Psychology Curriculum

The *ISPA Guidelines for the Preparation of School Psychologists* (Cunningham & Oakland, 1998) describes a model curriculum for a school psychology program. Coursework includes core courses in psychology, including developmental, educational, social, and personality psychology; learning and cognition; and measurement, research design, and statistics. Courses in educational foundations promote knowledge of education. Specialization in school psychology is promoted through courses such as professional issues in school psychology, educational and psychological assessment, consultation, exceptional children, school-based interventions, and organizational and program development. The model program also includes provisions for research activities, together with supervised practica and internships.

Ethics Codes

Ethics codes are developed with the firm belief that professional conduct is expected to exemplify a profession's values. These typically include doing no harm; helping others derive benefit from professional services; promoting a client's freedom to think, choose, and act; displaying loyalty; and promoting justice. Professionals are expected to transcend narrow personal, social, and cultural values and attitudes; adopt positions that benefit professional–client relationships; and act in ways consistent with the best interests of students, educators, parents, institutions, the community, and the profession. Most of these qualities are supported universally, permitting the approval of an ethics code by an international professional community.

The ISPA leadership recognized the need for an ethics code for school psychology. In 1990 its members approved a *Code of Ethics* (Oakland, Goldman, & Bischoff, 1997) that is similar to those published by the National Association of School Psychologists (2000a) and the American Psychological Association (2002). This ethics code addresses issues important to the following areas: professional responsibility, confidentiality, professional growth, professional limitations, professional relationships, assessment, and research. The following describe ethical approaches and actions by school psychologists based on the 1990 code.

Professional Responsibility. School psychologists familiarize themselves with the goals and philosophy of the school system, families, and other organizations within which they work, and work effectively within their organizational structure. They are knowledgeable of laws, administrative codes, and regulations. School psychologists should not allow personal prejudices or biases to interfere in their decision making, nor should they engage in discriminatory procedures or practices based on one's social or economic background, race, disability, age, gender, sexual preference, religion, or national origin.

Confidentiality. School psychologists safeguard confidential student information. Confidential information is discussed only for professional purposes and only with individuals clearly concerned with the case. Consent is obtained from parents or students before releasing confidential information.

Professional Growth. School psychologists recognize the need for and participate in continuing professional development. They maintain knowledge of current scientific and professional information.

Professional Limitations. School psychologists are aware of their professional limitations and offer only those services that are within their areas of professional competence.

Professional Relationships. The welfare of children and youth is of primary importance. School psychologists do not exploit their professional relationships for personal gain. They strive to develop harmonious and cooperative relationships with colleagues and school staff and attempt to resolve possible unethical practices of colleagues in a constructive manner.

Assessment. School psychologists typically administer tests according to published guidelines and interpret them in light of suitable norms, reliability, validity, and other well-established standards. They are accountable for the methods they use and are able to defend their use.

Research. School psychologists inform parents when their children are participating in research projects and ensure that students participating in research do not suffer any mental or physical distress as a result of the procedures. They communicate research results to educators, parents, students, and other interested parties in ways that ensure the exactness and limitations of the research findings. When conducting cross-national research, school psychologists abide by the research ethics of the countries in which they are working. They demonstrate respect for the host culture and avoid actions that violate cultural expectations or reveal culturally biased perspectives. Investigators are knowledgeable of cross-national methodology and are familiar with the cultural context of research settings.

FUTURE OF SCHOOL PSYCHOLOGY INTERNATIONALLY

The development of school psychology internationally is likely to remain uneven. School psychology is strong and stable in about 15 countries and can be expected to remain that way (those described as clusters 5 and 6 in an earlier section of this chapter, "The Influence of Regulations"). School psychology is emerging as a strong, stable profession in another 26 to 28 countries (those in clusters 3 and 4). School psychology is barely discernible in many other countries. For example, about 50% of the world's population of about 6.6 billion resides in China, India, Indonesia, and Pakistan, yet the number of school psychologists found in these countries is so small that they could be seated easily in a large auditorium. Furthermore, some countries with large populations lack programs for the preparation of school psychologists (e.g., China, Indonesia, and Pakistan). The profession's status is less clear in many of the remaining countries (Oakland & Wechsler, 1988). Some are experiencing significant improvements (e.g., Greece), whereas others are in a state of decline. For example, in Costa Rica and Venezuela, excellent earlier leadership in the development of viable professional associations was not followed by leadership needed to advance, or even sustain, this development.

Among the more than 190 countries in the world, information about school psychological practice is readily available on fewer than 60. Thus, little is known about the status of school psychology in most countries. The growing recognition that education serves as an important pathway to a country's financial prosperity and social stability, together with the growing prestige and importance of psychology, suggests bright futures for school psychology internationally (Oakland, 2003).

Among the more than 190 countries in the world, information about school psychological practice is readily available on fewer than 60. Thus, little is known about the status of school psychology in most countries.

Five External Qualities That Favorably Influence Growth

The future of school psychology in any country will be strongly influenced by five qualities external to psychology (Russell, 1984): the nation's economy, geography, language, needs and priorities, and cultural factors.

Economic Factors

Economic realities strongly influence psychology. Psychology as a profession is stronger in nations that have higher GNPs and are industrialized, in contrast to those that have lower GNPs and are dependent on agriculture or tourism. Moreover, within countries, psychology is stronger in urban areas than in rural areas, because of the former's concentration of wealth. Consequently, the growth of school psychology is likely to be stronger in countries that are more prosperous; and within those, growth will first occur in larger cities.

Geography

Geographic barriers between nations also influence the development of psychology. Psychology reaches countries that are most closely linked politically, geographically, and by transportation and communication. The birth and rapid growth of psychology in Germany, France, and England occurred, in part, because of their close links. In contrast, the growth of psychology in Arab countries has been slower. Thus, growth of school psychology is likely to be stronger in countries that have fewer geographic barriers between them and when psychology is strong in neighboring countries.

Language

Language, an important component of communication, is important in transporting psychology. German, French, and English historically constituted the international languages of scientific and professional practice. English has become the most prominent language of science and the scientific professions. Psychology can be expected to remain less developed in countries in which English is not widely used as a second language. English-language countries, especially the United States, have numerous outstanding graduate and research programs from which school psychologists in almost all countries have benefited. Many world leaders in school psychology have been educated in English-language countries, and later returned home to assume leadership roles as professors and researchers. These leaders maintain close contacts with their English-speaking colleagues and rely on English-language scholarly publications for much of their continued professional development. Much of the theory and research that form the basis for preparing school psychologists comes from the United States. Most scientific scholarship in psychology appears in English. All international conferences use English as their primary language. As a result, many graduate programs in psychology, including school psychology, now require their students to read English. Thus, the growth of school psychology is likely to be stronger in countries that encourage students to acquire facility with English.

National Needs and Priorities

National needs and priorities strongly influence the degree to which psychological services are initiated and sustained. School psychology services always emerge because national leaders and the public see value associated with the provision of these services. Services are initiated in response to national needs, and services are sustained if they are seen as continuing to provide value. For example, the goal of school psychology in socialist countries is to help promote social values in children. The goals of school psychology in the United States, for example, to promote children as strong and independent citizens, also are consistent with its national priorities. The growth of school psychology is likely to be stronger when the profession is responding to important national needs and priorities.

Cultural Conditions

Cultural conditions have a decisive influence on the emergence of and support for psychology and its professional specialties. Professions emerge and remain strong when they are seen by others as providing technically sophisticated and relevant services within a context that respects cultural values and mores. Psychology has a decided Western emphasis. This limits its influence in many regions of the world, such as in the Middle East and in the Pacific Rim countries. The acceptance of the discipline and practice of psychology depends, in part, on the extent to which psychology expands to embrace cultural conditions and beliefs that are important in non-Western nations, particularly in regard to child growth and development in educational, social, and cultural contexts. School psychology will become stronger internationally when its theory and research go beyond the current dependency on Canadian, European, and U.S. sources.

Five Internal Actions That Favorably Influence Growth

Many of the five qualities described above are beyond the control of the school psychology profession. However, other conditions over which members of the profession have more control also can influence its future (Oakland & Saigh, 1989; Oakland, 1992; Oakland & Cunningham, 1999). Five of these actions, described in the following sections, include promoting professionalism, codifying the scope and functions of school psychology, expanding professional activities, improving its interface with education, and promoting scholarship and technical contributions.

Promote Professionalism

Professional associations representing school psychologists are needed to help promote high standards for the preparation of school psychologists and the delivery of services, yet they exist in less than 10% of countries. Leaders of professional associations serve as the profession's spokespersons, provide vision and direction, and work to ensure that needed services are supported during periods of economic, social, and political turmoil. Achieving the remaining four actions depends, in part, on the formation of strong and viable national associations of school psychology.

Codify the Scope and Functions of School Psychology

Statements that describe the scope and functions of service can be prepared and endorsed by national professional associations. Such statements establish the boundaries of service and provide strong direction to academic and professional preparation.

Expand Professional Activities

In many countries, services are restricted to caring for the needs of the mentally retarded and to providing assessments. Although these services are important, they constitute a limited range of the necessary services the profession could provide. Leaders in the field can help expand school psychological services by demonstrating the profession's ability to meet national needs and priorities and by emphasizing primary prevention (Oakland, 1990; Wechsler & Oakland, 1990), intervention, consultation, organizational and program development, and supervision.

Improve School Psychology's Interface With Education

School psychology straddles two fields: education and psychology. School psychologists often wonder to which field they owe their primary allegiance. Internationally, most school psychologists work in and for schools. Their primary allegiance must be to education because it provides the context and financial compensation for their work. Those who work in the private sector may align themselves more closely with psychology. Educators often determine whether school psychologists become viable members of the education establishment. Moreover, the growth of school psychology generally follows a discernible pattern. In a country's development, general education services from elementary through postsecondary levels typically are offered first, followed by special education services. Thereafter, school psychology services develop (Catterall, 1979b; Saigh & Oakland, 1989). Leaders in special education often serve as gatekeepers for school psychological services and strongly influence whether such services are provided. Their views are most critical when federal laws governing special education services are vague or absent.

Within most countries of Sub-Saharan Africa, with the exception of South Africa, the practice of school psychology is marginal, at best. To gauge whether school psychology is likely to grow in this important region, Mpofu, Zindi, Oakland, and Peresuh (1997) surveyed directors and other leaders within special education in 12 eastern and southern African countries to determine their views as to whether they would endorse the inclusion of school psychology services in their countries. Respondents reported that the availability, regulation, and utilization of school psychology services were low. Visibility and utilization are higher when school psychology is recognized formally and regulated at a national level. The services of school psychologists who were prepared abroad were seen as less relevant and less supportable than the services of those prepared in the subjects' region. Those who were prepared abroad were assumed to lack an understanding of the sociocultural context of education.

Promote Scholarship and Technical Contributions

School psychology practices are needed that would reflect a country's sociocultural conditions. However, scholarship on sociocultural conditions, which is readily available in developed countries, is greatly needed in less developed countries (Oakland & Wechsler, 1990). Psychologists in the United States may assume that most knowledge comes from their country. They often are unaware of important scholars or scholarship from other countries. For example, most school psychologists are unlikely to know the names of any scholar in psychology who lives in a country other than Canada or the United States. However, scholars from other countries have contributed important research and knowledge to the professional literature on issues pertaining to bullying, mediated learning experiences, and children's rights. (See, respectively, *School Psychology Review*, Vol. 21, No. 1, 2000; *School Psychology International*, Vol. 23, No. 1, 2002; and *School Psychology Review*, Vol. 22, No. 2, 2001.)

Nationally developed psychological and educational tests also are critical to improving professional services (Hu & Oakland, 1991; Oakland & Hu, 1989, 1991, 1992; Oakland & Hambleton, 1995). Tests to assess children's achievement, intelligence, personality and temperament, and other qualities and to identify children with learning disabilities would stimulate the provision of services to address these problems. This is what happened when, in the 1930s, school psychologists in New Zealand set about expanding scholarship and test availability in their country. They were instrumental in forming the New Zealand Council for Educational Research to assist in the promotion of scholarship and test development. More recent models are available to help countries and regions promote the scholarship and technical contributions necessary for providing school psychology services in most regions.

Proposed Changes in Professional Preparation in Europe

The psychology profession, including school psychology, is experiencing considerable growth throughout Europe, with an average growth rate of about 5%. Italy, Germany, the United Kingdom, France, and Spain have the largest number of psychologists. The total number of psychologists in relation to inhabitants is 1 per 1,850 people. Nineteen European Union member states protect the title of psychologist. The European Union Task Force on Training in Applied Psychology is attempting to develop somewhat uniform standards for the preparation of psychologists, including school psychologists. The task force has recommended that all applied psychology programs include a 3-year undergraduate degree in psychology. Those who desire professional preparation would enter a 3-year professional training program that includes a 1-year internship (Tikkanen, 2006).

Education and School Psychology in Mexico[1]

Immigration from Mexico into the United States is occurring at record levels, resulting in many Mexican children enrolling in U.S. schools. Their presence has been most noticeable in U.S. border states. However, record numbers also are enrolled in schools in many northern states (e.g., Colorado, Illinois). Knowing some features of immigrants' education through age 18, as well as school psychology programs within Mexico, may help school psychologists understand these students.

Mexico's population is about 107 million, about a third of the U.S population of 300 million. Approximately 40% is below the age of 18; 70% live with their nuclear families and another 30% live with their extended families or in institutions (INEGI, 2000). Health care, education, and labor policies for children fall far short of international standards (Bollin, 2003). Approximately 60% of Mexico's population is Mestizo (i.e., persons of mixed Spanish and Indian ancestry), 30% is American Indian, 9% is European, and 1% is other. Although Spanish is the official language, 62 dialects also are used, often to the exclusion of Spanish in rural areas. Although Mexico does not have a state-endorsed religion, almost 90% of the people are Roman Catholic.

Mexico's education system is federally controlled, with the intention of promoting national unity and a sense of patriotism. The publicly supported state system provides education through preschool and elementary (grades 1–6), junior high (grades 7–9), and high school or technical school (grades 10–12). The curricula are uniform throughout every grade and in every school. Students who fail a grade repeat the same curriculum the following year. However, not all Mexican children attend school, usually because they have to work. Approximately 3.5 million children ages 6–18 work. Among those who enter school, approximately 50% do not complete an elementary education (Bollin, 2003). Special education services are provided to approximately 110,000 students, mainly those with motor disabilities and visual and mental disorders. Services for students with emotional and social disorders are uncommon. Assuming that Mexico has 40 million children, less than 1% receive special education services.

Educational systems differ considerably in urban and rural areas. Elementary schools are classified as either A or B; the B schools commonly are in rural areas. The A schools have one teacher per class. In B schools, teachers instruct two or more grades and may have as many as six different grades (e.g., a one-room school).

[1]Appreciation is expressed to Hilda Zubiria and Rolando Diaz-Loving for providing much of the information found in this section.

Professionals working in rural areas often are compensated at a rate 50% below that of colleagues working in urban areas. Families in rural areas generally feel isolated from mainstream society and are poorly nourished. Adults tend to be illiterate; many never attend school and often do not speak Spanish.

Twelve universities in Mexico offer school psychology programs that lead to a 4-year undergraduate degree or a 2-year graduate degree. Two universities offer doctoral degrees in school psychology. Those with graduate degrees typically teach at the undergraduate and postgraduate levels. Thus, most psychologists who provide services in schools are trained at an undergraduate level. Moreover, given the popularity of clinical psychology preparation in Mexico, many—perhaps most—psychologists who work in schools are trained as clinical, not school, psychologists. Psychologists who work in schools earn an estimated average of approximately $800 per month.

Psychological services offered in schools typically include educational planning, evaluation, teaching, vocational guidance, and intervention for students with learning problems. Tests used include the Wechsler Scales, Raven's Progressive Matrices, Cattell's 16 Personality Factor model, and the Minnesota Multiphasic Personality Inventory. These tests have national norms, and their reliability and validity estimates have been established through research. Mexico has no national association dedicated to the interests of school psychology; thus, there is little national leadership dedicated to promoting a strong infrastructure for this specialty.

CONCLUSIONS

Knowing the international dimensions of school psychology can enrich students' and practitioners' understanding of the specialty. Participating in the field in an international setting can further broaden professional experience.

How to Become Involved in International School Psychology

Many school psychologists want to combine travel with professional work and service and thus seek opportunities to live and work abroad. Some live and work abroad for a few months; others do so for years. Employment opportunities can be found through various sources (see Gerner, 1990). One way is to meet foreign visitors at receptions and annual meetings of NASP and the APA. Initial collegial relationships may evolve into friendships and then into work opportunities. Other organizations also hire school psychologists. The U.S. Department of Defense Overseas Schools has been a large employer of school psychologists. Their schools are located at large military installations in areas other than war zones. The Institute for International Education, a division of the U.S. Department of State, has long-established programs that provide support for graduate students to study abroad and for teachers, school psychologists, and other professionals to work abroad. There is considerable prestige associated with this Fulbright program. In addition, more than 700 international schools provide services in expatriate communities. The organizations described can be contacted through their websites:

- International School Psychology Association, *www.ispaweb.org*
- U.S. Department of Defense Overseas Schools *www.military.com/Resources/ResourcesContent/0,13964,31992,00.html*
- Institute for International Education (*www.iie.org*) is a division of the U.S. Department of State
- International Schools Services: *www.iss.edu*
- Search Associates at *www.search-associates.com/schools.html*
- University of Northern Iowa Overseas Placement Service: *www.uni.edu/placement/overseas*
- European Council for International Schools: *www.ecis.org/home.asp/*

Some of these organizations hold recruitment fairs annually to inform professionals of work opportunities. Students seeking internships abroad are unlikely to find suitable locations, in part because of a lack of properly credentialed supervisors.

Looking Ahead

The practice of school psychology is found in most nations with advanced educational systems. The nature of school psychology services reflects a country's social, economic, and educational systems. The numbers of school psychology programs and school psychology practitioners is expected to increase, as well as the scope of their services. ISPA, with its 23 national member organizations, has helped establish a professional infrastructure that has raised the level of professionalism in the field of school psychology. The continued growth of school psychology internationally will depend heavily on the profession's success in establishing viable national associations that can provide leadership within other countries.

Chapter 11

Perspectives on the Future of School Psychology

Throughout, this book has reported the progress and accomplishments of school psychology: its roles, practices, credentialing, training, accreditation, and organizational and professional development. From the ideas, technological developments, and practices of a few individuals in the late 19th and early 20th centuries, school psychology has developed into a major specialty of professional psychology. Most, if not all, of the major symbols of professional development have been realized. What about school psychology's future? This final chapter addresses the future of school psychology from several perspectives: first, by revisiting the futuristic perspectives written before 1970; second, by answering many of the questions posed in chapter 1; and third, by discussing more recent viewpoints and predictions and making some general recommendations and guidelines for approaching the future. Finally, this book argues again for the profession to take a cautious approach to affecting a future characterized by increasing diversity of roles, functions, and practice settings.

PRE-1970 VIEWS OF THE FUTURE

Because school psychology in its early years was enmeshed within generic clinical psychology in most settings, the field was without an identity that would have fostered discussions of its future. Before the 1940s, few futuristic writings existed. However, Hollingworth (1933) made the following predictions about what psychological services would be rendered in the next quarter-century, that is, by 1958.

> Judging the future from the past, we venture to predict that this service will become a part of scholastic routine everywhere. It will become inconceivable that once upon a time the American people forcibly seized the children of the nation and subjected them from seven to fourteen or sixteen years of age indiscriminately to undifferentiated education, without knowledge of their abilities, their mental contents, or their emotional problems.
>
> By means of scientific psychological service education will become differentiated on the rational basis of individual differences in biological nature. The school will be fitted to the child. Suicide of pupils, in despair at failure, will be unknown. Truancy will become a thing of the past. The uneducable will be impersonally recognized as such. The gifted will be selected for the extraordinary opportunity which suits them by nature. Special talents and defects will be considered in school placements.

> It is surely inconceivable that the blind *wish* to believe all men created equal will finally prevail over demonstrated truth. Chaos will not be permitted to continue where order has been made possible.
>
> The more scientific (precise, disinterested, and verifiable) psychological service becomes, the more humanitarian does it automatically become. Without *impersonal* knowledge of the child, idealists do mainly "good deeds which are harmful." True idealism demands impersonal truth as a basis for action. In the field which we are considering, the pioneers have done their work of acquiring new knowledge, preparing themselves to use it, charting a departure, and showing the way to found education on a scientific knowledge of childhood. It is for the psychological service of the future to develop this work by continuing to discover and apply impersonal knowledge of the child's nature and deeds (p. 379).

Now, almost 70 years since her predictions, Hollingworth would probably be content with the current knowledge base of what was then generic clinical and applied psychology, but its limited application in education would be disconcerting. She probably would be very disappointed with the nature of the educational order established and the persistent problems of student academic learning, emotional–behavioral disorders, truancy, and violence.

With the founding of the APA's Division of School Psychology (Division 16) in 1945, a separate identity for school psychology began to crystallize and authors looked more closely at the future prospects of the field. In her presidential address to Division 16, Bertha Luckey (1951) stated:

> The psychologist of the future should have a thorough grounding in clinical psychology, group tests, and other devices which furnish crude means of sifting the population, but the real contribution and real pressures of school psychologists will always be in the specialized fields that require more basic knowledge of human development and its variations. This includes special approaches to various subjects, and especially those tool subjects that must constantly be used in the educational situation, as reading, writing, arithmetic, etc. (p. 10)

In 1955, the Thayer Conference proceedings (Cutts, 1955) stressed recommendations and predictions for the future. These included (a) two levels of training and practice in the schools, with the master's-level practitioner offering limited, supervised services (the two levels were also to be reflected in training, with accreditation available at both levels); (b) increased availability of part-time doctoral study for in-service psychological workers; and (c) certification by state departments of education (SDE) at two levels commensurate with training and accreditation. The proceedings also predicted a future with continued high demand for school psychologists. The conference was an agenda for Division 16, which set about the business of accomplishing its recommendations. Although the two levels of school psychology never gained widespread acceptance, they can be observed in some states (e.g., Maine and Texas), and Division 16 was successful in producing certification guidelines, training guidelines for the doctoral and master's level, achieving American Board of Professional Psychology certification, and APA accreditation (Fagan, 1993, 2005b).

In the 1960s, the growth of school psychology was reflected in a wave of books discussing its roles and functions and the future of the field (see appendix B). O'Shea (1960) painted the future with a broad brush, declaring that "the day has long since past [sic] when any psychologist relies upon a 'one-shot' testing period" (p. 280). O'Shea's future school psychologist would be involved with what is now considered undertaking an ecological assessment of the classroom, contributing to the decision-making process of school district affairs (e.g., curriculum planning and personnel policies), performing consultation and interventions with the school staff, working more effectively with parents, collaborating with nonschool agencies, initiating psychotherapy in the school setting, creating more effective learning environments, advocating respect for the social sciences in an era dominated by a need for mathematicians and physical scientists, and contributing to knowledge through research. She even suggested that every school building in the larger cities should have a well-trained doctoral-level school psychologist, echoing a plea made many years before (Symonds, 1933). Rural areas might have a single psychologist supervising the work of lesser-trained personnel in several districts.

Hirst (1963) predicted a strong need for school psychologists, substantial increases in the doctoral force over the next 20 years, the rising involvement of school psychologists in the diagnosis of learning disabilities, and greater involvement in counseling and psychotherapy as school psychologists acquired training in those areas. Hirst also predicted increased roles of in-service education, prevention, research, and program evaluation. Gray (1963a) advocated a broad future of applications of psychology to education and the necessity of maintaining the scientist–professional model of training and practice.

Authors of the 1960s overestimated the rise of doctoral training and doctoral credentialing and the breadth of functioning that school psychologists would achieve . . . and they failed to see the impact that emerging legislation for exceptional children would later have . . . and the impact of NASP.

Among the more comprehensive discussions was that of Magary (1967a). Blending others' preferences for the future with his own, Magary predicted the emergence of treatment-oriented roles and consultation, the school psychologist as a high school (and even elementary school) teacher of psychology, the legal and ethical problems facing school psychologists in private practice, the need for well-established training models and program growth, and improved internship and certification models. Although he praised the growth of school psychology, Magary felt there were already too many professional associations and journals and that consolidation was needed in the future. He stated that school psychologists needed to establish a stronger identity as pupil personnel services (PPS) workers and members of the school faculty, rather than seek a separate identity just for themselves. Magary's desire for greater cooperative efforts and PPS teamwork has been only partially realized. It was true that school psychologists shared areas of knowledge and practice with school counselors and social workers, but the "hardening of the categories approach in pupil personnel services" that Magary deplored became a hallmark of each PPS area in the

1970s. School psychology's categorization was effectively augmented by the joint efforts of the National Association of School Psychologists (NASP), which was formed a few years after Magary's book appeared, and APA Division 16, in which Magary was very active. Magary's chapter in the 1967 handbook is an excellent description of school psychology's overall professional development in the 1960s.

Finally, a little-known work by Gelinas and Gelinas (1968) depicted a very positive future for school psychologists from the standpoint of employment alternatives within the school system. The authors foresaw opportunities for advancement to administrative positions, including those of director of psychological services, principal, assistant superintendent for pupil services, and superintendent. Their discussion of the advantages for women in choosing a future as a school psychologist is instructive with regard to how much the status of women has changed since the 1960s (see "Family Life," in Gelinas & Gelinas, 1968).

Authors of the 1960s overestimated the rise of doctoral training and doctoral credentialing and the breadth of functioning that school psychologists would achieve. They were writing in an era of rapid growth in school psychology, and they failed to see the impact that emerging legislation for exceptional children would later have. The impact of NASP was also unforeseen. As a major advocate for non-doctoral-level school psychologists, NASP may have inadvertently impeded the rise of doctoral-level school psychology. Clearly the authors of the 1960s did not foresee either the growth of the field since 1970 or the persistence of its traditions.

POST-1970 VIEWS OF THE FUTURE

Bardon and Bennett (1974) suggested that the future would include better trained school psychologists able to offer a wider variety of services than the child-centered services of the past. Their discussion of a developmental educational approach exhibits the influence of earlier writers and previews the prototype of Bardon's later position supporting school psychologists' involvement with a psychology of schooling (Bardon, 1983). Another future perspective was provided by Tindall (1979), who expressed concern about the lack of role expansion that had been predicted by earlier writers. He foresaw serious conflicts over the differences between the APA and NASP policies on training and credentialing. He considered it probable that specializations would develop within school psychology and expressed the need for accountability in accordance with APA and NASP standards and ethics. Tindall felt that most of Magary's earlier predictions were not yet realized and that the field needed to avoid divisiveness that would draw school psychology away from the larger profession of psychology, leaving the school psychologist with a "meaningless title and a bag of techniques" (p. 22).

In the 1980s, Herron, Herron, and Handron (1984) expressed concern about continuing identity problems, doctoral versus nondoctoral issues, the proliferation of training at the nondoctoral level, and decreasing job demand. They sensed a future based on the doctoral level in school psychology, with fewer but better training programs, limited job demand, expanded service settings, and more indirect service provision, such as consultation. Another perspective viewed the future in terms of the content and process changes needed in school psychology (Reynolds, Gutkin, Elliott, & Witt, 1984). Blending traditional approaches and necessary changes, they called for reanalysis of assessment, diagnosis, and treatment, and of the methods and vehicles for delivering services, including the need for more follow-up services. They also called for a reconsideration of the sources of power in service delivery. Their changes were conceptualized within the framework of *reciprocal determinism* (in which a child's behavior is both influenced by and influences his or her cognitive skills, attitudes, and behavior and the environment), and they forecast the need for much broader applications of psychological science. For example, assessment in the future was described as being much broader than traditional normative approaches applied to internal characteristics, and it would include behavioral and environmental assessment. The Herron et al. (1984) predictions have not materialized, whereas those of Reynolds et al. (1984) have come into use.

Bergan (1985) considered the major future scientific advances to be associated with cognitive psychology and developments in behavioral and path-referenced assessment. Drawing heavily from the discussions at the Spring Hill Symposium in 1980 (Ysseldyke & Weinberg, 1981) and the Olympia Conference in 1981 (Brown, Cardon, Coulter, & Meyers, 1982), Bergan mentioned several professional developments, including training specialization, expanded practice settings, increased legal influences on practice, greater accountability, and role expansion into other settings, including the private practice sector. The Spring Hill and Olympia conferences were the most concentrated discussions of the future of school psychology since the Thayer Conference. As at Thayer, many subjects were discussed and many plans for action were considered, but recommendations far exceeded predictions for the future. The proceedings described comprehensively the issues and anxieties of the field in the early 1980s. The Olympia Conference also provided a process for considering the future at subsequent conferences held by numerous state school psychology associations.

The National School Psychology Inservice Training Network (1984) published its *School Psychology: A Blueprint for Training and Practice*, which advocated broader roles for school psychologists, primarily in school settings. In conjunction with greater inclusion of exceptional children in regular education, the recommended domains of school psychology leadership and function were class management, interpersonal communication and consultation, basic academic skills, basic life skills, affective and social skills, parental involvement, classroom organization and social structures, systems development and planning, personnel development, individual differences in development and learning, school–community relations, instruction, legal/ethical and professional issues, assessment, multicultural concerns, and research. The domains formed the basis for recommendations regarding future training. The *Blueprint* was revised in 1997 and 2006 and is discussed below.

After an optimistic discussion of the field generally, Phillips (1990b) cautiously considered the future of school psychology:

> School psychology is at a turning point, and several possibilities exist for its future. Will school psychology be an occupation that continues to play a role limited largely to assessment and determinations of special education eligibility? Will school psychology become a two-tiered occupation,

> consisting of doctoral school psychologists increasingly engaged in a variety of nontraditional (and non-school) roles and non-doctoral school psychologists who continue to be engaged in the traditional assessment role? Or will school psychology become a specialty and profession that reaches for new roles, that raises the academic standards of training programs and the practical competence of its members, thus engendering prestige, compensation, and working conditions good enough to be recognized as a specialty and profession of first class? (p. 252)

Phillips's preferred future for school psychology is characterized by greater professionalization as a doctoral specialty of psychology, with an increased sociocultural orientation to behavior and learning. He cautioned against school psychology establishing its primary orientation with education instead of with psychology. His predictions for expansion into the nonschool sector have yet to materialize, but he likely would be concerned about school psychology's continued educational orientation.

Woody, LaVoie, and Epps (1992) identified a future with the continued need for school psychological services with schoolchildren and possibly with adults, a broader role that would engage the entire school population, a need for continuing education beyond training and credentialing, an increase in the number of school psychologists in private practice, and increased feminization and concern for women's and minority issues in training and practice.

Among the most recent perspectives on the future are those provided by the revised *Blueprint* (Ysseldyke et al., 1997, 2006) and a chapter by Oakland and Cunningham (1999). The 1997 *Blueprint* identified several domains of practice that were tied to training in school psychology and formed the basis of the revision of the NASP training standards of 2000. The 10 domains were data-based decision making and accountability; interpersonal communication, collaboration, and consultation; effective instruction and development of cognitive/academic skills; socialization and development of life competencies; student diversity in development and learning; school structure, organization, and climate; prevention, wellness promotion, and crisis intervention; home–school–community collaboration; research and program evaluation; and legal, ethical practice, and professional development. The domains of the 2006 revision were developed from the *Blueprint*'s model of practice and are covered in two broad areas: (a) foundational competencies—interpersonal and collaborative skills; diversity awareness and sensitive service delivery; technological applications; professional, legal, ethical, and social responsibility; and (b) functional competencies—data-based decision making and accountability; systems-based service delivery; enhancing the development of cognitive and academic skills; enhancing the development of wellness, social skills, mental health, and life competencies. These domains will influence the next revision of NASP training standards in 2010.

Oakland and Cunningham (1999) described models for understanding the future of school psychology and identified potential changes in terms of the areas over which school psychology has most, some, and little control. Most control was identified in guild areas such as membership, associations, literature and standards, credentialing, and preparation. Some control was identified in areas such as school finance, federal and state laws and regulations, school-based service provision, expansion of services beyond the schools, the number of training programs and practitioners, and public perceptions of the field. Little control was identified in broader areas such as cultural, political, and social components of employment settings, or knowledge produced from unrelated disciplines.

Oakland and Cunningham identified several areas of future tension, among which was the yielding of the historical unity of the field—in terms of training, services, and practice settings—to a growing plurality of aspects that threaten the solidarity and identity of school psychology. They also foresaw tension between the current lengthy training period of school psychologists compared with other professionals and the need for extending preparation to keep up with the growth of service needs; the need for more services in an atmosphere of tight or diminishing financial resources; the possibility of being replaced by other professionals as schools try to provide unattainable services that exceed the skills of the available school psychologists; the need to shift the emphasis from remediation to prevention; practitioner desires to expand services beyond special education to general education; and the shift from traditional to emerging assessment strategies. Overall, they forecast a fairly stable future for school psychology and suggested that "a retrospective view of school psychology in 10 years is likely to find the number of significant changes to be far less than its consistencies over this period" (p. 51).

A miniseries in the *School Psychology Review* (2000, Vol. 29, No. 4) explored several aspects of school psychology in the 21st century (Fagan & Sheridan, 2000). Across the contributing articles is a call for less traditional services and a need to better prepare for and deliver services in an ecological model. The authors raised numerous concerns about barriers to improved service delivery, including systemic barriers in training and in service settings. Future needs in mental health and instructional services, as well as training and research, were discussed. The series also considered the future of the relationship between APA Division 16 and NASP. The commentaries to the main articles provided additional perspectives on why change would continue to be slow.

The 2002 School Psychology Futures Conference contained very similar themes, and its participants have promoted follow-up materials and training modules. Although the conference focused on goals for professional advancement rather than on predictions, the goals are compatible with the above predictions, and the viewpoints of several conference presenters are cited elsewhere in this book. Finally, Merrell, Ervin, and Gimpel (2006) made several predictions, but it is too soon to evaluate their outcomes. Their predictions for the future are consistent with those presented below, especially regarding personnel needs, diversity of services and providers, and continued expansion of settings and models of practice. Thus, the two most recent school psychology texts have similar viewpoints on the future.

PESSIMISTIC VIEWS ON THE FUTURE

In the 1960s and 1970s several doomsday publications predicted school psychology's demise for one or more of the following reasons:

1. The narrow conceptualization of psychology's contributions as clinical services (Lighthall, 1963)

2. The profession's failure to keep up with the changing needs of education and to become psychologists of schooling instead of school psychologists (White, 1968–1969)
3. School psychologists' lack of proper training and identity (Clair & Kiraly, 1971)
4. The conflicting interests in being a child advocate and agent of change for the schools while being a school employee (Silberberg & Silberberg, 1971)
5. School psychologists' lack of training in response to federal legislative mandates for the handicapped (Hayes & Clair, 1978)
6. The adverse impact of service provision through contracting (Hirsch, 1979)

Owing to the forces discussed in chapter 7, school psychology has survived these pessimistic predictions with roles that are broader but still entrenched in tradition. Perhaps such forecasts served as stimuli to draw a vital field in new directions. Now in the 21st century, dire predictions about the future of school psychology are rare. For the most part, the sense seems to be that school psychology has a bright future despite some areas in need of improvement.

Collectively, the discussions of the future of the profession have suggested a need for greater unification around a theoretical identity; expanded doctoral training and workforce; role expansion; expansion of work settings; and increased research, evaluation, accountability, preparedness for changes in psychology and education, and improved direct and functional assessments. If there is a single theme throughout all of the discussions since the Thayer Conference, it is the desire and need to expand, that is, in practitioner numbers, settings, and especially roles and functions. Other recent discussions on the future have followed this theme and place it in the context of changes observed in psychology and education (Cobb, 1990; Fagan, Gorin, & Tharinger, 2000; Jackson, 1990; Knoff, Curtis, & Batsche, 1997; Oakland & Cunningham, 1999; Phillips, 1990b; Pryzwansky, 1990). Cobb (1992) and Conoley (1992) suggested that school psychology may cease to be a specialty, becoming more generically a part of applied and professional psychology. As professional psychology specialties mature they would become more alike in what Phillips (1990b) called "inter specialty ecumenism," a process that could be augmented by changes in specialty recognition (DeMers, 1993). In these viewpoints, school psychology would be more closely aligned with the contributions of educational psychology and consultation models, pursuing prevention as well as intervention goals (e.g., Alpert, 1985). Although the changes predicted by several of these perspectives are occurring, professional psychology and school psychology continue to maintain separate specialty identities.

Collectively, the discussions of the future of the profession have suggested a need for greater unification around a theoretical identity; expanded doctoral training and workforce; role expansion; expansion of work settings; and increased research, evaluation, accountability, preparedness for changes in psychology and education, and improved direct and functional assessments.

THE AUTHORS' VIEWS ON THE FUTURE

As long as the context remains the same, the best predictor of future behavior is present behavior. In considering what the field of school psychology might look like 6 months or a few years from now, its present description is probably a good predictor. This is true because there exists a substantial database about the present, including the conditions under which school psychological services are perceived as needed, practiced, and regulated. What about 10, 20, or 50 years from now? Predicting the future that far ahead is very risky. A publication from 1900, "What May Happen in the Next Hundred Years," is remarkable for what it predicted and for what it failed to predict (Watkins, 1900). Although Watkins predicted global use of telephones and televising of events, he incorrectly predicted that there would be no C, X, or Q in the English alphabet and that science would practically exterminate mosquitoes, houseflies, and roaches. Although he predicted the use of airplanes, especially in war, he incorrectly predicted that cities would be free from noise because of subways and overhead roadways. He spoke of the use of medical inspectors in schools but not psychologists.

General Views on the Accomplishments of the Field

To achieve its current level, school psychology has successfully straddled education and psychology to impose a sphere of influence that is interdependent with both areas. School psychology now has strong professional organizations; a large workforce of trainers and practitioners; codes of ethics; standards for training, credentialing, and practice; credentials for the school and nonschool sectors; and its own literature. Issues of survival and identity are largely in the past. Now is a period of stability, contending with perceptions of which future directions will have the most beneficial outcomes. The present diversity of opinions is considerably different than in the 1960s. Then, the issues were being debated among individuals who were often not trained or identified with school psychology; many came from strong clinical or educational psychology backgrounds. In more recent times the issues are debated by school psychologists who have both training and credentialing. We have arrived at a point at which the argument can take place without fear of serious professional division.

The major growth period of school psychology is probably past. What lies ahead is substantial qualitative growth and only modest quantitative growth.

Another difference is the kind of future that is being considered. School psychology has evolved through the emergence of new services, the forging of an identity, and periods of growth and stability, and it is now entering a period of maturity and revision. The major growth period of school psychology, quantitatively, is probably past. What lies ahead is substantial qualitative growth and only modest quantitative growth. For example, public education enrollments, including those of special education, will not change as dramatically as in the past 25 years, but how special education is provided could change in significant ways. Moreover, the number of training institutions will remain stable, while training will continue to change. The following questions, discussed in chapter 1, provide some predictions for the profession over the next 20 years.

How Many School Psychologists Will There Be?

Given the problems of supply and demand, the relatively stable number of training programs, the expectations for growth in school enrollment, and the recommended and existing service ratios, the overall size of the workforce will probably not exceed 35,000–40,000. The growth over the past 35 years (from 5,000 to 30,000) is not likely to recur in the next few decades. Nevertheless, an increase to 35,000–40,000 would represent substantial growth in the number of school psychologists and continue the expansion of settings and roles. Although such growth would improve the overall service ratio, it would continue to be short of NASP's currently recommended ratio of 1:1,000 schoolchildren (NASP, 2000b).

The number of school psychologists over the next 20 years also will reflect the fact that school psychologists in the second wave of employment (1950–1970) will be retiring over the next two decades (Curtis, Grier, & Hunley, 2004; Fagan, 1988b). Training programs will need to produce enough graduates to fill the need for replacement and new positions. This shortage is already being reported in some states and also is seen in some training programs that are having difficulty finding faculty replacements. Thus, it is conceivable that the actual quantitative growth could be smaller than the range cited above. In 1994, the first edition of this book predicted a total number of 30,000–35,000 practitioners in 2014, which remains fairly accurate.

Diversity of the Field

The field of school psychology will continue to be disproportionately female over the next 20 years. Up considerably from the 46% estimate of Smith (1984), women now make up about 75% of the workforce, and this could rise to as high as 80–85%. The phenomenon is part of a broader feminization of the entire field of psychology. The field is expected to have a stronger presence of women in the organizational leadership, more women appointed to editorial positions, and a steady increase in women among training program faculty. To a large extent, the future of school psychology will be in the hands of its female leadership. The trend will be attended by concerns about gender issues, such as differential treatment, salaries, and sexual harassment, and issues of domestic impact (e.g., balancing work and family, violence, and abuse). Discussing the importance of affirmative action in employment, Woody et al. (1992) raised the specter that "the enthusiasm for righting past wrongs against women and minorities can be a breeding ground for reverse discrimination against males, especially if they are older and Caucasian" (p. 14). However, no evidence has been seen that men are being discriminated against in trainee selections or employment. Perhaps the more important

Women now make up about 75% of the workforce, and this could rise to as high as 80–85%.

issues are why men have chosen other fields and how the profession can attract more men into school psychology. It would not be surprising to see in the next decade student recruitment and employment notices encouraging males to apply. The 1994 edition predicted that the female representation might rise to 75–80%, which is about where the field is today.

The field over the next 20 years will continue to have difficulties in achieving greater minority representation because it is unlikely there will be a sufficient pool of minority undergraduates from which to draw training program applicants. Unless considerably more minority students enter undergraduate training in psychology and other related fields, the current 6–7% minority representation in the field is not likely to grow beyond 10%. A 1992 series of articles on multicultural issues in school psychology discussed the lack of empirical knowledge regarding African American and Hispanic students (Gopaul-McNicol, 1992) and the complex and variable nature of multicultural training in school psychology graduate programs (Rogers, Ponterotto, Conoley, & Wiese, 1992). The Division 16 newsletter, *The School Psychologist,* also ran a series of multicultural articles in 1995 (Vol. 49, No. 4, and Vol. 50, No. 1). More recently, the *Journal of Applied School Psychology* (2006, Vol. 22, No. 2) discussed multicultural training in terms of assessment, interventions, home–school partnerships, and systems-level interventions. Certain training programs make greater contributions in this area than others. Increased knowledge, experience, and sensitivity of training programs and practitioners may be the most important gains to be made in the near future. Rogers et al. (1999) provide excellent practice recommendations to improve sensitivity and to better serve diverse student groups. The 1994 edition of this book predicted that in 20 years the field would probably not have more than 10% minority representation, so the current figure of about 8% is consistent with that estimate.

Unless considerably more minority students enter undergraduate training in psychology and other fields from which training programs attract graduate students, it is unlikely that the present 6–7% minority representation will grow beyond 10%.

In addition to gender and minority representation within the profession, the future will include more practitioners who themselves have disabilities. Although some of this increase may result from aging practitioners' ailments and disabilities, graduate trainees with disabilities and more emphasis on specialized training programs will account for some of the increase.

At What Levels Will School Psychologists Be Trained?

The current number of institutions offering training in the United States is between 230 and 250. That number is not likely to change much, although it is possible that budgetary problems, regulatory requirements, program duplication, and other factors will lead to a reduction in the number of program institutions. For example, if specialist-level programs are forced to continue adding requirements to be accredited by the National Council for Accreditation of Teacher Education (NCATE) and NASP, it could become impractical for some institutions to continue offering programs. Several institutions have discontinued their programs, although other institutions have entered the field. Over the next 20 years, the number of doctoral programs will rise to about 100, and the pursuit of national accreditation will increase in importance. Unless NASP emerges as an independent accreditor, the APA will continue to be seen as the most representative and desired accreditor at the doctoral level. Nondoctoral program accreditation will continue to be managed by NCATE/NASP or possibly by NASP alone. The state partnership effort in NCATE will have an impact on how NASP standards are implemented locally. It is possible that NASP could join forces with APA in a joint accreditation agreement for doctoral programs. Similar predictions were made in 1994 and were accurate, with the exception that the number of doctoral institutions has not increased. The likelihood of NASP becoming an independent accreditor or joining with APA for accreditation continues to be improbable.

The proportions of specialist- or nondoctoral-level practitioners and doctoral-level practitioners in the workforce were predicted to change toward a more balanced condition; however, the percentage of the field holding doctoral degrees appears to be growing more slowly than anticipated. Since the 1994 edition of this textbook, the percentage has gone from about 21–28% to 33%. Incentives to acquire the doctoral degree do not seem strong enough to achieve a balanced workforce in the next 10 years. Specializations, primarily among the doctoral-level workforce, will continue to increase.

The long-standing affiliation of school psychology training programs with 4-year institutions may weaken. The 1994 edition stated that school psychology might follow the shift to a professional school model (then very visible in clinical psychology; Pion, 1992), bringing about greater sensitivity to practitioner issues and much greater availability of doctoral-program training for practicing school psychologists (Brown, 1989). That shift is clearly occurring both in freestanding professional schools and Internet-based programs. One concern is that training may drift away from the traditional scientist–practitioner model, creating a schism between trainers and practitioners. Such a shift could affect licensing by state boards of examiners in psychology but would probably be felt less in SDE licensing, where the standards for the Nationally Certified School Psychologist (NCSP) credential could provide the glue to hold NASP's training ideology together. However, NASP training standards undergo periodic review and revision, and a stronger practitioner orientation could emerge in the future. Although the number of persons holding the NCSP has dropped in recent years, with perhaps 50% of school psychologists holding the NCSP, there is a strong likelihood of CPD activity to maintain this credential. If more states were to require the NCSP for credentialing, and provide additional salary incentives to NCSP holders, it would better ensure CPD activity.

School psychology can learn from clinical psychology what the potential impact of the professional school model might be. This effect is more than merely an increase in the number of PsyD graduates from institutions unable to grant the EdD or PhD degree. In clinical psychology, the shift has been away from traditional academic institution roots to freestanding professional schools. As predicted in 1994, this shift has been gaining ground in school psychology. Suggestions for retaining the scientist–practitioner model within the future of doctoral and nondoctoral training programs were provided by Knoff, Curtis, and Batsche (1997). They provided suggestions for program administration and content, as well as faculty and student characteristics.

Another potential change is the preparation of school psychologists with greater identity with education than with psychology. Although the distinctions between training programs within educational psychology and those in psychology departments may not be clear, there are differences. The rapid growth of training programs in the 1960s and 1970s, and changes in accreditation requirements, moved the profession more in the direction of education academic units than psychology units. Although earlier orientations of trainers and programs may have been overly psychological (i.e., clinical), school psychology leaders must strive to maintain an appropriate balance of both psychology and education, with an identity as psychologists. Education-based programs, even doctoral programs, are too readily influenced by institutional changes made in response to state or national reforms that are more directed toward instruction than psychological practice. This is evident in the No Child Left Behind Act and the response-to-intervention methods of the IDEA reauthorization. School psychology trainers may argue that improving instruction is a laudable goal for all school psychologists; but such goals are more closely related to educational psychology than to the traditional and even contemporary practice of professional psychologists. The overlaps and differences signify the continuing influence of the profession's Witmerian and Hallian roots and the distinctions between what Bardon and others have referred to as school psychology in contrast to applied educational psychology (or a psychology of schooling).

Although distance learning technology may be useful in meeting many course requirements, the faculty–student interaction that is a necessary part of training, especially in field experiences, will never be eliminated completely.

Although distance learning technology may be useful in meeting many course requirements, the faculty–student interaction that is a necessary part of training, especially in field experiences, will never be eliminated completely. Such programs will need to pay close attention to NCATE/NASP and APA accreditation guidelines for survival, and those guidelines will continue to require direct contact and supervision. A recent discussion of these concerns and issues for professional psychology accreditation appeared in Murphy, Levant, Hall, and Glueckauf (2007).

How Will Practitioners Be Credentialed for Practice?

Because all states have some form of credentialing for the school and nonschool sectors, there is little room for quantitative growth in credentialing. The qualitative issues of the future revolve around the changing requirements for these credentials and their titles. The school sector will continue to require nondoctoral training, and the nonschool sector will continue to move in the directions set by the APA at the doctoral and postdoctoral levels. SDE credentialing will increasingly rely on the specialist degree and the NCSP for reciprocity. State boards of examiners in psychology will continue to license at the doctoral level in most states, and requirements for postdoctoral training or additional years of supervised experience will be more widespread. What remains to be seen is the impact of the APA resolution calling for 2 years of supervised experience but not requiring one of those years to be postdoctoral.

In nonschool practice, nondoctoral credentials will continue to be limited and fought by various forces. The doctoral degree will continue to be the choice primarily for practitioners who want to be employed with the fewest professional and legal restrictions. For individuals who want full-time employment in school districts, the forecast is for continued high demand for nondoctoral practitioners in most states, though such persons will experience restricted, and often prohibited, nonschool practice. If more SDEs relinquish their credentialing authority, more states will experience problems granting the title of school psychologist and perhaps end up with the title of specialist in school psychology. The long-term reciprocal impact of accreditation and credentialing, and wider recognition of the NCSP, will be greater state-to-state reciprocity in credentialing.

For individuals who want full-time employment in school districts, the forecast is for continued high demand for nondoctoral practitioners.

What Is the Employment Outlook?

The 1994 edition of this book predicted that school psychologists would continue to find that public school districts and cooperative agreement districts are their most common employment settings and that nontraditional settings, including private practice, would continue to increase and perhaps include 25% of the workforce. The best employment opportunities were predicted for practitioners with specializations and those with mobility, as well as for those interested in working in rural and developing areas, certain urban districts, many nonschool settings, and perhaps private practice. Although school psychologists have found employment opportunities in the nonschool sector, the prediction of 25% of the workforce in private practice fell far short of the mark. At least 90% of NASP members are in public and private school settings, and private practice continues to account for less then 5% of practitioners. At this point it appears that nonschool settings will likely remain in the 10–15% range, and private practice will likely account for about half of that.

The shortage of school-based practitioners that was observed in several states almost two decades ago has continued (Connolly & Reschly, 1990; National Association of State Consultants for School Psychological Services, 1987). The market for specialist-level practitioners should remain high for many years. However, school districts will never be willing or able to employ large numbers of doctoral-level school psychologists at appropriate salaries. With the substantial growth in training programs that occurred in the 1960s, large-scale numbers of retirements are anticipated with many senior-level academic positions continuing to be vacated. However, such positions are likely to be replaced by junior-level positions (assistant professorships). In some instances, training programs that were managed by a single senior-level faculty member may be discontinued when that person retires. These predictions are in reaction to tighter education budgets, lower student demand for training, duplication of programs among state institutions, and the cost of replacement and additional faculty to meet accreditation standards that did not exist when these programs were started. Nevertheless, the outlook for academic positions should be highly favorable. Many training programs are having difficulty filling available faculty positions, and only a small proportion of new doctoral-level professionals seem interested in such positions.

Training programs must continue to recruit more students in order to offset the gap between supply and demand and to avoid potentially negative influences of that gap on the profession. To offset the gap, universities will have to stretch existing resources and tight budgets or provide additional resources, such as faculty, student financial aid, and equipment.

Will the Service Ratio Improve?

The remarkable improvement of the service ratio of school psychologists to school-age children in the past 35 years will not be matched in the next 20 years. Now hovering around 1:1,500, the ratio improved from approximately 1:5,000 in 1970, but further improvement could be hampered by increasing school enrollments, stable or decreasing enrollment in training programs, faculty and practitioner retirements, and expanded service settings available to graduates. The 1994 edition predicted that the nationwide ratio would probably not improve beyond 1:1,500, and the prediction was accurate. Of course, many settings have much better ratios, and the range is expected to be reduced, so that few settings will exceed 1:4,000. For the coming decade, the ratio is not expected to improve beyond 1:1,400. As more school psychologists seek nonschool employment and private practice, the traditional calculation methods of the service ratio will need to include school and nonschool practitioners, and perhaps all school-age children in the community.

For the coming decade, the ratio is not expected to improve beyond 1:1,400.

How Has the Profession Changed, and How Should It Change?

School psychology has gradually evolved from very narrow testing roles and functions to much broader conceptualizations of assessment and the factors influencing child development and education (Fagan, 2008, in press). Target behaviors have shifted from precisely measured reaction times and physical attributes to less precise but more instructionally relevant attributes of children and the learning environment, especially ability and school achievement. As a result, the instrumentation has changed from laboratory equipment to test kits for almost every conceivable psychoeducational ability and skill.

Over the past decades, as regulations for special education became more widespread, the use of tests and trained examiners was increasingly accepted. The shift in assessment technology to the testing of various traits influenced the special education eligibility model of normative deviance (i.e., judging exceptionalities by comparisons to group averages on specific traits, behaviors, and skills). A model of nationally normative deviance for special education eligibility was widely established by 1930 and persists to the present. Tests have improved as a result of greater attention to standardization, reliability, validity, and cultural sensitivity. The assessment context has broadened beyond child-centered models to ecological conceptualizations, and child study instrumentation and methods have expanded accordingly. Although school psychology practice continues to be dominated by the assessment role, the assessment functions have shifted to more direct methods (e.g., curriculum-based), and a problem-solving model linking assessment to interventions has become widely accepted. Practitioners are more aware of the limitations of the assessment role, employ instruments that are more technologically adequate and culturally sensitive, and have outcome data on traditional school psychology functions. From a medical model of assessment that is focused heavily on what is wrong with the child, the profession has moved to concepts of ecological, family, and systems assessment.

Could a future shift occur in which eligibility is individually driven and in which eligibility assessment and placement are done irrespective of national norms? Perhaps, but it would not be a technological change; rather, it would be an ideological change, because the technology already exists. With the reauthorization of IDEA and its emphasis (for learning disabilities) on a response-to-intervention (RTI) model, less emphasis on normative assessment seems likely. However, wide-scale abandonment of normative assessment for special education placement is unlikely. Nor will test developers and corporations abandon their normative pursuits. Furthermore, how would special services for children be controlled and funded without normative criteria for eligibility that set limits on behaviors or traits? Even the RTI model relies on deviance from norms, albeit not based on national norms. There has not been, nor will there be, enough money in education to allow for a system in which a child can be declared eligible for special services (involving state and federal funds) based only on the judgment of the local team members, without some level of deviation from local or national normative data. Furthermore, to suggest that parents and educators in the future will not be interested in national normative comparisons is shortsighted. In fact, as a result of the No Child Left Behind Act, American education has moved in the direction of increased normative assessment as it tries to cope with public criticism. Although more local norms and practices may drive some areas of special education (e.g., learning disabilities), national norms will continue to be important, especially in the regular education sector.

Despite the continued dominance of the assessment role, that role is much better understood and has broadened to a variety of assessment models, settings, problems, and clients.

Thus, to the question, How has the profession changed? Even though the practice of school psychology has consistencies across its history, several things have changed, and the circumstances within which the field exists have changed as well. Despite the continued dominance of the assessment role, that role is much better understood and has broadened to a variety of assessment models, settings, problems, and clients. A comparison study by Reschly (1998) found that although roles had shifted negligibly over a 10-year period, some shifts in assessment functions were more easily observed. In fact, Reschly found that nontraditional assessment functions appeared to consume as much practitioner time as traditional functions. (This finding is supported by the data reported in Curtis, Lopez, Batsche, & Smith, 2006.)

As posited in chapter 1, the assessment role applies to almost all aspects of school psychology practice. School psychologists, regardless of their practice settings, will continue to be identified with, and respected for, their expertise in assessment. Thus, the use of normative testing will continue, but a broadened and more sophisticated, intervention-oriented assessment role is expected to gain wider acceptance. The future practitioner must continue to use assessment practices that lead to effective interventions in remediation, consultation, therapy, systems changes, and so forth. This need for an assessment–intervention link requires an ongoing examination of approaches to assessment. The newer forms of assessment, which shift the emphasis from trait to state, from internal to observable behaviors, and from nationally normative to locally compared progress, warrant serious consideration. Future school psychologists will be capable of providing measurable, assessment-based interventions that have instructional as well as mental health utility.

Changes That Arrive as Bandwagons, Buzzwords, and Trends

School psychologists should avoid being drawn onto practice bandwagons that result in trendy changes in service functions. Practices that are trends come and go in education and school psychology, for example, the initial teaching alphabet (ITA), perceptual–motor and neurological interventions (e.g., Frostig, Doman-Delacato), modality assessment and intervention (e.g., the Illinois Test of Psycholinguistic Abilities), certain projective techniques (e.g., Draw-A-Person), and profile analysis from ability scales. Some trendy practices are ushered in by well-intended but fleeting political movements. For example, aligning school psychology with the school reform bandwagon of the National Educational Goals of America 2000 may have enhanced visibility, but the goals were more politically correct than attainable (Sullivan, 1999). Practices that arise from political movements quickly become old news when political forces change. America 2000 had only vague goals related to children with disabilities and the importance of mental health services.

Aligning school psychology's future with that of education may help to place the "school" in school psychology, but it risks diminishing the profession's identification with psychology. School psychology should align itself with trends or movements that are clearly in the interests of children, as long as those movements are consistent with the tenets and ethics of the profession itself. Working with others to ban corporal punishment and the efforts for home–school collaboration are positive examples. In the assessment arena, the advice of Trachtman (1981) has not been heeded: to avoid bandwagons, to understand the person as well as the interaction, and to appreciate the complementary nature of various assessment techniques (p. 149). Lambert (1981, 1998) offered additional insights about the profession's tendency to be drawn to bandwagons and to accept as true others' criticisms of school psychology practice. It seems always in the midst of some bandwagon. It remains to be seen whether No Child Left Behind or RTI will be just another trend in public education and school psychology.

In the career of the practicing school psychologist, trends come and go; wheels are invented and reinvented. Special education labels have changed from disabled, to handicapped, and back to disabled (and some prefer the gentler term, *challenged*). The evolution of theories and their applications can be traced through lineage, such as *minimal brain dysfunction* becoming *hyperactivity* becoming *attention deficit hyperactivity disorder.* The lineage can be seen between Watsonian behaviorism and Skinnerian theory, Albert Ellis's rational–emotive therapy and cognitive–behavioral modification, and between mainstreaming, the regular education initiative, and inclusion. The recent outcome-based education seems to be a new form of individually guided education or mastery learning. Diagnostic teaching is traceable to Witmer's use of the term in the early 1900s. The major tests of intelligence and achievement also have discernible lineages. In the past decade criterion-referenced assessment has been repackaged, in apparently improved formulations, under the names *portfolio assessment*, *authentic assessment*, and *curriculum-based assessment.* Now there is a renewed emphasis on reading and literacy and the DIBELS curriculum. RTI will be a dominant aspect of school psychology practice, at least for the category of learning disabilities. These buzzwords and acronyms just may become more than new expressions of the earlier buzzword *accountability.*

NASP's and other professional groups' recent advocacy of intervention-linked assessment holds promise not because it is something new, but because it gives priority to the intervention role of the school psychologist. These newer approaches may have staying power, if research can provide a means of judging their utility for the practice of school psychology. Underlying these changes is the debate over the merits of traditional assessment versus nontraditional assessment. These different approaches have existed in the assessment literature for decades—traditional assessment, with its process, trait, and aptitude orientations, and nontraditional assessment, with its behavioral, situational and contextual, and outcome orientations—and they are not likely to be resolved in the foreseeable future. The third position is to believe that the two orientations are complementary, and that both have contributions to make to practice.

Changes Toward a Mental Health Orientation

Although schools continue to have a strong need for mental health–related services, school psychologists appear to be far more connected to special education and assessment. The schools have historically underserved the so-called emotionally disturbed (and socioemotionally or behaviorally disordered) children, but national studies have drawn greater attention to this category and have recommended that services to such children be improved (Dwyer, 1991). To move significantly in the direction of mental health prevention and intervention will require specialized training as well as a shift in perception among school authorities toward viewing the school setting as an appropriate arena for promoting mental health. Once the need for such services become widely accepted, schools would be thought of as centers for academic and personal social learning. However, it is unlikely that most school psychologists could effectively manage mental health services along with their academic assessment and intervention services without additional training, experience, and personnel. More likely is

To move significantly in the direction of mental health prevention and intervention will require specialized training as well as a shift in perception among school authorities toward viewing the school setting as an appropriate arena for promoting mental health.

the differential staffing of school psychologists by training, specialization, and interest, and possibly a greater infusion of counseling and clinical psychologists along with school social workers and school counselors, into the mental health services area of education. Such practices have been promoted under the topics of school-linked and school-based comprehensive clinic models (Pfeiffer & Reddy, 1998; Tyson, 1999; Vance & Pumariega, 1999).

Cautious Approaches to Change

Can school psychologists survive operating within a traditional assessment (refer–test–report) model? Certainly some can, in settings where such narrow practice is expected or accepted. However, school psychologists need assessment models that are linked to behavioral change intervention and instruction, mental health remediation, and academic improvement. Although the dominant role of the school psychologist has traditionally been assessment, that role will continue to broaden. Change will be in the direction of interventions and consultation, roles that are readily compatible with traditional roles, have long traditions in many places, are practiced to some extent by almost all school psychologists, and can be expanded within regular education or special education. Furthermore, the technology of the newer methods (e.g., curriculum-based assessment) is familiar to many school psychologists, and since it is not difficult to learn, it may open doors further to include consultation with those teachers and support personnel who would be involved in intervention implementation. The intervention-linked assessment approaches also fit well with the prereferral assessment and functional–behavioral assessment aspects of service delivery. Gredler (1992) cautioned that we cannot change to nontraditional roles and functions without addressing the need for traditional forms of service. The history of school psychology practice has been very closely related to that of special education; thus, if it moved in directions incongruent with educators' perceptions of schoolchildren's needs, the relationship could quickly dissolve. Changes in the regulation of special education could also have implications for the continuation of this relationship. If the eligibility model for school placement shifted to something that no longer required traditional assessment or any psychological services, many school psychology positions would be lost. However, these traditional roles are likely to persist, despite ongoing internal protest, because employers continue to perceive school psychologists' roles—that of sorters and repairers—as important. Challenging those perceptions, on the other hand, by giving educators the impression that school psychologists no longer want to do the things they have done for more than half a century could threaten job security. Advocating change also could encourage the state and federal government to no longer perceive as important what practitioners have historically done. Of course, some in the profession contend that there are risks in maintaining the status quo; still, a more patient, calculated, and documented approach to change is warranted.

Challenging employers' perceptions, on the other hand, by giving educators the impression that school psychologists no longer want to do the things they have done for more than half a century, could threaten job security.

The Future of Association Development

For the foreseeable future, the major issues for state associations will be their capacity to attract dedicated professionals into leadership roles and to effectively manage and represent the expanded training and practice of school psychology professionals. At the national level, both Division 16 (APA) and NASP seem to have secure futures (Fagan, 1993; Fagan, Gorin, & Tharinger, 2000). At the international level, the International School Psychology Association is without peer and should continue to grow and gain in importance in the future. At the state level, every state now has a state association for school psychologists, separate from the state psychological association in most instances.

The leadership of national and state associations will increasingly be women, and a higher representation of practitioners (as opposed to trainers) will be seen in the highest offices, especially in NASP and its affiliated state associations. Minority representation in leadership is not likely to increase unless a means can be found to increase minority recruitment and representation in the field generally. NASP president Deborah Crockett (1997–1998) was the first African American to hold a national school psychology association presidency.

PRESCRIPTIONS FOR CHANGE

Many times in books such as this, authors offer glimpses of the future without providing a list of suggestions to help readers participate in bringing about that future. Although this book does not claim to have all or even most of the answers, it does recommend certain steps that may help move the profession of school psychology productively into the future.

Questioning a Unifying Theoretical Orientation

Over the past 40 years, various unifying themes for school psychology have been suggested: Gray's (1963b) data-oriented problem solver; Reger's (1965) educational programmer; White's (1968–1969) psychology of schooling; Bardon's (1983) applied educational psychology; Elliott and Witt's (1986a) reciprocal determinism; and finally developmental, family, and social systems approaches (e.g., Medway & Cafferty, 1992; Plas, 1986; Woody et al., 1992). All are useful viewpoints for some, but not necessarily all, school psychologists. However, does the profession really need a single unifying theory of practice to establish its professional identity further? Other specialties lack a unifying theory of practice, and it should not be a cause for concern for school psychologists. What is the unifying theory of counseling psychology, or clinical psychology? A profession with diverse settings and practices will inevitably have diverse theoretical viewpoints and orientations, such as behavioral, psychodynamic, developmental, psychoneurological, family systems, organizational development, Cattell-Horn-Carroll assessment theory, and so on.

Accepting this considerable diversity is not the same as advocating that the profession should have a future of theoretical chaos. Rather, the strongest future for school psychology is one that allows several types of school psychologists to be unified around a very broad theme based on the contributions of psychological science to education. This theme can embrace practice involving traditional and nontraditional assessment, consultation, counseling and psychotherapy, remedial interventions, curriculum development and evaluation, family systems, school systems, and community educational issues. Unity should be provided by the focus on psychological applications to education and not be limited to particular theoretical orientations or the omission of certain roles and functions. Just as clients and practice settings do not benefit from a single approach, the future for school psychologists can have many orientations, traditional and nontraditional.

Just as clients and practice settings do not benefit from a single approach, the future for school psychologists can have many orientations, traditional and nontraditional.

Avoiding Dichotomies and Polarizations

A challenge for future leadership is the task of effectively representing the increasing diversity of the field. Several dichotomies are seen by some as dividing and polarizing the profession: doctoral versus nondoctoral training and credentialing, the regular education initiative and inclusion versus more traditional special education, the school psychologist as consultant versus traditional service provider, professionals aligned with education versus those aligned with psychology, practitioners aligned with academic learning versus those aligned with mental health, or school-based employees versus non-school-based practitioners, among others. Special interest groups may gravitate toward associations outside NASP and Division 16, potentially dividing the field. The first group to defect could be the school psychologists in the non-school-based sector, especially those in private practice. This threat seems even more acute in the academic learning versus mental health dichotomy.

Another divide threatens to develop over the use of response-to-intervention models, with advocates of curriculum-based and criterion-referenced assessment pitted against the normative assessment traditions of the field. Although advocates of curriculum-based assessment have a very important message to deliver about the links between assessment and intervention, some discuss it in ways that suggest normative assessment is obsolete (which it is not), that most school psychologists are heavily into the new approach (which they are not), and that those who are not into it, or about to get into it, are part of the problem in school psychology's future (which they are not). Those messages do not effectively convey the nature of normative and criterion-referenced assessment and the different, yet complementary, purposes of each approach. Unless these new approaches are advocated in a more realistic context, they will suffer the fate that behavior analysis in education suffered in the 1970s (Baer & Bushell, 1981).

Effective long-term change is more likely to occur when blended into the training and practice realities of the present (see, e.g., *Psychology in the Schools*, Vol. 43, Nos. 7 & 8, 2006). The newer forms of assessment and the RTI model have demonstrated their effectiveness (Burns & Ysseldyke, 2006; Grimes, Kurns, & Tilley, 2006;

Ranes, 1992; Rosenfield & Kuralt, 1990; Shapiro, 1989; Shinn, 1989; Shinn, Nolet, & Knutson, 1990). This book cautions against widespread polarization that would diminish either of them.

Bridging Ideology–Reality Gaps

Every profession experiences tension between its ideologies and its realities. Both APA and NASP set standards that represent the current ideologies of the field of school psychology. However, in some areas the profession's ideologies are ahead of the realities of training, credentialing, and practice. Many training programs are not in line with accreditation standards. Many states are out of line with credentialing standards.

Guidelines and standards are ideals or models, sometimes referred to as *best practices*, to which practitioners should aspire. They do not necessarily represent the norm of existing practices. An example is NASP's recommended service ratio, which is 1 practitioner to 1,000 clients or students, even as NASP survey data indicate that the typical ratio is about 1:1,500. It is important to have ideals as guides to the future. However, when they are portrayed as reality or as what the present must soon become, there is a risk of alienating practitioners and trainers for whom the ideology may be neither acceptable nor possible.

Preventing Professional Burnout

Often it seems that the best, brightest, and most caring members of the profession are the most likely to become frustrated during their first few years on the job. Many school psychologists, particularly those in rural areas, have few if any regular contacts with other school psychologists. Professional organizations, publications, and telecommunications technology can provide the framework for creating networks of school psychologists to provide collegial support and understanding. Various e-mail discussion lists now supplement traditional resources of communication for practitioners and bring together local, state, regional, and national professional contacts.

Expanding Services in the School and Community

The school psychology profession could have a future in emphasizing the broader use of skills to serve the entire school population, not limit professional services to those who might qualify for special education under IDEA. Children who are gifted and talented, children who are experiencing temporary difficulties because of stresses at home or at school, and children who fall in the "low average range" on a variety of assessment instruments should be regarded as being within the appropriate domain of the school psychologist. In the recent past, there has been renewed interest in the drawing together of regular and special education. A resurgence of remedial academic and mental health services, positioned between regular and special education, could provide the link for this relationship. The No Child Left Behind Act has also drawn practitioners into the regular education sector and helped to bridge services to special education and the need for accountability in both sectors.

The profession must continue to expand the age range of the clients it serves, in response to growing interest in children in the birth to kindergarten years and the years 18–21. For the younger age range, goals should include serving the needs of children already experiencing difficulties while preventing difficulties for children who are at risk because of congenital problems, family background, or socioeconomic status. The growing use of early literacy programs (e.g., DIBELS) is an example of these efforts. For the older age range, addressing issues related to why students drop out of school and vocational training work-study programs could be part of transition programs from school to community settings. Beyond secondary school, the notion of school psychologists working in junior colleges and in 4-year institutions is a logical expansion of school psychology services as well.

Using Resources Wisely, Continuing Professional Development, and Ensuring Accountability

School psychologists can accomplish their professional goals by using all their available resources in creative ways. Reducing or simplifying paperwork or cutting back on other time-consuming activities will recover lost time for addressing more important concerns. Preventive approaches can be used to deal with small problems before they escalate into major crises. Human resources (associates, clients, and the public) can be enlisted to help each other, such as retirees, the unemployed, college students, and even other students in the classroom.

Human resources also include school psychologists themselves when they discover the advantages of continuing education. Continued learning is an important means of keeping up with new developments, improving existing skills, acquiring new skills, having an opportunity to reflect on personal and professional development, and increasing awareness of what others are doing.

The school psychologist of the future must be concerned with accountability data not only to protect necessary services, but also to demonstrate how some services are more necessary than others.

Professional accountability provides an accurate picture of how practitioners spend their time. Demonstrating accountability for the effectiveness of processes and the accuracy of outcomes can bring about positive changes within the profession, thus enhancing the profession's image in the eyes of the public. The school psychologist of the future must be concerned with accountability data not only to protect necessary services, but also to demonstrate how some services are more necessary than others.

A PATIENT APPROACH TO CHANGE

The delivery systems for education and school psychology are ready for change. However, change that is emerging in the context of a century of compulsory schooling and psychological services will have to occur gradually, the result of planning that reflects the current context. Any change in the U.S. educational system in the next 20 years will be within the context of continued state-level responsibility and regulation, the lobbying power of more than 3 million teachers, the physical facilities of more than 90,000 school buildings, and funding mechanisms that continue to be strained. Those who are investing in such changes will need to be patient and recognize that the future will not come uniformly across the country. In a system of professional regulation that has no overarching authoritative agency, change will be characterized by uneven quantitative and qualitative development. Another factor is that all the regulatory agencies and influences are managed by people of varying competencies, who come and go. The quality of services statewide or districtwide can be seriously affected by individuals in key positions. Having high-quality services in the present does not guarantee that future services will be of such quality. Having accomplished certain goals in the present does not preclude their urgency in the future. Professional issues and problems are not permanently solved. Because this profession is people intensive, problems cannot be solved once and left behind. School psychologists are continuously educating and reeducating key administrative individuals and clients about the services of school psychologists. This attention is especially necessary in an era of high turnover of educational administrators, organizational leadership, budgetary constraints, and societal change.

Roles Clarification

A clarification of the whole spectrum of school psychologists' roles and functions is needed so that consumers (e.g., parents, teachers, and students) will have a better understanding of what practitioners can do. Although efforts at public relations by national and state organizations have increased greatly, school psychology still needs greater visibility.

Another need in role clarification is to distinguish between the terms "role" and "function." We should refrain from interchanging these terms and consider more closely what are the roles of the school psychologist and their attendant functions. Roles are not the things we do but rather the service conceptualizations within which we perform our functions. The distinction helps us to understand that the traditional role of the school psychologist is often victimized by concerns that are really directed at its functions. When critics contend that the profession must abandon the traditional assessment role of intelligence testing, what they mean is that school psychologists need to adjust the functions of the assessment role to include more instructionally relevant forms of testing or appraisal. The assessment role is central to most of the school psychologist's practice in traditional and nontraditional areas. Specializations such as neuropsychology, preschool, or vocational school psychology offer more modern functions to the traditional roles.

To fulfill the two historical roles of "child sorter" and "child repairer," school psychologists have developed functions such as remedial teaching, behavior modification, counseling and psychotherapy, and consultation. Repairs included the home as well as the learning environment. In more recent decades, school psychologists have expanded their roles to the study of systemic problems, becoming engineers to perform functions such as design, appraisal, consultation, advocacy, and systems change.

Every role school psychologists have filled has engaged them in areas of schooling where problems were perceived to exist, and their alleviation was expected to have positive instructional and mental health outcomes for children. These are central aspects of the education industry to which school psychologists are attached.

Technology

All roles and their attendant functions are influenced by technological advancements, especially in communications, assessment instrumentation, and interventions that rely on increasing medical and pharmaceutical discoveries. The 1994 and 2000 editions predicted that almost all practitioners would have incorporated the use of personal computers into their daily functions. Since then a communications revolution has occurred. Challenges of maintaining electronic confidentiality are rewarded with the greater ease of easily sharing observations and results. In addition, forthcoming breakthroughs in medical technology and pharmaceuticals will necessitate close relationships between school psychologists and the medical community.

Tolerance of Service Models and the Employment Context

School psychology is an important but small ship on the sea of education. We comprise about one-half of 1% of public school employees. We are hardly the center of the education universe. To school administrators, our role and function problems must appear relatively minor on a Monday morning when the buses are not running on time, the air conditioning is out at some buildings, and the teachers are threatening to go on strike. As a source of professional influence, school psychologists can only hope to achieve a position where they can provide sage counsel to the forces which make the waves on the sea. Beyond such counsel, school psychologists must be prepared to sail their ships on the calmest or the stormiest of seas, and to continue service provision in many modes as advocates for children and for psychological applications to education. Perhaps the same could be said for our relative status within psychology. However, we perceive school psychology to have a strong presence and status in both psychology and education. School psychology is expanding outward from center, away from its past of traditional roles, functions, and settings. Almost every conceivable type of school psychologist will exist in the coming decades. Roles and functions may be defined more by setting than in the past. We have expanded from a small group of clinic-based psychologists to a diverse field of practitioners in every school district nationwide, and in other settings as well. In our conceptualization, school psychology's future would be adversely restricted by selecting a minimum number of ideologies or models for the future and alienating the growth of others.

School psychologists must continue to appreciate their place in the employment context. School psychologists are associated with the education industry, among the largest industries in the nation. Most school psychologists have highly specific roles in the education industry despite the fact that some have other, perhaps even more preferred, roles. Critical appraisals of school psychologists as technicians versus professionals (e.g., Ysseldyke, 1986) imply that they should deny their traditional roles and functions in the system and assume similar roles (e.g., as professionals instead of as technicians). The technician–professional comparison is similar to the discussion by Phillips (1990b) of employing mechanistic and probabilistic paradigms in practice. Although we agree that many of the problems addressed by school psychologists do not lend themselves to simple technical solutions, some do, and the needs may change over time. Phillips (1990b) stated, "School psychologists apply their knowledge and skills in different ways, in different settings, and at different times, in accordance with current ideas within school psychology in particular and psychology in general, and within the public schools in particular and education in general" (p. 22). Bardon and Bennett (1974) viewed school psychology in three stages, with the Stage III practitioner of the present having emerged from earlier times when Stages I (tester) and II (clinician making diagnoses and recommendations) were more necessary, desirable, or convenient. Ysseldyke's and Phillips' conceptualization of the school psychologist as a professional is akin to Bardon and Bennett's Stage III "psychologist with a variety of skills and knowledge who applies his knowledge broadly and in diverse ways to a specific setting—the school" (p. 20). The same conceptualization permeates the three editions of the *School Psychology: Blueprint for Training and Practice*. We believe that for the foreseeable future there will continue to be school psychologists at various levels of role and function development. Such diversity has been typical of school psychology practice and may form the basis for two or more levels of training, credentialing, and practice in the future.

Considering the magnitude of the education industry in which school psychologists are employed, some comparisons to positions in other service industries may be instructive. If school psychologists were in the law enforcement system, would they be police officers, supervisors, or chiefs of police? In the postal system, would they be letter carriers, inspectors, or postmasters? Would they be flight attendants, pilots, or air traffic controllers? School psychologists should understand their roles in the educational system and perform them well while working to improve the opportunities for some school psychologists to perform other roles in the system. We need recognition of this diversity instead of the constant clamor that we should *all* be doing something more glamorous. Surely, school psychologists in Illinois or Wisconsin did not lobby for the right to administrative certification so that *all school psychologists would* become administrators! They did so in order that *some school psychologists could* become administrators (and if they wanted to, they could count their school psychology experience toward the attainment of that certificate).

In the future, most school psychologists will continue in the sorting and repairing roles but with new functions; many will also serve consultation roles, and some will serve research and evaluation or administrative roles.

We also wish to raise the question, *What's wrong with the sorter and repairer roles of the school psychologist?* We are not necessarily sanctioning the traditional functions here, but rather the roles. Are there not thousands of school psychologists satisfied with these roles? If you review the role and function studies of the past 40 years, when asked what they would *ideally* have as their roles, school psychologists persistently indicate one-third or more of their time in assessment, a higher proportion of time if you include preferences for traditional intervention roles. These surveys also reveal fairly high degrees of job satisfaction. If we abandoned traditional roles would we be serving the best interests of children or the education industry? The role and function critics refuse to recognize that every school psychologist cannot have a position analogous to a police chief, a postmaster, or an air traffic controller.

Every year or so our literature reports another study advocating the need for practitioners to provide particular services (Fagan, 2002). If a list were prepared of the articles about the importance of certain roles and functions of the school psychologist, it would make even the most competent practitioner feel deficient. The fact is that practitioners cannot be all things to all people and cannot all be experts in everything. In the future, most school psychologists will continue in the sorting and repairing roles but with new functions; many will also serve consultation roles, and some will serve research and evaluation or administrative roles. Is there not a need for various roles, and is there not room in the system for them all? If there is not, then the future of school psychology will be plagued with dissension and segmentation.

Roland Kaser (1993), a Swiss school psychologist, reviewed the desire by school psychologists to be something different than what they have been. Kaser raises an ethical issue stating, "Psychologists commit themselves, according to the ethical code of their profession, to make all efforts to protect the emotional and physical well-being of the individual. Renunciation of problem oriented, individual case work in favor of preventive work exclusively at the level of the school would be in violation of the basic ethical principles of the profession"(pp. 12–13). He raises several important issues including the absence of traditional services in the nonschool sector to which schools might turn for help, the illusion that individual problems of children can be avoided through even the best preventive services, and that role development needs to be conceptualized in a career context where experience and continuing education facilitate the expansion of roles and functions. In his developmental model, four foci of activity (diagnosis, counseling and consultation, supervision, and directing teaching or research) emerge over time in one's career as a function of additional training and experience. Thus practitioner careers move in the direction from diagnostic child study activities to broader activities such as consultation and supervision. Kaser's analysis is a stark contrast to conceptualizations of role change which imply that we should drop what we are now doing, and that even entry-level practitioners should pursue consultant, supervisor, and administrator roles in the absence of traditional experience.

CLOSING THOUGHTS

The future of school psychology appears to be very favorable. School psychology, positioned between psychology and education, has survived more than a century of change and growth and will continue to do so. As long-time trainers of school psychologists we have seen several changes in the profession come and go. Some were "flashes in the pan" while others lingered and have even become part of the practitioner's repertoire of skills. The profession as a whole has not changed that much over the past several decades. Many of the innovations were simply the things that the most effective school psychologists were already doing, such as working as a team member, consulting with parents and teachers, and serving the entire school population, not just students in need of special education. For perhaps the first time in our experience we are sensing a more permanent change for the future of school psychology practice. We believe that the models of flexible service delivery, response to intervention, outcome-based assessment in the schools, and others may permanently change the role that current students will be assuming in the future. We hope that school psychology will continue to be based on a strong foundation of data-based problem solving coupled with perhaps an increased emphasis on individual and group communication skills. Right now some of our alumni report dramatically changing roles, while others are still following a very traditional set of roles and functions. The profession will learn to accommodate both groups.

We have looked at the future along several of the dimensions on which we have described our past and our present. School psychology has a rich past, an unprecedented present, and a very promising future under almost any scenario drawn for psychology and education. The United States is increasing in its diversity in many ways. We are more culturally diverse. We have increasing diversity in products and services. Our telecommunications are also more diverse; phones are used for traditional one-to-one communication as well as conferences, data transmission, and even entertainment; and television seems to have a channel for every conceivable constituency. School psychology must find the means to manage its own inevitable diversity. There must be room for those whose jobs depend on traditional assessment functions; those who consult; those who do curriculum-based assessment, therapy, in-service education, or junior college work; those who work in rural or urban areas, in schools, agencies or independent practice; and those who work with all ages of people engaged in schooling.

School psychology has a rich past, an unprecedented present, and a very promising future under almost any scenario drawn for psychology and education.

James Gibson, an experimental psychologist, once noted that the world, when viewed from the caboose of a forward moving train, seems to flow inward while from the locomotive the world seems to flow outward (Neisser, 1981). Where we are positioned gives the impression of convergence or expansion even though looking at the same terrain. School psychology has always had to ride two trains at the same time: the train of psychology and that of education. Only recently has school psychology had a train of its own. At least on our own train, we need to view the future from the front. If there is no room for viewing the future as expanding, we will have a future that is little more than our past. If the field is fractionated in the next 20 years, it will be the result of trying to manage its future by ignoring its past.

> I do not know all the duties that the future will hold for the school psychologist but I will agree that it is a challenging array, never the same, with constantly new avenues of research opening up. There are large rewards in friendships and social contacts. The school psychologist is on the line of skirmish. There may be a lot of dust and noise, humor and pathos, but I guarantee it will never be a quiet or dull life. (Luckey, 1951, p. 10)

Discussion Questions and Practical Exercises

CHAPTER 1

Throughout, this book encourages readers to gather information about school psychology. Information related to the material in this chapter can be used to complete the data sheet in appendix A. The data sheet provides a convenient source of information from national and state levels for use during training and practice. It will provide up-to-date information about national and state organizations, training, and credentialing, as well as an overview of the practice of school psychology in a state and local area or region of interest. The data sheet will help readers respond to or complete the following.

1. How are school psychology services defined in your state and training program?
2. What are the results of state-level surveys of school psychologists' services in your state or local area?
3. How are school psychologists in your state dispersed, and what impact does this have on practice and state association activity?
4. What is the service ratio of school psychologists to children in your community and state?
5. What school psychology and related journals are available in your training institution's library?
6. What codes of ethics are employed by your state and local groups?
7. What state associations are in your state, and why are memberships in professional associations important?
8. How do salaries in your state and district compare with those reported in this chapter?
9. How do job prospects appear in your state?
10. Conduct a class discussion on the authors' assertion that assessment is the primary role of the school psychologist.

CHAPTER 2

1. Have members of your school psychology class select a name of an important contributor to school psychology and report on that person's career.
2. Explore the history of your local or state association of school psychologists.
3. Explore the history of your school psychology training program or the district in which area practitioners are employed.
4. Choose a 1- or 2-year period in the history of school psychology and review the literature of that time. What significant events occurred that had a lasting impact on the field?
5. Review the proceedings of one or more of the national school psychology conferences.
6. Compare this text on school psychology with that of Hildreth (1930) or one of the books of the 1960s.
7. Interview a senior member of the field to get personal perspectives on changes in practices over time.
8. Describe how recent practices (e.g., evidence-based intervention, functional–behavioral assessment, the response-to-intervention model) are being implemented in your local school system.

CHAPTER 3

1. Ask a local school administrator to visit your class and discuss the goals of the district and where psychological services fit into such goals.
2. How are school psychological services represented in your state department of education? Are they a part of pupil services or special education? Under whose authority are psychological services in your local district?
3. How are public schools financed in your state? What portions of local district financing are from federal, state, and local sources?
4. Diagram the organizational relationship of psychologists, including a school psychologist if employed, in a local or regional mental health center serving your community.
5. Discuss issues of power and authority, administrative organization, and clientage with a school psychologist in private practice.
6. What is the official policy position of school psychologists in your state or local district regarding collective bargaining and work stoppages?
7. Attend a meeting of the local school board, and report to your class on the issues discussed and their relevance to psychological services.

8. Diagram the administrative structure of education in your state and local district. Place the names of key administrators on your chart. Describe where school psychologists are located in this structure.
9. How has your district or agency complied with federal and state regulations regarding services for children with disabilities?
10. See how many reasons you can generate for the legitimate claim to clientage by children, parents, teachers, and administrators. Conduct an in-class debate on the topic.
11. Conduct a panel discussion on the structure of service delivery with school psychologists from public school, private school, mental health agency, and independent practice settings.
12. Create a file of community resources in a school district and community of your choosing. Note the commonality of resources to those gathered by others in your class.

CHAPTER 4

1. Make arrangements to shadow a school psychologist for a day, either in the area around your university or in your hometown. How does that person's day compare with the scenarios described above?
2. If your training program has an intern return day, ask the interns to describe a typical day. You might even ask all of the interns "What did you do yesterday?" to get a snapshot view of their activities.
3. After reading the three scenarios in Boxes 4.1–4.3, ask yourself which of the settings is most appealing to you and why.
4. Ask your program director if any recent alumni data show how graduates of your program spend their time.
5. If you have the opportunity to meet with experienced school psychologists, either in class or elsewhere, ask them how things have changed and are continuing to change over time.

CHAPTER 5

1. Review the statements listed in item "a".
   a. How could you define each statement sufficiently in order to measure a given individual's level of expertise?
      i. An excellent school psychologist administers tests quickly and accurately.

ii. An excellent school psychologist has superb interpersonal skills: People talk freely and listen to you, and people cooperate with you.
iii. An excellent school psychologist is committed to helping children.
iv. An excellent school psychologist writes excellent reports.
v. An excellent school psychologist performs in an exemplary manner even under less than perfect circumstances (e.g., outdated test kits, unreasonable number of students to serve, less than excellent team members).
vi. An excellent school psychologist performs in an exemplary manner in all professional settings (e.g., preschool through high school; assessment, counseling, and consultation).

b. Rank order each of the statements in terms of its importance to the practice of school psychology. Which one is most important? Which one is least important?

c. Are there items in the above list that you would like to have added or omitted?

2. Identify the characteristics of an excellent school psychology graduate student. How does an "excellent" student differ from an "adequate" student? Write a brief description evaluating your own strengths and weaknesses as a student in a school psychology program. Are you an excellent student? What evidence do you have to support your excellence? If you were asked to document your skills in the form of a personal portfolio, what materials would you include?

3. If you asked your family members, your friends, your professors, and your classmates whether or not you are an excellent student, would their answers agree? Why or why not?

4. In your state or national newsletters, locate the most recent recipient of the School Psychologist of the Year awards. What characteristics set the winner apart from other school psychologists?

5. Ask a school psychologist in your area to comment on the implementation of the response-to-intervention model in a local school district.

6. Discuss the difficulties inherent in developing a manual of evidence-based interventions.

CHAPTER 6

1. Prepare a summary of the history of the training program in which you are enrolled.

2. Would you describe your program's model of preparation as scientist–practitioner, professional, or pragmatic?

3. What is the nature of the accreditation(s) held by your program?

4. What are the characteristics and backgrounds of students in your program?
5. By sampling school psychologists in your area, develop a list of desirable personal characteristics of the school psychologist. What characteristics are considered critical by the faculty in your training program, and how are you judged on such characteristics?
6. Using the factors identified in Figure 6.1 and Table 6.3, provide a brief statement of the model employed by your training program.
7. How does your program ensure that students gain familiarity and understanding of the settings in which they will be employed and that they are exposed to multicultural influences on education?
8. What resources does your program offer for selecting advanced training programs and for reviewing SDE and SBEP licensing requirements?
9. How do the emphases in content areas in your program compare with those of Table 6.4?
10. Are paraprofessionals used in your local school districts? If so, how are they trained, what tasks do they perform, and what has been the impact on the supervising school psychologist?
11. In districts with both doctoral and nondoctoral practitioners, what differences in their respective roles and functions might be identified?

CHAPTER 7

1. What is the accreditation status of your training program and that of other programs in your state?
2. Survey other students in your program to determine in what states they intend to practice and whether they intend to work in school or nonschool settings.
3. What are the practice and nonpractice credentials of the faculty in your program and department?
4. Report to your class on the requirements of the ABSP and the National Certification System in school psychology.
5. What are the certification and licensure requirements in the state in which your training program is located?
6. What do practitioners in your area describe as the main determinants of their role and function?
7. What additional determinants can you think of, and where would they fit into Table 7.1?
8. What do practitioners in your area describe as their main legal or ethical problems?

9. How are alleged ethical violations adjudicated by practitioners in your state?
10. What have been the results of state and federal monitoring visits to your local school district? Are the district and its psychological services considered to be in compliance with the provisions of IDEA and the NCLB?
11. What types of liability insurance are carried by the school psychologists in your local district?

CHAPTER 8

The following questions should be completed by students on the basis of written or oral information from training program faculty, former students, area practitioners, and the state department of education.

1. Requirements
   a. Does this state require an internship in order to become a certified school psychologist?
   b. What are the state requirements for field experience and internship?
   c. Must I complete my internship in this state if I want to be certified here?
   d. What happens if, for a variety of reasons (e.g., health, personal crisis, incompatibility with a supervisor), I do not complete the full internship?
   e. How is the internship graded and who does the grading?
   f. What if I do not pass? Can I complete another internship?
   g. Must I complete my internship in a public school setting?
   h. Do I need to take some sort of state or national certification test in addition to the internship in order to be certified as a school psychologist?
2. Practical considerations
   a. What kinds of supervision will I get from the university?
   b. What kinds of supervision should I expect from my site supervisor?
   c. Are certain internship sites considered exemplary?
   d. Are certain internship sites considered unacceptable?
   e. How do exemplary internship sites differ from unacceptable sites?
   f. If I want to be employed in a certain state eventually, would I be better off doing my internship there or waiting until after the internship to move?
   g. If I complete my internship here and then decide to move to another state, how easy will it be for me to find employment and to become certified?
   h. Should I complete an internship even if I want to get my doctorate and teach at a university?
   i. Can I wait and complete my internship in a few years, or must I complete it at a particular time in the program?
   j. If I want to or need to stay in this immediate area, what kind of internship will I be able to find?
   k. How much do internships in this state typically pay? How is this salary determined?

3. Ask your program coordinator or other program faculty about nontraditional jobs that program alumni have taken. Check with the faculty to see if one or more of the nontraditional school psychologists could be invited to speak to students in the program. Come up with questions to ask the individuals regarding the advantages and disadvantages of their jobs compared with the more traditional job of a school psychologist.
4. Ask the faculty members in your program why they decided to become faculty members rather than practicing school psychologists.
5. Find out what practitioners in your area are planning after retirement.

Appendix A

School Psychology Data Sheet

NATIONAL LEVEL

National Association of School Psychologists (NASP)
4340 East West Highway, Suite 402
Bethesda, MD 20814-9457
Phone: (301) 657-0270; FAX (301) 657-0275
Website: *http://www.nasponline.org*

Executive Director: ____________________

President: ____________________

Dates and location of next convention: ____________________

____

Current membership total: __________

Annual dues: Member rate: __________ Student rate: __________

Journal: *School Psychology Review*, Editor contact: ____________________

Newspaper *Communiqué*, Editor contact: ____________________

NASP region in which your state is located: ____________________

Name of your regional delegate representative: ____________________

Name of your NASP state delegate: ____________________

Current number of NASP members in your state: __________

American Psychological Association (APA)
750 First St. NE
Washington, DC 20002-4242
(202) 336-5500
Website: *http://www.apa.org*

Executive Director: ______________________________

President: ______________________________

Division 16 President: ______________________________

Dates and location of next convention: ______________________________

____

Current membership total: ____________ (APA) ____________ (Div. 16)

Annual dues: Member rate: ____________ (APA) ____________ (Div. 16)

Student rate: ____________ (APA) ____________ (Div. 16)

APA journals:

American Psychologist, Editor contact: ______________________________

School Psychology Quarterly, Editor contact: ______________________________

GradPsych (for students), contact: *www.gradpsych.apags.org*

APA newsletters:

Monitor on Psychology, Editor contact: ______________________________

The School Psychologist, Editor contact: ______________________________

STATE LEVEL

State School Psychology Association

Name: ______________________________

Address: ______________________________

____

____

Phone: ______________________________

Website: ______________________________

President: ______________________________

President-Elect: ______________________________

Dates and location of next convention: ______________________________

____

Newsletter: ______________ Editor contact: ______________

Number of members: ______________

Annual dues: Member rate: ____________ Student rate: ____________

State Psychology Association

Name: ______________________________

Address: ______________________________

____

Phone: ______________________________

Website: ______________________________

President: ______________________________

President-Elect: ______________________________

Dates and location of next convention: ______________________________

____

Newsletter: ______________ Editor contact: ______________

Number of members: ______________

Annual dues: Member rate: ____________ Student rate: ____________

State Department of Education

Name: ____

Address: ____

____

Phone: ______________________________

SDE Website: ____

State Commissioner: ___________________________________

State Consultant for School Psychology: ___________________

State's definition of school psychologist: __________________

____

____

School Psychology Training Programs in Your State

Names of Programs *Available Degrees*

1. ____
2. ____
3. ____
4. ____
5. ____

Credentialing in Your State

State education agency name: __________________________

Credentials offered: ______________________________

Website: _______________________________________

State psychology board name: __________________________

Credentials offered: ____

Website: ____

Other agency name: ____

Credentials offered: ____

Website: ____

Other Information

Number of practitioners in the United States: ______________________

Number of practitioners in your state: __________________________

Number of practitioners in your city/county: _____________________

Number of practitioners in your school district: ___________________

Appendix B

Primary Journals and Books on School Psychology

JOURNALS ON SCHOOL PSYCHOLOGY

California Journal of School Psychology, CASP Office, 1400 K St., Suite 311, Sacramento, CA 95814.

Canadian Journal of School Psychology, Division of Applied Psychology, University of Calgary, 2500 University Dr. NW, Calgary, Alberta, T2N 1N4 Canada.

Journal of Applied School Psychology, Haworth Press, 10 Alice St., Binghamton, NY 13904-1580.

Journal of Educational and Psychological Consultation, Lawrence Erlbaum Associates, 10 Industrial Ave., Mahwah, NJ 07430-2262.

Journal of School Psychology, Elsevier, 6277 Sea Harbor Dr., Orlando, FL 32887-4800.

Psychology in the Schools, John Wiley and Sons, 111 River St., Hoboken, NJ 07030-5774.

School Psychology Forum: Research in Practice. An online journal available to members at the NASP website; first issue published in November 2006.

School Psychology International, Sage Publications, 2455 Teller Rd., Thousand Oaks, CA 91320-2218.

School Psychology Quarterly (formerly *Professional School Psychology*), American Psychological Association, 750 First St. NE, Washington, DC 20002-4242.

School Psychology Review (formerly *School Psychology Digest*), National Association of School Psychologists, 4340 East West Highway, Suite 402, Bethesda, MD 20814-9457.

BOOKS ON SCHOOL PSYCHOLOGY

This list was prepared in part from citations appearing in Fagan, Delugach, Mellon, and Schlitt (1985); Fagan (1986b); French (1986); Whelan and Carlson (1986), and Kraus and Mclaughlin (1997). All of the references cited are maintained in Tom Fagan's collection of school psychology literature.

Alpert, J. L., & Associates. (1982). *Psychological consultation in educational settings.* San Francisco: Jossey-Bass.

Attwell, A. A. (1972). *The school psychologist's handbook* (Rev. in 1976). Los Angeles: Western Psychological Services.

Bardon, J. I., & Bennett, V. C. (1974). *School psychology.* Englewood Cliffs, NJ: Prentice Hall.

Bergan, J. R. (Ed.). (1985). *School psychology in contemporary society: An introduction.* Columbus, OH: Charles E. Merrill.

Blanco, R. F., & Rosenfeld, J. G. (1978). *Case studies in clinical and school psychology.* Springfield, IL: Charles C. Thomas.

Brown, D., Pryzwansky, W. B., & Schulte, A. C. (1998). *Psychological consultation: Introduction to theory and practice.* Boston: Allyn & Bacon.

Carroll, J. L. (Ed.). (1978). *Contemporary school psychology* (*Selected readings from* Psychology in the Schools).Brandon, VT: Clinical Psychology Publishing Co. Selected readings in three topic areas: The Role of the School Psychologist: An Historical Perspective; Functioning as a School Psychologist; and Legal and Ethical Issues

Carroll, J. L. (Ed.). (1981). *Contemporary school psychology* (*Readings from* Psychology in the Schools). Brandon, VT: Clinical Psychology Publishing Co. Selected reading in three topic areas: The Role of the School Psychologist: Action and Reaction; Functioning as a School Psychologist: Divergent Directions; and Legal and Ethical Issues: Muddying the Waters.

Catterall, C. D. (Ed.). (1976–1979). *Psychology in the schools in international perspective* (Vols. 1–3). Columbus, OH: Author (92 S. Dawson Ave., 43209).

Claiborn, W. L., & Cohen, R. (Eds.). (1973). *School intervention* (Vol. 1). New York: Behavioral Publications. (Volume in a continuing series in community-clinical psychology.)

Cole, E., & Siegel, J. A. (Eds.). (1992). *Effective consultation in school psychology.* Toronto: Hogrefe & Huber.

Conoley, J. C., & Conoley, C. W. (1982). *School consultation: A guide to practice and training*. New York: Pergamon Press.

Conoley, J. C., & Conoley, C. W. (1992). *School consultation: Practice and training* (2nd ed.). New York: Macmillan.

Cull, J. G., & Golden, L. B. (Eds.). (1984). *Psychotherapeutic techniques in school psychology.* Springfield, IL: Charles C. Thomas.

Curtis, M. J., & Zins, J. E. (Eds.). (1981). *The theory and practice of school consultation*. Springfield, IL: Charles C. Thomas. (All but a few of the chapters are previously published articles in school psychology and related journals.)

Cutts, N. E. (Ed.). (1955). *School psychologists at mid-century.* Washington, DC: American Psychological Association.

D'Amato, R. C., & Dean, R. S. (Eds.). (1989). *The school psychologist in nontraditional settings: Integrating clients, services, and setting*. Hillsdale, NJ: Erlbaum.

Educational Testing Service. (2003). *Study guide: School leaders and services.* Princeton, NJ: Author.

Eiserer, P. E. (1963). *The school psychologist.* Washington, DC: Center for Applied Research in Education.

Elliott, S. N., & Witt, J. C. (Eds.). (1986). *The delivery of psychological services in schools: Concepts, processes, and issues*. Hillsdale, NJ: Erlbaum.

Erchul, W. P., & Martens, B. K. (1997). *School consultation: Conceptual and empirical bases of practice*. New York: Plenum Press.

Esquivel, G. B., Lopez, E. C., & Nahari, S. G. (Eds.). (2006). *Handbook of multicultural school psychology: An interdisciplinary perspective*. Mahwah, NJ: Erlbaum.

Fagan, T. K., Delugach, F. J., Mellon, M., & Schlitt, P. (1986). *A bibliographic guide to the literature of professional school psychology 1890-1985*. Washington, DC: National Association of School Psychologists.

Fagan, T. K., & Warden, P. G. (Eds.). (1996). *Historical encyclopedia of school psychology.* Westport, CT: Greenwood.

Fagan, T. K., & Wise, P. S. (1994). *School psychology: Past, present, and future*. White Plains, NY: Longman.

Fagan, T. K., & Wise, P. S. (2000). *School psychology: Past, present, and future* (2nd ed.). Bethesda, MD: National Association of School Psychologists.

Fagan, T. K., & Wise, P. S. (2007). *School psychology: Past, present, and future* (3rd ed.). Bethesda, MD: National Association of School Psychologists.

Fairchild, T. N. (Ed.). (1977). *Accountability for school psychologists: Selected readings.* Washington, DC: University Press of America. (A collection of articles published in school psychology journals and some nonpublished speeches, etc.)

Fein, L. G. (1974). *The changing school scene: Challenge to psychology.* New York: Wiley.

Fine, M. J. (Ed.). (1989). *School psychology: Cutting edges in research and practice.* Washington, DC: National Education Association and the National Association of School Psychologists.

Fischer, L., & Sorenson, G. P. (1991). *School law for counselors, psychologists, and social workers.* New York: Longman.

Frisby, C. L., & Reynolds, C. R. (Eds.). (2005). *Comprehensive handbook of multicultural school psychology.* Hoboken, NJ: Wiley.

Gelinas, P. J., & Gelinas, R. P. (1968). *A definitive study of your future in school psychology.* New York: Richards Rosen Press.

Gottsegen, M. G., & Gottsegen, G. B. (Eds.). (1960–1969). *Professional school psychology* (Vol. 1–3). New York: Grune & Stratton.

Gray, S. W. (1963). *The psychologist in the schools.* New York: Holt-Rinehart & Winston.

Gredler, G. R. (Ed.). (1972). *Ethical and legal factors in the practice of school psychology: Proceedings of the First Annual Conference in School Psychology.* Philadelphia, PA: Temple University.

Gutkin, T. B., & Reynolds, C. R. (Eds.). (1990). *The handbook of school psychology* (2nd ed.). New York: Wiley.

Harvey, V. S., & Struzziero, J. (2000). *Effective supervision in school psychology.* Bethesda, MD: National Association of School Psychologists.

Herron, W. G., Green, M., Guild, M., Smith, A., & Kantor, R. E. (1970). *Contemporary school psychology.* Scranton, PA: Intext.

Herron, W. G., Herron, M. J., & Handron, J. (1984). *Contemporary school psychology: Handbook of practice, theory, and research.* Cranston, RI: Carroll Press.

Hildreth, G. H. (1930). *Psychological service for school problems.* Yonkers-On-Hudson, NY: World Book Co. (Perhaps the earliest book on school psychology that employs the term *school psychologist.*)

Hirst, W. E. (1963). *Know your school psychologist.* New York: Grune & Stratton.

Holt, F. D., & Kicklighter, R. H. (Eds.). (1971). *Psychological services in the schools: Readings in preparation, organization and practice.* Dubuque, IA: Wm. C. Brown. (Mostly reprints from school psychology and related journals.)

Hynd, G. W. (Ed.). (1983). *The school psychologist: An introduction.* Syracuse, NY: Syracuse University Press.

International Bureau of Education. (1948). *School psychologists.* (Publication No. 105). Paris: UNESCO.

Jackson, J. H., & Bernauer, M. (Eds.). (1968). *The psychologist as a therapist.* Milwaukee, WI: Milwaukee Public Schools.

Jacob, S., & Hartshorne, T. (1991). *Ethics and law for school psychologists.* Brandon, VT: Clinical Psychology Publishing.

Jacob-Timm, S., & Hartshorne, T. S. (1994). *Ethics and law for school psychologists* (2nd ed.). Brandon, VT: Clinical Psychology Publishing Company.

Jacob-Timm, S., & Hartshorne, T. S. (1998). *Ethics and law for school psychologists* (3rd ed.). New York: Wiley.

Jacob, S., & Hartshorne, T. S. (2003). *Ethics and law for school psychologists* (4th ed.). New York: Wiley.

Jacob, S., & Hartshorne, T. S. (2007). *Ethics and law for school psychologists* (5th ed.). Hoboken, NJ: Wiley.

Jimerson, S. R., Oakland, T. D., & Farrell, P. T. (Eds.). (2006). *The handbook of international school psychology.* Thousand Oaks, CA: Sage.

Kratochwill, T. R. (Ed.). (1981–1990). *Advances in school psychology* (Vols. 1–7). Hillsdale, NJ: Erlbaum.

Kratochwill, T. R., Elliott, S. N., & Gettinger, M. (Eds.). (1992). *Advances in school psychology* (Vol. 8). Hillsdale, NJ: Erlbaum.

Lawrence, M. M. (1971). *The mental health team in the schools.* New York: Behavioral Publications.

Lee, S. W. (Ed.). (2005). *Encyclopedia of school psychology.* Thousand Oaks, CA: Sage.

Magary, J. F. (Ed.). (1967). *School psychological services in theory and practice, a handbook.* Englewood Cliffs, NJ: Prentice Hall.

Maher, C.A., Illback, R. J., & Zins, J. E. (Eds.). (1984). *Organizational psychology in the schools: A handbook for professionals.* Springfield, IL: Charles C. Thomas.

Marzolf, S. S. (1956). *Psychological diagnosis and counseling in the schools.* New York: Holt, Rinehart & Winston.

Medway, F. J., & Cafferty, T. P. (1992). *School psychology: A social psychological perspective.* Hillsdale, NJ: Erlbaum.

Merrell, K. W., Ervin, R. A., & Gimpel, G. A. (2006). *School psychology for the 21st century.* New York: Guilford.

Meyers, J., Martin, R., & Hyman, I. (Eds.). (1977). *School consultation: Readings about preventive techniques for pupil personnel workers.* Springfield, IL: Charles C. Thomas.

Meyers, J., Parsons, R. D., & Martin, R. (1979). *Mental health consultation in the schools.* San Francisco: Jossey-Bass.

Miezitis, S., & Orme, M. (Eds.). (1977). *Innovation in school psychology.* Toronto: The Ontario Institute for Studies in Education.

Milofsky, C. (1989). *Testers and testing: The sociology of school psychology.* New Brunswick, NJ: Rutgers University Press.

Mok, P. P. (1962). *A view from within: American education at the crossroads of individualism.* New York: Carlton Press.

Nolen, P. A. (1983). *School psychologist's handbook: Writing the educational report.* Springfield, IL: Charles C. Thomas.

Phillips, B. N. (1990). *School psychology at a turning point: Ensuring a bright future for the profession.* San Francisco: Jossey-Bass.

Phye, G. D., & Reschly, D. J. (Eds.). (1979). *School psychology perspectives and issues.* New York: Academic Press.

Plas, J. M. (1986). *Systems psychology in the schools.* New York, NY: Pergamon Press.

Reger, R. (1965). *School psychology.* Springfield, IL: Charles C. Thomas.

Reynolds, C. R., & Gutkin, T. B. (Eds.). (1982). *The handbook of school psychology.* New York: Wiley.

Reynolds, C. R., & Gutkin, T. B. (Eds.). (1999). *The handbook of school psychology* (3rd ed.). New York: Wiley.

Reynolds, C. R., Gutkin, T. B., Elliott, S. N., & Witt, J. C. (1984). *School psychology: Essentials of theory and practice.* New York: Wiley.

Rosenbaum, D. S., & Toepfer, C. F. (1966). *Curriculum planning and school psychology: The coordinated approach.* Buffalo, NY: Hertillon Press.

Saigh, P., & Oakland, T. (Eds.). (1989). *International perspectives on psychology in the schools.* Hillsdale, NJ: Erlbaum.

Schmuck, R. A., & Miles, M. B. (Eds.). (1971). *Organization development in schools.* Palo Alto, CA: National Press Books.

Scholl, G. T. (Ed.). (1985). *The school psychologist and the exceptional child.* Reston, VA: Council for Exceptional Children.

Shapiro, E. S. (1987). *Behavioral assessment in school psychology.* Hillsdale, NJ: Erlbaum.

Spadafore, G. J. (Ed.). (1981). *School psychology: Issues and answers.* Muncie, IN: Accelerated Development, Inc. (The readings are previously published articles or presentations.)

Talley, R. C., Kubiszyn, T., Brassard, M., & Short, R. J. (Eds.). (1996). *Making psychologists in schools indispensable: Critical questions and emerging perspectives.* Washington, DC: American Psychological Association.

Thomas, A., & Grimes, J. (Eds.). (1985). *Best practices in school psychology.* Washington, DC: National Association of School Psychologists.

Thomas, A., & Grimes, J. (Eds.). (1990). *Best practices in school psychology II.* Silver Spring, MD: National Association of School Psychologists.

Thomas, A., & Grimes, J. (Eds.). (1995). *Best practices in school psychology III.* Washington, DC: National Association of School Psychologists.

Thomas, A., & Grimes, J. (Eds.). (2002). *Best practices in school psychology IV* (Vols. 1 & 2). Bethesda, MD: National Association of School Psychologists.

Thomas, A., & Grimes, J. (Eds.). (2008). *Best practices in school psychology V.* Bethesda, MD: National Association of School Psychologists.

United Nations Educational, Scientific and Cultural Organization. (1948). *School psychologists* (International Bureau of Education Publication No. 105). Geneva, Switzerland: Author.

Valett, R. E. (1963). *The practice of school psychology: Professional problems.* New York: Wiley.

Wall, W. D. (Ed.). (1956). *Psychological services for schools.* New York: New York University Press.

Wallin, J. E. W. (1914). *The mental health of the school child (The psycho-educational clinic in relation to child welfare, contributions to a new science of orthophrenics and orthosomatics).* New Haven, CT: Yale University Press. (Some of the chapters were previously published but were substantially revised.)

Watson, S. T., & Skinner, C. H. (Eds.). (2004). *Encyclopedia of school psychology.* Cambridge, MA: Springer.

White, M. A., & Harris, M. W. (1961). *The school psychologist.* New York: Harper.

Woody, R. H., LaVoie, J. C., & Epps, S. (1992). *School psychology: A developmental and social systems approach.* Boston: Allyn & Bacon.

Ysseldyke, J. E. (Ed.). (1984). *School psychology: The state of the art.* Minneapolis, MN: University of Minnesota, National School Psychology Inservice Training Network.

Appendix C

American Psychological Association Ethical Principles of Psychologists and Code of Conduct

CONTENTS

2.05 Delegation of Work to Others
2.06 Personal Problems and Conflicts

3. Human Relations
3.01 Unfair Discrimination
3.02 Sexual Harassment
3.03 Other Harassment
3.04 Avoiding Harm
3.05 Multiple Relationships
3.06 Conflict of Interest
3.07 Third-Party Requests for Services
3.08 Exploitative Relationships
3.09 Cooperation With Other Professionals
3.10 Informed Consent
3.11 Psychological Services Delivered to or Through Organizations
3.12 Interruption of Psychological Services

4. Privacy and Confidentiality
4.01 Maintaining Confidentiality
4.02 Discussing the Limits of Confidentiality
4.03 Recording
4.04 Minimizing Intrusions on Privacy
4.05 Disclosures
4.06 Consultations
4.07 Use of Confidential Information for Didactic or Other Purposes

5. Advertising and Other Public Statements
5.01 Avoidance of False or Deceptive Statements
5.02 Statements by Others
5.03 Descriptions of Workshops and Non-Degree-Granting Educational Programs
5.04 Media Presentations
5.05 Testimonials
5.06 In-Person Solicitation

6. Record Keeping and Fees
6.01 Documentation of Professional and Scientific Work and Maintenance of Records
6.02 Maintenance, Dissemination, and Disposal of Confidential Records of Professional and Scientific Work
6.03 Withholding Records for Nonpayment
6.04 Fees and Financial Arrangements
6.05 Barter With Clients/Patients
6.06 Accuracy in Reports to Payors and Funding Sources
6.07 Referrals and Fees

7. Education and Training
   - 7.01 Design of Education and Training Programs
   - 7.02 Descriptions of Education and Training Programs
   - 7.03 Accuracy in Teaching
   - 7.04 Student Disclosure of Personal Information
   - 7.05 Mandatory Individual or Group Therapy
   - 7.06 Assessing Student and Supervisee Performance
   - 7.07 Sexual Relationships With Students and Supervisees

8. Research and Publication
   - 8.01 Institutional Approval
   - 8.02 Informed Consent to Research
   - 8.03 Informed Consent for Recording Voices and Images in Research
   - 8.04 Client/Patient, Student, and Subordinate Research Participants
   - 8.05 Dispensing With Informed Consent for Research
   - 8.06 Offering Inducements for Research Participation
   - 8.07 Deception in Research
   - 8.08 Debriefing
   - 8.09 Humane Care and Use of Animals in Research
   - 8.10 Reporting Research Results
   - 8.11 Plagiarism
   - 8.12 Publication Credit
   - 8.13 Duplicate Publication of Data
   - 8.14 Sharing Research Data for Verification
   - 8.15 Reviewers

9. Assessment
   - 9.01 Bases for Assessments
   - 9.02 Use of Assessments
   - 9.03 Informed Consent in Assessments
   - 9.04 Release of Test Data
   - 9.05 Test Construction
   - 9.06 Interpreting Assessment Results
   - 9.07 Assessment by Unqualified Persons
   - 9.08 Obsolete Tests and Outdated Test Results
   - 9.09 Test Scoring and Interpretation Services
   - 9.10 Explaining Assessment Results
   - 9.11. Maintaining Test Security

10. Therapy
    - 10.01 Informed Consent to Therapy
    - 10.02 Therapy Involving Couples or Families
    - 10.03 Group Therapy
    - 10.04 Providing Therapy to Those Served by Others
    - 10.05 Sexual Intimacies With Current Therapy Clients/Patients

10.06 Sexual Intimacies With Relatives or Significant Others of Current Therapy Clients/Patients
10.07 Therapy With Former Sexual Partners
10.08 Sexual Intimacies With Former Therapy Clients/Patients
10.09 Interruption of Therapy
10.10 Terminating Therapy

INTRODUCTION AND APPLICABILITY

The American Psychological Association's (APA's) Ethical Principles of Psychologists and Code of Conduct (hereinafter referred to as the *Ethics Code*) consists of an Introduction, a Preamble, five General Principles (A–E), and specific Ethical Standards. The Introduction discusses the intent, organization, procedural considerations, and scope of application of the Ethics Code. The Preamble and General Principles are aspirational goals to guide psychologists toward the highest ideals of psychology. Although the Preamble and General Principles are not themselves enforceable rules, they should be considered by psychologists in arriving at an ethical course of action. The Ethical Standards set forth enforceable rules for conduct as psychologists. Most of the Ethical Standards are written broadly, in order to apply to psychologists in varied roles, although the application of an Ethical Standard may vary depending on the context. The Ethical Standards are not exhaustive. The fact that a given conduct is not specifically addressed by an Ethical Standard does not mean that it is necessarily either ethical or unethical.

This Ethics Code applies only to psychologists' activities that are part of their scientific, educational, or professional roles as psychologists. Areas covered include but are not limited to the clinical, counseling, and school practice of psychology; research; teaching; supervision of trainees; public service; policy development; social intervention; development of assessment instruments; conducting assessments; educational counseling; organizational consulting; forensic activities; program design and evaluation; and administration. This Ethics Code applies to these activities across a variety of contexts, such as in person, postal, telephone, Internet, and other electronic transmissions. These activities shall be distinguished from the purely private conduct of psychologists, which is not within the purview of the Ethics Code.

Membership in the APA commits members and student affiliates to comply with the standards of the APA Ethics Code and to the rules and procedures used to enforce them. Lack of awareness or misunderstanding of an Ethical Standard is not itself a defense to a charge of unethical conduct.

The procedures for filing, investigating, and resolving complaints of unethical conduct are described in the current Rules and Procedures of the APA Ethics Committee. APA may impose sanctions on its members for violations of the standards of the Ethics Code, including termination of APA membership, and may notify other bodies and individuals of its actions. Actions that violate the standards of the Ethics Code may also lead to the imposition of sanctions on psychologists or students whether or not they are APA members by bodies other than APA, including state psychological associations, other professional groups, psychology boards, other state or federal agencies, and payors for health services. In addition, APA may take action against a member after his or her conviction of a felony, expulsion or suspension from an affiliated state psychological association, or suspension or loss of licensure. When the sanction to be imposed by APA is less than expulsion, the 2001 Rules and Procedures do not guarantee an opportunity for an in-person hearing, but generally provide that complaints will be resolved only on the basis of a submitted record.

The Ethics Code is intended to provide guidance for psychologists and standards of professional conduct that can be applied by the APA and by other bodies that choose to adopt them. The Ethics Code is not intended to be a basis of civil liability. Whether a psychologist has violated the Ethics Code standards does not by itself determine whether the psychologist is legally liable in a court action, whether a contract is enforceable, or whether other legal consequences occur.

The modifiers used in some of the standards of this Ethics Code (e.g., reasonably, appropriate, potentially) are included in the standards when they would (1) allow professional judgment on the part of psychologists, (2) eliminate injustice or inequality that would occur without the modifier, (3) ensure applicability across the broad range of activities conducted by psychologists, or (4) guard against a set of rigid rules that might be quickly outdated. As used in this Ethics Code, the term *reasonable* means the prevailing professional judgment of psychologists engaged in similar activities in similar circumstances, given the knowledge the psychologist had or should have had at the time.

In the process of making decisions regarding their professional behavior, psychologists must consider this Ethics Code in addition to applicable laws and psychology board regulations. In applying the Ethics Code to their professional work, psychologists may consider other materials and guidelines that have been adopted or endorsed by scientific and professional psychological organizations and the dictates of their own conscience, as well as consult with others within the field. If this Ethics Code establishes a higher standard of conduct than is required by law, psychologists must meet the higher ethical standard. If psychologists' ethical responsibilities conflict with law, regulations, or other governing legal authority, psychologists make known their commitment to this Ethics Code and take steps to resolve the conflict in a responsible manner. If the conflict is unresolvable via such means, psychologists may adhere to the requirements of the law, regulations, or other governing authority in keeping with basic principles of human rights.

PREAMBLE

Psychologists are committed to increasing scientific and professional knowledge of behavior and people's understanding of themselves and others and to the use of such knowledge to improve the condition of individuals, organizations, and society. Psychologists respect and protect civil and human rights and the central importance of freedom of inquiry and expression in research, teaching, and publication. They strive to help the public in developing informed judgments and choices concerning human behavior. In doing so, they perform many roles, such as researcher, educator, diagnostician, therapist, supervisor, consultant, administrator, social interventionist, and expert witness. This Ethics Code provides a common set of principles and standards upon which psychologists build their professional and scientific work.

This Ethics Code is intended to provide specific standards to cover most situations encountered by psychologists. It has as its goals the welfare and protection of the individuals and groups with whom psychologists work and the education of members, students, and the public regarding ethical standards of the discipline.

The development of a dynamic set of ethical standards for psychologists' work-related conduct requires a personal commitment and lifelong effort to act ethically;

to encourage ethical behavior by students, supervisees, employees, and colleagues; and to consult with others concerning ethical problems.

GENERAL PRINCIPLES

This section consists of General Principles. General Principles, as opposed to Ethical Standards, are aspirational in nature. Their intent is to guide and inspire psychologists toward the very highest ethical ideals of the profession. General Principles, in contrast to Ethical Standards, do not represent obligations and should not form the basis for imposing sanctions. Relying upon General Principles for either of these reasons distorts both their meaning and purpose.

Principle A: Beneficence and Nonmaleficence

Psychologists strive to benefit those with whom they work and take care to do no harm. In their professional actions, psychologists seek to safeguard the welfare and rights of those with whom they interact professionally and other affected persons, and the welfare of animal subjects of research. When conflicts occur among psychologists' obligations or concerns, they attempt to resolve these conflicts in a responsible fashion that avoids or minimizes harm. Because psychologists' scientific and professional judgments and actions may affect the lives of others, they are alert to and guard against personal, financial, social, organizational, or political factors that might lead to misuse of their influence. Psychologists strive to be aware of the possible effect of their own physical and mental health on their ability to help those with whom they work.

Principle B: Fidelity and Responsibility

Psychologists establish relationships of trust with those with whom they work. They are aware of their professional and scientific responsibilities to society and to the specific communities in which they work. Psychologists uphold professional standards of conduct, clarify their professional roles and obligations, accept appropriate responsibility for their behavior, and seek to manage conflicts of interest that could lead to exploitation or harm. Psychologists consult with, refer to, or cooperate with other professionals and institutions to the extent needed to serve the best interests of those with whom they work. They are concerned about the ethical compliance of their colleagues' scientific and professional conduct. Psychologists strive to contribute a portion of their professional time for little or no compensation or personal advantage.

Principle C: Integrity

Psychologists seek to promote accuracy, honesty, and truthfulness in the science, teaching, and practice of psychology. In these activities psychologists do not steal, cheat, or engage in fraud, subterfuge, or intentional misrepresentation of fact.

Psychologists strive to keep their promises and to avoid unwise or unclear commitments. In situations in which deception may be ethically justifiable to maximize benefits and minimize harm, psychologists have a serious obligation to consider the need for, the possible consequences of, and their responsibility to correct any resulting mistrust or other harmful effects that arise from the use of such techniques.

Principle D: Justice

Psychologists recognize that fairness and justice entitle all persons to access to and benefit from the contributions of psychology and to equal quality in the processes, procedures, and services being conducted by psychologists. Psychologists exercise reasonable judgment and take precautions to ensure that their potential biases, the boundaries of their competence, and the limitations of their expertise do not lead to or condone unjust practices.

Principle E: Respect for People's Rights and Dignity

Psychologists respect the dignity and worth of all people, and the rights of individuals to privacy, confidentiality, and self-determination. Psychologists are aware that special safeguards may be necessary to protect the rights and welfare of persons or communities whose vulnerabilities impair autonomous decision making. Psychologists are aware of and respect cultural, individual, and role differences, including those based on age, gender, gender identity, race, ethnicity, culture, national origin, religion, sexual orientation, disability, language, and socioeconomic status, and consider these factors when working with members of such groups. Psychologists try to eliminate the effect on their work of biases based on those factors, and they do not knowingly participate in or condone activities of others based upon such prejudices.

ETHICAL STANDARDS

1. Resolving Ethical Issues

1.01 Misuse of Psychologists' Work

If psychologists learn of misuse or misrepresentation of their work, they take reasonable steps to correct or minimize the misuse or misrepresentation.

1.02 Conflicts Between Ethics and Law, Regulations, or Other Governing Legal Authority

If psychologists' ethical responsibilities conflict with law, regulations, or other governing legal authority, psychologists make known their commitment to the Ethics Code and take steps to resolve the conflict. If the conflict is unresolvable via such means, psychologists may adhere to the requirements of the law, regulations, or other governing legal authority.

1.03 Conflicts Between Ethics and Organizational Demands

If the demands of an organization with which psychologists are affiliated or for whom they are working conflict with this Ethics Code, psychologists clarify the nature of the conflict, make known their commitment to the Ethics Code, and to the extent feasible, resolve the conflict in a way that permits adherence to the Ethics Code.

1.04 Informal Resolution of Ethical Violations

When psychologists believe that there may have been an ethical violation by another psychologist, they attempt to resolve the issue by bringing it to the attention of that individual, if an informal resolution appears appropriate and the intervention does not violate any confidentiality rights that may be involved. (See also Standards 1.02, Conflicts Between Ethics and Law, Regulations, or Other Governing Legal Authority, and 1.03, Conflicts Between Ethics and Organizational Demands.)

1.05 Reporting Ethical Violations

If an apparent ethical violation has substantially harmed or is likely to substantially harm a person or organization and is not appropriate for informal resolution under Standard 1.04, Informal Resolution of Ethical Violations, or is not resolved properly in that fashion, psychologists take further action appropriate to the situation. Such action might include referral to state or national committees on professional ethics, to state licensing boards, or to the appropriate institutional authorities. This standard does not apply when an intervention would violate confidentiality rights or when psychologists have been retained to review the work of another psychologist whose professional conduct is in question. (See also Standard 1.02, Conflicts Between Ethics and Law, Regulations, or Other Governing Legal Authority.)

1.06 Cooperating With Ethics Committees

Psychologists cooperate in ethics investigations, proceedings, and resulting requirements of the APA or any affiliated state psychological association to which they belong. In doing so, they address any confidentiality issues. Failure to cooperate is itself an ethics violation. However, making a request for deferment of adjudication of an ethics complaint pending the outcome of litigation does not alone constitute noncooperation.

1.07 Improper Complaints

Psychologists do not file or encourage the filing of ethics complaints that are made with reckless disregard for or willful ignorance of facts that would disprove the allegation.

1.08 Unfair Discrimination Against Complainants and Respondents

Psychologists do not deny persons employment, advancement, admissions to academic or other programs, tenure, or promotion, based solely upon their having made or their being the subject of an ethics complaint. This does not preclude taking action based upon the outcome of such proceedings or considering other appropriate information.

2. Competence

2.01 Boundaries of Competence

(a) Psychologists provide services, teach, and conduct research with populations and in areas only within the boundaries of their competence, based on their education, training, supervised experience, consultation, study, or professional experience.

(b) Where scientific or professional knowledge in the discipline of psychology establishes that an understanding of factors associated with age, gender, gender identity, race, ethnicity, culture, national origin, religion, sexual orientation, disability, language, or socioeconomic status is essential for effective implementation of their services or research, psychologists have or obtain the training, experience, consultation, or supervision necessary to ensure the competence of their services, or they make appropriate referrals, except as provided in Standard 2.02, Providing Services in Emergencies.

(c) Psychologists planning to provide services, teach, or conduct research involving populations, areas, techniques, or technologies new to them undertake relevant education, training, supervised experience, consultation, or study.

(d) When psychologists are asked to provide services to individuals for whom appropriate mental health services are not available and for which psychologists have not obtained the competence necessary, psychologists with closely related prior training or experience may provide such services in order to ensure that services are not denied if they make a reasonable effort to obtain the competence required by using relevant research, training, consultation, or study.

(e) In those emerging areas in which generally recognized standards for preparatory training do not yet exist, psychologists nevertheless take reasonable steps to ensure the competence of their work and to protect clients/patients, students, supervisees, research participants, organizational clients, and others from harm.

(f) When assuming forensic roles, psychologists are or become reasonably familiar with the judicial or administrative rules governing their roles.

2.02 Providing Services in Emergencies

In emergencies, when psychologists provide services to individuals for whom other mental health services are not available and for which psychologists have not obtained the necessary training, psychologists may provide such services in order to ensure that services are not denied. The services are discontinued as soon as the emergency has ended or appropriate services are available.

2.03 Maintaining Competence

Psychologists undertake ongoing efforts to develop and maintain their competence.

2.04 Bases for Scientific and Professional Judgments

Psychologists' work is based upon established scientific and professional knowledge of the discipline. (See also Standards 2.01e, Boundaries of Competence, and 10.01b, Informed Consent to Therapy.)

2.05 Delegation of Work to Others

Psychologists who delegate work to employees, supervisees, or research or teaching assistants or who use the services of others, such as interpreters, take reasonable steps to (1) avoid delegating such work to persons who have a multiple relationship with those being served that would likely lead to exploitation or loss of objectivity; (2) authorize only those responsibilities that such persons can be expected to perform competently on the basis of their education, training, or experience, either independently or with the level of supervision being provided; and (3) see that such persons perform these services competently. (See also Standards 2.02, Providing Services in Emergencies; 3.05, Multiple Relationships; 4.01, Maintaining Confidentiality; 9.01, Bases for Assessments; 9.02, Use of Assessments; 9.03, Informed Consent in Assessments; and 9.07, Assessment by Unqualified Persons.)

2.06 Personal Problems and Conflicts

(a) Psychologists refrain from initiating an activity when they know or should know that there is a substantial likelihood that their personal problems will prevent them from performing their work-related activities in a competent manner.

(b) When psychologists become aware of personal problems that may interfere with their performing work-related duties adequately, they take appropriate measures, such as obtaining professional consultation or assistance, and determine whether they should limit, suspend, or terminate their work-related duties. (See also Standard 10.10, Terminating Therapy.)

3. Human Relations

3.01 Unfair Discrimination

In their work-related activities, psychologists do not engage in unfair discrimination based on age, gender, gender identity, race, ethnicity, culture, national origin, religion, sexual orientation, disability, socioeconomic status, or any basis proscribed by law.

3.02 Sexual Harassment

Psychologists do not engage in sexual harassment. Sexual harassment is sexual solicitation, physical advances, or verbal or nonverbal conduct that is sexual in nature, that occurs in connection with the psychologist's activities or roles as a psychologist, and that either (1) is unwelcome, is offensive, or creates a hostile workplace or educational environment, and the psychologist knows or is told this or (2) is sufficiently severe or intense to be abusive to a reasonable person in the context. Sexual harassment can consist of a single intense or severe act or of multiple persistent or pervasive acts. (See also Standard 1.08, Unfair Discrimination Against Complainants and Respondents.)

3.03 Other Harassment

Psychologists do not knowingly engage in behavior that is harassing or demeaning to persons with whom they interact in their work based on factors such as those persons' age, gender, gender identity, race, ethnicity, culture, national origin, religion, sexual orientation, disability, language, or socioeconomic status.

3.04 Avoiding Harm

Psychologists take reasonable steps to avoid harming their clients/patients, students, supervisees, research participants, organizational clients, and others with whom they work, and to minimize harm where it is foreseeable and unavoidable.

3.05 Multiple Relationships

(a) A multiple relationship occurs when a psychologist is in a professional role with a person and (1) at the same time is in another role with the same person, (2) at the same time is in a relationship with a person closely associated with or related to the person with whom the psychologist has the professional relationship, or (3) promises to enter into another relationship in the future with the person or a person closely associated with or related to the person.

A psychologist refrains from entering into a multiple relationship if the multiple relationship could reasonably be expected to impair the psychologist's objectivity, competence, or effectiveness in performing his or her functions as a psychologist, or otherwise risks exploitation or harm to the person with whom the professional relationship exists.

Multiple relationships that would not reasonably be expected to cause impairment or risk exploitation or harm are not unethical.

(b) If a psychologist finds that, due to unforeseen factors, a potentially harmful multiple relationship has arisen, the psychologist takes reasonable steps to resolve it with due regard for the best interests of the affected person and maximal compliance with the Ethics Code.

(c) When psychologists are required by law, institutional policy, or extraordinary circumstances to serve in more than one role in judicial or administrative proceedings, at the outset they clarify role expectations and the extent of confidentiality and thereafter as changes occur. (See also Standards 3.04, Avoiding Harm, and 3.07, Third-Party Requests for Services.)

3.06 Conflict of Interest

Psychologists refrain from taking on a professional role when personal, scientific, professional, legal, financial, or other interests or relationships could reasonably be expected to (1) impair their objectivity, competence, or effectiveness in performing their functions as psychologists or (2) expose the person or organization with whom the professional relationship exists to harm or exploitation.

3.07 Third-Party Requests for Services

When psychologists agree to provide services to a person or entity at the request of a third party, psychologists attempt to clarify at the outset of the service the nature of the relationship with all individuals or organizations involved. This clarification includes the role of the psychologist (e.g., therapist, consultant, diagnostician, or expert witness), an identification of who is the client, the probable uses of the services provided or the information obtained, and the fact that there may be limits to confidentiality. (See also Standards 3.05, Multiple Relationships, and 4.02, Discussing the Limits of Confidentiality.)

3.08 Exploitative Relationships

Psychologists do not exploit persons over whom they have supervisory, evaluative, or other authority such as clients/patients, students, supervisees, research participants, and employees. (See also Standards 3.05, Multiple Relationships; 6.04, Fees and Financial Arrangements; 6.05, Barter With Clients/Patients; 7.07, Sexual Relationships With Students and Supervisees; 10.05, Sexual Intimacies With Current Therapy Clients/Patients; 10.06, Sexual Intimacies With Relatives or Significant Others of Current Therapy Clients/Patients; 10.07, Therapy With Former Sexual Partners; and 10.08, Sexual Intimacies With Former Therapy Clients/Patients.)

3.09 Cooperation With Other Professionals

When indicated and professionally appropriate, psychologists cooperate with other professionals in order to serve their clients/patients effectively and appropriately. (See also Standard 4.05, Disclosures.)

3.10 Informed Consent

(a) When psychologists conduct research or provide assessment, therapy, counseling, or consulting services in person or via electronic transmission or other forms of communication, they obtain the informed consent of the individual or individuals using language that is reasonably understandable to that person or persons except when conducting such activities without consent is mandated by law or governmental regulation or as otherwise provided in this Ethics Code.

(See also Standards 8.02, Informed Consent to Research; 9.03, Informed Consent in Assessments; and 10.01, Informed Consent to Therapy.)

(b) For persons who are legally incapable of giving informed consent, psychologists nevertheless (1) provide an appropriate explanation, (2) seek the individual's assent, (3) consider such persons' preferences and best interests, and (4) obtain appropriate permission from a legally authorized person, if such substitute consent is permitted or required by law. When consent by a legally authorized person is not permitted or required by law, psychologists take reasonable steps to protect the individual's rights and welfare.

(c) When psychological services are court ordered or otherwise mandated, psychologists inform the individual of the nature of the anticipated services, including whether the services are court ordered or mandated and any limits of confidentiality, before proceeding.

(d) Psychologists appropriately document written or oral consent, permission, and assent. (See also Standards 8.02, Informed Consent to Research; 9.03, Informed Consent in Assessments; and 10.01, Informed Consent to Therapy.)

3.11 Psychological Services Delivered to or Through Organizations

(a) Psychologists delivering services to or through organizations provide information beforehand to clients and when appropriate those directly affected by the services about (1) the nature and objectives of the services, (2) the intended recipients, (3) which of the individuals are clients, (4) the relationship the psychologist will have with each person and the organization, (5) the probable uses of services provided and information obtained, (6) who will have access to the information, and (7) limits of confidentiality. As soon as feasible, they provide information about the results and conclusions of such services to appropriate persons.

(b) If psychologists will be precluded by law or by organizational roles from providing such information to particular individuals or groups, they so inform those individuals or groups at the outset of the service.

3.12 Interruption of Psychological Services

Unless otherwise covered by contract, psychologists make reasonable efforts to plan for facilitating services in the event that psychological services are interrupted by factors such as the psychologist's illness, death, unavailability, relocation, or retirement or by the client's/patient's relocation or financial limitations. (See also Standard 6.02c, Maintenance, Dissemination, and Disposal of Confidential Records of Professional and Scientific Work.)

4. Privacy and Confidentiality

4.01 Maintaining Confidentiality

Psychologists have a primary obligation and take reasonable precautions to protect confidential information obtained through or stored in any medium, recognizing that the extent and limits of confidentiality may be regulated by law or established by institutional rules or professional or scientific relationship. (See also Standard 2.05, Delegation of Work to Others.)

4.02 Discussing the Limits of Confidentiality

(a) Psychologists discuss with persons (including, to the extent feasible, persons who are legally incapable of giving informed consent and their legal representatives) and organizations with whom they establish a scientific or professional relationship (1) the relevant limits of confidentiality and (2) the foreseeable uses of the information generated through their psychological activities. (See also Standard 3.10, Informed Consent.)

(b) Unless it is not feasible or is contraindicated, the discussion of confidentiality occurs at the outset of the relationship and thereafter as new circumstances may warrant.

(c) Psychologists who offer services, products, or information via electronic transmission inform clients/patients of the risks to privacy and limits of confidentiality.

4.03 Recording

Before recording the voices or images of individuals to whom they provide services, psychologists obtain permission from all such persons or their legal representatives. (See also Standards 8.03, Informed Consent for Recording Voices and Images in Research; 8.05, Dispensing With Informed Consent for Research; and 8.07, Deception in Research.)

4.04 Minimizing Intrusions on Privacy

(a) Psychologists include in written and oral reports and consultations, only information germane to the purpose for which the communication is made.

(b) Psychologists discuss confidential information obtained in their work only for appropriate scientific or professional purposes and only with persons clearly concerned with such matters.

4.05 Disclosures

(a) Psychologists may disclose confidential information with the appropriate consent of the organizational client, the individual client/patient, or another legally authorized person on behalf of the client/patient unless prohibited by law.

(b) Psychologists disclose confidential information without the consent of the individual only as mandated by law, or where permitted by law for a valid purpose such as to (1) provide needed professional services; (2) obtain appropriate professional consultations; (3) protect the client/patient, psychologist, or others from harm; or (4) obtain payment for services from a client/patient, in which instance disclosure is limited to the minimum that is necessary to achieve the purpose. (See also Standard 6.04e, Fees and Financial Arrangements.)

4.06 Consultations

When consulting with colleagues, (1) psychologists do not disclose confidential information that reasonably could lead to the identification of a client/patient, research participant, or other person or organization with whom they have a confidential relationship unless they have obtained the prior consent of the person or organization or the disclosure cannot be avoided, and (2) they disclose information only to the extent necessary to achieve the purposes of the consultation. (See also Standard 4.01, Maintaining Confidentiality.)

4.07 Use of Confidential Information for Didactic or Other Purposes

Psychologists do not disclose in their writings, lectures, or other public media, confidential, personally identifiable information concerning their clients/patients, students, research participants, organizational clients, or other recipients of their services that they obtained during the course of their work, unless (1) they take reasonable steps to disguise the person or organization, (2) the person or organization has consented in writing, or (3) there is legal authorization for doing so.

5. Advertising and Other Public Statements

5.01 Avoidance of False or Deceptive Statements

(a) Public statements include but are not limited to paid or unpaid advertising, product endorsements, grant applications, licensing applications, other credentialing applications, brochures, printed matter, directory listings, personal resumes or curricula vitae, or comments for use in media such as print or electronic transmission, statements in legal proceedings, lectures and public oral presentations, and published materials. Psychologists do not knowingly make public statements that are false, deceptive, or fraudulent concerning their research, practice, or other work activities or those of persons or organizations with which they are affiliated.

(b) Psychologists do not make false, deceptive, or fraudulent statements concerning (1) their training, experience, or competence; (2) their academic degrees; (3) their credentials; (4) their institutional or association affiliations; (5) their services; (6) the scientific or clinical basis for, or results or degree of success of, their services; (7) their fees; or (8) their publications or research findings.

(c) Psychologists claim degrees as credentials for their health services only if those degrees (1) were earned from a regionally accredited educational institution or (2) were the basis for psychology licensure by the state in which they practice.

5.02 Statements by Others

(a) Psychologists who engage others to create or place public statements that promote their professional practice, products, or activities retain professional responsibility for such statements.

(b) Psychologists do not compensate employees of press, radio, television, or other communication media in return for publicity in a news item. (See also Standard 1.01, Misuse of Psychologists' Work.)

(c) A paid advertisement relating to psychologists' activities must be identified or clearly recognizable as such.

5.03 Descriptions of Workshops and Non-Degree-Granting Educational Programs

To the degree to which they exercise control, psychologists responsible for announcements, catalogs, brochures, or advertisements describing workshops, seminars, or other non-degree-granting educational programs ensure that they accurately describe the audience for which the program is intended, the educational objectives, the presenters, and the fees involved.

5.04 Media Presentations

When psychologists provide public advice or comment via print, Internet, or other electronic transmission, they take precautions to ensure that statements (1) are based on their professional knowledge, training, or experience in accord with appropriate psychological literature and practice; (2) are otherwise consistent with this Ethics Code; and (3) do not indicate that a professional relationship has been established with the recipient. (See also Standard 2.04, Bases for Scientific and Professional Judgments.)

5.05 Testimonials

Psychologists do not solicit testimonials from current therapy clients/patients or other persons who because of their particular circumstances are vulnerable to undue influence.

5.06 In-Person Solicitation

Psychologists do not engage, directly or through agents, in uninvited in-person solicitation of business from actual or potential therapy clients/patients or other persons who because of their particular circumstances are vulnerable to undue influence. However, this prohibition does not preclude (1) attempting to implement appropriate collateral contacts for the purpose of benefiting an already engaged therapy client/patient or (2) providing disaster or community outreach services.

6. Record Keeping and Fees

6.01 Documentation of Professional and Scientific Work and Maintenance of Records

Psychologists create, and to the extent the records are under their control, maintain, disseminate, store, retain, and dispose of records and data relating to their professional and scientific work in order to (1) facilitate provision of services later by them or by other professionals, (2) allow for replication of research design and analyses, (3) meet institutional requirements, (4) ensure accuracy of billing and payments, and (5) ensure compliance with law. (See also Standard 4.01, Maintaining Confidentiality.)

6.02 Maintenance, Dissemination, and Disposal of Confidential Records of Professional and Scientific Work

(a) Psychologists maintain confidentiality in creating, storing, accessing, transferring, and disposing of records under their control, whether these are written, automated, or in any other medium. (See also Standards 4.01, Maintaining Confidentiality, and 6.01, Documentation of Professional and Scientific Work and Maintenance of Records.)

(b) If confidential information concerning recipients of psychological services is entered into databases or systems of records available to persons whose access has not been consented to by the recipient, psychologists use coding or other techniques to avoid the inclusion of personal identifiers.

(c) Psychologists make plans in advance to facilitate the appropriate transfer and to protect the confidentiality of records and data in the event of psychologists' withdrawal from positions or practice. (See also Standards 3.12, Interruption of Psychological Services, and 10.09, Interruption of Therapy.)

6.03 Withholding Records for Nonpayment

Psychologists may not withhold records under their control that are requested and needed for a client's/patient's emergency treatment solely because payment has not been received.

6.04 Fees and Financial Arrangements

(a) As early as is feasible in a professional or scientific relationship, psychologists and recipients of psychological services reach an agreement specifying compensation and billing arrangements.

(b) Psychologists' fee practices are consistent with law.

(c) Psychologists do not misrepresent their fees.

(d) If limitations to services can be anticipated because of limitations in financing, this is discussed with the recipient of services as early as is feasible. (See also Standards 10.09, Interruption of Therapy, and 10.10, Terminating Therapy.)

(e) If the recipient of services does not pay for services as agreed, and if psychologists intend to use collection agencies or legal measures to collect the fees, psychologists first inform the person that such measures will be taken and provide that person an opportunity to make prompt payment. (See also Standards 4.05, Disclosures, 6.03, Withholding Records for Nonpayment, and 10.01, Informed Consent to Therapy.)

6.05 Barter With Clients/Patients

Barter is the acceptance of goods, services, or other nonmonetary remuneration from clients/patients in return for psychological services. Psychologists may barter only if (1) it is not clinically contraindicated, and (2) the resulting arrangement is not exploitative. (See also Standards 3.05, Multiple Relationships, and 6.04, Fees and Financial Arrangements.)

6.06 Accuracy in Reports to Payors and Funding Sources

In their reports to payors for services or sources of research funding, psychologists take reasonable steps to ensure the accurate reporting of the nature of the service provided or research conducted, the fees, charges, or payments, and where applicable, the identity of the provider, the findings, and the diagnosis. (See also Standards 4.01, Maintaining Confidentiality, 4.04, Minimizing Intrusions on Privacy, and 4.05, Disclosures.)

6.07 Referrals and Fees

When psychologists pay, receive payment from, or divide fees with another professional, other than in an employer-employee relationship, the payment to each is based on the services provided (clinical, consultative, administrative, or other) and is not based on the referral itself. (See also Standard 3.09, Cooperation With Other Professionals.)

7. Education and Training

7.01 Design of Education and Training Programs

Psychologists responsible for education and training programs take reasonable steps to ensure that the programs are designed to provide the appropriate knowledge and proper experiences, and to meet the requirements for licensure, certification, or other goals for which claims are made by the program. (See also Standard 5.03, Descriptions of Workshops and Non-Degree-Granting Educational Programs.)

7.02 Descriptions of Education and Training Programs

Psychologists responsible for education and training programs take reasonable steps to ensure that there is a current and accurate description of the program content (including participation in required course- or program-related counseling, psychotherapy, experiential groups, consulting projects, or community service), training goals and objectives, stipends and benefits, and requirements that must be met for satisfactory completion of the program. This information must be made readily available to all interested parties.

7.03 Accuracy in Teaching

(a) Psychologists take reasonable steps to ensure that course syllabi are accurate regarding the subject matter to be covered, bases for evaluating progress, and the nature of course experiences. This standard does not preclude an instructor from modifying course content or requirements when the instructor considers it pedagogically necessary or desirable, so long as students are made aware of these modifications in a manner that enables them to fulfill course requirements. (See also Standard 5.01, Avoidance of False or Deceptive Statements.)

(b) When engaged in teaching or training, psychologists present psychological information accurately. (See also Standard 2.03, Maintaining Competence.)

7.04 Student Disclosure of Personal Information

Psychologists do not require students or supervisees to disclose personal information in course- or program-related activities, either orally or in writing, regarding sexual history, history of abuse and neglect, psychological treatment, and relationships with parents, peers, and spouses or significant others except if (1) the program or training facility has clearly identified this requirement in its admissions and program materials or (2) the information is necessary to evaluate or obtain assistance for students whose personal problems could reasonably be judged to be preventing them from performing their training- or professionally related activities in a competent manner or posing a threat to the students or others.

7.05 Mandatory Individual or Group Therapy

(a) When individual or group therapy is a program or course requirement, psychologists responsible for that program allow students in undergraduate and graduate programs the option of selecting such therapy from practitioners unaffiliated with the program. (See also Standard 7.02, Descriptions of Education and Training Programs.)

(b) Faculty who are or are likely to be responsible for evaluating students' academic performance do not themselves provide that therapy. (See also Standard 3.05, Multiple Relationships.)

7.06 Assessing Student and Supervisee Performance

(a) In academic and supervisory relationships, psychologists establish a timely and specific process for providing feedback to students and supervisees. Information regarding the process is provided to the student at the beginning of supervision.

(b) Psychologists evaluate students and supervisees on the basis of their actual performance on relevant and established program requirements.

7.07 Sexual Relationships With Students and Supervisees

Psychologists do not engage in sexual relationships with students or supervisees who are in their department, agency, or training center or over whom psychologists have or are likely to have evaluative authority. (See also Standard 3.05, Multiple Relationships.)

8. Research and Publication

8.01 Institutional Approval

When institutional approval is required, psychologists provide accurate information about their research proposals and obtain approval prior to conducting the research. They conduct the research in accordance with the approved research protocol.

8.02 Informed Consent to Research

(a) When obtaining informed consent as required in Standard 3.10, Informed Consent, psychologists inform participants about (1) the purpose of the research, expected duration, and procedures; (2) their right to decline to participate and to withdraw from the research once participation has begun; (3) the foreseeable consequences of declining or withdrawing; (4) reasonably foreseeable factors that may be expected to influence their willingness to participate such as potential risks, discomfort, or adverse effects; (5) any prospective research benefits; (6) limits of confidentiality; (7) incentives for participation; and (8) whom to contact for questions about the research and research participants' rights. They provide opportunity for the prospective participants to ask questions and receive answers. (See also Standards 8.03, Informed Consent for Recording Voices and Images in Research; 8.05, Dispensing With Informed Consent for Research; and 8.07, Deception in Research.)

(b) Psychologists conducting intervention research involving the use of experimental treatments clarify to participants at the outset of the research (1) the experimental nature of the treatment; (2) the services that will or will not be available to the control group(s) if appropriate; (3) the means by which assignment to treatment and control groups will be made; (4) available treatment alternatives if an individual does not wish to participate in the research or wishes to withdraw once a study has begun; and (5) compensation for or monetary costs of participating including, if appropriate, whether reimbursement from the participant or a third-party payor will be sought. (See also Standard 8.02a, Informed Consent to Research.)

8.03 Informed Consent for Recording Voices and Images in Research

Psychologists obtain informed consent from research participants prior to recording their voices or images for data collection unless (1) the research consists solely of naturalistic observations in public places, and it is not anticipated that the recording will be used in a manner that could cause personal identification or harm, or (2) the research design includes deception, and consent for the use of the recording is obtained during debriefing. (See also Standard 8.07, Deception in Research.)

8.04 Client/Patient, Student, and Subordinate Research Participants

(a) When psychologists conduct research with clients/patients, students, or subordinates as participants, psychologists take steps to protect the prospective participants from adverse consequences of declining or withdrawing from participation.

(b) When research participation is a course requirement or an opportunity for extra credit, the prospective participant is given the choice of equitable alternative activities.

8.05 Dispensing With Informed Consent for Research

Psychologists may dispense with informed consent only (1) where research would not reasonably be assumed to create distress or harm and involves (a) the study of normal educational practices, curricula, or classroom management methods conducted in educational settings; (b) only anonymous questionnaires, naturalistic observations, or archival research for which disclosure of responses would not place participants at risk of criminal or civil liability or damage their financial standing, employability, or reputation, and confidentiality is protected; or (c) the study of factors related to job or organization effectiveness conducted in organizational settings for which there is no risk to participants' employability, and confidentiality is protected or (2) where otherwise permitted by law or federal or institutional regulations.

8.06 Offering Inducements for Research Participation

(a) Psychologists make reasonable efforts to avoid offering excessive or inappropriate financial or other inducements for research participation when such inducements are likely to coerce participation.

(b) When offering professional services as an inducement for research participation, psychologists clarify the nature of the services, as well as the risks, obligations, and limitations. (See also Standard 6.05, Barter With Clients/Patients.)

8.07 Deception in Research

(a) Psychologists do not conduct a study involving deception unless they have determined that the use of deceptive techniques is justified by the study's significant prospective scientific, educational, or applied value and that effective nondeceptive alternative procedures are not feasible.

(b) Psychologists do not deceive prospective participants about research that is reasonably expected to cause physical pain or severe emotional distress.

(c) Psychologists explain any deception that is an integral feature of the design and conduct of an experiment to participants as early as is feasible, preferably at the conclusion of their participation, but no later than at the conclusion of the data collection, and permit participants to withdraw their data. (See also Standard 8.08, Debriefing.)

8.08 Debriefing

(a) Psychologists provide a prompt opportunity for participants to obtain appropriate information about the nature, results, and conclusions of the research, and they take reasonable steps to correct any misconceptions that participants may have of which the psychologists are aware.

(b) If scientific or humane values justify delaying or withholding this information, psychologists take reasonable measures to reduce the risk of harm.

(c) When psychologists become aware that research procedures have harmed a participant, they take reasonable steps to minimize the harm.

8.09 Humane Care and Use of Animals in Research

(a) Psychologists acquire, care for, use, and dispose of animals in compliance with current federal, state, and local laws and regulations, and with professional standards.

(b) Psychologists trained in research methods and experienced in the care of laboratory animals supervise all procedures involving animals and are responsible for ensuring appropriate consideration of their comfort, health, and humane treatment.

(c) Psychologists ensure that all individuals under their supervision who are using animals have received instruction in research methods and in the care, maintenance, and handling of the species being used, to the extent appropriate to their role. (See also Standard 2.05, Delegation of Work to Others.)

(d) Psychologists make reasonable efforts to minimize the discomfort, infection, illness, and pain of animal subjects.

(e) Psychologists use a procedure subjecting animals to pain, stress, or privation only when an alternative procedure is unavailable and the goal is justified by its prospective scientific, educational, or applied value.

(f) Psychologists perform surgical procedures under appropriate anesthesia and follow techniques to avoid infection and minimize pain during and after surgery.

(g) When it is appropriate that an animal's life be terminated, psychologists proceed rapidly, with an effort to minimize pain and in accordance with accepted procedures.

8.10 Reporting Research Results

(a) Psychologists do not fabricate data. (See also Standard 5.01a, Avoidance of False or Deceptive Statements.)

(b) If psychologists discover significant errors in their published data, they take reasonable steps to correct such errors in a correction, retraction, erratum, or other appropriate publication means.

8.11 Plagiarism

Psychologists do not present portions of another's work or data as their own, even if the other work or data source is cited occasionally.

8.12 Publication Credit

(a) Psychologists take responsibility and credit, including authorship credit, only for work they have actually performed or to which they have substantially contributed. (See also Standard 8.12b, Publication Credit.)

(b) Principal authorship and other publication credits accurately reflect the relative scientific or professional contributions of the individuals involved, regardless of their relative status. Mere possession of an institutional position, such as department chair, does not justify authorship credit. Minor contributions to the research or to the writing for publications are acknowledged appropriately, such as in footnotes or in an introductory statement.

(c) Except under exceptional circumstances, a student is listed as principal author on any multiple-authored article that is substantially based on the student's doctoral dissertation. Faculty advisors discuss publication credit with students as early as feasible and throughout the research and publication process as appropriate. (See also Standard 8.12b, Publication Credit.)

8.13 Duplicate Publication of Data

Psychologists do not publish, as original data, data that have been previously published. This does not preclude republishing data when they are accompanied by proper acknowledgment.

8.14 Sharing Research Data for Verification

(a) After research results are published, psychologists do not withhold the data on which their conclusions are based from other competent professionals who seek to verify the substantive claims through reanalysis and who intend to use such data only for that purpose, provided that the confidentiality of the participants can be protected and unless legal rights concerning proprietary data preclude their release. This does not preclude psychologists from requiring that such individuals or groups be responsible for costs associated with the provision of such information.

(b) Psychologists who request data from other psychologists to verify the substantive claims through reanalysis may use shared data only for the declared purpose. Requesting psychologists obtain prior written agreement for all other uses of the data.

8.15 Reviewers

Psychologists who review material submitted for presentation, publication, grant, or research proposal review respect the confidentiality of and the proprietary rights in such information of those who submitted it.

9. Assessment

9.01 Bases for Assessments

(a) Psychologists base the opinions contained in their recommendations, reports, and diagnostic or evaluative statements, including forensic testimony, on information and techniques sufficient to substantiate their findings. (See also Standard 2.04, Bases for Scientific and Professional Judgments.)

(b) Except as noted in 9.01c, psychologists provide opinions of the psychological characteristics of individuals only after they have conducted an examination of the individuals adequate to support their statements or conclusions. When, despite reasonable efforts, such an examination is not practical, psychologists document the efforts they made and the result of those efforts, clarify the probable impact of their limited information on the reliability and validity of their opinions, and appropriately limit the nature and extent of their conclusions or recommendations. (See also Standards 2.01, Boundaries of Competence, and 9.06, Interpreting Assessment Results.)

(c) When psychologists conduct a record review or provide consultation or supervision and an individual examination is not warranted or necessary for the opinion, psychologists explain this and the sources of information on which they based their conclusions and recommendations.

9.02 Use of Assessments

(a) Psychologists administer, adapt, score, interpret, or use assessment techniques, interviews, tests, or instruments in a manner and for purposes that are appropriate in light of the research on or evidence of the usefulness and proper application of the techniques.

(b) Psychologists use assessment instruments whose validity and reliability have been established for use with members of the population tested. When such validity or reliability has not been established, psychologists describe the strengths and limitations of test results and interpretation.

(c) Psychologists use assessment methods that are appropriate to an individual's language preference and competence, unless the use of an alternative language is relevant to the assessment issues.

9.03 Informed Consent in Assessments

(a) Psychologists obtain informed consent for assessments, evaluations, or diagnostic services, as described in Standard 3.10, Informed Consent, except when (1) testing is mandated by law or governmental regulations; (2) informed consent is implied because testing is conducted as a routine educational, institutional, or organizational activity (e.g., when participants voluntarily agree to assessment when applying for a job); or (3) one purpose of the testing is to evaluate decisional capacity. Informed consent includes an explanation of the nature and purpose of the assessment, fees, involvement of third parties, and limits of confidentiality and sufficient opportunity for the client/patient to ask questions and receive answers.

(b) Psychologists inform persons with questionable capacity to consent or for whom testing is mandated by law or governmental regulations about the nature and purpose of the proposed assessment services, using language that is reasonably understandable to the person being assessed.

(c) Psychologists using the services of an interpreter obtain informed consent from the client/patient to use that interpreter, ensure that confidentiality of test results and test security are maintained, and include in their recommendations, reports, and diagnostic or evaluative statements, including forensic testimony, discussion of any limitations on the data obtained. (See also Standards 2.05, Delegation of Work to Others, 4.01, Maintaining Confidentiality, 9.01, Bases for Assessments, 9.06, Interpreting Assessment Results, and 9.07, Assessment by Unqualified Persons.)

9.04 Release of Test Data

(a) The term *test data* refers to raw and scaled scores, client/patient responses to test questions or stimuli, and psychologists' notes and recordings concerning client/patient statements and behavior during an examination. Those portions of test materials that include client/patient responses are included in the definition of test data. Pursuant to a client/patient release, psychologists provide test data to the client/patient or other persons identified in the release. Psychologists may refrain from releasing test data to protect a client/patient or others from substantial harm or misuse or misrepresentation of the data or the test, recognizing that in many instances release of confidential information under these circumstances is regulated by law. (See also Standard 9.11, Maintaining Test Security.)

(b) In the absence of a client/patient release, psychologists provide test data only as required by law or court order.

9.05 Test Construction

Psychologists who develop tests and other assessment techniques use appropriate psychometric procedures and current scientific or professional knowledge for test design, standardization, validation, reduction or elimination of bias, and recommendations for use.

9.06 Interpreting Assessment Results

When interpreting assessment results, including automated interpretations, psychologists take into account the purpose of the assessment as well as the various test factors, test-taking abilities, and other characteristics of the person being assessed, such as situational, personal, linguistic, and cultural differences, that might affect psychologists' judgments or reduce the accuracy of their interpretations. They indicate any significant limitations of their interpretations. (See also Standards 2.01b and c, Boundaries of Competence, and 3.01, Unfair Discrimination.)

9.07 Assessment by Unqualified Persons

Psychologists do not promote the use of psychological assessment techniques by unqualified persons, except when such use is conducted for training purposes with appropriate supervision. (See also Standard 2.05, Delegation of Work to Others.)

9.08 Obsolete Tests and Outdated Test Results

(a) Psychologists do not base their assessment or intervention decisions or recommendations on data or test results that are outdated for the current purpose.

(b) Psychologists do not base such decisions or recommendations on tests and measures that are obsolete and not useful for the current purpose.

9.09 Test Scoring and Interpretation Services

(a) Psychologists who offer assessment or scoring services to other professionals accurately describe the purpose, norms, validity, reliability, and applications of the procedures and any special qualifications applicable to their use.

(b) Psychologists select scoring and interpretation services (including automated services) on the basis of evidence of the validity of the program and procedures as well as on other appropriate considerations. (See also Standard 2.01b and c, Boundaries of Competence.)

(c) Psychologists retain responsibility for the appropriate application, interpretation, and use of assessment instruments, whether they score and interpret such tests themselves or use automated or other services.

9.10 Explaining Assessment Results

Regardless of whether the scoring and interpretation are done by psychologists, by employees or assistants, or by automated or other outside services, psychologists take reasonable steps to ensure that explanations of results are given to the individual or designated representative unless the nature of the relationship precludes provision of an explanation of results (such as in some organizational consulting, preemployment or security screenings, and forensic evaluations), and this fact has been clearly explained to the person being assessed in advance.

9.11. Maintaining Test Security

The term *test materials* refers to manuals, instruments, protocols, and test questions or stimuli and does not include test data as defined in Standard 9.04, Release of Test Data. Psychologists make reasonable efforts to maintain the integrity and security of test materials and other assessment techniques consistent with law and contractual obligations, and in a manner that permits adherence to this Ethics Code.

10. Therapy

10.01 Informed Consent to Therapy

(a) When obtaining informed consent to therapy as required in Standard 3.10, Informed Consent, psychologists inform clients/patients as early as is feasible in the therapeutic relationship about the nature and anticipated course of therapy, fees, involvement of third parties, and limits of confidentiality and provide sufficient opportunity for the client/patient to ask questions and receive answers. (See also Standards 4.02, Discussing the Limits of Confidentiality, and 6.04, Fees and Financial Arrangements.)

(b) When obtaining informed consent for treatment for which generally recognized techniques and procedures have not been established, psychologists inform their clients/patients of the developing nature of the treatment, the potential risks involved, alternative treatments that may be available, and the voluntary nature of their participation. (See also Standards 2.01e, Boundaries of Competence, and 3.10, Informed Consent.)

(c) When the therapist is a trainee and the legal responsibility for the treatment provided resides with the supervisor, the client/patient, as part of the informed consent procedure, is informed that the therapist is in training and is being supervised and is given the name of the supervisor.

10.02 Therapy Involving Couples or Families

(a) When psychologists agree to provide services to several persons who have a relationship (such as spouses, significant others, or parents and children), they take reasonable steps to clarify at the outset (1) which of the individuals are clients/patients and (2) the relationship the psychologist will have with each person. This clarification includes the psychologist's role and the probable uses of the services provided or the information obtained. (See also Standard 4.02, Discussing the Limits of Confidentiality.)

(b) If it becomes apparent that psychologists may be called on to perform potentially conflicting roles (such as family therapist and then witness for one party in divorce proceedings), psychologists take reasonable steps to clarify and modify, or withdraw from, roles appropriately. (See also Standard 3.05c, Multiple Relationships.)

10.03 Group Therapy

When psychologists provide services to several persons in a group setting, they describe at the outset the roles and responsibilities of all parties and the limits of confidentiality.

10.04 Providing Therapy to Those Served by Others

In deciding whether to offer or provide services to those already receiving mental health services elsewhere, psychologists carefully consider the treatment issues and the potential client's/patient's welfare. Psychologists discuss these issues with the client/patient or another legally authorized person on behalf of the client/patient in order to minimize the risk of confusion and conflict, consult with the other service providers when appropriate, and proceed with caution and sensitivity to the therapeutic issues.

10.05 Sexual Intimacies With Current Therapy Clients/Patients

Psychologists do not engage in sexual intimacies with current therapy clients/patients.

10.06 Sexual Intimacies With Relatives or Significant Others of Current Therapy Clients/Patients

Psychologists do not engage in sexual intimacies with individuals they know to be close relatives, guardians, or significant others of current clients/patients. Psychologists do not terminate therapy to circumvent this standard.

10.07 Therapy With Former Sexual Partners

Psychologists do not accept as therapy clients/patients persons with whom they have engaged in sexual intimacies.

10.08 Sexual Intimacies With Former Therapy Clients/Patients

(a) Psychologists do not engage in sexual intimacies with former clients/patients for at least two years after cessation or termination of therapy.

(b) Psychologists do not engage in sexual intimacies with former clients/patients even after a two-year interval except in the most unusual circumstances. Psychologists who engage in such activity after the two years following cessation or termination of therapy and of having no sexual contact with the former client/patient bear the burden of demonstrating that there has been no exploitation, in light of all relevant factors, including (1) the amount of time that has passed since therapy terminated; (2) the nature, duration, and intensity of the therapy; (3) the circumstances of termination; (4) the client's/patient's personal history; (5) the client's/patient's current mental status; (6) the likelihood of adverse impact on the client/patient; and (7) any statements or actions made by the therapist during the course of therapy suggesting or inviting the possibility of a posttermination sexual or romantic relationship with the client/patient. (See also Standard 3.05, Multiple Relationships.)

10.09 Interruption of Therapy

When entering into employment or contractual relationships, psychologists make reasonable efforts to provide for orderly and appropriate resolution of responsibility for client/patient care in the event that the employment or contractual relationship ends, with paramount consideration given to the welfare of the client/patient. (See also Standard 3.12, Interruption of Psychological Services.)

10.10 Terminating Therapy

(a) Psychologists terminate therapy when it becomes reasonably clear that the client/patient no longer needs the service, is not likely to benefit, or is being harmed by continued service.

(b) Psychologists may terminate therapy when threatened or otherwise endangered by the client/patient or another person with whom the client/patient has a relationship.

(c) Except where precluded by the actions of clients/patients or third-party payors, prior to termination psychologists provide pretermination counseling and suggest alternative service providers as appropriate.

History and Effective Date Footnote

This version of the APA Ethics Code was adopted by the American Psychological Association's Council of Representatives during its meeting, August 21, 2002, and is effective beginning June 1, 2003. Inquiries concerning the substance or interpretation of the APA Ethics Code should be addressed to the Director, Office of Ethics, American Psychological Association, 750 First Street, NE, Washington, DC 20002-4242. The Ethics Code and information regarding the Code can be found on the APA website, *http://www.apa.org/ethics*. The standards in this Ethics Code will be used to adjudicate complaints brought concerning alleged conduct occurring on or after the effective date. Complaints regarding conduct occurring prior to the effective date will be adjudicated on the basis of the version of the Ethics Code that was in effect at the time the conduct occurred.

The APA has previously published its Ethics Code as follows:

American Psychological Association. (1953). Ethical standards of psychologists. Washington, DC: Author.

American Psychological Association. (1959). Ethical standards of psychologists. *American Psychologist, 14*, 279-282.

American Psychological Association. (1963). Ethical standards of psychologists. *American Psychologist, 18*, 56-60.

American Psychological Association. (1968). Ethical standards of psychologists. *American Psychologist, 23*, 357-361.

American Psychological Association. (1977, March). Ethical standards of psychologists. *APA Monitor*, 22-23.

American Psychological Association. (1979). Ethical standards of psychologists. Washington, DC: Author.

American Psychological Association. (1981). Ethical principles of psychologists. *American Psychologist, 36*, 633-638.

American Psychological Association. (1990). Ethical principles of psychologists (Amended June 2, 1989). *American Psychologist, 45*, 390-395.

American Psychological Association. (1992). Ethical principles of psychologists and code of conduct. *American Psychologist, 47*, 1597-1611.

Request copies of the APA's Ethical Principles of Psychologists and Code of Conduct from the APA Order Department, 750 First Street, NE, Washington, DC 20002-4242, or phone (202) 336-5510.

Appendix D

NASP Principles for Professional Ethics

2010

INTRODUCTION

The mission of the National Association of School Psychologists (NASP) is to represent school psychology and support school psychologists to enhance the learning and mental health of all children and youth. NASP's mission is accomplished through identification of appropriate evidence-based education and mental health services for all children; implementation of professional practices that are empirically supported, data driven, and culturally competent; promotion of professional competence of school psychologists; recognition of the essential components of high-quality graduate education and professional development in school psychology; preparation of school psychologists to deliver a continuum of services for children, youth, families, and schools; and advocacy for the value of school psychological services, among other important initiatives.

School psychologists provide effective services to help children and youth succeed academically, socially, behaviorally, and emotionally. School psychologists provide direct educational and mental health services for children and youth, as well as work with parents, educators, and other professionals to create supportive learning and social environments for all children. School psychologists apply their knowledge of both psychology and education during consultation and collaboration with others. They conduct effective decision making using a foundation of assessment and data collection. School psychologists engage in specific services for students, such as direct and indirect interventions that focus on academic skills, learning, socialization, and mental health. School psychologists provide services to schools and families that enhance the competence and well-being of children, including promotion of effective and safe learning environments, prevention of academic and behavior problems, response to crises, and improvement of family–school collaboration. The key foundations for all services by school psychologists are understanding of diversity in development and learning; research and program evaluation; and legal, ethical, and professional practice. All of these components and their relationships are depicted in Figure D.1, a graphic representation of a national model for comprehensive and integrated services by school psychologists. School psychologists are credentialed by state education agencies or other similar state entities that have the statutory authority to regulate and establish credentialing requirements for professional practice within a state. School psychologists typically work in public or private schools or other educational contexts.

The NASP *Principles for Professional Ethics* is designed to be used in conjunction with the *NASP Standards for Graduate Preparation of School Psychologists, Standards for the Credentialing of School Psychologists,* and *Model for Comprehensive and Integrated School Psychological Services* to provide a unified set of national principles that guide graduate education, credentialing, professional practices, and ethical behavior of effective school psychologists. These NASP policy documents are intended to define contemporary school psychology; promote school psychologists' services for children, families, and schools; and provide a foundation for the future of school psychology. These NASP policy documents are used to communicate NASP's positions and advocate for qualifications and practices of school psychologists with stakeholders, policy makers, and other professional groups at the national, state, and local levels.

The formal principles that elucidate the proper conduct of a professional school psychologist are known as *ethics*. In 1974, NASP adopted its first code of ethics, the *Principles for Professional Ethics (Principles),* and revisions were made in 1984, 1992, 1997, and 2000. The purpose of the *Principles* is to protect the public and those who receive school psychological services by sensitizing school psychologists to the ethical aspects of their work, educating them about appropriate conduct, helping them monitor their own behavior, and providing standards to be used in the resolution of complaints of unethical conduct.[1] NASP members and school psychologists who are certified by the National School Psychologist Certification System are bound to abide by NASP's code of ethics.[2]

The NASP *Principles for Professional Ethics* were developed to address the unique circumstances associated with providing school psychological services. The duty to educate children and the legal authority to do so rests with state governments. When school psychologists employed by a school board make decisions in their official roles, such acts are seen as actions by state government. As state actors, school-based practitioners have special obligations to all students. They must know and respect the rights of students under the U.S. Constitution and federal and state statutory law. They must balance the authority of parents to make decisions about their children with the needs and rights of those children, and the purposes and authority of schools. Furthermore, as school employees, school psychologists have a legal as well as an ethical obligation to take steps to protect all students from reasonably foreseeable risk of harm. Finally, school-based practitioners work in a context that emphasizes multidisciplinary problem solving and intervention.[3] For these reasons, psychologists employed by the schools may have less control over aspects of service delivery than practitioners in private practice. However, within this framework, it is expected that school psychologists will make careful, reasoned, and principled ethical choices[4] based on knowledge of this code, recognizing that responsibility for ethical conduct rests with the individual practitioner.

School psychologists are committed to the application of their professional expertise for the purpose of promoting improvement in the quality of life for students, families, and school communities. This objective is pursued in ways that protect the dignity and rights of those involved. School psychologists consider the interests and rights of children and youth to be their highest priority in decision making, and act as advocates for all students. These assumptions necessitate that school psychologists "speak up" for the needs and rights of students even when it may be difficult to do so.

The *Principles for Professional Ethics*, like all codes of ethics, provide only limited guidance in making ethical choices. Individual judgment is necessary to apply the code to situations that arise in professional practice. Ethical dilemmas may be created by situations involving competing ethical principles, conflicts between ethics and law, the conflicting interests of multiple parties, the dual roles of employee and pupil advocate, or because it is difficult to decide how statements in the ethics code apply to a particular situation.[5] Such situations are often complicated and may require a nuanced application of these *Principles* to effect a resolution that results in the greatest benefit for the student and concerned others. When difficult situations arise, school psychologists are advised to use a systematic problem-solving process to identify the best course of action. This process should include identifying the ethical issues involved, consulting these *Principles*, consulting colleagues with greater expertise, evaluating the rights and welfare of all affected parties, considering alternative solutions and their consequences, and accepting responsibility for the decisions made.[6, 7]

The NASP Principles for Professional Ethics may require a more stringent standard of conduct than law, and in those situations in which both apply, school psychologists are expected to adhere to the *Principles*. When conflicts between ethics and law occur, school psychologists are expected to take steps to resolve conflicts by problem solving with others and through positive, respected, and legal channels. If not able to resolve the conflict in this manner, they may abide by the law, as long as the resulting actions do not violate basic human rights.[8]

In addition to providing services to public and private schools, school psychologists may be employed in a variety of other settings, including juvenile justice institutions, colleges and universities, mental health clinics, hospitals, and private practice. The principles in this code should be considered by school psychologists in their ethical decision making regardless of employment setting. However, this revision of the code, like its precursors, focuses on the special challenges associated with providing school psychological services in schools and to students. School psychologists who provide services directly to children, parents, and other clients as private practitioners, and those who work in health and mental health settings, are encouraged to be knowledgeable of federal and state law regulating mental health providers, and to consult the American Psychological Association's (2002) *Ethical Principles of Psychologists and Code of Conduct* for guidance on issues not directly addressed in this code.

Four broad ethical themes[9] provide the organizational framework for the 2010 *Principles for Professional Ethics*. The four broad ethical themes subsume 17 ethical principles. Each principle is then further articulated by multiple specific standards of conduct. The broad themes, corollary principles, and ethical standards are to be considered in decision making. NASP will seek to enforce the 17 ethical principles and corollary standards that appear in the *Principles for Professional Ethics* with its members and school psychologists who hold the Nationally Certified School Psychologist (NCSP) credential in accordance with NASP's *Ethical and Professional Practices*

Committee Procedures (2008). Regardless of role, clientele, or setting, school psychologists should reflect on the theme and intent of each ethical principle and standard to determine its application to his or her individual situation.

The decisions made by school psychologists affect the welfare of children and families and can enhance their schools and communities. For this reason, school psychologists are encouraged to strive for excellence rather than simply meeting the minimum obligations outlined in the NASP *Principles for Professional Ethics*,[10] and to engage in the lifelong learning that is necessary to achieve and maintain expertise in applied professional ethics.

DEFINITION OF TERMS AS USED IN THE PRINCIPLES FOR PROFESSIONAL ETHICS

Client: The *client* is the person or persons with whom the school psychologist establishes a professional relationship for the purpose of providing school psychological services. A school psychologist–client professional relationship is established by an informed agreement with client(s) about the school psychologist's ethical and other duties to each party.[11] While not clients per se, classrooms, schools, and school systems also may be recipients of school psychological services and often are parties with an interest in the actions of school psychologists.

Child: A *child,* as defined in law, generally refers to a minor, a person younger than the age of majority. Although this term may be regarded as demeaning when applied to teenagers, it is used in this document when necessary to denote minor status. The term *student* is used when a less precise term is adequate.

Informed Consent: Informed consent means that the person giving consent has the legal authority to make a consent decision, a clear understanding of what it is he or she is consenting to, and that his or her consent is freely given and may be withdrawn without prejudice.[12]

Assent: The term *assent* refers to a minor's affirmative agreement to participate in psychological services or research.

Parent: The term *parent* may be defined in law or district policy, and can include the birth or adoptive parent, an individual acting in the place of a natural or adoptive parent (a grandparent or other relative, stepparent, or domestic partner), and/or an individual who is legally responsible for the child's welfare.

Advocacy: School psychologists have a special obligation to speak up for the rights and welfare of students and families, and to provide a voice to clients who cannot or do not wish to speak for themselves. *Advocacy* also occurs when school psychologists use their expertise in psychology and education to promote changes in schools, systems, and laws that will benefit schoolchildren, other students, and families.[13] Nothing in this code of ethics, however, should be construed as requiring school psychologists to engage in insubordination (willful disregard of an employer's lawful instructions) or to file a complaint about school district practices with a federal or state regulatory agency as part of their advocacy efforts.

School-Based Versus Private Practice: School-based practice refers to the provision of school psychological services under the authority of a state, regional, or local educational agency. School-based practice occurs if the school psychologist is an employee of the schools or contracted by the schools on a per case or consultative basis. *Private practice* occurs when a school psychologist enters into an agreement with a client(s) rather than an educational agency to provide school psychological services and the school psychologist's fee for services is the responsibility of the client or his or her representative.

I. RESPECTING THE DIGNITY AND RIGHTS OF ALL PERSONS

School psychologists engage only in professional practices that maintain the dignity of all with whom they work. In their words and actions, school psychologists demonstrate respect for the autonomy of persons and their right to self-determination, respect for privacy, and a commitment to just and fair treatment of all persons.

Principle I.1. Autonomy and Self- Determination (Consent and Assent)

School psychologists respect the right of persons to participate in decisions affecting their own welfare.

Standard I.1.1

School psychologists encourage and promote parental participation in school decisions affecting their children (see Standard II.3.10). However, where school psychologists are members of the school's educational support staff, not all of their services require informed parent consent. It is ethically permissible to provide school based consultation services regarding a child or adolescent to a student assistance team or teacher without informed parent consent as long as the resulting interventions are under the authority of the teacher and within the scope of typical classroom interventions.[14] Parent consent is not ethically required for a school based school psychologist to review a student's educational records, conduct classroom observations, assist in within-classroom interventions and progress monitoring, or to participate in educational screenings conducted as part of a regular program of instruction. Parent consent is required if the consultation about a particular child or adolescent is likely to be extensive and ongoing and/or if school actions may result in a significant intrusion on student or family privacy beyond what might be expected in the course of ordinary school activities.[15] Parents must be notified prior to the administration of school- or classroom-wide screenings for mental health problems and given the opportunity to remove their child or adolescent from participation in such screenings.

Standard I.1.2

Except for urgent situations or self-referrals by a minor student, school psychologists seek parent consent (or the consent of an adult student) prior to establishing a school psychologist–client relationship for the purpose of psychological diagnosis, assessment of eligibility for special education or disability accommodations, or to provide ongoing individual or group counseling or other non-classroom therapeutic intervention.*

- It is ethically permissible to provide psychological assistance without parent notice or consent in emergency situations or if there is reason to believe a student may pose a danger to others; is at risk for self-harm; or is in danger of injury, exploitation, or maltreatment.
- When a student who is a minor self-refers for assistance, it is ethically permissible to provide psychological assistance without parent notice or consent for one or several meetings to establish the nature and degree of the need for services and assure the child is safe and not in danger. It is ethically permissible to provide services to mature minors without parent consent where allowed by state law and school district policy. However, if the student is not old enough to receive school psychological assistance independent of parent consent, the school psychologist obtains parent consent to provide continuing assistance to the student beyond the preliminary meetings or refers the student to alternative sources of assistance that do not require parent notice or consent.

Standard I.1.3

School psychologists ensure that an individual providing consent for school psychological services is fully informed about the nature and scope of services offered, assessment/intervention goals and procedures, any foreseeable risks, the cost of services to the parent or student (if any), and the benefits that reasonably can be expected. The explanation includes discussion of the limits of confidentiality, who will receive information about assessment or intervention outcomes, and the possible consequences of the assessment/intervention services being offered. Available alternative services are identified, if appropriate. This explanation takes into account language and cultural differences, cognitive capabilities, developmental level, age, and other relevant factors so that it may be understood by the individual providing consent. School psychologists appropriately document written or oral consent. Any service provision by interns, practicum students, or other trainees is explained and agreed to in advance, and the identity and responsibilities of the supervising school psychologist are explained prior to the provision of services.[16]

Standard I.1.4

School psychologists encourage a minor student's voluntary participation in decision making about school psychological services as much as feasible. Ordinarily,

*It is recommended that school district parent handbooks and websites advise parents that a minor student may be seen by school health or mental health professionals (e.g., school nurse, counselor, social worker, school psychologist) without parent notice or consent to ensure that the student is safe or is not a danger to others. Parents should also be advised that district school psychologists routinely assist teachers in planning classroom instruction and monitoring its effectiveness and do not need to notify parents of, or seek consent for, such involvement in student support.

school psychologists seek the student's assent to services; however, it is ethically permissible to bypass student assent to services if the service is considered to be of direct benefit to the student and/or is required by law.[17]

- If a student's assent for services is not solicited, school psychologists nevertheless honor the student's right to be informed about the services provided.
- When a student is given a choice regarding whether to accept or refuse services, the school psychologist ensures the student understands what is being offered, honors the student's stated choice, and guards against overwhelming the student with choices he or she does not wish or is not able to make.[18]

Standard I.1.5

School psychologists respect the wishes of parents who object to school psychological services and attempt to guide parents to alternative resources.

Principle I.2. Privacy and Confidentiality

School psychologists respect the right of persons to choose for themselves whether to disclose their private thoughts, feelings, beliefs, and behaviors.

Standard I.2.1

School psychologists respect the right of persons to self determine whether to disclose private information.

Standard I.2.2

School psychologists minimize intrusions on privacy. They do not seek or store private information about clients that is not needed in the provision of services. School psychologists recognize that client–school psychologist communications are privileged in most jurisdictions and do not disclose information that would put the student or family at legal, social, or other risk if shared with third parties, except as permitted by the mental health provider–client privilege laws in their state.[19]

Standard I.2.3

School psychologists inform students and other clients of the boundaries of confidentiality at the outset of establishing a professional relationship. They seek a shared understanding with clients regarding the types of information that will and will not be shared with third parties. However, if a child or adolescent is in immediate need of assistance, it is permissible to delay the discussion of confidentiality until the immediate crisis is resolved. School psychologists recognize that it may be necessary to discuss confidentiality at multiple points in a professional relationship to ensure client understanding and agreement regarding how sensitive disclosures will be handled.

Standard I.2.4

School psychologists respect the confidentiality of information obtained during their professional work. Information is not revealed to third parties without the agreement of a minor child's parent or legal guardian (or an adult student), except in those situations in which failure to release information would result in danger to the student or others, or where otherwise required by law. Whenever feasible, student assent is obtained prior to disclosure of his or her confidences to third parties, including disclosures to the student's parents.

Standard I.2.5

School psychologists discuss and/or release confidential information only for professional purposes and only with persons who have a legitimate need to know. They do so within the strict boundaries of relevant privacy statutes.

Standard I.2.6

School psychologists respect the right of privacy of students, parents, and colleagues with regard to sexual orientation, gender identity, or transgender status. They do not share information about the sexual orientation, gender identity, or transgender status of a student (including minors), parent, or school employee with anyone without that individual's permission.[20]

Standard I.2.7

School psychologists respect the right of privacy of students, their parents and other family members, and colleagues with regard to sensitive health information (e.g., presence of a communicable disease). They do not share sensitive health information about a student, parent, or school employee with others without that individual's permission (or the permission of a parent or guardian in the case of a minor). School psychologists consult their state laws and department of public health for guidance if they believe a client poses a health risk to others.[21]

Principle I.3. Fairness and Justice

In their words and actions, school psychologists promote fairness and justice. They use their expertise to cultivate school climates that are safe and welcoming to all persons regardless of actual or perceived characteristics, including race, ethnicity, color, religion, ancestry, national origin, immigration status, socioeconomic status, primary language, gender, sexual orientation, gender identity, gender expression, disability, or any other distinguishing characteristics.

Standard I.3.1

School psychologists do not engage in or condone actions or policies that discriminate against persons, including students and their families, other recipients of service, supervisees, and colleagues based on actual or perceived characteristics including race; ethnicity; color; religion; ancestry; national origin; immigration status; socioeconomic status; primary language; gender; sexual orientation, gender identity, or gender expression; mental, physical, or sensory disability; or any other distinguishing characteristics.

Standard I.3.2

School psychologists pursue awareness and knowledge of how diversity factors may influence child development, behavior, and school learning. In conducting psychological, educational, or behavioral evaluations or in providing interventions, therapy, counseling, or consultation services, the school psychologist takes into account individual characteristics as enumerated in Standard I.3.1 so as to provide effective services.[22]

Standard I.3.3

School psychologists work to correct school practices that are unjustly discriminatory or that deny students, parents, or others their legal rights. They take steps to foster a school climate that is safe, accepting, and respectful of all persons.

Standard I.3.4

School psychologists strive to ensure that all children have equal opportunity to participate in and benefit from school programs and that all students and families have access to and can benefit from school psychological services.[23]

II. PROFESSIONAL COMPETENCE AND RESPONSIBILITY

Beneficence, or responsible caring, means that the school psychologist acts to benefit others. To do this, school psychologists must practice within the boundaries of their competence, use scientific knowledge from psychology and education to help clients and others make informed choices, and accept responsibility for their work.[24]

Principle II.1. Competence

To benefit clients, school psychologists engage only in practices for which they are qualified and competent.

Standard II.1.1

School psychologists recognize the strengths and limitations of their training and experience, engaging only in practices for which they are qualified. They enlist the assistance of other specialists in supervisory, consultative, or referral roles as appropriate in providing effective services.

Standard II.1.2

Practitioners are obligated to pursue knowledge and understanding of the diverse cultural, linguistic, and experiential backgrounds of students, families, and other clients. When knowledge and understanding of diversity characteristics are essential to ensure competent assessment, intervention, or consultation, school psychologists have or obtain the training or supervision necessary to provide effective services, or they make appropriate referrals.

Standard II.1.3

School psychologists refrain from any activity in which their personal problems may interfere with professional effectiveness. They seek assistance when personal problems threaten to compromise their professional effectiveness (also see III.4.2).

Standard II.1.4

School psychologists engage in continuing professional development. They remain current regarding developments in research, training, and professional practices that benefit children, families, and schools. They also understand that professional skill development beyond that of the novice practitioner requires well-planned continuing professional development and professional supervision.

Principle II.2. Accepting Responsibility for Actions

School psychologists accept responsibility for their professional work, monitor the effectiveness of their services, and work to correct ineffective recommendations.

Standard II.2.1

School psychologists review all of their written documents for accuracy, signing them only when correct. They may add an addendum, dated and signed, to a previously submitted report if information is found to be inaccurate or incomplete.

Standard II.2.2

School psychologists actively monitor the impact of their recommendations and intervention plans. They revise a recommendation, or modify or terminate an intervention plan, when data indicate the desired outcomes are not being attained. School psychologists seek the assistance of others in supervisory, consultative, or referral roles when progress monitoring indicates that their recommendations and interventions are not effective in assisting a client.

Standard II.2.3

School psychologists accept responsibility for the appropriateness of their professional practices, decisions, and recommendations. They correct misunderstandings resulting from their recommendations, advice, or information and take affirmative steps to offset any harmful consequences of ineffective or inappropriate recommendations.

Standard II.2.4

When supervising graduate students' field experiences or internships, school psychologists are responsible for the work of their supervisees.

Principle II.3. Responsible Assessment and Intervention Practices

School psychologists maintain the highest standard for responsible professional practices in educational and psychological assessment and direct and indirect interventions.

Standard II.3.1

Prior to the consideration of a disability label or category, the effects of current behavior management and/or instructional practices on the student's school performance are considered.

Standard II.3.2

School psychologists use assessment techniques and practices that the profession considers to be responsible, research-based practice.

- School psychologists select assessment instruments and strategies that are reliable and valid for the child and the purpose of the assessment. When using standardized measures, school psychologists adhere to the procedures for administration of the instrument that are provided by the author or publisher or the instrument. If modifications are made in the administration procedures for standardized tests or other instruments, such modifications are identified and discussed in the interpretation of the results.
- If using norm-referenced measures, school psychologists choose instruments with up-to-date normative data.
- When using computer-administered assessments, computer-assisted scoring, and/or interpretation programs, school psychologists choose programs that meet professional standards for accuracy and validity. School psychologists use professional judgment in evaluating the accuracy of computer-assisted assessment findings for the examinee.

Standard II.3.3

A psychological or psychoeducational assessment is based on a variety of different types of information from different sources.

Standard II.3.4

Consistent with education law and sound professional practice, children with suspected disabilities are assessed in all areas related to the suspected disability

Standard II.3.5

School psychologists conduct valid and fair assessments. They actively pursue knowledge of the student's disabilities and developmental, cultural, linguistic, and experiential background and then select, administer, and interpret assessment instruments and procedures in light of those characteristics (see Standard I.3.1. and I.3.2).

Standard II.3.6

When interpreters are used to facilitate the provision of assessment and intervention services, school psychologists take steps to ensure that the interpreters are appropriately trained and are acceptable to clients.[25]

Standard II.3.7

It is permissible for school psychologists to make recommendations based solely on a review of existing records. However, they should utilize a representative sample of records and explain the basis for, and the limitations of, their recommendations.[26]

Standard II.3.8

School psychologists adequately interpret findings and present results in clear, understandable terms so that the recipient can make informed choices.

Standard II.3.9

School psychologists use intervention, counseling and therapy procedures, consultation techniques, and other direct and indirect service methods that the profession considers to be responsible, research-based practice:

- School psychologists use a problem-solving process to develop interventions appropriate to the presenting problems and that are consistent with data collected.
- Preference is given to interventions described in the peer-reviewed professional research literature and found to be efficacious.

Standard II.3.10

School psychologists encourage and promote parental participation in designing interventions for their children. When appropriate, this includes linking interventions between the school and the home, tailoring parental involvement to the skills of the family, and helping parents gain the skills needed to help their children.

- School psychologists discuss with parents the recommendations and plans for assisting their children. This discussion takes into account the ethnic/cultural values of the family and includes alternatives that may be available. Subsequent recommendations for program changes or additional services are discussed with parents, including any alternatives that may be available.
- Parents are informed of sources of support available at school and in the community.

Standard II.3.11

School psychologists discuss with students the recommendations and plans for assisting them. To the maximum extent appropriate, students are invited to participate in selecting and planning interventions.[27]

Principle II.4 Responsible School-Based Record Keeping

School psychologists safeguard the privacy of school psychological records and ensure parent access to the records of their own children.

Standard II.4.1

School psychologists discuss with parents and adult students their rights regarding creation, modification, storage, and disposal of psychological and educational records that result from the provision of services. Parents and adult students are notified of the electronic storage and transmission of personally identifiable school psychological records and the associated risks to privacy.[28]

Standard II.4.2

School psychologists maintain school-based psychological and educational records with sufficient detail to be useful in decision making by another professional and with sufficient detail to withstand scrutiny if challenged in a due process or other legal procedure.[29]

Standard II.4.3

School psychologists include only documented and relevant information from reliable sources in school psychological records.

Standard II.4.4

School psychologists ensure that parents have appropriate access to the psychological and educational records of their child.

- Parents have a right to access any and all information that is used to make educational decisions about their child.
- School psychologists respect the right of parents to inspect, but not necessarily to copy, their child's answers to school psychological test questions, even if those answers are recorded on a test protocol (also see II.5.1).[30]

Standard II.4.5

School psychologists take steps to ensure that information in school psychological records is not released to persons or agencies outside of the school without the consent of the parent except as required and permitted by law.

Standard II.4.6

To the extent that school psychological records are under their control, school psychologists ensure that only those school personnel who have a legitimate educational interest in a student are given access to the student's school psychological records without prior parent permission or the permission of an adult student.

Standard II.4.7

To the extent that school psychological records are under their control, school psychologists protect electronic files from unauthorized release or modification (e.g., by using passwords and encryption), and they take reasonable steps to ensure that school psychological records are not lost due to equipment failure.

Standard II.4.8

It is ethically permissible for school psychologists to keep private notes to use as a memory aid that are not made accessible to others. However, as noted in Standard II.4.4, any and all information that is used to make educational decisions about a student must be accessible to parents and adult students.

Standard II.4.9

School psychologists, in collaboration with administrator and other school staff, work to establish district policies regarding the storage and disposal of school psychological records that are consistent with law and sound professional practice. They advocate for school district policies and practices that:

- safeguard the security of school psychological records while facilitating appropriate parent access to those records
- identify time lines for the periodic review and disposal of outdated school psychological records that are consistent with law and sound professional practice
- seek parent or other appropriate permission prior to the destruction of obsolete school psychological records of current students
- ensure that obsolete school psychology records are destroyed in a way that the information cannot be recovered

Principle II.5 Responsible Use of Materials

School psychologists respect the intellectual property rights of those who produce tests, intervention materials, scholarly works, and other materials.

Standard II.5.1

School psychologists maintain test security, preventing the release of underlying principles and specific content that would undermine or invalidate the use of the instrument. Unless otherwise required by law or district policy, school psychologists provide parents with the opportunity to inspect and review their child's test answers rather than providing them with copies of the their child's test protocols. However, on parent request, it is permissible to provide copies of a child's test protocols to a professional who is qualified to interpret them.

Standard II.5.2

School psychologists do not promote or condone the use of restricted psychological and educational tests or other assessment tools or procedures by individuals who are not qualified to use them.

Standard II.5.3

School psychologists recognize the effort and expense involved in the development and publication of psychological and educational tests, intervention materials, and scholarly works. They respect the intellectual property rights and copyright interests of the producers of such materials, whether the materials are published in print or digital formats. They do not duplicate copyright-protected test manuals, testing materials, or unused test protocols without the permission of the producer. However, school psychologists understand that, at times, parents' rights to examine their child's test answers may supersede the interests of test publishers.[31, 32]

III. HONESTY AND INTEGRITY IN PROFESSIONAL RELATIONSHIPS

To foster and maintain trust, school psychologists must be faithful to the truth and adhere to their professional promises. They are forthright about their qualifications, competencies, and roles; work in full cooperation with other professional disciplines to meet the needs of students and families; and avoid multiple relationships that diminish their professional effectiveness.

Principle III.1. Accurate Presentation of Professional Qualifications

School psychologists accurately identify their professional qualifications to others.

Standard III.1.1

Competency levels, education, training, experience, and certification and licensing credentials are accurately represented to clients, recipients of services, and others. School psychologists correct any misperceptions of their qualifications. School psychologists do not represent themselves as specialists in a particular domain without verifiable training and supervised experience in the specialty.

Standard III.1.2

School psychologists do not use affiliations with persons, associations, or institutions to imply a level of professional competence that exceeds that which has actually been achieved.

Principle III.2. Forthright Explanation of Professional Services, Roles, and Priorities

School psychologists are candid about the nature and scope of their services.

Standard III.2.1

School psychologists explain their professional competencies, roles, assignments, and working relationships to recipients of services and others in their work setting in a forthright and understandable manner. School psychologists explain all professional services to clients in a clear, understandable manner (see I.1.2).

Standard III.2.2

School psychologists make reasonable efforts to become integral members of the client service systems to which they are assigned. They establish clear roles for themselves within those systems while respecting the various roles of colleagues in other professions.

Standard III.2.3

The school psychologist's commitment to protecting the rights and welfare of children is communicated to the school administration, staff, and others as the highestpriority in determining services.

Standard III.2.4

School psychologists who provide services to several different groups (e.g., families, teachers, classrooms) may encounter situations in which loyalties are conflicted. As much as possible, school psychologists make known their priorities and commitments in advance to all parties to prevent misunderstandings.

Standard III.2.5

School psychologists ensure that announcements and advertisements of the availability of their publications, products, and services for sale are factual and professional. They do not misrepresent their degree of responsibility for the development and distribution of publications, products, and services.

Principle III.3. Respecting Other Professionals

To best meet the needs of children, school psychologists cooperate with other professionals in relationships based on mutual respect.

Standard III.3.1

To meet the needs of children and other clients most effectively, school psychologists cooperate with other psychologists and professionals from other disciplines in relationships based on mutual respect. They encourage and support the use of all resources to serve the interests of students. If a child or other client is receiving similar services from another professional, school psychologists promote coordination of services.

Standard III.3.2

If a child or other client is referred to another professional for services, school psychologists ensure that all relevant and appropriate individuals, including the client, are notified of the change and reasons for the change. When referring clients to other professionals, school psychologists provide clients with lists of suitable practitioners from whom the client may seek services.

Standard III.3.3

Except when supervising graduate students, school psychologists do not alter reports completed by another professional without his or her permission to do so.

Principle III.4. Multiple Relationships and Conflicts of Interest

School psychologists avoid multiple relationships and conflicts of interest that diminish their professional effectiveness.

Standard III.4.1

The Principles for Professional Ethics provide standards for professional conduct. School psychologists, in their private lives, are free to pursue their personal interests, except to the degree that those interests compromise professional effectiveness.

Standard III.4.2

School psychologists refrain from any activity in which conflicts of interest or multiple relationships with a client or a client's family may interfere with professional effectiveness. School psychologists attempt to resolve such situations in a manner that provides greatest benefit to the client. School psychologists whose personal or religious beliefs or commitments may influence the nature of their professional services or their willingness to provide certain services inform clients and responsible parties of this fact. When personal beliefs, conflicts of interests, or multiple relationships threaten to diminish professional effectiveness or would be viewed by the public as inappropriate, school psychologists ask their supervisor for reassignment of responsibilities, or they direct the client to alternative services.[33]

Standard III.4.3

School psychologists do not exploit clients, supervisees, or graduate students through professional relationships or condone these actions by their colleagues. They do not participate in or condone sexual harassment of children, parents, other clients, colleagues, employees, trainees, supervisees, or research participants. School psychologists do not engage in sexual relationships with individuals over whom they have evaluation authority, including college students in their classes or program, or any other trainees, or supervisees. School psychologists do not engage in sexual relationships with their current or former pupil-clients; the parents, siblings, or other close family members of current pupil-clients; or current consultees.

Standard III.4.4

School psychologists are cautious about business and other relationships with clients that could interfere with professional judgment and effectiveness or potentially result in exploitation of a client.

Standard III.4.5

NASP requires that any action taken by its officers, members of the Executive Council or Delegate Assembly, or other committee members be free from the appearance of impropriety and free from any conflict of interest. NASP leaders recuse themselves from decisions regarding proposed NASP initiatives if they may gain an economic benefit from the proposed venture.

Standard III.4.6

A school psychologist's financial interests in a product (e.g., tests, computer software, professional materials) or service can influence his or her objectivity or the perception of his or her objectivity regarding that product or service. For this reason, school psychologists are obligated to disclose any significant financial interest in the products or services they discuss in their presentations or writings if that interest is not obvious in the authorship/ownership citations provided.

Standard III.4.7

School psychologists neither give nor receive any remuneration for referring children and other clients for professional services.

Standard III.4.8

School psychologists do not accept any remuneration in exchange for data from their client database without the permission of their employer and a determination of whether the data release ethically requires informed client consent.

Standard III.4.9

School psychologists who provide school-based services and also engage in the provision of private practice services (dual setting practitioners) recognize the potential for conflicts of interests between their two roles and take steps to avoid such conflicts. Dual setting practitioners:

- are obligated to inform parents or other potential clients of any psychological and educational services available at no cost from the schools prior to offering such services for remuneration
- may not offer or provide private practice services to a student of a school or special school program where the practitioner is currently assigned
- may not offer or provide private practice services to the parents or family members of a student eligible to attend a school or special school program where the practitioner is currently assigned
- may not offer or provide an independent evaluation as defined in special education law for a student who attends a local or cooperative school district where the practitioner is employed
- do not use tests, materials, equipment, facilities, secretarial assistance, or other services belonging to the public sector employer unless approved in advance by the employer
- conduct all private practice outside of the hours of contracted public employment
- hold appropriate credentials for practice in both the public and private sectors

IV. RESPONSIBILITY TO SCHOOLS, FAMILIES, COMMUNITIES, THE PROFESSION, AND SOCIETY

School psychologists promote healthy school, family, and community environments. They assume a proactive role in identifying social injustices that affect children and schools and strive to reform systems-level patterns of injustice. They maintain the public trust in school psychologists by respecting law and encouraging ethical conduct. School psychologists advance professional excellence by mentoring less experienced practitioners and contributing to the school psychology knowledge base.

Principle IV.1. Promoting Healthy School, Family, and Community Environments

School psychologists use their expertise in psychology and education to promote school, family, and community environments that are safe and healthy for children.

Standard IV.1.1

To provide effective services and systems consultation, school psychologists are knowledgeable about the organization, philosophy, goals, objectives, culture, and methodologies of the settings in which they provide services. In addition, school psychologists develop partnerships and networks with community service providers and agencies to provide seamless services to children and families.

Standard IV.1.2

School psychologists use their professional expertise to promote changes in schools and community service systems that will benefit children and other clients. They advocate for school policies and practices that are in the best interests of children and that respect and protect the legal rights of students and parents.[34]

Principle IV.2. Respect for Law and the Relationship of Law and Ethics

School psychologists are knowledgeable of and respect laws pertinent to the practice of school psychology. In choosing an appropriate course of action, they consider the relationship between law and the Principles for Professional Ethics.

Standard IV.2.1

School psychologists recognize that an understanding of the goals, procedures, and legal requirements of their particular workplace is essential for effective functioning within that setting.

Standard IV.2.2

School psychologists respect the law and the civil and legal rights of students and other clients. The *Principles for Professional Ethics* may require a more stringent standard of conduct than law, and in those situations school psychologists are expected to adhere to the *Principles*.

Standard IV.2.3

When conflicts between ethics and law occur, school psychologists take steps to resolve the conflict through positive, respected, and legal channels. If not able to resolve the conflict in this manner, they may abide by the law, as long as the resulting actions do not violate basic human rights.[35]

Standard IV.2.4

School psychologists may act as individual citizens to bring about change in a lawful manner. They identify when they are speaking as private citizens rather than as employees. They also identify when they speak as individual professionals rather than as representatives of a professional association.

Principle IV.3. Maintaining Public Trust by Self-Monitoring and Peer Monitoring

School psychologists accept responsibility to monitor their own conduct and the conduct of other school psychologists to ensure it conforms to ethical standards.

Standard IV.3.1

School psychologists know the *Principles for Professional Ethics* and thoughtfully apply them to situations within their employment context. In difficult situations, school psychologists consult experienced school psychologists or state associations or NASP.

Standard IV.3.2

When a school psychologist suspects that another school psychologist or another professional has engaged in unethical practices, he or she attempts to resolve the suspected problem through a collegial problem-solving process, if feasible.

Standard IV.3.3

If a collegial problem-solving process is not possible or productive, school psychologists take further action appropriate to the situation, including discussing the situation with a supervisor in the employment setting, consulting state association ethics committees, and, if necessary, filing a formal ethical violation complaint with state associations, state credentialing bodies, or the NASP Ethical and Professional Practices Committee in accordance with their procedures.

Standard IV.3.4

When school psychologists are concerned about unethical practices by professionals who are not NASP members or do not hold the NCSP, informal contact is made to discuss the concern if feasible. If the situation cannot be resolved in this manner, discussing the situation with the professional's supervisor should be considered. If necessary, an appropriate professional organization or state credentialing agency could be contacted to determine the procedures established by that professional association or agency for examining the practices in question.

Principle IV.4. Contributing to the Profession by Mentoring, Teaching, and Supervision

As part of their obligation to students, schools, society, and their profession, school psychologists mentor less experienced practitioners and graduate students to assure high quality services, and they serve as role models for sound ethical and professional practices and decision making.

Standard IV.4.1

School psychologists who serve as directors of graduate education programs provide current and prospective graduate students with accurate information regarding program accreditation, goals and objectives, graduate program policies and requirements, and likely outcomes and benefits.

Standard IV.4.2

School psychologists who supervise practicum students and interns are responsible for all professional practices of the supervisees. They ensure that practicum students and interns are adequately supervised as outlined in the NASP Graduate Preparation Standards for School Psychologists. Interns and graduate students are identified as such, and their work is cosigned by the supervising school psychologist.

Standard IV.4.3

School psychologists who employ, supervise, or train professionals provide appropriate working conditions, fair and timely evaluation, constructive supervision, and continuing professional development opportunities.

Standard IV.4.4

School psychologists who are faculty members at universities or who supervise graduate education field experiences apply these ethical principles in all work with school psychology graduate students. In addition, they promote the ethical practice of graduate students by providing specific and comprehensive instruction, feedback, and mentoring.

Principle IV.5. Contributing to the School Psychology Knowledge Base

To improve services to children, families, and schools, and to promote the welfare of children, school psychologists are encouraged to contribute to the school psychology knowledge base by participating in, assisting in, or conducting and disseminating research.

Standard IV.5.1

When designing and conducting research in schools, school psychologists choose topics and employ research methodology, research participant selection procedures, data-gathering methods, and analysis and reporting techniques that are grounded in sound research practice. School psychologists identify their level of training and graduate degree to potential research participants.

Standard IV.5.2

School psychologists respect the rights, and protect the well-being, of research participants. School psychologists obtain appropriate review and approval of proposed research prior to beginning their data collection.

- Prior to initiating research, school psychologists and graduate students affiliated with a university, hospital, or other agency subject to the U.S. Department of Health and Human Services (DHHS) regulation of research first obtain approval for their research from their Institutional Review Board for Research Involving Human Subjects (IRB) as well as the school or other agency in which the research will be conducted. Research proposals that have not been subject to IRB approval should be reviewed by individuals knowledgeable about research methodology and ethics and approved by the school administration or other appropriate authority.
- In planning research, school psychologists are ethically obligated to consider carefully whether the informed consent of research participants is needed for their study, recognizing that research involving more than minimum risk requires informed consent, and that research with students involving activities that are not part of ordinary, typical schooling requires informed consent. Consent and assent protocols provide the information necessary for potential research participants to make an informed and voluntary choice about participation. School psychologists evaluate the potential risks (including risks of physical or psychological harm, intrusions on privacy, breach of confidentiality) and benefits of their research and only conduct studies in which the risks to participants are minimized and acceptable.

Standard IV.5.3

School psychologists who use their assessment, intervention, or consultation cases in lectures, presentations, or publications obtain written prior client consent or they remove and disguise identifying client information.

Standard IV.5.4

School psychologists do not publish or present fabricated or falsified data or results in their publications and presentations.

Standard IV.5.5

School psychologists make available their data or other information that provided the basis for findings and conclusions reported in publications and presentations, if such data are needed to address a legitimate concern or need and under the condition that the confidentiality and other rights of research participants are protected.

Standard IV.5.6

If errors are discovered after the publication or presentation of research or other information, school psychologists make efforts to correct errors by publishing errata, retractions, or corrections.

Standard IV.5.7

School psychologists only publish data or other information that make original contributions to the professional literature. They do not report the same study in a second publication without acknowledging previous publication of the same data. They do not duplicate significant portions of their own or others' previous publications without permission of copyright holders.

Standard IV.5.8

When publishing or presenting research or other work, school psychologists do not plagiarize the works or ideas of others. They appropriately cite and reference all sources, print or digital, and assign credit to those whose ideas are reflected. In inservice or conference presentations, school psychologists give credit to others whose ideas have been used or adapted.

Standard IV.5.9

School psychologists accurately reflect the contributions of authors and other individuals who contributed to presentations and publications. Authorship credit is given only to individuals who have made a substantial professional contribution to the research, publication, or presentation. Authors discuss and resolve issues related to publication credit as early as feasible in the research and publication process.

Standard IV.5.10

School psychologists who participate in reviews of manuscripts, proposals, and other materials respect the confidentiality and proprietary rights of the authors. They limit their use of the materials to the activities relevant to the purposes of the professional review. School psychologists who review professional materials do not communicate the identity of the author, quote from the materials, or duplicate or circulate copies of the materials without the author's permission.

Figure D.1.

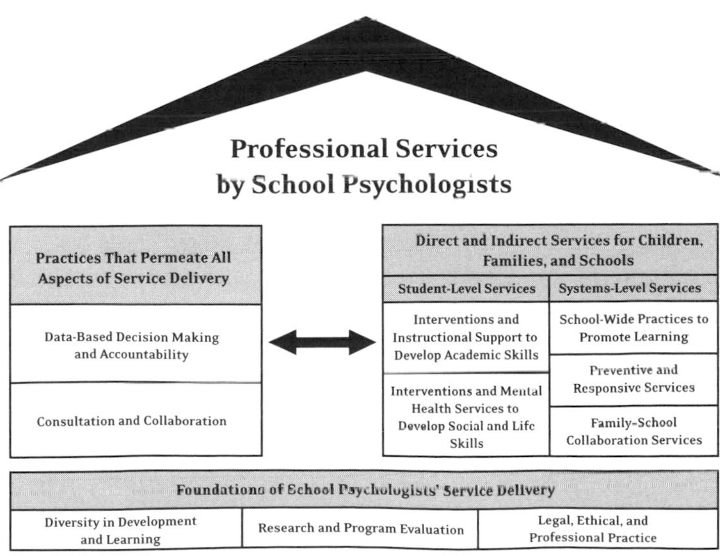

---

[1]Jacob, S., Decker, D. M., & Hartshorne, T. S. (in press). *Ethics and law for school psychologists* (6th ed.). Hoboken, NJ: John Wiley & Sons.

[2]National Association of School Psychologists. (2008). *Ethical and Professional Practices Committee Procedures.* Available: http://www.nasponline.org.

[3]Russo, C. J. (2006). *Reutter's the law of public education* (6th ed.). New York: Foundation Press.

[4]Haas, L. J., & Malouf, J. L. (2005). *Keeping up the good work: A practitioner's guide to mental health ethics* (4th ed.). Sarasota, FL: Professional Resource Press.

[5]Jacob-Timm, S. (1999). Ethical dilemmas encountered by members of the National Association of School Psychologists. *Psychology in the Schools, 36,* 205–217.

[6]McNamara, K. (2008). *Best practices in the application of professional ethics.* In A. Thomas & J. Grimes (Eds.), *Best practices in school psychology V* (pp. 1933–1941). Bethesda, MD: National Association of School Psychologists.

[7]Williams, B., Armistead, L., & Jacob, S. (2008). *Professional ethics for school psychologists: A problem-solving model casebook.* Bethesda, MD: National Association of School Psychologists.

[8]American Psychological Association. (2002). Ethical principles of psychologists and code of conduct. *American Psychologist, 57,* 1060–1073.

[9]Adapted from the Canadian Psychological Association. (2000). *Canadian code of ethics for psychologists* (3rd ed.). Available: http://www.cpa.ca.

[10]Knapp, S., & VandeCreek, L. (2006). *Practical ethics for psychologists: A positive approach.* Washington, DC: American Psychological Association.

[11]Fisher, M. A. (2009). Replacing "who is the client" with a different ethical question. *Professional Psychology: Research and Practice, 40,* 1–7.

[12]Dekraai, M., Sales, B., & Hall, S. (1998). *Informed consent, confidentiality, and duty to report laws in the conduct of child therapy.* In T. R. Kratochwill & R. J. Morris (Eds.), *The practice of child therapy* (3rd ed., pp. 540–559). Boston: Allyn & Bacon.

[13]Masner, C. M. (2007). *The ethic of advocacy.* Doctoral dissertation, University of Denver. Available: http://www/dissertation.com.

[14]Burns, M. K., Jacob, S., & Wagner, A. (2008). Ethical and legal issues associated with using responsiveness-to-intervention to assess learning disabilities. *Journal of School Psychology, 46,* 263–279.

[15]Corrao, J., & Melton, G. B. (1985). *Legal issues in school-based therapy.* In J. C. Witt, S. N. Elliot & F.M. Gresham (Eds.), *Handbook of behavior therapy in education* (pp. 377–399). New York: Plenum Press.

[16]Weithorn, L. A. (1983). *Involving children in decisions affecting their own welfare: Guidelines for professionals.* In G. B. Melton, G. P. Koocher & M. J. Saks (Eds.), *Children's competence to consent* (pp. 235–260). New York: Plenum Press.

[17]Weithorn, L. A. (1983). *Involving children in decisions affecting their own welfare: Guidelines for professionals.* In G. B. Melton, G. P. Koocher & M. J. Saks (Eds.), *Children's competence to consent* (pp. 235–260). New York: Plenum Press.

[18]Weithorn, L. A. (1983). *Involving children in decisions affecting their own welfare: Guidelines for professionals.* In G. B. Melton, G. P. Koocher & M. J. Saks (Eds.), *Children's competence to consent* (pp. 235–260). New York: Plenum Press.

[19]Jacob, S., & Powers, K. E. (2009). Privileged communication in the school psychologist–client relationship. *Psychology in the Schools, 46,* 307–318.

[20]Sterling v. Borough of Minersville, 232 F.3d 190, 2000 U.S. App. LEXIS 27855 (3rd Cir. 2000)

[21]Jacob, S., Decker, D. M., & Hartshorne, T. S. (in press). *Ethics and law for school psychologists* (6th ed.). Hoboken, NJ: John Wiley & Sons.

[22]Flanagan, R., Miller, J. A., & Jacob, S. (2005). The 2002 revision of APA's ethics code: Implications for school psychologists. *Psychology in the Schools, 42,* 433–444.

[23]Flanagan, R., Miller, J. A., & Jacob, S. (2005). The 2002 revision of APA's ethics code: Implications for school psychologists. *Psychology in the Schools, 42,* 433–445.

[24]Jacob, S., Decker, D. M., & Hartshorne, T. S. (in press). *Ethics and law for school psychologists* (6th ed.). Hoboken, NJ: John Wiley & Sons.

[25]American Psychological Association. (2002). Ethical principles of psychologists and code of conduct. *American Psychologist, 57,* 1060–1073.

[26]American Psychological Association. (2002). Ethical principles of psychologists and code of conduct. *American Psychologist, 57,* 1060–1073.

[27]Weithorn, L. A. (1983). *Involving children in decisions affecting their own welfare: Guidelines for professionals.* In G. B. Melton, G. P. Koocher & M. J. Saks (Eds.), *Children's competence to consent* (pp. 235–260). New York: Plenum Press.

[28]American Psychological Association. (2002). Ethical principles of psychologists and code of conduct. *American Psychologist, 57,* 1060–1073.

[29]Nagy, T. F. (2000). *Ethics in plain English.* Washington, DC: American Psychological Association.

[30]Reschly, D. J., & Bersoff, D. N. (1999). *Law and school psychology.* In C. R. Reynolds & T. B. Gutkin (Eds.), *Handbook of school psychology* (3rd ed., pp. 1077–1112). New York: Wiley. Note: this chapter summarizes Department of Education policy letters on the matter of parent inspection of test protocols.

[31]Reschly, D. J., & Bersoff, D. N. (1999). *Law and school psychology.* In C. R. Reynolds & T. B. Gutkin (Eds.), (Eds.), *Handbook of school psychology* (3rd ed., pp. 1077–1112). New York: Wiley. Note: this chapter summarizes Department of Education policy letters on the matter of parent inspection of test protocols.

[32]Newport-Mesa Unified School District v. State of California Department of Education, 371 F. Supp. 2d 1170; 2005 U.S. Dist. LEXIS 10290 (C.D. Cal. 2005).

[33]American Psychological Association. (2002). Ethical principles of psychologists and code of conduct. *American Psychologist, 57,* 1060–1073.

[34]Prilleltensky, I. (1991). The social ethics of school psychology: A priority for the 1990s. *School Psychology Quarterly, 6,* 200–222.

[35]American Psychological Association. (2002). Ethical principles of psychologists and code of conduct. *American Psychologist, 57,* 1060–1073.

NASP MODEL FOR COMPREHENSIVE AND INTEGRATED SCHOOL PSYCHOLOGICAL SERVICES 2010

INTRODUCTION

The mission of the National Association of School Psychologists (NASP) is to represent school psychology and support school psychologists to enhance the learning and mental health of all children and youth. NASP's mission is accomplished through identification of appropriate evidence-based education and mental health services for all children; implementation of professional practices that are empirically supported, data driven, and culturally competent; promotion of professional competence of school psychologists; recognition of the essential components of high-quality graduate education and professional development in school psychology; preparation of school psychologists to deliver a continuum of services for children, youth, families, and schools; and advocacy for the value of school psychological services, among other important initiatives.

School psychologists provide effective services to help children and youth succeed academically, socially, behaviorally, and emotionally. School psychologists provide direct educational and mental health services for children and youth, as well as work with parents, educators, and other professionals to create supportive learning and social environments for all children. School psychologists apply their knowledge of both psychology and education during consultation and collaboration with others. They conduct effective decision making using a foundation of assessment and data collection. School psychologists engage in specific services for students, such as direct and indirect interventions that focus on academic skills, learning, socialization, and mental health. School psychologists provide services to schools and families that enhance the competence and well-being of children, including promotion of effective and safe learning environments, prevention of academic and behavior problems, response to crises, and improvement of family–school collaboration. The key foundations for all services by school psychologists are understanding of diversity in development and learning; research and program evaluation; and legal, ethical, and professional practice. All of these components and their relationships are depicted in Figure 1, a graphic representation of a national model for comprehensive and integrated services by school psychologists. School psychologists are credentialed by state education agencies or other similar state entities that have the statutory authority to regulate and establish credentialing requirements for professional practice within a state. School psychologists typically work in public or private schools or other educational contexts.

The NASP *Model for Comprehensive and Integrated School Psychological Services* is designed to be used in conjunction with the NASP *Standards for Graduate Preparation of School Psychologists, Standards for the Credentialing of School Psychologists,* and *Principles for Professional Ethics* to provide a unified set of national principles that guide graduate education, credentialing, professional practice and services, and ethical behavior of effective school psychologists. These NASP policy documents are intended to define contemporary school psychology; promote school psychologists' services for children, families, and schools; and provide a foundation for the future of school psychology. These NASP policy documents are used to communicate NASP's positions and advocate for qualifications and practices of school psychologists with stakeholders, policy makers, and other professional groups at the national, state, and local levels.

The *Model for Comprehensive and Integrated School Psychological Services* represents the official policy of NASP regarding the delivery of comprehensive school psychological services. First written in 1978 as the *Guidelines for the Provision of School Psychological Services*, revised in 1984, 1992, 1997, 2000, and 2010, the model serves as a guide to the organization and delivery of school psychological services at the federal, state, and local levels. The model provides direction to school psychologists, students, and faculty in school psychology, administrators of school psychological services, and consumers of school psychological services regarding excellence in professional school psychology. It also delineates what services might reasonably be expected to be available from most school psychologists and, thus, should help to further define the field. In addition, the model is intended to educate the profession and the public regarding appropriate professional practices and, hopefully, will stimulate the continued development of the profession.

The Model *for Comprehensive* and *Integrated School Psychological Services* addresses the delivery of school psychological services within the context of educational programs and educational settings. In addition to providing services to public and private schools, school psychologists are employed in a variety of other settings, including juvenile justice institutions, colleges and universities, mental health clinics, hospitals, and in private practice. This revision of the *Guidelines for the Provision of School Psychological Services*, like its precursors, focuses on the special challenges associated with providing school psychological services in schools and to schoolchildren. School psychologists who provide services directly to children, parents, and other clients as private practitioners, and those who work

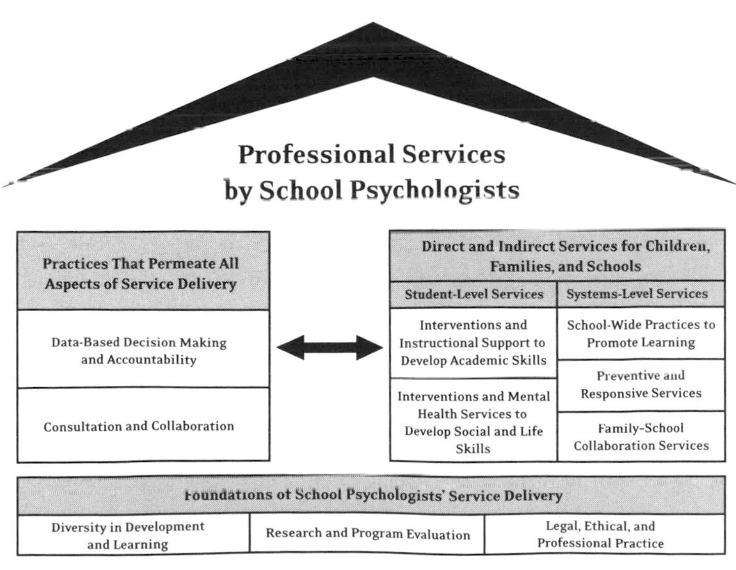

in health and mental health settings, are encouraged to be knowledgeable of federal and state law regulating mental health providers, and to consult the National Association of School Psychologists's (2010) *Principles for Professional Ethics* and the American Psychological Association's (2002) *Ethical Principles of Psychologists and Code of Conduct* for guidance on issues not addressed in the model.

The model includes two major sections, which describe responsibilities of individual school psychologists and the responsibilities of school systems to support comprehensive school psychological services. The first section describes *Professional Practices* aligned with each of 10 domains of practice that are the core components of this model of school psychological services. The second section outlines *Organizational Principles* that should be assumed by the organizations that employ school psychologists. These principles describe the organizational conditions that must be met in order to ensure effective delivery of school psychological services for children, families, and schools.

Not all school psychologists or school systems will be able to meet every standard contained within this document. Nevertheless, it is anticipated that these guidelines will serve as a model for effective program development and professional practice on federal, state, and local levels. The 10 domains provide a *general framework of basic competencies* that practitioners should possess upon beginning practice as school psychologists. School psychologists will perceive that it is in their own best interest—and that of the agencies, parents, and children they serve—to adhere to and support the model. NASP encourages state and federal legislators, local school boards, and the administrative leaders of federal, state, and local education agencies to support the concepts contained within the model.

NASP acknowledges that this model sets requirements for services not presently mandated by federal law or regulation and not always mandated in state laws and administrative rules. Future amendments of such statues and rules, and the state and local plans resulting from them, should incorporate the recommendations contained in this document. Furthermore, NASP understands that school psychological services are provided within the context of ethical and legal mandates. Nothing in the model should be construed as superseding such relevant rules and regulations.

The model provides flexibility, permitting agencies and professionals to develop procedures, polices, and administrative organizations that meet both the needs of the agency and the professional's desire to operate within recognized professional standards of practice. At the same time, the model has sufficient specificity to ensure appropriate and comprehensive service provision.

COMPREHENSIVE AND INTEGRATED SERVICES: DOMAINS OF SCHOOL PSYCHOLOGY PRACTICE

School psychologists provide comprehensive and integrated services across 10 general domains of school psychology, as illustrated in Figure 1 on page 2 of this document. Graduate education in school psychology prepares practitioners with basic professional competencies, including both *knowledge* and *skills*, in the 10 domains of school psychology, as well as the ability to integrate knowledge and apply professional skills across domains in the practice of school psychology. The 10 domains of school psychology reflect the following principles:

- School psychologists have a foundation in the knowledge bases for both psychology and education, including theories, models, research, empirical findings, and techniques in the domains, and the ability to explain important principles and concepts.
- School psychologists use effective strategies and skills in the domains to help students succeed academically, socially, behaviorally, and emotionally.
- School psychologists apply their knowledge and skills by creating and maintaining safe, supportive, fair, and effective learning environments and enhancing family–school collaboration for *all* students.
- School psychologists demonstrate knowledge and skills relevant for professional practices and work characteristics in their field.
- School psychologists ensure that their knowledge, skills, and professional practices reflect understanding and respect for human diversity and promote effective services, advocacy, and social justice for all children, families, and schools.
- School psychologists integrate knowledge and professional skills across the 10 domains of school psychology in delivering a comprehensive range of services in professional practice that result in direct, measurable outcomes for children, families, schools, and/or other consumers.

The domains are highly interrelated and not mutually exclusive. The brief descriptions and examples of professional practices in each of the domains provided below outline major areas of knowledge and skill, but are not intended to reflect the possible full range of competencies of school psychologists. Figure 1 represents the 10 domains within a model of comprehensive and integrated services by school psychologists. It is important to emphasize that the 10 domains provide a *general frame of reference for basic competencies* that program graduates should possess upon beginning practice as school psychologists.

The *Model for Comprehensive and Integrated School Psychological Services* describes the services provided by school psychologists to children, families, and schools. Because these services are based on the needs of children, families, and schools, the model generally does not differentiate the services provided by school psychologists prepared at the doctoral and specialist levels. Rather, the model promotes a high level of services to meet the academic, social, behavioral, and emotional needs of all children and youth. It may be noted, however, that work experience and advanced graduate education will result in areas of specialization by individual school psychologists. Among groups of school psychologists, not everyone will acquire skills to the same degree across all domains of practice. However, all school psychologists are expected to possess at least a basic level of competency in all of the 10 domains of practice described in this model.

PART I: PROFESSIONAL PRACTICES

PRACTICES THAT PERMEATE ALL ASPECTS OF SERVICE DELIVERY

Data-Based Decision Making and Accountability

School psychologists have knowledge of varied models and methods of assessment and data collection methods for identifying strengths and needs, developing effective services and programs, and measuring progress and outcomes. As part of a systematic and comprehensive process of effective decision making and problem solving that permeates all aspects of service delivery, school psychologists demonstrate skills to use psychological and educational assessment, data collection strategies, and technology resources and apply results to design, implement, and evaluate response to services and programs. Examples of professional practices associated with data-based decision making and accountability include the following:

- School psychologists use a problem-solving framework as the basis for all professional activities.
- School psychologists systematically collect data from multiple sources as a foundation for decision-making and consider ecological factors (e.g., classroom, family, community characteristics) as a context for assessment and intervention in general and special education settings.
- School psychologists collect and use assessment data to understand students' problems and to select and implement evidence-based instructional and mental health services.
- School psychologists, as part of an interdisciplinary team, conduct assessments to identify students' eligibility for special education and other educational services.
- School psychologists use valid and reliable assessment techniques to assess progress toward academic and behavioral goals, to measure responses to interventions, and to revise interventions as necessary.
- School psychologists assist with design and implementation of assessment procedures to determine the degree to which recommended interventions have been implemented (i.e., treatment fidelity).
- School psychologists use systematic and valid data collection procedures for evaluating the effectiveness and/or need for modification of school-based interventions and programs.
- School psychologists use systematic and valid data collection procedures to evaluate and document the effectiveness of their own services.
- School psychologists use information and technology resources to enhance data collection and decision making.

Consultation and Collaboration

School psychologists have knowledge of varied models and strategies of consultation, collaboration, and communication applicable to individuals, families, groups, and systems and methods to promote effective implementation of services. As part of a systematic and comprehensive process of effective decision making and problem solving that permeates all aspects of service delivery, school psychologists demonstrate skills to consult, collaborate, and communicate effectively with others. Examples of professional practices associated with consultation and collaboration include the following:

- School psychologists use a consultative problem solving process as a vehicle for planning, implementing, and evaluating academic and mental health services.
- School psychologists effectively communicate information for diverse audiences, such as parents, teachers and other school personnel, policy makers, community leaders, and others.
- School psychologists consult and collaborate at the individual, family, group, and systems levels
- School psychologists facilitate communication and collaboration among diverse school personnel, families, community professionals, and others
- School psychologists function as change agents, using their skills in communication, collaboration, and consultation to promote necessary change at the individual student, classroom, building, and district, state, and federal levels.
- School psychologists apply psychological and educational principles necessary to enhance collaboration and achieve effectiveness in provision of services.

DIRECT AND INDIRECT SERVICES FOR CHILDREN, FAMILIES, AND SCHOOLS

Student-Level Services

Interventions and Instructional Support to Develop Academic Skills

School psychologists have knowledge of biological, cultural, and social influences on academic skills; human learning, cognitive, and developmental processes; and evidence-based curricula and instructional strategies. School psychologists, in collaboration with others, demonstrate skills to use assessment and data collection methods and to implement and evaluate services that support cognitive and academic skills. Examples of direct and indirect services that support the development of cognitive and academic skills include the following:

- School psychologists use assessment data to develop and implement evidence-based instructional strategies that are intended to improve student performance.
- School psychologists promote the principles of student-centered learning to help students develop their individual abilities to be self-regulated learners, including the ability to set individual learning goals, design a learning process

to achieve those goals, and assess outcomes to determine whether the goals were achieved.

- School psychologists work with other school personnel to ensure the attainment of state and local academic benchmarks by all students.
- School psychologists apply current empirically based research on learning and cognition to the development of effective instructional strategies to promote student learning at the individual group, and systems level.
- School psychologists work with other school personnel to develop, implement, and evaluate effective interventions for increasing the amount of time students are engaged in learning.
- School psychologists incorporate all available assessment information in developing instructional strategies to meet the individual learning needs of children.
- School psychologists share information about research in curriculum and instruction with educators, parents, and the community to promote improvement in instruction, student achievement, and healthy lifestyles.
- School psychologists facilitate design and delivery of curriculum and instructional strategies that promote children's academic achievement, including, for example, literacy instruction, teacher-directed instruction, peer tutoring, interventions for self regulation and planning/organization, etc.
- School psychologists use information and assistive technology resources to enhance students' cognitive and academic skills.
- School psychologists address intervention acceptability and fidelity during development, implementation, and evaluation of instructional interventions.

Interventions and Mental Health Services to Develop Social and Life Skills

School psychologists have knowledge of biological, cultural, developmental, and social influences on behavior and mental health, behavioral and emotional impacts on learning and life skills, and evidence-based strategies to promote social–emotional functioning and mental health. School psychologists, in collaboration with others, demonstrate skills to use assessment and data-collection methods and to implement and evaluate services that support socialization, learning, and mental health. Examples of professional practices associated with development of social, emotional, behavioral, and life skills include the following:

- School psychologists integrate behavioral supports and mental health services with academic and learning goals for children.
- School psychologists facilitate design and delivery of curricula to help students develop effective behaviors, such as self-regulation and self-monitoring, planning/organization, empathy, and healthy decision-making.

- School psychologists use systematic decision-making to consider the antecedents, consequences, functions, and potential causes of behavioral difficulties that may impede learning or socialization.
- School psychologists address intervention acceptability and fidelity during development, implementation, and evaluation of behavioral and mental health interventions.
- School psychologists provide a continuum of developmentally appropriate mental health services, including individual and group counseling, behavioral coaching, classroom and school-wide social–emotional learning programs, positive behavioral support, and parent education and support; this may include attention to issues such as life skills and personal safety for students with lower levels of functioning.
- School psychologists develop and implement behavior change programs at individual, group, classroom, and school-wide levels that demonstrate the use of appropriate ecological and behavioral approaches (e.g., positive reinforcement, social skills training, and positive psychology) to student discipline and classroom management.
- School psychologists evaluate implementation and outcomes of behavioral and mental health interventions for individuals and groups.

Systems-Level Services

School-Wide Practices to Promote Learning

School psychologists have knowledge of school and systems structure, organization, and theory; general and special education; technology resources; and evidence-based school practices that promote learning and mental health. School psychologists, in collaboration with others, demonstrate skills to develop and implement practices and strategies to create and maintain effective and supportive learning environments for children and others. Professional practices associated with school-wide promotion of learning include the following:

- School psychologists, in collaboration with others, incorporate evidence-based strategies in the design, implementation, and evaluation of effective policies and practices in areas such as discipline, instructional support, staff training, school and other agency improvement activities, program evaluation, student transitions at all levels of schooling, grading, home– school partnerships, and more.
- School psychologists use their knowledge of organizational development and systems theory to assist in promoting a respectful and supportive atmosphere for decision making and collaboration, and a commitment to quality instruction and services.
- School psychologists are actively involved in the development of school improvement plans that impact the programs and services available to children,

youth, and families, and the manner in which school psychologists deliver their services.

- School psychologists incorporate evidence-based strategies when developing and delivering intervention programs to facilitate successful transitions of students from one environment to another environment (e.g., program to program, school to school, age-level changes, and school to work transitions).
- School psychologists promote the development and maintenance of learning environments that support resilience and academic growth, promote high rates of academic engaged time, and reduce negative influences on learning and behavior.
- School psychologists participate in designing and implementing universal screening programs to identify students in need of additional instructional or behavioral support services, as well as progress monitoring systems to ensure successful learning and school adjustment.
- School psychologists work collaboratively with other school personnel to create and maintain a multitiered continuum of services to support all students' attainment of academic, social, emotional, and behavioral goals.
- School psychologists apply the problem-solving process to broader research and systems-level problems that result in the identification of factors that influence learning and behavior, the evaluation of the outcomes of classroom, building, and system initiatives and the implementation of decision-making practices designed to meet general public accountability responsibilities.

Preventive and Responsive Services

School psychologists have knowledge of principles and research related to resilience and risk factors in learning and mental health, services in schools and communities to support multitiered prevention, and evidence-based strategies for effective crisis response. School psychologists, in collaboration with others, demonstrate skills to promote services that enhance learning, mental health, safety, and physical well-being through protective and adaptive factors and to implement effective crisis preparation, response, and recovery. Examples of effective practices associated with preventive and responsive services include the following:

- School psychologists promote recognition of risk and protective factors that are vital to understanding and addressing systemic problems such as school failure, truancy, dropout, bullying, youth suicide, or school violence.
- School psychologists participate in school crisis teams and use data-based decision making methods, problem-solving strategies, consultation, collaboration, and direct services in the context of crisis prevention, preparation, response, and recovery.
- School psychologists provide direct counseling, behavioral coaching, and indirect interventions through consultation for students who experience mental health problems that impair learning and/or socialization.

- School psychologists develop, implement, and evaluate prevention and intervention programs based on risk and protective factors that are precursors to severe learning and behavioral problems.
- School psychologists collaborate with school personnel, parents, students, and community resources to provide competent mental health support during and after crisis situations.
- School psychologists promote wellness and resilience by (a) collaborating with other healthcare professionals to provide a basic knowledge of behaviors that lead to good health for children; (b) facilitating environmental changes conducive to good health and adjustment of children; and (c) accessing resources to address a wide variety of behavioral, learning, mental, and physical needs.
- School psychologists participate in the implementation and evaluation of programs that promote safe and violence-free schools and communities.

Family–School Collaboration Services

School psychologists have knowledge of principles and research related to family systems, strengths, needs, and culture; evidence-based strategies to support family influences on children's learning and mental health; and strategies to develop collaboration between families and schools. School psychologists, in collaboration with others, demonstrate skills to design, implement, and evaluate services that respond to culture and context and facilitate family and school partnerships and interactions with community agencies for enhancement of academic and social–behavioral outcomes for children. Examples of professional practices associated with family–school collaboration include the following:

- School psychologists use evidence-based strategies to design, implement, and evaluate effective policies and practices that promote family, school, and community partnerships to enhance learning and mental health outcomes for students.
- School psychologists identify diverse cultural issues, contexts, and other factors that have an impact on family–school partnerships and interactions with community providers, and address these factors when developing and providing services for families.
- School psychologists promote strategies for safe, nurturing, and dependable parenting and home interventions to facilitate children's healthy development.
- School psychologists advocate for families and support parents in their involvement in school activities, for both addressing individual students' needs and participating in classroom and school events.
- School psychologists educate the school community regarding the influence of family involvement on school achievement and advocate for parent involvement in school governance and policy development whenever feasible.

- School psychologists help create linkages between schools, families, and community providers, and help coordinate services when programming for children involves multiple agencies.

FOUNDATIONS OF SCHOOL PSYCHOLOGICAL SERVICE DELIVERY

Diversity in Development and Learning

School psychologists have knowledge of individual differences, abilities, disabilities, and other diverse characteristics; principles and research related to diversity factors for children, families, and schools, including factors related to culture, context, and individual and role differences; and evidence-based strategies to enhance services and address potential influences related to diversity. School psychologists demonstrate skills to provide effective professional services that promote effective functioning for individuals, families, and schools with diverse characteristics, cultures, and backgrounds and across multiple contexts, with recognition that an understanding and respect for diversity in development and learning and advocacy for social justice are foundations for all aspects of service delivery. Examples of professional practices that promote and respect diversity include:

- School psychologists apply their understanding of the influence of culture, background, an individual learning characteristics (e.g., age, gender or gender identity, cognitive capabilities, social–emotional skills, developmental level, race, ethnicity, national origin, religion, sexual an gender orientation, disability, chronic illness, language, socioeconomic status) when designing and implementing interventions to achieve learning and behavioral outcomes.
- School psychologists, in collaboration with others, address individual differences, strengths, backgrounds, talents, and needs in the design, implementation, and evaluation of services in order to improve learning and mental health outcomes for all children in family, school, and community contexts.
- School psychologists provide culturally competent and effective practices in all areas of school psychology service delivery and in the contexts of diverse individual, family, school, and community characteristics.
- School psychologists work collaboratively with cultural brokers or community liaisons to understand and address the needs of diverse learners.
- School psychologists utilize a problem solving framework for addressing the needs of English language learners.
- School psychologists recognize in themselves and others the subtle racial, class, gender, cultural and other biases they may bring to their work and the way these biases influence decision-making, instruction, behavior, and long-term outcomes for students.
- School psychologists promote fairness and social justice in educational programs and services.

Research and Program Evaluation

School psychologists have knowledge of research design, statistics, measurement, varied data collection and analysis techniques, and program evaluation sufficient for understanding research and interpreting data in applied settings. School psychologists demonstrate skills to evaluate and apply research as a foundation for service delivery and, in collaboration with others, use various techniques and technology resources for data collection, measurement, and analysis to support effective practices at the individual, group, and/or systems levels. Examples of professional practices associated with research and program evaluation include the following:

- School psychologists evaluate and synthesize a cumulative body of research findings as a foundation for effective service delivery.
- School psychologists incorporate techniques for data collection, analyses, and accountability in evaluation of services at the individual, group, and system levels.
- School psychologists, in collaboration with others, collect, analyze, and interpret program evaluation data in applied settings.
- School psychologists provide support for classroom teachers in collecting and analyzing progress monitoring data.
- School psychologists apply knowledge of evidence based interventions and programs in designing, implementing, and evaluating the fidelity and effectiveness of school-based intervention plans.
- School psychologists provide assistance in schools and other settings for analyzing, interpreting, and using empirical foundations for effective practices at the individual, group, and/or systems levels.
- School psychologists incorporate various techniques for data collection, measurement, analysis, accountability, and use of technology resources in evaluation of services at the individual, group, and/or systems levels.

Legal, Ethical, and Professional Practice

School psychologists have knowledge of the history and foundations of school psychology; multiple service models and methods; ethical, legal, and professional standards; and other factors related to professional identity and effective practice as school psychologists. School psychologists demonstrate skills to provide services consistent with ethical, legal, and professional standards; engage in responsive ethical and professional decision-making; collaborate with other professionals; and apply professional work characteristics needed for effective practice as school psychologists, including respect for human diversity and social justice, communication skills, effective interpersonal skills, responsibility, adaptability, initiative, dependability, and technology skills. Examples of legal, ethical, and professional practice include the following:

- School psychologists practice in ways that are consistent with ethical, professional, and legal standards and regulations.
- School psychologists engage in effective, collaborative, and ethical professional relationships.
- School psychologists use supervision and mentoring for effective practice.
- School psychologists access, evaluate, and utilize information sources and technology in ways that safeguard and enhance the quality of services and responsible record keeping. N School psychologists assist administrators, teachers, other school personnel, and parents in understanding and adhering to legislation and regulations relevant to regular education and special education.
- School psychologists advocate for professional roles as providers of effective services that enhance the learning and mental health of all children and youth.
- School psychologists engage in lifelong learning and formulate personal plans for ongoing professional growth.
- School psychologists participate in continuing education activities at a level consistent with maintenance of the NCSP credential (i.e., a minimum of 25 hours of professional development per year).

PART II: ORGANIZATIONAL PRINCIPLES

ORGANIZATIONAL PRINCIPLE 1: ORGANIZATION OF SERVICE DELIVERY

School psychological services are provided in a coordinated, organized fashion and are delivered in a manner that ensures the provision of a comprehensive and seamless continuum of services. Services are delivered in accordance with a strategic planning process that considers the needs of consumers and utilizes an evidence-based program evaluation model.

1.1 School psychological services are planned and delivered on the basis of a systematic assessment of the educational and psychological needs of the students and families in the local community. School systems ensure that services provided directly by school psychologists are based on a strategic plan. The plan is developed based on the collective needs of the school system and community, with the primary focus being the specific needs of the students served by individual school psychologists.

1.2 School psychological services are available to all students on an equal basis and are not determined by a specific funding source. Services are provided to students based on their need, not based on their eligibility to generate specific funding.

1.3 School psychological services are integrated with other school and community services. Students and their families should not be responsible for the integration of these services based on funding, setting, or program location. Therefore, school psychological and mental health services are provided through a "seamless" system of care. When school psychological services are provided by outside consultants, the school system maintains responsibility for the quality of services and for oversight of planning and implementation of services.

1.4 Contractual school psychological services are provided in a manner consistent with this model, *NASP Principles for Professional Ethics*, and other relevant professional guidelines and standards. Contractual school psychological services are not used as a means to decrease the type, amount, and quality of school psychological services provided by an employing agency. They may be used to augment and enhance programs.

1.5 School systems conduct regular evaluations of the collective delivery of educational, mental health, and other student services as well as those services provided by individual school psychologists. The evaluation process focuses on both the nature and extent of the services provided (process) and the student- or family-focused effects of those services (outcomes). Evaluation of services from outside consultants who provide school psychological services is the responsibility of the school system, and the evaluation process should be consistent with that used for services provided by school psychologists who are school district employees.

1.6 The school system provides a range of services to meet the academic and mental health needs of students. As indicated in this model, school psychologists collaborate with other school personnel to provide both direct and indirect services to students and families. The consumers of and participants in these services include the following: students, teachers, counselors, social workers, administrators, other school personnel, families, care providers, other community and regional agencies, and resources that support the educational process.

1.7 School systems support the provision of consultative and other services by school psychologists to teachers, administrators, and other school personnel for the purpose of improving student outcomes.

ORGANIZATIONAL PRINCIPLE 2: CLIMATE

It is the responsibility of the school system to create a climate in which school psychological services can be delivered with mutual respect for all parties. Employees have the freedom to advocate for the services that are necessary to meet the needs of consumers and are free from artificial, administrative, or political constraints that might hinder or alter the provision of appropriate services.

2.1 School systems promote cooperative and collaborative relationships among staff members in the best mutual interests of students and families. Conflicts are resolved in a constructive and professional manner.

2.2 School systems provide an organizational climate in which school psychologists and other personnel may advocate in a professional manner for the most appropriate services for students and families, without fear of reprisal from supervisors or administrators.

2.3 School systems promote work environments that maximize job satisfaction of employees in order to maintain a high quality of services provided to students. Measures of work climate are included in organizational self-evaluation.

2.4 School systems promote and advocate for balance between professional and personal lives of employees. Supervisors monitor work and stress levels of employees and take steps to reduce pressure when the well-being of the employee is at risk. Supervisors are available to employees to problem solve when personal factors may adversely affect job performance and when job expectations may adversely affect the personal life of the employee.

ORGANIZATIONAL PRINCIPLE 3: PHYSICAL, PERSONNEL, AND FISCAL SUPPORT SYSTEMS

School systems ensure that (a) an adequate recruitment and retention plan for employees exists to ensure adequate personnel to meet the needs of the system; (b) all sources of funding, both public and private, are used and maximized to ensure the fiscal support necessary to provide adequate services; (c) all employees have adequate technology, clerical services, and a physical work environment; and (d) employees have adequate personnel benefits necessary to support their work, including continuing educational professional development.

3.1 School systems assume professional responsibility and accountability for services through the recruitment of qualified and diverse staff and the assurance that staff function only in their areas of competency.

3.2 School systems support recruitment and retention of qualified staff by advocating for appropriate ratios of school psychology services staff to students. The ratio of school psychologists to students is a critical aspect of the quality of services to students. This ratio should be determined by the level of staffing needed to provide comprehensive school psychological services in accordance with the system's needs assessment. Generally, the ratio should not exceed 1,000 students to 1 school psychologist. When school psychologists are providing comprehensive and preventive services (i.e., evaluations, consultation, individual/group counseling, crisis response, behavioral interventions, etc), this ratio should not exceed 500 to 700 students for 1 school psychologist in order to ensure quality of student outcomes. Similarly, when school psychologists are assigned to work primarily with student populations that have particularly intensive special needs (e.g., students with significant emotional or behavioral disorders, or students with autism spectrum disorders), this student to school psychologist ratio should be even lower.

3.3 School systems provide advanced technological resources in time management, communication systems, data management systems, and service delivery.

3.4 School systems provide staff with access to adequate clerical assistance, appropriate professional work materials, sufficient office and work space, adequate technology support (e.g., e-mail, computer), and general working conditions that enhance the delivery of effective services. Included are assessment and intervention materials, access to private telephone and office, clerical services, therapeutic aids, and access to professional literature.

ORGANIZATIONAL PRINCIPLE 4: PROFESSIONAL COMMUNICATION

School systems ensure that policies and practices exist that result in positive, proactive communication among employees at all administrative levels of the organization.

4.1 School systems provide opportunities for employees to communicate with each other about issues of mutual professional interest on a regular basis.

4.2 School systems support collaborative problem solving approaches to the planning and delivery of school psychological services. Decision making and strategic planning regarding school psychological services is done in collaboration with other departments and outside agencies to ensure optimal services for students.

4.3 School systems ensure that staff members have access to the technology necessary to perform their jobs adequately and to maintain appropriate and confidential communication with students, families, and service providers within and outside the system.

4.4 The school system's policy on student records is consistent with state and federal rules and laws and ensures the protection of the confidentiality of the student and his or her family. The policy specifies the types of data developed by the school psychologist that are classified as school or pupil records. The policy gives clear guidance (consistent with *the Family Educational Records and Privacy Act* or similar state/court regulations) regarding which documents belong to the school and the student/ guardian and which documents (such as clinical notes) are the personal property of the school psychologist. Although test protocols are part of the student's record, the school system ensures that test security is protected and copyright restrictions are observed. Release of records and protocols is consistent with state and federal regulations. The policy on student records includes procedures for maintaining student confidentiality and privacy in the use of electronic communications. The NASP *Principles for Professional Ethics* provides additional guidance for schools with regard to responsible school-based record keeping.

ORGANIZATIONAL PRINCIPLE 5: SUPERVISION AND MENTORING

The school system ensures that all personnel have levels and types of supervision and/or mentoring adequate to ensure the provision of effective and accountable services. Supervision and mentoring are provided through an ongoing, positive, systematic, collaborative process between the school psychologist and a school psychology supervisor or other school psychology colleagues. This process focuses on promoting professional growth and exemplary professional practice leading to improved performance by all concerned, including the school psychologist, supervisor, students, and the entire school community.

5.1 Supervisors have a valid state school psychologist credential for the setting in which they are employed, and have a minimum of 3 years of experience as a practicing school psychologist. Education and/or experience in the supervision of school personnel are desirable.

5.2 Supervision methods should match the developmental level of the school psychologist. Interns and novice school psychologists require more intensive supervisory modalities, including regularly scheduled face-to-face sessions. Alternative methods, such as supervision groups, mentoring and/or peer support can be utilized with more experienced school psychologists to ensure continued professional growth and support for complex or difficult cases.

5.3 School systems allow time for school psychologists to participate in supervision and mentoring. In small or rural systems, where a supervising school psychologist may not be available, the school system ensures that school psychologists are given opportunities to seek supervision and/or peer support outside the district (e.g., through regional, state, or national school psychologist networks).

5.4 The school system should develop and implement a coordinated plan for the accountability and evaluation of all school psychological services. This plan should address evaluation of both implementation and outcomes of services.

5.5 Supervisors ensure that practica and internship experiences occur under conditions of appropriate supervision including (a) access to professional school psychologists who will serve as appropriate role models, (b) provision of supervision by an appropriately credentialed school psychologist, and (c) provision of supervision within the guidelines of the training institution and *NASP Graduate Preparation Standards for School Psychology*.

5.6 Supervisors provide professional leadership through participation in school psychology professional organizations and active involvement in local, state, and federal public policy development.

ORGANIZATIONAL PRINCIPLE 6: PROFESSIONAL DEVELOPMENT AND RECOGNITION SYSTEMS

Individual school psychologists and school systems develop professional development plans annually. The school system ensures that continuing

professional development of its personnel is both adequate for and relevant to the service delivery priorities of the school system. School systems recognize the need for a variety of professional development activities. These activities could include those provided by the school system, NASP-approved providers, other educational entities, or other activities such as online training, formal self-study, and professional learning communities.

6.1 **Professional Development Responsibilities**

- The school system provides support (e.g., funding, time, supervision) to ensure that school psychologists have sufficient access to continuing professional development at a level necessary to remain current regarding developments in professional practices that benefit children, families, and schools.
- The school system provides technology and personnel resources to assist in providing a system for documenting professional development activities.

6.2 **Professional Development Plans and Application of New Skills**

- The school system provides supervision of school psychologists by an appropriately credentialed and experienced school psychologist, so that the development of professional skills is continued and maintained over time. School psychologists seek and use appropriate types and levels of supervision as they acquire new knowledge, skills, and abilities by creating and following a personal plan of professional development.
- Supervision supported by the school system makes available the opportunities to provide feedback to the school psychologist about the quality of new skill applications.

6.3 **Advanced Recognition of Professional Development:** The school system provides levels of recognition (e.g., salary, opportunity to use new skills) that reflect the professional growth of individual school psychologists.

References

Accredited doctoral programs in professional psychology: 2005. (2005). *American Psychologist, 60*(9), 1002–1016.

Accredited internship and postdoctoral programs for training in psychology: 2005. (2005). *American Psychologist, 60*(9), 979–1001.

Agin, T. (1979). The school psychologist and collective bargaining: The brokerage of influence and professional concerns. *School Psychology Digest, 8,* 187–192.

Akin-Little, K. A., Bray, M. A., Eckert, T. L., & Kehle, T. J. (2006). The perceptions of academic women in school psychology: A national survey. *School Psychology Quarterly, 19,* 327–341.

Akin-Little, K. A., Little, S. G., & Eckert, T. L. (2006, March). *Men and women in academic school psychology: A national survey.* Paper presented at the annual convention of the National Association of School Psychologists, Anaheim, CA.

Albayrak-Kaymak, D., & Dolek, N. (1997). New challenges facing school psychologists in Turkey. *World-Go-Round, 24*(5), 4.

Albee, G. W. (1998). Fifty years of clinical psychology: Selling our soul to the devil. *Applied and Preventive Psychology, 7,* 189–194.

Allen, W. (1993). Comprehensive contracted services: Assets to the field of school psychology. *Communiqué, 22*(1), 3–4.

Allensworth, D., Lawson, E., Nicholson, L., & Wyche, J. (Eds.). (1997). *Schools and health: Our nation's investment.* Washington, DC: National Academy Press.

Alpert, J. L. (1985). Change within a profession: Change, future, prevention, and school psychology. *American Psychologist, 40,* 1112–1121.

America's Best Graduate Schools. (1995, March 20). U.S. News & World Report, p. 109.

American Counseling Association. (2005). *ACA code of ethics.* Alexandria, VA: Author.

American Educational Research Association, American Psychological Association, & National Council on Measurement in Education. (1999). *Standards for educational and psychological testing.* Washington, DC: Author.

American Psychiatric Association. (2000). *Diagnostic and statistical manual of mental disorders, text revision* (4th ed.) Washington, DC: Author.

American Psychological Association. (1953). *Ethical standards of psychologists.* Washington, DC: Author.

American Psychological Association. (1981). Specialty guidelines for the delivery of services by school psychologists. In APA, *Specialty guidelines for the delivery of services* (pp. 33–44). Washington, DC: Author. See also *American Psychologist, 36,* 640–681.

American Psychological Association. (1986). *Guidelines for computer-based tests and interpretations.* Washington, DC: Author.

American Psychological Association. (1987a). Model act for state licensure of psychologists. *American Psychologist, 42,* 696–703.

American Psychological Association. (1987b). *General guidelines for providers of psychological services*. Washington, DC: Author.

American Psychological Association. (1995). *Guidelines for engaging in the contractual provision of psychological services in schools*. Washington, DC: Author.

American Psychological Association. (1998, May). *Surviving and thriving in academia: A guide for women and ethnic minorities*. Washington, DC: Author.

American Psychological Association. (2002). *Ethical principles of psychologists and code of conduct*. Washington, DC: Author. See also *American Psychologist, 57*(12), 1060–1073.

American Psychological Association. (2003, November). *Psychology: Scientific problem solvers: Careers for the twenty-first century*. Washington, DC: Author.

American Psychological Association, Commission for the Recognition of Specialties and Proficiencies in Professional Psychology. (2006.) *Archival Description of School Psychology*. Retrieved February 24, 2006 from APA Online website: http://www.apa.org/crsppp/schpsych.html

American Psychological Association, Committee on Employment and Human Resources. (1986). The changing face of American psychology. *American Psychologist, 41*, 1311–1327.

American Psychological Association, Committee on Psychological Tests and Assessment. (1996). *Statement on the disclosure of tests data*. Washington, DC: Author.

American Psychological Association, Office of Program Consultation and Accreditation, Education Directorate. (2005). *Guidelines and principles for accreditation of programs in professional psychology*. Washington, DC: Author.

American Psychological Association and American Association for Applied Psychology Committee on Graduate and Professional Training (APA & AAAP). (1945). Subcommittee report on graduate internship training in psychology. *Journal of Consulting Psychology, 9*, 243–266.

Americans With Disabilities Act of 1990, Pub. L. 101-336, 42 U.S.C.A.:12101 et seq.

Anastasi, A. (1992, August). *A century of psychological testing: Origins, problems, and progress*. Paper presented at the annual meeting of the American Psychological Association, Washington, DC.

Anderson, W. T., Hohenshil, T. H., & Brown, D. T. (1984). Job satisfaction among practicing school psychologists: A national study. *School Psychology Review, 13*, 225–230.

Andrews, J. (2002). In search of professional identity or accepting what we do and getting better at it? *In-Psyghts, 13*(2), 13–15.

Andrews, J., & Saklofske, D. (2007). *Special education in Canada*. Unpublished manuscript, Division of Applied Psychology, University of Calgary.

Andrews, J., Saklofske, D. H., & Janzen, H. L. (Eds). (2001). *Handbook of psychoeducational assessment: Ability, achievement, and behaviour in children*. San Diego, CA: Academic Press.

Andrews, T. J., Wisniewski, J. J., & Mulick, J. A. (1997). Variables influencing teachers' decisions to refer children for school psychological assessment services. *Psychology in the Schools, 34*, 239–244.

Annie E. Casey Foundation. (2002). *Children at risk: State trends 1990–2000*. Baltimore, MD: Author.

Arthur, A. Z. (1971). Applied training programmes of psychology in Canada: A survey. *The Canadian Psychologist, 12*, 46–65.

Association of Psychology Postdoctoral and Internship Centers. (2001). *APPIC membership criteria: Doctoral psychology internship programs.* Washington, DC: Author. Retrieved from http://www.appic.org

Association of Psychology Postdoctoral and Internship Centers. (2005). *APPIC directory 2005–2006.* Washington, DC: Author. Retrieved from http://www.appic.org

Association of State and Provincial Psychology Boards. (1998). *ASPPB model act for licensing psychologists.* Montgomery, AL: Author.

Association of State and Provincial Psychology Boards (2005). *Code of conduct.* Montgomery, AL: Author.

Baer, D. M., & Bushell, D. (1981). The future of behavior analysis in the schools? Consider its recent past, and then ask a different question. *School Psychology Review, 10,* 259–270.

Bahr, M. W. (1996). Are school psychologists reform-minded? *Psychology in the Schools, 33,* 295–307.

Baker, J. A. (2006). Council of Directors of School Psychology Programs Student Survey 2006. Unpublished study, contact author at 434 Erickson Hall, Michigan State University, East Lansing, MI 48824.

Barbarin, O. A. (1992). Family functioning and school adjustment: Family systems perspectives. In F. J. Medway and T. P. Cafferty (Eds.), *School psychology: A social psychological perspective* (pp. 137–163). Hillsdale, NJ: Erlbaum.

Bardon, J. I. (1979). How best to establish the identity of professional school psychology. *School Psychology Digest, 8*, 162–167.

Bardon, J. I. (1983). Psychology applied to education: A specialty in search of an identity. *American Psychologist, 38*, 185–196.

Bardon, J. I. (1986). Psychology and schooling: The interrelationships among persons, processes, and products. In S. N. Elliott & J. C. Witt (Eds.), *The delivery of psychological services in schools: Concepts, processes, and issues* (pp. 53–79). Hillsdale, NJ: Erlbaum.

Bardon, J. I. (1987). The translation of research into practice in school psychology. *School Psychology Review, 16*, 317–328.

Bardon, J. I., & Bennett, V. C. (1974). *School psychology.* Englewood Cliffs, NJ: Prentice Hall.

Barona, A., & Garcia, E. E. (Eds.). (1990). *Children at risk: Poverty, minority status, and other issues in educational equity.* Washington, DC: National Association of School Psychologists.

Bartell, R. (1995). Historical perspective on the role and practice of school psychology. *Canadian Journal of School Psychology, 11,* 133–137.

Bartell, R. (1996a). The argument for a paradigm shift or what's in a name? *Canadian Journal of School Psychology, 12*, 86–90.

Bartell, R. (1996b, August). *Will the real school psychologist stand up? The psychologist of the school or the psychologist in the school.* Paper presented at the Third School Psychology Institute, 104th Convention of the American Psychological Association, Toronto, Ontario, Canada.

Bartell, R. (2003, November). *Creating positive school environments: Toward optimal learning and well-being of school children.* Paper presented at the Manitoba Educational Network Research Forum on Improving Learning Outcomes, Brandon, Manitoba, Canada.

Bartell, R. (2006). *Contemplating the future course for school psychology in Manitoba: To contextualize or decontextualize?* Unpublished manuscript, University of Manitoba, Winnepeg, Manitoba, Canada.

Bartell, R., & Saklofske, D. (1998). *Proposal for national standards for Canadian school psychologists* (Draft). Adopted by the Canadian Association of School Psychologists, Winnipeg, Manitoba.

Batsche, G. M. (1996). National certification in school psychology. In T. K. Fagan & P. G. Warden (Eds.), *Historical encyclopedia of school psychology* (pp. 223–225). Westport, CT: Greenwood Press.

Batsche, G. M., Knoff, H. M., & Peterson, D. W. (1989). Trends in credentialing and practice standards. *School Psychology Review, 18,* 193–202.

Batts, J., & Grossman, F. (1997). Frequently asked questions (FAQs): Ethics and standards. *Communiqué, 25*(6), 16.

Beal, A. L., & Service, J. (1995). Submission to an Ontario Board of Education concerning proposed reduction in psychological services. *Canadian Journal of School Psychology, 11,* 90–92.

Bender, R. H. (1991). If you can count it, you can improve it: Total quality transformation tools sculpt better handle on system. *The School Administrator, 9*(48), 24–26, 35.

Benjamin, L. T., & Baker, D. B. (2004). *From séance to science: A history of the profession of psychology in America.* Belmont, CA: Wadsworth/Thompson Learning.

Benjamin, L. T., & Shields, S. A. (1990). Leta Stetter Hollingworth (1886–1939). In A. N. O'Connell & N. F. Russo (Eds.), *Women in psychology: A bio-bibliographic sourcebook* (pp. 173–183). Westport, CT: Greenwood Press.

Benson, A. J. (1985). School psychology service configurations: A regional approach. *School Psychology Review, 14,* 421–428.

Bent, R. J., Packard, R. E., & Goldberg, R. W. (1999). The American Board of Professional Psychology, 1947 to 1997: A historical perspective. *Professional Psychology: Research and Practice, 30,* 65–73.

Beran, T., & Tutty, L. (2002). Children's reports of bullying and safety at school. *Canadian Journal of School Psychology, 17,* 1–14.

Beran, T., Tutty, L., & Steinwrath, G. (2004). An evaluation of a bullying prevention program for elementary schools. *Canadian Journal of School Psychology, 19* (1/2), 99–116.

Bergan, J. R. (1985). The future of school psychology. In J. R. Bergan (Ed.), *School psychology in contemporary society: An introduction* (pp. 421–437). Columbus, OH: Charles E. Merrill.

Bernard, J. L. (1975). Due process in dropping the unsuitable clinical student. *Professional Psychology, 6,* 275–278.

Berne, E. (1964). *Games people play: The psychology of human relationships.* New York: Grove Press.

Bersoff, D. N. (1981). Testing and the law. *American Psychologist, 36,* 1047–1056.

Bersoff, D. N. (1982a). Larry P. and PASE: Judicial report cards on the validity of individual intelligence tests. In T. Kratochwill (Ed.), *Advances in school psychology* (Vol. 2, pp. 61–95). Hillsdale, NJ: Erlbaum.

Bersoff, D. N. (1982b). The legal regulation of school psychology. In C. R. Reynolds & T. B. Gutkin (Eds.), *The handbook of school psychology* (pp. 1043–1074). New York: Wiley.

Beutler, L. E., & Fisher, D. (1994). Combined specialty training in counseling, clinical, and school psychology: An idea whose time has returned. *Professional Psychology: Research and Practice*, *25*, 62–69.

Bevan, W. (1981). On coming of age among the professions. *School Psychology Review*, *10*, 127–137.

Biddle, B. J. (1997). Foolishness, dangerous nonsense, and real correlates of state differences in achievement. *Phi Delta Kappan*, *79*(1), 9–13.

Binet, A., & Henri, V. (1894). De la suggestibilite naturelle chez les enfants (On natural suggestibility in children). *Review Philosophique*, *38*, 337–347.

Blagg, D., Durbin, K., Kelly, C., McHugh, C., & Safranski, S. (1997). School psychologists as administrators: Five journeys. *Communiqué*, *25*(8), 14–15.

Blakely, D. L., & Wells, N. (2001). School psychology in the Northwest Territories. *Canadian Journal of School Psychology*, *16*, 87–88.

Bollin, G. (2003). The realities of middle school for Mexican children. *The Clearing House*, *76*(4), 198–203.

Bonham, S. J., & Grover, E. C. (1961). *The history and development of school psychology in Ohio.* Columbus: Ohio Department of Education.

Bontrager, T., & Wilczenski, F. L. (1997). School psychology practice in an era of educational reform. *Communiqué*, *25*(8) 28–29.

Bose, J. (2003). *Testing environments of school psychologists: Are they adequate?* Unpublished master's thesis, University of Memphis, Memphis, Tennessee.

Bowers, J. E. (1962). Wanted: Trained psychologists for employment in school systems. *The Canadian Psychologist*, *3*, 51–52.

Boxley, R., Drew, C., & Rangel, D. (1986). Clinical trainee impairment in APA approved internship programs. *The Clinical Psychologist*, *39*, 49–52.

Bradley-Klug, K. L., & Powell-Smith, K. A. (2001, January). *Web-based courses in graduate training programs: An overview.* Presented at the annual meeting of the Council of Directors of School Psychology Programs, Deerfield Beach, FL.

Bradshaw, J. (2005, May/June). CPQs improve mobility for psychologists. *The National Psychologist*, *14*(3), 1, 3.

Bramlett, R. K., Murphy, J. J., Johnson, J., Wallingsford, L., & Hall, J. D. (2002). Contemporary practices in school psychology: A national survey of roles and referral problems. *Psychology in the Schools*, *39*, 327–335.

Brandt, J. E. (1996). Prereferral assessment. In T. K. Fagan & P. G. Warden (Eds.), *Historical encyclopedia of school psychology.* Westport, CT: Greenwood Press.

Bronfenbrenner, U. (1979). *The ecology of human development.* Cambridge, MA: Harvard University Press.

Brooks, B., & Seigel, P. (1996). *The scared child: Helping kids overcome traumatic events.* New York: Wiley.

Brotemarkle, R. A. (Ed.). (1931). *Clinical psychology: Studies in honor of Lightner Witmer to commemorate the thirty-fifth anniversary of the founding of the first psychological clinic.* Philadelphia: University of Pennsylvania Press.

Brown, D. T. (1989). The evolution of entry-level training in school psychology: Are we now approaching the doctoral level? *School Psychology Review, 18,* 11–15.

Brown, D. T., Cardon, B. W., Coulter, W. A., & Meyers, J. (Eds.). (1982). The Olympia proceedings [Special issue]. *School Psychology Review, 11*(2).

Brown, D. T., & Lindstrom, J. P. (1977). *Directory of school psychology training programs in the United States and Canada.* Washington, DC: National Association of School Psychologists.

Brown, D. T., & Minke, K. M. (1984). *Directory of school psychology training programs.* Washington, DC: National Association of School Psychologists.

Brown, D. T., & Minke, K. M. (1986). School psychology graduate training: A comprehensive analysis. *American Psychologist, 41,* 1328–1338.

Brown, M., & Hohenshil, T. (2004, March). *Job satisfaction of school psychologists.* Paper presented at the annual convention of the National Association of School Psychologists, Dallas, TX.

Brown, M. B., Hohenshil, T. H., & Brown, D. T. (1998). Job satisfaction of school psychologists in the United States. *School Psychology International, 19*(1), 79–89.

Brown, M. B., Kissell, S., & Bolen, L. M. (2003). Doctoral school psychology internships in non-school settings in the United States. *School Psychology International, 24*(4), 394–404.

Brown, M. B., Swigart, M. L., Bolen, L. M., Hall, C. W., & Webster, R. T. (1998). Doctoral and nondoctoral practicing school psychologists: Are there differences? *Psychology in the Schools, 35,* 347–354.

Brown-Chidsey, R., & Steege, M. W. (2005). *Response to intervention: Principles and strategies for effective practice.* New York: Guilford Press.

Bruner, J. S., Oliver, R. R., & Greenfield, P. M. (1966). *Studies in cognitive growth.* New York: Wiley.

Bucy, J. E., Meyers, A. B., & Swerdlik, M. E. (2002). Best practices in working in full-service schools. In A. Thomas & J. Grimes (Eds.), *Best practices in school psychology* (pp. 281–291). Bethesda, MD: National Association of School Psychologists.

Burns, M. K., & Ysseldyke, J. E. (2006, February). Comparison of existing response-to-intervention models to identify and answer implementation questions. *Communiqué, 34*(5), 1, 5.

Butler, A. S., & Maher, C. A. (1981). Conflict and special service teams: Perspectives and suggestions for school psychologists. *Journal of School Psychology, 19,* 62–70.

California Association of School Psychologists. (1991). CASP position paper. The role of assessment in California schools: Ensuring student success. *CASP Today, 4*(August), 7.

Canadian Psychological Association. (2000). *Canadian code of ethics for psychologists* (3rd. ed.). Ottawa, Ontario: Author.

Canadian Psychological Association. (2002). *Enhancing the experience of children and youth in today's schools: The role of psychology in Canadian schools.* Ottawa, Ontario: Author.

Canter, A. (1990a). Issues related to third-party reimbursement. *Communiqué, 19*(3), 14.

Canter, A. (1990b). Policy needed for handling parents' requests for protocols. *Communiqué, 19*(2), 2.

Canter, A. (1991a). Alternative sources of funding may be mixed blessing. *Communiqué, 19*(6), 16.

Canter, A. S. (1991b). Effective psychological services for all students: A data-based model of service delivery. In G. Stoner, M. R. Shinn, & H. M. Walker (Eds.), *Interventions for achievement and behavior problems* (pp. 49–78). Washington, DC: National Association of School Psychologists.

Canter, A. S., & Carroll, S. A. (Eds.). (1998). *Helping children at home and school: Handouts from your school psychologist.* Bethesda, MD: National Association of School Psychologists.

Canter A., & Crandall, A. (Eds.). (1994) *Professional advocacy resource manual: Preserving school-based positions.* Washington, DC: National Association of School Psychologists.

Canter, A. S., Paige, L. Z., Roth, M. D., Romero, I., and Carroll, S. A. (Eds.). (2004). *Helping children at home and school II: Handouts for families and educators.* Bethesda, MD: National Association of School Psychologists.

Caplan, G. (1970). *The theory and practice of mental health consultation.* New York: Basic Books.

Cardon, B., Kuriloff, P., & Phillips, B. N. (Eds.). (1975). Law and the school psychologist: Challenge and opportunity [Special issue]. *Journal of School Psychology, 13.*

Carlson, C. I., & Sincavage, J. M. (1987). Family-oriented school psychology practice: Results of a national survey of NASP members. *School Psychology Review, 16,* 519–526.

Carlson, H. S. (1978). The AASPB story. *American Psychologist, 33,* 486–495.

Carlson, J. F., & Martin, S. P. (1997, April). *Responsible use of computer-based test interpretation and report generation software: Implications for practice.* Paper presented at the annual meeting of the National Association of School Psychologists, Anaheim, CA.

Carlson, J. S., Demaray, M. K., & Oehmke, S. (2006). A survey of school psychologists' knowledge and training in child psychopharmacology. *Psychology in the Schools, 43,* 623–633.

Carlson, J. S., Thaler, C. L., & Hirsch, A. J. (2005). Psychotropic medication consultation in schools: An ethical and legal dilemma for school psychologists. *Journal of Applied School Psychology, 22*(1), 29–41.

Carney, P. (1995a). Symposium: School psychology at the intersection of societal change. *Canadian Journal of School Psychology, 11,* 81–82.

Carney, P. (1995b). Submission to an Ontario Board of Education from the Canadian Association of School Psychologists. *Canadian Journal of School Psychology, 11,* 89.

Carney, P. (2001). The practice of psychology in Ontario schools. *Canadian Journal of School Psychology, 16*, 47–57.

Carney, P., & Cole, E. (1995). Editorial: Advocacy issues and events in school psychology. *Canadian Journal of School Psychology, 11*, i.

Carper, R. M., & Williams, R. L. (2004). Article publications, journal outlets, and article themes for current faculty in APA-accredited school psychology programs: 1995–1999. *School Psychology Quarterly, 19*, 141–165.

Cattell, J. McK. (1890). Mental tests and measurement. *Mind, 15*, 373–380.

Catterall, C. D. (1967). *Strategies for prescriptive interventions.* Santa Clara, CA: Santa Clara Unified School District.

Catterall, C. (Ed.). (1976–1979a). *Psychology in the schools in international perspectives* (Vols.1–3). Columbus, OH: Author.

Catterall, C. (1979b). State of the art. In C. Catterall (Ed.), *Psychology in the schools in international perspective: Vol. 3* (pp. 193–219). Columbus, OH: Author. (Now available from International School Psychology Association.)

CDSPP doctoral level internship guidelines. (1998). *CDSPP Press, 16*(2), 7–8.

Ceci, S. J., Papierno, P. B., & Mueller-Johnson, K. U. (2002). The twisted relationship between school spending and academic outputs: In search of a new metaphor. *Journal of School Psychology, 40*, 477–484.

Centra, J. A., & Potter, D. A. (1980). School and teacher effects: An inter-relational model. *Review of Educational Research, 50*, 273–291.

Chamberlin, J. (2006). Psychologist, professor among top 10 U.S. jobs. *GradPSYCH, 4*(3), 7.

Charvat, J. L. (2005). NASP study: How many school psychologists are there? *Communiqué, 33*(6). 12–14.

Charvat, J., & Feinberg, T. (2003, October). The school psychologist shortage: Evidence for effective advocacy. *Communiqué, 32*(2), 1, 4–5.

Christenson, S. L. (1995). Supporting home-school collaboration. In A. Thomas & J. Grimes (Eds.), *Best practices in school psychology III* (pp. 253–267). Washington, DC: National Association of School Psychologists.

Christenson, S. L. (2004). The family-school partnership: An opportunity to promote the learning competence of all students. *School Psychology Review, 33*, 83–104.

Christenson, S. L., & Conoley, J. C. (Eds.). (1992). *Home-school collaboration: Enhancing children's academic and social competence.* Washington, DC: National Association of School Psychologists.

Christenson, S. L., Rounds, T., & Gorney, D. (1992). Family factors and student achievement: An avenue to students' success. *School Psychology Quarterly, 7*, 178–206.

Christie, K. (2005). Stateline: Paraprofessionals on the front line. *Phi Delta Kappan, 87*(3), 181–182.

Cincinnati Public Schools, Board of Education. (1912). *83rd annual report of the board of education.* Cincinnati, OH: Author.

City of Chicago, Board of Education. (1941). *Bureau of Child Study and the Chicago adjustment service plan.* Chicago: Author.

City of New York, Board of Education. (1938). *Bureau of Child Guidance five year report 1932–1937.* New York: Author.

Clair, T. N., & Kiraly, J. (1971). Can school psychology survive in the 70's? *Professional Psychology, 2*, 383–388.

Clay, R. A. (1996, June). New state laws jeopardize fate of school psychology. *APA Monitor, 27*(6), 25.

Cleveland Public Schools. (ca. 1928). Psychological clinic: Brief survey. Cleveland, OH: Author.

Clinchy, E. (1998). The educationally challenged American school district. *Phi Delta Kappan, 80*(4), 272–277.

Cobb, C. T. (1990). School psychology in the 1980s and 1990s: A context for change and definition. In T. B. Gutkin & C. R. Reynolds (Eds.), *The handbook of school psychology* (pp. 21 31). New York: Wiley.

Cobb, C. T. (1992, August). *Will there be a school psychology symposium at the 150th APA convention?* Paper presented at the annual meeting of the American Psychological Association, Washington, DC.

Cohen, R. D. (1985). Child-saving and progressivism, 1885–1915. In J. M. Hawes & N. R. Hiner (Eds.), *American childhood: A research guide and historical handbook* (pp. 273–309). Westport, CT: Greenwood Press.

Cohen, R. J., Swerdlik, M. E., & Phillips, S. M. (1996). *Psychological testing and assessment: An introduction to tests and measurement* (3rd ed.). Mountain View, CA: Mayfield Press.

Cole, E. (1992). Characteristics of students referred to school teams: Implications for preventive psychological services. *Canadian Journal of School Psychology, 8*, 23–36.

Cole, E. (1995). Responding to school violence: Understanding today and tomorrow. *Canadian Journal of School Psychology, 11*, 108–116.

Cole, E. (1996). An integrative perspective on school psychology. *Canadian Journal of School Psychology, 6*, 115–121.

Cole, E. (1998). Immigrant and refugee children: Challenges for education and mental health services. *Canadian Journal of School Psychology, 14*, 36–50.

Cole, E., & Siegel, J. A. (Eds.). (1990). *Effective consultation in school psychology.* Toronto, Ontario, Canada: Hogrefe & Huber.

Cole, E., & Siegel, J. A. (Eds.). (2003). *Effective consultation in school psychology* (2nd ed.). Toronto, Ontario, Canada: Hogrefe & Huber.

Committee on Professional Practice and Standards. (2003). Legal issues in the professional practice of psychology. *American Psychologist, 34*(6), 595–600.

Connolly, L. M., & Reschly, D. (1990). The school psychology crisis of the 1990s. *Communiqué, 19*(3), 1–12.

Conoley, J. C. (1989). The school psychologist as a community/family service provider. In R. C. D'Amato & R. S. Dean (Eds.), *The school psychologist in nontraditional settings: Integrating clients, services, and settings* (pp. 33–65). Hillsdale, NJ: Erlbaum.

Conoley, J. C. (1992, August). 2042: *A prospective look at school psychology.* Paper presented at the annual meeting of the American Psychological Association, Washington, DC.

Conoley, J. C., & Conoley, C. W. (1992). *School consultation: Practice and training* (2nd ed.). New York: Macmillan.

Conoley, J. C., & Gutkin, T. B. (1986). Educating school psychologists for the real world. *School Psychology Review, 15*, 457–465.

Conoley, J. C., & Henning-Stout, M. (1990). Gender issues and school psychology. In T. R. Kratochwill (Ed.), *Advances in school psychology* (Vol. 7, pp. 7–31). Hillsdale, NJ: Erlbaum.

Constable, R., McDonald, S., & Flynn, J. P. (Eds.). (1999). *School social work: Practice, policy & research perspectives* (4th ed.). Chicago: Lyceum Books.

Cornwall, A. (1990). Social validation of psycho-educational assessment reports. *Journal of Learning Disabilities, 23*, 413–416.

Cournoyer, K. L. R. (2004, Spring). The assessment of professional work characteristics and the practice of school psychology. *The School Psychologist, 58*(2), 65–68.

Cravens, H. (1985). Child-saving in the age of professionalism, 1915–1930. In J. M. Hawes & N. R. Hiner (Eds.), *American childhood. A research guide and historical handbook* (pp. 415–488). Westport, CT: Greenwood Press.

Cravens, H. (1987). Applied science and public policy: The Ohio Bureau of Juvenile Research and the problem of juvenile delinquency 1913–1930. In M. M. Sokal (Ed.), *Psychological testing and American society 1890–1930* (pp. 158–194). New Brunswick, NJ: Rutgers University Press.

Cremin, L. A. (1988). *American education: The metropolitan experience 1876–1980.* New York: Harper & Row.

Crespi, T. D. (1998). Considerations for clinical supervision. *The Texas School Psychologist, 15*(2), 14–15.

Crespi, T. D. (1999). Post-doctoral respecialization as a school psychologist: Cultivating competence for school-based practice. *The School Psychologist*, 53(4), 111–113, 116.

Crespi, T. D., & Fischetti, B. A. (1997). Counseling licensure: An emerging credential for health care professionals. *Communiqué, 25*(5), 17–18.

Crossland, C. L., Fox, B. J., & Baker, R. (1982). Differential perceptions of role responsibilities among professionals in the public school. *Exceptional Children, 48*, 536–537.

Cubberley, E. P. (1909). *Changing conceptions of education.* Cambridge, MA: Riverside Press.

Cubberley, E. P. (Ed.). (1920). *Readings in the history of education.* Boston: Riverside Press.

Culbertson, F. (1975). Average students' needs and perceptions of school psychologists. *Psychology in the Schools, 12,* 191–196.

Cummings, J. (2005). Division of School Psychology (Division 16). In S. W. Lee (Ed.), *Encyclopedia of school psychology* (pp. 169–170). Thousand Oaks, CA: Sage.

Cummings, J. A., Huebner, E. S., & McLeskey, J. (1985). Issues in the preservice preparation of school psychologists for rural settings. *School Psychology Review, 14*, 429–437.

Cunningham, J. (1994). *A contextual investigation of the international development of psychology in the schools.* Unpublished doctoral dissertation, University of Texas at Austin.

Cunningham, J. (2006). Centripetal and centrifugal trends influencing school psychology's international development. In S. R. Jimerson, T. D. Oakland, & P. T. Farrell (Eds.), *The handbook of international school psychology* (pp. 463–474). Thousand Oaks, CA: Sage.

Cunningham, J., & Oakland, T. (1998). International School Psychology Association guidelines for the preparation of school psychologists. *School Psychology International, 19*, 19–30.

Curtis, M. J., & Batsche, G. M. (1991). Meeting the needs of children and families: Opportunities and challenges for school psychology training programs. *School Psychology Review, 20*, 565–577.

Curtis, M., Batsche, G., & Tanous, J. (1996). Nondoctoral school psychology threatened: The Texas experience. *Communiqué, 24*(8), 1, 6–8.

Curtis, M., Graden, J., & Reschly, D. (1992). *School psychology as a profession: Demographics, professional practices, and job satisfaction.* Symposium conducted at the annual meeting of the National Association of School Psychologists, Nashville, TN.

Curtis, M. J., Grier, J. E. C., & Hunley, S. A. (2004). The changing face of school psychology: Trends in data and projections for the future. *School Psychology Review, 33*, 49–66.

Curtis, M. J., Hunley, S. A., & Grier, J. E. C. (2002). Relationships among the professional practices and demographic characteristics of school psychologists. *School Psychology Review, 31*, 30–42.

Curtis, M. J., Hunley, S. A., & Prus, J. R. (Eds.). (1998). *Credentialing requirements for school psychologists.* Bethesda, MD: National Association of School Psychologists.

Curtis, M. J., Hunley, S. A., Walker, K. J., & Baker, A. C. (1999). Demographic characteristics and professional practices in school psychology. *School Psychology Review, 28*, 104–116.

Curtis, M. J., Lopez, A. D., Batsche, G. M., & Smith, J. C. (2006, March). *School psychology 2005: A national perspective.* Paper presented at the annual convention of the National Association of School Psychologists, Anaheim, CA.

Curtis, M. J., & Meyers, J. (1985). Best practices in school-based consultation: Guidelines for effective practice. In A. Thomas & J. Grimes (Eds.), *Best practices in school psychology* (pp. 79–94). Kent, OH: National Association of School Psychologists.

Curtis, M. J., & Zins, J. E. (1986). The organization and structuring of psychological services within educational settings. In S. N. Elliott & J. C. Witt (Eds.), *The delivery of psychological services in schools: Concepts, processes, and issues* (pp. 109–138). Hillsdale, NJ: Erlbaum.

Curtis, M. J., & Zins, J. E. (1989). Trends in training and accreditation. *School Psychology Review, 18*, 182–192.

Cutts, N. E. (Ed.). (1955). *School psychologists at mid-century.* Washington, DC: American Psychological Association.

Daley, C. E., Nagle, R. J., & Onwuegbuzie, A. J. (1998, April). *Ethics training in school psychology in the United States.* Paper presented at the annual meeting of the National Association of School Psychologists, Orlando, FL.

D'Amato, R. C., & Dean, R. S. (Eds.). (1989). *The school psychologist in nontraditional settings: Integrating clients, services, and settings.* Hillsdale, NJ: Erlbaum.

Da Silva, T. A. (2003). An evaluation of the Structured Success Program from the students' point of view. *Canadian Journal of School Psychology, 18*, 129–152.

Davis, J. M. (1988). The school psychologist in a community mental health center. *School Psychology Review, 17*, 435–439.

Dawson, D. (1980). Editorial. *The Alberta School Psychologist, 1*(2), 1.

Dawson, D. (1981, August). Editorial. *NASP Canada/Mexico Newsletter, 1*, 4–6.

Dawson, D. (1982, January). The future of school psychology in Canada. *NASP Canada/Mexico Newsletter, 2*, 4–8.

Dawson, P., Mendez, P., & Hyman, A. (1994). Average school psychologist's salary tops $43,000. *Communiqué, 23*(1), 1, 6.

DeAngelis, T. (2006, May). A culture of inclusion. *Monitor on Psychology, 37*(5), 30–33.

Demaray, M. K., Carlson, J. S., & Hodgson, K. K. (2003). Assistant professors of school psychology: A national survey of program directors and job applicants. *Psychology in the Schools, 40*, 691–698.

DeMers, S. T. (1993). The changing face of specialization in psychology. *The School Psychologist, 47*(1), 3, 8.

Deno, E. (1970). Special education as developmental capital. *Exceptional Children, 37*, 229–237.

De Vaney Olvey, C., Hogg, A., & Counts, W. (2002). Licensure requirements: Have we raised the bar too far? *Professional Psychology: Research and Practice, 33*, 323–329.

DiVerde-Nushawg, N., & Walls, G. B. (1998). The implication of pager use for the therapeutic relationship in independent practice. *Professional Psychology: Research and Practice, 29*, 368–372.

Division 44/Commission on Lesbian, Gay, and Bisexual Concerns Joint Task Force. (2000). Guidelines for psychotherapy with lesbian, gay, and bisexual clients. *American Psychologist, 55*(12), 1440–1451.

Dobson, K., & Dobson, D. (Eds.). (1993). *Professional psychology in Canada.* Toronto: Hogrefe & Huber.

Dorken, H. (1958). The functions of psychologists in mental health services. *The Canadian Psychologist, 7*, 89–95.

Dorken, H., Walker, C. B., & Wake, F. R. (1960). A 15-year review of Canadian trained psychologists. *The Canadian Psychologist, 1*, 123–130.

Duis, S., Rothlisberg, B., & Hargrove, L. (1995). *Collaborative consultation: Are both school psychologists and teachers equally trained?* Paper presented at the annual meeting of the Council for Exceptional Children, Indianapolis, IN.

Dumont, F. (1989). School psychology in Canada: Views on its status. In P. Saigh & T. Oakland (Eds.), *International perspectives on psychology in the schools* (pp. 211–222). Hillsdale, NJ: Erlbaum.

Dunn, L. M. (1973). An overview. In L. M. Dunn (Ed.), *Exceptional children in the schools: Special education in transition* (pp. 1–62). New York: Holt, Rinehart & Winston.

Dwyer, K. (1991). Children with emotional and behavioral disorders: An underserved population. *Communiqué, 20*(1), 21.

Dwyer, K., Osher, D., & Warger, C. (1998). *Early warning, timely response: A guide to safe schools.* Washington, DC: U.S. Department of Education, Special Education and Rehabilitative Services.

Eberst, N. D. (1984). *Sources of funding of school psychologists.* Washington, DC: National Association of School Psychologists.

Education for All Handicapped Children Act of 1975, Pub. L. 94-142 (20 U.S.C. and 34 C.F.R.).

Education of the Handicapped Amendments of 1986, Pub. L. 99-457 (20 U.S.C. 1470).

Education of the Handicapped Act Amendments of 1990, Pub. L. 101-476 (104 Stat. 1103).

Educational Testing Service. (2003). Study guide: School leaders and services. Princeton, NJ: Author.

Elias, C. L. (1999). The school psychologist as expert witness: Strategies and issues in the courtroom. *School Psychology Review, 28*, 44–59.

Elias, M. J., Zins, J. E., Graczyk, P. A., & Weissberg, R. P. (2003). Implementation, sustainability and scaling up of social-emotional and academic innovations in public schools. *School Psychology Review, 32,* 303–319.

Elliott, S. N., & Witt, J. C. (Eds.). (1986a). *The delivery of psychological services in schools: Concepts, processes, and issues.* Hillsdale, NJ: Erlbaum.

Elliott, S. N., & Witt, J. C. (1986b). Fundamental questions and dimensions of psychological service delivery in schools. In S. N. Elliott & J. C. Witt (Eds.), *The delivery of psychological services in schools: Concepts, processes, and issues* (pp. 1–26). Hillsdale, NJ: Erlbaum.

Elliott, S. N., Witt, J. C., & Kratochwill, T. R. (1991). Selecting, implementing, and evaluating classroom interventions. In G. Stoner, M. R. Shinn, & H. M. Walker (Eds.), *Interventions for achievement and behavior problems* (pp. 99–135). Silver Spring, MD: National Association of School Psychologists.

Engin, A. W. (1983). National organizations: Professional identity. In G. W. Hynd (Ed.), *The school psychologist: An introduction* (pp. 27–44). Syracuse, NY: Syracuse University Press.

Engin, A. W., & Johnson, R. (1983). School psychology training and practice: The NASP perspective. In T. R. Kratochwill (Ed.), *Advances in school psychology* (Vol. 3, pp. 21–44). Hillsdale, NJ: Erlbaum.

English, H. B. (1938). Organization of the American Association of Applied Psychologists. *Journal of Consulting Psychology, 2*, 7–16.

English, H. B., & English, A. C. (1958). *A comprehensive dictionary of psychological and psychoanalytic terms: A guide to usage.* New York: Longmans, Green.

Erchul, W. P. (1992). Social psychological perspectives on the school psychologist's involvement with parents. In F. J. Medway & T. P. Cafferty (Eds.), *School psychology: A social psychological perspective* (pp. 425–448). Hillsdale, NJ: Erlbaum.

Erchul, W. P., & Raven, B. H. (1997). Social power in school consultation: A contemporary view of French and Raven's bases of power model. *Journal of School Psychology, 35*, 137–171.

Erchul, W. P., Scott, S. S., Dombalis, A. O., & Schulte, A. C. (1989). Characteristics and perceptions of beginning doctoral students in school psychology. *Professional School Psychology, 4*(2), 103–111.

Esquivel, G. B., Lopez, E. C., & Nahari, S. G. (Eds.). (2006). *Handbook of multicultural school psychology: An interdisciplinary perspective.* Mahwah, NJ: Erlbaum.

Examination for License as Psychologist (announcement). (1925, December 29). Department of Education, City of New York, Office of the Board of Examiners.

Fagan, T. K. (1985). Sources for the delivery of school psychological services during 1890–1930. *School Psychology Review, 14*, 378–382.

Fagan, T. K. (1986a). The evolving literature of school psychology. *School Psychology Review, 15*, 430–440.

Fagan, T. K. (1986b). The historical origins and growth of programs to prepare school psychologists in the United States. *Journal of School Psychology, 24*, 9–22.

Fagan, T. K. (1986c). School psychology's dilemma: Reappraising solutions and directing attention to the future. *American Psychologist, 41*, 851–861. See also *School Psychology Review, 16*(l).

Fagan, T. K. (1987a). Gesell: The first school psychologist. Part II. Practice and significance. *School Psychology Review, 16*, 399–409.

Fagan, T. K. (1987b). *Trends in the development of United States school psychology with implications for Canadian school psychology.* Paper presented at the first annual meeting of the Canadian Association of School Psychologists, Winnipeg, Manitoba.

Fagan, T. K. (1988a). The first school psychologist in Oklahoma. *Communiqué, 17*(3), 19.

Fagan, T. K. (1988b). The historical improvement of the school psychology service ratio: Implications for future employment. *School Psychology Review, 17*, 447–458.

Fagan, T. K. (1989a). Obituary: Norma Estelle Cutts. *American Psychologist, 44*, 1236.

Fagan, T. K. (1989b). School psychology: Where next? *Canadian Journal of School Psychology, 5*, 1–7.

Fagan, T. K. (1990a). Best practices in the training of school psychologists: Considerations for trainers, prospective entry-level and advanced students. In A. Thomas & J. Grimes (Eds.), *Best practices in school psychology II* (pp. 723–741). Silver Spring, MD: National Association of School Psychologists.

Fagan, T. K. (1990b). Contributions of Leta Hollingworth to school psychology. *Roeper Review, 12*(3), 157–161.

Fagan, T. K. (1990c). Research on the history of school psychology: Recent developments, significance, resources, and future directions. In T. R. Kratochwill (Ed.), *Advances in school psychology* (Vol. 7, pp. 151–182). Hillsdale, NJ: Erlbaum.

Fagan, T. K. (1992). Compulsory schooling, child study, clinical psychology, and special education: Origins of school psychology. *American Psychologist, 47*, 236–243.

Fagan, T. K. (1993). Separate but equal: School psychology's search for organizational identity. *Journal of School Psychology, 31*, 3–90.

Fagan, T. K. (1994). A critical appraisal of the NASP's first 25 years. *School Psychology Review, 23*, 604–618.

Fagan, T. K. (1996a). A history of Division 16 (School Psychology): Running twice as fast. In D. A. Dewsbury (Ed.), *Unification through division: Histories of the divisions of the American Psychological Association* (Vol. 1, pp. 101–135). Washington, DC: American Psychological Association.

Fagan, T. K. (1996b). Historical perspective on the role and practice of school psychology. *Canadian Journal of School Psychology, 6*, 83–85.

Fagan, T. K. (1997). Culminating experiences in NASP approved non-doctoral school psychology training programs [Insert]. *Trainers' Forum, 16*(1).

Fagan, T. K. (1999). Training school psychologists before there were school psychologist training programs: A history 1890–1930. In C. R. Reynolds & T. B. Gutkin (Eds.), *The handbook of school psychology* (pp. 2–33). New York: Wiley.

Fagan, T. K. (2002). School psychology: Recent descriptions, continued expansion, and an ongoing paradox. *School Psychology Review, 31*, 5–10.

Fagan, T. K. (2004a). First school psychology ABPP, Virginia Bennett, dies. *The School Psychologist, 58*(1), 25–27.

Fagan, T. K. (2004b). School psychology's significant discrepancy: Historical perspectives on personnel shortages. *Psychology in the Schools, 41*, 419–430.

Fagan, T. K. (2005a). Literary origins of the term, "school psychologist," revisited. *School Psychology Review, 34*, 432–434.

Fagan, T. K. (2005b). The 50th Anniversary of the Thayer Conference: Historical perspectives and accomplishments. *School Psychology Quarterly, 20*(3), 224–251.

Fagan, T. K. (2005c). Results of on-line survey of Praxis test usage. *Trainer's Forum, 24*(4), 8, 10.

Fagan, T. K. (2005d). National Association of School Psychologists. In S. W. Lee (Ed.), *Encyclopedia of school psychology* (pp. 345–348). Thousand Oaks, CA: Sage.

Fagan, T. K. (in press). Trends in the history of school psychology in the United States. In A. Thomas & J. Grimes (Eds.), *Best practices in school psychology V.* Bethesda, MD: National Association of School Psychologists.

Fagan, T. K., & Bischoff, H. (1984). In memoriam: Calvin D. Catterall, 1925–1984. *Communiqué, 13*(1), 1, 4.

Fagan, T. K., & Delugach, F. J. (1984). Literary origins of the term "school psychologist." *School Psychology Review, 13*, 216–220.

Fagan, T. K., Delugach, F. J., Mellon, M., & Schlitt, P. (1985). *A bibliographic guide to the literature of professional school psychology 1890–1985.* Washington, DC: National Association of School Psychologists.

Fagan, T. K., Gorin, S., & Tharinger, D. (2000). The National Association of School Psychologists and the Division of School Psychology–APA: Now and beyond. *School Psychology Review, 29*, 525–535.

Fagan, T. K., Hensley, L. T., & Delugach, F. J. (1986). The evolution of organizations for school psychologists in the United States. *School Psychology Review, 15*, 127–135.

Fagan, T. K., & Schicke, M. C. (1994). The service ratio in large school districts: Historical and contemporary perspectives. *Journal of School Psychology, 32*, 305–312.

Fagan, T. K., & Sheridan, S. M. (Guest Eds.). (2000). Miniseries: School psychology in the 21st century. *School Psychology Review, 29*(4).

Fagan, T. K., & Warden, P. G. (Eds.). (1996). *Historical encyclopedia of school psychology.* Westport, CT: Greenwood Press.

Fagan, T. K., & Wells, P. D. (1999). Frances Mullen: Her life and contributions to school psychology. *School Psychology International, 20*, 91–102.

Fagan, T. K., & Wells, P. D. (2000). History and status of school psychology accreditation in the United States. *School Psychology Review, 29*, 28–58.

Fagan, T. K., & Wise, P. S. (1994). *School psychology: Past, present, and future.* White Plains, NY: Longman.

Fagan, T. K., & Wise, P. S. (2000). *School psychology: Past, present, and future* (2nd ed.). Bethesda, MD: National Association of School Psychologists.

Fairchild, T. N. (1975). Accountability: Practical suggestions for school psychologists. *Journal of School Psychology, 13*, 149–159.

Fairchild, T. N., & Seeley, T. J. (1996). Evaluation of school psychological services: A case illustration. *Psychology in the Schools, 33*, 46–55.

Fairchild, T. N., & Zins, J. E. (1992). Accountability practices of school psychologists: 1991 national survey. *School Psychology Review, 21*, 617–627,

Fairchild, T. N., Zins, J. E., & Grimes, J. (1983). *Improving school psychology through accountability* [Filmstrip and manual]. Washington, DC: National Association of School Psychologists.

Family Educational Rights and Privacy Act of 1974, Pub. L. 93-380 (20 U.S.C. and 34 C.F.R.).

Farling, W. H., & Hoedt, K. C. (1971). *National survey of school psychologists.* Washington, DC: National Association of School Psychologists.

Featherstone, H. (1980). *A difference in the family: Living with a disabled child.* New York: Penguin.

Feinberg, T., Nujiens, K. L., & Canter A. (2005). Workload vs. caseload: There's more to school psychology than numbers. *Communiqué, 33*(6), 38–39.

Feller, B. (2004, May 30). School counselors stretched too thin. *The Commercial Appeal*, p. A18.

Ferguson, D. G. (1963). *Pupil personnel services.* New York: Center for Applied Research in Education.

Field, A. J. (1976). Educational expansion in mid-nineteenth-century Massachusetts: Human capital formation or structural reinforcement? *Harvard Educational Review, 46*, 521–552.

Fine, M. J. (Ed.). (1991). *Collaboration with parents of exceptional children.* Brandon, VT: Clinical Psychology Publishing.

Finn, C. A., Heath, N. L., Petrakos, H., & McLean-Heywood, D. (2002). A comparison of school service models for children at risk for emotional and behavioural disorders. *Canadian Journal of School Psychology, 17*, 61–68.

Fireoved, R., & Cancelleri, R. (1985). What training programs need to emphasize: Notes from the field. *Trainers' Forum, 5*(1), 1, 4–5.

Fischer, L., & Sorenson, G. P. (1991). *School law for counselors, psychologists, and social workers.* New York: Longman.

Fischetti, B. A., & Crespi, T. D. (1997). Clinical supervision: School psychology at a crossroad. *Communiqué, 25*(6), 18.

Fischetti, B. A., & Crespi, T. D. (1999). Clinical supervision for school psychologists: National practices, trends, and future implications. *School Psychology International, 20*(3), 278–288.

Fish, M. (2002). Best practices in collaborating with parents of children with disabilities. In A. Thomas & J. Grimes (Eds.), *Best practices in school psychology IV* (pp. 363–376). Bethesda, MD: National Association of School Psychologists.

Fish, M. C., & Massey, R. (1991). Systems in school psychology practice: A preliminary investigation. *Journal of School Psychology, 29*, 361–366.

Flanagan, R., Miller, J. A., & Jacob, S. (2005). The 2002 revision of the American Psychological Association's ethics code: Implications for school psychologists. *Psychology in the Schools, 42*, 433–445.

Fly, B. J., van Bark, W. P., Weinman, L., Kitchener, K. S., & Lang, P. R. (1997). Ethical transgressions of psychology graduate students: Critical incidents with implications for training. *Professional Psychology: Research and Practice, 28*, 492–495.

Forrest v. *Ambach*, 436 N.Y.S. 2d 119 (1980); 463 N.Y.S. 2d 84 (1983).

Fournier, C. J., & Perry, J. D. (1998). The report of the U.S. Commission on Child and Family Welfare: Implications for psychologists working with children and families. *Children's Services: Social Policy, Research, and Practice, 2*, 45–56.

Fowler, E., & Harrison, P. L. (2001). Continuing professional development needs and activities of school psychologists. *Psychology in the Schools, 38*, 75–88.

Fox, R. E., Barclay, A. G., & Rodgers, D. A. (1982). The foundations of professional psychology. *American Psychologist, 37*, 306–312.

Frank, G. (1984). The Boulder model: History, rationale, and critique. *Professional Psychology: Research and Practice, 15*, 417–435.

French, J. L. (1984). On the conception, birth, and early development of school psychology: With special reference to Pennsylvania. *American Psychologist, 39*, 976–987.

French, J. L. (1986). Books in school psychology: The first forty years. *Professional School Psychology, 1*, 267–277.

French, J. L. (1988). Grandmothers I wish I knew: Contributions of women to the history of school psychology. *Professional School Psychology, 3*, 51–68.

French, J. L. (1990). History of school psychology. In T. B. Gutkin & C. R. Reynolds (Eds.), *Handbook of school psychology* (pp. 3–20). New York: Wiley.

Frisby, C. L. (1998). Formal communication within school psychology: A 1990–1994 journal citation analysis. *School Psychology Review, 27*, 304–316.

Frisby, C. L., & Reynolds, C. R. (Eds.). (2005). *Comprehensive handbook of multicultural school psychology.* Hoboken, NJ: Wiley.

Fry, M. A. (1986). The connections among educational and psychological research and the practice of school psychology. In S. N. Elliott & J. C. Witt (Eds.), *The delivery of psychological services in schools: Concepts, processes and issues* (pp. 305–327). Hillsdale, NJ: Erlbaum.

Gale, B., & Gale, L. (1989). *Stay or leave.* New York: Harper & Row.

Gallagher, J. J. (Ed.). (1980). *Parents and families of handicapped children* [Special issue]. *New Directions for Exceptional Children.* San Francisco: Jossey-Bass.

Gallagher, J. J., & Vietze, P. M. (Eds.). (1986). *Families of handicapped persons: Research, programs, and policy issues.* Baltimore, MD: Brookes.

Gargiulo, R. M. (1985). *Working with parents of exceptional children: A guide for professionals.* Boston: Houghton Mifflin.

Gelinas, P. J., & Gelinas, R. P. (1968). *A definitive study of your future in school psychology.* New York: Richards Rosen Press.

Georgas, J., Weiss, L. G., van de Vijver, F. J. R., & Saklofske, D. H. (2003). (Eds.). *Culture and children's intelligence: Cross-cultural analysis of the WISC-III.* San Diego, CA: Academic Press.

Gerken, K. C. (1981). The paraprofessional and the school psychologist: Can this be an effective team? *School Psychology Review, 10,* 470–479.

Gerner, M. (1981). The necessity of a teacher background for school psychologists. *Professional Psychology, 12,* 216–223.

Gerner, M. (1983). When face validity is only skin deep: Teaching experience and school psychology. *Communiqué, 11*(8), 2.

Gerner, M. (1990). Living and working overseas: School psychologists in American international schools. *School Psychology Quarterly, 20,* 91–102.

Gerner, M., & Genshaft, J. (1981). *Selecting a school psychology training program,* Washington, DC: National Association of School Psychologists.

Gibson, G., & Chard, K. M. (1994). Quantifying the effects of community mental health consultation interventions. *Consulting Psychology Journal: Practice and Research, 46*(4), 13–25.

Gickling, E. E., & Rosenfield, S. (1995). Best practices in curriculum-based assessment. In A. Thomas and J. Grimes (Eds.), *Best practices in school psychology III* (pp. 587–595). Silver Spring, MD: National Association of School Psychologists.

Gilman, R., & Teague, T. L. (2005). School psychologists in non-traditional settings: Alternative roles and functions in psychological service delivery. In R. D. Morgan, T. L. Kuther, & C. J. Habben (Eds.), *Life after graduate school in psychology* (pp. 167–180). Oxford, England: Psychology Press.

Givner, A., & Furlong, M. (2003). Relevance of the combined-integrated model of training to school psychology: The Yeshiva Program. *The School Psychologist, 57*(4), 145–154.

Glasser, W. (1990). *The quality school: Managing schools without coercion.* New York: Harper & Row.

Goddard, H. H. (1914). *The research department: What it is, what it is doing, what it hopes to do.* Vineland, NJ: The Training School.

Goh, D. S. (1977). Graduate training in school psychology. *Journal of School Psychology, 15,* 207–218.

Goldstein, A. P., Harootunian, B., & Conoley, J. C. (1994). *Student aggression: Prevention, management, and replacement training.* New York: Guilford Press.

Goldwasser, E., Meyers, J., Christenson, S., & Graden, J. (1983). The impact of P.L. 94–142 on the practice of school psychology: A national survey. *Psychology in the Schools, 20,* 153–165.

Goodman, M. (1973). Psychological services to schools: Meeting educational needs of tomorrow. *The Canadian Psychologist, 14*, 249–255.

Gopaul-McNicol, S. (1992). Guest editor's comments: Understanding and meeting the psychological and educational needs of African-American and Spanish-speaking students. *School Psychology Review, 21*, 529–531.

Gopaul-McNicol, S. A. (1997). A theoretical framework for training monolingual school psychologists to work with multilingual/multicultural children: An exploration of the major competencies. *Psychology in the Schools, 34*, 17–29.

Goslin, D. A. (1965). *The school in contemporary society.* Glenview, IL: Pearson Scott Foresman.

Goslin, D. A. (1969). *Guidelines for the collection, maintenance and dissemination of pupil records.* Troy, NY: Russell Sage Foundation.

Gottsegen, G. B., & Gottsegen, M. B. (1960). *Professional school psychology* (Vol. 1). New York: Grune and Stratton.

Graden, J. L. (1989). Redefining "prereferral" intervention as intervention assistance: Collaboration between general and special education. *Exceptional Children, 56*, 227–231.

Graden, J. L., Casey, A., & Bonstrom, O. (1985). Implementing a prereferral intervention system. Part II: The data. *Exceptional Children, 51*, 487–496.

Graden, J. L., Casey, A., & Christenson, S. L. (1985). Implementing a prereferral intervention system. Part I: The model. *Exceptional Children, 51*, 377–384.

Graden, J., & Curtis, M. (1991). *A demographic profile of school psychology: A report to the Delegate Assembly of the National Association of School Psychologists.* Washington, DC: National Association of School Psychologists.

Gray, S. (1963a). *The internship in school psychology: Proceedings of the Peabody Conference, March 21–22, 1963.* Nashville, TN: George Peabody College for Teachers, Department of Psychology.

Gray, S. W. (1963b). *The psychologist in the schools.* New York: Holt, Rinehart & Winston.

Gredler, G. R. (Ed.). (1972). *Ethical and legal factors in the practice of school psychology: Proceedings of the First Annual Conference in School Psychology.* Philadelphia: Temple University Press.

Gredler, G. R. (1992). [Review of the book *Effective consultation in school psychology.*] *Psychology in the Schools, 29*, 192–195.

Greenough, P., Schwean, V. L., & Saklofske, D. H. (1993). School psychology services in northern Saskatchewan: A collaborative-consultation model. *Canadian Journal of Special Education, 9*, 1–12.

Greenspoon, P. J. (1998). *Toward an integration of subjective well-being and psychopathology.* Unpublished doctoral dissertation, University of Saskatchewan, Saskatoon.

Greer, M. (2005, January). Career center, Postgrad growth area: School psychology. *GradPSYCH, 31*(1), 32–33.

Greif, J. L., & Greif, G. L. (2004). Including fathers in school psychology literature: A review of four school psychology journals. *Psychology in the Schools, 41*, 575–580.

Grimes, J., Kurns, S., & Tilley, D. (2006). Sustainability: An enduring commitment to success. *School Psychology Review, 35*, 224–244.

Grossman, F. (1992). Ethical dilemma: What do you do when your boss asks you to do something you're not trained for? *Communiqué, 24*(4), 18.

Guadalupe Organizations, Inc. v. *Tempe Elementary School District No. 3*, Civ. No. 71–435 (D. Ariz. 1972).

Gutkin, T. B., & Curtis, M. J. (1990). School-based consultation: Theory, techniques, and research. In T. B. Gutkin & C. R. Reynolds (Eds.), *Handbook of school psychology* (pp. 577–611). New York: Wiley.

Gutkin, T. B., & Curtis, M. J. (1999). School-based consultation theory and practice: The art and science of indirect service delivery. In C. R. Reynolds & T. B. Gutkin (Eds.), *Handbook of school psychology* (3rd ed., pp. 598–637). New York: Wiley.

Gutkin, T. B., & Reynolds, C. R. (Eds.). (1990). *The handbook of school psychology.* New York: Wiley.

Hagemeier, C., Bischoff, L., Jacobs, J., & Osmon, W. (1998, April). *Role perceptions of the school psychologist by school personnel.* Poster session presented at the annual meeting of the National Association of School Psychologists.

Haggan, D., & Dunham, M. (2002, Summer). Non-doctoral respecialization as a school psychologist. *Trainers' Forum, 21*(4), 5–6, 11.

Hagin, R. A. (1993). Contributions of women in school psychology: The Thayer report and thereafter. *Journal of School Psychology, 31,* 123–141.

Hall, G. S. (1911). *Educational Problems* (Vols. 1–2). New York: D. Appleton.

Hall, J. D., Howerton, D. L., & Bolin, A. U. (2005). The use of testing technicians: Critical issues for professional psychology. *International Journal of Testing, 5*(4), 357–375.

Hall, J. E., & Lunt, I. (2005). Global mobility for psychologists: The role of psychology organizations in the United States, Canada, Europe, and other regions. *American Psychologist, 60*(7), 712–726.

Hamovitch, G. (1995). Submission to the chair and members of the Education and Finance Committee of an Ontario Board of Education. *Canadian Journal of School Psychology, 11,* 96–98.

Hann, G. S. (2001). School psychology in Nova Scotia. *Canadian Journal of School Psychology, 16*(2), 19–24.

Happe, D. (1990). Best practices in identifying community resources. In A. Thomas & J. Grimes (Eds.), *Best practices in school psychology II* (pp. 1009–1047). Silver Spring, MD: National Association of School Psychologists.

Harrington, R. G. (1985). Best practices in facilitating organizational change in the schools. In A. Thomas & J. Grimes (Eds.), *Best practices in school psychology* (pp. 193–206). Kent, OH: National Association of School Psychologists.

Harris, J. D., Gray, B. A., Rees-McGee, S., Carroll, J. L., & Zaremba, E. T. (1987). Referrals to school psychologists: A national survey. *Journal of School Psychology, 25,* 343–354.

Harrison, P. L. (2000). *School Psychology Review*: Ending the 20th century and looking ahead to the future. *School Psychology Review, 29,* 473–482.

Harrison, P. L., & McCloskey, G. (1989). School psychology applied to business. In R. C. D'Amato & R. S. Dean (Eds.), *The school psychologist in nontraditional settings: Integrating clients, services, and settings* (pp. 107–137). Hillsdale, NJ: Erlbaum.

Hart, S. (1991). From property to person status: Historical perspective on children's rights. *American Psychologist, 46*, 53–59.

Harvey, V. S. (2005). *Hybrid School Psychology Programs: Online and Web-supported on-campus courses.* Paper presented at the annual convention of the National Association of School Psychologists, Atlanta, GA.

Harvey, V. S., & Carlson, J. F. (2003). Ethical and professional issues with computer-related technology. *School Psychology Review, 32*, 92–107.

Hass, M., & Osborn, J. (2002). Using a formative program portfolio to enhance graduate school psychology programs. *The California School Psychologist, 7*, 75–84.

Hatch, N. O. (1988). Introduction: The professions in a democratic culture. In N. O. Hatch (Ed.), *The professions in American history* (pp. 1–13). Notre Dame, IN: University of Notre Dame Press.

Havey, M. (1999). School psychologists' involvement in special education due process hearings. *Psychology in the Schools, 36*, 117–123.

Hayes, M. E., & Clair, T. N. (1978). School psychology: Why is the profession dying? *Psychology in the Schools, 15,* 518–521.

Helton, G. B., & Ray, B. A. (2005). Strategies school practitioners report they would use to resist pressures to practice unethically. *Journal of Applied School Psychology, 22*(1), 45–67.

Henning-Stout, M. (1992). *Practitioners describe the gender climates of their workplaces: Graduates of an M.S. program.* Paper presented at the annual meeting of the National Association of School Psychologists, Nashville, TN.

Hermann, D. L., & Kush, J. C. (1995, Spring). Survey of projective assessment training practices in school psychology graduate programs. *Insight, 15*(3), 15–16.

Herron, W. G., Herron, M. J., & Handron, J. (1984). *Contemporary school psychology: Handbook of practice, theory, and research.* Cranston, RI: Carroll Press.

Hershey, J. M., Kopplin, D. A., & Cornell, J. E. (1991). Doctors of psychology: Their career experiences and attitudes toward degree and training. *Professional Psychology: Research and Practice, 22*, 351–356.

Hildreth, G. H. (1930). *Psychological service for school problems.* Yonkers-on-Hudson, NY: World Book.

Hill, J. G., & Johnson, F. (2005). *Revenues and expenditures for public elementary and secondary education: School year 2002–03 (NCES 2005-353).* Washington, DC: U.S. Department of Education, National Center for Education Statistics.

Hintze, J. M., & Shapiro, E. S. (1995). Best practices in the systematic observation of classroom behavior. In A. Thomas and J. Grimes (Eds.), *Best Practices in School Psychology III* (pp. 651–660). Washington, DC: National Association of School Psychologists.

Hirsch, B. Z. (1979). Is school psychology doomed? *The School Psychologist, 33*(4), 1.

Hirst, W. E. (1963). *Know your school psychologist.* New York: Grune & Stratton.

Hoagwood, K., & Erwin, H. D. (1997). Effectiveness of school-based mental health services for children: A 10-year research review. *Journal of Child and Family Studies, 6*(4), 435–451.

Hobson v. *Hansen*, 269 F. Supp. 401, 514 (D.D.C. 1967), *aff 'd. sub nom, Smuck* v. *Hobson*, 408 F.2d 175 (D.C. Cir. 1969).

Hogan, D. B. (1983). The effectiveness of licensing: History, evidence, and recommendations. *Law and Human Behavior, 7*(2/3), 117–138.

Hollingworth, L. S. (1918). Tentative suggestions for the certification of practicing psychologists. *Journal of Applied Psychology, 2*, 280–284.

Hollingworth, L. S. (1933). Psychological service for public schools. *Teachers College Record, 34*, 368–379.

Holmes, B. J. (1986, December). *Task force on school psychology report.* Paper submitted to the British Columbia Psychological Association, Vancouver, BC, Canada.

Holmes, B. (1993). Issues in training and credentialing in school psychology. In K. S. Dobson & D. J. G. Dobson (Eds.), *Professional psychology in Canada* (pp. 123–146). Toronto: Hogrefe & Huber.

Hosp, J. L., & Reschly, D. J. (2002). Regional differences in school psychology practice. *School Psychology Review, 31*, 11–29.

House, A. E. (2002). *DSM-IV diagnosis in the schools.* New York: Guilford Press.

Hu, S., & Oakland, T. (1991). Global and regional perspective on testing children and youth: An international survey. *International Journal of Psychology, 26*(3), 329–344.

Hubbard, D. D., & Adams, J. (2002). Best practices in facilitating meaningful family involvement in educational decision making. In A. Thomas & J. Grimes (Eds.). *Best practices in school psychology IV* (pp. 377–387). Bethesda, MD: National Association of School Psychologists.

Huebner, E. S. (1992). Burnout among school psychologists: An exploratory investigation into its nature, extent, and correlates. *School Psychology Quarterly, 7*, 129–136.

Huebner, E. S., & Hahn, B. M. (1990). Best practices in coordinating multidisciplinary teams. In A. Thomas & J. Grimes (Eds.), *Best practices in school psychology II* (pp. 193–206). Silver Spring, MD: National Association of School Psychologists.

Huebner, E. S., & Mills, L. B. (1998). A prospective study of personality characteristics, occupational stressors, and burnout among school psychology practitioners. *Journal of School Psychology, 36*, 103–120.

Huerta, L.A., d'Entremont, C., & Gonzalez, M. (2006). Cyber charter schools: Can accountability keep pace with innovation? *Phi Delta Kappan, 88*(1), 23–30.

Hughes, J. N. (1979). Consistency of administrators' and psychologists' actual and ideal perceptions of school psychologists' activities. *Psychology in the Schools, 16*, 234–239.

Hughes, J. N. (1986). Ethical issues in school consultation. *School Psychology Review, 15*, 489–499.

Hughes, J. N. (1996). Guilty as charged: Division 16 represents the specialty of doctoral school psychology. *Communiqué, 25*(1), 8, 10.

Hummel, D. L., & Humes, D. W. (1984). *Pupil services: Development, coordination, and administration.* New York: Macmillan.

Humphreys, K., Winzelberg, A., & Klaw, E. (2000). Psychologists' ethical responsibilities in Internet-based groups: Issues, strategies, and a call for dialogue. *Professional Psychology: Research and Practice, 31*(5), 493–496.

Hunley, S. A, & Curtis, M. J. (1998). The changing face of school psychology: Demographic trends, 1990–1995. *Communiqué, 27*(1), 16.

Hunley, S., Harvey, V., Curtis, M., Portnoy, L., Grier, E. C., & Helffrich, D. (2000, June). School psychology supervisors: A national study of demographics and professional practices. *Communiqué, 28*(8), 32–33.

Hutt, R. B. W. (1923). The school psychologist. *The Psychological Clinic, 15*, 48–51.

Hyman, I., Bilker, S., Freidman, M., Marino, M., & Roessner, P. (1973, November). National survey of school psychologists: Salaries, contracts, professional issues and practices. *The School Psychologist, 28*(2), 14–19.

Hyman, I., Flynn, A., Kowalcyk, R., & Marcus, M. (1998, April). *The status of school psychology trainers with regard to licensing and ABPP.* Paper presented at the meeting of Trainers of School Psychologists, Orlando, FL.

Hyman, I., Friel, P., & Parsons, R. (1975). Summary of a national survey on collective bargaining, salaries, and professional problems of school psychologists. *Communiqué, 4*(3), 1–2.

Hynd, G. W., Cannon, S. B., & Haussmann, S. E. (1983). The exceptional child. In G. W. Hynd (Ed.), *The school psychologist: An introduction* (pp. 121–144). Syracuse, NY: Syracuse University Press.

Icove, M. S., & Palomares, R. S. (2003). HIPAA, psychologists and schools. *The School Psychologist, 57*(2), 54.

Illback, R. J. (1992). Organizational influences on the practice of psychology in the schools. In F. J. Medway & T. P. Cafferty (Eds.), *School psychology: A social psychological perspective* (pp. 165–191). Hillsdale, NJ: Erlbaum.

Illback, R. J., Zins, J. E., & Maher, C. A. (1999). Program planning and evaluation: Principles, procedures, and planned change. In C. R. Reynolds & T. B. Gutkin (Eds.), *The handbook of school psychology* (3rd ed., pp. 907–932). New York: Wiley.

Individuals with Disabilities Education Act of 1997, Pub. L. 105-117.

Individuals with Disabilities Education Improvement Act of 2004, Pub. L. 108-446., 118 Stat. 2647 (2006).

Instituto Nacional de Estadistica Geografia e Informatica [National Institute for Geographic Statistics and Information]. (2006). Mexico. Retrieved at http://www.inegi.gob.mx/inegi/default.asp

International Union of Life Insurance Agents. (1983). *Our Voice, 47*(8), 1.

Iowa School Psychologists Association (1983, June 25). *Provision of school psychological services in the private sector.* Unpublished paper.

Itkin, W. (1966). The school psychologist and his training. *Psychology in the Schools, 3*, 348–354.

Jackson, J. H. (1990). School psychology after the 1980s: Envisioning a possible future. In T. B. Gutkin & C. R. Reynolds (Eds.), *The handbook of school psychology* (pp. 40–50). New York: Wiley.

Jackson, J. H. (1992). Trials, tribulations, and triumphs of minorities in psychology: Reflections at century's end. *Professional Psychology: Research and Practice, 23*, 80–86.

Jacob, S., & Hartshorne, T. S. (2007). *Ethics and law for school psychologists* (5th ed.). Hoboken, NJ: Wiley.

Jacob-Timm, S. (1999). Ethically challenging situations encountered by school psychologists. *Psychology in the Schools, 36*, 205–217.

Jacobsen, R. L. (1980, June 16). The great accreditation debate: What role for the government? *The Chronicle of Higher Education, 20*(16), 1.

Jann, R. J. (1991). Research indicates employers pressure members to act unethically. *Communiqué, 20*(4), 11–12.

Janzen, H. L. (1976). Psychology in the schools in English speaking Canada. In C. D. Catterall (Ed.), *Psychology in the schools in international perspective* (Vol. 1, pp. 163–183). Columbus, OH: Author.

Janzen, H. L. (1980, June). Psychological services to schools: Meeting educational and psychological needs of tomorrow. *The Alberta School Psychologist, 1*, 1.

Janzen, H. L., & Carter, S. (2001). State of the art of school psychology in Alberta. *Canadian Journal of School Psychology, 16*, 79–84.

Jay, B. (1989, January). Managing a crisis in the schools. *National Association of Secondary School Principals Bulletin, 3*, 14–17.

Jimerson, S. R., Graydon, K., Farrell, P., Kikas, E., Hatzichristou, C., Boce, E., et al. (2004). The international school psychology survey: Development and data from Albania, Cyprus, Estonia, Greece, and Northern England. *School Psychology International, 25*(3), 259–286.

Jimerson, S. R., Oakland, T. D., & Farrell, P. T. (Eds.). (2006). *The handbook of international school psychology.* Thousand Oaks, CA: Sage.

Jobin, H. (1995). Deputation to the trustees of an Ontario board of education. *Canadian Journal of School Psychology, 11*, 99–100.

Johnson, D. B., Malone, P. J., & Hightower, A. D. (1997). Barriers to primary prevention efforts in the schools: Are we the biggest obstacle to the transfer of knowledge? *Applied and Preventive Psychology, 6*, 81–90.

Johnson, P. M., Lubker, B. B., & Fowler, M. G. (1988). Teacher needs assessment for the educational management of children with chronic illnesses. *Journal of School Health, 58*, 232–235.

Johnson, W. B., & Campbell, C. D. (2004). Character and fitness requirements for professional psychologists: Training directors' perspectives. *Professional Psychology: Research and Practice, 35*(4), 405–411.

Joint Committee on Internships for the Council of Directors of School Psychology Programs; APA Division of School Psychology and the National Association of School Psychologists. (2006). *Directory of internships for doctoral students in school psychology.* (Available from Dr. James DiPerna, 125 Cedar Bldg., Pennsylvania State University, University Park, PA 16802.)

Jordan, K. F., & Lyons, T. S. (1992). *Financing public education in an era of change.* Bloomington, IN: Phi Delta Kappa Education Foundation.

Kaplan, M. S., & Kaplan, H. E. (1985). School psychology: Its educational and societal connections. *Journal of School Psychology, 23*, 319–325.

Kaser, R. (1993). A change in focus ... without losing sight of the child. *School psychology International, 14,* 5–19.

Kaufman, F., & Smith, T. (1998, June). *The roles and function of Canadian psychological service providers.* Poster session presented at the annual meeting of the Canadian Psychological Association, Edmonton, Alberta, Canada.

Keating, A. C. (1962). A counselling psychologist in an Ontario junior high school. *Canadian Psychologist, 3*, 14–17.

Kehle, T. J., Clark, E., & Jenson, W. R. (1993). The development of testing as applied to school psychology. *Journal of School Psychology, 31*, 143–161.

Keilin, W. G. (1998). Internship selection 30 years later: An overview of the APPIC matching program. *Professional Psychology: Research and Practice, 29*(6), 599–603.

Kikas, E. (2003). Pupils as consumers of school psychological services. *School Psychology International, 24*(1), 20–32.

Kimball, P., & Bansilal, S. (1998, December). School psychologists and due process hearings. *VASP Bulletin, 26*(3), 5–7.

King, C. R. (1993). *Children's health in America: A history.* New York: Twayne.

Kirby, J. L., & Keon, W. J. (November, 2004). *Mental health, mental illness and addiction; issues and options for Canada: Report 3.* Interim report of the Standing Senate Committee on Social Affairs, Science and Technology, Government of Canada.

Knapp, S. J., Vandecreek, L., & Zirkel, P. A. (1985). Legal research techniques: What the psychologist needs to know. *Professional Psychology: Research and Practice, 16,* 363–372.

Knoff, H. M., Curtis, M. J., & Batsche, G. M. (1997). The future of school psychology: Perspectives on effective training. *School Psychology Review, 26,* 93–103.

Knoff, H. M., McKenna, A. F., & Riser, K. (1991). Toward a consultant effectiveness scale: Investigating the characteristics of effective consultants. *School Psychology Review, 20,* 81–96.

Knoff, H., & Prout, H. (1985). Terminating students from professional psychology programs: Criteria, procedures, and legal issues. *Professional Psychology: Research and Practice, 16,* 789–797.

Koocher, G. P., & Keith-Spiegel, P. (1998). *Ethics in psychology.* New York: Oxford.

Korman, M. (1974). National Conference on Levels and Patterns of Professional Training in Psychology. *American Psychologist, 29*, 441–449.

Kratochwill, T. R., Elliott, S. N., & Callan-Stoiber, K. (2002). Best practices in school-based problem-solving consultation. In A. Thomas & J. Grimes (Eds.), *Best practices in school psychology IV* (pp. 583–608). Bethesda, MD: National Association of School Psychologists.

Kratochwill, T., Elliot, S., & Carrington-Rotto, P. (1995). School-based behavioral consultation. In A. Thomas & J. Grimes (Eds.), *Best practices in school psychology III* (pp. 519–538). Washington, DC: National Association of School Psychologists.

Kratochwill, T. R., Shernoff, E. S., & Sanetti, L. (2004). Promotion of academic careers in school psychology: A conceptual framework of impact points, recommendations, strategies, and hopeful outcomes. *School Psychology Quarterly, 19,* 342–364.

Kraus, T., & Mcloughlin, C. S. (1997). An essential library in school psychology. *School Psychology International, 18*, 343–349.

Kruger, L., Bennett, J., & Farkis, J. (2006). Developing leadership skills in school psychology graduate students. Poster presentation at the annual convention of the National Association of School Psychologists, Anaheim, CA.

Kubiszyn, T., Brown, R., Landau, S., DeMers, S., & Reynolds, C. (1992, August). *APA Division 16 Task Force preliminary report: Psychopharmacology in the schools.* Washington, DC: American Psychological Association, Division of School Psychology.

LaCayo, N., Sherwood, G., & Morris, J. (1981). Daily activities of school psychologists: A national survey. *Psychology in the Schools, 18,* 184–190.

Lamb, D. H., Cochran, D. J., & Jackson, V. R. (1991). Training and organizational issues associated with identifying and responding to intern impairment. *Professional Psychology: Research and Practice, 22,* 291–296.

Lambert, N. M. (1981). School psychology training for the decades ahead, or rivers, streams and creeks: Currents and tributaries to the sea. *School Psychology Review, 10,* 194–205.

Lambert, N. M. (1993). Historical perspective on school psychology as a scientist-practitioner specialization in school psychology. *Journal of School Psychology, 31,* 163–193.

Lambert, N. M. (1998). *School psychology: The whole is more than the sum of its parts.* Paper presented at the annual meeting of the National Association of School Psychologists, Orlando, FL.

Larry P. v. *Riles,* 343 F. Supp. 1306 (N.D. Cal. 1972); *aff'd.,* 502 F. 2d 963 (9th Cir. 191/ 4); 495 F. Supp. 926 (N.D. Cal. 1979); *aff'd.,* 793 F.2d 969 (9th Cir. 1984).

Lawrence, E. C., & Heller, M. B. (2001). Parent-school collaboration: The utility of a competence lens. *Canadian Journal of School Psychology, 17,* 5–15.

Lecavalier, L., Tassé, M. J., & Lévesque, S. (2001). Assessment of mental retardation by school psychologists. *Canadian Journal of School Psychology, 17,* 97–107.

Lee, S. W. (Ed.). (2005). *Encyclopedia of school psychology.* Thousand Oaks, CA: Sage.

Levinson, E. M., Fetchkan, R., & Hohenshil, T. H. (1988). Job satisfaction among practicing school psychologists revisited. *School Psychology Review, 17,* 101–112.

Lichtenstein, R., & Fischetti, B. A. (1998). How long does a psychoeducational evaluation take? An urban Connecticut study. *Professional Psychology: Research and Practice, 29,* 144–148.

Lighthall, F. F. (1963). School psychology: An alien guild. *Elementary School Journal, 63,* 361–374.

Little, S. G. (1997). Graduate education of the top contributors to the school psychology literature: 1987–1995. *School Psychology International, 18,* 15–27.

Little, S. G., Akin-Little, K. A., & Tingstrom, D. H. (2004). An analysis of school psychology faculty by graduating university. *School Psychology Quarterly, 19,* 299–310.

Little, S. G., Lee, H. B., & Akin-Little, A. (2003). Education in statistics and research design in school psychology. *School Psychology International, 24*(4), 437–448.

Loe, S. A., & Miranda, A. H. (2005). An examination of ethnic incongruence in school-based psychological services and diversity-training experiences among school psychologists. *Psychology in the Schools, 42,* 419–432.

Logsdon-Conradsen, S., Sirl, K., Battle, J., Stapel, J., Anderson, P., Ventura-Cook, E., et al. (2001). Formalized postdoctoral fellowships: A national survey of postdoctoral fellows. *Professional Psychology: Research and Practice, 32*(3), 312–318.

Luckey, B. M. (1951, May). Duties of the school psychologist: Past, present, and future. *Division of School Psychologists Newsletter,* 4–10.

Lund, A. R., Reschly, D. J., & Connolly Martin, L. M. (1998). School psychology personnel needs: Correlates of current patterns and historical trends. *School Psychology Review, 27,* 106–120.

Lupart, J. L., Goddard, T., Hebert, Y., Jacobsen, M., & Timmons, V. (2001). *Students at risk in Canadian schools and communities.* Hull, Quebec: HRDC Publications Centre.

MacLeod, R. B. (1955). *Psychology in Canadian universities and colleges.* Ottawa, Ontario, Canada: Canadian Social Science Research Council.

Magary, J. F. (1966). A school psychologist is ... *Psychology in the Schools, 3,* 340–341.

Magary, J. F. (1967a). Emerging viewpoints in school psychological services. In J. F. Magary (Ed.), *School psychological services in theory and practice: A handbook* (pp. 671–755). Englewood Cliffs, NJ: Prentice Hall.

Magary, J. F. (Ed.). (1967b). *School psychological services in theory and practice: A handbook.* Englewood Cliffs, NJ: Prentice Hall.

Maher, C. A., & Greenberg, R. E. (1988). The school psychologist in business and industry. *School Psychology Review, 17,* 440–446.

Maher, C. A., Illback, R. J., & Zins, J. E. (Eds.). (1984). *Organizational psychology in the schools: A handbook for practitioners.* Springfield, IL: Charles C. Thomas.

Maher, C. A., & Zins, J. E. (1987). *Psychoeducational interventions in the schools: Methods and procedures for enhancing student competence.* New York: Pergamon Press.

Maier, H. W. (1969). *Three theories of child development.* New York: Harper & Row.

Marshall et al. v. *Georgia.* U.S. District Court for the Southern District of Georgia, CV482–233, June 28, 1984; *aff'd* (11th Cir. no. 84-8771, October 29, 1985).

Martens, B. K., & Keller, H. R. (1987). Training school psychologists in the scientific tradition. *School Psychology Review, 16,* 329–337.

Martens, E. H. (1939). *Clinical organization for child guidance within the schools* (Office of Education Bulletin No. 15). Washington, DC: Government Printing Office.

Martin, R. (1978). Expert and referent power: A framework for understanding and maximizing consultation effectiveness. *Journal of School Psychology, 16,* 49–55.

Martin, R. P. (1983). Consultation in the schools. In G. Hynd (Ed.), *The school psychologist: An introduction* (pp. 269–292). Syracuse, NY: Syracuse University Press.

Martin, R. (2001). Educational psychology in Newfoundland and Labrador: A thirty year history. *Canadian Journal of School Psychology, 16,* 5–17.

Martin, S. (2005). Healthy kids make better students. *Monitor on Psychology, 36*(9), 24–26.

Marzano, R. J., (2003). *What works in schools: Translating research into action.* Alexandria, VA: Association for Supervision and Curriculum Development.

Mash, E. J., & Dozois, J. A. (1999). Theory and research in the study of childhood exceptionalities. In V. L. Schwean & D. H. Saklofske (Eds.), *Handbook of psychosocial characteristics of exceptional children* (pp. 3–39). New York: Kluwer Academic/Plenum Publishers.

Maslach, C. (1976, September). Burned-out. *Human Behavior*, 16–22.

Maslach, C. M., & Jackson, S. E. (1986). *Maslach Burnout Inventory* (2nd ed.). Palo Alto, CA: Consulting Psychologists Press.

Matines, D. (2004). A quantitative coding system for evaluating the effects of multicultural training in schools using the consultation model. *Trainer's Forum, 23* (4, Summer), 10–12.

Mattie T. v. *Holladay* (D.C. 75 31 S, N.D. Miss. 1979).

May, J. V. (1976). *Professionals and clients: A constitutional struggle.* Beverly Hills, CA: Sage.

McCarney, S. B., Wunderlich, K. C., & Bauer, A. M. (1993). *The pre-referral intervention manual* (2nd ed.). Columbia, MO: Hawthorne Educational Services.

McDaid, J. L., & Reifman, A. (1996, November). What school psychologists do: Time study of psychologists' services in San Diego. *Communiqué, 25*(3), 8, 10.

McGuire, P. A. (1998). The freedom to move from state to state. *APA Monitor, 29*(8), 27.

McIntosh, David E. (Ed.). (2004). Addressing the shortage of school psychologists [Special issue]. *Psychology in the Schools*, 41(4).

McKee, W. T. (1996). Legislation, certification, and licensing of school psychologists. *Canadian Journal of School Psychology, 12*, 103–114.

McKinley, D. L., & Hayes, M. (1987). Moving ahead in professional psychology. *The Counseling Psychologist, 15*, 261–266.

McLaughlin, M., Vogt, M. E., Anderson, J. A., DuMez, J., Peter, M. G., & Hunter, A. (1998). *Portfolio models across the teaching profession.* Norwood, MA: Christopher-Gordon.

Mcloughlin, C. S., Leless, D. B., & Thomas, A. (1998). The school psychologist in Ohio: Additional results from OSPA's 1997 omnibus survey. *The Ohio School Psychologist, 43*(3), 3–5.

McManus, J. L. (1986). Student paraprofessionals in school psychology: Practices and possibilities. *School Psychology Review, 15*, 9–23.

McMaster, M. D., Reschly, D. J., & Peters, J. M. (1989). *Directory of school psychology graduate programs.* Washington, DC: National Association of School Psychologists.

McMinn, M. R., Buchanan, T., Ellens, B. M., & Ryan, M. K. (1999). Technology, professional practice, and ethics: Survey findings and implications. *Professional Psychology: Research and Practice, 30*, 165–172.

McMurray, J. G. (1967). Two decades of school psychology: Past and future. *Canadian Psychologist, 8*, 207–217.

McReynolds, P. (1997). *Lightner Witmer: His life and times.* Washington, DC: American Psychological Association.

Medway, F. J. (1996) Turning imperfection into perfection: Some advice for making psychology indispensable in the schools. In R. C. Talley, T. Kubiszyn,

M. Brassard, & R. J. Short (Eds.), *Making psychologists in schools indispensable: Critical questions and emerging perspectives* (pp. 111–116). Washington, DC: American Psychological Association.

Medway, F. J., & Cafferty, T. P. (Eds.). (1992). *School psychology: A social psychological perspective*. Hillsdale, NJ: Erlbaum.

Merrell, K. W., Ervin, R. A., & Gimpel, G. A. (2006). *School psychology for the 21st century: Foundations and practices*. New York: Guilford Press.

Meyers, J., Alpert, J. L., & Fleisher, B. D. (1983). *Training in consultation: Perspectives from mental health, behavioral and organizational consultation*. Springfield, IL: Charles C. Thomas.

Miller, C. D., Witt, J. C., & Finley, J. L. (1981). School psychologists' perceptions of their work: Satisfactions and dissatisfactions in the United States. *School Psychology International, 2*(2), 1–3.

Miller, D. C. (2001). The shortage of school psychologists: Issues and actions. *Communiqué 30*(1), 34, 36–38.

Miller, D. C. (2007). School Psychology Training Programs in the United States and Canada. Unpublished Paper Posted on the Internet, May 31, 2007.

Miller, D. C., & Masten, W. (2000). *Trainers of school psychologists survey*. Unpublished study.

Miller, D. C., & Palomares, R. S. (2000). Growth in school psychology: A necessary blueprint. *Communiqué, 28*(6), 1, 6–7.

Millman, J. (Ed.). (1981). *Handbook of teacher evaluation*. Beverly Hills, CA: Sage.

Mills v. *Board of Education of the District of Columbia*, 348 F. Supp. 866(1972); *contempt proceedings*, EHLE 551:643 (D.D.C. 1980).

Minke, K. M., & Brown, D. T. (1996). Preparing psychologists to work with children: A comparison of curricula in child-clinical and school psychology programs. *Professional Psychology: Research and Practice, 27*, 631–634.

Miranda, A. H., & Gutter, P. B. (2002). Diversity research literature in school psychology. *Psychology in the Schools, 39*, 597–604.

Monroe. V. (1979). Roles and status of school psychology. In G. Phye & D. Reschly (Eds.), *School psychology: Perspectives and issues* (pp. 25–47). New York: Academic Press.

Moore, M. T., Strang, E. W., Schwartz, M., & Braddock, M. (1988). *Patterns in special education service delivery and cost*. Washington, DC: Decision Resources Corporation.

Mordock, J. B. (1988). The school psychologist working in residential and day treatment centers. *School Psychology Review, 17*, 421–428.

Morgan, E. M. (1998). *A complete guide to the advanced study in and profession of school psychology*. Delaware, OH: Author.

Morris, R. J., & Morris, Y. P. (1989). School psychology in residential treatment facilities. In R. C. D'Amato & R. S. Dean (Eds.), *The school psychologist in nontraditional settings: Integrating clients, services, and settings* (pp. 159–183). Hillsdale, NJ: Erlbaum.

Morrow, W. R. (1946). The development of psychological internship training. *Journal of Consulting Psychology, 10*, 165–183.

Moss, J. A., & Wilson, M. S. (1998). School psychology services preferred by principals. *CASP Today, 48*(1), 15–17.

Mpofu, E., Zindi, F., Oakland, T., & Peresuh, M. (1997). School psychology practices in East and Southern Africa: Special educators' perspectives. *The Journal of Special Education, 31*, 387–402.

Mullen, F. A. (1967). The role of the school psychologist in the urban school system. In J. F. Magary (Ed.), *School psychological services in theory and practice: A handbook* (pp. 30–67). Englewood Cliffs, NJ: Prentice Hall.

Mullen, F. A. (1981). School psychology in the USA: Reminiscences of its origin. *Journal of School Psychology, 19*, 103–119.

Munsterberg, H. (1898). Psychology and education. *Educational Review, 16*, 105–132.

Mureika, J. M. K. (2007). School psychology: The new kid on the CPA block. *Psynopsis, 29*(1), 3.

Mureika, J. M. K., Falconer, R. D., & Howard, B. M. (2004, Spring). The changing role of the school psychologist: From tester to collaborator. *Canadian Association of School Psychologists/Canadian Psychological Association Joint Newsletter.*

Mureika, J. M. K., French, F., & Service, J. (2002a). Enhancing the experience of children and youth in today's schools: The role of psychology in Canadian Schools. Position paper prepared for the Canadian Psychological Association. Retrieved from http://www.cap.ca/documents/school%5F2.pdf

Mureika, J. M. K., French, F., & Service J. (2002b). Enhancing the experience of children and youth in today's schools: The contribution of the school psychologist. Position paper prepared for the Canadian Psychological Association. Retrieved from http://www.cap.ca/documents/school%5F2.pdf

Murphy, M. J., Levant, R. F., Hall, J. E., & Glueckauf, R. L. (2007). Distance education in professional training in psychology. *Professional Psychology: Research and Practice, 38*(1), 97–103.

Murray, B. (1995). APA recognizes areas of expertise in practice. *APA Monitor, 26*(4), 45.

Murray, B. (1998, December). The authorship dilemma: Who gets credit for what? *APA Monitor, 29*(12), 1.

Murray, J. (1985). Best practices in working with families of handicapped children. In A. Thomas & J. Grimes (Eds.), *Best practices in school psychology* (pp. 321–330). Kent, OH: National Association of School Psychologists.

Mussell, B., Cardiff, K., & White, J. (2004). *The mental health and well-being of aboriginal children and youth: Guidance for new approaches and services.* Report prepared for the British Columbia Ministry of Children and Family Development, British Columbia, Canada.

Myers, R. (1958). Professional psychology in Canada. *Canadian Psychologist, 7*, 27–36.

Mykota D., & Schwean, V. L. (2006). Moderator factors in First Nations students at risk for psychosocial problems. *Canadian Journal of School Psychology, 21*, 4–17.

Nagle, R. J., & Medway, F. J. (Guest Eds.). (1982). Psychological services in the high school. *School Psychology Review, 11*, 357–416.

Nagle, R. J., Suldo, S. M., Christenson, S. L., & Hansen, A. L. (2004). Graduate students' perspectives of academic positions in school psychology. *School Psychology Quarterly, 19*, 311–326.

Napoli, D. S. (1981). *Architects of adjustment: The history of the psychological profession in the United States.* Port Washington, NY: Kennikat.

NASP adopts position on testing and strikes. (1973). *Communiqué, 1*(3), 1.

Nastasi, B. K. (2004). Meeting the challenges of the future: Integrating public health and public education for mental health promotion. *Journal of Educational and Psychological Consultation, 15*(3/4), 295–312.

National Association of School Psychologists. (1972). *Guidelines for training programs in school psychology.* Washington, DC: Author.

National Association of School Psychologists. (1973). *Competency continuum for school psychologists and support personnel.* Washington, DC: Author.

National Association of School Psychologists. (1974). *Principles for professional ethics.* Washington, DC: Author.

National Association of School Psychologists. (1984a). *Principles for professional ethics.* Washington, DC: Author.

National Association of School Psychologists. (1984b). *Standards for the provision of school psychological services.* Washington, DC: Author.

National Association of School Psychologists. (1989). *Membership directory.* Washington, DC: Author.

National Association of School Psychologists. (2000a). *Principles for professional ethics.* Bethesda, MD: Author. See also *School Psychology Review, 29,* 616–629.

National Association of School Psychologists. (2000b). *Guidelines for the provision of school psychological services.* Bethesda, MD: Author. See also *School Psychology Review, 29,* 630–638.

National Association of School Psychologists. (2000c). *Standards for training and field placement programs in school psychology.* Bethesda, MD: Author.

National Association of School Psychologists. (2000d). *Standards for credentialing of school psychologists.* Bethesda, MD: Author.

National Association of School Psychologists, Multicultural Affairs Committee. (1998). *Directory of bilingual school psychologists.* Bethesda, MD: Author.

National Association of State Consultants for School Psychological Services. (1987, August). Committee report on personnel shortages in school psychology. Available from NASP, Bethesda, MD.

National Council for Accreditation of Teacher Education. (2002). *NCATE Unit Standards.* Washington, DC: Author.

National School Psychology Inservice Training Network. (1984). *School psychology. A blueprint for training and practice.* Minneapolis, MN: Author.

Neisser, U. (1981). Obituary: James J. Gibson (1904–1979). *American Psychologist, 36,* 214–215.

Nelson, J. R., Peterson, L., & Strader, H. (1997). The use of school psychological services by charter schools. *Communiqué, 26*(1), 12.

Neudorf, J. (1989). *The role and tasks of educational psychologists in Saskatchewan.* Unpublished master's thesis, University of Regina, Saskatchewan, Canada.

New Brunswick Department of Education. (2001). *Keeping our schools safe: A protocol for violence prevention and crisis response in New Brunswick Schools.* Fredericton, New Brunswick, Canada: Author.

New Brunswick Department of Education. (2004). *Meeting behavioural challenges.* Fredericton, New Brunswick, Canada: Author.

New Brunswick Department of Education & Canadian Psychological Association. (2001). *Guidelines for professional practice for school psychologists.* Fredericton, New Brunswick, Canada: Department of Education.

New Brunswick Department of Education & Canadian Psychological Association. (2004). *Guidelines for referrals for school psychological consultation.* Fredericton, New Brunswick, Canada: Department of Education.

New Jersey Coalition of Child Study Teams. (2002) Position statement on roles and functions of child study team members. *New Jersey School Psychologist, 24*(8), 9–10.

New York State Association for Applied Psychology, Special Committee on School Psychologists. (1943). Report on the functions, training and employment opportunities of school psychologists. *Journal of Consulting Psychology, 7*, 230–243.

Newland, T. E. (1980). Psychological assessment of exceptional children and youth. In W. M. Cruickshank (Ed.), *Psychology of exceptional children and youth* (pp. 74–135). Englewood Cliffs, NJ: Prentice Hall.

Norcross, J. C., Castle, P. H., Sayette, M. A., & Mayne, T. J. (2004). The PsyD: Heterogeneity in practitioner training. *Professional Psychology: Research and Practice, 35*(4), 412–419.

Oakland, T. (1986). Fare well, Journal of School Psychology. *Journal of School Psychology, 24*, 321–323.

Oakland, T. (1990). Psicologia escolar no Brazil: Passado, presente, e futuro [School psychology in Brazil: Past, present, and future]. *Psicologia: Tedria ePesquisa, 5*(2), 191–201.

Oakland, T. (1992). Formulating priorities for international school psychology toward the turn of the twentieth century. *School Psychology International, 13*, 171–177.

Oakland, T. (1993). A brief history of international school psychology. *Journal of School Psychology, 31*, 109–122.

Oakland, T. (2003). International school psychology: Psychology's worldwide portal to children and youth. *American Psychologist, 58*(11), 985–992.

Oakland, T. (2005). International School Psychology Association. In S. W. Lee (Ed.), *Encyclopedia of school psychology* (pp. 272–273). Thousand Oaks, CA: Sage.

Oakland, T. D., & Cunningham, J. L. (1992). A survey of school psychology in developed and developing countries. *School Psychology International, 13*, 99–129.

Oakland, T., & Cunningham, J. (1997). International School Psychology Association definition of school psychology. *School Psychology International, 18*, 195–200.

Oakland, T., & Cunningham, J. (1999). The futures of school psychology: Conceptual models for its development and examples of their applications. In C. R. Reynolds & T. B. Gutkin (Eds.), *The handbook of school psychology* (pp. 34–53). New York: Wiley.

Oakland, T., Cunningham, J., Poulsen, A., & Meazzini, P. (1991). An examination of policies governing the normalization of handicapped pupils in Denmark, Italy, and the United States. *International Journal of Special Education, 6*(2), 386–402.

Oakland, T., Feldman, N., & Leon De Viloria, C. (1995). School psychology in Venezuela: Three decades of progress and futures of great potential. *School Psychology International, 16*, 29–42.

Oakland, T., Goldman, S., & Bischoff, H. (1997). Code of ethics of the International School Psychology Association. *School Psychology International, 18*, 291–298.

Oakland, T., & Hambleton, R. (Eds.). (1995) *International perspectives on assessment of academic achievement*. Norwell, MA: Kluwer.

Oakland, T., & Hu, S. (1989). Psychology in the schools of four Asian countries. *Psychologia, 32*, 71–80.

Oakland, T., & Hu, S. (1991). Professionals who administer tests with children and youth: An international survey. *Journal of Psychoeducational Assessment, 9*(2), 108–120.

Oakland, T., & Hu, S. (1992). The top ten tests used with children and youth worldwide. *Bulletin of the International Test Commission, 5*, 99–120.

Oakland, T., Mpofu, E., Gregoire, G., & Faulkner, M. (in press). An exploration of learning disabilities in four countries: Implications for test development and use in developing countries. *International Journal of Testing, 7*(1), 53–69.

Oakland, T., & Phillips, B. (1997). *Addressing the needs of children with learning disabilities: Advocacy by the International School Psychology Association*. Paper presented to UNESCO's Committee on the Rights of the Child, Geneva, Switzerland

Oakland, T., & Saigh, P. (1989). Psychology in the schools: An introduction to international perspectives. In P. Saigh & T. Oakland (Eds.), *International perspectives on psychology in the schools* (pp. 1–22). Hillsdale, NJ: Erlbaum.

Oakland, T., & Wechsler, S. (1988). School psychology in five South American countries: A 1989 perspective. *Revista Interamericana dePsicologia/Interamerican Journal of Psychology, 22*, 41–55.

Oakland, T., & Wechsler, S. (1990). School psychology in Brazil: An examination of its research infrastructure. *School Psychology International, 11*, 287–293.

Ochoa, S. H., Rivera, B., & Ford, L. (1997). An investigation of school psychology training pertaining to bilingual psycho educational assessment of primarily Hispanic students: Twenty-five years after *Diana* v. *California*. *Journal of School Psychology, 35*, 329–349.

Orlosky, D. E., McCleary, L. E., Shapiro, A., & Webb, L. D. (1984). *Educational administration today*. Columbus, OH: Charles E. Merrill.

Ormrod, J. E., Saklofske, D. H., Schwean, V. L., Harrison, G., & Andrews, J. (2005). *Principles of educational psychology* (Canadian ed.). Toronto, Ontario, Canada: Pearson.

Ormrod, J. E., Saklofske, D. H., Schwean, V. L., Harrison, G., & Andrews, J. (2006). *Educational psychology: Developing learners*. Toronto, Ontario, Canada: Pearson.

O'Shea, H. E. (1960). The future of school psychology. In M. G. Gottsegen & G. B. Gottsegen (Eds.), *Professional school psychology* (pp. 275–283). New York: Grune & Stratton.

Ownby, R. (1991). *Psychological reports: A guide to report writing in professional psychology* (2nd ed.). Brandon, VT: Clinical Psychology Publishing.

P.A.R.C. [Pennsylvania Association for Retarded Citizens] v. *Commonwealth of Pennsylvania*, 334 F. Supp. 1257 (1971), 343 F. Supp. 279 (1972).

P.A.S.E. [Parents in Action in Special Education] v. *Hannon*, 506 F. Supp. 831 (N.D. Ill. 1980).

Perkins, M. (1990). School psychology in Ontario. *Canadian Journal of School Psychology, 6*(1), 34–38.

Pesce v. *J. Sterling Morton High School District*, 651 F. Supp. 152 (N.D. Ill. 1986).

Petersen, D. R. (1976). Is psychology a profession? *American Psychologist, 38*, 572–581.

Peterson, K. A., Waldron, D. J., & Paulson, S. E. (1998, April). *Teachers' perceptions of school psychologists' existing and potential roles.* Paper presented at the annual meeting of the National Association of School Psychologists, Orlando, FL.

Peterson, R. L., Peterson, D. R., Abrams, J. C., & Stricker, G. (1997). The National Council of Schools and Programs of Professional Psychology educational model. *Professional Psychology: Research and Practice, 28*, 373–386.

Petition for reaffirmation of the specialty of school psychology. (2005, August). Washington, DC: American Psychological Association.

Pfeiffer, S. I. (1980). The school-based interprofessional team: Recurring problems and some possible solutions. *Journal of School Psychology, 18*, 388–394.

Pfeiffer, S. I., & Marmo, P. (1981). The status of training in school psychology and trends toward the future. *Journal of School Psychology, 19*, 211–216.

Pfeiffer, S. I., & Reddy, L. A. (1998). School-based mental health programs in the United States: Present status and a blueprint for the future. *School Psychology Review, 27*, 84–96.

Pfeiffer, S. I., & Reddy, L. A. (Eds.). (1999). Inclusion practices with special needs students: Theory, research, and application [Special issue]. *Special Services in the Schools, 15*(1–2).

Pfohl, W., & Pfohl, V. A. (2002). Best practices in technology. In A. Thomas & J. Grimes (Eds.), *Best practices in school psychology IV* (pp. 195–207). Bethesda, MD: National Association of School Psychologists.

Phelps, L. (1998, November). CRSPPP and recognition of school psychology as a specialty. *CDSPP Press, 17*(1), 7–10.

Phelps, L. (2005). Council of Directors of School Psychology Programs. In S. W. Lee (Ed.), *Encyclopedia of school psychology* (pp. 122–123). Thousand Oaks, CA: Sage.

Phelps, L., Brown, R. T., & Power, T. J. (2002). *Pediatric psychopharmacology: Combining medical and psychosocial interventions.* Washington, DC: American Psychological Association.

Philips, D., Schwean, V. L., & Saklofske, D.H. (1997). Treatment effects of a school-based cognitive-behavioral program for aggressive children. *Canadian Journal of School Psychology, 13*, 60–67.

Phillips, B. (1985). Education and training. In J. R. Bergan (Ed.), *School psychology in contemporary society: An introduction* (pp. 92–115). Columbus, OH: Charles E. Merrill.

Phillips, B. N. (1990a). Law, psychology, and education. In T. R. Kratochwill (Ed.), *Advances in school psychology* (Vol. 7, pp. 79–130). Hillsdale, NJ: Erlbaum.

Phillips, B. N. (1990b). *School psychology at a turning point: Ensuring a bright future for the profession.* San Francisco: Jossey-Bass.

Phillips, B. N. (1993). Trainers of school psychologists and council of directors of school psychology programs: A new chapter in the history of school psychology. *Journal of School Psychology, 31,* 91–108.

Phillips, B. N. (1999). Strengthening the links between science and practice: Reading, evaluating, and applying research in school psychology. In C. R. Reynolds & T. B. Gutkin (Eds.), *Handbook of School Psychology* (3rd ed., pp. 56–77). New York: Wiley.

Phillips, V., & McCullough, L. (1990). Consultation-based programming: Instituting the collaborative ethic in schools. *Exceptional Children, 56,* 291–304.

Pickover, B., Barbrack, C., & Glat, M. (1982). Preventive and educative programs within the high school. *School Psychology Review, 11,* 399–408.

Pion, G. M. (1992, April). *Professional psychology's human resources: Scientists, practitioners, scientist-practitioners, or none of the above?* Paper presented at the 1992 Accreditation Summit, American Psychological Society, Chicago.

Pion, G. M., Bramblett, J. P., & Wicherski, M. (1987). *Preliminary report: 1985 doctorate employment survey.* Washington, DC: American Psychological Association.

Pipho, C. (1999, February). The profit side of education. *Phi Delta Kappan, 80*(6), 421–422.

Pitcher, G. D., & Poland, S. (1992). *Crisis intervention in the schools.* New York: Guilford Press.

Plas, J. M. (1986). *Systems psychology in the schools.* New York: Pergamon Press.

Plas, J. M., & Williams, B. (1985). Best practices in working with community agencies. In A. Thomas & J. Grimes (Eds.), *Best practices in school psychology* (pp. 331–340). Kent, OH: National Association of School Psychologists.

Poland, S. (1998). Jonesboro turns to school psychologists for leadership. NASP *Communiqué, 26*(8), 5–6.

Poland, S., Pitcher, G., & Lazarus, P. (1995). Crisis intervention. In A. Thomas & J. Grimes (Eds.), *Best practices in school psychology III* (pp. 445–458). Washington, DC: National Association of School Psychologists.

Pope, K. S., & Vetter, V. A. (1992). Ethical dilemmas encountered by members of the American Psychological Association. *American Psychologist, 47,* 397–411.

Power, T. J., DuPaul, G. J., Shapiro, E. S., & Parrish, J. M. (1998). Role of the school-based professional in health-related services. In L. Phelps (Ed.), *Health-related disorders in children and adolescents* (pp. 15–26). Washington, DC: American Psychological Association.

Prasse, D. P. (1988). Licensing, school psychology, and independent private practice. In T. R. Kratochwill (Ed.), *Advances in school psychology* (Vol. 6, pp. 49–80). Hillsdale, NJ: Erlbaum.

Prasse, D. (1995). Best practices in school psychology and the law. In A. Thomas & J. Grimes (Eds.), *Best practices in school psychology III* (pp. 41–50) Washington, DC: National Association of School Psychologists.

Prifitera, A., Saklofske, D. H., & Weiss, L. G. (Eds.). (2005). *WISC-IV Clinical use and interpretation: Scientist-practitioner perspectives.* San Diego, CA: Elsevier.

Proctor, B. E., & Steadman, T. (2003). Job satisfaction, burnout, and perceived effectiveness of "in-house" versus traditional school psychologists. *Psychology in the Schools, 40*(2), 237–243.

Prout, H. T., Meyers, J., & Greggo, S. P. (1989). *The acceptability of PsyD graduates in the academic job market.* Unpublished. (Available from the authors at ED 233, SUNY Albany, Albany, NY 12222.)

Pryzwansky, W. B. (1982). School psychology training and practice: The APA perspective. In T. R. Kratochwill (Ed.), *Advances in school psychology* (Vol. 2, pp. 19–39). Hillsdale, NJ: Erlbaum.

Pryzwansky, W. B. (1989). Private practice as an alternative setting for school psychologists. In R. C. D'Amato & R. S. Dean (Eds.), *The school psychologist in nontraditional settings: Integrating clients, services, and settings* (pp. 76–85). Hillsdale, NJ: Erlbaum.

Pryzwansky, W. B. (1990). School psychology in the next decade: A period of some difficult decisions. In T. B. Gutkin & C. R. Reynolds (Eds.), *The handbook of school psychology* (pp. 32–40). New York: Wiley.

Pryzwansky, W. B. (1993). The regulation of school psychology: A historical perspective on certification, licensure, and accreditation. *Journal of School Psychology, 31,* 219–235.

Pryzwansky, W. (1998). Task Force on Post-Doctoral Education and Training in School Psychology purpose statement. *CDSPP Press, 16*(2), 9–11.

Pryzwansky, W. (1999). Accreditation and credentialing systems in school psychology. In C. R. Reynolds & T. B. Gutkin (Eds.), *The handbook of school psychology* (pp. 1145–1158). New York: Wiley.

Pryzwansky, W. B., & Wendt, R. N. (1987). *Psychology as a profession: Foundations of practice.* New York: Pergamon Press.

Raimy, V. C. (Ed.). (1950). *Training in clinical psychology.* New York: Prentice Hall.

Ranes, R. G. (1992). District-wide implementation of curriculum based measurement: First year outcomes. *CASP Today, 51*(4), 7.

Ranseen, J. D. (1998). Lawyers with ADHD: The special test accommodation controversy. *Professional Psychology: Research and Practice, 29*, 450–459.

Rathvon, N. (1999). *Effective school interventions: Strategies for enhancing academic achievement and social competence.* New York: Guilford Press.

Reeder, G. D., Maccow, G. C., Shaw, S. R., Swerdlik, M. E., Horton, C. B., & Foster, P. (1997). School psychologists and full-service schools: Partnerships with medical, mental health, and social services. *School Psychology Review, 26*, 603–621.

Reger, R. (1965). *School psychology.* Springfield, IL: Charles C. Thomas.

Rehabilitation Act of 1973, Pub. L. 93-112, 87 Stat. 394 (1973).

Reinhardt, J., & Martin, M. (1991). Ethics forum. *Communiqué, 20*(2), 10–11.

Reschly, D. J. (1979). Nonbiased assessment. In G. D. Phye & D. J. Reschly (Eds.), *School psychology: Perspectives and issues* (pp. 215–256). New York: Academic Press.

Reschly, D. J. (1983). Legal issues in psychoeducational assessment. In G. W. Hynd (Ed.), *The school psychologist: An introduction* (pp. 67–93). Syracuse, NY: Syracuse University Press.

Reschly, D. J. (1998, August). *School psychology practice: Is there change?* Paper presented at the annual meeting of the American Psychological Association, San Francisco, CA.

Reschly, D. J. (2000). The present and future status of school psychology in the United States. *School Psychology Review, 29*, 507–522.

Reschly, D. J., & Bersoff, D. N. (1999). Law and school psychology. In C. R. Reynolds & T. B. Gutkin (Eds.), *The handbook of school psychology* (pp. 1077–1112). New York: Wiley.

Reschly, D. J., & Connolly, L. M. (1990). Comparisons of school psychologists in the city and country: Is there a "rural" school psychology? *School Psychology Review, 19,* 534–549.

Reschly, D. J., Kicklighter, R. H., & McKee, P. (1988a). Recent placement litigation: Part 1. Regular education grouping: Comparison of *Marshall* (1984, 1985) and *Hobson* (1967, 1969). *School Psychology Review, 17*, 9–21.

Reschly, D. J., Kicklighter, R. H., & McKee, P. (1988b). Recent placement litigation: Part 2. Minority EMR over-representation: Comparison of *Larry P.* (1979, 1984, 1986) with *Marshall* (1984, 1985) and *S-1* (1986). *School Psychology Review, 17*, 22–38.

Reschly, D. J., Kicklighter, R. H., & McKee, P. (1988c). Recent placement litigation: Part 3. Analysis of differences in *Larry P., Marshall,* and *S-1* and implications for future practices. *School Psychology Review, 17,* 39–50.

Reschly, D. J., & McMaster-Beyer, M. (1991). Influences of degree level, institutional orientation, college affiliation, and accreditation status on school psychology graduate education. *Professional Psychology: Research and Practice, 22,* 368–374.

Reschly, D. J., & Wilson, M. S. (1992). *School psychology faculty and practitioners: 1986 to 1991 trends in demographic characteristics, roles, satisfaction, and system reform.* Unedited manuscript.

Reschly, D. J., & Wilson, M. S. (1995). School psychology practitioners and faculty: 1986 to 1991–92 trends in demographics, roles, satisfaction, and system reform. *School Psychology Review, 24*, 62–80.

Reschly, D. J., & Wilson, M. S. (1997). Characteristics of school psychology graduate education: Implications for the entry-level discussion and doctoral-level specialty definition. *School Psychology Review, 26*, 74–92.

Reynolds, C. R., & Gutkin, T. B. (Eds.). (1982). *The handbook of school psychology.* New York: Wiley.

Reynolds, C. R., & Gutkin, T. B. (Eds.). (1999). *Handbook of school psychology* (3rd ed.). New York: Wiley.

Reynolds, C. R., Gutkin, T. B., Elliott, S. N., & Witt, J. C. (1984). *School psychology: Essentials of theory and practice.* New York: Wiley.

Roberts, G. A., Gerrard-Morris, A., Zanger, D., Davis, K. S., & Robinson, D. H. (2006). Trends in female authorships, editorial board memberships, and editorships in school psychology journals from 1991–2004. *The School Psychologist, 60*(1), 5–10.

Roberts, R. D. (1970). Perceptions of actual and desired role functions of school psychologists by psychologists and teachers. *Psychology in the Schools, 7*, 175–178.

Roberts, R. D., & Solomons, G. (1970). Perceptions of the duties and functions of the school psychologist. *American Psychologist, 25*, 544–549.

Rogers, M. R., Ingraham, C. L., Bursztyn, A., Cajigas-Segrede, N., Esquivel, G., Hess, R., et al. (1999). Providing psychological services to racially, ethnically, culturally, and linguistically diverse individuals in the schools: Recommendations for practice. *School Psychology International, 20*, 243–264.

Rogers, M. R., Ponterotto, J. G., Conoley, J. C., & Wiese, M. J. (1992). Multicultural training in school psychology: A national survey. *School Psychology Review, 21,* 603–616.

Romans, J. S. C., Boswell, D. L., Carlozzi, A. F., & Ferguson, D. B. (1995). Training and supervision practices in clinical, counseling, and school psychology programs. *Professional Psychology: Research and Practice, 26*, 407–412.

Rosebrook, W. M. (1942). Psychological service for schools on a regional basis. *Journal of Consulting Psychology, 6,* 196–200.

Rosenberg, R. (1982). *Beyond separate spheres: Intellectual roots of modern feminism.* New Haven, CT: Yale University Press.

Rosenberg, S. L. (1995). Maintaining an independent practice. In A. Thomas & J. Grimes (Eds.), *Best practices in school psychology III* (pp. 145–152). Washington, DC: National Association of School Psychologists.

Rosenberg, S. L., & McNamara, K. M. (1988). *Independent practice of school psychology: Annotated bibliography and reference list.* Washington, DC: National Association of School Psychologists.

Rosenfeld, J. G., & Blanco, R. F. (1974). Incompetence in school psychology: The case of "Dr. Gestalt." *Psychology in the Schools, 11*, 263–269.

Rosenfield, S. (1996). The school psychologist as citizen of the learning community. In R. C. Talley, T. Kubiszyn, M. Brassard, & R. J. Short (Eds.), *Making psychologists in schools indispensable: Critical questions and emerging perspectives* (pp. 83–88). Washington, DC: American Psychological Association.

Rosenfield, S. (2002). Best practices in instructional consultation. In A. Thomas & J. Grimes (Eds.), *Best practices in school psychology IV* (pp. 609–623). Bethesda, MD: National Association of School Psychologists.

Rosenfield, S. (2004). Academia: It's a wonderful life—Isn't it? *School Psychology Quarterly, 19*(4), 398–408.

Rosenfield, S., & Gravois, T. (1999). Working with teams in the school. In C. R. Reynolds & T. B. Gutkin (Eds.), *The handbook of school psychology* (pp. 1025–1040). New York: Wiley.

Rosenfield, S., & Kuralt, S. K. (1990). Best practices in curriculum-based assessment. In A. Thomas & J. Grimes (Eds.), *Best practices in school psychology II* (pp. 275–286). Silver Spring, MD: National Association of School Psychologists.

Ross, D. (1972). *G. Stanley Hall: The psychologist as prophet.* Chicago: University of Chicago Press.

Ross, M. J., Holzman, L. A., Handal, P. J., & Gilner, F. H. (1991). Performance on the Examination for the Professional Practice of Psychology as a function of specialty, degree, administrative housing, and accreditation status. *Professional Psychology: Research and Practice, 22*, 347–350.

Ross, R. P. (1995). Best practices in implementing intervention assistance teams. In A. Thomas & J. Grimes (Eds.), *Best practices in school psychology III* (pp. 227–237). Washington, DC: National Association of School Psychologists.

Ross-Reynolds, G. (1990). Best practices in report writing. In A. Thomas & J. Grimes (Eds.), *Best practices in school psychology II* (pp. 621–633). Silver Spring, MD: National Association of School Psychologists.

Russell, R. (1984). Psychology in its world context. *American Psychologist, 39*, 1027–1025.

Sacken, D. M., & Overcast, T. D. (1999). The legal rights of students. In C. R. Reynolds & T. B. Gutkin (Eds.), *The handbook of school psychology* (pp. 1113–1144). New York: Wiley.

Sagan, C. (1977). *The dragons of Eden: Speculations on the evolution of human intelligence*. New York: Random House.

Saigh, P., & Oakland, T. (Eds.). (1989). *International perspectives on psychology in the schools*. Hillsdale, NJ: Erlbaum.

Saklofske, D. H. (1996). Moving toward a core curriculum for training school psychologists. *Canadian Journal of School Psychology, 12*, 91–96.

Saklofske, D. H., Bartell, R., Derevensky, J., Hann, S. G., Holmes, B., & Janzen, H. L. (2000). School psychology in Canada: Past, present, and future perspectives. In T. K. Fagan & P. S. Wise, *School psychology: Past, present, and future* (2nd ed., pp. 313–354). Bethesda, MD: National Association of School Psychologists.

Saklofske, D. H., & Grainger, J. (1990). School psychology in Saskatchewan. *Canadian Journal of School Psychology, 6*, 15–21.

Saklofske, D. H., & Grainger, J. (2001). School psychology in Saskatchewan: The end of a decade, the start of a century. *Canadian Journal of School Psychology, 16*, 67–77.

Saklofske, D. H., Hildebrand, D. K., Reynolds, C. R., & Wilson, V. L. (1998). Substituting symbol search for coding on the WISC-III: Canadian normative tables for performance and full scale IQ scores. *Canadian Journal of Behavioural Science, 20*(2) 57–68.

Saklofske, D. H., & Janzen, H. L. (1990). School-based assessment research in Canada. *McGill Journal of Education, 25*(1), 5–23.

Saklofske, D. H., & Janzen, H. L. (1993). Contemporary issues in school psychology. In K. S. Dobson & D. J. G. Dobson (Eds.), *Professional psychology in Canada* (pp. 313–350). Toronto: Hogrefe & Huber.

Saklofske, D. H., Schwean, V. L., Harrison, G. L., & Mureika, J. (2006). School psychology in Canada. In S. R. Jimerson, T. D. Oakland, & P. T. Farrell (Eds.), *The handbook of international school psychology* (pp. 39–51). Thousand Oaks, CA: Sage.

Sales, B. D., Krauss, D. A., Sacken, D. M., & Overcast, T. D. (1999). The legal rights of students. In C. R. Reynolds & T. B. Gutkin (Eds.), *The handbook of school psychology* (pp. 1113–1144). New York: Wiley.

Salvia, J., & Ysseldyke, J. E. (2007). *Assessment in special and inclusive education* (10th ed.). Boston: Houghton-Mifflin.

Sandoval, J. (1988). The school psychologist in higher education. *School Psychology Review, 17*, 391–396.

Sandoval, J. (1993). The history of interventions in school psychology. *Journal of School Psychology, 31,* 195–217.

Sarason, S. B. (1971). *The culture of the school and the problem of change.* Boston: Allyn & Bacon.

Sattler, J. M. (1998). *Clinical and forensic interviewing of children and families: Guidelines for the mental health, education, pediatric, and child maltreatment fields.* San Diego, CA: Author.

Sattler, J. M. (2001). *Assessment of children: Cognitive applications.* San Diego: CA: Author.

Sattler, J. M. (2002). *Assessment of children: Behavioral and clinical applications* (4th ed.). La Mesa, CA: Author.

Schmidt, W. H. O. (1976, November). The training of educational psychologists in Canada. *CSSE News,* 4–8.

Schmuck, R. A., & Miles, M. B. (1971). *Organization development in schools.* Palo Alto, CA: National Press Books.

Schudson, M. (1980). [Review of the book *The rise of professionalism: A sociological analysis.*] *Theory and Society, 9,* 215–229.

Schwarz, J. (1986). *Radical feminists of heterodoxy: Greenwich Village 1912–1940.* Norwich, VT: New Victoria.

Schwean, V. L. (2006, June). *Systems of care: Promoting healthy developmental outcomes.* Paper presented at the annual convention of the Canadian Psychological Association, Calgary, Alberta.

Schwean, V. L., Saklofske, D. H., Shatz, E., & Folk, G. (1996). Achieving supportive integration for children with behavioral disorders in Canada: Multiple paths to realization. *Canadian Journal of Special Education, 11*(1), 35–50.

Section 504 Amendment to the Rehabilitation Act of 1973 (enacted under the Workforce Investment Act of 1998, Pub. L. 105-220, 112 Stat. 936 [1998]).

Seligman, M. (Ed.). (1991). *The family with a handicapped child.* Boston: Allyn & Bacon.

Seligman, M., & Darling, R. B. (1997). *Ordinary families, special children.* New York: Guilford Press.

Sewell, T. E. (1981). Shaping the future of school psychology: Another perspective. *School Psychology Review, 10,* 232–242.

Shapiro, E. S. (1989). *Academic skills problems: Direct assessment and intervention.* New York: Guilford Press.

Shapiro, E. S. (1995). *School Psychology Review*: Past, present, future revisited. *School Psychology Review, 24,* 529–536.

Shaw, S. (2002, Fall). Post-doctoral residency in school psychology: Perspectives and proposals. *Trainer's Forum, 22*(1), 4–6.

Shaw, S. R., & Swerdlik, M. E. (1995). Best practices in facilitating team functioning. In A. Thomas and J. Grimes (Eds.), *Best Practices in School Psychology III* (pp. 153–159). Washington, DC: National Association of School Psychologists.

Shellenberger, S. (1988). Family medicine: The school psychologist's influence. *School Psychology Review, 17,* 405–410.

Sheridan, S. M., & Gutkin, T. B. (2000). The ecology of school psychology: Examining and changing our paradigm for the 21st century. *School Psychology Review, 29*, 485–502.

Shernoff, E. S., Kratochwill, T. R., & Stoiber, K. C. (2003). Training in evidence-based interventions (EBIs): What are school psychology programs teaching? *Journal of School Psychology, 41*, 467–483.

Shinn, M. R. (Ed.). (1989). *Curriculum-based measurement: Assessing special children.* New York: Guilford Press.

Shinn, M. R. (Ed.). (1995). Curriculum-based measurement and its use in a problem-solving model. In A. Thomas & J. Grimes (Eds.), *Best practices in school psychology III* (pp. 547–567). Washington, DC: National Association of School Psychologists.

Shinn, M. R., Nolet, V., & Knutson, N. (1990). Best practices in curriculum-based measurement. In A. Thomas & J. Grimes (Eds.), *Best practices in school psychology II* (pp. 287–307). Silver Spring, MD: National Association of School Psychologists.

Siegel, A. W., & White, S. H. (1982). The child study movement: Early growth and development of the symbolized child. In H. W. Reese & L. Lipsitt (Eds.), *Advances in child development and behavior* (Vol. 17, pp. 233–285). New York: Academic Press.

Silberberg, N. E., & Silberberg, M. C. (1971). Should schools have psychologists? *Journal of School Psychology, 9*, 321–328.

Sinclair, C., Simon, N. P., & Pettifor, J. L. (1996). The history of ethical codes and licensure. In L. Bass, S. DeMers, J. Ogloff, C. Peterson, R. Reaves, T. Retfalvi, et al. (Eds.), *Professional conduct and discipline in psychology* (pp. 1–15). Washington, DC: American Psychological Association; and Montgomery, AL: Association of State and Provincial Psychology Boards.

Singleton, D., Tate, A., & Randall, G. (2003, January). *Salaries in psychology 2001: Report of the 2001 APA salary survey.* Washington, DC: American Psychological Association, Research Office.

Skinner, C. H., Robinson, S. L., Brown, C. S., & Cates, G. L. (1999). Female publication patterns in *School Psychology Review, Journal of School Psychology,* and *School Psychology Quarterly* from 1985–1994. *School Psychology Review, 28*, 76–83.

Sladeczek, I., & Heath, N. (1997). Consultation in Canada. *Canadian Journal of School Psychology, 13*, 1–14.

Slater, R. (1980). The organizational origins of public school psychology. *Educational Studies, 2*, 1–11.

Smith, D. K. (1984). Practicing school psychologists: Their characteristics, activities, and populations served. *Professional Psychology: Research and Practice, 15*, 798–810.

Smith, D. K., Clifford, E. S., Hesley, J., & Leifgren, M. (1992). *The school psychologist of 1991: A survey of practitioners.* Paper presented at the annual meeting of the National Association of School Psychologists, Nashville, TN.

Smith, D. K., & Mealy, N. S. (1988). *Changes in school psychology practice: A five-year update.* Paper presented at the annual meeting of the American Psychological Association, Atlanta, GA.

Smith, F. (1997). Comparisons of state associations. *The Louisiana School Psychologist, 8*(5), 3–4.

Snyder, T. D., Hoffman, C. M., & Geddes, C. M. (1997). *Digest of educational statistics 1997*. Washington, DC: U.S. Department of Education, Office of Educational Research and Improvement.

Social Security Administration. (2000). *Social security: Understanding supplemental security income*. Washington, DC: Author.

Sokal, M. M. (1982). The Committee on the Certification of Consulting Psychologists: A failure of applied psychology in the 1920s. In C. J. Adkins & B. A. Winstead (Eds.), *History of applied psychology: Department of Psychology Colloquium Series II* (pp. 71–90). Norfolk, VA: Old Dominion University, Department of Psychology, Center for Applied Psychological Studies.

Solly, D. C., & Hohenshil, T. H. (1986). Job satisfaction among school psychologists in a primarily rural state. *School Psychology Review, 15*, 119–126.

Solway, K. S. (1985). Transition from graduate school to internship: A potential crisis. *Professional Psychology: Research and Practice, 16*, 50–54.

Sorenson, J. L., Masson, C. L., Clark, W. W., & Morin, S. F. (1998). Providing public testimony: A guide for psychologists. *Professional Psychology: Research and Practice, 29*, 588–593.

Spring, J. (1989). *American education: An introduction to social and political aspects*. New York: Longman.

Stanhope, V. (1995). Congress targets children's SSI benefits. *Communiqué, 23*(7), 3.

Statistics Canada. (2001). *A profile of disability in Canada, 2001* (Catalogue no. 89-577-X1E). Ottawa: Author.

Steil, D. A. (1994). Post secondary school psychology: Come on in, the water's fine. *Communiqué, 22*(8), 28–30.

Stein, H. L. (1964). *The status and role of school psychologists in Canada*. Unpublished manuscript.

Steingart, S. K. (2005). *The Web-connected school psychologist: A busy person's guide to school psychology on the Internet*. Boston: Sopris West.

Stern, W. D. (1910). Ubernormale kind. *Der Saemann Monatschrift Fuer Paedagogische Reform*. Jahrg, s. 97-72 U.S. 160–167.

Stern, W. (1911). The supernormal child: II. *Journal of Educational Psychology, 2*, 181–190.

Stern, W. (1914). *The psychological methods of testing intelligence*. Baltimore, MD: Warwick & York.

Stewart, K. J. (1986). Disentangling the complexities of clientage. In S. N. Elliott & J. C. Witt (Eds.), *The delivery of psychological services in schools: Concepts, processes, and issues* (pp. 81–107). Hillsdale, NJ: Erlbaum.

Stirtzinger, R., Campbell, L., Green, A., DeSouza, C., & Dawe, I. (2001). Multimodal school-based intervention for at-risk, aggressive, latency-age youth. *Canadian Journal of School Psychology, 17*(1), 27–46.

Stoiber, K. C., & Kratochwill, T. R. (2000). Empirically supported interventions and school psychology: Rationale and methodological issues, Pt 1. *School Psychology Quarterly, 15*, 75–105.

Stoner, G., & Green, S. K. (1992). Reconsidering the scientist-practitioner model for school psychology practice. *School Psychology Review, 21,* 155–166.

Strein, W. (1996a). Administrative supervision. In T. K. Fagan & P. J. Warden (Eds.), *Historical encyclopedia of school psychology* (pp. 12–13). Westport, CT: Greenwood Press.

Strein, W. (1996b). Professional supervision. In T. K. Fagan & P. J. Warden (Eds.), *Historical encyclopedia of school psychology* (pp. 297–298). Westport, CT: Greenwood Press.

Strein, W., Cramer, K., & Lawser, M. (2003). School psychology research and scholarship: USA status, international explorations. *School Psychology International, 24*(4), 421–436.

Stringfield, S. (Guest Ed.). (1991). Looking to the future of Chapter 1. *Phi Delta Kappan, 72,* 576–607.

Stumme, J. M. (1995). Best practices in serving as an expert witness. In A. Thomas & J. Grimes (Eds.), *Best practices in school psychology III* (pp. 179–190). Washington, DC: National Association of School Psychologists.

Sullivan, L. (1999). Progress: The national education goals. *Communiqué, 27*(6), 12.

Supplement to listing of accredited doctoral, internship, and post-doctoral training programs in professional psychology. (2006). *American Psychologist, 61*(5), 554–555.

Sutkiewicz, F. (1997, May). Ethical issues involved with computer use: How to avoid the pitfalls. *The Wisconsin School Psychologist, 96*(3), 1, 6–7.

Sweet, T. (1990). School psychology in British Columbia: The state of the art. *Canadian Journal of School Psychology, 6,* 1–8.

Swenson, E. V. (1998, Winter). Applications of the APA ethics code to the training of school psychologists in the classroom. *Trainers' Forum, 16*(2), 12–15.

Symonds, P. M. (1933). Every school should have a psychologist. *School and Society, 38*(976), 321–329.

Symonds, P. M. (Ed.). (1942). [Special issue]. *Journal of Consulting Psychology, 6*(4).

Tallent, N. (1993). *Psychological report writing* (4th ed.). Englewood Cliffs, NJ: Prentice Hall.

Talley, R. C., Kubiszyn, T., Brassard, M., & Short, R. J. (Eds.). (1996). *Making psychologists in schools indispensable: Critical questions and emerging perspectives.* Washington, DC: American Psychological Association.

Tarasoff v. Regents of California, 529 P.2d 553 (1974); 551 P.2d 334 (1976).

Tarquin, K. M., & Truscott, S. D. (2006). School psychology students' perceptions of their practicum experiences. *Psychology in the Schools, 43,* 727–736.

Telzrow, C. F. (1999). IDEA amendments of 1997: Promise or pitfall for special education reform? *Journal of School Psychology, 37,* 7–28.

Tenure . . . Questions & Answers. (1997, Spring). *CASP Today, 46*(3), 12.

Terman, L. M. (1916). *The measurement of intelligence: An explanation of and complete guide for the use of the Stanford revision and extension of the Binet-Simon Intelligence Scale.* Boston: Houghton Mifflin.

Tharinger, D. J. (1996). Psychologists in the schools: Routes to becoming indispensable. In R. C. Talley, T. Kubiszyn, M. Brassard, & R. J. Short (Eds.), *Making psychologists in schools indispensable: Critical questions and emerging perspectives* (pp. 105–110). Washington, DC: American Psychological Association.

Thomas, A. (Ed.). (1998). *Directory of school psychology graduate programs*. Bethesda, MD: National Association of School Psychologists.

Thomas, A. (1999a). School psychology 2000: A national database. *Communiqué, 28*(1), 26.

Thomas, A. (1999b). School psychology 2000. *Communiqué, 28*(2), 28.

Thomas, A. (2000). School psychology 2000: What is average? *Communiqué, 28*(7), 32–33.

Thomas, A., & Grimes, J. (Eds.). (1985). *Best practices in school psychology*. Kent, OH: National Association of School Psychologists.

Thomas, A., & Grimes, J. (Eds.). (1990). *Best practices in school psychology II*. Silver Spring, MD: National Association of School Psychologists.

Thomas, A., & Grimes, J. (Eds.). (1995). *Best practices in school psychology III*. Washington, DC: National Association of School Psychologists.

Thomas, A., & Grimes, J. (Eds.). (2002). *Best practices in school psychology IV* (Vol. 1–2). Bethesda, MD: National Association of School Psychologists.

Thomas, A., & Grimes, J. (Eds.). (2008). *Best practices in school psychology V* Bethesda, MD: National Association of School Psychologists.

Thomas, A., & Pinciotti, D. (1992). *Administrators' satisfaction with school psychologists: Implications for practice*. Paper presented at the annual meeting of the National Association of School Psychologists, Nashville, TN.

Thomas, A., & Witte, R. (1996). A study of gender differences among school psychologists. *Psychology in the Schools, 33*, 351–359.

Thompson, P. (2004). *The school psychology licensure exam guide: The most effective guide to prepare for the National Association of School Psychologists (NASP) exam*. New York: iUniverse, Inc.

Thorndike, E. L. (1912). *Education: A first book*. New York: Macmillan.

Tikkanen, T. (2006). *The present status and future prospects of the profession of psychology in Europe*. Paper presented at the International Congress of Applied Psychology, Athens, Greece.

Tindall, R. H. (1964). Trends in the development of psychological services in the schools. *Journal of School Psychology, 3*, 1–12.

Tindall, R. H. (1979). School psychology: The development of a profession. In G. D. Phye & D. J. Reschly (Eds.), *School psychology: Perspectives and issues* (pp. 3–24). New York: Academic Press.

Tingstrom, D. H. (2000). Academic positions in school psychology: Fall 2000. *The School Psychologist, 54*(1), 12–13.

Tingstrom, D. (2006, January). *Academic positions in school psychology: Fall 2006*. Paper presented at the annual meeting of the Council of Directors of School Psychology Programs.

Tolan, P. H., & Dodge, K. A. (2005). Children's mental health as a primary care and concern: A system for comprehensive support and service. *American Psychologist, 60*(6), 601–614.

Trachtman, G. M. (1981). On such a full sea. *School Psychology Review, 10*, 138–181.

Trachtman, G. M. (1996). Indispensability: The holy grail. In R. C. Talley, T. Kubiszyn, M. Brassard, & R. J. Short (Eds.), *Making psychologists in schools indispensable: Critical questions and emerging perspectives* (pp. 9–13). Washington, DC: American Psychological Association.

Tracy, M. (1998). Be aware of malpractice risks when using electronic devices. *The National Psychologist*, *7*(1), 17.

Truch, S. (2006). *The WISC–IV Companion: A guide to interpretation and educational intervention.* Austin, TX: Pro-Ed Inc.

Tulsky, D., Saklofske, D. H., Chelune, G. J., Heaton, R. K., Ivnik, R. J., Bornstein, R., et al. (Eds.). (2003). *Clinical interpretation of the WAIS-III and WMS-III.* San Diego, CA: Academic Press.

Turner, S. M., DeMers, S. T., Fox, H. R., & Reed, G. M. (2001). APA's guidelines for test user qualifications. *American Psychologist*, *56*(12), 1099–1113.

Tyack, D. B. (1976). Ways of seeing: An essay on the history of compulsory schooling. *Harvard Educational Review, 46,* 355–389.

Tyson, H. (1999). Kappan special report: A load off the teachers' backs: Coordinated school health programs. *Phi Delta Kappan*, *80*(5), K1–K8.

UNESCO (1948). *School psychologists* (UNESCO and IBE Publication No. 105). Paper presented at the XI International Congress on Public Education. Geneva: UN Educational, Scientific, and Cultural Organization, International Bureau of Education.

U.S. Department of Education. (1998, August). *Early warning, timely response: A guide to safe schools.* Washington, DC: Author.

U.S. Department of Education. (2002). *To assure the free appropriate public education of all children with disabilities: 24th annual report to Congress on the implementation of the IDEA.* Washington, DC: Author.

U.S. Department of Education, National Center for Education Statistics (2003). *Overview of public elementary and secondary schools and districts: School year 2001–02* (NCES 2003-411). Retrieved from http://nces.ed.gov/pubs2003/overview03/

U.S. Department of Education, National Center for Education Statistics. (2004). Institute of Education Sciences *Statistical Analysis Report.* Retrieved from http://nces.ed.gov/pubs2003/snf_report03/table_03_1.asp

U.S. Department of Education, National Center for Education Statistics. (2004). Institute of Education Sciences Survey of Private Schools data tables. Retrieved from http://nces.ed.gov/surveys/pss/tables.asp

Valesky, T. C., Forsythe, G., & Hall, M. L. (1992). *Principal perceptions of school based decision making in Tennessee schools* (Policy Practice Brief No. 9201). Memphis, TN: Memphis State University, Center for Research in Educational Policy.

Valett, R. E. (1963). *The practice of school psychology: Professional problems.* New York: Wiley.

Valett, R. E. (1967). *The remediation of learning disabilities: A handbook of psychoeducational resource programs.* Palo Alto, CA: Fearon.

Van Sickle, J. H., Witmer, L., & Ayres, L. P. (1911). *Provision for exceptional children in the public schools.* (U.S. Bureau of Education Bulletin No. 14). Washington, DC: Government Printing Office.

Van Strein, P. J. (1998). Early applied psychology between essentialism and pragmatism: The dynamics of theory, tools, and clients. *History of Psychology, 1,* 205–234.

Vance, H. R., & Pumariega, A. J. (Guest Eds.). (1999). School-based mental health services [Special issue]. *Psychology in the Schools, 36*(5).

VanVoorhis, R. W., & Levinson, E. M. (2006). Job satisfaction among school psychologists: A meta-analysis. *School Psychology Quarterly, 21,* 77–90.

Vazquez, E., & Dunham, M. (2004). TSP in Dallas. *Trainer's Forum, 23*(4), 17–19.

Veatch, B. A. (1978). *Historical and demographic influences in the development of a situation specific model of school psychological services* (Vol. 39-09-A, 5423). Calgary, Alberta, Canada: University of Calgary.

Waddell, C., McEwan, K., Shepherd, C.A., Offord, D. R., & Hua, J. M. (2005). A public health strategy to improve the mental health of Canadian children. *Canadian Journal of Psychiatry, 50,* 226–233.

Waguespack, A., Stewart, W. T., & Dupre, C. (1992). *Consulting with teachers about interventions: How much do teachers remember?* Paper presented at the annual meeting of the National Association of School Psychologists, Nashville, TN.

Waizenhofer, R. N. (2002, June). Marketing and promoting school psychology in today's schools, Part 1. *School Psych Scene, 35*(6), 1, 4–6. Part 2 appears in *36*(1), August 2002, pp. 1, 4, 6.

Waldron, N. L., McLeskey, J., Skiba, R. J., Jancaus, J., & Schulmeyer, C. (1998). High and low referring teachers: Two types of teachers-as-tests? *School Psychology International, 19,* 31–41.

Wall, W. (1955). School psychological services in Europe. In N. E. Cutts (Ed.), *School psychologists at mid-century: A report of the Thayer conference* (pp. 183–194). Washington, DC: American Psychological Association.

Wall, W. (1956). *Psychological services for schools.* New York: University Press for UNESCO Institute for Education.

Wallin, J. E. W. (1914). *The mental health of the school child.* New Haven, CT: Yale University Press.

Wallin, J. E. W. (1919). The field of the clinical psychologist and the kind of training needed by the psychological examiner. *School and Society, 9,* 463–470.

Wallin, J. E. W. (1920). The problems confronting a psycho-educational clinic in a large municipality. *Mental Hygiene, 4,* 103–136.

Wallin, J. E. W., & Ferguson, D. G. (1967). The development of school psychological services. In J. F. Magary (Ed.), *School psychological services in theory and practice: A handbook* (pp. 1–29). Englewood Cliffs, NJ: Prentice Hall.

Walter, R. (1925). The functions of a school psychologist. *American Education, 29,* 167–170.

Watkins, C. E., Tipton, R. M., Manus, M., & Hunton-Shoup, J. (1991). Role relevance and role engagement in contemporary school psychology. *Professional Psychology: Research and Practice, 22,* 328–332.

Watkins, J. E. (1900, December). What may happen in the next hundred years. *The Ladies Home Journal.* For a popular analysis of this, see Roberts, R. (1993–1994). 20th century predictions: What came true, what didn't—and why. *The Elks Magazine*, *72*(6), 30–41.

Watkins, S. J., Dobson, S., & Berube, D. (2006). Professional psychology in Alberta. *Psymposium, 15*(3), 18–23.

Watson, S. T., & Skinner, C. H. (Eds.). (2004). *Encyclopedia of school psychology.* Cambridge, MA: Springer.

Wechsler, D. (1996). *WISC-III Manual, Canadian supplement.* Toronto: The Psychological Corporation.

Wechsler, S., & Oakland, T. (1990). Preventive strategies for promoting the education of low income Brazilian children: Implications for school psychologists from other Third World nations. *School Psychology International, 11*, 83–90.

Weininger, O. (1971). The school psychologist as chameleon. *Canadian Counsellor, 5*(2), 125–134.

Weiss, L. G., Saklofske, D. H., Prifitera, A., Chen, H. Y., & Hildebrand, D. K. (1999). The calculation of the WISC-III General Ability Index using Canadian norms. *Canadian Journal of School Psychology, 14*(2), 1–10.

Weiss, L. G., Saklofske, D. H., Prifitera, A., & Holdnack, J. (2006). *WISC-IV advanced clinical interpretation.* San Diego, CA: Elsevier.

Wells, P. D. (1999). A comparison of recent graduates of APA- and non-APA-accredited doctoral training programs in school psychology. Unpublished master's thesis, University of Memphis, Memphis, TN.

Whelan, T., & Carlson, C. (1986). Books in school psychology: 1970 to the present. *Professional School Psychology, 1*, 279–289.

Whipple, G. M. (1914). *Manual of mental and physical tests: Part 1. Simpler processes.* Baltimore, MD: Warwick & York.

Whipple, G. M. (1915). *Manual of mental and physical tests: Part 2. Complex processes.* Baltimore, MD: Warwick & York.

White, M. A. (1968–1969). Will school psychology exist? *Journal of School Psychology, 7*(2), 53–57.

Wicherski, M., & Kohout, J. (2005, August). *2003 Doctorate employment survey.* Washington, DC: American Psychological Associaion, Research Office.

Wilczenski, F. L., Phelps, L., & Lawler, M. (1992). Publishing guidelines for school psychologists. *Communiqué, 21*(4), 14.

Will, M. (1989, January). *The role of school psychology in providing services to all children.* Washington, DC: U.S. Department of Education, Office of Special Programs and Rehabilitative Services.

Williams, K. J., & Williams, G. M. (1992). Applications of social psychology to school employee evaluation and appraisal. In F. J. Medway & T. P. Cafferty (Eds.), *School psychology: A social psychological perspective* (pp. 333–354). Hillsdale, NJ: Erlbaum.

Wilson, M. S., & Reschly, D. J. (1995). Gender and school psychology: Issues, questions, and answers. *School Psychology Review, 24*, 45–61.

Wilson, M., & Reschly, D. (1996). Assessment in school psychology training and practice. *School Psychology Review, 25*, 9–23.

Wise, C. L., Li, C-Y, & Smith, R. C. (2000, March 31). *Assessment of workspace conditions for school psychologists: A three state comparison.* Paper presented at the annual convention of the National Association of School Psychologists, New Orleans, LA.

Wise, P. S. (1985). School psychologists' ratings of stressful events. *Journal of School Psychology, 23*, 31–41.

Wise, P. S. (1986). *Better parent conferences: A manual for school psychologists.* Washington, DC: National Association of School Psychologists.

Wise, P. S. (1995). Communicating with parents. In A. Thomas and J. Grimes (Eds.), *Best Practices in School Psychology III* (pp. 279–287). Washington, DC: National Association of School Psychologists.

Wise, P. S., Smead, V. S., & Huebner, E. S. (1987). Crisis intervention: Involvement and training needs of school psychology personnel. *Journal of School Psychology, 25*, 185–187.

Wishy, B. (1968). *The child and the republic: The dawn of modern American child nurture.* Philadelphia: University of Pennsylvania Press.

Witmer, L. (1897). The organization of practical work in psychology. *Psychological Review, 4*, 116–117.

Witmer, L. (1907). Clinical psychology. *The Psychological Clinic, 1*(1), 1–9.

Witt, J. C., & Elliott, S. N. (1985). Acceptability of classroom intervention strategies. In T. R. Kratochwill (Ed.), *Advances in school psychology* (Vol. 4, pp. 251–288). Hillsdale, NJ: Erlbaum.

Wodrich, D. L. (1988). School psychological practice in a department of pediatrics. *School Psychology Review, 17*, 411–415.

Wodrich, D. L., & Schmitt, A. J. (2003). Pediatric topics in the school psychology literature: Publications since 1981. *Journal of School Psychology, 41*(2), 131–141.

Wonderly, D. M., & Mcloughlin, C. (1984). Contractual services: A viable alternative. *School Psychology International, 5*(2), 107–113.

Woody, R. H. (1998). Copyright law in school psychology training. *Trainers' Forum, 16*(3), 1, 4–7.

Woody, R. H., & Davenport, J. (1998). The *Blueprint I* revisited: Training and practice in school psychology. *Psychology in the Schools, 35*(1), 49–55.

Woody, R. H., LaVoie, J. C., & Epps, S. (1992). *School psychology: A developmental and social systems approach.* Boston: Allyn & Bacon.

Woolfolk, A. E., Winnie, P. H., & Perry, N. E. (2006). Educational psychology (3rd Canadian ed.). Toronto: Pearson Education Canada.

Worrell, T. G., Skaggs, G. E., & Brown, M. B. (2006). School psychologists' job satisfaction: A 22-year perspective in the USA. *School Psychology International, 27*(2), 131–145.

Wrobel, G., & Krieg, F. (1998, September). Health care report. *NASP Executive Committee Minutes.* Washington, DC: National Association of School Psychologists.

York, L. (2001). NCSP stock on the rise. *School Psychology in Illinois, 22*(3), 18.

Yoshida, R. K., Fenton, K. S., Maxwell, J. P., & Kaufman, M. J. (1978). Group decision making in the planning team process: Myth or reality? *Journal of School Psychology, 16*, 237–244.

Ysseldyke, J. E. (1986). Current practice in school psychology. In S. N. Elliott & J. C. Witt (Eds.), *The delivery of psychological services in schools: Concepts, processes, and issues* (pp. 27–51). Hillsdale, NJ: Erlbaum.

Ysseldyke, J. E. (2005). Assessment and decision making for students with learning disabilities: What if this is as good as it gets? *Learning Disability Quarterly, 28*(2), 125–128.

Ysseldyke, J., Burns, M., Dawson, P., Kelley, B., Morrison, D., Ortiz, S., et al. (2006). *School psychology: A blueprint for training and practice III.* Bethesda, MD: National Association of School Psychologists.

Ysseldyke, J. E., & Christenson, S. L. (1988). Linking assessment to intervention. In J. L. Graden, J. E. Zins, & M. J. Curtis (Eds.), *Alternative educational delivery systems: Enhancing instructional options for all students* (pp. 91–109). Washington, DC: National Association of School Psychologists.

Ysseldyke, J., Dawson, P., Lehr, C., Reschly, D., Reynolds, M., & Telzrow, C. (1997). *School psychology: A blueprint for training and practice II.* Bethesda, MD: National Association of School Psychologists.

Ysseldyke, J., & Elliott, J. (1999). Effective instructional practices: Implications for assessing educational environments. In C. R. Reynolds and T. B. Gutkin (Eds.), *The handbook of school psychology* (3rd ed., pp. 497–518). New York: Wiley.

Ysseldyke, J. E., & Weinberg, R. A. (Eds.). (1981). The future of psychology in the schools: Proceedings of the Spring Hill Symposium [Special issue]. *School Psychology Review, 10*(2).

Zelizer, V. A. (1985). *Pricing the priceless child: The changing social value of children.* New York: Basic Books.

Zins, J. (1982). *Accountability for school psychologists: Developing trends.* Washington, DC: National Association of School Psychologists.

Zins. J. E. (1990). Best practices in developing accountability procedures. In A. Thomas & J. Grimes (Eds.), *Best practices in school psychology II* (pp. 323–337). Silver Spring, MD: National Association of School Psychologists.

Zins, J. E., Curtis, M. J., Graden, J. L., & Ponti, C. R. (1988). *Helping students succeed in the regular classroom: A guide for developing intervention assistance programs.* San Francisco: Jossey-Bass.

Zins, J. E., & Erchul, W. P. (2002). Best practices in school consultation. In A. Thomas & J. Grimes, (Eds.), *Best practices in school psychology IV* (pp. 625–643). Bethesda, MD: National Association of School Psychologists.

Zins, J. E., & Halsell, A. (1986). Status of ethnic minority group members in school psychology training programs. *School Psychology Review, 15,* 76–83.

Zins, J., Kratochwill, T., & Elliott, S. (Eds.). (1993). *Handbook of consultation services for children.* San Francisco: Jossey-Bass.

Zins, J. E., Maher, C. A., Murphy, J. J., & Wess, B. P. (1988). The peer support group: A means to facilitate professional development. *School Psychology Review, 17,* 138–146.

Zins, J. E., & Ponti, C. R. (1990). Best practices in school-based consultation. In A. Thomas & J. Grimes (Eds.), *Best practices in school psychology II* (pp. 673–693). Silver Spring, MD: National Association of School Psychologists.

Zirkel, P. A. (1992). Confident about confidences? *Phi Delta Kappan, 73,* 732–734.

Zirkel, P. A. (2001). Tips on testifying for school personnel [Insert]. *Communiqué, 29*(6).

Index

D

O

P

R

S